Market!

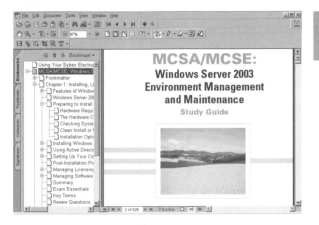

Search through the complete book in PDF!

- Access the entire *MCSA/MCSE: Windows Server 2003 Environment Management and Maintenance Study Guide*, complete with figures and tables, in electronic format.

- Search the *MCSA/MCSE: Windows Server 2003 Environment Management and Maintenance Study Guide* chapters to find information on any topic in seconds.

- Look up any Key Term, along with other general terms, in the Glossary.

Use the Electronic Flashcards for PCs, Pocket PCs, or Palm devices to jog your memory and prep last-minute for the exam!

- Reinforce your understanding of key concepts with these hardcore flashcard-style questions.

- Download the Flashcards to your Palm device, and go on the road. Now you can study anywhere, any time.

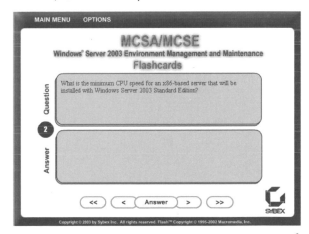

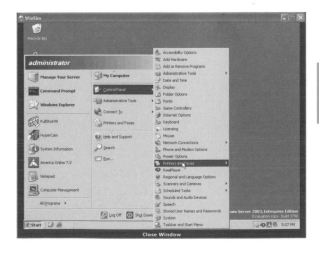

Prepare for Microsoft's tough simulation questions with the WinSim 2003 program!

- Use the simulators to guide you through real-world tasks step-by-step, or watch the movies to see the "invisible hand" perform the tasks for you.

SYBEX

MCSA/MCSE: Windows Server 2003 Environment Management and Maintenance Study Guide

Exam 70-290

OBJECTIVE	CHAPTER
Managing and Maintaining Physical and Logical Devices	
Manage basic disks and dynamic disks.	4
Monitor server hardware. Tools might include Device Manager, the Hardware Troubleshooting Wizard, and appropriate Control Panel items.	2
Optimize server disk performance.	4
Implement a RAID solution.	4
Defragment volumes and partitions.	4
Troubleshoot server hardware devices.	2
Diagnose and resolve issues related to hardware settings.	2
Diagnose and resolve issues related to server hardware and hardware driver upgrades.	2
Install and configure server hardware devices.	2
Configure driver signing options.	2
Configure resource settings for a device.	2
Configure device properties and settings.	2
Managing Users, Computers, and Groups	
Manage local, roaming, and mandatory user profiles.	3
Create and manage computer accounts in an Active Directory environment.	3
Create and manage groups.	3
Identify and modify the scope of a group.	3
Find domain groups in which a user is a member.	3
Manage group membership.	3
Create and modify groups by using the Active Directory Users and Computers Microsoft Management Console (MMC) snap-in.	3
Create and modify groups by using automation.	3
Create and manage user accounts.	3
Create and modify user accounts by using the Active Directory Users and Computers MMC snap-in.	3
Create and modify user accounts by using automation.	3
Import user accounts.	3
Troubleshoot computer accounts.	3
Diagnose and resolve issues related to computer accounts by using the Active Directory Users and Computers MMC snap-in.	3
Reset computer accounts.	3
Troubleshoot user accounts.	3
Diagnose and resolve account lockouts.	3
Diagnose and resolve issues related to user account properties.	3
Troubleshoot user authentication issues.	3

SYBEX

SYBEX

MCSA/MCSE:

Windows Server 2003 Environment Management and Maintenance

Study Guide

MCSA/MCSE:
Windows® Server 2003 Environment Management and Maintenance
Study Guide

Lisa Donald

with Suzan Sage London and James Chellis

San Francisco • London

SYBEX®

Associate Publisher: Neil Edde
Acquisitions and Developmental Editor: Jeff Kellum
Production Editor: Elizabeth Campbell
Technical Editors: Donald Fuller, Craig Vazquez
Copyeditor: Suzanne Goraj
Compositor: Interactive Composition Corporation
Graphic Illustrator: Interactive Composition Corporation
CD Coordinator: Dan Mummert
CD Technician: Kevin Ly
Proofreaders: Laurie O'Connell, Nancy Riddiough, Monique Vandenberg
Indexer: Nancy Guenther
Book Designer: Bill Gibson
Cover Designer: Archer Design
Cover Photographer: Colin Paterson, PhotoDisc

Library of Congress Card Number: 2003104318

ISBN: 0-7821-4260-5

SYBEX and the SYBEX logo are either registered trademarks or trademarks of SYBEX Inc. in the United States and/or other countries.

Screen reproductions produced with FullShot 99. FullShot 99 © 1991–1999 Inbit Incorporated. All rights reserved. FullShot is a trademark of Inbit Incorporated.

The CD interface was created using Macromedia Director, COPYRIGHT 1994, 1997–1999 Macromedia Inc. For more information on Macromedia and Macromedia Director, visit http://www.macromedia.com.

Microsoft, the Microsoft Internet Explorer logo, Windows, Windows XP Professional, Windows Server 2003, and the Windows logo are either registered trademarks or trademarks of Microsoft Corporation in the United States and/or other countries.

SYBEX is an independent entity from Microsoft Corporation, and not affiliated with Microsoft Corporation in any manner. This publication may be used in assisting students to prepare for a Microsoft Certified Professional Exam. Neither Microsoft Corporation, its designated review company, nor SYBEX warrants that use of this publication will ensure passing the relevant exam. Microsoft is either a registered trademark or trademark of Microsoft Corporation in the United States and/or other countries.

TRADEMARKS: SYBEX has attempted throughout this book to distinguish proprietary trademarks from descriptive terms by following the capitalization style used by the manufacturer.

The author and publisher have made their best efforts to prepare this book, and the content is based upon final release software whenever possible. Portions of the manuscript may be based upon pre-release versions supplied by software manufacturer(s). The author and the publisher make no representation or warranties of any kind with regard to the completeness or accuracy of the contents herein and accept no liability of any kind including but not limited to performance, merchantability, fitness for any particular purpose, or any losses or damages of any kind caused or alleged to be caused directly or indirectly from this book.

Manufactured in the United States of America

10 9 8 7 6 5 4 3 2 1

SYBEX

To Our Valued Readers:

Thank you for looking to Sybex for your Microsoft Windows 2003 certification exam prep needs. We at Sybex are proud of the reputation we've established for providing certification candidates with the practical knowledge and skills needed to succeed in the highly competitive IT marketplace. Sybex is proud to have helped thousands of Microsoft certification candidates prepare for their exams over the years, and we are excited about the opportunity to continue to provide computer and networking professionals with the skills they'll need to succeed in the highly competitive IT industry.

With its release of Windows Server 2003, and the revised MCSA and MCSE tracks, Microsoft has raised the bar for IT certifications yet again. The new programs better reflect the skill set demanded of IT administrators in today's marketplace and offers candidates a clearer structure for acquiring the skills necessary to advance their careers.

The authors and editors have worked hard to ensure that the Study Guide you hold in your hand is comprehensive, in-depth, and pedagogically sound. We're confident that this book will exceed the demanding standards of the certification marketplace and help you, the Microsoft certification candidate, succeed in your endeavors.

As always, your feedback is important to us. Please send comments, questions, or suggestions to support@sybex.com. At Sybex we're continually striving to meet the needs of individuals preparing for IT certification exams.

Good luck in pursuit of your Microsoft certification!

Neil Edde
Associate Publisher—Certification
Sybex, Inc.

For Kevin, the amazing genius!

Acknowledgments

This book is the work of a great team. First I'd like to thank my editor Suzanne Goraj for her excellent job on the editing process. The production editor Elizabeth Campbell was always a pleasure to work with and kept the book moving along and on schedule. Thanks also to technical editor Donald Fuller for his thorough edit and for keeping me honest.

I would like to thank Neil Edde, associate publisher and James Chellis who both helped develop and nurtured the MCSE series of books since the beginning. Jeff Kellum, acquisitions and developmental editor for all of his hard work on the initial development of the book and its format and keeping the project on track.

I'd also like to thank the second technical editors Don Fuller and Craig Vazquez, the proofreaders Laurie O'Connell, Nancy Riddiough, and Monique Vandenberg, and the indexer Nancy Guenther.

Finally, I want to thank my family for all of their support.

Contents at a Glance

Contents

Table of Exercises

Introduction

Microsoft's Microsoft Certified Systems Administrator (MCSA) and Microsoft Certified Systems Engineer (MCSE) tracks for Windows Server 2003 are the premier certifications for computer industry professionals. Covering the core technologies around which Microsoft's future will be built, this program provides powerful credentials for career advancement.

This book has been developed to give you the critical skills and knowledge you need to prepare for one of the core requirements of both the MCSA and MCSE certifications in the new Windows Server 2003 track: Managing and Maintaining a Microsoft Windows Server 2003 Environment (Exam 70-290).

The Microsoft Certified Professional Program

Since the inception of its certification program, Microsoft has certified almost 1.5 million people. As the computer network industry increases in both size and complexity, this number is sure to grow—and the need for *proven* ability will also increase. Companies rely on certifications to verify the skills of prospective employees and contractors.

Microsoft has developed its Microsoft Certified Professional (MCP) program to give you credentials that verify your ability to work with Microsoft products effectively and professionally. Obtaining your MCP certification requires that you pass any one Microsoft certification exam. Several levels of certification are available based on specific suites of exams. Depending on your areas of interest or experience, you can obtain any of the following MCP credentials:

Microsoft Certified Systems Administrator (MCSA) on Windows Server 2003 The MCSA certification is the latest certification track from Microsoft. This certification targets systems and network administrators with roughly 6 to 12 months of desktop and network administration experience. The MCSA can be considered the entry-level certification. You must take and pass a total of four exams to obtain your MCSA. Or, if you are an MCSA on Windows 2000, you can take one Upgrade exam to obtain your MCSA on Windows Server 2003.

Microsoft Certified Systems Engineer (MCSE) on Windows Server 2003 This certification track is designed for network and systems administrators, network and systems analysts, and technical consultants who work with Microsoft Windows XP and Server 2003 software. You must take and pass seven exams to obtain your MCSE. Or, if you are an MCSE on Windows 2000, you can take two Upgrade exams to obtain your MCSE on Windows Server 2003.

MCSE versus MCSA

In an effort to provide those just starting off in the IT world a chance to prove their skills, Microsoft introduced its Microsoft Certified Systems Administrator (MCSA) program.

Targeted at those with less than a year's experience, the MCSA program focuses primarily on the administration portion of an IT professional's duties. Therefore, there are certain Windows exams that satisfy both MCSA and MCSE requirements, namely exams 70-270, 70-290, and 70-291.

> Of course, it should be any MCSA's goal to eventually obtain his or her MCSE. However, don't assume that, because the MCSA has to take two exams that also satisfy an MCSE requirement, the two programs are similar. An MCSE must also know how to design a network. Beyond these two exams, the remaining MCSE required exams require the candidate to have much more hands-on experience.

Microsoft Certified Application Developer (MCAD)   This track is designed for application developers and technical consultants who primarily use Microsoft development tools. Currently, you can take exams on Visual Basic .NET or Visual C# .NET. You must take and pass three exams to obtain your MCSD.

Microsoft Certified Solution Developer (MCSD)   This track is designed for software engineers and developers and technical consultants who primarily use Microsoft development tools. As of this printing, you can get your MCSD in either Visual Studio 6 or Visual Studio .NET. In Visual Studio 6, you need to take and pass three exams to obtain your MCSD. In Visual Studio .NET, you must take and pass five exams.

Microsoft Certified Database Administrator (MCDBA)   This track is designed for database administrators, developers, and analysts who work with Microsoft SQL Server. As of this printing, you can take exams on either SQL Server 7 or SQL Server 2000. You must take and pass four exams to achieve MCDBA status.

Microsoft Certified Trainer (MCT)   The MCT track is designed for any IT professional who develops and teaches Microsoft-approved courses. To become an MCT, you must first obtain your MCSE, MCSD, or MCDBA, then you must take a class at one of the Certified Technical Training Centers. You will also be required to prove your instructional ability. You can do this in various ways: by taking a skills-building or train-the-trainer class, by achieving certification as a trainer from any of several vendors, or by becoming a Certified Technical Trainer through CompTIA. Last of all, you will need to complete an MCT application.

Microsoft recently announced two new certification tracks for Windows 2000: MCSA: Security and MCSE: Security. In addition to the core operating system requirements, candidates must take two security specialization core exams, one of which can be CompTIA's Security+ exam. MCSE: Security candidates must also take a security specialization design exam. As of this printing, no announcement had been made on the track for Windows Server 2003. Check out Microsoft's Web site at www.microsoft.com/traincert.com for more information.

How Do You Become Certified on Windows Server 2003?

Attaining an MCSA or MCSE certification has always been a challenge. In the past, students have been able to acquire detailed exam information—even most of the exam questions—from online "brain dumps" and third-party "cram" books or software products. For the new MCSE exams, this is simply not the case.

Microsoft has taken strong steps to protect the security and integrity of its certification tracks. Now prospective candidates must complete a course of study that develops detailed knowledge about a wide range of topics. It supplies them with the true skills needed, derived from working with Windows XP, Server 2003, and related software products.

The Windows Server 2003 certification programs are heavily weighted toward hands-on skills and experience. Microsoft has stated that "nearly half of the core required exams' content demands that the candidate have troubleshooting skills acquired through hands-on experience and working knowledge."

Fortunately, if you are willing to dedicate the time and effort to learn Windows XP and Server 2003, you can prepare yourself well for the exams by using the proper tools. By working through this book, you can successfully meet the exam requirements to pass the Windows Server 2003 management and maintenance exam.

This book is part of a complete series of MCSA and MCSE Study Guides, published by Sybex Inc., that together cover the core MCSA and MCSE operating system requirements, as well as the Design requirements needed to complete your MCSE track. Please visit the Sybex website at www.sybex.com for complete program and product details.

MCSA Exam Requirements

Candidates for MCSA certification on Windows Server 2003 must pass four exams.

For a more detailed description of the Microsoft certification programs, including a list of all the exams, visit Microsoft's Training and Certification website at www.microsoft.com/traincert.

You must take one of the following client operating system exams:

- Installing, Configuring, and Administering Microsoft Windows 2000 Professional (70-210)
- Installing, Configuring, and Administering Microsoft Windows XP Professional (70-270)

plus the following networking operating system exams:

- Managing and Maintaining a Microsoft Windows Server 2003 Environment (70-290)
- Implementing, Managing, and Maintaining a Microsoft Windows Server 2003 Network Infrastructure (70-291)

plus one of a number of electives, including:

- Implementing and Supporting Microsoft Systems Management Server 2.0 (70-086)
- Installing, Configuring, and Administering Microsoft Internet Security and Acceleration (ISA) Server 2000, Enterprise Edition (70-227)
- Installing, Configuring, and Administering Microsoft SQL Server 2000 Enterprise Edition (70-228)

- CompTIA's A+ and Network+ exams
- CompTIA's A+ and Server+ exams

Also, if you are an MCSA on Windows 2000, you can take one Upgrade exam: Managing and Maintaining a Microsoft Windows Server 2003 Environment for an MCSA Certified on Windows 2000 (70-292).

MCSE Exam Requirements

Candidates for MCSE certification on Windows Server 2003 must pass seven exams, including one client operating system exam, three networking operating system exams, one design exam, and two electives.

 For a more detailed description of the Microsoft certification programs, visit Microsoft's Training and Certification website at www.microsoft.com/ traincert.

You must take one of the following client operating system exams:

- Installing, Configuring, and Administering Microsoft Windows 2000 Professional (70-210)
- Installing, Configuring, and Administering Microsoft Windows XP Professional (70-270)

plus the following networking operating system exams:

- Managing and Maintaining a Microsoft Windows Server 2003 Environment (70-290)
- Implementing, Managing, and Maintaining a Microsoft Windows Server 2003 Network Infrastructure (70-291)
- Planning and Maintaining a Microsoft Windows Server 2003 Network Infrastructure (70-293)
- Planning, Implementing, and Maintaining a Microsoft Windows Server 2003 Active Directory Infrastructure (70-294)

plus one of the following Design exams:

- Designing a Microsoft Windows Server 2003 Active Directory and Network Infrastructure (70-297)
- Designing Security for a Microsoft Windows Server 2003 Network 2000 Server Technologies (70-298)

plus one of a number of electives, including:

- Implementing and Supporting Microsoft Systems Management Server 2.0 (70-086)
- Installing, Configuring, and Administering Microsoft Internet Security and Acceleration (ISA) Server 2000, Enterprise Edition (70-227)

- Installing, Configuring, and Administering Microsoft SQL Server 2000 Enterprise Edition (70-228)
- Designing and Implementing Databases with Microsoft SQL Server 2000 Enterprise Edition (70-229)
- The Design exam not taken as a requirement

Also, if you are an MCSE on Windows 2000, you can take two Upgrade exams: Managing and Maintaining a Microsoft Windows Server 2003 Environment for an MCSA Certified on Windows 2000 and Planning, Implementing, and Maintaining a Microsoft Windows Server 2003 Environment for an MCSE Certified on Windows 2000. In addition, if you are an MCSE in Windows NT, you do not have to take the client requirement, but you do have to take the networking operating system, design, and an elective.

Windows 2000 and Windows 2003 Certification

Microsoft recently announced that they will distinguish between Windows 2000 and Windows Server 2003 certifications. Those who have their MCSA or MCSE certification in Windows 2000 will be referred to as "certified on Windows 2000." Those who obtained their MCSA or MCSE in the Windows Server 2003 will be referred to as "certified on Windows Server 2003."

If you are certified in Windows 2000, you can take either one Upgrade exam (for MCSA) or two Upgrade exams (for MCSE) to obtain your certification on Windows 2003.

Microsoft also introduced a clearer distinction between the MCSA and MCSE certifications, by more sharply focusing each certification. In the new Windows 2003 track, the objectives covered by the MCSA exams relate primarily to administrative tasks. The exams that relate specifically to the MCSE, however, deal mostly with design-level concepts. So, MCSA job tasks are considered to be more hands-on, while the MCSE job tasks involve more strategic concerns of design and planning.

The *Managing and Maintaining a Microsoft Windows Server 2003 Environment* Exam

The Managing and Maintaining a Microsoft Windows Server 2003 Environment exam covers concepts and skills related to managing and maintaining a Windows Server 2003 environment. It emphasizes the following elements of server management:

- Managing and maintaining physical and logical devices
- Managing users, computers, and groups
- Managing and maintaining access to resources

- Managing and maintaining a server environment
- Managing and implementing disaster recovery

This exam is quite specific regarding the Windows Server 2003 environment configuration and operational settings, and it can be particular about how administrative tasks are performed within the operating system. It also focuses on fundamental concepts of Windows Server 2003's operation. Careful study of this book, along with hands-on experience, will help you prepare for this exam.

Microsoft provides exam objectives to give you a general overview of possible areas of coverage on the Microsoft exams. Keep in mind, however, that exam objectives are subject to change at any time without prior notice and at Microsoft's sole discretion. Please visit Microsoft's Training and Certification website (www.microsoft.com/traincert) for the most current listing of exam objectives.

Types of Exam Questions

In an effort to both refine the testing process and protect the quality of its certifications, Microsoft has focused its Windows XP and Server 2003 exams on real experience and hands-on proficiency. There is a greater emphasis on your past working environments and responsibilities, and less emphasis on how well you can memorize. In fact, Microsoft says a certification candidate should have at least six months of hands-on experience.

Microsoft will accomplish its goal of protecting the exams' integrity by regularly adding and removing exam questions, limiting the number of questions that any individual sees in a beta exam, and adding new exam elements.

Exam questions may be in a variety of formats: Depending on which exam you take, you'll see multiple-choice questions, as well as select-and-place and prioritize-a-list questions. Simulations and case study–based formats are included as well. Let's take a look at the types of exam questions and examine the adaptive testing technique, so you'll be prepared for all of the possibilities.

With the release of Windows 2000, Microsoft stopped providing a detailed score breakdown. This is mostly because of the various and complex question formats. Previously, each question focused on one objective. The Windows Server 2003 exams, however, contain questions that may be tied to one or more objectives from one or more objective sets. Therefore, grading by objective is almost impossible. Also, Microsoft no longer offers a score. Now you will only be told if you pass or fail.

For more information on the various exam question types, go to www.microsoft
.com/traincert/mcpexams/policies/innovations.asp.

MULTIPLE-CHOICE QUESTIONS

Multiple-choice questions come in two main forms. One is a straightforward question followed
by several possible answers, of which one or more is correct. The other type of multiple-choice
question is more complex and based on a specific scenario. The scenario may focus on several
areas or objectives.

SELECT-AND-PLACE QUESTIONS

Select-and-place exam questions involve graphical elements that you must manipulate to successfully answer the question. For example, you might see a diagram of a computer network, as
shown in the following graphic taken from the select-and-place demo downloaded from
Microsoft's website.

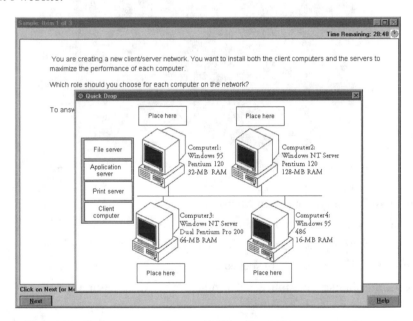

A typical diagram will show computers and other components next to boxes that contain
the text "Place here." The labels for the boxes represent various computer roles on a network,
such as a print server and a file server. Based on information given for each computer, you
are asked to select each label and place it in the correct box. You need to place *all* of the labels
correctly. No credit is given for the question if you correctly label only some of the boxes.

In another select-and-place problem you might be asked to put a series of steps in order, by
dragging items from boxes on the left to boxes on the right, and placing them in the correct order.

SIMULATIONS

Simulations are the kinds of questions that most closely represent actual situations and test
the skills you use while working with Microsoft software interfaces. These exam questions

include a mock interface on which you are asked to perform certain actions according to a given scenario. The simulated interfaces look nearly identical to what you see in the actual product, as shown in this example:

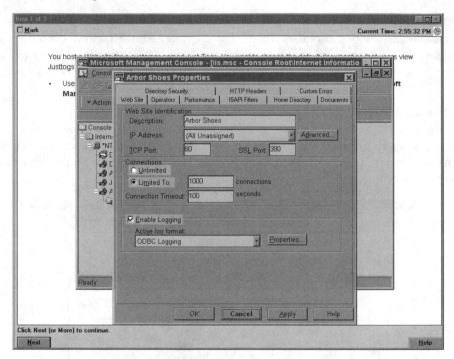

Because of the number of possible errors that can be made on simulations, be sure to consider the following recommendations from Microsoft:

- Do not change any simulation settings that don't pertain to the solution directly.

- When related information has not been provided, assume that the default settings are used.

- Make sure that your entries are spelled correctly.

- Close all the simulation application windows after completing the set of tasks in the simulation.

The best way to prepare for simulation questions is to spend time working with the graphical interface of the product on which you will be tested.

 We recommend that you study with the WinSim 2003 product, which is included on the CD that accompanies this Study Guide. By completing the exercises in this Study Guide and working with the WinSim 2003 software, you will greatly improve your level of preparation for simulation questions.

CASE STUDY–BASED QUESTIONS

Case study–based questions first appeared in the MCSD program. These questions present a scenario with a range of requirements. Based on the information provided, you answer a series of multiple-choice and select-and-place questions. The interface for case study–based questions has a number of tabs, each of which contains information about the scenario.

At present, this type of question appears only in most of the Design exams.

Microsoft will regularly add and remove questions from the exams. This is called *item seeding*. It is part of the effort to make it more difficult for individuals to merely memorize exam questions that were passed along by previous test-takers.

Exam Question Development

Microsoft follows an exam-development process consisting of eight mandatory phases. The process takes an average of seven months and involves more than 150 specific steps. The MCP exam development consists of the following phases:

Phase 1: Job Analysis Phase 1 is an analysis of all the tasks that make up a specific job function, based on tasks performed by people who are currently performing that job function. This phase also identifies the knowledge, skills, and abilities that relate specifically to the performance area being certified.

Phase 2: Objective Domain Definition The results of the job analysis phase provide the framework used to develop objectives. Development of objectives involves translating the job-function tasks into a comprehensive package of specific and measurable knowledge, skills, and abilities. The resulting list of objectives—the *objective domain*—is the basis for the development of both the certification exams and the training materials.

Phase 3: Blueprint Survey The final objective domain is transformed into a blueprint survey in which contributors are asked to rate each objective. These contributors may be MCP candidates, appropriately skilled exam-development volunteers, or Microsoft employees. Based on the contributors' input, the objectives are prioritized and weighted. The actual exam items are written according to the prioritized objectives. Contributors are queried about how they spend their time on the job. If a contributor doesn't spend an adequate amount of time actually performing the specified job function, his or her data are eliminated from the analysis. The blueprint survey phase helps determine which objectives to measure, as well as the appropriate number and types of items to include on the exam.

Phase 4: Item Development A pool of items is developed to measure the blueprinted objective domain. The number and types of items to be written are based on the results of the blueprint survey.

Phase 5: Alpha Review and Item Revision   During this phase, a panel of technical and job-function experts reviews each item for technical accuracy. The panel then answers each item and reaches a consensus on all technical issues. Once the items have been verified as being technically accurate, they are edited to ensure that they are expressed in the clearest language possible.

Phase 6: Beta Exam   The reviewed and edited items are collected into beta exams. Based on the responses of all beta participants, Microsoft performs a statistical analysis to verify the validity of the exam items and to determine which items will be used in the certification exam. Once the analysis has been completed, the items are distributed into multiple parallel forms, or *versions*, of the final certification exam.

Phase 7: Item Selection and Cut-Score Setting   The results of the beta exams are analyzed to determine which items will be included in the certification exam. This determination is based on many factors, including item difficulty and relevance. During this phase, a panel of job-function experts determines the *cut score* (minimum passing score) for the exams. The cut score differs from exam to exam because it is based on an item-by-item determination of the percentage of candidates who answered the item correctly and who would be expected to answer the item correctly.

Phase 8: Live Exam   In the final phase, the exams are given to candidates. MCP exams are administered by Prometric and Virtual University Enterprises (VUE).

Tips for Taking the Managing and Maintaining a Microsoft Windows Server 2003 Environment Exam

Here are some general tips for achieving success on your certification exam:

- Arrive early at the exam center so that you can relax and review your study materials. During this final review, you can look over tables and lists of exam-related information.

- Read the questions carefully. Don't be tempted to jump to an early conclusion. Make sure you know *exactly* what the question is asking.

- On simulations, do not change settings that are not directly related to the question. Also, assume default settings if the question does not specify or imply which settings are used.

- For questions you're not sure about, use a process of elimination to get rid of the obviously incorrect answers first. This improves your odds of selecting the correct answer when you need to make an educated guess.

Exam Registration

You may take the Microsoft exams at any of more than 1000 Authorized Prometric Testing Centers (APTCs) and VUE Testing Centers around the world. For the location of a testing center near you, call Prometric at 800-755-EXAM (755-3926), or call VUE at 888-837-8616. Outside the United States and Canada, contact your local Prometric or VUE registration center.

Find out the number of the exam you want to take, and then register with the Prometric or VUE registration center nearest to you. At this point, you will be asked for advance payment for the exam. The exams are $125 each and you must take them within one year of payment. You can schedule exams up to six weeks in advance or as late as one working day prior to the date of the exam. You can cancel or reschedule your exam if you contact the center at least two working days prior to the exam. Same-day registration is available in some locations, subject to space availability. Where same-day registration is available, you must register a minimum of two hours before test time.

You may also register for your exams online at www.prometric.com or www.vue.com.

When you schedule the exam, you will be provided with instructions regarding appointment and cancellation procedures, ID requirements, and information about the testing center location. In addition, you will receive a registration and payment confirmation letter from Prometric or VUE.

Microsoft requires certification candidates to accept the terms of a Non-Disclosure Agreement before taking certification exams.

Is This Book for You?

If you want to acquire a solid foundation in managing and maintaining a Windows Server 2003 environment, and your goal is to prepare for the exam by learning how to use and manage the new operating system, this book is for you. You'll find clear explanations of the fundamental concepts you need to grasp, and plenty of help to achieve the high level of professional competency you need to succeed in your chosen field.

If you want to become certified as an MCSE or MCSA, this book is definitely for you. However, if you just want to attempt to pass the exam without really understanding Windows Server 2003 management and maintenance, this Study Guide is *not* for you. It is written for people who want to acquire hands-on skills and in-depth knowledge of Windows Server 2003 management and maintenance exam.

What's in the Book?

What makes a Sybex Study Guide the book of choice for over 100,000 MCPs? We took into account not only what you need to know to pass the exam, but what you need to know to take what you've learned and apply it in the real world. Each book contains the following:

Objective-by-objective coverage of the topics you need to know Each chapter lists the objectives covered in that chapter.

The topics covered in this Study Guide map directly to Microsoft's official exam objectives. Each exam objective is covered completely.

Assessment Test Directly following this introduction is an Assessment Test that you should take. It is designed to help you determine how much you already know about Windows Server 2003 management and maintenance. Each question is tied to a topic discussed in the book. Using the results of the Assessment Test, you can figure out the areas where you need to focus your study. Of course, we do recommend you read the entire book.

Exam Essentials   To highlight what you learn, you'll find a list of Exam Essentials at the end of each chapter. The Exam Essentials section briefly highlights the topics that need your particular attention as you prepare for the exam.

Key Terms and Glossary   Throughout each chapter, you will be introduced to important terms and concepts that you will need to know for the exam. These terms appear in italic within the chapters, and a list of the Key Terms appears just after the Exam Essentials. At the end of the book, a detailed Glossary gives definitions for these terms, as well as other general terms you should know.

Review questions, complete with detailed explanations   Each chapter is followed by a set of Review Questions that test what you learned in the chapter. The questions are written with the exam in mind, meaning that they are designed to have the same look and feel as what you'll see on the exam. Question types are just like the exam, including multiple choice, exhibits, and select-and-place.

Hands-on exercises   In each chapter, you'll find exercises designed to give you the important hands-on experience that is critical for your exam preparation. The exercises support the topics of the chapter, and they walk you through the steps necessary to perform a particular function.

Real World Scenarios   Because reading a book isn't enough for you to learn how to apply these topics in your everyday duties, we have provided Real World Scenarios in special sidebars. These explain when and why a particular solution would make sense, in a working environment you'd actually encounter.

Interactive CD   Every Sybex Study Guide comes with a CD complete with additional questions, flashcards for use with an interactive device, a Windows simulation program, and the book in electronic format. Details are in the following section.

What's on the CD?

With this new member of our best-selling MCSE Study Guide series, we are including quite an array of training resources. The CD offers numerous simulations, bonus exams, and flashcards to help you study for the exam. We have also included the complete contents of the Study Guide in electronic form. The CD's resources are described here:

The Sybex E-book for MCSA/MCSE: Windows Server 2003 Environment Management and Maintenance Study Guide   Many people like the convenience of being able to carry their whole Study Guide on a CD. They also like being able to search the text via computer to find specific information quickly and easily. For these reasons, the entire contents of this Study Guide are supplied on the CD, in PDF. We've also included Adobe Acrobat Reader, which provides the interface for the PDF contents as well as the search capabilities.

WinSim 2003   We developed the WinSim 2003 product to allow you to experience the multimedia and interactive operation of working with Windows Server 2003. WinSim 2003 provides both audio/video files and hands-on experience with key features of Windows Server 2003. Built around the Study Guide's exercises, WinSim 2003 will help you attain the knowledge and hands-on skills you must have in order to understand Windows Server 2003 (and pass the exam). Here is a sample screen from WinSim 2003:

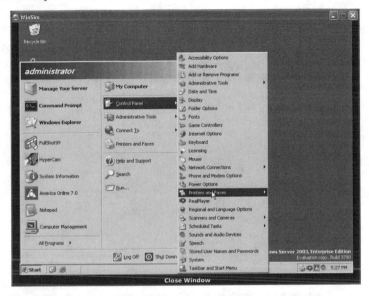

The Sybex Test Engine   This is a collection of multiple-choice questions that will help you prepare for your exam. There are four sets of questions:

- Two bonus exams designed to simulate the actual live exam.
- All the questions from the Study Guide, presented in a test engine for your review. You can review questions by chapter or by objective, or you can take a random test.
- The Assessment Test.

Here is a sample screen from the Sybex Test Engine:

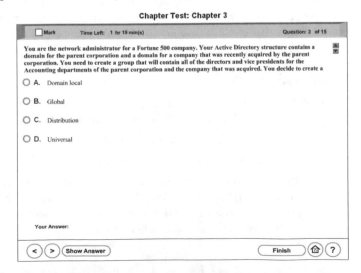

Sybex MCSE Flashcards for PCs and Handheld Devices   The "flashcard" style of question offers an effective way to quickly and efficiently test your understanding of the fundamental concepts covered in the exam. The Sybex Flashcards set consists of more than 100 questions presented in a special engine developed specifically for this Study Guide series. Here's what the Sybex Flashcards interface looks like:

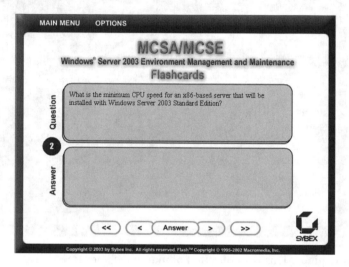

Because of the high demand for a product that will run on handheld devices, we have also developed, in conjunction with Land-J Technologies, a version of the flashcard questions that you can take with you on your Palm OS PDA (including the PalmPilot and Handspring's Visor).

 In addition, if you bought this book as part of the *MCSA: Windows 2003 Core Requirements* or the *MCSE: Windows 2003 Certification Kit* box set, you will find two bonus CDs—one including an 180-day evaluation version of Windows Server 2003 and another including two additional practice exams per book. Further information can be found in the readme files on the CDs, and instructions on how to install Windows Server 2003 can be found on the bottom of the box set.

How Do You Use This Book?

This book provides a solid foundation for the serious effort of preparing for the exam. To best benefit from this book, you may wish to use the following study method:

1. Take the Assessment Test to identify your weak areas.

2. Study each chapter carefully. Do your best to fully understand the information.

3. Complete all the hands-on exercises in the chapter, referring back to the text as necessary so that you understand each step you take. If you don't have access to a lab environment in which you can complete the exercises, install and work with the exercises available in the WinSim 2003 software included with this Study Guide.

To do the exercises in this book, your hardware should meet the minimum hardware requirements for Windows Server 2003. See below for a list of recommended hardware and software we think you should have in your home lab.

4. Read over the Real World Scenarios to improve your understanding of how to use what you learn in the book.

5. Study the Exam Essentials and Key Terms to make sure you are familiar with the areas you need to focus on.

6. Answer the review questions at the end of each chapter. If you prefer to answer the questions in a timed and graded format, install the Sybex Test Engine from the book's CD and answer the chapter questions there instead of in the book.

7. Take note of the questions you did not understand, and study the corresponding sections of the book again.

8. Go back over the Exam Essentials and Key Terms.

9. Go through the Study Guide's other training resources, which are included on the book's CD. These include WinSim 2003, electronic flashcards, the electronic version of the chapter review questions (try taking them by objective), and the two bonus exams.

To learn all the material covered in this book, you will need to study regularly and with discipline. Try to set aside the same time every day to study, and select a comfortable and quiet place in which to do it. If you work hard, you will be surprised at how quickly you learn this material. Good luck!

Hardware and Software Requirements

You should verify that your computer meets the minimum requirements for installing Windows Server 2003. We suggest that your computer meet or exceed the recommended requirements for a more enjoyable experience.

The exercises in this book assume that you have two computers, a Windows Server 2003 domain controller and a Windows XP Professional computer that is part of the domain.

Contacts and Resources

To find out more about Microsoft Education and Certification materials and programs, to register with Prometric or VUE, or to obtain other useful certification information and additional study resources, check the following resources:

Microsoft Training and Certification Home Page

www.microsoft.com/traincert

This website provides information about the MCP program and exams. You can also order the latest Microsoft Roadmap to Education and Certification.

Microsoft TechNet Technical Information Network

www.microsoft.com/technet

800-344-2121

Use this website or phone number to contact support professionals and system administrators. Outside the United States and Canada, contact your local Microsoft subsidiary for information.

Prometric

www.prometric.com

800-755-3936

Contact Prometric to register to take an MCP exam at any of more than 800 Prometric Testing Centers around the world.

Virtual University Enterprises (VUE)

www.vue.com

888-837-8616

Contact the VUE registration center to register to take an MCP exam at one of the VUE Testing Centers.

MCP Magazine Online

www.mcpmag.com

Microsoft Certified Professional Magazine is a well-respected publication that focuses on Windows certification. This site hosts chats and discussion forums, and tracks news related to the MCSE program. Some of the services cost a fee, but they are well worth it.

Windows & .NET Magazine

www.windows2000mag.com

You can subscribe to this magazine or read free articles at the website. The study resource provides general information on Windows Server 2003, Windows XP, Windows 2000 Server.

Cramsession on Brainbuzz.com

cramsession.brainbuzz.com

Cramsession is an online community focusing on all IT certification programs. In addition to discussion boards and job locators, you can download one of several free cram sessions, which are nice supplements to any study approach you take.

Assessment Test

1. You are responsible for managing all of the Windows licenses in your organization. You currently have a server called Server1 that is configured as the site license server. You want to centrally manage all of the Windows licenses from a server called Server2. How do you configure Server2 to be the site license server?

   A. Control Panel ➤ Licensing

   B. Administrative Tools ➤ Licensing

   C. Administrative Tools ➤ Services

   D. Administrative Tools ➤ Active Directory Sites and Services

2. You are the network administrator of a large network. You use a SUS server to manage all of the updates to the Windows computers within the network. As part of your general maintenance, you manually approve which updates will be applied to the network after you have tested the update. Which of the following actions would you use to view the SUS server's synchronization log?

   A. Administrative Tools ➤ SUSAdmin

   B. `http://yourservername/SUSAdmin`

   C. Administrative Tools ➤ SUS Administrator

   D. `http://yourservername/SUS`

3. You are the network administrator of a large network. You want to use MBSA to verify that the computers' operating systems and applications have the latest security updates. Which of the following operating systems and applications are scanned by MBSA? (Choose all that apply.)

   A. Windows NT 4

   B. Windows 2000

   C. Windows XP

   D. Windows Server 2003

   E. IIS 4 and 5

   F. Internet Explorer, versions 5.01 and higher

   G. SQL Server 7 and SQL Server 2000

   H. Microsoft Office 2000 and Microsoft Office XP

4. You are a network administrator in charge of all of the servers within the sales group. As part of your general maintenance of the servers, you want to verify that all of the drivers installed on each server are digitally signed and verified. You also want to ensure that you have the latest version of each driver. Which of the following utilities should you use to determine file signature verification?

   A. `sigverif`

   B. `verifsig`

   C. `dsv`

   D. `fsv`

5. You are the network administrator of a large network. You are in charge of all of the Sales servers. All of your servers use standardized hardware. You recently discovered that the network cards used by your servers have an updated driver. You obtained the updated driver and have verified that the driver is digitally signed by Microsoft. Which of the following utilities or processes should you use to install the updated driver?

   A. Control Panel ➢ Add Or Remove Hardware.

   B. Device Manager.

   C. Hardware Manager.

   D. Remove the hardware device, then reinstall it using the new driver.

6. You are the network administrator responsible for all of the servers within your organization. As a part of general maintenance you want to collect information about all of the servers' configurations, which will be stored as a part of the Help Desk database. The data you require includes the OS version, any Service Packs that have been applied, and the BIOS version and date for the server. Which of the following utilities will provide the information you require?

   A. Device Manager

   B. Hardware Manager

   C. System Information Utility

   D. Windows Diagnostics

7. Which of the following group types is not supported if your Windows 2003 domain is configured for mixed mode?

   A. Domain local group

   B. Global group

   C. Universal group

   D. Distribution group

8. You are the network administrator for your company. Your company recently acquired a smaller company that has 100 employees. You need to add the 100 new users to the Users domain on your Windows 2003 network. Which of the following command-line utilities will allow you to automate this process through a batch script?

 A. `Dsget`

 B. `Dsadd`

 C. `Dsuser`

 D. `Dscreate`

9. You are the network administrator for a large network. All of the marketing users use Windows XP Professional computers with a Windows 2003 domain. Each user within the group should use a standardized profile. You decide to implement a mandatory profile that will be shared by all users. After you copy the profile to a shared network location, which of the following steps should you take?

 A. Rename the `Ntuser.dat` file to `Ntuser.man`.

 B. Rename the `Ntuser.dat` file to `Ntuser.sav`.

 C. Change the file attributes in the `Ntuser.dat` file to Read-Only.

 D. Change the file attributes in the `Ntuser.dat` file to Mandatory.

10. You are the network administrator of a large network. You have a Windows Server 2003 member server that is currently experiencing a shortage of disk space on the D: drive. You add a new hard drive to the server and want to create a spanned volume to increase the space on the D: drive. Which of the following command-line utilities should you use?

 A. `Diskpart add`

 B. `Diskpart extend`

 C. `Dmanage add`

 D. `Dmanage extend`

11. You are the network administrator for a Windows 2003 network. You have decided to implement shadow copies on the Sales server on the D: volume, which is configured to use the NTFS file system. After you configure the volume to use shadow copies, you want to configure several client computers to be able to access the shadow copies. Which of the following steps must be taken before the clients can access the shadow copies?

 A. The users who will access the shadow copies must be given Full Control access to the shadow copy volume.

 B. The users who will access the shadow copies must be added to the Shadow Users group.

 C. The users who will access the shadow copies must be added to the Server Operators group.

 D. The users who will access the shadow copies must install the Shadow Copies Of Shared Folders software from the *windir*\system32\clients\twclient folder (located on a Windows Server 2003 share).

12. Select and Place. You are the network administrator of a Windows 2003 network. You have implemented disk mirroring on your Windows Server 2003 computers for fault tolerance. One of your servers experiences a failed mirrored volume. Which of the following actions should you take to repair the mirrored volume?

	Replace the failed drive
	From Disk Management right-click the mirrored volume and select Remove Mirror
	Recreate the mirror set
	Select Repair The Mirror Set through Disk Management

13. In Windows Server 2003, what default permissions are applied to NTFS volumes by default? (Choose all that apply.)

   A. The Everyone group has Full Control.

   B. The Administrators group has Full Control.

   C. The System group has Full Control.

   D. The Users group has Read & Execute, List Folder Contents, and Read.

14. In Windows Server 2003, what default permissions are applied to shared folders volumes by default? (Choose all that apply.)

   A. The Everyone group has Full Control.

   B. The Administrators group has Full Control.

   C. The System group has Full Control.

   D. The Everyone group has Read.

15. You are the network administrator of a large network. You want to create a shared folder on the Accounting server for the C:\2003 folder. You do not want this folder to be visible from any browse lists. What special character should you put behind the share name so that it will be hidden?

   A. *

   B. $

   C. %

   D. !

16. You have installed IIS on a Windows Server 2003 member server that will act as a clearing house for public information about your company. Which of the following Windows 2003 user accounts will be used when the website is accessed anonymously?

    A. IUSR_*computername*

    B. Guest

    C. IIS_Guest

    D. IIS_*computername*

17. You are in charge of configuring IIS security for your internal website. Which of the following methods of authentication are supported by IIS 6.0? (Choose all that apply.)

    A. Integrated Windows Authentication

    B. Digest Authentication For Windows Domain Servers

    C. MS-CHAP Authentication

    D. .NET Passport Authentication

18. Your company offers third-party hosting for websites. Websites are hosted on Windows Server 2003 member servers running IIS 6.0. Each server hosts multiple websites. You want to ensure that no single website consumes excessive bandwidth. Which of the following options should you configure for each website?

    A. Bandwidth throttling

    B. Process throttling

    C. Bandwidth allocation

    D. Network allocation

19. You have configured two printers for the marketing department, Laser1 and Laser2. The print device that was used by Laser1 experienced a breakdown that required it be sent out for maintenance. How can you configure Laser1 so that any print jobs that are sent to Laser1 are automatically redirected to Laser2?

    A. In the Port Name dialog box, type the UNC name of the printer that you want to redirect the jobs to, in the format *computername**printer_sharename*.

    B. In the Sharing Name dialog box, type the UNC name of the printer that you want to redirect the jobs to, in the format *computername**printer_sharename*.

    C. In the Sharing Name dialog box, type in the IP address of the printer that you want to redirect the jobs to.

    D. You can't redirect the print jobs; instruct all of the users to send their print jobs to Laser2.

20. You are the network administrator for a Windows 2003 network. You need to install five print devices that will be shared by the marketing department. You want the users to be able to have their jobs go to the first available print device, so you decide to implement a printer pool. Which of the following conditions must be met in order to use a printer pool?

A. All of the print devices must be of the same make and model.

B. All of the print devices must be able to use the same print driver.

C. You must create a printer for each print device, then link them through the Printer Pool configuration tab.

D. All of the printers must be network printers.

21. You are the network administrator for a medium-sized company. The administrative assistant for the Vice President of Marketing has a color laser printer attached to her computer. Two other users need occasional access to this printer. You share the network printer but want to make sure no other users can access the printer. What two actions should you take?

A. Assign the Everyone group No Access to the printer.

B. Remove the Everyone group Print permission to the printer.

C. Add the two users who need to access the printer to a group and grant their group Print permission to the printer.

D. Disable the browser service on the computer that the printer is attached to so that the printer will not be displayed within any browse lists.

22. You are the network administrator of a large company. You recently decided to integrate the Shipping department into the corporate network. The computers used by the Shipping department are older PCs. You decide to implement Terminal Services so users in the Shipping department can access the standard suite of corporate applications. In order to support Terminal Services, you need to configure Terminal Services licensing. Which of the following options will allow you to install Terminal Services Licensing?

A. Control Panel ➢ Add or Remove Programs ➢ Add/Remove Windows Components

B. Administrative Tools ➢ Terminal Services Manager

C. Administrative Tools ➢ Terminal Licensing Manager

D. Administrative Tools ➢ Licensing

23. You recently decided to implement Terminal Services to support a wide variety of legacy hardware still used within your corporation. When you tested the new configuration, some of the Terminal Service clients could connect to the Terminal Services server and some of the clients could not connect. You suspect that the problem is related to security settings. Which of the following settings should you use to promote a balance between connectivity and security for the Terminal Service clients?

A. No Security

B. Low

C. Client Compatible

D. FIPS Compatible

24. You are the network administrator of a Windows 2003 network. One of the Help Desk managers uses Windows 2000 Professional as their desktop operating system and wants to use Remote Desktop Connection (RDC) to make a Remote Desktop For Administration connection to Windows Server 2003 computers. What software needs to be installed on his client computer?

    A. *Windir*\System32\Clients\RDC\Win32 from a share on a Windows Server 2003 computer.

    B. *Windir*\System32\Clients\Tsclient\Win32 from a share on a Windows Server 2003 computer.

    C. Install the RDC software through Add Or Remove Programs in Control Panel.

    D. Install the Tsclient software through Add Or Remove Programs in Control Panel.

25. You are the network administrator for a large company. You want to allow members of the Help Desk to track, monitor, edit, and manage performance-related counters through System Monitor. Which of the following groups do the Help Desk members need to be added to that will allow them to complete this task without granting them excessive administrative rights?

    A. Power Users

    B. Server Operators

    C. Performance Log Users

    D. Performance Monitor Users

26. You are the network administrator of a large network. You are currently helping an administrator in a remote office troubleshoot a performance problem on one of the remote servers. The remote administrator is currently experiencing the performance-related problem. The System Monitor utility has been configured with key counters. Which of the following command-line utilities will allow the remote administrator to take the performance data that is in the current command window and write it to a data log file so that it can be e-mailed to you for analysis?

    A. Logman

    B. Relog

    C. Tracerpt

    D. Typeperf

27. You are the network administrator of a large network. You are running Windows Server 2003 on a member server in the Accounting department that appears to be performing sluggishly. You run System Monitor with counters for all of the key subsystems. When you analyze the data, you see the following averages reported for the following counters:

PhysicalDisk > Current Disk Queue Length: 6

Process > %Processor Time: 65

Memory > Available Mbytes: 8

Paging File > %Usage: 65

Based on the data, which of the following counters indicates a potential bottleneck?

A. PhysicalDisk > Current Disk Queue Length

B. Process > %Processor Time

C. Memory > Available Mbytes

D. Paging File > %Usage

28. You are the network administrator of a large network. One of your Windows Server 2003 domain controllers recently failed. You reinstalled Windows Server 2003 and now need to restore the System State data and the Active Directory. Which of the following steps should you take? (Choose all that apply.)

A. Restart the server in Directory Services Restore Mode.

B. Perform an authoritative restore using the `Ntdsutil.exe` command.

C. Perform a non-authoritative restore using the `Ntdsutil.exe` command.

D. Perform an authoritative restore using the `Ntdsrestore.exe` command.

29. You are the network administrator of a large network. You are designing a network backup strategy for all of the servers within the domain. Every Friday, you will perform a complete backup. On Saturday through Thursday you want to create backups at 1 A.M. and 1 P.M. that use the minimum amount of space. Which of the following backup options should you use?

A. Copy

B. Differential

C. Incremental

D. Daily

30. You are the network administrator of a large network. You want to configure all of the Windows Server 2003 member servers within the Active Directory so that whenever an Event Viewer event reports that there is less than 10% free disk space, the Disk Cleanup utility automatically runs. Which of the following utilities can be configured to trigger this event?

A. Eventcreate

B. Eventquery

C. Eventtriggers

D. Eventexecute

Answers to Assessment Test

1. **D.** The *site license server* is responsible for managing all of the Windows licenses for the site. The default license server is the first domain controller in the site. The site license server does not have to be a domain controller, but for best performance it is recommended that site license server and domain controller be in the same site. To determine which server is the site license server, you would take the following steps from a domain controller: Select Start ➢ Administrative Tools ➢ Active Directory Sites And Services. The Active Directory Sites And Services window will be displayed. Expand Sites and click on Default-First-Site. In the right-hand pane, you will see Licensing Site Settings. See Chapter 1 for more information.

2. **B.** In order to install and manage SUS, you must use IIS. You manage the SUS server through `http://yourservername/SUSAdmin` that starts the Software Update Services screen. See Chapter 1 for more information.

3. **A, B, C, D, E, F, G, H.** The Microsoft Baseline Security Analyzer (MBSA) is a security assessment utility that can be downloaded from the Microsoft website. It verifies whether your computer has the latest security updates and whether there are any common security violation configurations (configurations that could allow security breaches) that have been applied to your computer. The programs that are scanned by MBSA include all of those listed above. See Chapter 1 for more information.

4. **A.** Windows Server 2003 includes a File Signature Verification utility that you can use to verify that system files have been digitally signed. The installation of unsigned drivers can cause random lockups on a server. To run this utility, select Start ➢ Run; in the Run dialog box, type in **sigverif** and click OK. See Chapter 2 for more information.

5. **B.** Device manufacturers periodically update device drivers to add functionality or enhance driver performance. The updated drivers are typically posted on the device manufacturer's website. If you have an updated device driver, you can upgrade your device driver through the Device Manager utility. To update a driver, double-click the device in Device Manager and click the Driver tab. From the Driver tab, click the Update Driver button and the Hardware Update Wizard will start. You can let the wizard search for a newer driver or you can specify the new device driver's location. Once the wizard locates the updated files, they will be copied to your computer. See Chapter 2 for more information.

6. **C.** The *System Information utility* is used to collect and display configuration information for your server. The information can be viewed for the local server or a computer that you are connected to. You access the System Information utility through Start ➢ All Programs ➢ Accessories ➢ System Tools ➢ System Information. See Chapter 2 for more information.

7. **C.** In order to support universal groups, the domain must be configured for Windows 2000/2003 native mode. If the domain is configured for Windows 2000/2003 mixed mode (which supports Windows NT 4.0), universal groups are not supported. See Chapter 3 for more information.

8. **B.** Windows Server 2003 includes several command-line utilities for managing objects within the Active Directory. You can automate the process of creating users, groups, and computers through the `Dsadd` command-line utility. See Chapter 3 for more information.

9.   A.   A *mandatory profile* is a profile that can't be modified by the user. Only members of the Administrators group can manage mandatory profiles. You might consider creating mandatory profiles for users who should maintain consistent Desktops. By default the user profile is stored in a file called `Ntuser.dat`. You can create mandatory profiles for a single user or a group of users. The mandatory profile is stored in a file named `Ntuser.man`. A user with a mandatory profile can set different Desktop preferences while logged on, but those settings will not be saved when the user logs off. See Chapter 3 for more information.

10.   B.   The `DiskPart` command-line utility can be used to manage disks, partitions, and volumes from a command prompt or through the use of automated scripts. The `Diskpart extend` option is used to extend the specified volume. See Chapter 4 for more information.

11.   D.   You can configure the Client for Shadow Copies on Windows XP and Window Server 2003 computers. In order to use shadow copies, the client must install the Shadow Copies Of Shared Folders software. Windows Server 2003 computers have this software installed in the *windir*\system32\clients\twclient folder. See Chapter 4 for more information.

12.

From Disk Management, right-click the mirrored volume and select Remove Mirror
Replace the failed drive
Recreate the mirror set

If you have a mirrored volume fail, you would take the following steps: 1. In the Disk Management utility, right-click the failed mirrored volume (marked as Failed Redundancy) and choose Remove Mirror from the pop-up menu. 2. The Remove Mirror dialog box appears. Select the disk that will be removed from the mirrored volume and click the Remove Mirror button. 3. You will see a dialog box asking you to confirm that you want to remove the mirror. Click the Yes button. The remaining drive will become a simple volume. 4. Remove the failed hard drive from the computer and replace the drive, or use a spare drive. 5. Use the Disk Management utility to re-create the mirrored volume. See Chapter 4 for more information.

13.   B, C, D.   Default NTFS permissions have changed significantly from Windows NT and Windows 2000, which by default assigned the Everyone group Full Control permissions. In Windows Server 2003, the following permissions are applied to NTFS folders by default: Administrators group has Full Control (default permission inherited from the root folder, unless root folder permissions have been modified). System group has Full Control (default permission inherited from the root folder, unless root folder permissions have been modified). Users group has Read & Execute, List Folder Contents, and Read (default permission inherited from the root folder, unless root folder permissions have been modified). See Chapter 5 for more information.

14.   D.   Read is the default permission on shared folders for the Everyone group. In previous versions of Windows, the default permission for the Everyone group was Full Control. See Chapter 5 for more information.

15. B.   A share that is followed by a dollar sign ($) indicates that the share is hidden from view when users access utilities such as My Network Places and browse network resources. See Chapter 5 for more information.

16. A.   In order to access IIS, you must be logged in with a valid Windows 2003 user account. If you choose to allow anonymous access, your users will access your website through a user account called IUSR_*computername*. This user account is created when you install IIS, and can be viewed and managed through Active Directory Users And Computers. See Chapter 6 for more information.

17. A, B, D.   When users log on to your website through a valid Windows 2003 user account, you can specify that one of the following authentication methods be used: Integrated Windows Authentication, Digest Authentication For Windows Domain Servers, Basic Authentication (Password Is Sent In Clear Text), and .NET Passport Authentication. See Chapter 6 for more information.

18. A.   Bandwidth is defined as the total capacity of your transmission media. IIS allows you to limit how much network bandwidth can be used by a given website. This is called *bandwidth throttling*, and it prevents a particular website from hogging bandwidth and adversely affecting the performance of the other sites on the web server. When bandwidth throttling is enabled, IIS sets it to 1024 bytes per second (minimum); the maximum is 32,767 bytes per second. See Chapter 6 for more information.

19. A.   If your print device fails, you can redirect all of the jobs that are scheduled to be printed to that print device to another print device that has been configured as a printer. For this redirection to work, the new print device must be able to use the same print driver as the old print device. To redirect print jobs, click the Add Port button in the Ports tab, highlight Local Port, and choose New Port. In the Port Name dialog box, type the UNC name of the printer that you want to redirect the jobs to, in the format *computername**printer_sharename*. See Chapter 7 for more information.

20. B.   Printer pools are used to associate multiple physical print devices with a single logical printer. To configure a printer pool, click the Enable Printer Pooling checkbox at the bottom of the Ports tab and then check all of the ports that the print devices in the printer pool will attach to. If you do not select the Enable Printer Pooling option, you can select only one port per printer. All of the print devices within a printer pool must be able to use the same print driver. See Chapter 7 for more information.

21. B, C.   You can control which users and groups can access Windows Server 2003 printers by configuring the print permissions. In Windows Server 2003, you can allow or deny access to a printer. If you deny access, the user or group will not be able to use the printer. Deny permissions override allow permissions. By default, group Everyone has print permissions, so you need to remove this group's permissions, then explicitly assign permissions to the users who should be able to access the printer. See Chapter 7 for more information.

22. A.   You can enable Terminal Services Licensing when you install Windows Server 2003 or later, through the Add Or Remove Programs icon in Control Panel. When you enable Terminal Services Licensing, you can select between two types of license servers, an enterprise license server or a domain license server. See Chapter 8 for more information.

23. C. The Client Compatible setting encrypts data between the server and the client at the highest security level that can be negotiated between the server and the client. This encryption level is used with environments that support a mixture of Windows 2000 and higher and older legacy clients. See Chapter 8 for more information.

24. B. RDC is installed by default on Windows XP Professional and Windows Server 2003 computers. For other clients, you can install the software by creating a share on the *Windir*\System32\Clients\Tsclient\Win32 folder and then running the Setup program. See Chapter 8 for more information.

25. C. The Performance Log Users group is a security group that allows members to manage performance-related counters through System Monitor, or logs and alerts through Performance Logs And Alerts, on a local server or on a remote computer without having to be a member of the Administrators or Server Operators group. See Chapter 9 for more information.

26. D. Windows Server 2003 added new command-line utilities that allow you to manage system monitoring. The Typeperf command line utility takes performance counter data that is in the current command window and writes it to a counter data log file. See Chapter 9 for more information.

27. A. The PhysicalDisk > Current Disk Queue Length counter indicates the number of outstanding disk requests that are waiting to be processed. This value should be less than 2. A value greater than 2 indicates a disk bottleneck. See Chapter 9 for more information.

28. A, B. If you need to restore System State data on a domain controller, you should restart your computer with the advanced startup option Directory Services Restore Mode. This allows the Active Directory directory service database and the SYSVOL directory to be restored. If the System State data is restored on a domain controller that is a part of a domain where data is replicated to other domain controllers, you must perform an authoritative restore. For an authoritative restore, you use the Ntdsutil.exe command, then restart the computer. See Chapter 10 for more information.

29. C. Incremental backups will back up only the files that have not been marked as archived and sets the archive bit for each file that is backed up. Requires the last normal backup set and all of the incremental tapes that have been created since the last normal backup for the restore process. See Chapter 10 for more information.

30. C. There are several command-line utilities that can be used to manage event logs. Eventtriggers is used to configure or display an event trigger. For example, you could create an event trigger that monitors the percentage of free disk space and, when the number is below 10%, starts the Disk Cleanup utility. See Chapter 10 for more information.

Chapter 1

Installing, Licensing, and Updating Windows Server 2003

MICROSOFT EXAM OBJECTIVES COVERED IN THIS CHAPTER:

- ✓ Manage software update infrastructure.
- ✓ Manage software site licensing.

Windows Server 2003 provides the highest level of features and security compared to previous versions of Windows servers. This chapter will begin by introducing you to Windows Server 2003. You will start by learning about the features of Windows Server 2003 and the key features and differences between the versions within the Windows Server 2003 family of operating systems.

Before you can use Windows Server 2003, you have to install it. You need to know what the basic hardware requirements are, how to check for system compatibility, determine whether you will upgrade or use a clean installation, and understand the installation options. Once you have considered the options for installing Windows Server 2003, you are ready for the installation. To take advantage of Active Directory, you will need to upgrade your server to a domain controller after it is installed.

After your computer has been installed with Windows Server 2003 and configured as a domain controller, you will need to complete post-installation activation. This ensures that you are running a valid copy of Windows Server 2003.

In addition to activating Windows Server 2003, you need to ensure that the clients that connect to the server are properly licensed. You can manage licensing through a single server or through enterprise management using a site license server.

You also need to manage software installation and maintenance for your network. You can keep your software up-to-date through Windows Update, Windows Automatic Updates, and Software Update Services. The Microsoft Baseline Security Analyzer is used to ensure that your computer is configured in a secure manner.

Features of Windows Server 2003

The Windows Server 2003 family was originally going to be called Windows .NET Server. Early in 2003, Microsoft announced that the product family would be called Windows Server 2003. Windows .NET is a set of Microsoft technologies and software that are designed to work together to provide a high level of services, compatibility, and XML (Extensible Markup Language) Web services. Windows Server 2003 is the server component of .NET services. Windows Server 2003 builds upon the features of Windows NT and Windows 2000.

The main features of Windows Server 2003 include:

- Active Directory
- File and Print Services
- Security
- Networking and Communications

- Application Services
- Management Services
- Storage Management Services
- Internet Information Server (IIS) 6.0
- Terminal Services
- Windows Media Services
- Universal Description, Discovery, and Integration (UDDI) Services

In the following sections, you will learn more about the enhancements and new features that have been added to Windows Server 2003 compared to Windows NT Server 4 and Windows 2000 Server.

Active Directory

Active Directory has been enhanced so that it supports easier deployment and management, increased security, and improved performance and dependability. New features within Windows Server 2003 for Active Directory include:

- Active Directory Migration Tool (ADMT) 2.0, which allows migration of users and passwords from Windows NT 4.0 domains or Windows 2000 domains to Windows 2003 domains.

- New support for renaming DNS and/or NetBIOS names of existing domains within a forest. This allows greater support for companies that merge or are restructured.

- New group policy management tool called Microsoft Group Policy Management Console (GPMC), which allows users to manage group policy for multiple domains and sites within a specified forest. The User Interface (UI) is simplified and allows drag-and-drop support and functionality for backup, restore, copy, import, and reporting of Group Policy Objects (GPOs).

- Improvement to the MMC, which allows administrators to have better drag-and-drop capability, ability to save and reuse queries, and the ability to select and manage multiple objects concurrently.

- Support for cross-forest authentication, which allows secure access for a user who is located in one forest accessing resources in another forest.

- Support for inter-forest permissions, which allows administrators in one forest to add users and groups to Discretionary Access Control Lists (DACLs) from trusted forests.

- Support for cross-certification, if cross-forest trusts have been configured. This allows Internet Authentication Service/ Remote Authentication Dial-In User Server (IAS/RADIUS) authentication for user accounts from the trusted forests. RADIUS (Microsoft's IAS) is equipment-to-equipment authentication. The equipment is authenticated first and then the user is authenticated. For example, two routers verify password authentication and then the user account can be authenticated in a normal manner.

- Improved Credential Manager, which allows a secure store of user password and X.509 certificates.

- Software restriction policies, which are lists of software that is allowed to be installed on client computers through the use of GPOs. You can specify that software that is not on the list can't be installed.

- Enhanced logon for remote sites, which increases the speed by which remote users can log on.

- Better management of how group membership changes are replicated. Only the delta changes are replicated as compared to replicating all group information when changes are made.

- Ability of the Active Directory database to be initially replicated from media as opposed to being populated from the network.

- Better dependability through a new feature called Health Monitoring, which is used to verify replications between domain controllers. Improved scaling of forests and sites (compared to Windows 2000) with the use of an improved Inter-Site Topology Generator (ISTG). The speed and dependability of global catalog replication has also been enhanced.

 The Active Directory is covered in great detail in *MCSE: Windows 2003 Active Directory Planning, Implementation, and Maintenance Study Guide* by Anil Desai with James Chellis (Sybex, 2003).

File and Print Services

File and print management is one of the most critical server roles. Windows Server 2003 improves file and print services through higher dependability, increased productivity, and better connectivity. New features for file and print services include:

- Improved reliability with enhanced Automated System Recovery (ASR), which is used to recover the system and restore files in the event of system failure. The key improvement in ASR is one-step restore of the operating system, system state, and hardware configuration. ASR is covered in greater detail in Chapter 10, "Performing System Recovery Functions."

- Ability to support remote document sharing over the Internet through Web Distributed Authoring and Versioning (WebDAV).

- New command-line utilities for supporting disk management tasks and file system tuning. The new command-line utilities for disk management are covered in greater detail in Chapter 4, "Managing Disks."

- New GUID Partition Table (GPT) that is used with Windows Server 2003 64-bit edition, which replaces the Master Boot Record (MBR) used with 32-bit versions of Windows. With GPT partitions there are redundant primary and backup partition tables for better data structure integrity.

- Improved Windows Defragmenter Tool, which is faster and more efficient than the version that was used with Windows 2000. The Disk Defragmenter utility is covered in greater detail in Chapter 4.

- Enhanced Distributed File System (DFS), which now can be used with Active Directory to publish DFS objects as Volume objects and allow delegation of administration for DFS objects. There is also a new service called DFS File Replication Service (FRS), which is used to replicate DFS within the Active Directory.

- Improved Encrypting File System (EFS), which now runs as an integrated system service. EFS is covered in greater detail in Chapter 4.

- New kernel APIs, which provide new support for antivirus applications.

- Faster CHKDSK, which runs 20% to 38% faster after an unplanned disk shutdown or disk failure than it did in Windows 2000. CHKDSK is covered in greater detail in Chapter 4.

- New feature called shadow copies, which creates copies of network shares, and is used to roll back to a previous copy of a file in the event that a shared file is overwritten, deleted, or corrupted. Shadow copies are covered in greater detail in Chapter 4.

- New command-line utilities for managing printing. The new command-line utilities for managing printing are covered in Chapter 7, "Managing Printing."

- New 64-bit print drivers for 64-bit editions of Windows Server 2003. The new Point-n-Print 64-bit drivers can support both 32-bit and 64-bit clients.

- Added support for over 3,800 print devices.

- Improved support for publishing printers to Active Directory.

- New support for wireless (IEEE 802.11 and 802.1X, and Bluetooth) devices.

- Broader support for cross-platform printing support for AppleTalk, LPR/LPD, and IPX print protocols. Cross-platform printing support is covered in Chapter 7.

Security

Windows Server 2003 provides the highest level of security of any of the Windows platforms to date. Security enhancements have been added through general improvements in security, public key infrastructure, and secure Internet accessibility. Specific enhancements to security include:

- Improved Internet Connection Firewall (ICF), which is designed to act as a firewall for computers directly connected to the Internet.

- Better support for authentication of users who connect to the network via wireless and Ethernet LANs. New support is also included for IEEE 802.11 protocols.

- New support for IAS, which is used by RADIUS to manage remote user connections and authentication.

- New software restriction policies, which are used by administrators to specify policy or execution enforcement. For example, through software restriction policies specific applications can only be run from specified directories, which is used to prevent Trojan viruses from running.

- Improved web server security through IIS 6.0. IIS is covered in Chapter 6, "Managing Internet Information Services."

- New options to support the encryption of off-line files.

- Protocol support for RFC 2617 and RFC 2222, which is a digest authentication protocol and is used with IIS and the Active Directory.

- Better system security performance with Secure Sockets Layer (SSL), which is 35% faster with Windows Server 2003 compared to Windows 2000 Server.

- Ability of SSL session cache to be used by multiple processes, which increases performance by reducing the number of times reauthentication is required by applications.

- Automatic enrollment and deployment of X.509 certificates to users. Certificates can also be automatically renewed as they expire.

- Improved support for digital signatures in conjunction with Windows Installer packages.

- Through the Certificate Server that ships with Windows Server 2003, support for delta Certificate Revocation Lists (CRLs), which makes the publication of revoked X.509 certificates more efficient.

- New support for Microsoft Passport integration with Active Directory and Windows Server 2003.

- Support for cross-forest trusts.

Networking and Communications

Windows Server 2003 makes significant improvements to networking and security, which are critical to network operations. Some of the key improvements are extended versatility, better reliability and security, and more simplified management. Specific improvements include:

- Support for the latest generation of TCP/IP, which is IPv6. IPv6 makes improvements over IPv4 in the areas of address depletion, auto-configuration capabilities, and enhanced security. Windows Server 2003 supports IPv6 through an enhanced Internet Explorer (IE), IIS, and Internet file and print sharing utilities such as telnet and the ftp client software.

- A new Point-to-Point Protocol over Ethernet (PPPoE) driver that is used to make broadband connections to Internet Service Providers (ISPs) without requiring additional software.

- Better support for network bridging when using wireless adapters, Ethernet adapters, or dial-up adapters.

- Ability to support IPSec-based VPNs or IPSec-protected applications across Network Address Translation (NAT). Also allows support of Layer Two Tunneling Protocol (L2T2) over IPSec.

- Support for DNS client settings through Group Policy.

- Enhanced Connection Manager Administration Kit (CMAK) for providing remote access to clients running Windows XP, Windows 2000, Windows NT 4, Windows Me, or Windows 98.

- Enhancements to IAS, which allows you to better support wireless network deployments using RADIUS servers.

- New Network Load Balancing Manager that is used to load-balance TCP/IP traffic on an IEEE 1394 serial bus.

The networking and communications technologies are covered in greater detail in *MCSA/MCSE: Windows Server 2003 Network Infrastructure Implementation, Management, and Maintenance Study Guide* by Michael Chacon with James Chellis (Sybex, 2003).

Application Services

Windows Server 2003 is designed to better support application integration and interoperability, help developers produce better applications, increase efficiency, improve scalability and reliability, provide a high level of application security, and provide efficient deployment and management of applications. To help support these goals, the following options have been added or improved in Windows Server 2003:

- Native support for XML Web services, for standards including XML, Simple Object Access Protocol (SOAP), Universal Description, Discovery, and Integration (UDDI), and Web Services Description Language (WSDL).

- Enterprise UDDI support that allows companies to use their own custom UDDI services for internal or external use.

- A common .NET framework, which makes it easier for software developers to develop applications across Windows platforms.

- Integrated support for applications through IIS 6.0.

- Improved ASP .NET cacheing model, which improves performance.

- Improved security for applications through integration with Active Directory, plus added support for .NET Passport.

- New support for application-installed tools, such as Fusion, which makes deploying applications easier and more reliable.

Management Services

The new management services in Windows Server 2003 are designed to make management more dependable, provide greater productivity, and provide greater connectivity. Specific improvements to management services include:

- The Group Policy Editor has been added, which makes it easier to manage the Active Directory.

- A new tool, the Resultant Set of Policy (RSoP). The RSoP snap-in is used to determine what the effective policies are when Group Policies have been applied at many layers of Active Directory to a user or computer.

- New policy settings that are used to manage configurations such as Remote Assistance, AutoUpdating, and Error Reporting.

- Improved help features within the Group Policy Editor that explain functions and supported environments for group policy objects.

- New support for creation and management of cross-forests.

- More comprehensive software restriction policies.

- Updated Remote Installation Services (RIS) to support remote installations of XP Professional and 32-bit/64-bit editions of Windows Server 2003, with the exception of Windows Server 2003, Datacenter Edition.

- New Windows Server 2003 tools, including remote server operation via an /s switch on the command-line utility.

- Improved Windows Update to more fully support keeping all of your Windows files up-to-date. Windows Update can also be configured for Automatic Updating, manually or through Group Policy. Windows Update is covered in greater detail later in this chapter in the section, "Using Windows Update."

 The management services related to Active Directory are covered in greater detail in *MCSE: Windows 2003 Active Directory Planning, Implementation, and Maintenance Study Guide* by Anil Desai with James Chellis (Sybex, 2003).

Storage Management Services

Storage management services are used to manage volumes and disks, backup and restore operations, and access to Storage Area Networks (SANs). Windows Server 2003 adds the following features and improvements in storage management services:

- A new service called Virtual Disk Service (VDS), which enables support for multi-vendor storage devices through native Windows support.

- The Volume Shadow Copy service, which can be used to create shadow copies in conjunction with SANs.

- Ability for offline files to be encrypted with EFS.

- Support for open file backups, which allow you to back up a file without it being closed, in conjunction with shadow copies. Backups are covered in Chapter 10.

- A new command-line utility, Diskpart.exe, that includes all of the functionality of Disk Manager, an MMC snap-in.

- Enhanced DFS to allow support for multiple DFS roots on a single server.

Internet Information Server (IIS) 6.0

Internet Information Server is included with Windows Server 2003 to provide scalable, integrated Web services. By default, IIS is not loaded on Windows Server 2003 during installation, and must be manually installed through Add/Remove Programs. The enhancements to IIS 6.0 include:

- Application health monitoring and automatic application recycling.

- Improved security and manageability over previous versions of IIS. By default, maximum security settings are applied.
- A new kernel mode driver, `http.sys`, used to improve scalability and performance.
- URL authorization in conjunction with Authorization Manager, used to control access and manage administrator delegation.
- Ability for IIS to use URLs that are encoded with Unicode, which is used to support multi-languages.

IIS is covered in greater detail in Chapter 6.

Terminal Services

Terminal Server is used to provide Windows-based applications to clients, even if the client computer is not capable of running Windows. This allows you to leverage server processing power for client computers. The improvements to Terminal Server in Windows Server 2003 include:

- Better scalability; more users are supported than were with Windows 2000.
- Improved user interface for the client software, the Remote Desktop Connection. Additionally, users can more easily set up and save connections, and switch between windowed and full mode screens.
- Enhanced Remote Desktop Protocol (RDP) giving better support for accessing resources, such as printers.
- Ability to set color depth and screen resolution higher than with previous versions on Terminal Server.
- Terminal Server now better able to take advantage of Windows Server 2003 features such as software restriction policies, enhancements to roaming profiles, and new application compatibility modes.

Terminal Services are covered in greater detail in Chapter 8, "Administering Terminal Services."

Windows Media Services

Windows Media Services are used for distribution of digital media content over an intranet or the Internet. Advances to Windows Media Services include:

- Fast stream technology, which bypasses buffering delays, to provide instant-on playback capabilities.

- Always-on Fast Cache, which streams playback to the client computer via streaming content as fast as the player's cache and network will allow.

- Fast recovery, which is used to reduce or eliminate packet corruption through local packet correction technology.

- Fast reconnect technology, which reconnects a connection to the Internet faster if a client is disconnected during a broadcast.

- Support now provided for integrating with third-party AD servers, and support for advanced usage reporting.

- Improved wizards that provide scenario-based help for completing common management activities for audio and video streaming needs.

Universal Description, Discovery, and Integration (UDDI) Services

UDDI services are used to provide dynamic and flexible XML Web services. UDDI provides web developers with the ability to create applications more easily and make the applications easier to manage through Windows Server 2003. Some of the key improvements to UDDI services include:

- Enterprise service based on the Microsoft .NET framework. UDDI services can be automatically published and discovered through web-based interfaces.

- Can take advantage of Active Directory features such as authentication and authorization.

- Supports programming inquiries through the UDDI API or a web interface.

- Active monitoring to allow auditing of all authenticated activities including the username and the activity that was completed.

Windows Server 2003 Family Features

Windows Server 2003 is available in four different versions:

- Windows Server 2003, Standard Edition
- Windows Server 2003, Enterprise Edition
- Windows Server 2003, Datacenter Edition
- Windows Server 2003, Web Edition

Windows Server 2003, Standard Edition is designed for the most common server environments. Windows Server 2003, Enterprise Edition is designed for larger enterprise environments or businesses that require higher reliability and performance. Windows Server 2003, Datacenter Edition is designed for businesses that use mission-critical applications and also need a higher level of scalability and reliability. Windows Server 2003, Web Edition is designed to be optimized for hosting web servers. By offering different editions, Microsoft ensures that consumers and businesses can select the product family that best suits their needs and budget.

Table 1.1 summarizes the features found in the different Server 2003 families:

TABLE 1.1   Windows Server 2003 Feature Comparison

Feature	Web Edition	Standard Edition	Enterprise Edition	Datacenter Edition
.NET Framework	Yes	Yes	Yes	Yes
Act as a Domain Controller in the Active Directory	No	Yes	Yes	Yes
Microsoft Metadirectory Services (MMS) support	No	No	Yes	Yes
Internet Information Services (IIS) 6.0	Yes	Yes	Yes	Yes
ASP .NET	Yes	Yes	Yes	Yes
Enterprise UDDI services	No	Yes	Yes	Yes
Network load balancing	Yes	Yes	Yes	Yes
Server clusters	No	No	Yes	Yes
Virtual Private Network (VPN) support	Only supports one connection per media type	Yes	Yes	Yes
Internet Authentication Services (IAS)	No	Yes	Yes	Yes
Ipv6	Yes	Yes	Yes	Yes
Distributed File System (DFS)	Yes	Yes	Yes	Yes
Encrypting File System (EFS)	Yes	Yes	Yes	Yes
Shadow Copy Restore	Yes	Yes	Yes	Yes
Removable and Remote Storage	No	Yes	Yes	Yes
Fax services	No	Yes	Yes	Yes
Services for Macintosh	No	Yes	Yes	Yes
Print Services for Unix	Yes	Yes	Yes	Yes

TABLE 1.1   Windows Server 2003 Feature Comparison *(continued)*

Feature	Web Edition	Standard Edition	Enterprise Edition	Datacenter Edition
Terminal Services	No	Yes	Yes	Yes
IntelliMirror	Yes	Yes	Yes	Yes
Remote OS Installation (RIS)	Yes	Yes	Yes	Yes
64-bit support for Itanium-based computers	No	No	Yes	Yes
Datacenter Program	No	No	No	Yes

In addition to providing different product families, Windows Server 2003 also comes in 32-bit editions, which are used with Pentium-based computers (also referred to as *x*86-based computers), and a 64-bit edition (for Windows Server 2003 Enterprise Edition and Windows Server 2003 Datacenter Edition). The 64-bit edition of Windows Server is compatible only with Itanium-based systems and can't be installed on 32-bit *x*86-based systems. Previously known by the code name Merced, the Itanium processor employs a 64-bit architecture and enhanced instruction handling to greatly increase the performance of computational and multimedia operations, and supports clock speeds of up to 800MHz. The Itanium 2 processor uses a 128-bit architecture and supports speeds of 900MHz and 1GHz.

Preparing to Install Windows Server 2003

Planning and preparation are key to making your Windows Server 2003 installation proceed smoothly. Before you begin the installation, you should know what is required for a successful installation and have all the pieces of information you'll need to supply during the installation process. In preparing for the installation, you should make sure you have the following information:

- What the hardware requirements are for Windows Server 2003
- How to determine whether your hardware is supported by Windows Server 2003
- Determine whether your system is compatible with Windows Server 2003
- The difference between a clean installation and an upgrade
- What installation options are suitable for your system, such as which disk-partitioning scheme and file system you should select for Windows Server 2003 to use

Hardware Requirements

In order to install Windows Server 2003 successfully, your system must meet certain hardware requirements. Table 1.2 lists the minimum requirements as well as the more realistic recommended requirements.

 The hardware requirements listed in Table 1.2 were those specified at the time this book was published. Check Microsoft's website for the most current information.

TABLE 1.2   Hardware Requirements for Windows Server 2003

	Web Edition	Standard Edition	Enterprise Edition	Datacenter Edition
Minimum RAM	128MB	128MB	128MB	512MB
Recommended RAM	256MB	256MB	256MB	1GB
Maximum RAM	2GB	4GB	32GB for *x*86-based computers, 64GB for Itanium-based computers	64GB for *x*86-based computers, 512GB for Itanium-based computers
Minimum CPU Speed	133MHz	133MHz	133MHz for *x*86-based computers, 733MHz for Itanium-based computers	400MHz for *x*86-based computers, 733MHz for Itanium-based computers
Recommended minimum CPU speed	550MHz	550MHz	733MHz	733MHz
Multiprocessor Support	Up to 2	Up to 4	Up to 8	Minimum of 8, maximum of 32 for 32-bit version, 64 for Itanium-based computer
Free disk storage for setup	1.5GB	1.5GB	1.5GB for *x*86-based computers, 2GB for Itanium-based computers	1.5GB for *x*86-based computers, 2GB for Itanium-based computers
Cluster nodes	No	No	Up to 8	Up to 8

These requirements represent the operating system requirements. If you are running any processor- or memory-intensive tasks or applications, factor those requirements separately. When determining disk-space requirements for add-on software and data, a good rule of thumb is to plan what you need for the next 12 months, then double that number.

Depending on the installation method you choose, other devices may be required:

- If you are installing Windows Server 2003 from the CD, you should have at least a 12x CD-ROM drive.

- If you choose to install Windows Server 2003 from the network, you need a network connection and a server with the distribution files.

The Hardware Compatibility List (HCL)

Along with meeting the minimum requirements, your hardware should appear on the *Hardware Compatibility List (HCL)*. The HCL is an extensive list of computers and peripheral hardware that have been tested with the Windows Server 2003 operating system.

The Windows Server 2003 operating system requires control of the hardware for stability, efficiency, and security. The hardware and supported drivers on the HCL have been put through rigorous tests. If you call Microsoft for support, the first thing a Microsoft support engineer will ask about is your configuration. If you have any hardware that is not on the HCL, there is no guarantee of support.

To determine if your computer and peripherals are on the HCL, check the most up-to-date list at www.microsoft.com/hcl.

Checking System Compatibility

The Windows Server 2003 CD comes with a utility to check system compatibility. When you launch the CD, you'll see several options, one being Check System Compatibility.

When you check system compatibility, you can select:

- Check My System Automatically

- Visit The Compatibility Web Site

If your computer is not connected to the Internet, you would select Check My System Automatically. If you are connected to the Internet, selecting Visit The Compatibility Web Site will allow your computer to be checked against the most updated information.

The Windows compatibility check will determine whether your system meets the minimum requirements for Windows Server 2003 and whether the hardware components that are installed are compatible. If any errors are found, a report will be created and details can be viewed.

Clean Install or Upgrade

Once you've determined that your hardware not only meets the minimum requirements but is also on the HCL, you need to decide whether you want to do a clean install or an upgrade. A clean install installs Windows Server 2003 in a new folder and uses all of the Windows Server 2003 default settings. An upgrade preserves existing settings from an operating system that is on the upgrade list.

If you already have Windows NT Server 4 or Windows 2000 Server installed on your computer, you might want to upgrade that system to Windows Server 2003. In an upgrade, you retain previous settings such as the Desktop, users and groups, and program groups and items. During an upgrade, you point to a prior operating system, and the Windows Server 2003 files are loaded into the same folder that contained the former operating system.

The only operating systems that can be directly upgraded to Windows Server 2003 are Windows NT Server 4 SP5 or greater and Windows 2000 Server. Any other operating systems cannot be upgraded, but they may be able to coexist with Windows Server 2003 in a multi-boot environment.

If you don't have Windows NT Server 4 or Windows 2000 Server, you need to perform a clean install. A clean install puts the operating system into a new folder and uses its default settings the first time the operating system is loaded. You should perform a clean install if any of the following conditions are true:

- There is no operating system currently installed.
- You have an operating system installed that does not support an upgrade to Windows Server 2003 (such as DOS, Windows 3.*x*, Windows 9*x*, Windows XP, Windows NT 3.51 Server, or Windows 2000 Professional).
- You want to start from scratch, without keeping any existing preferences.
- You want to be able to dual-boot between Windows Server 2003 and your previous operating system.

Installation Options

There are many choices that you will need to make during the Windows Server 2003 installation process. The following are some of the options that you will configure:

- How your hard disk space will be partitioned
- The file system your partitions will use
- The licensing method the computer will use
- Whether the computer will be a part of a workgroup or a domain
- The language and locale for the computer's settings

    The process for a clean installation is described in the next section.

Installing Windows Server 2003

Before you install Windows Server 2003, you should check for system compatibility. Once you have ensured that your computer is compatible, you can begin the Windows Server 2003 installation process.

The Windows Server 2003 installation process consists of five main stages:

- Collecting information
- Updating dynamically
- Preparing installation
- Installing Windows
- Finalizing installation

The stages you see during your installation will vary based on the installation option you are using. For example, if you boot to the Window Server 2003 CD and start a new installation, you will not use Dynamic Update. If you are upgrading or starting the installation from an existing operating system, you would see the Dynamic Update stage.

Steps for Windows Server 2003 Installation

If you are installing Windows Server 2003 on an Itanium processor, you would insert the Windows Server 2003 Itanium CD and restart the computer. When the EFI Boot manager appears, select the CD-ROM option, and select Windows Server 2003 CD. You will then boot from the CD-ROM and follow the onscreen instructions as if you were installing a 32-bit version of Windows Server 2003.

The steps in the following sections assume that the disk drive is clean and that you are starting the installation using the Windows Server 2003 CD.

The following sections give the details of the installation process to show how the process works. But you should not actually install Windows Server 2003 until you reach the "Setting Up Your Computers for Hands-on Exercises" section. In the exercises in that section, you'll set up a domain controller and a Windows XP Professional computer, which you'll use to complete the rest of the exercises in this book.

If you have installed previous versions of Windows, you will notice that this is the most streamlined installation to date. Installing Windows Server 2003 can be broken into three phases:

1. Collecting information and preparing for the installation
2. Installing Windows
3. Finalizing the installation

We will look at each of these phases in the following sections.

Collecting Information and Preparing Installation

To start collecting information and preparing for the installation, follow these steps:

1. Boot your computer using the Windows Server 2003 distribution CD.

2. The text mode portion of Setup will start, and through the process will advise you to press F6 if you need to install any additional SCSI or RAID device drivers or F2 if you want to run the Automated System Recovery (ASR) utility. If you have a SCSI or RAID driver that is not provided through the Windows Server 2003 CD, you would press F6; otherwise ignore these prompts and setup will continue.

3. The Welcome To Setup dialog box will appear. You can set up Windows by pressing Enter, repair an existing Windows installation by pressing R to run the Recovery Console, or quit Windows Setup by pressing F3. In this example, you would press Enter to continue.

4. The Windows License Agreement dialog box appears. You can accept the license agreement by pressing F8, or Esc if you do not agree. If you do not agree to the license agreement, the installation process will terminate. In this case, you would press F8 to continue.

5. The next dialog box asks you which partition you want to use to set up Windows Server 2003. You can pick a partition that already exists, or you can choose free space and create a new partition. To set up Windows Server 2003 on an existing partition, you would highlight the partition you want to use for installation and press Enter. To create a new partition, you would press C. To delete an existing partition, you would press D. If you create a new partition, you can format it as NTFS or FAT32.

6. After you select your partition and it is formatted, the installation files will be automatically copied to your computer. This requires no user intervention. Once this process is complete, the computer will reboot.

Installing Windows

To actually start installing Windows, follow these steps.

1. Once the computer has rebooted, the Windows installation will automatically continue using the Setup Wizard. The installation process will detect and install device drivers and copy any needed files. This process will take several minutes, and during this process, your screen may flicker.

2. The Regional And Language Options dialog box will appear. From this dialog box, you choose your locale and keyboard settings. Locale settings are used to configure international options for numbers, currencies, times, and dates. Keyboard settings allow you to configure your keyboard to support different local characters or keyboard layouts. For example, you can choose Danish or United States–Dvorak through this option. Once you make your selection, click Next to continue.

3. The Personalize Your Software dialog box appears. In this dialog box, you fill in the Name and Organization boxes. This information is used to personalize your operating system

software and the applications that you install. If you install Windows Server 2003 in a workgroup, the Name entry here is used for the initial user. Type in your information and click the Next button.

4. The Your Product Key dialog box appears. From the product key located on the yellow sticker on the back of the Windows Server 2003 CD folder, type in the 25-character product key and click the Next button.

5. The Licensing Modes dialog box appears. You can choose from Per Server licensing or Per Seat licensing. Licensing is covered in greater detail in the "Managing Licensing" section later in this chapter. Make your selection and click the Next button. If you're unsure which licensing mode to use, select Per Server.

6. The Computer Name And Administrator Password dialog box appears. Here you specify a name that will uniquely identify your computer on the network. The Setup Wizard will suggest a name, but you can change it to another name. In this dialog box, you also type and confirm the Administrator password. An account called Administrator will automatically be created as a part of the installation process. Verify that the computer name is correct or specify a name and an Administrator password and click the Next button to continue. If you do not use a complex password (upper case, lower case, number, or symbol) a warning will appear.

Be sure that the computer name is a unique name within your network. If you are part of a corporate network, you should also verify that the computer name follows the naming convention specified by your Information Services (IS) department.

7. If you have a Plug and Play modem installed, you will see the Modem Dialing Information dialog box. Here, you specify your country/region, your area code (or city code), whether you dial a number to get an outside line, and whether the telephone system uses tone dialing or pulse dialing. Select the applicable options and click the Next button.

8. The Date And Time Settings dialog box will appear. In this dialog box, you set your date and time settings and the time zone in which your computer is located. You can also configure the computer to automatically adjust for daylight savings time (recommended). Verify that the correct settings are selected and click the Next button.

9. The Network Settings dialog box appears. This dialog box is used to specify how you want to connect to other computers, networks, and the Internet. You have two choices:

   ▪ Typical Settings installs network connections for Client for Microsoft Networks, as well as File and Print Sharing for Microsoft Networks. It also installs the TCP/IP protocol with an automatically (DHCP) assigned address.

   ▪ Custom Settings allows you to customize your network settings. You can choose whether or not you want to use Client for Microsoft Networks, File and Print Sharing for Microsoft Networks, and the TCP/IP protocol. You should use the custom settings if you need to specify particular network settings, such as a specific IP address and subnet mask (rather than using an automatically assigned address).

   Once you make your selection, click the Next button to continue.

10. The Workgroup Or Computer Domain dialog box appears. In this dialog box, you specify whether your computer will be installed as a part of a local workgroup or as a part of a domain. Once you make your selection, click the Next button.

11. Based on your selections, the Windows installation process will automatically copy any needed files. The computer will also perform some final tasks, including installing Start menu items, registering components, saving settings, and removing any temporary files. This will take several minutes (there is a countdown clock) and is fully automated. After this process is complete, your computer will automatically restart.

Finalizing Installation

To finalize the installation, follow these steps:

1. Windows Server 2003 will automatically start. Press Ctrl+Alt+Delete to access the Log On To Windows dialog box. By default, Administrator will be specified for the User Name. Type in your Administrator password and click the OK button.

2. The Manage Your Server dialog box will automatically appear.

You will learn how to upgrade a member server to a domain controller using the Manage Your Server utility in the next section.

Using Active Directory and Domain Controllers

While the Active Directory is not a focus of this exam, you should have a basic understanding of what it is and how it is organized. In this section, you will learn about the Active Directory through an overview of Active Directory, and then you will learn how to promote a Windows Server 2003 member server to a domain controller.

 Active Directory will be covered in greater detail in the *MCSE: Windows 2003 Active Directory Planning, Implementation, and Maintenance Study Guide* by Anil Desai with James Chellis (Sybex, 2003).

Overview of Active Directory

The Windows 2003 *Active Directory (AD)* is designed to be a scalable network structure. The logical structure of the Active Directory consists of *containers*, *domains*, and *organizational units (OUs)*.

A container is an Active Directory object that holds other Active Directory objects. Domains and OUs are examples of container objects.

A domain is the main logical unit of organization in the Active Directory. The objects in a domain share common security and account information. Each domain must have at least one domain controller. The *domain controller* is a Windows Server 2003 computer that stores the complete domain database.

Each domain can consist of multiple OUs, logically organized in a hierarchical structure. OUs may contain users, groups, security policies, computers, printers, file shares, and other Active Directory objects.

Domains are connected to one another through logical structure relationships. The relationships are implemented through domain trees and domain forests.

A domain tree is a hierarchical organization of domains in a single, contiguous namespace. In the Active Directory, a tree is a hierarchy of domains that are connected to each other through a series of trust relationships (logical links that combine two or more domains into a single administrative unit). The advantage of using trust relationships between domains is that they allow users in one domain to access resources in another domain, assuming the users have the proper access rights.

A forest is a set of trees that does not form a contiguous namespace. For example, you might have a forest if your company merged with another company. With a forest, you could each maintain a separate corporate identity through your namespace, but share information across Active Directory.

An example of an Active Directory structure is shown in Figure 1.1.

FIGURE 1.1   Active Directory Structure

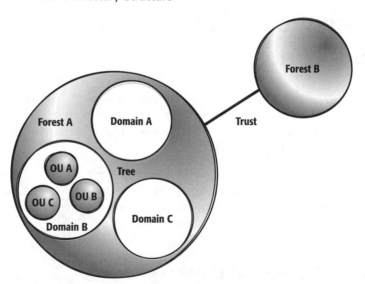

In the following sections, you will learn about domains, organizational units, and trees and forests in more detail.

Domains

The most basic Windows 2003 security structure is the domain. Domains are independent administrative units, with their own security and administrative policies. All domain controllers within a domain replicate their information to each other automatically. This is known as a multi-master replication model. Any domain controller can receive changes and then replicate these out to other domain controllers within the domain.

To allow for an orderly migration from NT 4 to Windows 2003 domains, the Windows 2003 domain includes Active Directory support for communication with existing NT domain structures and security. This is done through the use of a mixed-mode domain model. Then, after all your domains have been upgraded to Windows 2003 domains, you can perform a onetime conversion to native mode. Native-mode domains have additional features that are unavailable to mixed-mode domains, but no longer support NT 4 domain controllers.

Since Windows 2000 and Windows 2003 share the same directory services model, the upgrade from Windows 2000 Server to Windows Server 2003 requires no special configuration.

Organizational Units (OUs)

Within the Active Directory, you can categorize the objects in the domain by using organizational units (OUs). Organizational units are typically defined based on geography or function and the scope of administrative authority, such as the following examples:

Limiting administrative authority within the domain   If your company has three campuses (buildings within different geographic locations), you can create an OU for each, and assign a different administrator to each.

Organizing users by function   OUs can be created for Sales, Accounting, Manufacturing, etc. Users and resources can then be added to these and can be managed as a group. In Figure 1.2, users and resources have been arranged using organizational units.

FIGURE 1.2   Organizational units by function

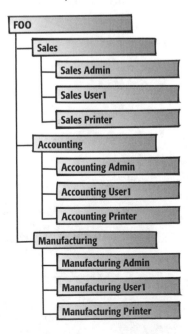

The beauty of combining Active Directory's capability to support millions of objects and its capability to subdivide domains into organizational units is that a single domain will be all that many companies ever need.

Trees and Forests

Microsoft's use of the words *tree* and *forest* can be confusing. You do not, for instance, need a bunch of trees to make a forest. A tree is simply a set of domains that all have a similar DNS naming structure, and a forest consists of all the trees within a single organization.

When the first server is installed in a new domain (for instance, foo.com), it becomes a domain controller within that domain and also is the parent domain of a new tree. If you are not adding to an existing forest, this tree also becomes the root tree of a new forest. Although you have installed only one server, you now have a domain, a tree, and even a forest.

The real difference between a tree and a forest is not in the numbers. Within a single tree, all the domains must fall under a contiguous namespace. Assume that you have created the domain called foo.com in your New York office, and now want to create additional geographically based domains in Hong Kong, Rome, and Fargo. If you want to allow permissions to flow without the use of trusts, you need to put the new domains into the same tree. To do this, the new domains will need to incorporate the existing DNS name.

In the next section, you will learn about trees and forests in more detail.

Trees

In the top graphic in Figure 1.3, notice how the DNS namespaces are in different branches. These, therefore, cannot be in a single tree. In the bottom graphic, the three new domains nest under the foo.com parent domain and share its DNS namespace. They are able to incorporate into the tree.

FIGURE 1.3   Sample DNS namespaces

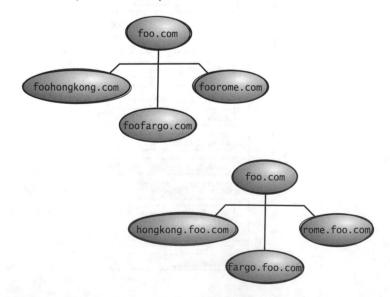

What all of this means is that if you have a company with four offices, you may want to split up network administration by using four autonomous domains in a tree. As long as the naming structure is not an issue, this is the easiest and most integrated approach to adding domains.

Forests

Forests are similar to trees in that both are ways of connecting domains. Forests are created to connect domains whose naming conventions make them incompatible for use in a single tree, or can also be used to keep two domains distinct from each other.

The first tree you create also becomes the root tree of a new forest. As new domains are added, you have three choices:

- Create the new domain as a child domain in the existing tree. If you simply create the new domain as a child domain, permissions and other configuration information automatically are shared between the domains.

- Create the new domain as a new tree in the existing forest. Configuration data—the schema and global catalog—will be shared, but the domains will be separate administrative entities. The new tree will have automatic two-way transitive trusts with the old tree.

- Create the new domain as a new tree in a new forest. This provides the greatest degree of administrative separation and makes interaction between the domains more difficult. No configuration data is shared, and trusts must be set up to share resources between forests.

Remember that Windows 2003 Active Directory will support millions of users and other objects. You should begin by assuming a single domain/tree/forest is best, and only modify this plan based on particular requirements of your company or client.

Upgrading a Server to a Domain Controller

Once a server has been installed with Windows Server 2003, you can upgrade it to a domain controller through the Dcpromo utility. The following steps assume that the server will be the first server installed into the domain and DNS is not already installed.

To upgrade a Windows Server 2003 member server to a domain controller, take the following steps:

1. Select Start ➢ Run. In the Run dialog box, type **Dcpromo** and click the OK button.

2. You will see the Welcome To The Active Directory Installation Wizard dialog box. Click the Next button.

3. The Operating System Compatibility dialog box will appear notifying you that Windows Server 2003 domain security does not support Windows 95 or Windows NT 4.0 Service Pack 3 or earlier clients. Click the Next button.

4. The Domain Controller Type dialog box will appear, as shown in Figure 1.4. Verify that Domain Controller For A New Domain is selected and click the Next button.

FIGURE 1.4   Domain Controller Type dialog box

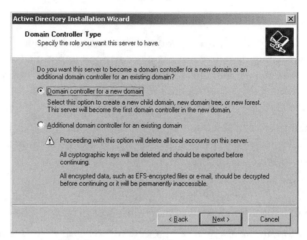

5. The Create New Domain dialog box will appear, as shown in Figure 1.5. Verify that Domain In A New Forest is selected and click the Next button.

FIGURE 1.5   Create New Domain dialog box

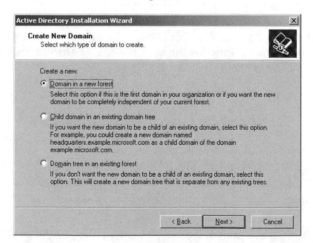

6. The New Domain Name dialog box will appear, as shown in Figure 1.6. Type in whatever domain name you wish to use. In this example, we are using Sybex.local. (The .local extension is not a legal extension and therefore cannot be connected directly to the Internet. If you are going to connect directly to the Internet, you must use a registered domain name.) Once you have specified your Active Directory domain name, click the Next button.

FIGURE 1.6   New Domain Name dialog box

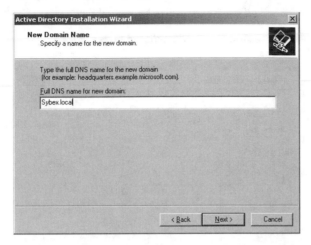

7. The NetBIOS Name dialog box will appear, as shown in Figure 1.7. NetBIOS names are used for compatibility with other Windows clients that are not using Windows 2000, Windows XP, or Windows Server 2003. You would typically accept the default values in this dialog box, then click the Next button.

FIGURE 1.7   NetBIOS Name dialog box

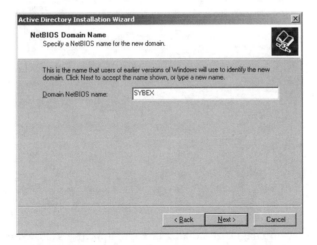

8. The Database And Log Folders dialog box will appear, as shown in Figure 1.8. You can accept the default values for the location of the Database folder and the Log folder or you can manually specify the location of these folders. Once you make your selection, click the Next button.

9. The Shared System Volume name dialog box will appear, as shown in Figure 1.9. The shared system volume is called SYSVOL and contains the domain's public files. You can accept the default location or manually specify the location of the SYSVOL folder. The SYSVOL folder must be installed on a NTFS partition. Once you make your selection, click the Next button.

FIGURE 1.8   Database And Log Folders dialog box

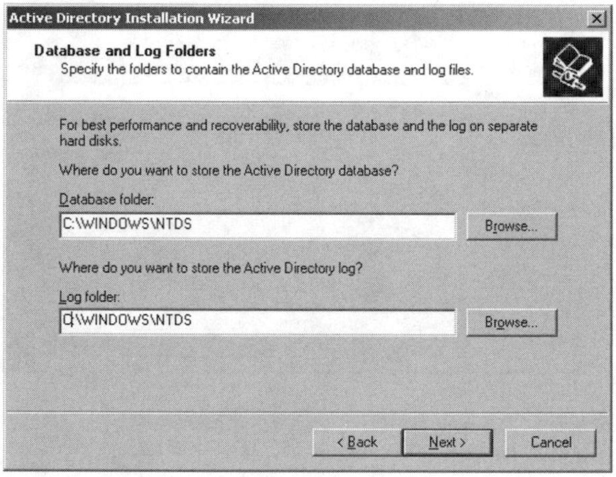

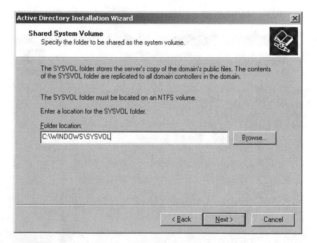

FIGURE 1.9   Shared System Volume dialog box

10. The DNS Registration Diagnostics dialog box will appear, as shown in Figure 1.10. This dialog box appears because DNS has not been installed in the network. Select Install And Configure The DNS Server On This Computer, And Set This Computer To Use This DNS Server As Its Preferred Server and click the Next button.

11. The Permissions dialog box will appear, as shown in Figure 1.11. You can select Permissions Compatible With Pre-Windows 2000 Server Operating Systems or Permissions Compatible Only With Windows 2000 or Windows Server 2003 Operating Systems. Make your selection and click the Next button.

FIGURE 1.10   DNS Registration Diagnostics dialog box

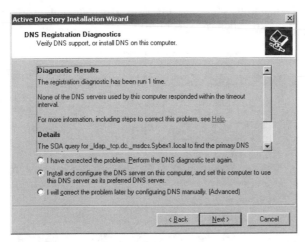

FIGURE 1.11   Permissions dialog box

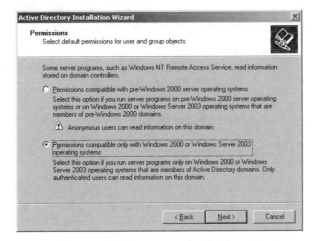

12. The Directory Services Restore Mode Administrator Password dialog box will appear, as shown in Figure 1.12. This password is associated with restoring Directory Services if it becomes corrupt or can not be accessed. Type in and confirm the Restore Mode Password and click the Next button.

13. The Summary dialog box will appear. Verify that your selections are correct and click the Next button.

14. The Active Directory Installation Wizard will configure the Active Directory, which will take several minutes. During this process you will need to insert the Windows Server 2003 distribution CD.

15. If the server was installed with a dynamic IP address you will see an Optional Networking Components dialog box notifying you that for DNS you must use a static IP address. Click the OK button. The Local Area Connection Properties dialog box will appear. If this is not a practice server, you should configure an IP address based on your corporate standards. Make your selections and click the OK button.

FIGURE 1.12   Directory Services Restore Mode Administrator Password dialog box

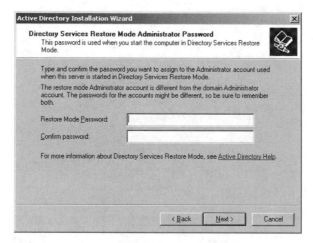

16. The Completing the Active Directory Installation Wizard dialog box will appear. Click the Finish button. You will be prompted to restart your computer. Click the Restart Now button.

Setting Up Your Computers for Hands-On Exercises

The exercises in this book assume that you have two computers configured in a specified manner. In order to complete all of the exercises throughout the book, you will install Windows Server 2003 on one computer as a domain controller within Active Directory, and Windows XP Professional on a second computer, which will act as a member computer of the domain. Both computers need to be networked and your Windows Server 2003 computer will require Internet access.

You should make a complete backup of your computer before doing any repartitioning or installation of new operating systems. All data will be lost during this process!

Installing Windows Server 2003 as a Domain Controller

For the exercises to work properly, you should make sure that the computer that will act as your server meets the list of requirements specified in Table 1.2. Your server should have a network card installed, and it should have at least a 2.5GB drive that is configured with the minimum space requirements and partitions. Other exercises in this book assume that your server is configured as follows:

- 2GB (about 2000MB) C: primary partition with the NTFS file system
- 500MB of free space (you will create a new partition with this free space in Chapter 4)

Of course, you can allocate more space to your partitions if it is available. Exercise 1.1 assumes that you are not currently running any previous versions of Windows and that you are performing a clean install and not an upgrade. Your partitions should be created and formatted, or you can create the primary partition through the installation process.

In Exercise 1.1, you will install Windows Server 2003, then upgrade the server to a domain controller. Before you start, you should note what values you will use for the following options for the domain controller:

- Name and organization
- Computer name
- Workgroup name
- Administrator password (if one will be assigned)
- Domain name

In this chapter the installation process assumes that you are using a 32-bit edition of Windows Server 2003. If you are using a 64-bit Itanium-based server, then refer to the Microsoft website for installation instructions.

EXERCISE 1.1

Installing Windows Server 2003 as a Domain Controller

Collecting Information and Preparing Installation

1. Boot your computer using the Windows Server 2003 distribution CD.

2. The text mode portion of Setup will start. If you have a SCSI or RAID driver that is not provided through the Windows Server 2003 CD, you would press F6; otherwise ignore these prompts and setup will continue.

3. The Welcome To Setup dialog box will appear. Press Enter to continue.

4. The Windows License Agreement dialog box appears. Press F8 to continue.

5. In the next dialog box, you can pick a partition that already exists, or you can choose free space and create a new partition. The partition you use must be formatted with NTFS since you will be upgrading this server to a domain controller.

6. After you select your partition (and it is formatted), the installation files will be automatically copied to your computer. This requires no user intervention. Once this process is complete, the computer will reboot.

EXERCISE 1.1 *(continued)*

Installing Windows

7. After the installation process detects and installs device drivers and copies any needed files, the Regional And Language Options dialog box will appear. Make your selections and click Next to continue.

8. The Personalize Your Software dialog box appears. Fill in the Name and Organization boxes and click the Next button.

9. The Your Product Key dialog box appears. From the product key located on the yellow sticker on the back of the Windows Server 2003 CD folder, type in the 25-character product key and click the Next button.

10. The Licensing Modes dialog box appears. Accept the default values and click the Next button.

11. The Computer Name And Administrator Password dialog box appears. Specify the computer name you want to use and type and confirm the Administrator password. Click the Next button to continue.

12. If you have a Plug and Play modem installed, you will see the Modem Dialing Information dialog box. Select the applicable options and click the Next button.

13. The Date And Time Settings dialog box will appear. Configure the appropriate date and time settings and click the Next button.

14. The Network Settings dialog box appears. Specify Typical Settings and click the Next button to continue.

15. The Workgroup Or Computer Domain dialog box appears. Select the No, This Computer Is Not On A Network, Or Is On A Network Without A Domain. Make this computer a member of the following workgroup: Workgroup. Click the Next button to continue.

16. Based on your selections, the Windows installation process will automatically copy any needed files, perform some final tasks, and automatically restart.

Upgrading Your Server to a Domain Controller

17. Select Start ➢ Run. In the Run dialog box, type **Dcpromo** and click the OK button.

18. You will see the Welcome To The Active Directory Installation Wizard dialog box. Click the Next button.

19. The Operating System Compatibility dialog box will appear notifying you that Windows Server 2003 domain security does not support Windows 95 or Windows NT 4.0 Service Pack 3 or earlier clients. Click the Next button.

20. The Domain Controller Type dialog box will appear. Verify that Domain Controller For A New Domain is selected and click the Next button.

21. The Create New Domain dialog box will appear. Verify that Domain In A New Forest is selected and click the Next button.

22. The New Domain Name dialog box will appear. Type in whatever domain name you wish to use. In this example, we are using Sybex.local. If you are going to connect directly to the Internet, you must use a registered domain name. Once you have specified your Active Directory domain name, click the Next button.

23. The NetBIOS Name dialog box will appear. Accept the default values in this dialog box, then click the Next button.

24. The Database And Log Folders dialog box will appear. Accept the default values for the location of the Database folder and the Log folder and click the Next button.

25. The Shared System Volume name dialog box will appear. Ensure SYSVOL is pointing to an NTFS partition, and accept the default location and click the Next button.

26. The DNS Registration Diagnostics dialog box will appear. Select Install And Configure The DNS Server On This Computer, And Set This Computer To Use This DNS Server As Its Preferred Server and click the Next button.

27. The Permissions dialog box will appear. Select Permissions Compatible Only With Windows 2000 or Windows 2003 Operating Systems and click the Next button.

28. The Directory Service Restore Mode Administration Password dialog box will appear. Leave the password as blank and click the Next button.

29. The Summary dialog box will appear. Verify that your selections are correct and click the Next button.

30. The Active Directory Installation Wizard will configure the Active Directory, which will take several minutes. During this process you will need to insert the Windows Server 2003 distribution CD.

31. Since the server was installed with a dynamic IP address you will see an Optional Networking Components dialog box notifying you that for DNS you must use a static IP address. Click the OK button. The Local Area Connection Properties dialog box will appear. Without assigning a static IP address, click the OK button. You will see a notification dialog box that you have chosen not to use a static IP address. Click the OK button.

32. The Completing the Active Directory Installation Wizard dialog box will appear. Click the Finish button. You will be prompted to restart your computer. Click the Restart Now button.

33. After the server restarts, log on as Administrator.

Installing Windows XP Professional within the Windows 2003 Domain

Once Windows Server 2003 has been installed and configured as a domain controller, you will install Windows XP Professional. The computer that will be installed with Windows XP Professional must meet the minimum requirements listed in Table 1.3.

TABLE 1.3   Hardware Requirements for Windows XP Professional

Component	Minimum Requirement	Recommended Requirement
Processor	Intel Pentium (or compatible) 233MHz or higher	Intel Pentium II (or compatible) 300MHz or higher
Memory	64MB	128MB
Disk space	1.5GB of free disk space	2GB or more of free disk space
Network	None	Network card and any other hardware required by your network topology if you want to connect to a network or if you will install over the network
Display	Video adapter and monitor with VGA resolution	Video adapter and monitor with SVGA resolution or higher
Peripheral devices	Keyboard, mouse, or other pointing device	Keyboard, mouse, or other pointing device
Removable storage	CD-ROM or DVD-ROM drive	12x or faster CD-ROM or DVD-ROM

Windows XP Professional is covered in *MCSE: Windows XP Professional Study Guide, Second Edition*, by Lisa Donald with James Chellis (Sybex, 2003).

If you do not have a computer already installed with Windows XP Professional, you will use Exercise 1.2 to install Windows XP Professional on a computer within the domain you created in Exercise 1.1 as part of the Windows Server 2003 installation. If you already have Windows XP Professional installed on a computer, use Exercise 1.3 to join your existing Windows XP Professional computer to the domain you created in Exercise 1.1. Before you start, note the following information that you will need to provide as a part of the installation process:

- Windows XP Professional Product Key
- Name of the registered user

- Organization name
- Computer name
- Administrator password

EXERCISE 1.2

Installing Windows XP Professional as a part of a Windows 2003 Domain

Information Collection

1. Boot your computer with the Windows XP CD inserted into your CD-ROM drive.

2. The Welcome To Setup screen appears. Press Enter to set up Windows XP Professional.

3. The License Agreement dialog box appears. Press F8 to agree to the license terms if you wish to continue.

4. In the next dialog box, if needed, create a partition, and then specify the C: partition as the one you want to use to set up Windows XP Professional. Then press Enter.

5. If you create a partition, in the next dialog box choose NTFS (Quick Format) for the file system and press Enter to continue. The file copying will take a few minutes to complete and your computer will reboot automatically.

Installing Windows

6. You will see a series of informational screens as the system does some background installation tasks.

7. The Regional And Language Options dialog box will appear. Verify that the settings are correct, and click the Next button.

8. In the Personalize Your Software dialog box, type your name and organization. Click the Next button.

9. In the Your Product Key dialog box, type the 25-character product key (this key can be found on a yellow sticker on the installation folder). Click the Next button.

10. The Computer Name And Administrator Password dialog box appears. Type in the computer name. You can also specify an Administrator password (or, since this computer will be used for practice, you can leave the Password field blank if you want to). Click the Next button.

11. If you have a Plug and Play modem installed, the Modem Dialing Information dialog box appears. Specify the settings for your environment and click the Next button.

12. The Date And Time Settings dialog box appears. Verify that all of the settings are correct, and click the Next button.

13. After the Networking Component files are copied (which takes a few minutes), the Network Settings dialog box appears. Confirm that the Typical Settings radio button is selected. Then click the Next button.

14. In the Workgroup And Computer Domain dialog box, select Yes, Make This Computer A Member Of The Following Domain and specify the domain name you specified in Exercise 1.1 (for example, sybex.local), then click the Next button.

15. The Join Computer To Domain dialog box will appear. For User Name, specify Administrator and for Password, the password you specified in Exercise 1.1. Click the OK button. The Setup components will be installed, which takes several minutes, and your computer will reboot as part of this process.

Finalizing Installation

16. The Welcome To Network Identification Wizard will start. Click the Next button to continue.

17. The User Account dialog box will appear. Click the Do Not Add A User At This Time radio button and click the Next button.

18. The Completing The Network Identification Wizard dialog box will appear. Click the Finish button.

19. In the Welcome To Windows dialog box, press Ctrl+Alt+Delete to start the logon process.

20. In the Log On To Windows dialog box, confirm that the username is Administrator and type in the password you specified in Exercise 1.1. Click the Options button. In the Log On To field, click the arrow to the right of the dialog box, and from the drop-down menu select the domain you specified in Exercise 1.1. Then click the OK button.

If you already have Windows XP Professional installed on a computer, you would use Exercise 1.3 to join the existing computer to the domain you created in Exercise 1.1.

Joining an Existing Windows XP Professional Computer to a Windows 2003 Domain

1. From Windows XP Professional, select Start, right-click My Computer, and select Properties.

2. From the System Properties dialog box, select the Computer Name tab, then click the Network ID button.

3.   The Network Identification Wizard will start. Click the Next button.

4.   In the Connecting To The Network dialog box, verify that the This Computer Is Part Of A Business Network, And I Use It To Connect To Other Computers At Work option is selected and click the Next button.

5.   The next question will ask what kind of network you use. Verify that the My Company Uses A Network With A Domain option is selected and click the Next button.

6.   The Network Information dialog box will appear. Click the Next button.

7.   The User Account And Domain Information dialog box will appear. For User Name, specify Administrator, and for Password and Domain, specify the options you configured in Exercise 1.1, then click the Next button.

8.   The User Account dialog box will appear. Click the Do Not Add A User At This Time option and click the Next button.

9.   The Completing The Network Identification Wizard dialog box will appear. Click the Finish button.

10. The Computer Name Changes dialog box will appear, notifying you that you need to restart the computer for the changes to take effect. Restart the computer and log on as Administrator to the domain you created.

Post-Installation Product Activation

Product activation is Microsoft's way of reducing software piracy. Unless you have a volume corporate license for Windows Server 2003 or are using a 64-bit version of Windows Server 2003 (which does not use product activation), you will need to perform post-installation activation. This can be done online or through a telephone call.

After Windows Server 2003 is installed, you will have 14 days to activate the license. After the 14-day grace period expires, you will not be able to restart Windows Server 2003 normally if you log out of the computer or if the computer is restarted. However, you can start Windows Server 2003 to Safe Mode. With Safe Mode, you will not have any networking capabilities, but you would have access to any folders or files located on the server.

When you activate Windows Server 2003, product activation uses the 25-character product key you provided during the Windows Server 2003 installation to create a product ID, which is a unique 20-character ID for your computer. A non-unique hardware hash will also be created based on general information for your server's hardware configuration, which creates a hardware identifier. Based on product ID and the hardware identifier, a unique installation ID is created. The installation ID is what activates Windows Server 2003.

When the installation ID is generated, you should store it in a safe place—for example, within the Windows Server 2003 installation folder. Then, if you need to re-install Windows Server 2003 on the same computer, you can use the installation ID that was previously generated. However, if you install Windows Server 2003 on a different computer, using a product key that has already been used, a new installation ID will need to be generated, as the hardware hash will not match.

 Microsoft scans no personal information during product activation. This process is completely anonymous.

To activate Windows Server 2003 over the Internet, you would take the following steps:

1. Select Start ➢ All Programs ➢ Activate Windows.

2. The Let's Activate Windows dialog box will appear, as shown in Figure 1.13. Select Yes, Let's Activate Windows Over The Internet Now and click the Next button.

FIGURE 1.13   Let's Activate Windows dialog box

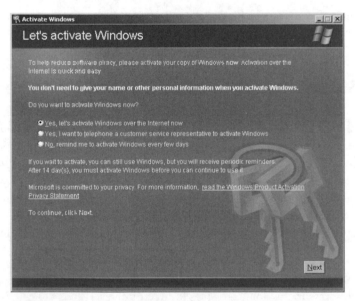

3. The Register With Microsoft? dialog box will appear, as shown in Figure 1.14, which gives you the option of registering Windows Server 2003 at the same time you activate it. In this example, we will skip registering Windows by clicking the No, I Don't Want To Register Now; Let's Just Activate Windows and click the Next button.

FIGURE 1.14 Register With Microsoft? dialog box

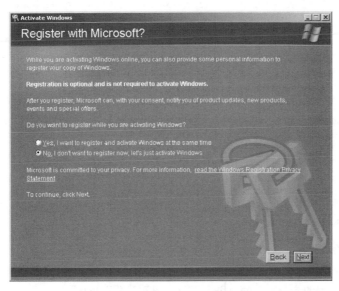

4. You will see a Thank You! dialog box indicating that you have successfully activated your copy of Windows.

Once Windows Server 2003 has been activated, you can see the Product ID listed through the properties of My Computer as shown in Figure 1.15.

FIGURE 1.15 Product ID shown through My Computer Properties dialog box

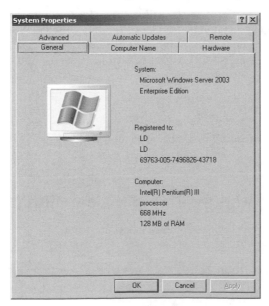

You can verify that Windows Server 2003 has been activated through Event Viewer in the Application Event Log. Event Viewer is covered in greater detail in Chapter 10.

You will need an Internet connection to complete Exercise 1.4. In this exercise, you will activate Windows Server 2003.

EXERCISE 1.4

Activating Windows Server 2003

1. Select Start ➤ All Programs ➤ Activate Windows.

2. The Let's Activate Windows dialog box will appear. Select Yes, Let's Activate Windows Over The Internet Now and click the Next button.

3. The Register With Microsoft? dialog box will appear. Click the No, I Don't Want To Register Now; Let's Just Activate Windows and click the Next button.

4. You will see a Thank You! dialog box indicating that you have successfully activated your copy of Windows.

Managing Licensing

Each Microsoft client must have a local client license. For example, if you have 100 computers running Windows 2000 Professional and 100 computers running Windows XP Professional, all 200 computers would have to have an appropriate client license. Additional licensing is required if the client computers will connect to Windows Server 2003 servers.

In the following sections you will learn:

- How to select a licensing mode
- How to configure the License Logging service
- How to administer licensing in a local environment
- How to administer licensing in an enterprise environment

Understanding and Selecting a Licensing Mode

Windows Server 2003 supports two types of client licensing:

- Per Server licensing
- Per Seat licensing (which includes Per Device or Per User licensing)

In the following sections, you will learn how to select which licensing option is right for your network and how to administer licensing.

Using Per Server Licensing

The *Per Server licensing* mode is the traditional method for client licensing. In this mode, the server must be licensed for each concurrent connection. For example, assume that you have five users and three servers, as shown in Figure 1.16. All five users need to access each of the three servers. Each of the three servers must be licensed per server, supporting five connections. If you added more users, they could technically access the server as long as no more than five concurrent users were accessing a single server at the same time. With Per Server licensing, clients are granted access on a first-come, first-served basis. Once the maximum number of clients for the license has been reached, any additional clients attempting to access the server will be denied access.

FIGURE 1.16 Per Server Licensing

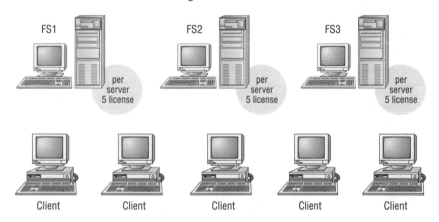

In an enterprise environment, where users need to access resources on multiple servers, Per Server licensing can be very expensive. However, in small companies where clients only need to access a single server, the per-server mode of licensing is less expensive than the Per Seat licensing mode. This option is also useful if you are supporting remote clients or your server is providing Internet services, and clients are only accessing a single server.

Using Per Seat (Per Device or Per User) Licensing

The *Per Seat licensing* mode is more practical for the enterprise environment. By purchasing a *Client Access License (CAL)* for each device or user, each client is licensed at the client side to access as many servers as needed.

When using the Per Seat licensing mode, you record the CALs. In Figure 1.17, note that the servers are only licensed for the server software, and the right to access the server is licensed at the client.

FIGURE 1.17 Per Seat Licensing

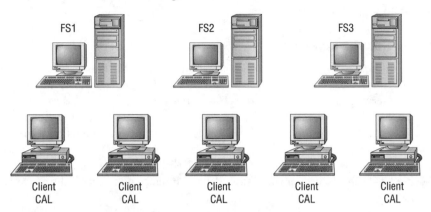

In environments where one user uses a computer, this would be referred to as Per Seat usage. However, some environments have special considerations and must require you to create license groups for Per Device and Per User licensing. You would create licensing groups in the following scenarios:

- You may have more than one user using a computer—if, for example, your organization has workers in shifts and users from different shifts all share a computer.
- You have many users who share many devices—for example, students working in a school computer lab.
- You have a single user who accesses many computers—for example, someone working in a test lab.

The licensing that would be required in these scenarios is as follows:

- If 10 or fewer users are sharing a single computer, then you only need one CAL.
- If one user is accessing multiple devices, you will need a CAL for each device.

You will learn how to create license groups in the "Administering Licensing in an Enterprise" section.

Administering the License Logging Service

If the *License Logging service* is running, Administrators can manage and track licensing through the Licensing option in Control Panel or the Licensing utility in Administrative Tools. If you were managing licenses for a single server, you would use the Licensing option in Control Panel. If you were managing licenses for an enterprise environment, you would use the Licensing Tools within Administrative Tools.

If the License Logging service has not been started, then licensing is not monitored, although it is still enforced. You can view the status and manage the License Logging service from Start ➢ Administrative Tools ➢ Services. From Services, you would double-click the License Logging service to see the dialog box shown in Figure 1.18.

FIGURE 1.18   License Logging Properties dialog box

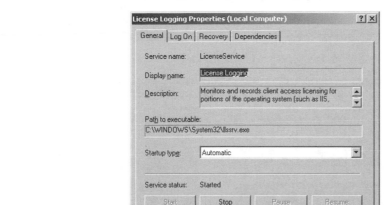

In order to use license logging, the following settings should be applied:

- Configure Startup Type as Automatic.
- If the Service Status is Stopped, click the Start button to start the service.

WARNING   Failure to start the License Logging service will prevent you from managing licenses through the Licensing option in Control Panel or through the Licensing utility in Administrative Tools.

In Exercise 1.5, you will configure the License Logging service.

EXERCISE 1.5

Configuring the License Logging Service

1. Select Start ➤ Administrative Tools ➤ Services.

2. Scroll down until you see the License Logging service, and double-click License Logging.

3. Click the Log On tab and under Log On As, click Local System Account.

4. Click the General tab. Under Startup Type, select Automatic.

5. Under Service Status, click the Start button. The service will start and the Service Status will display Started. Click the OK button.

6. Close the Service window.

Administering Licensing Locally

The Licensing option in Control Panel, as shown in Figure 1.19, is used to manage a local server's licensing. The following tasks can be managed:

▪ Add or remove CALs for the Per Server licensing mode

▪ Convert Per Server licensing to Per Device or Per User licensing (a onetime conversion from Per Server to Per Seat licensing is allowed, at no charge)

▪ Configuration of replication frequency if the server's licensing is managed on a centralized licensing server

FIGURE 1.19   Choose Licensing Mode dialog box

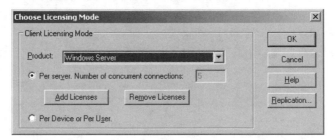

In the following sections, you will learn about managing specific tasks through the Licensing option in Control Panel.

Managing Per Server Connections

If you are using Per Server licensing, you can add or remove licenses with the Add Licenses and Remove Licenses buttons.

If you need to add additional licenses and you have purchased the Per Server licenses from Microsoft, you would click the Add Licenses radio button. This brings up the New Client Access License dialog box, shown in Figure 1.20. Within the Quantity field, specify how many additional licenses you are adding and click the OK button. You will need to agree that you have purchased the license and that you agree to the governing terms of the license agreement.

FIGURE 1.20   New Client Access License dialog box

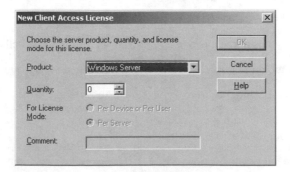

You would remove Per Server licenses from a server if you wanted to use them on another server. You would complete this task by clicking the Remove Licenses button. The Select Certificate To Remove Licenses dialog box will appear. Specify how many licenses you want to remove and click the Remove button.

Switching from Per Server Connections to Per Device or Per User Connections

Microsoft allows a one-time conversion from Per Server to Per Device or Per User Connections. If you want to switch from Per Server connections to Per Device or Per User connections, in the Choose Licensing Mode dialog box you would click the Per Device Or Per User radio button. You will see a License Violation dialog box warning you that your change may violate the license agreement. If you have met all of the terms of the license agreement, click the No button (so that the request is not cancelled) to complete the conversion process.

If you configure Per Server licensing, you can always convert to Per Device or Per User licensing. However, you can't convert from Per Device or Per User licensing to Per Server licensing.

In Exercise 1.6, you will administer Per Server licensing in a single server environment using the Licensing option in Control Panel.

EXERCISE 1.6

Managing Per Server Licensing in a Single Server Environment

1. Select Start ➤ Control Panel ➤ Licensing.

2. From the Choose Licensing Mode dialog box, click the Add Licenses button. (If you receive an error at this point, it's because the License Logging Service is not started.)

3. The New Client Access License dialog box will appear. In the Quantity field, select 1 and click the OK button.

4. The Per Server Licensing Agreement dialog box will appear. Click the I Agree That: dialog box and click the OK button.

5. In the Choose Licensing Mode dialog box, you will see that your Per Server concurrent connections are listed as 6.

If you are using a production server, as opposed to a practice server, verify that your license meets the Microsoft requirements.

Managing Per Device and Per Users are typically associated with enterprise environments and are covered in detail in the following section.

Administering Licensing in an Enterprise

If a network consists of multiple servers in an enterprise network (using Active Directory services), then licensing should be administered on an enterprise level. The following topics relate to administering licensing in an enterprise environment:

- Determining and specifying which server is the site license server
- Using the Licensing utility in Administrative Tools
- Viewing site licensing for a Windows 2000 or Windows 2003 site

Each of these topics is covered in greater detail in the following subsections.

Determining and Specifying the Site License Server

The *site license server* is responsible for managing all of the Windows licenses for the site. The default license server is the first domain controller in the site. The site license server does not have to be a domain controller but for best performance it is recommended that site license server and domain controller be in the same site.

To determine what server is the site license server, you would take the following steps from a domain controller:

1. Select Start ➤ Administrative Tools ➤ Active Directory Sites And Services.

2. The Active Directory Sites And Services window will be displayed. Expand Sites and click on Default-First-Site. In the right-hand pane, you will see Licensing Site Settings, as shown in Figure 1.21.

FIGURE 1.21   Active Directory Sites And Services window

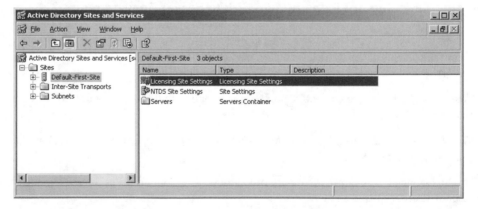

3. Double-click License Site Settings, and the Licensing Site Settings Properties dialog box will appear, as shown in Figure 1.22. In the lower half of the dialog box, under Licensing Computer, you will see the server that has been designated the site license server.

4. If you want to change the site license server, under Licensing Computer you click the Change button. The Select Computer dialog box appears and you can specify the computer name that will be the new site license server.

FIGURE 1.22   Licensing Site Settings Properties dialog box

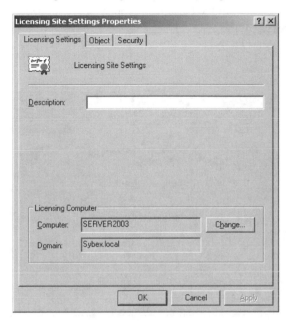

Once you have determined which server is the site license server, you can manage licensing for your site through the Licensing utility in Administrative Tools.

Using the Licensing

To access the Licensing utility, select Start ➢ Administrative Tools ➢ Licensing. This brings up the Licensing utility shown in Figure 1.23.

FIGURE 1.23   Licensing utility

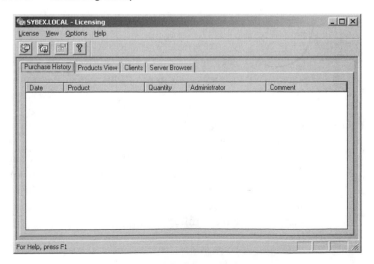

If you click the Server Browser tab, then expand your domain and your server, you will see an entry called Windows Server. Double-clicking Windows Server accesses the Choose Licensing Mode dialog box, as shown in Figure 1.24. This allows you to specify whether you will manage enterprise licensing through Per Server mode or Per Device or Per User mode.

FIGURE 1.24   Choose Licensing Mode dialog box

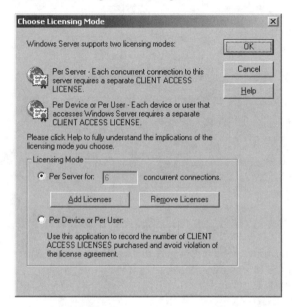

Once you have selected your licensing mode, you can manage licensing from the main dialog box of the Licensing utility, which contains four main tabs:

- Purchase History
- Products View
- Clients
- Server Browser

Each of these tabs and the processes for creating and editing licensing groups and for managing replication are covered in greater detail in the following subsections.

Purchase History

The Purchase History tab of Licensing (shown in Figure 1.23) displays the historical overview of all licenses that have been added or deleted for the site. Specifically, you can see the date the license was added or deleted, the product (Windows or other Microsoft product), the quantity (added or deleted), the user who added the licenses, and a comment (if one was added). If you click the heading for Date, Product, Quantity, Administrator, or Comment, the purchase history will be sorted based on the category you selected.

You would add new licenses through the following process:

1.   Select License ➢ New License.

2. The New Client Access License dialog box will appear. For Product, select Windows Server and then specify the quantity for the licenses you have purchased. You can add a descriptive comment in the comment field. Click the OK button when you are done.

3. The Per Device Or Per User Licensing dialog box will appear. You must agree that you have read and are bound to the license agreement for this product, then click the OK button.

4. The new licenses will appear in the Purchase History tab.

Products View

Through the Products View tab, shown in Figure 1.25, you can see the following information for each product that is licensed on the server:

- Per Device or Per User licenses that have been purchased
- Per Device or Per User licenses that have been allocated
- Per Server licenses that have been purchased
- The number of connections for Per Server that have been reached

FIGURE 1.25   Product View tab of the Licensing utility

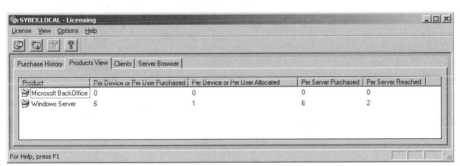

If you look on the left-hand side of the Products View tab, you will see the licensing status of each product. The following symbols are used to indicate license status:

Symbol	License Status
	License is in legal compliance.
	License is not in legal compliance.
	License has reached legal limit, and you should consider purchasing additional licenses.

Clients

Through the Clients tab, shown in Figure 1.26, you can see the following information for each client that has accessed the server:

- The username of each user who has accessed the server

- The licensed usage (access) to the server
- The unlicensed usage (access) to the server
- The product (for example, Windows Server or Windows BackOffice) that was accessed by the user

FIGURE 1.26   Clients tab of the Licensing utility

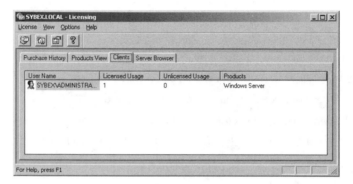

If you look on the left-hand side of the Clients tab, you will see the licensing status of each product. The following symbols are used to indicate license status:

Symbol	License Status
	User's license is in legal compliance.
	User's license is not in legal compliance.

Server Browser

The Server Browser tab, as shown in Figure 1.27, displays all of the sites, domains, and servers within the Active Directory structure. You can view and configure licensing for the servers that you have administrative rights to within the site.

FIGURE 1.27   Server Browser tab of the Licensing utility

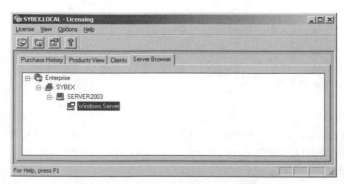

Creating and Editing Licensing Groups

You would create a license group if more than one person will be using a single computer.

In the following example, you will create a license group called WS1 that consists of three users (who work different shifts) who share a single computer.

1. Select Start ➢ Administrative Tools ➢ Licensing. In the main menu of the Licensing utility, select Options ➢ Advanced ➢ New License Group.

2. The New License Group dialog box will appear, as shown in Figure 1.28.

FIGURE 1.28   New License Group dialog box

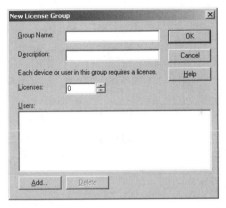

3. Specify a group name (in this example, it's WS1) and a description (optional).

4. In the Licenses drop-down box, you would specify 1, as up to 10 users can share a single computer.

5. To add users to this license group, click the Add button, which brings up the Add Users dialog box, shown in Figure 1.29. Select the users you want to add by highlighting them and then clicking the Add button. When you are done, click the OK button.

6. In the New License Group dialog box, click the OK button.

FIGURE 1.29   Add Users dialog box

Once a license group has been created, you can edit the licenses or group members for the license group through Options ➤ Advanced ➤ Edit License Group.

Managing Replication

In an enterprise environment, you can centrally manage licensing information by collecting and storing all license information on a central server (the site license server) through the License Logging service.

If your Windows Server 2003 server is not the site license server, you can configure how your server will replicate information to the site license server through the following steps:

1. Select Start ➤ Control Panel ➤ Licensing.

2. From the Choose Licensing Mode dialog box, click the Replication button.

3. The Replication Configuration dialog box will appear, as shown in Figure 1.30. You can configure replication to start at a specific time (every 24 hours) or specify that licensing information should be replicated every *x* (number specified) hours.

FIGURE 1.30   Replication Configuration dialog box

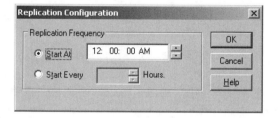

In sites with a large number of servers, staggering replication times on different servers can balance the load of traffic that is sent to a site license server.

Managing Software Installation and Maintenance

To keep your Windows operating systems up-to-date and secure, you use *Windows Update, Automatic Update, Software Update Services (SUS)*, and the *Microsoft Baseline Security Analyzer (MBSA)*:

Windows Update   This attaches to the Microsoft website through a user-initiated process and allows the Windows users to update their operating systems by downloading updated files (critical and non-critical software updates).

Automatic Update   This extends the functionality of Windows Update by automating the process of updating critical files. With Automatic Update, you can specify whether you want updates to be automatically downloaded and installed or whether you just want to be notified when updates are available.

Software Update Services (SUS)   This is used to deploy a limited version of Windows Update to a corporate server, which in turn provides the Windows updates to client computers within the corporate network. This allows clients that are limited to what they can access through a firewall to still keep their Windows operating systems up-to-date.

Microsoft Baseline Security Analyzer (MBSA)   This is a utility you can download from the Microsoft website to ensure that you have the most current security updates.

In the following sections you will learn how to use Windows Update, Automatic Update, Microsoft Software Update Services, and the Microsoft Baseline Security Analyzer.

Using Windows Update

Windows Update is available through the Microsoft website and is used to provide the most current files for the Windows operating systems. Examples of updates include security fixes, critical updates, updated help files, and updated drivers.

Sometimes the updates that are installed require that the computer be restarted before the update can take effect. In this event, Windows Update uses a technology called chained installation. With chained installation, all updates that require a computer restart are applied before the computer is restarted. This eliminates the need to restart the computer more than once.

If Windows Update detects any updates for your computer, you will see an update icon in the notification area of the Taskbar.

The following steps are used to setup Windows Update from a Windows Server 2003 server that is connected to the Internet:

1. Select Start ➤ Help And Support.

2. The Help And Support Center dialog box will appear, as shown in Figure 1.31.

3. Under Support Tasks, click the Windows Update option.

4. The Welcome To Windows Update will appear, as shown in Figure 1.32. Click Scan For Updates.

5. Windows Update will look for all available updates based on your computer's configuration. A list of all updates for your computer will be listed, and you can selectively pick which updates you want to download.

The results of the Windows Update search will be displayed on the left-hand side of the Windows Update screen. You will see options for:

-   Welcome, which describes what Windows Update is and provides an option to Scan For Updates

FIGURE 1.31   Help And Support Center dialog box

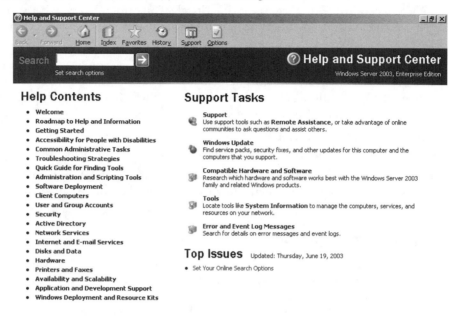

FIGURE 1.32   The Welcome To Windows Update window

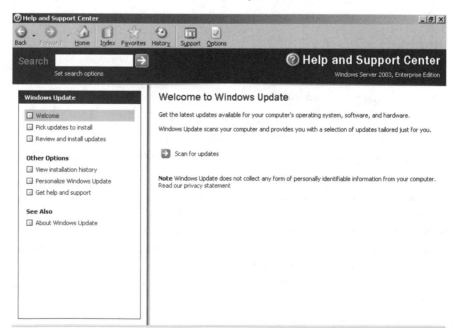

- Pick Updates To Install, which lists what updates are available for your computer and includes:
  - Critical Updates And Service Packs
  - Windows Server 2003 Family
  - Driver Updates
- Review And Install Updates, which allows you to view all updates you have selected to install and installs the updates
- View Installation History, which allows you to track all of the updates you have applied to your server
- Personalize Windows Update, which customizes what you see when you use Windows Update
- Get Help And Support, which displays help and support information about Windows Update
- About Windows Update, which displays information about what Windows Update is used for

The information that is collected by Windows Update includes operating system and version number, Internet Explorer version, the software version information for any software that can be updated through Windows Update, Plug and Play ID numbers for installed hardware, and region and language settings. Windows Update will also collect the Product ID and Product Key to confirm that you are running a licensed copy of Windows, but this information is only retained during the Windows Update session, and this information is not stored. No information that can be used to personally identify users of the Windows Update service is collected.

You will use Windows Update in Exercise 1.7.

EXERCISE 1.7

Using Windows Update

1. Select Start ➢ Help and Support.

2. The Help And Support Center dialog box will appear.

3. Under Support Tasks, click the Windows Update option.

4. The Welcome To Windows Update will appear. Click Scan For Updates.

5. Windows Update will look for all available updates based on your computer's configuration.

6. A list of all updates for your computer will be listed. Click each option for Critical Updates And Service Packs, Windows Server 2003 Family, and Driver Updates and check the updates you want to install.

7. Click Review And Install Updates. In the Total Selected Updates section, click the Install Now button.

Using Windows Automatic Updates

Windows Automatic Updates extends the functionality of Windows Update by automating the update process. With Automatic Updates, Windows Server 2003 recognizes when you have an Internet connection and will automatically search for any updates for your computer from the Windows Update website.

If any updates are identified, they will be downloaded using Background Intelligent Transfer Services (BITS). BITS is a bandwidth-throttling technology that only allows downloads to occur using idle bandwidth. This means that downloading Automatic Updates will not interfere with any other Internet traffic.

In order to configure Automatic Updates, you must have local administrative rights to the computer that Automatic Updates is being configured on. Requiring administrative rights prevents users from specifying that critical security updates not be installed. In addition, Microsoft will digitally sign any updates that are downloaded. Automatic Updates will not install files that do not contain a digital signature.

You configure Automatic Updates through the following process by selecting Start ➢ Control Panel ➢ System and click the Automatic Updates tab. You will see the dialog box shown in Figure 1.33.

FIGURE 1.33   Automatic Updates tab from System Properties

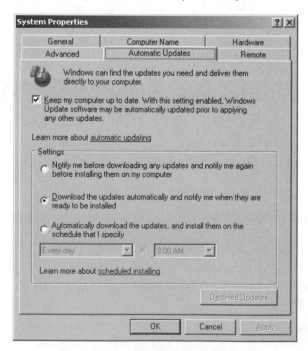

You enable Automatic Updates by checking the option Keep My Computer Up To Date. With This Setting Enabled, Windows Update Software May Be Automatically Updated Prior To Applying Any Other Updates.

The settings that can be applied to Automatic Updates include:

- Notify Me Before Downloading Any Updates And Notify Me Again Before Installing Them On My Computer. This option will prompt you to accept the downloading of any updates and you will be required to verify that you want the updates installed.

- Download The Updates Automatically And Notify Me When They Are Ready To Be Installed. This is the default setting and will automatically download updates as a background process; however, you must verify that you want to install the updates.

- Automatically Download The Updates, And Install Them On The Schedule That I Specify. This allows you to specify the days and times you want Windows to search for updates—for example, during non-business hours. You still have to verify that you want the updates installed prior to the updates being applied to your server.

The bottom of the Automatic Updates tab has a Declined Updates button. If Windows Update notifies you of an update and you decline the update—meaning you did not choose certain updates initially—you can click this button at a later time and still access the update, even if it was initially declined.

You will configure Automatic Updates in Exercise 1.8.

EXERCISE 1.8

Configuring Automatic Updates

1. Select Start ➢ Control Panel ➢ System and click the Automatic Updates tab.

2. Verify that the Keep My Computer Up To Date option is checked.

3. Under Settings, select the Automatically Download The Updates, And Install Them On The Schedule That I Specify option. Select Every Sunday at 2:00 A.M. and click the OK button.

Using Software Update Services

Software Update Services (SUS) is used to leverage the features of Windows Update within a corporate environment by downloading Windows Update to a corporate server, which in turn provides the updates to the internal corporate clients. This allows administrators to test and have full control over what updates are deployed within the corporate environment.

SUS is designed to work in medium-sized corporate networks that are not using Systems Management Server (SMS).

In the following sections, you will learn about:

- Advantages of using SUS
- SUS server requirements

- Installing and configuring the SUS servers
- SUS client requirements
- Configuration of the SUS clients

The current version of SUS, during the writing of this book, is SUS 1.0 with Service Pack 1.

🌐 Real World Scenario

Using SUS

You are the network administrator for a large company. You want to ensure that your Windows servers and clients are kept up-to-date. You have a process that specifies that all updates must be tested in a lab environment before they are deployed within the network. You want to streamline the update process as much as possible with minimum cost and setup.

All of your client computers are running Windows 2000 Professional or Windows XP Professional and all of the servers are running Windows 2000 Server or Windows Server 2003. They all have the current Service Packs applied.

You decide to use Software Update Services. The software can be downloaded from the Microsoft website at no charge and can be configured to automatically download any updates based on the schedule you specify. You can then test all of the updates before they are configured to be deployed within the internal network.

Advantages of Using SUS

There are many advantages to using SUS. The advantages include:

- SUS allows an internal server within a private intranet to act as a virtual Windows Update server.
- Administrators have selective control over what updates are posted and deployed from the public Windows Update site. No updates are deployed to client computers unless they are first approved by an administrator.
- Administrators can control the synchronization of updates from the public Windows Update site to the SUS server either manually or automatically.
- Automatic Updates can be configured on client computers to access the local SUS server as opposed to the public Windows Update site.
- Each update can be checked to verify that they are digitally signed by Microsoft, and any updates that are not digitally signed are discarded.
- Updates can be deployed to clients in multiple languages.

- You can configure the SUS statistics server to log update access, which allows an administrator to track which clients have installed updates. The SUS server and the SUS statistics server can coexist on the same computer.
- Administrators can manage SUS servers remotely using HTTP or HTTPS if their web browser is Internet Explorer 5.5 or higher.

SUS Server Requirements

In order to act as a SUS server, the server must meet the following requirements:

- Be running Windows 2000 Server with Service Pack 2 or higher or Windows Server 2003
- Be using Internet Explorer 5.5 or higher
- Have all of the most current security patches applied
- Be running Internet Information Services (IIS)
- Be connected to the network
- Have an NTFS partition with 100MB free disk space to install the SUS server software and 6GB of free space to store all of the update files

If your SUS server meets the following system requirements, it can support up to 15,000 SUS clients:

- Pentium III 700MHz processor
- 512MB of RAM

Installing and Configuring the SUS Server

The SUS server should run on a server that is dedicated to running SUS, meaning that it will not run any other applications other than IIS, which is required. Microsoft recommends that you install a clean or new version of Windows 2000 Server or Windows Server 2003 and apply any service packs or security-related patches.

 You should not have any virus-scanning software installed on the server. Virus scanners can mistake SUS activity for a virus.

Installing a SUS Server

The following steps are used to install the SUS server:

1. Download the SUS software from the Microsoft website. The URL for accessing the SUS homepage is: `http://go.Microsoft.com/fwlink/?linkid=6930`. The download file is called `SUS10SP1.exe`. The SUS software is available in English and Japanese.

2. Once SUS is downloaded, the Welcome To The Microsoft Software Update Services Setup Wizard screen will appear. Click the Next button.

 If IIS is not installed on the server, which is a prerequisite for SUS, you will receive an error. The installation of IIS is covered in Chapter 6.

3. The End-User License Agreement dialog box will appear. Accept the terms of the agreement and click the Next button.

4. The Choose Setup Type dialog box will appear. You can select Typical (which installs Microsoft Software Update Services with default settings) or Custom (which customizes the installation and settings of Microsoft Software Update Services). Click Typical to install the SUS with default settings.

5. The Ready To Install dialog box will appear and a download URL will be specified, as shown in Figure 1.34. The download URL is HTTP://*yourservername* by default. Computers running Automatic Updates must be configured to use this URL. Click the Install button.

FIGURE 1.34   Ready To Install dialog box

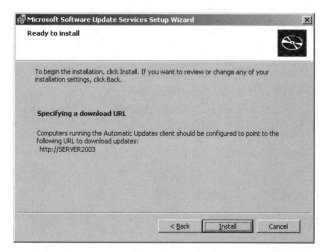

6. The Completing The Microsoft Software Update Services Setup Wizard dialog box will appear. Click the Finish button.

7. The SUS Administration website will automatically open in Internet Explorer.

Configuring a SUS Server

In the following sections, you will learn how to set the SUS server options, set synchronization, approve updates, view the synchronization log, view the approval log, and monitor the SUS server.

SETTING SUS SERVER OPTIONS

You can configure the SUS server through the following steps:

1. If the SUS Administration website is not open, you can open it from Internet Explorer through the URL http://*yourservername*/SUSAdmin.

2. The Software Update Services screen will appear, as shown in Figure 1.35. Under the Other Options section, click Set Options.

3. Within the Set Options selection, shown in Figure 1.36, you can select the following options:

    ▪ Select A Proxy Server Configuration

    ▪ Specify The Name Your Clients Use To Locate This Update Server

FIGURE 1.35   Microsoft Software Update Services

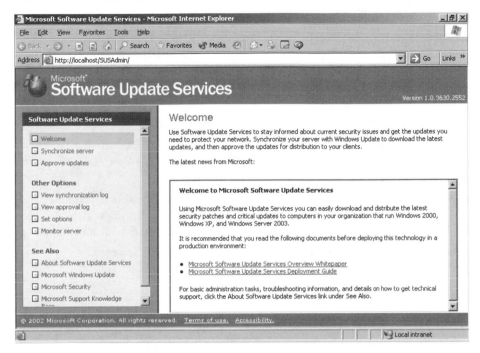

FIGURE 1.36   Set Options

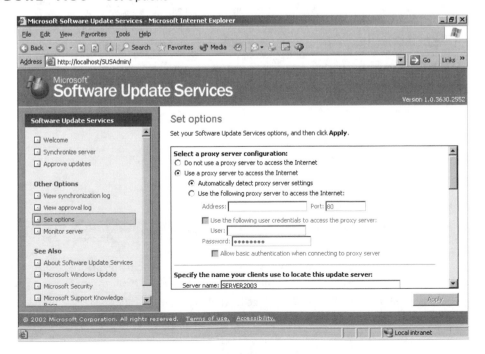

- Select Which Server To Synchronize Content From (Microsoft Windows Update Servers Or Local Software Update Server)

- Select How You Want To Handle New Versions Of Previously Approved Updates (Automatically Approve New Versions Of Previously Approved Updates, Do Not Automatically Approve New Versions Of Approved Updates, Default, or Recommended)

- Select Where You Want To Store Updates (You Can Maintain The Updates On A Microsoft Windows Update Server Or Save The Updates To A Local Update Folder)

- Synchronize Installation Packages Only For These Locales (Allows You To Specify Locales/Languages That You Are Storing Update Packages For)

Click the Apply button when you are done with your configuration settings.

SETTING SUS SERVER SYNCHRONIZATION

By default, SUS server synchronization is not defined. You can manually synchronize your server with the Windows Update server or you can set a synchronization schedule to automate the process. The following steps are used to configure SUS Server synchronization:

1. From the Software Update Services screen, click Synchronize Server.

2. The Synchronize Server screen will appear, as shown in Figure 1.37.

FIGURE 1.37   Synchronize Server

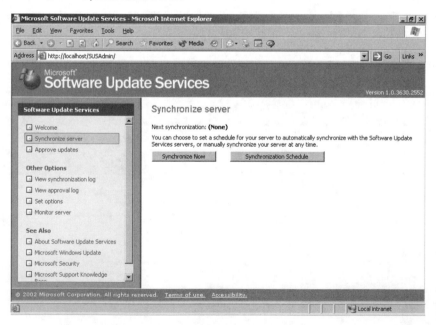

3. You can select Synchronize Now (which forces a manual synchronization) or Synchronization Schedule. To set a synchronization schedule, click the Synchronization Schedule button.

4. The Schedule Synchronization—Web Page Dialog dialog box will appear (see Figure 1.38). You can specify that you will not use a synchronization schedule (which means you will need to manually synchronize your server) or synchronize your server using the specified

schedule. You would typically schedule updates during non-peak network hours. When you are done, click the OK button.

FIGURE 1.38   Schedule Synchronization—Web Page Dialog dialog box

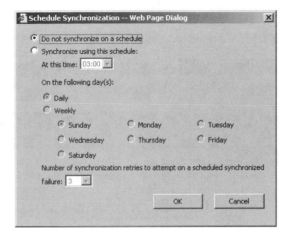

APPROVING UPDATES

Before updates can be deployed to SUS clients, the administrator must approve the updates. You approve updates through the following steps:

1. From the Software Update Services screen, click Approve Updates.

2. The Approve Updates screen will appear, as shown in Figure 1.39.

FIGURE 1.39   Approve Updates screen

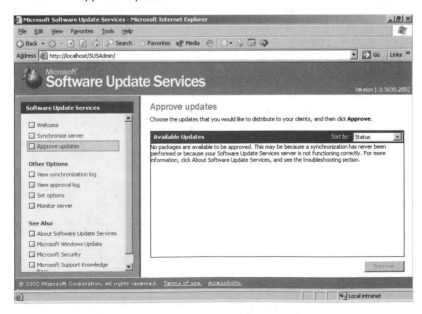

VIEWING THE SYNCHRONIZATION LOG

The following steps are used to view the synchronization log:

1. From the Software Update Services screen, click View Synchronization Log.

2. The Synchronization Log screen will appear, as shown in Figure 1.40.

FIGURE 1.40   Synchronization Log screen

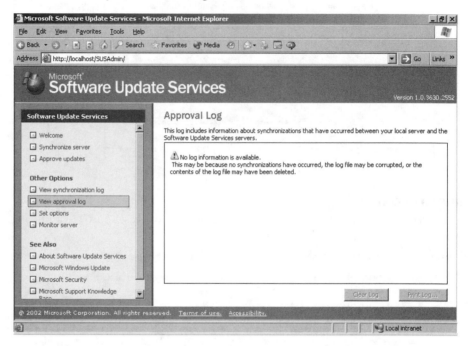

VIEW THE APPROVAL LOG

The approval log shows the update status for each item. Update status will be marked as New, Approved, Not Approved, Updated, or Temporarily Unavailable.

The following steps are used to view the approval log:

1. From the Software Update Services screen, click View Approval Log.

2. The Approval Log screen will appear, as shown in Figure 1.41.

MONITORING THE SUS SERVER

The Monitor Server option allows you to see what updates have been cached into the server memory. If the memory cache does not load automatically, you can click the Refresh button.

1. From the Software Update Services screen, click Monitor Server.

2. The Monitor Server screen will appear, as shown in Figure 1.42.

FIGURE 1.41   Approval Log screen

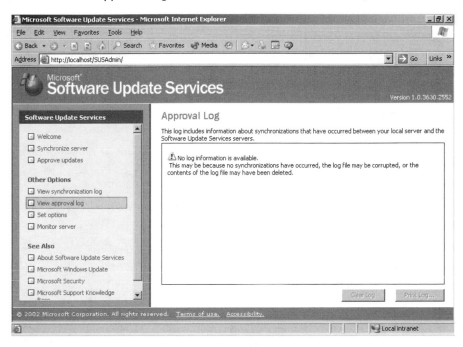

FIGURE 1.42   Monitor Server screen

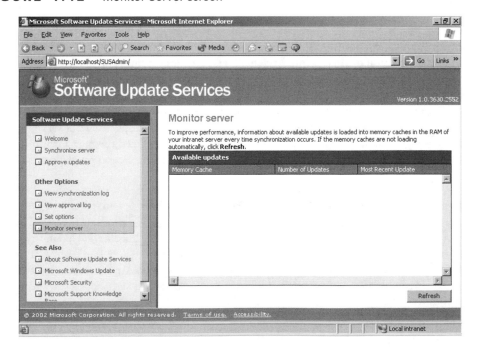

SUS Client Requirements

SUS clients run a special version of Automatic Updates that are designed to support SUS. The enhancements to Automatic Updates include:

- Support so that the client can receive updates from a SUS server as opposed to the public Microsoft Windows Update site
- Support so that the administrator can schedule when downloading of updated files will occur
- Configuration support so that clients can be configured via group policy or through editing the Registry
- Support for allowing updates when an administrative account or non-administrative account is logged on

    The only client platforms that SUS currently supports are:

- Windows 2000 Professional (with Service Pack 2 or higher)
- Windows 2000 Server (with Service Pack 2 or higher)
- Windows 2000 Advanced Server (with Service Pack 2 or higher)
- Windows XP Home Edition (with Service Pack 1 or higher)
- Windows XP Professional (with Service Pack 1 or higher)
- Windows Server 2003 (all platforms)

Configuration for the SUS Clients

There are two methods for configuring SUS clients. The method you use is dependent on whether your network uses Active Directory.

In a non-enterprise network (not running Active Directory), you would configure Automatic Updates through Control Panel using the same process that was defined in the "Using Automatic Updates" section of this chapter. Each client's Registry would then be edited to reflect the location of the server that will provide the Automatic Updates.

Within an enterprise network, using Active Directory, you would typically see Automatic Updates configured through group policy. Group policies are used to manage configuration and security settings via Active Directory. Group policy is also used to specify what server a client will use for Automatic Updates. If Automatic Updates are configured through Group Policy, then Automatic Updates settings through Control Panel ➤ System, Automatic Updates tab are disabled.

Configuring a Client in a Non-Active Directory Network

The easiest way to configure the client to use Automatic Updates is through Control Panel ➤ System, Automatic Updates tab. However, you can also configure Automatic Updates through the Registry. The Registry is a database of all of your server's settings and can be accessed by clicking Start ➤ Run and typing **Regedit** in the Run dialog box. Automatic Updates settings are defined through HKEY_LOCAL_MACHINE\Software\Policies\Microsoft\Windows\WindowsUpdate\AU.

The Registry options that can be configured for Automatic Updates are specified in Table 1.4.

TABLE 1.4 Registry Keys and Values for Automatic Updates

Registry Key	Options for Values
NoAutoUpdate	0 Automatic Updates are enabled (default) 1 Automatic Updates are disabled
AUOptions	2 Notify of download and installation 3 Auto download and notify of installation 4 Auto download and schedule installation
ScheduledInstallDay	0 Every day 1 Sunday 2 Monday 3 Tuesday 4 Wednesday 5 Thursday 6 Friday 7 Saturday
UseWUServer	0 Use public Microsoft Windows Update site 1 Use server specified in WUServer entry

To specify what server will be used as the Windows Update server, you edit two Registry keys, which are found at HKEY_LOCAL_MACHINE\Software\Policies\Microsoft\Windows\WindowsUpdate.

- The WUServer key sets the Windows Update server using the server's HTTP name—for example, http://intranetSUS

- The WUStatusServer key sets the Windows Update intranet SUS statistics server by using the server's HTTP name—for example, http://intranetSUS

Configuring a Client in an Active Directory Network

If the SUS client is a part of an enterprise network using Active Directory, you would configure the client via group policy. To configure group policy on a Windows Server 2003 domain controller, you would take the following steps:

1. Select Start ➢ Run. In the Run dialog box, type **MMC**.

2. From the MMC console, select File ➢ Add/Remove Snap-in.

3. In the Add/Remove Snap-in dialog box, click the Add button.

4. In the Add Standalone Snap-in dialog box, select Group Policy Object Editor and click the Add button.

5. For Group Policy Object, click the Browse button and select Default Domain Policy and click the OK button.

6. In the Select Group Policy Object dialog box, click the Finish button. In the Add Standalone Snap-in dialog box, click the Close button. In the Add/Remove Snap-in dialog box, click the OK button.

7. Expand `Default Domain Policy\Computer Configuration\Administrative Templates\ Windows Components\Windows Update` to access the Windows Update settings shown in Figure 1.43.

FIGURE 1.43   Group Policy Settings for Windows Update

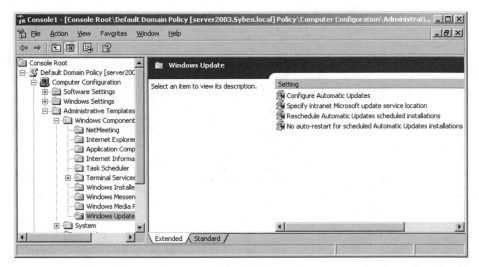

8. Double-click the Configure Automatic Updates option. The Configure Automatic Updates Properties dialog box will appear, as shown in Figure 1.44. The Automatic Update options that can be configured through group policy are:

- Whether Automatic Updates are Not Configured, Enabled, or Disabled

- How automatic updating is configured, either Notify For Download And Notify For Install, Auto Download And Notify For Install, or Auto Download And Schedule The Install

- The schedule that will be applied for the install day and the install time

9. To configure which server will provide automatic updates, you click the Next Setting button on the Configure Automatic Updates Properties dialog box. This brings up the Specify Intranet Microsoft Update Service Location Properties dialog box shown in Figure 1.45. The Specify Intranet Microsoft Update Service Location Properties that can be configured through group policy are:

- The status of the Intranet Microsoft Update Service location as Not Configured, Enabled, or Disabled

- The HTTP name of the server that will provide intranet service updates

- The HTTP name of the server that will act as the intranet SUS statistics server

FIGURE 1.44   Configure Automatic Updates Properties dialog box

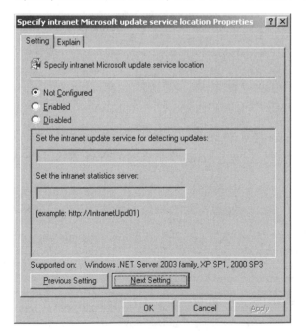

FIGURE 1.45   Specify Intranet Microsoft Update Service Location Properties dialog box

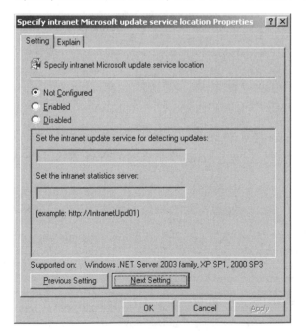

10. To configure rescheduling of automatic updates, you click Next Setting button on the Specify Intranet Microsoft Update Service Location Properties dialog box. This brings up the Reschedule Automatic Updates Scheduled Installation Properties dialog box shown in Figure 1.46. You can enable and schedule the amount of time that Automatic Updates waits after system startup to proceed with a scheduled installation that was previously missed.

FIGURE 1.46   Reschedule Automatic Updates Scheduled Installation Properties dialog box

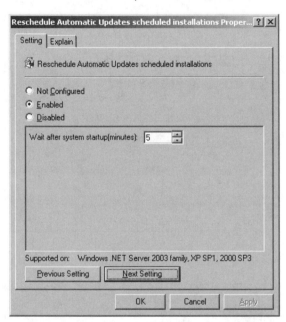

11. To configure auto-restart for scheduled Automatic Updates installations, you click Next Setting button on Reschedule Automatic Updates Scheduled Installation Properties dialog box. This brings up the No Auto-Restart For Scheduled Automatic Updates Installations dialog box shown in Figure 1.47. If an update requires the computer to restart, there are two configuration options available: the computer will be updated the next time the computer is restarted, or the restart is automatically performed as a part of the update.

There are security templates called Wuau.adm (for Windows 2000 Server, if you are using Service Pack 2 you will need to import this template. If you are using Service Pack 3 or higher, the template is included as a part of the Service Pack Update), which is available through the Software Update Services installation. If you are using Windows Server 2003 you would use the System.adm security template that automatically applies the group policy settings that are used by SUS. Group Policies and security templates are described in more detail in *MCSE: Windows 2003 Active Directory Planning, Implementation, and Maintenance Study Guide* by Anil Desai with James Chellis (Sybex, 2003)

FIGURE 1.47   No Auto-Restart Of Scheduled Automatic Updates Installations dialog box

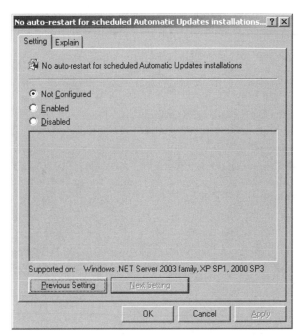

12. When you are done making setting changes, click the OK button.

Using the Microsoft Baseline Security Analyzer

The Microsoft Baseline Security Analyzer (MBSA) is a security assessment utility that can be downloaded from the Microsoft website. It verifies whether your computer has the latest security updates and whether there are any common security violation configurations (configurations that could allow security breaches) that have been applied to your computer. The programs that are scanned by MBSA include:

- Windows NT 4
- Windows 2000
- Windows XP
- Windows Server 2003
- IIS 4 and 5
- Internet Explorer, versions 5.01 and higher
- SQL Server 7 and SQL Server 2000
- Microsoft Office 2000 and Microsoft Office XP
- Windows Media Player, versions 6.4 and higher

In order to use MBSA, the computer must meet the following requirements:

- Be running Windows 2000, Windows XP, or Windows Server 2003 (MBSA is not supported by Windows 95, Windows 98, or Windows Me)
- Be running Windows Explorer 5.01 or higher
- Have an XML parser installed for full functionality
- Have the Workstation and the Server service enabled
- Have Client for Microsoft Networks installed

MSBA replaces the Microsoft Personal Security Advisor (MPSA), an application that was previously used to scan for possible security threats to your computer.

A GUI version of MBSA can be run from Start All Programs ➢ Microsoft Baseline Security Analyzer. You can also open a command prompt and changing the path to `Drive: Program Files\Microsoft Baseline Security Analyzer` and typing **mbsa** (after the `Mbsasetup.msi` has been downloaded and installed from the Microsoft site) or from the command line using `mbsacli.exe`.

 Real World Scenario

Using MBSA

You are the network administrator of a large company. In the past you have had problems with security as security holes have become public knowledge and hackers have tried to gain unauthorized access to your network. You also want to ensure that your configuration settings meet the current standards for security that have been defined by Microsoft.

You decided to use the Microsoft Baseline Security Analyzer. The utility is constantly being updated and will tell you if you have any configurations that could cause security problems or if there are any known security problems with your current software.

Using the GUI Version of MBSA

Once you have installed MBSA, you can access it from Start ➢ All Programs ➢ Microsoft Baseline Security Analyzer or by opening the command prompt and executing `mbsa.exe`. This brings up the Baseline Security Analyzer utility shown in Figure 1.48.

You can select from Scan A Computer, Scan More Than One Computer, or View Existing Security Reports.

When you click Scan A Computer, the Pick A Computer To Scan dialog box will appear, as shown in Figure 1.49. You can specify that you want to scan a computer based on computer name or IP address. You can also specify the name of the security report that will be generated. Options for the security scan include:

- Check for Windows vulnerabilities
- Check for weak passwords
- Check for IIS vulnerabilities

FIGURE 1.48 Baseline Security Analyzer

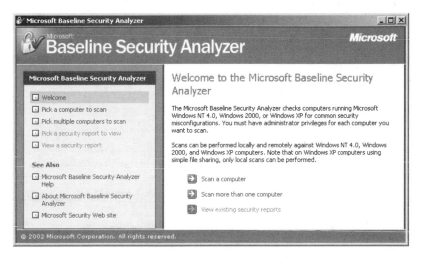

FIGURE 1.49 Pick A Computer To Scan dialog box

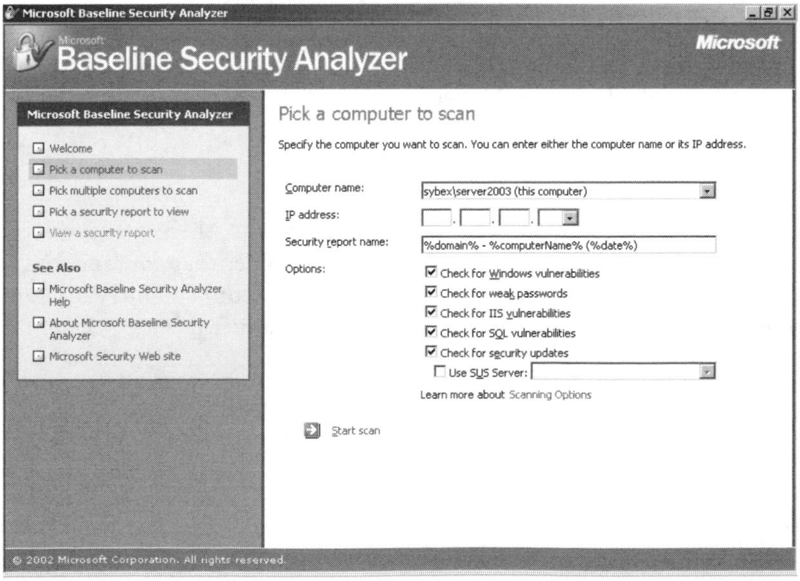

- Check for SQL vulnerabilities
- Check for security updates (if you use this option and are using SUS, you can specify the name of the SUS server that should be checked for the security updates)

Once you are done with your selections, click Start Scan.

Once the scan is complete, the security report will be automatically displayed, as shown in Figure 1.50.

FIGURE 1.50   View Security Report dialog box

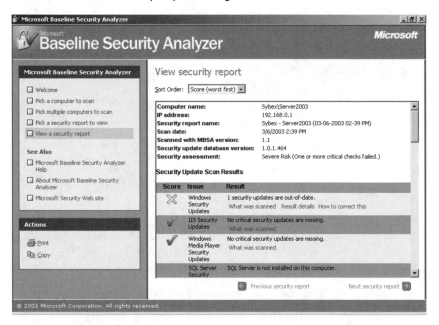

If you have scanned multiple computers, you can sort the security reports based on issue name, score (worst first), or score (best first).

Using *mbsacli.exe*

If you use MBSA from the command-line utility mbsacli.exe, there are several options that can be specified. You type **mbsacli.exe /hf** (from the folder that contains mbsacli.exe, which is *Drive*: Program Files\Microsoft Baseline Security Analyzer) and can then customize the command execution with the options defined in Table 1.5.

TABLE 1.5   mbsacli.exe /hf Command-line Options

Option	Description
-h *hostname*	Scans the specified host. You can specify that you want to scan multiple host computers by separating the hostnames with a comma.

TABLE 1.5   `mbsacli.exe /hf` Command-line Options *(continued)*

Option	Description
`-fh` *filename*	Scans the NetBIOS names of each computer that is to be scanned and saves the information as text within the filename you specify.
`-i` *xxxx.xxxx.xxxx.xxxx*	Scans a computer based on the specified IP address. You can scan multiple computers by IP address by separating each IP address with a comma.
`-fip` *filename*	Scans the computer's IP addresses within the text file that was specified, up to a maximum of 256 IP addresses.
`-d` *domainname*	Scans the specified domain.
`-n`	Specifies that all of the computers on the local network should be scanned.

Summary

In this chapter, you learned about basic features of Windows Server 2003, how to install Windows Server 2003, licensing for Windows Server 2003, and how to keep Windows Server 2003 up-to-date. We covered the following topics:

- The basic features of Windows Server 2003, which include Active Directory, file and print services, security, network and communications, application services, management services, Storage Management Services, Internet Information Services, Terminal Services, Universal Description, Discovery, and Integration services.

- Preparation needed for installing Windows Server 2003, which included verifying that your computer meets the hardware requirements for Windows Server 2003, making sure your hardware is on the Hardware Compatibility List, checking system compatibility, and understanding the installation options for Windows Server 2003.

- How to install Windows Server 2003 and configure the server as a domain controller.

- What post-installation activation is and how to activate Windows Server 2003.

- The options for managing licensing with Windows Server 2003 clients and how to administer licensing.

- How to manage software installation and maintenance through Windows Update, Windows Automatic Updates, Software Update Services, and Microsoft Baseline Security Analyzer.

Exam Essentials

Be able to manage Windows licensing.   You should understand the options for licensing Windows clients and how licensing can be administered in a local environment or within an enterprise environment.

Be able to keep Windows up-to-date and secure.   Understand the use of Windows Update, Windows Automatic Updates, Software Update Services, and Microsoft Baseline Security Analyzer. Be able to install and configure SUS servers and clients and administer software updates. Know how to use the Microsoft Baseline Security Analyzer to identify possible security weaknesses from a GUI interface and from the command line.

Key Terms

Before you take the exam, be certain you are familiar with the following terms:

Active Directory (AD)	Microsoft Baseline Security Analyzer (MBSA)
Automatic Update	organizational units (OUs)
Client Access License (CAL)	Per Seat licensing
containers	Per Server licensing
domain controller	product activation
domains	site license server
Hardware Compatibility List (HCL)	Software Update Services (SUS)
License Logging service	Windows Update

Review Questions

1. You are the network administrator for a Fortune 500 company. You are responsible for all client computers at the central campus. You want to make sure that all of the client computers have the most current software installed for their operating systems, including:

    Critical Updates and Service Packs

    Windows Server 2003 Family

    Driver Updates

    You want to automate the process as much as possible, and you want the client computers to download the updates from a central server that you are managing. You decide to use Software Update Services. You have several computers that you can use as the SUS server. Which of the following computers meet(s) the requirements for being a SUS server?

Computer Hardware/ Software	Computer A	Computer B	Computer C	Computer D
Operating System	Windows Server 2003	Windows 2000 Server (SP2)	Windows Server 2003	Windows 2000 Server (SP3)
Partitions	FAT32 with 10GB free space	NTFS with 10GB free space	NTFS with 8GB free space	FAT32 with 8GB free disk space
Additional software	Domain controller, most current IE	Domain controller, most current IE	Member server, IIS, most current IE	Member server, IIS, most current IE

    A. Computer A

    B. Computer B

    C. Computer C

    D. Computer D

2. You were recently hired to manage the network for the Wacky Widgets Corporation. One of your first tasks is to ensure that all of the operating systems and software that is being used is properly licensed. Your network consists of a Windows 2003 domain that includes 10 Windows Server 2003 servers and 250 Windows XP Professional client computers. All of the computers within the network are located in a single site. You create a licensing strategy that specifies that you will use a server called LicenseServer to manage all of the Windows licensing through Administrative Tools ➢ Licensing. You configure all of the servers with the License Logging service. The next step you need to complete is determining which server is acting as the site license server and changing the site license server to LicenseServer. Which of the following options will allow you to configure the site license server?

    A. Configure the site license server through the License Logging service.

    B. Configure the site license server using Administrative Tools ➢ Active Directory Sites And Services.

    C. Configure the site license server through Administrative Tools ➢ Licensing.

    D. Configure the site license server through Control Panel ➢ Licensing.

3. You are the network administrator for a Fortune 500 company. You are responsible for all client computers at the central campus. You want to make sure that all of the client computers have the most current software installed for their operating systems, including:

   Critical Updates and Service Packs

   Windows Server 2003 Family

   Driver Updates

   You want to automate the process as much as possible, and you want the client computers to download the updates from a central server that you are managing. You decide to use Software Update Services. Which of the following client computers (with their current configuration) can be used with Software Service Update? (Choose all that apply.)

   A. Windows 98 (with most current Service Pack)

   B. Windows Me (with most current Service Pack)

   C. Windows 2000 Professional (Service Pack 2)

   D. Windows XP Home Edition (Service Pack 1)

   E. Windows XP Professional (no Service Pack)

   F. Windows Server 2003 member server (no Service Pack)

4. You are the network administrator for a Fortune 500 company. You are responsible for all client computers at the central campus. You want to make sure that all of the client computers have the most current software installed for their operating systems, including:

   Critical Updates and Service Packs

   Windows Server 2003 Family

   Driver Updates

   You want to automate the process as much as possible, and you want the client computers to download the updates from a central server that you are managing. You decide to use Software Update Services. The SUS server software has been installed on a server called SUSServer. You want to test the SUS server before you set up group policy within the domain. You install Windows XP Professional with the latest Service Pack on a test client. Which of the following Registry entries needs to be made for the client in order to specify that the client should use SUSServer for Windows Update? (Choose all that apply.)

   A. HKEY_LOCAL_MACHINE\Software\Policies\Microsoft\Windows\WindowsUpdate\ AU\UseWUServer and specify 0 for data

   B. HKEY_LOCAL_MACHINE\Software\Policies\Microsoft\Windows\WindowsUpdate\ AU\UseWUServer and specify 1 for data

   C. HKEY_LOCAL_MACHINE\Software\Policies\Microsoft\Windows\WindowsUpdate\ AU\WUServer and specify http://SUSServer

   D. HKEY_LOCAL_MACHINE\Software\Policies\Microsoft\Windows\WindowsUpdate\ AU\WUServer and specify SUSServer

   E. HKEY_LOCAL_MACHINE\Software\Policies\Microsoft\Windows\WindowsUpdate\ WUServer and specify http://SUSServer

   F. HKEY_LOCAL_MACHINE\Software\Policies\Microsoft\Windows\WindowsUpdate\ WUServer and specify SUSServer

5. You are the network administrator for a small company. Your company has one Windows Server 2003 computer configured as a domain controller and 25 clients running Windows XP Professional. You want to ensure that your server stays up-to-date through Windows Automatic Update. Where should you configure your server to use Windows Automatic Update? (Choose all that apply.)

   A. Through the Registry

   B. Through Group Policy

   C. Start ➤ All Programs ➤ Accessories ➤ System Tools ➤ Windows Update

   D. Start ➤ Control Panel ➤ System and click the Automatic Updates tab

6. You are the network administrator for a Fortune 500 company. You are responsible for all client computers at the central campus. You want to make sure that all of the client computers have the most current software installed for their operating systems, including:

   Critical Updates and Service Packs

   Windows Server 2003 Family

   Driver Updates

   You want to automate the process as much as possible, and you want the client computers to download the updates from a central server that you are managing. You decide to use Software Update Services. The SUS server software has been installed on a server called SUSServer. You want to use group policy to define all of the Windows Update settings for the SUS clients. Where would you configure this information within Group Policy?

   A. `Computer Configuration\Administrative Templates\Windows Components\ Windows Update`

   B. `Computer Configuration\Windows Update`

   C. `Computer Configuration\Administrative Templates\SUS Settings\Windows Update`

   D. `Software Settings\SUS Settings\Windows Update`

7. You are the network administrator for a Fortune 500 company. You are responsible for all client computers at the central campus. You want to make sure that all of the client computers are secure. You decide to use MBSA to scan your client computers for possible security violations. Which of the following clients are supported by MBSA? (Choose all that apply.)

   A. Windows 98 (with most current Service Pack)

   B. Windows Me (with most current Service Pack)

   C. Windows 2000 Professional (Service Pack 2)

   D. Windows XP Home Edition (Service Pack 1)

   E. Windows XP Professional (no Service Pack)

   F. Windows Server 2003 member server (no Service Pack)

8. You are the network administrator for a Fortune 500 company. You are responsible for all client computers at the central campus. You want to make sure that all of the client computers have the most current software installed for their operating systems, including:

Critical Updates and Service Packs

Windows Server 2003 Family

Driver Updates

You want to automate the process as much as possible, and you want the client computers to download the updates from a central server that you are managing. You decide to use Software Update Services. The SUS server software has been installed on a Windows Server 2003 member server called SUSServer. You want to use group policy to define all of the Windows Update settings for the SUS clients. Which of the following template files should you use to apply the group policy settings?

A. `Wuau.adm`

B. `Sus.adm`

C. `System.adm`

D. `Security.adm`

9. You are the manager of a testing lab. Your company develops applications that will run with Windows Server 2003. As a part of your job, you install and configure servers that will be used for testing purposes. You recently installed a Windows Server 2003 member server for testing of a local application, but did not register the product. After 14 days, you still have not registered the product, and now you cannot access the server. The product key is being supplied through your corporate IT department, but you will not have access to the information for two more days. In the meantime, what process can you use to access local data on the computer?

A. Start the server using Automated System Recovery (ASR).

B. Boot the server using Safe Mode.

C. Start the server using the Recovery Console.

D. There is nothing you can do until you complete Windows Activation.

E. Boot the server using Safe Mode with Networking.

10. You are the network administrator for the computer lab at the University of Microsoft. Within the lab 250 students use 25 computers on a regular basis. When you manage the licensing for the lab, you receive error reports that you are out of licenses. You decide to implement license groups to manage licensing. Which of the following options can be used to create a license group?

A. Administrative Tools ➢ License Manager

B. Administrative Tools ➢ Licensing

C. Control Panel ➢ License Manager

D. Control Panel ➢ Licensing

11. You are the network administrator for a small company. Your network consists of one Windows Server 2003 server, which is configured as a domain controller, with 250 client computers. You want to make license management as easy as possible. Which of the following utilities should you use to configure licensing?

   A. Administrative Tools ➤ License Manager

   B. Administrative Tools ➤ Licensing

   C. Control Panel ➤ License Manager

   D. Control Panel ➤ Licensing

12. You are the network administrator for a Fortune 500 company. You are responsible for all client computers at the central campus. You want to make sure that all of the client computers have the most current software installed for their operating systems, including:

Critical Updates and Service Packs

Windows Server 2003 Family

Driver Updates

You want to automate the process as much as possible, and you want the client computers to download the updates from a central server that you are managing. You decide to use Software Update Services. The SUS server software has been installed on a server called SUSServer. Which of the following options would you use to remotely manage the SUS server?

   A. Start ➤ Administrative Tools ➤ SUSAdmin

   B. Start ➤ Administrative Tools ➤ Software Update Services

   C. From command-line through `SUSAdmin`

   D. Internet Explorer through the URL `http://yourservername/SUSadmin`

13. You are the network administrator for a Fortune 500 company. You are responsible for all client computers at the central campus. You want to make sure that all of the client computers are secure. You decide to use MBSA to scan your client computers for possible security violations. You want to use the command-line version of MBSA to scan all of the computers on the local network. Which of the following commands should you use?

   A. `mdsacli.exe /hf -n`

   B. `mbsacli.exe /hf -n`

   C. `mbsa.exe /hf -n`

   D. `mbsa.exe -n`

14. You are the network administrator for a small company. Your network consists of one Windows Server 2003 server, which is configured as a domain controller, and 250 client computers. You want to make license management as easy as possible. Which of the following requirements must be met before you can manage licensing?

A. You must have the License Management service running.

B. You must have the License Logging service running.

C. You must have the License Query service running.

D. Nothing, license management is inherent in Windows Server 2003.

15. You are the network administrator for a Fortune 500 company. You are responsible for all client computers at the central campus. You want to make sure that all of the client computers are secure. You decide to use MBSA to scan your client computers for possible security violations. You want to use the command-line version of MBSA to scan your computers based on IP address. Which of the following commands should you use?

A. `mbsacli.exe /hf -i` *xxxx.xxxx.xxxx.xxxx*

B. `mbsacli.exe /hf -ip` *xxxx.xxxx.xxxx.xxxx*

C. `mbsa.exe /hf -ip` *xxxx.xxxx.xxxx.xxxx*

D. `mbsa.exe /ip` *xxxx.xxxx.xxxx.xxxx*

Answers to Review Questions

1. C. In order to act as a SUS server, the following requirements must be met: the server must be running Windows 2000 Server with Service Pack 2 or higher or Windows Server 2003. The server must be using Internet Explorer 5.5 or higher. The server must have the most current security patches applied. The server must be running Internet Information Services (IIS). The server must be connected to the network. The server must have a NTFS partition with 100MB free disk space to install the SUS server software and 6GB of free space to store all of the update files.

2. B. You can view and configure the site license server by selecting Start ➢ Administrative Tools ➢ Active Directory Sites And Services. The Active Directory Sites And Services dialog box will be displayed. Expand Sites and click Default-First-Site. In the right-hand pane, you will see Licensing Site Settings. Double-click License Site Settings and the Licensing Site Setting Properties dialog box will appear. In the lower half of the dialog box, under Licensing Computer, you will see the server that has been designated the site license server. By default, the licensing server is the first domain controller installed in the site. You can change the site license server through the Licensing Computer dialog box.

3. C, D, F. The following clients can use Software Update Services: Windows 2000 Professional (with Service Pack 2 or higher), Windows 2000 Server (with Service Pack 2 or higher), Windows 2000 Advanced Server (with Service Pack 2 or higher), Windows XP Home Edition (with Service Pack 1 or higher), Windows XP Professional (with Service Pack 1 or higher), and Windows Server 2003 (all platforms). These clients use a special version of Automatic Updates that is required by Software Update Services.

4. B, E. The Registry key HKEY_LOCAL_MACHINE\Software\Policies\Microsoft\Windows\ WindowsUpdate\AU\UseWUServer can be set to 0, which uses the public Windows Update server, or 1, which specifies that you will specify the server for Windows Update in the HKEY_ LOCAL_MACHINE\Software\Policies\Microsoft\Windows\WindowsUpdate key. The WUServer key sets the Windows Update server using the server's HTTP name, for example, http://intranetSUS.

5. D. You configure Automatic Update by selecting Start ➢ Control Panel ➢ System and clicking the Automatic Updates tab. You can configure the schedule that your computer will use to scan for updates and how updates should be applied to your computer.

6. A. You can configure Windows Update settings that are used in conjunction with Software Update Services (SUS) through group policy. Within Group Policy, you edit Computer Configuration\Administrative Templates\Windows Components\Windows Update.

7. C, D, E, F. MBSA will scan the following clients: Windows NT 4, Windows 2000, Windows XP, and Windows Server 2003. Service packs are not required to use MBSA.

8. C. There are security templates called Wuau.adm (for Windows 2000 Server), which is available through the Software Update Services installation, and System.adm (for Windows Server 2003), which automatically applies the group policy settings that are used by SUS.

9. B. After Windows Server 2003 is installed, you will have 14 days to activate the license. After the 14-day grace period expires, you will not be able to restart Windows Server 2003 normally if you log out of the computer or if the computer is restarted. However, you can start Windows Server 2003 in Safe Mode (not Safe Mode with Networking). With Safe Mode, you will not have any networking capabilities, but you will have access to any folders or files located on the server.

10. B. Some environments have special considerations and will require you to create license groups for Per Device and Per User licensing. You would create licensing groups if you have more than one user using a computer—for example, if your organization has workers in shifts and users from different shifts all share a computer. Another possibility might be that you have many users who share many devices—for example, students working in a school computer lab. To create a license group you would use Administrative Tools ≻ Licensing. From the main menu, you would then select Options ≻ Advanced ≻ New License Group.

11. D. If you only have one server, then you will be using Per Server licensing in a non-enterprise environment. In this case, the preferred way to manage licensing is through Control Panel ≻ Licensing. In Enterprise Licensing, licensing considerations must be accomplished through Administrative Tools ≻ Licensing.

12. D. To remotely manage a SUS server, open http://*yourservername*/SUSadmin from Internet Explorer.

13. B. If you use MBSA from the command-line utility mbsacli.exe, there are several options that can be specified. You type **mbsacli.exe /hf** (from the folder that contains mbsacli.exe) and can then customize the command execution with an option such as -n, which specifies that all of the computers on the local network should be scanned.

14. B. If the License Logging service is running, Administrators can manage and track licensing through the Licensing option in Control Panel or the Licensing utility in Administrative Tools. If you were managing licenses for a single server, you would use the Licensing option in Control Panel. If you were managing licenses for an enterprise environment, you would use the Licensing within Administrative Tools.

15. A. If you use MBSA from the command-line utility mbsacli.exe, there are several options that can be specified. You type **mbsacli.exe /hf** from the folder (Drive: Program Files\ Microsoft Baseline Security Analyzer) that contains mbsacli.exe and can then customize the command execution with an option such as /hf -i *xxxx.xxxx.xxxx.xxxx*, which specifies that computers with the specified IP address should be scanned.

Chapter

2

Configuring Windows Server 2003 Hardware

MICROSOFT EXAM OBJECTIVES COVERED IN THIS CHAPTER:

✓ **Monitor server hardware. Tools might include Device Manager, the Hardware Troubleshooting Wizard, and appropriate Control Panel items.**

✓ **Troubleshoot server hardware devices.**

   ▪ Diagnose and resolve issues related to hardware settings.

   ▪ Diagnose and resolve issues related to server hardware and hardware driver upgrades.

✓ **Install and configure server hardware devices.**

   ▪ Configure driver signing options.

   ▪ Configure resource settings for a device.

   ▪ Configure device properties and settings.

After you've installed Windows Server 2003, you will need to know how to manage existing devices and install and configure new hardware. Windows Server 2003 supports Plug and Play hardware and will try to automatically install and configure new hardware devices for you. If Windows Server 2003 does not have a device driver for your new hardware device, you will have to manually install the device driver.

In this chapter, you will learn how to configure the Windows Server 2003 environment, beginning with an overview of hardware installation that includes detailed information on understanding hardware resources.

You will also learn about the Device Manager utility, which is a graphically-based utility that provides information about all of the devices that your computer currently recognizes. Through Device Manager, you can see a summary of all of the currently installed hardware; view and change hardware settings; view, uninstall, update, or roll back a device driver; disable and enable devices; and print a summary of all of the hardware devices that have been installed on your computer. You can also run the Hardware Troubleshooting Wizards from Device Manager.

This chapter also looks at managing device drivers, which involves understanding and being able to configure your server's driver signing options, updating drivers when necessary, and rolling back to older drivers if an upgraded driver does not work properly.

In addition, you will be introduced to the System Information utility. This is used to collect and display configuration information for your server. The information can be viewed for the local server or a computer that you are connected to. When the System Information utility is run, it will automatically collect information about your system settings. Administrators and Help Desk operators can save the data provided through System Information to a file, export the data to a text file, or print the collected information.

You will also learn how to manage server hardware through Control Panel. Control Panel is an item on the Start menu that contains options for configuring your computer's setup. A list of the options available in the Control Panel will expand by default.

Finally, you will learn about the Registry and how it can be edited through the Registry Editor. The Registry Editor is an advanced utility for managing a server's configuration.

Overview of Hardware Installation

You install new hardware (for instance, a network adapter or hard drive) through a multi-step configuration process. The fundamental steps are to first install the device at a physical level and then configure the device at one or more logical levels so that the system can communicate with the device. A device will not function properly unless it is correctly installed.

Configuring your computer hardware can be an easy or a difficult task to complete. Each hardware device must be configured with unique system resource settings. The resource settings enable the device to communicate with the computer's processor and memory without competing or conflicting with other devices. Most devices have the capability to accept various combinations of resource settings.

In the following sections, you will learn in greater detail about installing hardware and about how resources are used in Windows Server 2003.

Installing Hardware

There are two types of hardware devices that can be installed: *Plug and Play* and non–Plug and Play. If the hardware was manufactured after 1995, the device is most likely Plug and Play compatible. Prior to 1995, installing computer hardware was a tedious task that involved manually configuring the hardware and manually installing the device driver. The process became easier with the release of Windows 95, which introduced Plug and Play support.

With Plug and Play–compatible devices, an appropriate driver will be loaded for it or you can manually install the device driver (you would typically do this if Windows Server 2003 does not have the device driver for your device). A *device driver* is a piece of software that provides a software interface between a physical piece of hardware and the Windows Server 2003 operating system.

If your device is not Plug and Play compatible, you will need to install the device and manually install the device drivers. In addition, you may need to set configuration parameters for the device.

When Windows Server 2003 detects a new piece of hardware through Plug and Play technology, it will automatically try to install and configure the device. If Windows Server 2003 detects the device but isn't able to complete the hardware installation (for example, because the device driver is not on the Windows Server 2003 distribution CD), the Found New Hardware Wizard will start. The Found New Hardware Wizard will prompt you to insert the CD or floppy that came with the device for installation purposes, and any necessary files will automatically be copied and the installation process will be completed.

Windows Server 2003 Plug and Play support includes the following features:

- Automatic and dynamic recognition of hardware that is installed
- Automatic resource allocation (or reallocation, if necessary)
- Determination of the correct driver that must be loaded for hardware support
- Support for interaction with the Plug and Play system
- Support for power management features

 Microsoft has announced that they will no longer support non–Plug and Play hardware starting with the Windows XP Professional and Windows Server 2003 operating systems. However, if you have a non–Plug and Play device that has a Windows Server 2003 driver (which is supplied by the device manufacturer), it may still work with Windows Server 2003.

Understanding Hardware Resources

Each hardware device is unique and will have its own settings that you need to configure. You can specify hardware settings manually on the device or through software configuration programs (see the manufacturer documentation for setup instructions). Common configuration settings include interrupts, base memory, I/O memory, and direct memory access. These items are covered in more detail in the following sections.

Using Interrupts

Each device interacts with the computer by interrupting the processor so that the device can send or retrieve data or carry out a function. A device must have a method for telling the computer's processor that it needs attention. A hardware device tells the processor that it needs attention through an *interrupt request (IRQ)* line. By using this method of interruption, the processor can function without the need to ask a device every few seconds whether it needs service.

When a device interrupts the system processor, the processor stops what it is doing and handles the interrupt request. Because each device is assigned an IRQ number when the device is configured, the system knows which device needs attention. After the processor has attended to the device, it returns to the function it was performing before the interruption.

Traditionally, each device needed a unique IRQ. IRQs are used so that the processor knows what to attend to when a service request is called. Some devices are able to share IRQs; for instance, serial ports (also referred to as communication, or COM, ports) can share the same IRQ, but they must be assigned another unique identifier (I/O address). PCI devices also share IRQs. Plug and Play devices scan the system and determine an available interrupt request to assign to a new device during installation.

 The PCI bus standard enables devices connected to a PCI bus to communicate by using one common interrupt (IRQ 10).

Table 2.1 shows the standard interrupts that most systems use, including Windows XP Professional and Windows Server 2003. In the table, System Device refers to the device that is configured to use the specified interrupt; IRQ refers to the interrupt request line that the hardware device uses to notify the processor that it needs attention; and IRQ numbers that are listed as available can be allocated to new devices that are installed in the computer.

TABLE 2.1   Common IRQ Assignments

System Device	IRQ
System timer	0
Keyboard	1
Reserved	2
COMs 2, 4	3

TABLE 2.1   Common IRQ Assignments *(continued)*

System Device	IRQ
COMs 1, 3	4
LPT2 (usually available for other devices)	5
Floppy disk controller	6
LPT1	7
Real-time clock	8
Redirected or cascaded to IRQ 2	9
Available (also used for PCI common interrupt)	10
Available	11
PS/2 or bus mouse port (available if not used)	12
Math coprocessor	13
Hard disk controller	14
Available (also used for PCI secondary IDE controller)	15

Using Base Memory

Base memory (called memory in Windows Server 2003) refers to the reserved area in memory where devices can store data so that the processor can directly access that data. Some devices need this allocated memory range located in the system RAM. The area is typically located in the upper area of RAM memory called the *Upper Memory Area (UMA)*.

Table 2.2 shows some typical base memory address assignments. When configuring memory ranges, be sure that they do not overlap.

TABLE 2.2   Common Base Memory Assignments

System Device	Memory Range
Video RAM	A0000–BFFFF
Available	C0000–CFFFF
Available	D0000–DFFFF
System ROM	E0000–EFFFF

Using I/O Memory

Each device has a memory address called an I/O address, which is stored as a part of *I/O memory* (called I/O in Windows Server 2003). The address acts like a mailbox that the processor uses to send instructions to the device. The I/O address is also commonly called the *port address*.

When the CPU sends instructions to this address, the device reads the instructions and carries them out. But the device does not talk to the processor through the same mechanism. It uses the interrupt assigned to it to request service or additional instructions from the processor.

Each device must have a unique I/O address so that the correct device receives the instructions from the processor. Some older devices are coded to use only one I/O address and cannot be changed.

Most PCs are designed to support more than one I/O address for a device. This feature helps prevent a conflict between two similar devices, such as the COM ports that share the same interrupt. The two ports would have separate I/O addresses, thus preventing a clash between them.

If your device does not support an I/O address that is available (not in use by another device), you may select an address used by another device, provided you can change the other device's address to an available I/O address.

Table 2.3 shows the typical I/O address assignments.

TABLE 2.3   Common I/O Memory Assignments

System Device	I/O Address
DMA controller	000–01F
Interrupt controller	020–03F
Timer	040–05F
Keyboard	060–06F
Real-time clock	070–07F
DMA page register	080–09F
Second interrupt controller	0A0–0BF
DMA controller 2	0C0–0DF
Math coprocessor	0F0–0FF
Primary hard disk controller	1F0–1F8
Game controller	200–20F
XT expansion unit	210–217

TABLE 2.3   Common I/O Memory Assignments *(continued)*

System Device	I/O Address
FM synthesis interface	220–22F
CD-ROM I/O port	230–233
Bus mouse	238–23B
Plug-and-Play I/O port	274–277
LPT2 (second parallel port)	278–27F
COM 4 (serial port 4)	2E8–2EF
COM 2 (serial port 2)	2F8–2FF
Available	280–31F
XT hard disk controller	320–32F
MIDI port	330–33F
Alternate floppy controller	370–377
LPT1 (primary printer port)	378–37F
LPT3 (third parallel port)	3BC–3BF
Color graphics adapter (VGA)	3D0–3DF
COM 3 (serial port 3)	3E8–3EF
Floppy-disk controller	3F0–3F7
COM 1 (serial port 1)	3F8–3FF

Using DMA

Direct Memory Access (DMA) enables a device to transfer data directly to RAM by only using the processor during the transfer period. The result is a faster and more direct method of data transfer. This method was especially useful in older PCs, enabling the DMA channel to transfer data in the background, thus freeing the processor to tend to other duties. During a DMA cycle the CPU is placed in a hold state. This means that the CPU can execute internal instructions only and the external bus is disconnected (tri-stated) during the active DMA cycle. Devices such as floppy disks, hard disks, tape devices, and network cards typically use DMA.

Table 2.4 shows the standard DMA channels that most systems use. When two devices are configured to use the same DMA channel, neither device can transfer the data to memory correctly. The only available DMA channel on older PCs is DMA channel 3.

TABLE 2.4   Common DMA Assignments

System Device	DMA Channel
Available	0
Available	1
Floppy disk controller	2
Available	3
Not available (used for internal purposes or a second DMA controller)	4
Available	5
Available	6
Available	7

Assuming that the hardware has been installed, it can be managed through Device Manager, which is covered in the following section. If the hardware is non–Plug and Play compatible and needs to be manually installed, you would use the Add Hardware option in Control Panel to install it, which is covered in the "Using Control Panel" section of this chapter.

Using Device Manager

Device Manager is a graphically based utility that provides information about all of the devices—Plug and Play and non–Plug and Play—that your computer currently recognizes. Device Manager provides the following functionality:

- Provides a summary of all of the hardware that is installed on your computer and the status of each piece of hardware
- View and change hardware settings for a specific device (IRQ, base memory, I/O memory, and DMA)
- View, uninstall, update, or roll back the device driver that is used by each device
- If the device supports advanced settings, change advanced properties settings for a specific device
- Disable and enable devices
- Print a summary of all of the installed devices for your computer

You access Device Manager through Start ➤ Administrative Tools ➤ Computer Management. In the Computer Management window, select System Tools, and then select Device Manager, as shown in Figure 2.1.

FIGURE 2.1   Device Manager

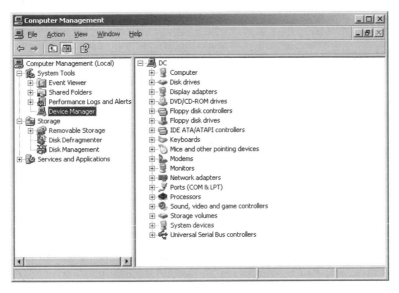

In the following sections you will learn how to use Device Manager to manage hardware, view devices, and print a report through Device Manager, as well as use the Hardware Troubleshooting Wizards.

Managing Hardware Devices through Device Manager

Along with displaying information about your hardware devices, the Device Manager utility provides configuration options for managing devices.

In the right pane of the Device Manager window, double-click the category of the device you wish to manage to see a list of the devices of that type recognized by your computer. Then right-click the specific device you wish to manage. You will see the options shown in Figure 2.2.

Update Driver   Used to install a more current version of the device driver.

Disable   Allows you to disable a device. This option is typically used with laptop computers that use different configurations associated with hardware profiles.

Uninstall   Allows you to uninstall the device driver.

Scan For Hardware Changes   Allows you to force a manual scan to see if any new hardware changes have been detected.

Properties   Allows you to configure the properties for the device. The device Properties dialog box that appears will have different tabs, depending on its type. Typically, most devices will have tabs for General, Driver, and Resources. These are covered in greater detail in the following sections.

FIGURE 2.2   Device management options

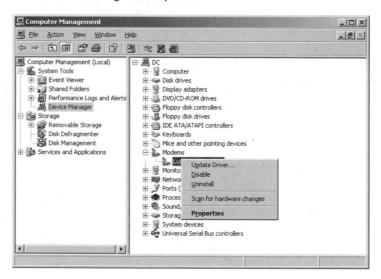

General Properties

The General tab, shown in Figure 2.3, lists the device type, manufacturer, and location. It also shows the device status, which indicates whether or not the device is working properly. If the device is not working properly, you can click the Troubleshoot button in the lower third of the dialog box to get some help with resolving the problem. Using the Troubleshoot option is covered in greater detail later, in the section, "Running the Hardware Troubleshooting Wizards."

FIGURE 2.3   The General tab of a device Properties dialog box

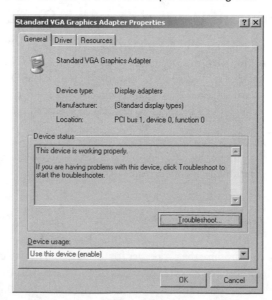

Driver Properties

The Driver tab, shown in Figure 2.4, displays information about the driver in the top half of the dialog box and allows you to manage the driver through the buttons in the lower half of the dialog box.

FIGURE 2.4   The Driver tab of a device Properties dialog box

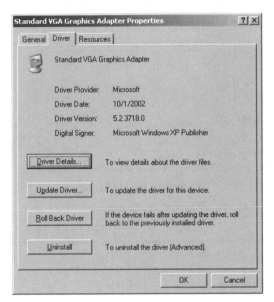

Through the information that is shown for the currently loaded driver, administrators can determine if they have the most current driver for their device and who has provided and signed the device driver. The information that is provided for each driver includes:

- Driver Provider
- Driver Date
- Driver Version
- Digital Signer

Through the bottom of the Driver tab, you see buttons for Driver Details, Update Driver, Roll Back Driver, and Uninstall.

Clicking the Driver Details button brings up the Driver File Details dialog box, shown in Figure 2.5. This is used to provide more information about the driver. You can see the location (within the file system) of the driver files, the provider, the file version, copyright information, and the digital signer for the driver.

The Update Driver and Roll Back Driver options allow you to update a device driver or roll back a device driver to a previous version in the event that an updated driver does not work properly. Each of these options is covered in detail in the "Managing Device Drivers" section of this chapter.

The Uninstall button is used to uninstall a device driver. This option is not typically used with Plug and Play devices, as the operating system will automatically re-install the hardware and device drivers on the next power up. However, this option might be used to uninstall a device driver for a non–Plug and Play device.

FIGURE 2.5   Driver File Details dialog box

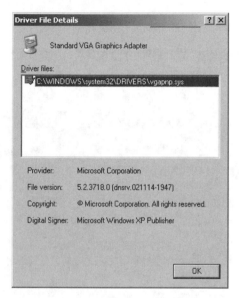

Resources Properties

If the server is using a device that allocates resources (IRQ, base memory, I/O memory, or DMA), then you will see a Resources tab, as shown in Figure 2.6.

FIGURE 2.6   The Resources tab of a device Properties dialog box

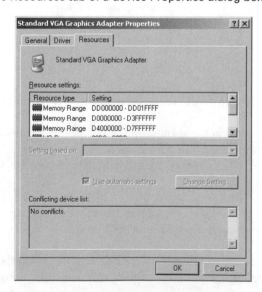

   In the top third of the screen, the Resources tab identifies all of the resources used by the device. The middle portion of the screen includes a Settings Based On drop-down list, which lists the hardware profiles that use the device. Servers will typically only use one hardware profile, so the Settings Based On list is normally inactive. The Use Automatic Settings checkbox allows you to edit settings on non-Plug and Play hardware to manually configure hardware devices.

Other Device Properties

The Properties dialog box for each device will contain will only applicable tabs, so you might not see the Resources tab on a built-in sound device, for instance. Some devices may also have additional tabs, based on the functionality that was coded into the driver. For example, the network adapter shown in Figure 2.7 lists two additional tabs: Advanced and Power Management. In this case, the Advanced tab allows you to set advanced features that are specific to the network adapter. The Power Management tab allows you to set power management options for the network adapter, such as bringing the computer out of standby (Wake On LAN).

FIGURE 2.7   The Power Management tab of a device Properties dialog box

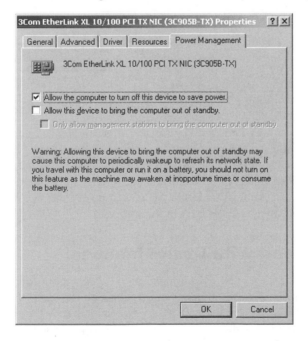

Viewing Resource Usage in Device Manager

In the previous section, you learned how to view resource use by device. Device Manager also allows you to view resource usage for DMA, I/O, IRQ, and Memory. This option is useful if you have a non–Plug and Play device and you are trying to determine what resources are available. To view resource usage, you would take the following steps:

1. From Device Manager, select View ➢ Resources by connection.

2. Device Manager displays a list of the current resources. Click a resource to see all of the resources of that type that have been allocated. Figure 2.8 shows an example of an IRQ listing in Device Manager.

FIGURE 2.8 Viewing resource allocation in Device Manager

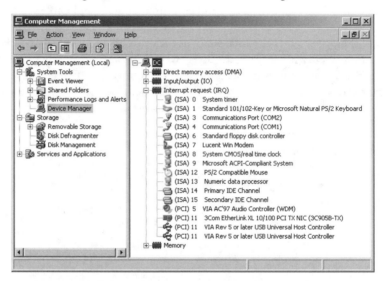

If you are installing a non–Plug and Play device, after you've configured the hardware resources, you can use the Add Hardware utility in Control Panel to add the new device to Windows Server 2003 and install the device driver. If the device is not listed, you will need to use a manufacturer-provided driver. Insert the disk that contains the driver and click the Have Disk button in Add Hardware. Adding hardware through Control Panel is covered in greater detail in the "Using Control Panel" section later in this chapter.

Printing a Report with Device Manager

One of the good practices for network administration is keeping thorough documentation for your servers, including configuration information. Through Device Manager, you can print reports, which can then be stored with other server documentation.

If you have a printer installed, you can print a report from Device Manager by selecting Action ➢ Print. This will access the Print dialog box, shown in Figure 2.9. At the bottom of the dialog box, you will see Report Type. From Report Type, you can select:

- System Summary

- Selected Class Or Device

- All Devices And System Summary

FIGURE 2.9   Print from Device Manager dialog box

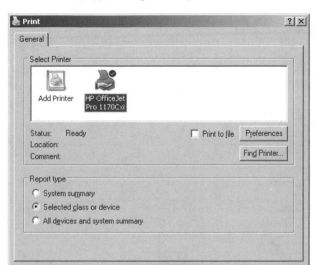

In Exercise 2.1, you will use Device Manager to view your server's configuration and to print a report of the configuration.

EXERCISE 2.1

Using Device Manager

1. Select Start ➢ Administrative Tools ➢ Computer Management. Expand System Tools, then Device Manager.

2. You will see a list of the devices that are installed on your computer. Expand Display Adapters, then double-click your display adapter.

3. Under the General tab, confirm that the Device Status is "This device is working properly."

4. Click the Driver tab, and note the digital signer for your driver.

5. Click the Resources tab and note the resources that are being used by your display adapter. Click OK to close the dialog box.

6. From the main dialog box, select View ➢ Resources By Connection. Expand Memory and you will see several memory ranges that have been used. Expand the memory range for PCI Bus and you should see the memory that is being used by your display adapter.

7. From the main dialog box, select View ➢ Devices by type.

8. From the main dialog box, select Action ➢ Print. If you have a printer configured for your server, select All Devices And System Summary and click the Print button.

Running the Hardware Troubleshooting Wizards

Hardware Troubleshooting Wizards are used to guide the user through a set of troubleshooting questions related to a specific piece of hardware. If your computer recognizes a device but can't properly access the device, you will see the device displayed through Device Manager with a yellow exclamation mark, as shown for the MPU-401 Compatible MIDI device in Figure 2.10.

FIGURE 2.10   Device Manager with incorrectly configured device

When you click on a device that is not running properly, you will see troubleshooting information in the Device Status section of the device's General tab, as shown in Figure 2.11.

FIGURE 2.11   General tab from Device Manager with incorrectly configured device

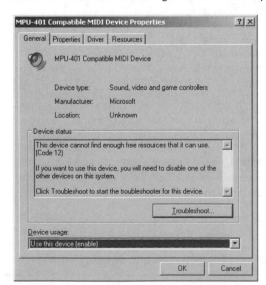

If you are not able to correct the problem based on the information provided through Device Status, you would click the Troubleshoot button to access the Hardware Troubleshooting Wizards, as shown in Figure 2.12.

FIGURE 2.12   The Hardware Troubleshooting Wizards

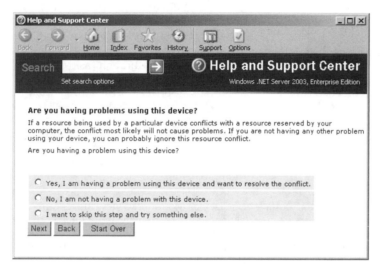

The Hardware Troubleshooting Wizards will lead you though a series of questions to help you resolve the specific problem you are having. The questions are arranged by category in a flowchart manner. Depending on how you answer each question, you will resolve the problem or be directed to try another logical troubleshooting step.

You should take notes of the selections you make within the Hardware Troubleshooting Wizards. Sometimes the wizard will ask you to reboot as a part of the troubleshooting process. By taking notes, you will be able to return to where the Hardware Troubleshooting Wizards left off when the reboot occurred.

In the next section, you will learn how to manage device drivers.

Device Driver Error Codes

If a device is not functioning properly, it will display an error code through Device Manager. The error code will display a message, which can then be used as a starting point in troubleshooting the device error.

Table 2.5 lists the error codes that have been defined for Device Manager, and steps for resolving the errors.

TABLE 2.5   Device Manager Error Codes and Resolutions

Error Code	Error Resolution
This device is not configured correctly. (Code 1)	Verify that the device is using the most current Windows Server 2003 driver. Verify that the device has been properly configured.
The driver for this device might be corrupted, or your system may be running low on memory or other resources. (Code 3)	Verify that your computer has sufficient memory. You can view memory usage through Task Manager. If your server is low on memory, close unused applications or add memory. If you think the driver is corrupted, uninstall the device driver and scan for new hardware to reinstall the driver.
This device cannot start. (Code 10)	Verify that the device is using the most current Windows Server 2003 driver. If the device still won't start, run the Hardware Troubleshooting Wizards for the device you are trying to install.
This device cannot find enough free resources that it can use. If you want to use this device, you will need to disable one of the other devices on this system. (Code 12)	Use Device Manager to view the resources that have been allocated. If two devices have been configured (through the system BIOS or Windows Server 2003) to use the same IRQ, I/O, memory, or DMA, then this error can occur. Disable the conflicting device.
This device cannot work properly until you restart the computer. (Code 14)	The installation of some devices requires the computer to be restarted so that the device will work properly, you need to restart your computer if you see this error code.
Windows cannot identify all of the resources this device uses. (Code 16)	The device is not properly configured. Within Device Manager look on the Resources tab for the device Properties. If the device can be manually configured, configure the device through the Change Settings button. If the device can't be manually configured, clear the Use Automatic Settings Checkbox.
Reinstall the drivers for this device. (Code 18)	The device driver for the device is missing or corrupt. Uninstall the driver and install the most current version of the device driver for Windows Server 2003. If the problem is a result of updating a driver, use the driver rollback option to roll the driver back to a previously known good device driver.
Windows cannot start this hardware device because its configuration information (in the Registry) is incomplete or damaged. To fix this problem you can first try running a troubleshooting wizard. If that does not work, you should uninstall and then reinstall the hardware device. (Code 19)	The hardware has a configuration error within the Registry. This error can occur if the device is configured to use more than one service or the driver name is not configured as a part of the service subkey. Uninstall the device driver and install the most current device driver for Windows Server 2003. If the problem is a result of updating a driver, use the driver rollback option to roll the driver back to a previously known good device driver.

TABLE 2.5   Device Manager Error Codes and Resolutions *(continued)*

Error Code	Error Resolution
Windows is removing this device. (Code 21)	Wait a minute and refresh the view in Device Manager. If the device does not appear, reinstall the device and install the most current driver for Windows Server 2003.
This device is disabled. (Code 22)	A user has disabled the device through Device Manager. Click Enable Device in Device Manager to enable the device.
This device is not present, is not working properly, or does not have all its drivers installed. (Code 24)	The device may have been prepared for removal. If it has been marked for removal, you should remove and reinsert the device, which will cause it to be recognized again. This error can also occur if the hardware is missing or misconfigured. Verify that the hardware has been properly installed and that the most current device driver has been loaded for Windows Server 2003. If the problem is a result of updating a driver, use the driver rollback option to roll the driver back to a previously known good device driver.
The drivers for this device are not installed. (Code 28)	Install the most current device driver for Windows Server 2003. If the problem is a result of updating a driver, use the driver rollback option to roll the driver back to a previously known good device driver.
This device is disabled because the firmware of the device did not give it the required resources. (Code 29)	Verify that the BIOS for the hardware device is enabled. Consult the documentation from the hardware vendor for instructions on configuring the hardware or enabling BIOS settings.
This device is not working properly because Windows cannot load the drivers required for this device. (Code 31)	Install the most current device driver for Windows Server 2003. If the problem is a result of updating a driver, use the driver rollback option to roll the driver back to a previously known good device driver.
A driver (service) for this device has been disabled. An alternate driver may be providing this functionality. (Code 32)	The start type for the service has been set to Disabled in the Registry. Uninstall the current driver and then select the Scan For Hardware Changes option in Device Manager to reinstall or upgrade the driver. If the driver is still not loading properly, check the Registry to see if the service start type is still marked as Disabled; if so, configure the start type as Start.
Windows cannot determine which resources are required for this device. (Code 33)	Verify that the hardware is compatible with Windows Server 2003 and that you have a Windows Server 2003 driver loaded for the device. The hardware may need to be manually configured or replaced.

TABLE 2.5   Device Manager Error Codes and Resolutions *(continued)*

Error Code	Error Resolution
Windows cannot determine the settings for this device. Consult the documentation that came with this device and use the Resource tab to set the configuration. (Code 34)	The device needs to be manually configured. Consult the documentation from the hardware vendor for instructions on configuring the hardware.
Your computer's system firmware does not include enough information to properly configure and use this device. To use this device, contact your computer manufacturer to obtain a firmware or BIOS update. (Code 35)	The computer's Multiprocessor System (MPS) table, which is used to store the resource assignment for the BIOS, does not support an entry for your device. Contact your computer manufacturer to obtain a BIOS update.
This device is requesting a PCI interrupt but is configured for an ISA interrupt (or vice versa). Please use the computer's system setup program to reconfigure the interrupt for this device. (Code 36)	The computer is not able to perform IRQ translation. See if you can configure the BIOS through the computer's Setup program, which may allow you to reserve an IRQ for a PCI or ISA device.
Windows cannot initialize the device driver for this hardware. (Code 37)	Uninstall the driver and install the most current version of the device driver for Windows Server 2003. If the problem is a result of updating a driver, use the driver rollback option to roll the driver back to a previously known good device driver.
Windows cannot load the device driver for this hardware because a previous instance of the device driver is still in memory. (Code 38)	Restart the computer and then install the new driver.
Windows cannot load the device driver for this hardware. The driver may be corrupt or missing. (Code 39)	Uninstall the current driver and then select the Scan For Hardware Changes option in Device Manager to reinstall or upgrade the driver. If the problem is a result of updating a driver, use the driver rollback option to roll the driver back to a previously known good device driver.
Windows cannot access this hardware because its service key information in the Registry is missing or recorded incorrectly. (Code 40)	The hardware has a configuration error within the Registry. This error can occur if the device is configured to use more than one service or the driver name is not configured as a part of the service subkey. Uninstall the device driver and use the Scan For Hardware Changes option within Device Manager to install the most current device driver for Windows Server 2003.

TABLE 2.5 Device Manager Error Codes and Resolutions *(continued)*

Error Code	Error Resolution
Windows successfully loaded the device driver for this hardware but cannot find the hardware device. (Code 41)	This error can occur when a driver is loaded for a non–Plug and Play device. Use the Add Hardware option in Control Panel to install the non–Plug and Play device.
Windows cannot load the device driver for this hardware because there is a duplicate device already running in the system. (Code 42)	This error can occur if the bus driver creates two identically named children for the same bus device. This can occur when a device is moved and it is recognized as a new device before the old device is deleted. Restarting the computer will correct this error.
Windows has stopped this device because it has reported problems. (Code 43)	The device has reported hardware errors. See the product documentation for the hardware device to try to resolve the hardware error.
An application or service has shut down this hardware device. (Code 44)	This error can occur if an application or service is in conflict with the device. Restarting the computer typically corrects this error.
Currently, this hardware device is not connected to the computer. (Code 45)	The device was previously connected to the computer, but the computer does not currently recognize the device. Reconnect the hardware device to the computer.
Windows cannot gain access to this hardware device because the operating system is in the process of shutting down. (Code 46)	Restart the computer. The device should work properly.
Windows cannot use this hardware device because it has been prepared for "safe removal" but has not been removed from the computer. (Code 47)	The device has been prepared for ejection. Remove and reinsert the device, which will cause it to be recognized again.
The software for this device has been blocked from starting because it is known to have problems with Windows. Contact the hardware vendor for a new driver. (Code 48)	Contact the hardware vendor to get a Windows Server 2003 approved device driver.
Windows cannot start new hardware devices because the system hive is too large (exceeds the Registry Size Limit). (Code 49)	Uninstall any hardware devices that are not being used to free up space within the Registry.

Managing Device Drivers

Most of the devices on the Microsoft Hardware Compatibility List (HCL) have device drivers that are included on the Windows Server 2003 distribution CD. Managing device drivers involves understanding and being able to configure your server's driver signing options, updating drivers when necessary, and rolling back to older drivers if an upgraded driver does not work properly. These options are all covered in greater detail in the following sections.

Managing Driver Signing

In the past, poorly written device drivers have caused problems with Windows operating systems. Microsoft is now promoting a mechanism called *driver signing* as a way of ensuring that drivers have passed Microsoft's testing process for compatibility with Windows Server 2003. By applying a digital signature, device drivers can't be altered after they have been signed.

In the following sections you will learn how to configure driver signing options and how to verify existing device driver signatures.

Configuring Driver Signing Options

You can specify how Windows Server 2003 will respond if you choose to install an unsigned driver through the Driver Signing Options dialog box. To access this dialog box, select Start ➤ Control Panel ➤ System, click the Hardware tab, and under the Device Manager section, click the Driver Signing button. This opens the Driver Signing Options dialog box, as shown in Figure 2.13.

FIGURE 2.13 The Driver Signing Options dialog box

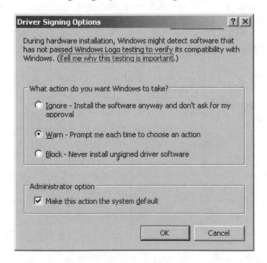

In the Driver Signing Options dialog box, you can select from three options for file system verification:

- The Ignore option has Windows Server 2003 install all of the files, whether or not they are signed. You will not see any type of message about driver signing.

- The Warn option has Windows Server 2003 display a warning message before installing an unsigned file. You can then choose to continue with the installation or cancel it. This is the default setting.

- The Block option has Windows Server 2003 prevent the installation of any unsigned file. You will see an error message when you attempt to install the unsigned driver, and you will not be able to continue.

If you check the Make This Action The System Default checkbox in the Administrator Option section, the settings that you apply will be used by all users who log on to the computer.

Verifying File Signature

Windows Server 2003 includes a File Signature Verification utility that you can use to verify that system files have been digitally signed. The installation of unsigned drivers can cause random lockups on a server. To run this utility, select Start ➢ Run and in the Run dialog box, type in `sigverif` and click OK. This starts the File Signature Verification utility, as shown in Figure 2.14.

FIGURE 2.14   The File Signature Verification utility

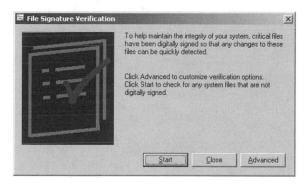

If you click the Start button in the File Signature Verification utility, your system will be scanned for any unsigned drivers. At the end of the scan process, the Signature Verification Results dialog box will appear, and will list any files that have not been digitally signed.

The Advanced button in the File Signature Verification utility allows you to configure advanced search and logging options, as shown in Figure 2.15.

Within the Advanced File Signature Verification Settings dialog box, the Search tab is configured to notify you if any system files are not digitally signed. You can also select the Look For Other Files That Are Not Digitally Signed option, which allows you to specify what file types you want to search for, which folder should be searched, and whether subfolders should be included within the search.

The Logging tab of Advanced File Signature Verification, shown in Figure 2.16, is used to specify whether you want to save the file signature verification results to a log file, and if so whether to append it to the existing log file or overwrite the existing log file. You can also specify the log file name that will be used. If logging is enabled, by default a log file called *windir*\\ `sigverif.txt` will be created. Figure 2.17 shows a sample log file that was created through the File Signature Verification utility.

FIGURE 2.15 Search tab of Advanced File Signature Verification Settings

FIGURE 2.16 Logging tab of Advanced File Signature Verification Settings

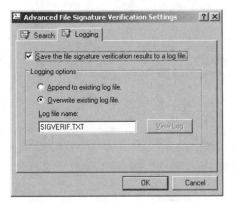

FIGURE 2.17 Sigverif.txt log file

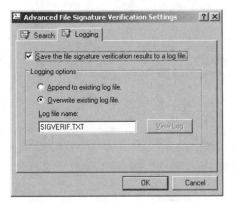

You can also see detailed information about driver signing through the System Information utility, which is covered in greater detail in the "Using the System Information Utility" section of this chapter.

In Exercise 2.2, you will check the setting for driver signing and run the File Signature Verification utility.

EXERCISE 2.2

Managing Driver Signing

1. Select Start ➤ Control Panel ➤ System, click the Hardware tab, and under the Device Manager section, click the Driver Signing button.

2. In the Driver Signing Options dialog box, verify that the Warn radio button is selected and the Make This Action The System Default checkbox is checked.

3. Click the OK button to close the dialog box. Click the OK button within the System Properties dialog box.

4. Select Start ➤ Run. In the Run dialog box, type **sigverif** and click the OK button.

5. In the File Signature Verification window, click the Start button.

6. When the results of the signature verification appear, note whether the utility detected any files that were not digitally signed. From the Signature Verification dialog box, click the Close button.

7. From the File Signature Verification window, click the Advanced button, then the Logging tab.

8. From the Logging tab, click the View Log button. View the log file, and when done, close the log file. From the Advanced File Signature Verification Settings dialog box, click the OK button, then the Close button in the File Signature Verification window.

Updating Drivers

Device manufacturers periodically update device drivers to add functionality or enhance driver performance. The updated drivers are typically posted on the device manufacturer's website.

If you have an updated device driver, you can upgrade your device driver through the Device Manager utility. To update a driver, double-click the device in Device Manager and click the Driver tab. From the Driver tab, click the Update Driver button and the Hardware Update Wizard will start. You can let the wizard search for a newer driver or you can specify the new device driver's location. Once the wizard locates the updated files, they will be copied to your computer.

In Exercise 2.3, you will update a driver using Device Manager.

EXERCISE 2.3

Updating a Device Driver

1.   Select Start ➤ Administrative Tools ➤ Computer Management. Expand System Tools, then Device Manager.

2.   The right side of the window lists all of the devices that are installed on your computer. Double-click the device whose driver you want to update.

3.   The device Properties dialog box appears. Click the Driver tab.

4.   The Driver tab appears. Click the Update Driver button.

5.   The Hardware Update Wizard starts. Select the Install From A List Or Specific Location (Advanced) radio button. Click the Next button.

6.   The Hardware Update Wizard will continue and you will be asked to choose your search and installation options. Specify the location of the new driver and click the Next button.

7.   The files will be installed for your driver. Then you will see the Completing The Upgrade Device Driver Wizard dialog box. Click the Finish button to close this dialog box.

8.   You may see a dialog box indicating that you must restart your computer before the change can be successfully implemented. If so, restart your computer.

Using Driver Rollback

Driver rollback is used to restore the previous device driver that your computer successfully used. You would use driver rollback if you installed or upgraded a driver and you encountered problems that you did not have with the previous driver. Some of the problems with drivers relate to the following errors:

- Use of unsigned drivers
- Resource conflicts
- Badly written drivers

The following steps would be used to roll back a driver:

1.   Select Start ➤ Administrative Tools ➤ Computer Management. Expand System Tools, then Device Manager.

2.   Expand the category for the device driver you want to roll back—for example, a network card—then double-click the device and select the Driver tab as previously shown in Figure 2.4. From the Driver tab, click the Roll Back Driver option.

3.   You will be prompted to confirm that you want to overwrite the current driver; click the Yes button. The rollback process will proceed or you will be notified that an older driver was not available for rollback.

Using the System Information Utility

The *System Information utility* is used to collect and display configuration information for your server. The information can be viewed for the local server or a computer that you are connected to. You access the System Information utility through Start ➤ All Programs ➤ Accessories ➤ System Tools ➤ System Information.

When the System Information utility is run, it will automatically collect information about your system settings. Once the information is collected, you will see a summary in the main dialog box of System Information, as shown in Figure 2.18. This utility is especially helpful for administrators or Help Desk operators who are working on servers they are not familiar with, giving them a quick overview of system configuration.

FIGURE 2.18   System Information dialog box

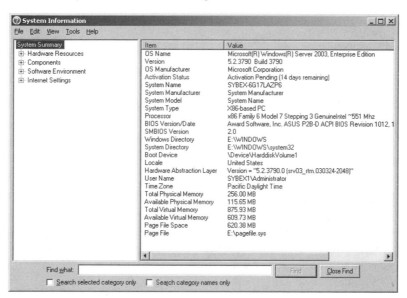

Administrators and Help Desk operators can save the data provided through System Information to a file (by default an `.nfo`—System Information—file, through File ➤ Save), export the data to a text file (through File ➤ Export), or print the collected information (through File ➤ Print), assuming that a printer has been installed. If you have administrative rights on the remote computer, you can also view system information for a remote computer (through View ➤ Remote Computer).

The information that is included in the System Information summary is as follows:

- OS name
- Version (including build number and any Service Packs that have been applied)
- OS Manufacturer
- Activation Status
- System name (same as computer name)

- System manufacturer
- System model
- System type
- Processor
- BIOS version/date
- SMBIOS version
- Windows directory
- System directory
- Boot device
- Locale
- Hardware Abstraction Layer
- User name
- Time zone
- Total physical memory
- Available physical memory
- Total virtual memory
- Available virtual memory
- Page file space
- Page file

Through the System Information utility, you can also see more specific information about hardware resources, components, software environment, Internet settings, and applications. The following sections will focus on the information relating to configuring Windows Server 2003 hardware using the System Information utility. This includes the Hardware Resources, Components, and Software Environment sections of System Information. You will also learn how to save, export, and print data. In addition, you will learn about using the command-line utility for System Information: `Msinfo32.exe`.

Viewing Hardware Resources

Through Hardware Resources in System Information, you can view detailed information on all of the resources that are in use by your server. Through Hardware Resources, you can view options for:

Conflicts/Sharing   Conflicts/Sharing lists all of the devices that are using the same DMA, IRQ, and memory resources. Windows Server 2003 generally manages resource sharing with no problems, but if a conflict did exist, this option would be useful in resolving it.

DMA   DMA lists all of the DMA resources that are currently in use for the computer.

Forced Hardware   Forced Hardware is used to list any hardware that you have configured manually. Typically, hardware is configured through Plug and Play technology and you will not see any entries under this option.

I/O   I/O lists all of the I/O memory resources that are currently in use for the computer.

IRQs   IRQs lists all of the IRQ resources that are currently in use for the computer.

Memory   Memory lists all of the base memory resources that are currently in use for the computer.

Viewing Components

Through Components in System Information, you can view verbose information about specific system components. The information that is displayed is dependant on the component you are viewing. You can see an example of information that would be provided through Components in Figure 2.19.

The components that you can see detailed information for include:

- Multimedia
- CD-ROM
- Sound device
- Display
- Infrared
- Input
- Modem
- Network
- Ports
- Storage
- Printing
- Problem devices
- USB

FIGURE 2.19   Components in the System Information dialog box

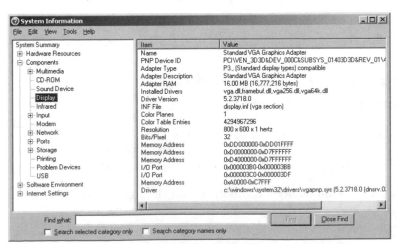

Viewing Software Environment

Through Software Environment in System Information, you can view verbose information about your software environment. The information that is displayed is dependant on the component you are viewing. In this section, we will focus on the software components that deal with hardware installation, which include the following:

System Drivers   System Drivers provides detailed information about all of the server's system drivers. Information includes the name, description, file location, type (for example, kernel driver or file system driver), whether the driver is started, the Start mode (for example, boot, manual, system, auto, or disabled), the current state (running or stopped), the status (should be OK), error control settings (for example, Normal or Ignore), whether to accept a user pause, and whether to accept a user stop.

Signed Drivers   Signed Drivers lists all of the signed drivers that have been installed on the server. A signed driver is a special driver that has been certified by Microsoft (these drivers are called Windows Hardware Quality Lab drivers or simply WHQL drivers) by going through a thorough testing process to ensure driver reliability. The information that you can see through Signed Drivers is the device name, the device class, the driver version, the driver date, the manufacturer, the INF name, the driver name, and the device ID.

Environment Variables   Environment Variables includes information about the server's computer environment, which consists of the number of processors the server is using, the path to the operating system, and the locations of temporary folders.

Saving, Exporting, and Printing Data

If you want to create a snapshot of the information that is collected through the System Information utility, you can save or export the data. The following options can be used to save System Information to a file or print the data:

- If you select File ➤ Save, the data will be saved as an .nfo file; when the file is opened, data will be displayed through the System Information interface.
- If you select File ➤ Export, the data will be saved as a text file.
- If you select File ➤ Print and you have configured a printer, you can print it.

Viewing Current or Historical Data and Remote Computer Data

By default, the System Information utility displays current information. To view historical data, select View ➤ System History from the main windows of System Information.

You will see all of the information that has changed in regard to system configuration information.

By default, the System Information utility displays information for the local computer. To view data on a remote computer, you would take the following steps:

1. From the main window of System Information, select View ➤ Remote Computer.

2. The Remote Computer dialog box appears. Select Remote Computer on the network dialog box and type in the name of the network computer you wish to view, then click the OK button.

In Exercise 2.4, you will use the System Information utility.

Using the System Information Utility

1. Select Start ➤ All Programs ➤ Accessories ➤ System Tools ➤ System Information.

2. Review the System Summary for your server.

3. Expand Hardware Resources. Expand Conflict/Sharing to see the resources that are shared and to verify that no conflicts exist.

4. Select File ➤ Save to create a System Information file. Give the filename today's date, *mmddyy*, and click the Save button. By default, an extension of .nfo will be applied.

5. Expand Software Environment. Expand Signed Drivers to see a detailed listing of driver configurations for the drivers installed on your server.

6. Close the System Information utility.

Using the *Msinfo32* Command-Line Utility

The *Msinfo32* command-line utility provides the same functionality as the System Information utility. Through the use of this command, you can:

- Gather information about computers through batch files

- Automatically create a System Information file (.nfo) or text file (.txt) with a snapshot of the computer's system information

- Create and save a System Information file, without ever opening the System Information utility on a local or remote computer

The options associated with Msinfo32 are defined in Table 2.6.

TABLE 2.6   Msinfo32 Command Line Switches Defined

Msinfo32 Switch	Description
/pch	Starts the System Information tool in System History view.
/nfo *path*	Creates an export file that collects data as a System Information file with an .nfo extension (unless another extension name is specified in *path*)

TABLE 2.6 Msinfo32 Command Line Switches Defined *(continued)*

Msinfo32 Switch	Description
/report *path*	Creates a report file that collects and stores the system information as text format.
/computer *ComputerName*	Assuming you have administrative rights on a remote computer, allows you to start the System Information tool on a remote computer.
/showcategories	Instead of starting System Information with friendly or localized names, starts System Information with all available categories displayed.
/categories *categoryID*	Starts the System Information utility and displays only the specified category. You can get a list of all categories from the /showcategories switch. If you want to display more than one category, you can add them to this switch with +*CategoryID*

The Msinfo32 command should be executed from the Run utility. If you use it from a command prompt window, you will generate an error message that the program is not recognized.

 Real World Scenario

Using the Msinfo32 Command for Troubleshooting

You are the corporate network administrator for a company that has the main corporate office in Atlanta and remote offices in Houston, San Jose, and New York. Each remote location has its own Windows Server 2003 domain controller (and a local administrator), which is connected to the corporate network. The local administrators can perform basic tasks, but require corporate support for complex administrative tasks or occasionally for troubleshooting.

In order to better support the remote administrators, you are collecting configuration information for each of the remote servers. You want the information to be as detailed as possible. You decide to use the Msinfo32 command to create .nfo files for each remote server. The information is then stored in a central location and accessed when any of the servers require hardware troubleshooting.

Using Control Panel

Control Panel is an item on the Start menu that contains options for configuring your computer's setup. In Windows Server 2003, you can access the Control Panel by selecting Start ➢ Control Panel. A list of the options available in the Control Panel will expand by default.

The Control Panel menu is logically organized by function, as shown in Figure 2.20. Table 2.7 provides brief descriptions of Control Panel options that are displayed by default on a Windows Server 2003 domain controller.

FIGURE 2.20   Control Panel Options

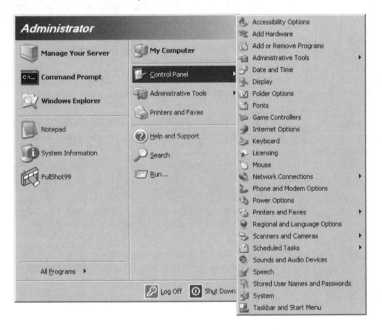

TABLE 2.7   Control Panel Options

Option	Description
Accessibility Options	Allows you to configure options that make Windows Server 2003 more accessible to users with limited sight, hearing, or mobility
Add Hardware	Allows you to install, remove, and troubleshoot your hardware (primarily used for non–Plug and Play hardware)
Add or Remove Programs	Allows you to change or remove programs that are currently installed on your computer, add new programs, and add or remove Windows Server 2003 components

TABLE 2.7   Control Panel Options *(continued)*

Option	Description
Administrative Tools	Provides access to Windows Server 2003 administrative utilities
Date and Time	Allows you to set the date, time, and time zone for your computer
Display	Allows you to configure your computer's display, including themes, desktop, screen saver, appearance, and settings
Folder Options	Allows you to configure folder options, such as general folder properties, view options, file types, and offline files and folders
Fonts	Allows you to manage the fonts installed on your computer
Game Controllers	Allows you to add, remove, and configure game controllers, including joysticks and game pads
Internet Options	Allows you to configure Internet connection properties, including security, content settings, and Internet programs
Keyboard	Allows you to configure keyboard settings, including speed, input locales (language and keyboard layout), and the keyboard driver
Licensing	Allows you to specify how many licenses have been purchased and can be used by clients attaching to the server
Mouse	Allows you to configure mouse settings, including button configuration, mouse pointers, motion settings, and the mouse driver
Network Connections	Contains settings for network connections and a Wizard to create new connections
Phone and Modem Options	Allows you to configure telephone dialing options and modem properties
Power Options	Allows you to configure power schemes, advanced options, hibernation, and UPS settings
Printers and Faxes	Allows you to install and manage printers and fax devices
Regional and Language Options	Allows you to set regional options, including numbers, currency, time, date, and input locales
Scanners and Cameras	Allows you to configure cameras and scanners
Scheduled Tasks	Allows you to configure tasks to be run at specific times or intervals

TABLE 2.7   Control Panel Options *(continued)*

Option	Description
Sounds and Audio Devices	Allows you to configure sound devices and to assign sounds to system events
Speech	Changes settings for text-to-speech and speech recognition
Stored User Names and Passwords	Allows you to store logon information for use with network locations and websites
System	Allows you to configure system properties, including network identification, hardware, user profiles, and advanced settings
Taskbar and Start Menu	Allows you to customize the Start menu and the Taskbar

The options that are related to hardware configuration—Add Hardware, Display, Keyboard, Mouse, Phone and Modem Options, and Sounds and Audio Devices—are covered in greater detail in the following subsections.

While other Control Panel options such as Game Controllers, and Scanners and Cameras are also hardware options, you would not typically add these devices to a Windows Server 2003 computer. These devices are typically associated with client computers. Therefore, we will not discuss these in the following sections.

Using Add Hardware

If you have non–Plug and Play hardware, you can install it through the Add Hardware icon in Control Panel, assuming that your device has a Windows Server 2003 driver. When you access the Add Hardware option, the Add Hardware Wizard will start automatically.

The following steps are used with the Add Hardware Wizard to add non–Plug and Play hardware:

1. Select Start ➤ Control Panel ➤ Add Hardware.

2. The Add Hardware Wizard will start and you will see the Welcome To The Add Hardware Wizard dialog box. Click the Next button to continue.

3. The Add Hardware Wizard will search for any new hardware. If no new hardware is detected, the Is The Hardware Connected? dialog box will appear, as shown in Figure 2.21. In order to proceed with the Add Hardware Wizard, the hardware must already be installed on the server. Select Yes, I Have Already Connected The Hardware and click the Next button.

FIGURE 2.21   Is The Hardware Connected dialog box

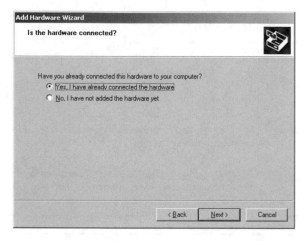

4.   The Add Hardware Wizard will display any hardware that is already installed on your computer through the The Following Hardware Is Already Installed On Your Computer dialog box, as shown in Figure 2.22. If the non–Plug and Play hardware is already listed, then you do not need to add the hardware. If the non–Plug and Play hardware is not listed, scroll down to the bottom of the dialog box until you see Add A New Hardware Device and highlight it. Click the Next button.

FIGURE 2.22   The Following Hardware Is Already Installed On Your Computer dialog box

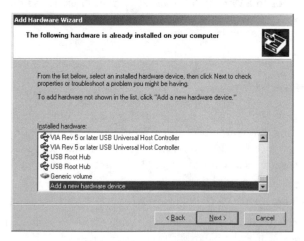

5.   The The Wizard Can Help You Install Other Hardware dialog box will appear, as shown in Figure 2.23. If Windows Server 2003 can't recognize your hardware, select Install The Hardware That I Manually Select From A List (Advanced) and click the Next button.

6.   The From The List Below, Select The Type Of Hardware You Are Installing dialog box will appear, as shown in Figure 2.24. Select the category for the hardware you are installing and click the Next button.

FIGURE 2.23   The Wizard Can Help You Install Other Hardware dialog box

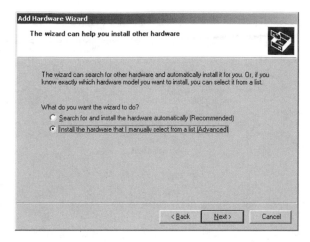

FIGURE 2.24   From The List Below, Select The Type Of Hardware You Are Installing
dialog box

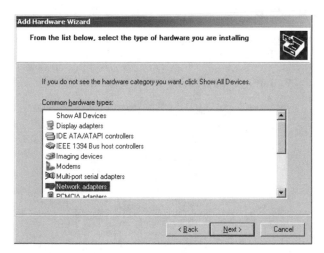

7. A dialog box will appear to prompt you to select a device, as shown in Figure 2.25. In this
   example, the Select Network Adapter dialog box will list the manufacturers and network
   adapters that are included with Windows Server 2003. If your device is not on the list, click
   the Have Disk button and specify the location of the manufacturer-provided Windows
   Server 2003 device driver. Then click the Next button.

8. The The Wizard Is Ready To Install Your Hardware dialog box will appear. If the hardware to install is listed properly, click the Next button and the needed files will be copied
   and installed.

9. The Completing The Add Hardware Wizard dialog box will appear. Click the Finish
   button.

FIGURE 2.25 Select Network Adapter dialog box

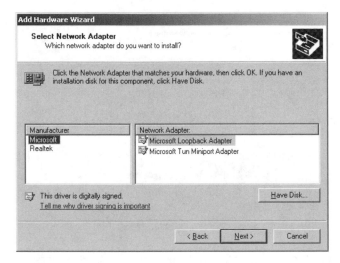

Configuring Display

You can configure your display adapter through the Display Properties dialog box (see Figure 2.26). To open it, choose Control Panel ➢ Display.

FIGURE 2.26 The Settings tab of the Display Properties dialog box

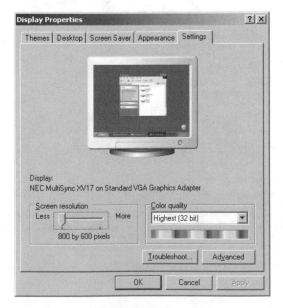

From the Settings tab, you can set screen resolution and color quality. The settings you can select are based on the display adapter your server is using.

The other tabs in the Display Properties dialog box allow you to customize the appearance of your Desktop.

To configure advanced settings for your video adapter, click the Advanced button in the lower-right corner of the Settings tab. This opens the monitor's Properties dialog box, as shown in Figure 2.27. The tabs in this dialog box can change because they are manufacturer specific, but usually there will be five of them with options for your video adapter and monitor:

- The General tab allows you to configure the DPI (dots per inch) setting for the display. You can also specify compatibility settings that are used with non–Windows Server 2003 compatible applications.

- The Adapter tab allows you to view and configure the properties of your video adapter.

- The Monitor tab allows you to view and configure the properties of your monitor, including the screen refresh rate (how often the screen is redrawn).

  A lower refresh frequency setting can cause your screen to flicker. Setting the refresh frequency too high can damage some monitors.

- The Troubleshoot tab allows you to configure how Windows Server 2003 uses your graphics hardware. For example, you can configure hardware acceleration settings.

- The Color Management tab allows you to select color profiles (the colors that are displayed on your monitor).

FIGURE 2.27   The monitor's Properties dialog box

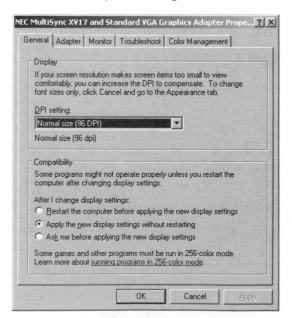

In Exercise 2.5, you will view the properties of your video adapter.

Usually, the video adapter is configured for typical use. Be careful if you change these settings, because improper settings may cause your display to be unreadable. You will get a chance to preview the settings before any changes are made to your configuration, so the chance for misconfiguration is minimized. However, if your video settings are unreadable, you can start your computer in Safe Mode.

EXERCISE 2.5

Viewing Video Adapter Properties

1. Select Start ➤ Control Panel ➤ Display and select the Settings tab.

2. Click the Advanced button at the bottom of the Settings tab. Note your current settings in the General tab.

3. Click the Adapter tab. Note your current settings.

4. Click the Monitor tab. Note your current settings.

5. Click the Troubleshoot tab. Note your current settings.

6. Click the OK button to close the monitor's Properties dialog box.

7. Click the OK button to close the Display Properties dialog box.

Configuring the Keyboard

You can configure keyboard options through the Keyboard Properties dialog box, shown in Figure 2.28. To access this dialog box, select the Keyboard option in Control Panel.

You must have a keyboard attached to your computer before you can install Windows Server 2003.

This dialog box has two tabs with options that control your keyboard's behavior:

- The Speed tab lets you configure how quickly characters are repeated when you hold down a key. You can also specify the cursor blink rate.

- The Hardware tab specifies the device settings for your keyboard.

FIGURE 2.28   The Keyboard Properties dialog box

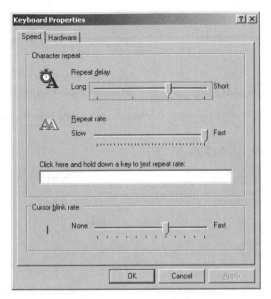

Configuring the Mouse

You can configure mouse options through the Mouse Properties dialog box, shown in Figure 2.29. To access this dialog box, select the Mouse option in Control Panel.

FIGURE 2.29   The Mouse Properties dialog box

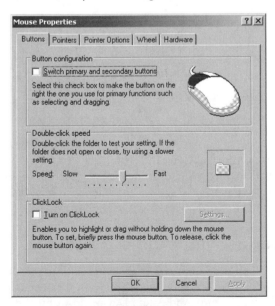

This dialog box has five tabs with options that control your mouse's behavior:

- The Buttons tab lets you configure the button configuration, double-click speed, and ClickLock (which allows you to highlight or drag an option without holding down the mouse button).

- The Pointers tab is used to select the mouse pointer scheme your server will use.

- The Pointer Options tab allows you to select motion, snap to, and visibility options.

- The Wheel tab allows you to select the scrolling options that will be used.

- The Hardware tab specifies the device you are using and the device properties.

Configuring the Modem

You can configure modem options through the Phone and Modem Options dialog box, shown in Figure 2.30. To access this dialog box, select the Phone And Modems option in Control Panel.

FIGURE 2.30   Modems tab in Phone And Modems Options dialog box

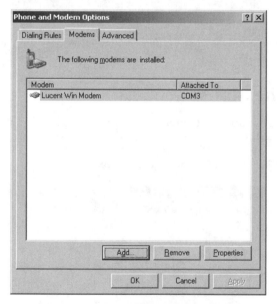

You can manage the modem properties by clicking on and selecting the modem you want to manage on the Modems tab, then clicking the Properties button. This brings up the Modem Properties dialog box, which allows you to configure general properties and modem properties, run diagnostics, set advanced parameters, view and manage the driver, and view the resources the modem is using.

Configuring Sounds and Audio Devices

By default, Windows Server 2003 does not enable audio. Through the Sounds And Audio Devices Properties dialog box, as shown in Figure 2.31, you can enable Windows Audio. To access this dialog box, select Sounds And Audio Devices in Control Panel.

FIGURE 2.31   Sounds And Audio Devices Properties dialog box

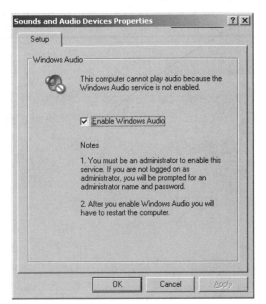

Only an administrator can enable this option; and once it is enabled, you need to restart the computer for the change to take effect.

Using the Registry Editor

The *Registry* is a database that the operating system uses to store configuration information, including hardware configuration. The Registry Editor program is used to edit the Registry. Normally, when you make changes to your configuration, you use other utilities, such as Control Panel. This utility is designed for advanced configuration of the system.

Only experienced administrators should use the Registry Editor. It should only be used to make configuration changes that cannot be made through more conventional means. For example, you might edit the Registry to specify an alternate location for a print spool folder. Improper changes to the Registry can cause the computer to fail to boot. You should use the Registry Editor with extreme caution.

Previous versions of Windows shipped with two versions of the Registry Editor, but Windows Server 2003 only ships with a single version, *Regedit*. To start the Registry Editor, Select Start ➢ Run, and type **regedit** in the Run dialog box.

You can also access the Registry Editor by entering **regedt32**, which was the name of one of the versions of the Registry Editor in Windows 2000. However, this is just a pointer to the actual regedit utility.

The Registry is organized in a hierarchical tree format of keys and subkeys that represent logical areas of computer configuration. By default, when you open the Registry Editor, you see five Registry key options, as shown in Figure 2.32. The five Registry keys are described in Table 2.8.

FIGURE 2.32   The Registry Editor

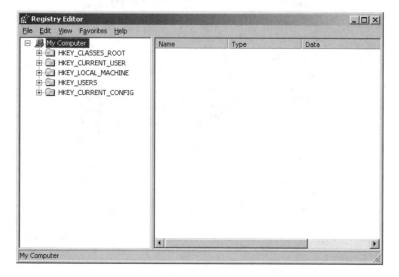

TABLE 2.8   Registry Keys

Registry Key	Description
HKEY_CURRENT_USER	Contains the configuration information for the user who is currently logged on to the computer. This key is a subkey of the HKEY_USERS key.
HKEY_USERS	Contains the configuration information for all users of the computer.
HKEY_LOCAL_MACHINE	Contains computer hardware configuration information. This computer configuration is used regardless of the user who is logged in.
HKEY_CLASSES_ROOT	Contains configuration information that is used by Windows Explorer to properly associate file types with applications.
HKEY_CURRENT_CONFIG	Contains the configuration of the hardware profile that is used during system startup.

Summary

In this chapter, you learned how to configure hardware for the Windows Server 2003 environment. We covered the following topics:

- An overview of installing Plug and Play and non–Plug and Play hardware, which included a section on understanding and using hardware resources.

- Using Device Manager to manage all of the hardware that is installed on your computer. Through Device Manager you can see an overview of the hardware that is installed, manage a specific device, manage device drivers, and troubleshoot hardware through the Hardware Troubleshooting Wizards.

- How to manage device drivers through configuring driver signing options, viewing file signatures, updating a device driver, and rolling back a device driver.

- Using the System Information utility to view verbose information about your server's configuration and how to run System Information through the command-line utility, Msinfo32.

- Using Control Panel to add non–Plug and Play hardware through the Add Hardware options and how to manage specific hardware such as a mouse, keyboard, and modems through Control Panel.

- An overview of the Registry Editor, Regedit, which is used to make manual Registry changes.

Exam Essentials

Be able to configure hardware devices for your server. Be aware of the different utilities that are used to install and configure hardware devices. Be able to successfully install Plug and Play hardware. Understand how devices use system resources. Use Device Manager and Control Panel to manage hardware devices.

Successfully manage driver signing. Understand the purpose of driver signing and the levels of driver signing that are offered. Be able to configure driver signing based on the requirements of your organization.

Be able to update device drivers. Understand the process of updating Windows Server 2003 device drivers. Know how to recover from failure due to updated drivers.

Successfully troubleshoot hardware errors. Understand what causes hardware failure and be able to list common errors that cause hardware errors. Use Hardware Troubleshooting Wizards to successfully troubleshoot and correct hardware errors.

Key Terms

Before you take the exam, be certain you are familiar with the following terms:

base memory	interrupt request (IRQ)
Control Panel	Msinfo32
device driver	Plug and Play
Device Manager	port address
Direct Memory Access (DMA)	Regedit
driver rollback	Registry
driver signing	System Information utility
Hardware Troubleshooting Wizards	Upper Memory Area (UMA)
I/O memory	

Review Questions

1. You are the network administrator for a large company. You are in charge of managing all of the IT servers. As a part of your documentation process, you want to create System Information files, as shown in the following exhibit for each server. Each of the files will be stored within a central database as well as having a hard copy printed for reference. Which of the following utilities would you use to create the System Information files?

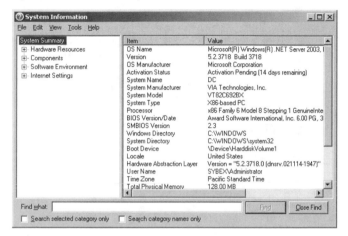

   A. `Msinfo32 /nfo` *path*

   B. `Msinfo32 /report` *path*

   C. `Sysinfo /nfo` *path*

   D. `Sysinfo /report` *path*

2. Your company produces a specialized video adapter that allows you to record video images, even if no operating system is running on the computer. Once the Windows Server 2003 operating system does load, the hardware needs to be loaded as a Windows device. The video adapter is not Plug and Play–compatible, but your company does provide a Windows Server 2003 device driver for the video adapter. The video adapter is currently configured to use the following resources:

   IRQ 5

   Memory A0000-BFFFF

   I/O 3D0-3DF

   You check through Device Manager and verify that the settings for the video adapter will not conflict with any existing settings. You manually install the card and restart the computer. The video adapter is not recognized through Device Manager. Which of the following options should you use through Windows Server 2003 to install the video adapter?

   A. From Device Manager, select Action ➢ Scan For New Hardware

   B. From Device Manager, select Action ➢ Install New Hardware

   C. From System Information, select Action ➢ Add New Hardware

   D. From Control Panel, use the Add Hardware option

3.   You are the network administrator of the Chocco Whacko Chocolate Company. One of your servers in the Sales department is not producing any audio. When you check Device Manager, your audio device displays the information shown in the following exhibit. When a computer with an identical hardware configuration is booted using Windows XP Professional, audio works. You suspect that the server has been left at default settings, which disable audio. Which of the following utilities should you use to enable the server's audio?

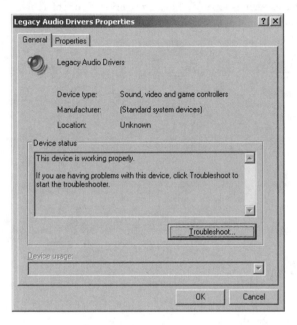

A. Device Manager

B. Control Panel ➤ Sounds and Audio Devices

C. System Information

D. `Msinfo32`

4.   You are the network administrator for a large network. You recently decided to monitor the network traffic on one of your subnets. When you tried to run the network monitoring utility, no network activity was reported. You verified that your network adapter was supported by the network monitoring utility. However, as part of your research, you realized that you needed to update your network adapter's driver to the most current version. Which of the following utilities can you use to update the driver?

A. Device Manager

B. Windows Server 2003 Diagnostics

C. System Information

D. Device Diagnostics

5. Your company is a hardware manufacturer of printers. You are developing updated drivers for your most popular printers. During the development stage, none of the drivers are signed. You want to be able to install these drivers on your test Windows 2003 server without getting any messages in regard to driver signing. Which driver signing option allows Windows Server 2003 to install all files, whether or not they are signed, and does not display any type of message about driver signing?

   A. Ignore

   B. Override

   C. Install

   D. None

6. You are the network administrator for the Wacky Widgets Corporation. Your corporate IT policy requires that all drivers used by production servers be digitally signed. You are in charge of verifying that servers already in use comply with this policy. Which of the following Windows utilities can be used to verify that system files have been digitally signed?

   A. `Sigverify`

   B. `Digsig`

   C. `Digmanage`

   D. `Sigverif`

7. You are the network administrator for a large corporation. You have a USB device that you need to add to a Windows Server 2003 computer. After you add the USB device to the USB hub, you switch to the Device Manager window to see what resources are being used by the USB device. However, the USB device is not listed through Device Manager. What course of action should you take?

   A. Restart the computer.

   B. Restart Device Manager.

   C. In Device Manager, select Action ➢ Scan For Hardware Changes.

   D. In Device Manager, select View ➢ Refresh.

8. You are the IT manager for a large company. All of the servers in the Sales department are configured with identical hardware. As a part of the corporate specification, you have been asked to install a non–Plug and Play device called ABC device to each server. You add the device to the first server and specify the Windows Server 2003 driver it should use. After you restart the computer, everything seems to be running properly. You want to verify which hardware resources are being used by the ABC device. Which of the following utilities can be used to view resources that are being used by a specific device? (Choose all that apply.)

   A. Device Manager

   B. Control Panel ➢ System Devices

   C. System Information utility

   D. `Msinfo32`

9. Your Windows Server 2003 computer is configured with several PCI devices. PCI devices share which of the following interrupts by default?

   A. IRQ 3

   B. IRQ 5

   C. IRQ 9

   D. IRQ 10

10. You are the network administrator for a medium-sized company. You use Device Manager to manage the hardware devices installed on your Windows Server 2003 computers. Which of the following tasks can be completed through Device Manager? (Choose all that apply.)

    A. Uninstall a device driver.

    B. Roll back a device driver.

    C. Verify that a device driver has been digitally signed.

    D. Set the driver signing options for installing new device drivers.

11. You are the network administrator for a small company. You recently installed a new USB device on your Windows Server 2003 computer. When you tried to access the new device, it did not work properly. You want to use the Hardware Troubleshooting Wizards to try to resolve the problem. Which of the following utilities will allow you to access the Hardware Troubleshooting Wizards?

    A. Device Manager

    B. Control Panel ➢ USB Devices

    C. System Information

    D. `Msinfo32`

12. You are the network administrator for a large corporation. The corporate office has asked you to verify that all of the servers that you manage are using signed device drivers. As a part of the corporate policy, you need to send the results of the file signature verification process back to the corporate office. After you use the File Signature Verification utility, what default file is created that shows the logged results of file signature verification?

    A. `\`*windir*`\Sigverif.txt`

    B. `\`*windir*`\Sigverif.log`

    C. `\`*windir*`\Filesigs.ncf`

    D. `\`*windir*`\Filesigs.log`

13. You are the network administrator for a small company. You recently updated the device driver for your network adapter and are now noticing that the network adapter is producing a large number of errors through your network monitoring utility. You decide you want to use the old driver for the network adapter instead of the new driver. What is the easiest process to fix this problem?

    A. Through Device Manager, uninstall the new driver and reinstall the old driver.

    B. Through Device Manager, select the Update Driver button and supply the old driver that was previously in use.

    C. Through Device Manager, use the Roll Back Driver option.

    D. Through Device Manager, use the Downgrade Driver option.

14. You are the network administrator for a small company. Your Windows Server 2003 computer does not currently have a sound card installed. You have a sound card that you want to install on your server that does not support Plug and Play. Which utility should you use to install the sound card?

   A. Device Manager

   B. System Information

   C. Control Panel ➤ Sounds and Audio Devices

   D. Control Panel ➤ Add Hardware

15. Your Windows Server 2003 computer has a generic video driver installed. You just updated the driver and now you want to set the display adapter's settings. Which utility should you use to set your display adapter's settings such as color and screen area?

   A. Display Manager

   B. Device Manager

   C. Control Panel ➤ Display

   D. Control Panel ➤ Video

Answers to Review Questions

1. **A.** The `Msinfo32` command-line utility provides the same functionality as System Information. Through the use of this command, you can gather information about computers through batch files and automatically create `.nfo` (System Information files) or `.txt` (text) files that contain the information you specify.

2. **D.** If you have non–Plug and Play hardware, you must install it through the Add Hardware icon in Control Panel, assuming that your device has a Windows Server 2003 driver. When you access the Add Hardware option, the Add Hardware Wizard will start automatically.

3. **B.** By default, Windows Server 2003 does not enable audio. Through the Sounds And Audio Devices option in Control Panel, you can enable Windows Audio. Only an administrator can enable this option, and once it is enabled, you need to restart the computer for the change to take effect.

4. **A.** You can update device drivers through the Device Manager utility. You should verify that Microsoft signed the driver you are updating for reliability purposes.

5. **A.** If you configure driver signing with the Ignore option, drivers will be installed even if they are unsigned. In production environments, it is not recommended to use unsigned drivers.

6. **D.** Windows Server 2003 includes the `Sigverif` command-line utility, which verifies that system files have been digitally signed.

7. **C.** If you add a Plug and Play device and currently have Device Manager open, you can force Device Manager to rescan your computer for changes by selecting Action ➢ Scan For Hardware Changes. This option may not work for non–Plug and Play devices.

8. **A, C, D.** You can view what resources are being used by a specific device through Device Manager, System Information, or `Msinfo32`. If you were using Device Manager, you would select View ➢ Resources by connection. If you used System Information or Msinfo32, you would look under Hardware Resources. The method given in option B does not exist.

9. **D.** Each device interacts with the computer by interrupting the processor so that it can send or retrieve data or carry out a function. A device must have a method for telling the computer's processor that it needs attention. The PCI bus standard enables devices connected to a PCI bus to communicate by using one common interrupt (IRQ 10).

10. **A, B, C.** Device Manager can be used to view, uninstall, update, or roll back the device driver that is used by each device. To set driver signing options, you use Control Panel ➢ System, click the Hardware tab, and under the Device Manager section, click the Driver Signing button.

11. **A.** If your computer recognizes a device, but can't properly access the device, you will see the device displayed through Device Manager with a yellow exclamation mark. Double-click on the device and in the General tab for the device you can click the Troubleshoot button to start the Hardware Troubleshooting Wizards.

12. **A.** By default, logging is enabled with the File Signature Verification utility. By default, a log file called `\windir\Sigverif.txt` is created.

13. C.   You would use driver rollback if you installed or upgraded a driver and you encountered problems that you did not have with the previous driver. Some of the problems with drivers relate to the following errors: use of unsigned drivers, resource conflicts, and badly written drivers.

14. D.   You use Control Panel ➤ Add Hardware to add any hardware that does not support Plug and Play. Any device that you install should have a Windows Server 2003–compatible device driver. Then you can enable sound through Control Panel ➤ Sounds and Audio Devices.

15. C.   Through Control Panel ➤ Display you can set colors, screen area, and advanced options such as display font size. These options can't be configured through Device Manager.

Chapter

3

Managing Users, Groups, and Computers

MICROSOFT EXAM OBJECTIVES COVERED IN THIS CHAPTER:

✓ **Manage local, roaming, and mandatory user profiles.**

✓ **Create and manage computer accounts in an Active Directory environment.**

✓ **Create and manage groups.**

- Identify and modify the scope of a group.
- Find domain groups in which a user is a member.
- Manage group membership.
- Create and modify groups by using the Active Directory Users and Computers Microsoft Management Console (MMC) snap-in.
- Create and modify groups by using automation.

✓ **Create and manage user accounts.**

- Create and modify user accounts by using the Active Directory Users and Computers MMC snap-in.
- Create and modify user accounts by using automation.
- Import user accounts.

✓ **Troubleshoot computer accounts.**

- Diagnose and resolve issues related to computer accounts by using the Active Directory Users and Computers MMC snap-in.
- Reset computer accounts.

✓ **Troubleshoot user accounts.**

- Diagnose and resolve account lockouts.
- Diagnose and resolve issues related to user account properties.

✓ **Troubleshoot user authentication issues.**

One of the most fundamental tasks in network management is the creation of user and group accounts. Without a user account, a user could not log on to a computer, a server, or a network. Without group accounts, an administrator would have a more difficult job of granting users' rights to network resources. Computer accounts are used to manage computers that are a part of the Active Directory.

Windows 2003 domains contain a limited number of default users. You will need to create a user account for each user within the domain. When you manage user accounts, you should first create a naming conventions standard that will be used to define the users' names that will be created. Managing users consists of common administrative tasks such as renaming user accounts and setting passwords as well as managing user properties.

Windows 2003 domains have several default groups already created that have all of the permissions needed to perform different administrative tasks. You can also create groups based on common rights requirements to network resources. When you use groups within a Windows 2003 domain, you must first select group type and group scope. You can configure properties for the group and, using the Active Directory Users And Computers snap-in, list what groups a particular user belongs to.

Each Windows NT, Windows 2000, Windows XP Professional, and Windows Server 2003 computer that is a part of the domain requires you to create a computer account for the computer within the Active Directory. Once the computer is created, you can manage the properties of the computer through the Active Directory Users And Computers utility.

Advanced user, group, and computer management allows you to locate objects within the Active Directory, move objects within the Active Directory, automate common administrative tasks through the use of command-line utilities, and import users from a Windows NT 4.0 domain.

Working with Active Directory User Accounts

Each user requires a user account to log on to the Windows 2003 domain. Once a user logs on, they can access resources based on the permissions that have been assigned to their user account and any groups that the user belongs to.

In the following sections, you will learn about working with Active Directory user accounts through the Active Directory Users And Computers utility. The specific topics that will be covered include:

- The default users that are created on Windows 2003 domains

- Username and password rules and conventions
- What usernames and security identifiers are
- How to create an Active Directory user
- How to disable or delete a user account
- How to rename a user account
- How to reset a user's password
- How to manage a user's properties
- What a user account template is and how to use a user account template
- What the Run As option is and why it should be used
- How to troubleshoot user authentication problems

Built-In Users Created in Active Directory

On a Windows Server 2003 domain, the Active Directory Users And Computers utility has a container called Users, which contains two built-in user accounts: Administrator and Guest. Each of the built-in accounts has rights and permissions automatically assigned.

Administrator Account

The *Administrator* account is created locally when you install a Windows Server 2003 member server or in the Active Directory when you install a Windows Server 2003 computer as the first server in the Active Directory domain. Administrator is a special account that has full control over the computer or the domain.

The Administrator account within the Active Directory has the following default settings:

- Administrators have full control over the domain and are able to assign user rights and access control to other users and groups.

- Administrators are members of the following groups: Administrators, Domain Admins, Enterprise Admins, Group Policy Creator Owners, and Schema Admins. Groups are covered later in this chapter in the "Working With Active Directory Group Accounts" section.

- The Administrator account can't be deleted or removed from the Administrators group. It can be renamed or disabled. For security purposes, it is recommended that you rename this account. If the Administrator account is disabled, it can still be used if the server is booted using Safe Mode.

By default, the name Administrator is given to the account with full control over the computer. You can increase the computer's security by renaming the Administrator account, and then creating an account named Administrator without any permissions. This way, even if a hacker is able to log on as Administrator, they won't be able to access any system resources.

Guest Account

The *Guest* account allows users to access the computer even if they do not have a unique username and password. Because of the inherent security risks associated with this type of account, this account is disabled by default. When this account is enabled, it is given very limited privileges.

When a Remote Assistance session is initiated, a HelpAssistance user account is automatically created. The Remote Desktop Help Session Manager service manages the HelpAssistance user account. HelpAssistance is automatically deleted when there are no Remote Assistance requests pending.

Username and Password Rules and Conventions

The only real requirement for creating a new user is that you must provide a valid username, meaning that the name must follow the Windows 2003 rules for usernames. However, it's also a good idea to have your own rules for usernames, which form your naming convention. These are the Windows 2003 rules for usernames:

- The username must be unique to the user, different from all other user and group names stored within the specified computer.

- If your users will log on from pre–Windows 2000 environments, then the username must be between 1 and 20 characters. If you are using only Windows 2000 and Windows 2003, the usernames can be longer.

- The username cannot contain any of these characters:

    * / \ [ ] : ; | = , + * ? < > "

- A username cannot consist exclusively of periods or spaces or combinations of the two.

Keeping these rules in mind, you should choose a naming convention, which is a consistent naming format. For example, consider a user named Kate Donald. One naming convention might use the last name and first initial, for the username DonaldK. Another naming convention might use the first initial and last name, for the username KDonald. Other user-naming conventions are based on the naming convention defined for e-mail names, so that the logon name and e-mail name match, although some environments might consider this a security breach. You should also provide a mechanism that would accommodate duplicate names. For example, if you had a user named Kate Donald and a user named Kevin Donald, you might use a middle initial, creating the usernames KLDonald and KMDonald.

The password rules are based on the security settings you define through Administrative Tools ➤ Domain Security Policy, Security Settings, Account Policies, Password Policy. You can set password policies as follows:

- Enforce Password History, specifies how many passwords are remembered and is used to prevent users from re-using the same password when they configure new passwords (default—24 passwords remembered)

- Maximum Password Age, defines how many days a user can keep the same password before having to create a new password (default—42 days)

- Minimum Password Age, defines the minimum number of days a user must keep a password before they can change the password (default—1 day)

- Minimum Password Length, specifies the minimum number of characters a password can contain (default—seven characters)

- Password Must Meet Complexity Requirements, specifies that passwords must not contain the user's account name, must be a minimum of six characters, and must contain characters from three of the following groups: English uppercase letters, English lowercase letters, numbers, and non-alphabetic numbers (default—enabled)

- Store Passwords Using Reversible Encryption, determines whether the operating system will store the user password using reversible encryption (default—disabled)

Microsoft recommends that all passwords contain an uppercase character, a lowercase character, and a symbol or a number; for example, instead of using oscar, you might use Osc@r.

Naming conventions should also be applied to objects such as groups, printers, and computers.

In Exercise 3.1, you will configure the default domain security settings for a user's password. Since this is a practice configuration, we will be easing the password restrictions to make the practice environment easier to use. You will also change the User Right Assignment so that non-Administrative users can log on to the domain controller. Normally you do not want regular users to log on to domain controllers so this action is not allowed by default. However, in this practice environment the option should be enabled. If the option is not enabled, when you create users in the following exercises and try to log on you will see the following error message: "The local policy of this system does not permit you to log on interactively."

EXERCISE 3.1

Setting Password Security Settings and User Rights Assignments

1. Select Start ➢ Administrative Tools ➢ Domain Security Policy.

2. Under Security Settings select Account Policies, Password Policy.

3. Double-click Minimum Password Length and in the Minimum Password Length Properties dialog box, set the Password Must Be At Least field to 0. Click the Apply button, then the OK button.

4. Double-click Password Must Meet Complexity Requirements and in the Password Must Meet Complexity Requirements Properties dialog box, click the Disabled radio button. Click the Apply button, then the OK button.

5. From the Default Domain Security Settings dialog box, select File ≻ Exit.

6. Select Start ≻ Administrative Tools ≻ Domain Controller Security Policy.

7. Under Security Settings, select Local Policies, User Right Assignment.

8. Double-click Allow Log On Locally.

9. The Allow Log On Locally Properties dialog box will appear. Click the Add User Or Group button. The Add User Or Group dialog box will appear. In the User And Group Names field, type in **Everyone** and click the OK button. In the Allow Log On Locally Properties dialog box, click the Apply button, then the OK button.

10. From the Default Domain Controller Security Settings dialog box, select File ≻ Exit.

11. To force the system to recognize your changes immediately select Start ≻ Command Prompt and from the Command Prompt window type **Gpupdate** and press Enter.

Usernames and Security Identifiers

When you create a new user, a *security identifier (SID)* is automatically created on the computer for the user account. The username is a property of the SID. For example, a user SID might look like this:

S-1-5-21-823518204-746137067-120266-629-500

It's apparent that using SIDs would make administration a nightmare. Fortunately for your administrative tasks, you see and use the username instead of the SID.

SIDs have several advantages. Because Windows 2003 uses the SID as the user object, you can easily rename a user while retaining all the properties of that user. SIDs also ensure that if you delete and re-create a user using the same username, the new user account will not have any of the properties of the old account, because it is based on a new, unique SID. Renaming and deleting user accounts are discussed later in this chapter.

Creating Active Directory Users

The Active Directory Users And Computers utility, shown in Figure 3.1, is the main tool for managing the Active Directory users, groups, and computers. You access this utility through Administrative Tools on a domain controller or a Windows 2000 Professional/Windows XP Professional/Windows Server 2003 member server with Administrative Tools (adminpak.msi) loaded.

FIGURE 3.1   The Active Directory Users And Computers window

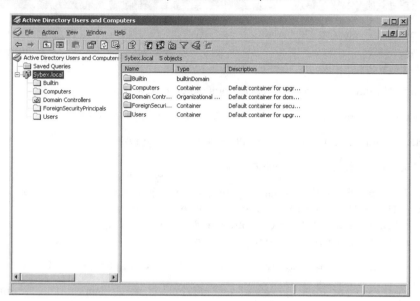

The options that can be configured for new users include:

First Name, Initials, Last Name, and Full Name   Allows you to provide more detailed information about this user. The Full Name field is automatically populated with the information you provide for the First Name, Initials, and Last Name fields. The full name (rather than the user logon name) will be displayed in the Active Directory Users And Computers utility under the container where the user is created.

User Logon Name   Defines the username for the new account that will be used with the logon process. Choose a name that is consistent with your naming convention (for example, WSmith). This field is required. User logon names are not case-sensitive within the logon process. The user principal name (UPN) is made up of the user logon name and the principal name suffix, which are connected with the @ sign. For example, the user logon name might be Kdonald and the principal suffix name might be Sybex.local. The UPN would then be Kdonald@Sybex.local.

User Logon Name (Pre–Windows 2000)   Enables a Windows 2003 domain to accept logon requests from clients running pre–Windows 2000 computers.

Password   Assigns the initial password for the user. For security purposes, it is not advisable to use readily available information about the user. If your clients are not exclusively Windows 2000/Windows XP/Windows 2003, passwords can contain up to 14 characters and are case-sensitive. If you operate in an exclusive Windows XP/Windows 2000/ Windows 2003 environment, passwords can be up to 127 characters.

Confirm Password   Confirms that you typed the password the same way two times, thus verifying that you entered the password correctly.

User Must Change Password At Next Logon   If selected, forces the user to change the password the first time they log on. This is done to increase security and moves password responsibility to the user and away from the administrator. By default, this option is selected.

User Cannot Change Password   If selected, prevents a user from changing the password. It is useful for accounts such as Guest and those that are shared by more than one user. By default, this option is not selected.

Password Never Expires   If selected, specifies that the password will never expire, even if a password policy has been specified. For example, you might select this option if this is a service account and you do not want the administrative overhead of managing and changing passwords. By default, this option is not selected.

Account Is Disabled   If selected, specifies that this account cannot be used for logon purposes. For example, you might select this option for template accounts or for an account that is not currently being used. It helps keep inactive accounts from posing security threats. By default, this option is not selected.

Make sure that your users know that usernames are not case-sensitive, but passwords are.

To create an Active Directory user, take the following steps:

1. Select Start ➤ Administrative Tools ➤ Active Directory Users And Computers.

2. The Active Directory Users And Computers window appears (refer to Figure 3.1). Right-click Users, select New from the pop-up menu, and select User.

3. The first New Object–User dialog box appears, as shown in Figure 3.2. Type in the user's first name, initials, last name, and logon name. The full name and pre–Windows 2000 logon name (for clients logging in from non–Windows 2000/2003 operating systems) will be filled in automatically when you enter the other information, but you can change them if desired. Click the Next button.

FIGURE 3.2   The New Object–User dialog box for username information

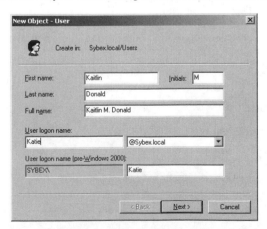

4. The second New Object–User dialog box appears, as shown in Figure 3.3. Type in and confirm the user's password. The checkboxes in this dialog box allow you to specify that the user must change the password when the user logs on, that the user cannot change the password, that the password never expires, or that the account is disabled. Click the Next button.

FIGURE 3.3   The New Object–User dialog box for password information

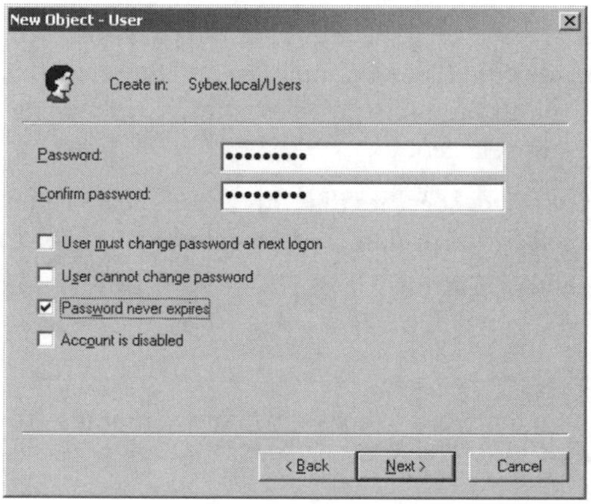

5. The final New Object–User dialog box appears. This dialog box shows the account you have configured. If all of the information is correct, click the Finish button.

In Exercise 3.2, you will create new domain user accounts. This exercise assumes you have completed Exercise 3.1.

EXERCISE 3.2

Creating Active Directory Users

1. Select Start ➤ Administrative Tools ➤ Active Directory Users And Computers.

2. In the Active Directory Users And Computers window, right-click Users, select New, and then select User.

3. In the first New Object–User dialog box, enter the following information:

> First Name: **Ginnie**
>
> Initial: **B**.
>
> Last Name: **Donald**
>
> User Logon Name: **Ginnie**

4. Click the Next button.

5. In the next New Object–User dialog box, type and confirm the password **girLYc@t**. Check the Password Never Expires checkbox and uncheck the User Must Change Password At Next Logon checkbox. Then click the Next button.

EXERCISE 3.2 *(continued)*

6. Create six more users. For each user, uncheck the User Must Change Password At Next Logon checkbox. Fill out the fields as follows:

First Name: **Robert**; Last Name: **Jones**; User Logon Name: **Robert**; Password: **b4tm4n**

First Name: **Terry**; Last Name: **Belle**; User Logon Name: **Terry**; Password: **b4tg1rl**

First Name: **Ron**; Last Name: **Klein**; User Logon Name: **Ron**; Password: **sup3rm4n**

First Name: **Wendy**; Last Name: **Smith**; User Logon Name: **Wendy**; Password: **sup3rg1rl**

First Name: **Emily**; Last Name: **Buras**; User Logon Name: **Emily**; Password: **p34ch**

First Name: **Michael**; Last Name: **Phillips**; User Logon Name: **Michael**; Password: **4ppl3**

Disabling or Deleting User Accounts

When a user account is no longer needed, the account should be disabled or deleted. If you choose to disable an account, you can later enable that account to restore it with all of its associated user properties and permissions. An account that is deleted can never be recovered.

WARNING

User accounts that are not in use pose a security threat because an intruder could access your network though an inactive account. For example, after inheriting a network, I ran a network security diagnostic and noticed several accounts for users who no longer worked for the company. These accounts had Administrative rights, including dial-in permissions. This was not a good situation, and the accounts were deleted on the spot.

You might disable an account because a user will not be using it for a period of time, perhaps because that employee is going on vacation or taking a leave of absence. Another reason to disable an account is if you're planning on putting another user in that same function. For example, suppose that Rick, the engineering manager, quit. If you disable his account, when your company hires a new engineering manager, you can simply rename the user account and password (from Rick to the username for the new manager) and enable that account. This ensures that the user who takes over Rick's position will have all of the user properties and own all of the resources that the original user Rick had.

Disabling accounts also provides a security mechanism for special situations. For example, if your company were laying off a group of people, a security measure would be to disable their accounts at the same time as these employees get their layoff notices. This prevents the users from inflicting any damage to the company's files on their way out. (Yes, this does seem cold-hearted, and the remaining employees are bound to fear for their jobs if they aren't able to log on later because the servers go down, but it does serve the purpose.)

You disable a user account by right-clicking the user account in the Active Directory Users And Computers utility and selecting the Disable Account option. You will see a confirmation dialog box stating that the selected object was deleted.

In Exercise 3.3, you will disable a user account. Before you follow this exercise, you should have already created the new users in Exercise 3.2.

EXERCISE 3.3

Disabling a User

1.   Select Start ➤ Administrative Tools ➤ Active Directory Users And Computers.

2.   In the Active Directory Users And Computers window, expand Users.

3.   Right-click user Robert and select Disable Account.

4.   You will see an Active Directory Users and Computers dialog box appear stating that Object Robert Has Been Disabled. Click the OK button.

5.   From your Windows XP Professional computer, attempt to log on as Robert to your domain. This will fail, since the account is now disabled.

You should delete a user account if you are sure that the account will never be needed again. In Exercise 3.4, you will delete a user account. This exercise assumes that you have completed the previous exercises in this chapter.

EXERCISE 3.4

Deleting a User

1.   Select Start ➤ Administrative Tools ➤ Active Directory Users And Computers.

2.   In the Active Directory Users And Computers window, expand Users.

3.   Right-click user Robert and select Delete.

4.   You will see an Active Directory Users and Computers dialog box appear asking you Are You Sure You Want To Delete This Object? Click the Yes button.

Renaming Users

Once an account has been created, you can rename the account at any time. Renaming a user account allows the user to retain all of the associated user properties and permissions of the previous username. As noted earlier in the chapter, the name is a property of the SID.

You might want to rename a user account because the user's name has changed (for example, the user got married) or because the name was spelled incorrectly. Also, as explained in

"Disabling and Deleting User Accounts" earlier in this chapter, you can rename an existing user's account for a new user whom you want to have the same properties, such as someone hired to take an ex-employee's position.

In Exercise 3.5, you will rename a user account. This exercise assumes that you have completed all of the previous exercises in this chapter.

EXERCISE 3.5

Renaming a User

1. Select Start ➢ Administrative Tools ➢ Active Directory Users And Computers.

2. In the Active Directory Users And Computers window, expand Users.

3. Right-click user Terry and select Rename.

4. Type in the username **Taralyn** and press Enter.

5. The Rename User dialog box will appear. Notice that the First Name retained the original property of Terry. Make any needed changes and click the OK button.

 Renaming a user does not change any "hard-coded" names, such as the user's home directory. If you want to change these names as well, you need to modify them manually.

Changing a User's Password

What do you do if a user forgot his or her password and can't log on? You can't just open a dialog box and see the old password. However, as an administrator, you can change a user's password, and then the user can use the new one.

In Exercise 3.6, you will change a user's password. This exercise assumes that you have completed all of the previous exercises in this chapter.

EXERCISE 3.6

Changing a User's Password

1. Select Start ➢ Administrative Tools ➢ Active Directory Users And Computers.

2. In the Active Directory Users And Computers window, expand Users.

3. Right-click user Ron and select Reset Password.

4. The Reset Password dialog box will appear. Type in the New Password **g01f** and Confirm Password **g01f**. Check the box User Must Change Password At Next Logon to force Ron to change his password the next time he logs on. Click the OK button.

5. You will see an Active Directory Users and Computers dialog box appear confirming The Password For Ron Has Been Changed. Click the OK button.

Managing Active Directory User Properties

For Active Directory users, you can configure a wide variety of properties. To access the Properties dialog box for an Active Directory user, open the Active Directory Users And Computers utility (by selecting Start ➤ Administrative Tools ➤ Active Directory Users And Computers), open the Users folder, and double-click the user account. The Active Directory user Properties dialog box has tabs for the 13 main categories of properties:

General	Terminal Services Profile
Address	COM+
Account	Member Of
Profile	Dial-in
Telephones	Environment
Organization	Sessions
Remote Control	

Four of the tabs in the Active Directory user Properties dialog box contain properties that relate to Terminal Services: Remote Control, Terminal Services Profile, Environment, and Sessions. Terminal Services is covered in Chapter 8, "Administering Terminal Services." In the following sections, we will look at the tabs commonly used for user administration.

Configuring General Active Directory User Properties

The General property tab, shown in Figure 3.4, contains the information that you supplied when you set up the new user account. You can add information in the Description and Office text boxes. You can also enter contact information for the user, including Telephone Number, E-mail, and Web Page URL.

Adding Active Directory User Address Information

You can provide address information for the user on the Address tab, as shown in Figure 3.5. This tab has text boxes for the user's street address, post office box number, city, state or province, and zip code. You can also select a country or region identifier from the Country/Region drop-down list.

FIGURE 3.4   The General tab of the Active Directory user Properties dialog box

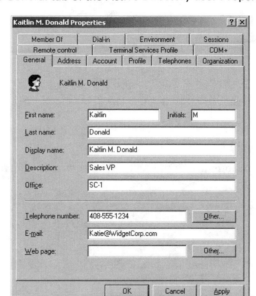

FIGURE 3.5   The Address tab of the Active Directory user Properties dialog box

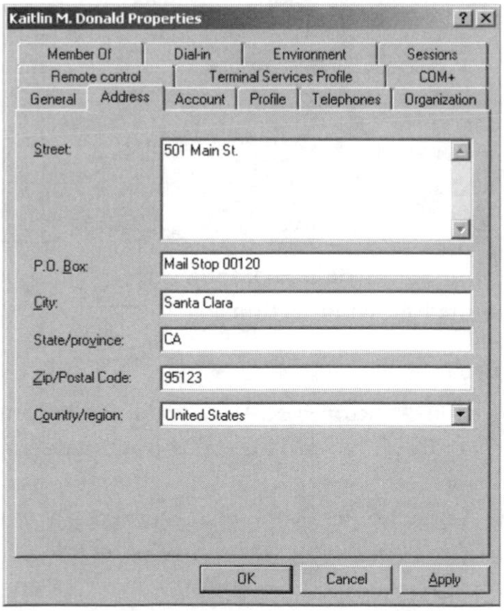

Controlling Active Directory Users' Accounts

Using the Account tab, shown in Figure 3.6, you can control the user's account. This tab shows the logon name information that you supplied when you set up the new user account and allows you to configure these settings:

- The user logon name and principal name suffix
- Pre–Windows 2000 user logon name
- The logon hours for the user
- The computers that the user is allowed to log on to
- Account lockout options
- Account options that apply to the user
- When the account expires

FIGURE 3.6 The Account tab of the Active Directory user Properties dialog box

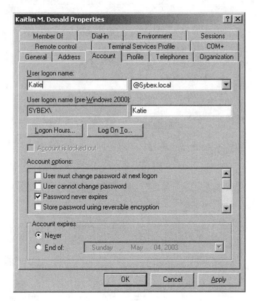

The settings for logon hours, controlling computer access, account options, and account expiration are described in the following sections.

Controlling Logon Hours

When you click the Logon Hours button, you'll see the Logon Hours dialog box, as shown in Figure 3.7. By default, users are allowed to log on 24 hours a day, 7 days a week. Logon hours are typically restricted during computer backups. You might also want to restrict logon hours for security reasons. A blue box indicates that logon is permitted. A white box indicates that logon is not permitted. You can change logon hours by selecting the hours you want to modify and clicking the Logon Permitted radio button or the Logon Denied radio button.

Controlling Computer Access

When you click the Log On To button, you'll see the Logon Workstations dialog box, as shown in Figure 3.8. This dialog box allows you to specify that the user can log on to all the computers in the domain (default) or limit the user to logging on to specific computers in the network.

For example, if the Administrator works in a secure environment, you might limit the Administrator account to log on only to a specific computer. You configure the computers that the user can log on to based on the computer's name. You add the computers that are allowed by typing in the computer name and clicking the Add button.

FIGURE 3.7   The Logon Hours dialog box

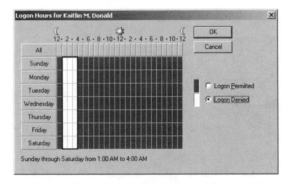

FIGURE 3.8   The Logon Workstations dialog box

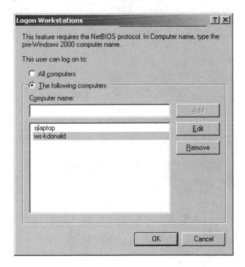

Managing Account Lockouts

You can configure account lockout settings through group policy. The account lockout policies that can be set include:

- Account Lockout Threshold, which specifies that the user gets a specific number of invalid login attempts before the account is locked
- Account Lockout Duration, which specifies how long the account will be locked in the event that the Account Lockout Threshold is exceeded
- Reset Account Lockout Counter After, which specifies in minutes how long the account lockout threshold will be tracked for

If you configure account lockout policies, you can unlock the account by unchecking the Account Is Locked Out checkbox (shown as inactive in Figure 3.6).

Setting Account Options

The account options listed in the Account tab allow you to control password security for the user account. You can specify these account options:

- User Must Change Password At Next Logon
- User Cannot Change Password
- Password Never Expires
- Store Password Using Reversible Encryption

Setting Account Expiration

By default, user accounts are set to Never Expire. The End Of radio button at the bottom of the Account tab lets you set account expiration for a specific date. You might want to set an expiration date if you have temporary employees and you want to disable their accounts on a specific date. This option is also useful in academic environments where students need user accounts, but their accounts should be disabled at the end of the academic period.

Setting Up the Active Directory User Environment

The Profile tab, shown in Figure 3.9, allows you to customize the user's environment. Here, you can specify these items for the user:

- User profile path
- Logon script
- Home folder

FIGURE 3.9 The Profile tab of the user Properties dialog box

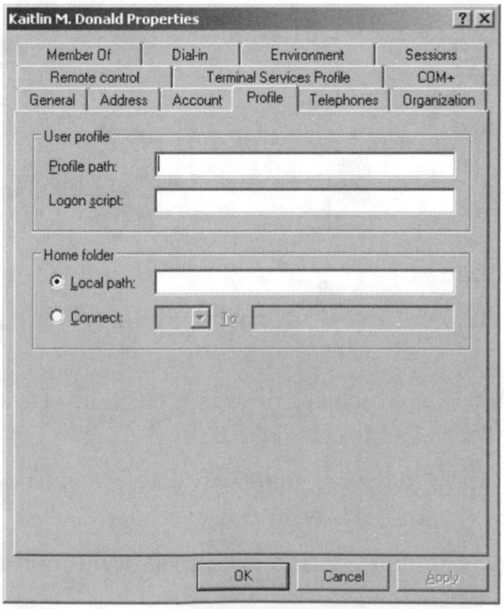

The following sections describe how these properties work and when you might want to use them.

Using User Profiles

User profiles contain information about the Windows 2003 environment for a specific user. For example, profile settings include the Desktop arrangement, program groups, and screen colors that users see when they log on.

If the configuration option is a personal preference, it is most likely a part of the user profile. Configuration options that relate to the computer are not a part of the user profile. For example, the mouse driver is not a part of a user profile. However, the properties of the mouse configuration—such as the speed, pointer, and mouse button settings—reflect the user's personal preferences and are a part of a user profile. In the following sections you will learn about local user profiles, roaming profiles, and mandatory profiles.

LOCAL USER PROFILES

By default, when a user logs on, a profile is opened for that user. The first time users log on, they receive a default user profile. A folder that matches the user's logon name is created for the user in the Documents And Settings folder. The user profile folder that is created holds a file called Ntuser.dat, as well as subfolders that contain directory links to the user's Desktop items.

Any changes that the user makes to the Desktop are stored in the user's profile when the user logs off. For example, suppose that user Kevin logs on, picks his wallpaper, creates shortcuts, and customizes the Desktop to his personal preference. When he logs off, his changes are stored in his user profile. If another user logs on at the same computer, that user's profile—not Kevin's—is loaded.

The Profile Path option in the Profile tab is used to point to another location for profile files other than the default local location. To specify a path, just type it in the Profile Path text box using Universal Naming Convention (UNC) format. This allows users to access profiles that have been stored on a shared network folder. This way, profiles are stored remotely and can be accessed from any machine in the system. Also, if a hard disk fails, the hard drive would be replaced and re-imaged, but the profile will be restored the first time the user logs on because it was stored remotely.

In Exercise 3.7, you will create and manage user profiles. This exercise assumes that you have completed Exercise 3.2.

EXERCISE 3.7

Using Local User Profiles

1. Log on to your domain as Administrator.

2. Select Start ➤ All Programs ➤ Accessories ➤ Windows Explorer; expand My Computer, then Local Disk (C:), then Documents And Settings. The folder will have subfolders for only those users who have logged in. Verify that no user profile folders exist for the users Emily and Michael (since they haven't logged on yet).

3. Log off as Administrator and log on as Emily (with the password **p34ch**).

EXERCISE 3.7 *(continued)*

4. Right-click an open area on the Desktop and select Properties. In the Display Properties dialog box, click the Desktop tab. Select the Follow Background, click the Apply button, and then click the OK button.

5. Right-click an open area on the Desktop and select New ➤ Shortcut. In the Create Shortcut dialog box, type **CALC and click Next**. Enter the name **Calculator** as the name for the shortcut and click the Finish button.

6. Log off as Emily and log on as Michael (with the password **4ppl3**). Notice that user Michael sees the Desktop configuration stored in the default user profile.

7. Log off as Michael and log on as Emily. Notice that Emily sees the Desktop configuration you set up in steps 4 and 5.

8. Log off as Emily and log on as Administrator. Select Start ➤ Windows Explorer; expand My Computer, then Local Disk (C:), then Documents And Settings. Verify that user profile folders now exist for Emily and Michael.

ROAMING USER PROFILES

A *roaming profile* is stored on a network server and allows users to access their user profile, regardless of the client computer to which they're logged on. Roaming profiles provide a consistent Desktop for users who move around, no matter which computer they access. Even if the server that stores the roaming profile is unavailable, the user can still log on using a local profile.

To create a roaming user profile, you create a network share that will store the roaming user profile, create the user profile, then copy the user profile to a shared network folder. You would use the following steps to create a roaming user profile:

1. Create a network share on the computer that will store the roaming profile. Assign NTFS permissions and share permissions to any users who will access the roaming profile. The creation of network shares and NTFS and share permissions are covered in Chapter 5, "Accessing Files and Folders." In this example, a share has been created called \\Server2003\Profiles.

2. Create a user using the Active Directory Users And Computers utility that will be used as a template account to create the roaming user profile. In this example, we are using a user called Test.

3. Log on as the Test user and create a local user profile with whatever settings the roaming user profile should have (for example, desktop environment, appearance settings, shortcuts, and Start menu options).

4. Log on as an administrator to the computer that is storing the local profile.

5. Select Start ➤ Control Panel ➤ System.

6. Select the Advanced tab and click the User Profiles Settings button to access the User Profiles dialog box shown in Figure 3.10.

7. Select the user's profile that you want to copy and click the Copy To button.

FIGURE 3.10   The User Profiles dialog box

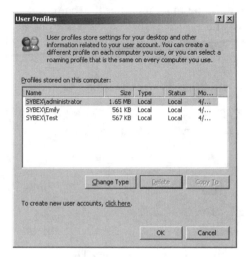

8. The Copy To dialog box will appear, as shown in Figure 3.11. Specify the network location where the roaming user profile will be stored. In this example, the roaming user profile is stored in \\Server2003\Profiles\Test.

FIGURE 3.11   The Copy To dialog box

9. At the bottom of the Copy To dialog box, you will see the Permitted To Use option. Click the Change button to specify which users can access this profile. The Select User Or Group dialog box will appear, as shown in Figure 3.12. In this example, user Michael is being permitted to use the profile. Click the OK button. And in the Copy To dialog box, click the OK button.

10. From the Active Directory Users And Computers utility, access the Test user's properties and click the Profile tab (shown in Figure 3.9), and under User Profile, Profile Path, specify the network share where the user profile was copied (in this example \\Server2003\Profiles\Test) and click the OK button.

11. You can test the roaming profile by logging in at a remote computer.

If you are using roaming profiles, the contents of the user's roaming profile from the shared network path folder will be copied to the local computer each time the roaming profile is accessed. If you have stored large files in any subfolders of your user profile folder, you may notice a significant delay when accessing your profile remotely as opposed to locally. If this problem occurs, you can reduce the amount of time the roaming profile takes to load by moving the subfolder to another location, such as the user's home directory, or you can use Group Policy Objects within the Active Directory to specify that specific folders should be excluded or loaded after the roaming profile is loaded.

FIGURE 3.12   The Select User Or Group dialog box

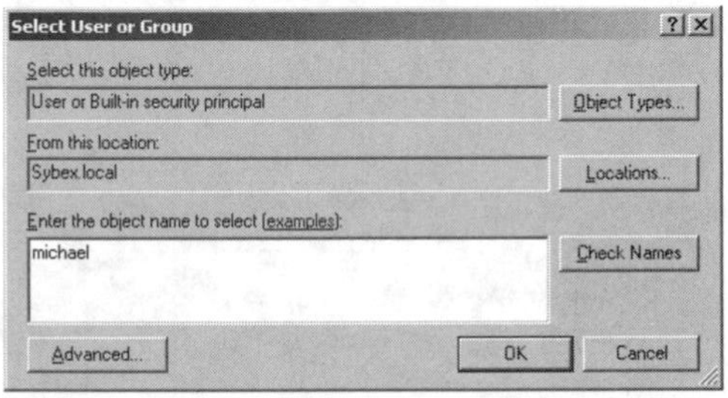

In Exercise 3.8, you will create a roaming profile. This exercise assumes that you are using two computers, one with Windows Server 2003 and one with Windows XP Professional.

EXERCISE 3.8

Using Roaming Profiles

1. Select Start ➢ Administrative Tools ➢ Active Directory Users And Computers.

2. In the Active Directory Users And Computers window, right-click Users, select New, and then select User.

3. In the first New Object—User dialog box, enter the following information:

    First Name: **Test**

    Last Name: **Account**

    User Logon Name: **Test**

4. Click the Next button.

5. In the next New Object—User dialog box, do not specify any password. Check the Password Never Expires checkbox. Then click the Next button and the Finish button.

6. Select Start ➢ Windows Explorer. Expand My Computer and Local Disk (C:). Select File ➢ New ➢ Folder and create a folder called **Profiles**.

7. Right-click the Profiles folder and select Sharing And Security. From the Sharing tab, click the Share This Folder radio button. Click the Permissions button.

8. The Permissions For Profiles dialog box will appear. Verify that group Everyone is highlighted and click Allow Full Control checkbox. Click the OK button.

9. Click the Security tab. Highlight the Users group and under Permissions For Users click the Allow Full Control checkbox. Click the OK button.

10. Log off as the Administrator and log on as Test.

11. Right-click an open area on the Desktop and select New ➤ Shortcut. In the Create Shortcut dialog box, type **CALC** and click Next. Enter the name **Calculator** as the name for the shortcut and click the Finish button.

12. Right-click an open area on the Desktop and select New ➤ Shortcut. In the Create Shortcut dialog box, type **Explorer** and click Next. Accept Explorer as the name for the shortcut and click the Finish button.

13. Log off as Test and log on as Administrator.

14. Select Start ➤ Control Panel ➤ System.

15. Select the Advanced tab and click the User Profiles Settings button to access the User Profiles dialog box.

16. Select the Test profile that you want to copy and click the Copy To button.

17. The Copy To dialog box will appear. Specify the network location where the roaming user profile will be stored as *yourservername*\Profiles\Test. At the bottom of the Copy To dialog box, you will see the Permitted To Use option. Click the Change button. The Select User Or Group dialog box will appear. In the Enter The Object Name To Select field, type in **Test** and click the OK button. In the Copy To dialog box, click the OK button.

18. Select Start ➤ Administrative Tools ➤ Active Directory Users And Computers. Expand Users and double-click Test.

19. Click the Profile tab and under User Profile, Profile Path, specify the network share *yourservername*\Profiles\Test and click the OK button.

20. From your Windows XP Professional computer, log on to your domain as Test. You will see the shortcuts on the desktop that were created as a part of the roaming profile.

USING MANDATORY PROFILES

A *mandatory profile* is a profile that can't be modified by the user. Only members of the Administrators group can manage mandatory profiles. You might consider creating mandatory profiles for users who should maintain consistent Desktops. For example, suppose that you have a group of 20 salespeople who know enough about system configuration to make changes, but not enough to fix any problems they create. For ease of support, you could use mandatory profiles. This way, all of the salespeople will always have the same profile and will not be able to change their profiles.

You can create mandatory profiles for a single user or a group of users. The mandatory profile is stored in a file named Ntuser.man. A user with a mandatory profile can set different Desktop preferences while logged on, but those settings will not be saved when the user logs off.

Only roaming profiles can be used as mandatory profiles. Mandatory profiles do not work for local user profiles.

Real World Scenario

Copying User Profiles

Within your company you have a user, Sharon, who logs in with two different user accounts. One account is a regular user account, and the other is an Administrator account used for administration tasks only.

When Sharon established all her Desktop preferences and installed the computer's applications, they were installed with the Administrator account. Now when she logs in with the regular user account, she can't access the Desktop and profile settings that were created for her as an administrative user.

To solve this problem, you can copy a local user profile from one user to another (for example, from Sharon's administrative account to her regular user account). Go to Control Panel ≻ System, Advanced tab, User Profiles Settings button, select the account and copy, then click the Copy To button. You will need to complete this task as an Administrator since you cannot copy an account that you are currently logged into. When you copy a user profile, the following items are copied: Favorites, Cookies, My Documents, Start menu items, and other unique user Registry settings.

Using Logon Scripts

Logon scripts are files that run every time a user logs on to the network. They are usually batch files, but they can be any type of executable file.

You might use logon scripts to set up drive mappings or to run a specific executable file each time a user logs on to the computer. For example, you could run an inventory management file that collects information about the computer's configuration and sends that data to a central management database. Logon scripts are also useful for compatibility with non–Windows 2000/ Windows XP/Windows 2003 clients who want to log on but still maintain consistent settings with their native operating system.

To run a logon script for a user, enter the path to the logon script in the Logon Script text box in the Profile tab of the user Properties dialog box.

 Logon scripts are not commonly used in Windows 2000/Windows XP/Windows 2003 networks. Windows 2000/Windows XP/Windows 2003 automates much of the user's configuration via group policy. In older NetWare environments, for example, this isn't the case, and administrators use logon scripts to configure the users' environment.

Setting Up Home Folders

Users normally store their personal files and information in a private folder called a *home folder*. In the Profile tab of the user Properties dialog box, you can specify the location of a home folder as a local folder or a network folder.

To specify a local path folder, choose the Local Path option in the Profile tab and type the path in the text box next to that option. To specify a network path for a folder, choose the Connect option and specify a network path using a UNC (Universal Naming Convention) path. In this case, the network folder should already be created and shared.

In Exercise 3.9, you will assign a home folder to a user. This exercise assumes that you have completed all of the previous exercises in this chapter.

EXERCISE 3.9

Assigning a Home Folder to a User

1. Select Start ➢ Administrative Tools ➢ Active Directory Users And Computers.

2. In the Active Directory Users And Computers window, expand the Users folder and double-click user Wendy. The user Properties dialog box appears.

3. Select the Profile tab and click the Local Path radio button to select it.

4. Specify the home folder path by typing **C:\Users\Wendy** in the text box for the Local Path option. Then click the OK button.

5. Use Windows Explorer to verify that this folder was created.

Adding Active Directory User Telephone Information

The Telephones tab, shown in Figure 3.13, allows you to configure the user's telephone numbers for home, pager, mobile, fax, and IP phone. You can also add notes such as "Don't call home after 10:00 P.M." The Other buttons allow you to specify alternate telephone numbers.

FIGURE 3.13   The Telephones tab of the Active Directory user Properties dialog box

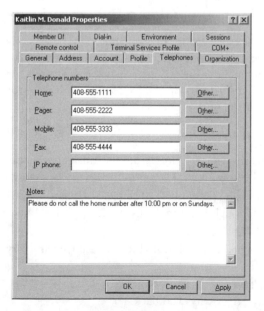

Adding Active Directory Organization Information

The Organization tab, shown in Figure 3.14, allows you to provide information about the user's role in your organization. You can enter the user's title, department, company, and manager. You can also view or add any users and contacts who directly report to the selected user account through the Direct Reports field.

FIGURE 3.14   The Organization tab of the Active Directory user Properties dialog box

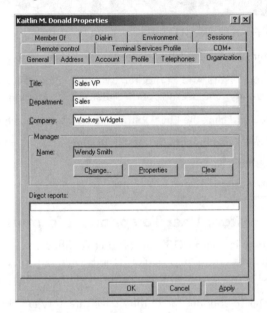

Managing Active Directory User Group Membership

The Member Of tab displays the groups that the user belongs to, as shown in Figure 3.15. You can add the user to an existing group by clicking the Add button. To remove the user from a group listed on this tab, highlight the group and click the Remove button.

If you are using Macintosh clients or POSIX-compliant applications, you can set the user's Primary Group at the bottom of the Member Of tab.

Configuring Dial-in Properties

Using the Dial-in tab, as shown in Figure 3.16, you configure the user's remote-access permissions for dial-in or VPN connections. The options that can be configured include:

- Remote Access Permission (Dial-in Or VPN). Here, you can set Allow Access, Deny Access, or Control Access Through Remote Access Policy (this last choice is available only if the domain is in native mode).

- Verify Caller ID (this option is not available if the Active Directory is configured to support a mixed-mode configuration).

- Callback Options. This can be set to No Callback, Set By Caller (Routing And Remote Access Service Only), or Always Callback To.

- Assign a Static IP Address.
- Apply Static Routes.

FIGURE 3.15   The Member Of tab of the Active Directory user Properties dialog box

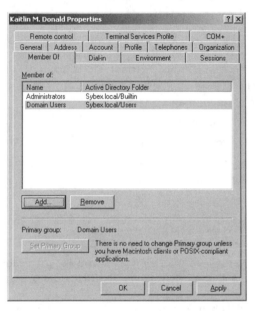

FIGURE 3.16   The Dial-in tab of the Active Directory user Properties dialog box

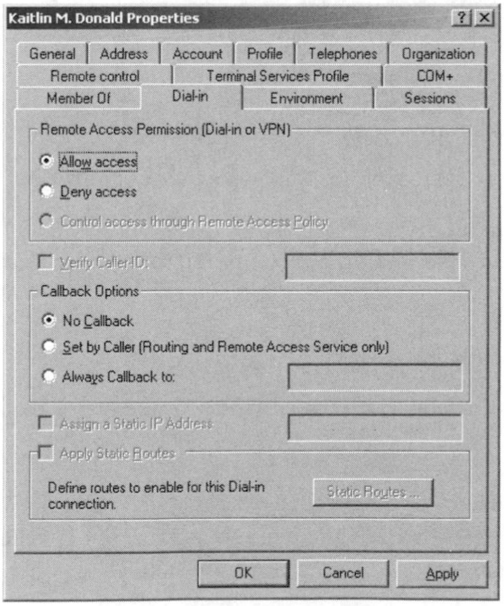

Remote access is covered in more detail in *MCSE: Windows XP Professional Study Guide, Second Edition*, by Lisa Donald with James Chellis (Sybex 2003).

Using User Account Templates

You can use user account templates to simplify user administration. For example, if you were managing the Sales organizational unit, you could create a user account template called #Sales (in this example, the # sign indicates that the user account is a user account template). You could then populate the following user properties any time you create a new account by copying the user account template:

- All Account properties except Logon Name
- All Address properties except Street Address
- Profile properties except for Profile Path and Home Folder (which are modified with the logon name of the user you are creating)
- Organization properties except for Title
- Member Of properties

If you use user account templates, you should disable the user account templates so that users cannot use them to log on to your network.

In Exercise 3.10, you will create a user account template and then create new users based on the template account.

EXERCISE 3.10

Using User Account Templates

1. Select Start ➢ Administrative Tools ➢ Active Directory Users And Computers.

2. In the Active Directory Users And Computers window, right-click Users, select New, and then select User.

3. In the first New Object–User dialog box, enter the following information:

    First Name: **#Sales**

    Last Name: **Template**

    User Logon Name: **#Sales**

4. Click the Next button.

5. In the next New Object–User dialog box, do not specify any password. Check the Password Never Expires checkbox and the Account Is Disabled checkbox. Then click the Next button. Click the Finish button.

6. Double-click #Sales to access the #Sales Template Properties dialog box.

7. Click the Address tab. For City, type in **Santa Cruz**. For State, type in **California**. For Zip/Postal Code, type in **95060**. For Country/Region, select United States from the pull-down list.

8. Click the Organization tab. For Department, type in **Sales**. For Company, type in **Wacky Widgets Corporation**. Click the OK button.

9. Right-click #Sales Template User and select Copy.

10. The Copy Object–User dialog box will appear. Enter the following information:

    First Name: **Dietrich**

    Last Name: **Moorehead**

    User Logon Name: **Dietrich**

11. Click the Next button.

12. In the next New Object–User dialog box, do not specify any password. Uncheck the Account Is Disabled option. Then click the Next button. Click the Finish button.

13. Double-click user Dietrich and click the Address tab and the Organization tab to verify that the information was populated based on the settings configured for the #Sales account template.

Using the Run As Option

The Run As option allows you to use a secondary logon process to log on to a computer using administrative credentials in order to perform a specific task. For security purposes, it is recommended that you use the Run As option when performing administrative tasks as opposed to logging into a computer or domain with an administrative account.

You can use the Run As option through most Windows programs, some Control Panel items, and the Microsoft Management Console (MMC). You can also use the Run As option with command-line utilities.

Assume that you were logged in as a regular user and you wanted to add a user through Active Directory Users And Computers utility using the Run As option with your administrative user account. You would take the following action:

1. Select Start ➤ Administrative Tools and then right-click Active Directory Users And Computers. Select Run As.

2. The Run As dialog box will appear. Select The Following User and specify the administrator username and password. Click the OK button.

Troubleshooting User Authentication

If a user can't log on, there are many possible causes. Logon failure can result from problems with the username, password, user account settings, or security settings.

The following are some common causes of domain logon errors:

Incorrect username   You can verify that the username is correct by checking the Microsoft Active Directory Users And Computers utility to verify that the name was spelled correctly.

Incorrect password As with local accounts, check that the password was entered in the proper case (and that the Caps Lock key isn't on), the password hasn't expired, and the account has not been locked out. If the password still doesn't work, you can assign a new password through the Microsoft Active Directory Users And Computers utility.

Prohibitive user rights Does the user have permission to log on locally at the computer? This assumes that the user is attempting to log on to the domain controller. Regular users do not have permission to log on locally at the domain controller. The assumption is that users will log on to the domain from network workstations. If the user has a legitimate reason to log on locally at the domain controller, that user should be assigned the Log On Locally user right in Domain Controller Security Policy.

A disabled or deleted account You can verify whether an account has been disabled or deleted by checking the account properties through the Microsoft Active Directory Users And Computers utility.

A local account logon at a domain computer Is the user trying to log on with a local user account name instead of a domain account name? Make sure that the user has selected to log on to a domain in the Logon dialog box.

The computer is not part of the domain Is the user sitting at a computer that is a part of the domain to which the user is trying to log on? If the client computer is not a part of the domain that contains the user account or does not have a trust relationship defined with the domain that contains the user account, the user will not be able to log on.

Unavailable domain controller, DNS Server, or Global Catalog Is the domain controller available to authenticate the user's request? If the domain controller is down for some reason, the user will not be able to log on until it comes back up (unless the user logs on using a local user account). A DNS server and the Global Catalog (if the Active Directory has multiple domains) for Active Directory are also required.

User unable to log on from their computer, but can log on from another computer Active Directory issues a new computer password every 30 days. If your computer does not receive that password for any reason you will not be able to log on. The symptom is that you cannot log on from your computer but you can log on from any other computer. To fix the problem, open Active Directory Users And Computers using Administrative privileges, open the Computers folder, right-click the computer account, and select Reset Account.

Working with Active Directory Group Accounts

Within the Active Directory a *group* is defined as a collection of user accounts, computer accounts, other group accounts, and contacts that can be managed as a single entity. Groups are used to simplify administration by allowing you to administer many accounts (through group membership) as opposed to manually administering individual user accounts.

In the following sections, you will learn about group scope and group type, default groups created on a Windows 2003 domain, how to create a new group, how to manage groups, and how to identify what groups a user belongs to.

Understanding Group Scope and Group Type

On a Windows 2003 domain controller in the Active Directory, groups are characterized by group scope and group type.

Group scope is used to determine if the group is limited to a single domain or if the group can span multiple domains. Group scopes are used to assign permissions to resources. The three types of group scopes are:

Domain Local Groups   *Domain local groups* are used to assign permissions to resources. Domain local groups can contain user accounts, universal groups, and global groups from any domain in the tree or forest. A domain local group can also contain other domain local groups from its own local domain. Microsoft recommends that global groups be added to domain local groups in a single domain environment and that universal groups are added to the domain local group in a multi-domain environment. User accounts should not be added to a domain local group.

Global Groups   *Global groups* are used to organize users who have similar network access requirements. A global group is simply a container of users. Global groups can contain users and global groups (in native mode) from the local domain.

Universal Groups   *Universal groups* are used to logically organize global groups and appear in the Global Catalog (a search engine that contains limited information about every object in the Active Directory). Universal groups can contain users (not recommended) from anywhere in the domain tree or forest, other universal groups, and global groups.

In order to support universal groups, the domain must be configured for Windows 2000/2003 native mode. If the domain is configured for Windows 2000/2003 mixed mode (which supports Windows NT 4.0), then universal groups are not supported.

Group type is used to organize users, computers, and other groups into logical objects that are used for management purposes. There are two group types:

Security Group   A *security group* is a logical group of users who need to access specific resources. Security groups are listed in Discretionary Access Control Lists (DACLs) to assign permissions to resources.

Distribution Group   A *distribution group* is a logical group of users who have common characteristics. Applications and e-mail programs (for example, Microsoft Exchange) can use distribution groups. Distribution groups can't be listed in DACLs and therefore have no permissions. This allows these groups to execute at very high speed.

Default Groups Created in Windows 2003 Domain

When you install Windows Server 2003, there are several built-in group accounts that are created by default. On a Windows Server 2003 domain controller, groups are located in the Users folder and the Builtin folder within the Active Directory Users And Computers utility. There are also special groups whose members are based on specific conditions being met.

Table 3.1 describes group accounts located in the Builtin folder.

TABLE 3.1   Default Group Accounts in the Builtin Folder

Builtin Group	Description
Account Operators	Members of the Account Operators group can create and manage domain user, group, and computer accounts within the Users or Computers containers (with the exception of the Domain Controllers container) or organizational units that have been created. Account Operators do not have rights to modify the Administrators or Domain Admins groups. This group has no default members.
Administrators	The Administrators group has full rights and privileges on all domain controllers within the domain. Its members can grant themselves any permissions they do not have by default to manage all of the objects on the computer. (Objects include the file system, printers, and account management.) By default, the Administrator user account and the Domain Admins and Enterprise Admins groups are members of the Administrators group. Because of the permissions associated with this group, you should add users to this group with caution.
Backup Operators	The members of the Backup Operators group have rights to back up and restore the file system, even if the file system is NTFS and they have not been assigned permissions to the file system. However, the members of Backup Operators can access the file system only through the Backup utility. To be able to directly access the file system, they must have explicit permissions assigned. By default, there are no members of the Backup Operators local group.
Guests	The Guests group has limited access to the computer. This group is provided so that you can let people who are not regular users have access to specific network resources. As a general rule, most administrators do not allow Guest access because it poses a potential security risk. By default, the Guest user account is a member of the Guests local group.
Incoming Forest Trust Builders	This group has special permissions to build one-way, incoming trusts to the forest root domain. This group has no default members.
Network Configuration Operators	This group has special permissions to manage TCP/IP networking configuration options. For example, members can renew and release TCP/IP addresses on domain controllers within the domain. This group does not have any default members.

TABLE 3.1   Default Group Accounts in the Builtin Folder *(continued)*

Builtin Group	Description
Performance Log Users	Members of this group have special permissions related to configuring and managing performance counters, logs, and alerts on domain controllers and computers within the domain. This group does not have any default members.
Performance Monitor Users	Members of this group have special permissions to remotely monitor (view) performance counters for all domain controllers and computers within the domain. This group does not have any default members.
Pre–Windows 2000 Compatible Access	This is a special group with backward compatibility for allowing read access to users and groups in the domain. By default, the Everyone group is a member of this group when the computer is loaded with pre–Windows 2000 permissions.
Print Operators	Print Operators group members can administer, create, delete, and share printers connected to domain controllers. In addition, members of this group can also manage printer objects within the Active Directory. This group does not have any default members.
Remote Desktop Users	This special group allows its members to log on to the server remotely. This group does not have any default members.
Replicator	The Replicator group is intended to support directory replication, which is a feature used by domain servers prior to Windows 2000 and 2003. Only domain users who will start the replication service should be assigned to this group. By default, there are no members of the Replicator local group.
Server Operators	The Server Operators group members can administer domain servers. Administration tasks include creating, managing, and deleting shared resources, starting and stopping services, formatting hard disks, backing up and restoring the file system, and shutting down domain controllers. By default, there are no members in this group.
Terminal Server License Servers	This group includes any Terminal Server License servers that have been installed within the domain.
Users	The Users group is used by end users who should have very limited system access. If you have installed a fresh copy of Windows Server 2003, the default settings for this group prohibit users from compromising the operating system or program files, changing the system time, and adding a local printer. By default, all users who have been created on the computer, except Guest, are members of the Users group.
Windows Authorization Access Group	Users of this group have been granted permissions to the TokenGroupsGlobalAndUniversal attribute on user objects. The Enterprise Domain Controllers group is added to this group by default.

Table 3.2 lists and describes the group accounts that are created in the Users folder by default.

TABLE 3.2 Default Group Accounts in the Users Folder

Users Group	Description
Cert Publishers	The Cert Publishers group members can manage enterprise certification and renewal agents for users and computers. There are no default members of this group.
DHCP Administrators	The DHCP Administrators group has administrative rights to manage Dynamic Host Configuration Protocol (DHCP) servers. Only available on DHCP servers.
DHCP Users	The DHCP Users group has read-only rights to the DHCP console. Only available on DHCP servers.
DnsAdmins	The DnsAdmins group has administrative rights to manage Domain Name System (DNS) servers. There are no default members of this group. (This group is installed with DNS.)
DnsUpdateProxy	The DnsUpdateProxy group has permissions that allow DNS clients to perform dynamic updates on behalf of other clients, such as DHCP servers. There are no default members of this group. (This group is installed with DNS.)
Domain Admins	The Domain Admins group has complete administrative rights over the domain. By default, the Administrator user account is a member of this group.
Domain Computers	The Domain Computers group contains all of the workstations and servers that are a part of the domain. Any computer that is added to the domain becomes a member of this group by default.
Domain Controllers	The Domain Controllers group contains all of the domain controllers in the domain. By default, any domain controller that is added to the domain becomes a member of this group.
Domain Guests	The Domain Guests group has limited access to the domain. This group is provided so that you can let people who are not regular users access specific network resources.
Domain Users	The Domain Users group contains all of the domain users. This group should have very limited system access. By default, any users who have been added to the domain become members of this group.
Enterprise Admins	The Enterprise Admins group has complete administrative rights over the enterprise (all domains within the forest). This group has the highest level of permissions of all groups and only exists in the forest root server.

TABLE 3.2   Default Group Accounts in the Users Folder *(continued)*

Users Group	Description
Group Policy Creator Owners	The Group Policy Creator Owners group has permissions to modify group policy for the domain. By default, the Administrator user account is a member of this group.
HelpServicesGroup	This group has special permissions to manage the Help and Support Center.
IIS_WPG (installed with IIS)	This group is used by the Internet Information Services worker process group. There are no default members of this group.
RAS and IAS Servers	The RAS and IAS Servers group contains the Remote Access Service (RAS) and Internet Authentication Service (IAS) servers in the domain. Servers in this group can access remote access properties of users.
Schema Admins	The Schema Admins group has special permissions to modify the schema of the Active Directory. By default, the Administrator user account is a member of this group.
TelnetClients	Members of this group have access to the Telnet server on this system.
WINS Users	The WINS Users group has special permissions to view information on the Windows Internet Name Service (WINS) server.

In addition to the default groups that are created, there are special groups used by Windows Server 2003. Membership in these groups is automatic if certain criteria are met. Special groups can't be managed through the Active Directory Users And Computers utility. Table 3.3 describes the special groups that are used by Windows Server 2003.

TABLE 3.3   Special Groups in Windows Server 2003

Group	Description
Creator Owner	The Creator Owner is the account that created or took ownership of the object. This is typically a user account. Each object (files, folders, printers, and print jobs) has an owner. Members of the Creator Owner group have special permissions to resources. For example, if you are a regular user who has submitted 12 print jobs to a printer, you can manipulate your print jobs as Creator Owner, but you can't manage any print jobs submitted by other users.

TABLE 3.3   Special Groups in Windows Server 2003 *(continued)*

Group	Description
Creator	The Creator group is the group that created or took ownership of the object (rather than an individual user). When a regular user creates an object or takes ownership of an object, the username becomes the Creator Owner. When a member of the Administrators group creates or takes ownership of an object, the group Administrators becomes the *Creator group.*
Everyone	This group includes anyone who could possibly access the computer. The Everyone group includes all users who have been defined on the computer (including Guest), plus (if your computer is a part of a domain) all users within the domain. If the domain has trust relationships with other domains, all users in the trusted domains are part of the Everyone group as well. The exception to automatic group membership with the Everyone group is that members of the Anonymous Logon group are no longer a part of the Everyone group.
Interactive	The Interactive group includes all users who use the computer's resources locally. Local users belong to the Interactive group.
Network	This group includes users who access the computer's resources over a network connection. Network users belong to the Network group.
Authenticated Users	The Authenticated Users group includes users who access the Windows Server 2003 operating system through a valid username and password. Users who can log on belong to this group.
Anonymous Logon	This group includes users who access the computer through anonymous logons. When users gain access through special accounts created for anonymous access to Windows Server 2003 services, they become members of the Anonymous Logon group.
Batch	This group includes users who log on as a user account that is only used to run a batch job. Batch job accounts are members of the Batch group.
Dialup	The Dialup group includes users who log on to the network from a dial-up connection. Dial-up users are members of the Dialup group.
Service	The Service group includes users who log on as a user account that is only used to run a service. You can configure the use of user accounts for logon through the Services program, and these accounts become members of the Service group.

TABLE 3.3   Special Groups in Windows Server 2003 *(continued)*

Group	Description
System	When the system accesses specific functions as a user, that process becomes a member of the System group. For example, say you have a virus scanner that runs as a service called abcscan; you want the service to run no matter what user is logged on and regardless of what the logged-on user's permissions are. You can create a special user—for example, abcscanuser—who has all of the permissions required to run the abcscan service each time the computer is started. The local user—for example, Katie—logs on. The user Katie is logged on as an interactive user. In addition, when the abcscan service was started, the abcscanuser was also logged on as a system user, which is a transparent process to user Katie.
Terminal Server User	This group includes users who log on through Terminal Services. These users become members of the Terminal Server User group.

Creating New Groups

To create a new group on a domain controller, take these steps (you must be logged in as Administrator or be given the right to create groups):

1. Select Start ➢ Administrative Tools ➢ Active Directory Users And Computers to open the Active Directory Users And Computers utility.

2. Right-click the Users folder, select New from the pop-up menu, and then select Group.

3. The New Object–Group dialog box appears, as shown in Figure 3.17. Type in the group name. The pre–Windows 2000 group name will be filled in automatically, but you can change it if desired.

FIGURE 3.17   The New Object–Group dialog box

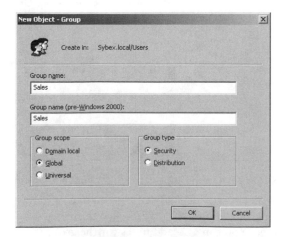

4. In the Group Scope section, select the scope for the group:

   ▪ Choose the Domain Local option if you want to use the group to assign permissions to resources. Domain local groups are always created where the resource resides.

   ▪ Choose the Global option if you want to use this group for users who require similar network access.

   ▪ Choose the Universal option if you want to assign permissions related to resources in multiple domains. This option is not active if the Active Directory is configured for Windows 2000/2003 mixed-mode support.

5. In the Group Type section, select the type of group that you want to create:

   ▪ Choose the Security option if this group is for users who need access to specific resources.

   ▪ Choose the Distribution option if this group is for users who have common characteristics (for example, users whom you may need to receive the same e-mail messages).

6. Click OK to close the dialog box and create the new group.

Managing Group Properties

You can manage an Active Directory group through the group Properties dialog box, shown in Figure 3.18. To access this dialog box, right-click the group in the Active Directory Users And Computers utility and select Properties from the pop-up menu.

FIGURE 3.18   The Active Directory group Properties dialog box

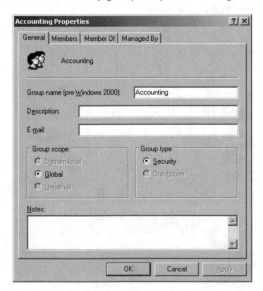

This dialog box has four tabs with options for managing the group:

▪ The General tab allows you to view and change the pre–Windows 2000 group name, the description, and the e-mail address. You can view the group scope and change group scope and group type. You can also add notes for the group.

- The Members tab, shown in Figure 3.19, allows you view and change group membership.

FIGURE 3.19   The Members tab of the Active Directory group Properties dialog box

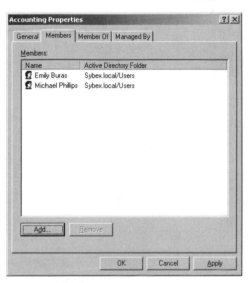

- The Member Of tab, shown in Figure 3.20, allows you to view group members and add groups to or remove groups from other groups, if the group type allows group nesting (one group contained within another group).

FIGURE 3.20   The Member Of tab of the Active Directory group Properties dialog box

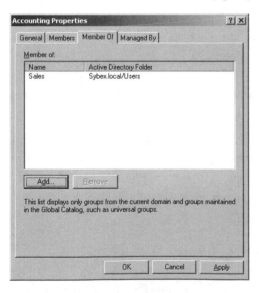

- The Managed By tab, shown in Figure 3.21, allows you to view and change the user who manages the group.

FIGURE 3.21 The Managed By tab of the Active Directory group Properties dialog box

In Exercise 3.11, you will create and manage an Active Directory group. This exercise assumes that you have completed the other exercises in this chapter.

EXERCISE 3.11

Creating and Managing an Active Directory Group

1. Select Start ≻ Administrative Tools ≻ Active Directory Users And Computers.

2. In the Active Directory Users And Computers utility, right-click the Users folder, select New, and then select Group.

3. In the New Object–Group dialog box, enter **Test Group** as the group name. Choose the Global option for the group scope and the Security option for the group type. Click the OK button.

4. In the Active Directory Users And Computers utility, right-click Test Group and select Properties.

5. In the Test Group Properties dialog box, click the Members tab and then click the Add button. Enter user **Ginnie** and click the Add button. Click the OK button. In the Test Group Properties dialog box, click the OK button.

6. Close the Active Directory Users And Computers utility.

Identifying Group Membership

You can easily identify what groups a user belongs to by viewing the user's properties and clicking the Member Of tab. For example, Figure 3.22 lists all of the groups that the Administrator user account belongs to. You can also use this dialog box to add or remove a user from a group through the Add and Remove buttons. The Set Primary Group button is used to support Macintosh and POSIX-compliant applications and is normally not used.

FIGURE   3.22   The Member Of tab for the Administrator user account

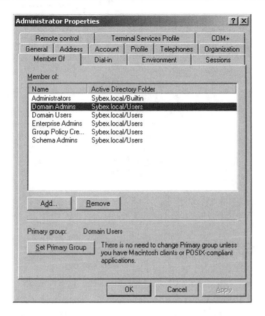

Working with Computer Accounts

Computer accounts are accounts stored in the Active Directory that are used to uniquely identify, authenticate, and manage computers within the domain. Computer accounts are created for any computer that joins the domain that is running Windows NT, Windows 2000, Windows XP Professional, or Windows Server 2003. You manage computer accounts through the Active Directory Users And Computers utility.

Windows 98, Windows Me, and Windows XP Home Edition operating systems do not have computer accounts created through the Active Directory. These operating systems do not have the ability to support the computer security requirements specified by Active Directory.

Creating Computer Accounts

You can create a computer account through two options. You can create the computer account in the Active Directory Users And Computers utility before the computer is joined to the domain or you can add the computer to the domain through the Computer Name tab of the computer's System Properties (see Figure 3.23).

FIGURE 3.23   The New Object–Computer dialog box

In order to add computers to the domain, you must be logged in as a member of the Account Operators group (which can only create new computer accounts in the Computers container or administrator-created organizational units), Domain Admins group, or Enterprise Admins group.

If you have administrative rights to add computer accounts to the domain and you are installing a new client computer, you would typically create the computer account as part of the installation process when you join the computer to the domain. If the client computer is already installed and configured and the user at the client computer will configure the computer to join the domain, you would pre-create the computer account in the Active Directory Users And Computers utility, since the local user would not have administrative rights to create a computer account in the domain.

Creating a Computer Account through Active Directory Users And Computers

To create a computer account in the Active Directory Users And Computers utility, you would take the following steps (you must be logged in as administrator or be given the right to add computers to the domain):

1. Select Start ➢ Administrative Tools ➢ Active Directory Users And Computers to open the Active Directory Users And Computers utility.

2. Right-click the Computers folder (or whatever location the computer will be created in), select New from the pop-up menu, and then select Computer.

3. The New Object–Computer dialog box will appear, as shown in Figure 3.23.

   The options that can be configured for a new computer object include:

- Computer Name, which uniquely identifies the object within the Active Directory.

- Computer Name (Pre–Windows 2000) specifies the backward-compatible computer name that will be used if the computer is using Windows NT.

- User or Group field specifies which user or group can manage this computer.

- Assign This Computer Account As A Pre–Windows 2000 Computer is used to assign a password to the computer that can be interpreted and used by a computer that is running Windows NT.

- Assign This Computer Account As A Backup Domain Controller is used if your domain is running in a mixed-mode configuration and you have a Windows NT 4.0 Backup Domain Controller (BDC) that will be added to the domain.

Creating a Computer Account through the Computer Name System Properties

You can add a computer to the domain through the Computer Name tab of the computer's System Properties dialog box. To add a Windows XP Professional computer to the domain, follow these steps:

1. On the computer that you are adding to the domain (for example a Windows XP Professional computer) select Start, right-click My Computer, and select Properties.

2. The System Properties dialog box will appear. Click the Computer Name tab.

3. To add the computer to the domain from the Computer Name tab, as shown in Figure 3.24, click the Network ID button to start the Network Identification Wizard, or click the Change button to manually add the computer to the domain. In this example, the computer is being manually added to the domain by clicking the Change button.

FIGURE 3.24   The Computer Name tab of the System Properties dialog box

4. The Computer Name Changes dialog box will appear, as shown in Figure 3.25. This dialog box can be used to change the computer's name or whether the computer is a part of a

domain or a workgroup. Under Member Of, specify the domain that you will join (in this example, sybex.local) and click the OK button.

FIGURE 3.25 The Computer Name Changes dialog box

5. The Computer Name Changes (request for username and password) dialog box will appear, as shown in Figure 3.26. Type in the username and password of a user who has rights to add the computer to the domain and click the OK button.

FIGURE 3.26 The Computer Name Changes (username and password) dialog box

6. You will see a confirmation dialog box welcoming you to the domain that you have joined. Click the OK button. If the attempt to join the domain fails, the first thing you need to check is the availability of a DNS server.

7. You will see a dialog box notifying you that the computer must be restarted for the change to take effect. Click the OK button. In the System Settings dialog box, click Yes to restart your computer.

Managing Computer Properties

To manage a computer through the Active Directory, you right-click the computer account in the Active Directory Users And Computers utility and select Properties.

The computer Properties dialog box has seven tabs for management, which include:

General   The General tab of a computer's properties, shown in Figure 3.27, is used to display the computer name (pre–Windows 2000), the DNS name for the computer (which will appear after the computer registers with DNS), and the role of the computer (Workstation Or Server). You can also specify a Description for the computer.

FIGURE 3.27   The General tab of the computer Properties dialog box

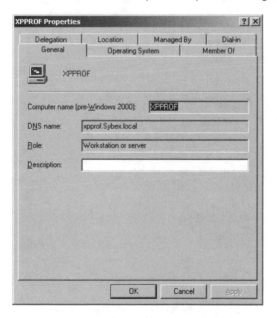

Operating System   The Operating System tab of a computer's properties, as shown in Figure 3.28, is used to display the name of the operating system, the version of the operating system, and the version of the service pack applied to the operating system.

Member Of   The Member Of tab of a computer's properties, as shown in Figure 3.29, is used to identify what groups within the local domain or any universal groups the computer object belongs to. You can also set the primary group for the computer if the computer is associated with running a Macintosh or POSIX-compliant application.

FIGURE 3.28 The Operating System tab of the computer Properties dialog box

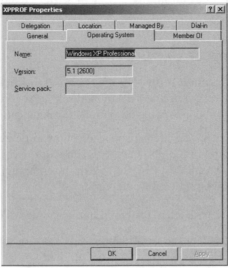

FIGURE 3.29 The Member Of tab of the computer Properties dialog box

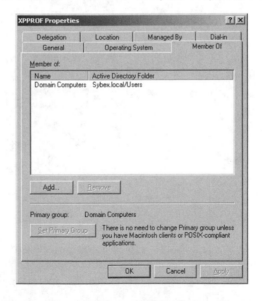

Delegation The Delegation tab of a computer's properties, as shown in Figure 3.30, is used to configure security delegation (which allows a service to act on behalf of another user or object) if the operating system is Windows 2000 or higher. The options that can be configured for delegation are:

- Do Not Trust This Computer For Delegation

- Trust This Computer For Delegation To Any Service (Kerberos Only)
- Trust This Computer For Delegation To Specified Services Only (Use Kerberos Only or Use Any Authentication Protocol).

FIGURE 3.30   The Delegation tab of the computer Properties dialog box

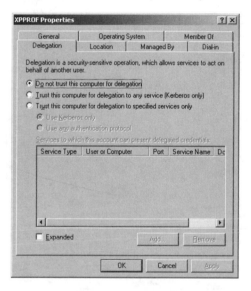

Location   The Location tab of a computer's properties, as shown in Figure 3.31, is used to provide descriptive text about where a computer is located.

FIGURE 3.31   The Location tab of the computer Properties dialog box

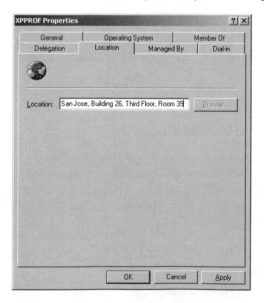

Managed By   The Managed By tab of a computer's properties, as shown in Figure 3.32, displays the user or contact who is responsible for managing the selected computer object.

FIGURE 3.32   The Managed By tab of the computer Properties dialog box

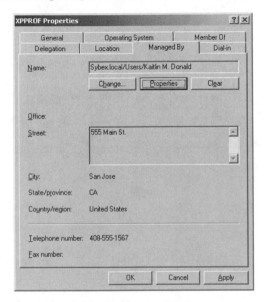

Dial-In   The Dial-In tab of a computer's properties, as shown in Figure 3.33, displays and allows the configuration of the following settings:

- Remote Access Permissions (Dial-In Or VPN)
- Verify Caller-ID
- Callback Options
- Assign A Static IP Address
- Apply Static Route

Resetting Computer Accounts

As a part of Active Directory security, computer accounts are assigned passwords that are changed every 30 days. This process is transparent to the user. If the computer password is reset and the computer crashes and is restored from a backup that contains an outdated computer password, the user who uses the computer will not be able to log on to the domain. In this case you will need to reset the computer account.

To reset a computer account, logon with administrative rights and take the following steps:

1. Select Start ➢ Administrative Tools ➢ Active Directory Users And Computers to open the Active Directory Users And Computers utility.

2. Expand the Computers folder (or whatever location the computer is located in).

FIGURE 3.33 The Dial-In tab of the computer Properties dialog box

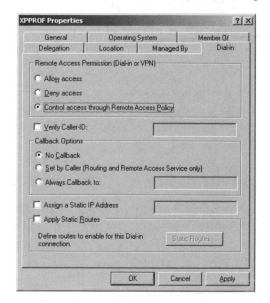

3. Right-click the computer that needs to be reset and select Reset Account.

4. You will see an Active Directory dialog box asking you to confirm that you want to reset the computer. Click the Yes button.

5. An Active Directory dialog box will appear confirming that the computer was successfully reset.

6. You will need to rejoin the computer to the domain, as covered in the Creating Computer Accounts section of this chapter.

Troubleshooting Computer Accounts

If you are having trouble connecting a computer account to a domain, you should ensure that the following conditions are met:

- The computer that is being joined to the domain must be running Windows NT, Windows 2000, Windows XP Professional, or Windows Server 2003.

- The computer that is joining the domain must have a valid network connection to the domain controller.

- The computer that is joining the domain must have a unique computer name.

- The user who is adding the computer to the domain must be logged in as a member of the Account Operators group (which can only create new computer accounts in the Computers container or administrator-created organizational units), Domain Admins group, or Enterprise Admins group.

- The computer that is being joined to the domain must have connectivity and an account in a DNS server.

Advanced User, Group, and Computer Management

Windows Server 2003 offers additional utilities for advanced user and group management. In the following sections, you will learn how to locate objects within the Active Directory, how to move objects within the Active Directory, how to create users, groups, and computers through automation, and how to import users from a Windows NT 4.0 domain or a Windows 2000 domain to a Windows 2003 domain.

Locating Objects within the Active Directory

If your Active Directory stores hundreds or thousands of users, it could potentially be time-consuming to locate a specific object. The Active Directory Users And Computers utility offers capabilities for searching for the following objects:

- Users, contacts, and groups
- Computers
- Printers
- Shared folders
- Organizational units
- Remote installation servers
- Remote installation clients
- Custom search
- Custom queries

In the following sections you will learn how to create a search for users, contacts and groups, and computers.

Locating Users, Contacts, and Groups

To locate a user, contact, or group, you would take the following steps:

1. From within Active Directory Users And Computers, right-click the domain you want to search and select Find. The Find Users, Contacts, And Groups dialog box will appear, as shown in Figure 3.34.

2. Type in the name of the user, group, or contact that you want to find and click the Find Now button.

3. The search results will be displayed in the bottom of the dialog box. You can double-click any objects that are found to bring up their properties.

4. If you need to perform a more advanced search, you would click the Advanced tab of the Find Users, Contacts, And Groups dialog box. This displays the dialog box shown in Figure 3.35.

FIGURE 3.34   The Find Users, Contacts, And Groups dialog box

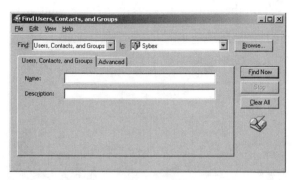

FIGURE 3.35   The Advanced tab of the Find Users, Contacts, And Groups dialog box

5.   From the Advanced tab click the Field button to specify the search criteria. You can search for a user, group, or contact. In this example, selecting User will list all of the user properties that can be searched—for example, Department or City. Once you specify the Field, you select the condition (Starts With, Ends With, Is, Is Not, Present, or Not Present) and value. For example, you could search for a user based on the Department Is Sales criteria. Once you have defined your search, click the Find Now button. The results of the search will be displayed in the Search Results section.

Locating Computers

Within the Find Users, Contacts, And Groups dialog box, you can specify that you want to search for a computer object by clicking the Find drop-down list and selecting Computer. The Find Computers dialog box will appear, as shown in Figure 3.36. The Computers tab allows you to define a search based on the computer name, owner, or role. The Advanced tab allows you to define a search based on any of the computer properties. Once you define your search criteria, click the Find Now button and the results of the search will be displayed at the bottom of the dialog box.

FIGURE 3.36   The Find Computers dialog box

Moving Objects within the Active Directory

The Active Directory is designed to allow flexibility in configuration. You can easily move objects within the Active Directory. For example, assume that you have designed your domain structure geographically and you have an OU called New York and an OU called London. You have a user in the New York office named Jsmith who transfers to the London office. You can easily move the Jsmith user object through the Active Directory Users And Computers utility.

To move an object, log on with administrative rights and take the following steps:

1. Select Start ➢ Administrative Tools ➢ Active Directory Users And Computers to open the Active Directory Users And Computers utility.

2. Expand the folder that contains the object you want to move.

3. Right-click the object that needs to be moved and select Move.

4. The Move dialog box will appear, as shown in Figure 3.37. Select the container that the object will be moved to and click the OK button.

FIGURE 3.37   The Move dialog box

In Exercise 3.12 you will move a user within the Active Directory.

EXERCISE 3.12

Moving Objects within the Active Directory

1. Select Start ➢ Administrative Tools ➢ Active Directory Users And Computers.

2. Right-click your domain and select New ➢ Organizational Unit. In the New Object–Organizational Unit dialog box, type in **New York** and click the OK button.

3. Right-click your domain and select New ➢ Organizational Unit. In the New Object–Organizational Unit dialog box, type in **London** and click the OK button.

4. Right-click New York and select New ➢ User.

5. In the New Object–User dialog box, enter the following information:

    First Name: **John**

    Initial: **B.**

    Last Name: **Jones**

    User Logon Name: **John**

6. Click the Next button.

7. In the next New Object–User dialog box, accept the default settings and click the Next button, then click the Finish button.

8. From within the New York folder, right-click John and select Move.

9. The Move dialog box will appear. Select the London folder and click the OK button.

Creating Users, Groups, and Computers through Automation

Windows Server 2003 includes several command-line utilities for managing objects within the Active Directory. They are Dsadd, Dsget, Dsmod, Dsmove, and Dsquery.

Dsadd

You can automate the process of creating users, groups, and computers through the Dsadd command-line utility. The Dsadd commands that can be used are:

- Dsadd computer
- Dsadd contact
- Dsadd group
- Dsadd ou
- Dsadd user
- Dsadd quota

Each `Dsadd` command offers a series of switches (which can be viewed from a command prompt window by typing `Dsadd /?`) that can be used to configure the object that is being created. For example, the `Dsadd user` command includes parameters for almost all of the options that can be configured for a user through the Active Directory Users And Computers utility.

Dsget

The `Dsget` command-line utility is used to display the selected properties of a specified object within the Active Directory. Each `Dsget` command has a unique set of parameters associated with the specified object.

The Active Directory objects that can have properties displayed through the `Dsget` command are:

- `Dsget computer`
- `Dsget contact`
- `Dsget group`
- `Dsget ou`
- `Dsget server`
- `Dsget user`
- `Dsget subnet`
- `Dsget site`
- `Dsget quota`
- `Dsget partition`

Dsmod

You can modify existing Active Directory objects through the `Dsmod` command-line utility. Each `Dsmod` command has a unique set of parameters based on the Active Directory object that is being modified. The objects that can be modified through the `Dsmod` command are:

- `Dsmod computer`
- `Dsmod contact`
- `Dsmod group`
- `Dsmod ou`
- `Dsmod server`
- `Dsmod user`
- `Dsmod quota`
- `Dsmod partition`

Dsmove

The `Dsmove` command-line utility is used to rename or move a single object within the Active Directory. When you use the `Dsmove` command-line utility, you specify the object's distinguished name, then the new name of the object (if you are changing the object's name) and the new location of the object.

Dsquery

You use the Dsquery command-line utility to query the Active Directory for objects that meet specified criteria. Each Dsquery command has a unique set of parameters based on the Active Directory object that is being modified. The objects that can be modified through the Dsquery command are:

- Dsquery computer
- Dsquery contact
- Dsquery group
- Dsquery ou
- Dsquery site
- Dsquery server
- Dsquery user
- Dsquery quota
- Dsquery partition
- Dsquery * (queries any type of object)

Importing Users

You can import users, groups, and computer accounts from a Windows NT 4.0 domain or a Windows 2000 domain to a Windows 2003 domain using the *Active Directory Migration Tool (ADMT)* v2.0. ADMT v2.0 can be downloaded from the Microsoft website. ADMT is a graphical utility that can be used to migrate users, groups, and computers. This utility allows the copying of accounts between separate forests and the moving of accounts within a forest. A new feature of ADMT v2.0 is the ability to maintain the old password during a user account migration.

Summary

In this chapter, you learned about managing users, groups, and computers. We covered the following topics:

- Managing user accounts including the default user accounts that are created within a Windows 2003 domain, an understanding of username and password rules and conventions, a description of usernames and security identifiers, how to create, disable, and delete user accounts, how to change a user's password, how to create and manage user accounts, how to use the Run As option, how to use user account templates, and troubleshooting user account authentication.

- Managing group accounts, which included understanding group scope and group type, the default groups created in a Windows 2003 domain, how to create and manage groups, and how to identify what groups a user belongs to.

- Working with the Active Directory Users And Computers utility to create computer accounts, manage a computer's properties, reset a computer account, or troubleshoot a computer account.

- Advanced user, group, and computer management, which is used to locate objects within the Active Directory, move objects within the Active Directory, create and manage users, groups, and computers through automation, and how to import user accounts from a Windows NT 4.0 domain or a Windows 2000 domain.

Exam Essentials

Be able to create and manage user accounts.   Know how to create user accounts from the Active Directory Users And Computers utility or through the command-line utility Dsadd. Be able to manage all of a user's properties. Know what utility is used to import user accounts from a Windows NT 4 domain or a Windows 2000 domain. Know how to troubleshoot user authentication problems. Know how to create a user through automation.

Be able to create roaming and mandatory user profiles.   Be able to create and configure local, roaming, and mandatory profiles.

Know how to create and manage group accounts.   Understand what group scope is and be able to create groups from the Active Directory Users And Computers utility or through the command-line utility Dsadd. Know what the default groups are and what the function of each default group is. Be able to determine what groups a user belongs to. Know how to create a group using automation.

Create and manage computers within the Active Directory.   Be able to create and manage computers within the Active Directory. Be able to troubleshoot and reset computer accounts when needed.

Key Terms

Before you take the exam, be certain you are familiar with the following terms:

Active Directory Migration Tool (ADMT)	Guest
Administrator	home folder
computer accounts	logon scripts
Creator group	mandatory profile
Distribution group	roaming profile
domain local groups	security group
global groups	security identifier (SID)
group	universal group
group scope	user profile
group type	

Review Questions

1. You are the administrator of a small network. Some of your users use a specific computer, while others use a bank of computers that are allocated to their department. Your company recently hired a user named Katie. You have created a user account called Katie within the Sales domain. Katie reports that she created a user profile on Computer 1 and that when she logs in to Computer 1 she gets her profile. However, Katie reports that when she logs in to Computer 2 she does not get the profile that she has customized. When you check the user properties for this user, you see the following exhibit. Based on the exhibit, what type of profile will Katie use when she logs in to Computer 2?

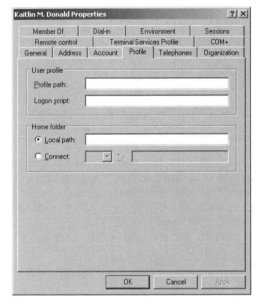

   A. She will use the default profile for the default_user that is stored on the domain controller.

   B. She will not have a user profile assigned to her.

   C. She will use the Katie user profile that is stored on the domain controller.

   D. She will use the Katie user profile that is stored on Computer 2.

2. You have just created an Active Directory user on a Windows 2003 domain controller. The security requirements for this user specify that the user should not be able to log on to the computer between 12:01 A.M. and 4:00 A.M. because this is when your company runs automated backups for the computer. You want to specify that the user account can log on only during specified hours. Which user Properties dialog box tab should you use to configure logon hours?

   A. The General tab.

   B. The Account tab.

   C. The Profile tab.

   D. You cannot restrict logon hours for an Active Directory user account.

3. You are the network administrator for a Fortune 500 company. Your Active Directory structure contains a domain for the parent corporation and a domain for a company that was recently acquired by the parent corporation. You need to create a group that will contain all of the directors and vice presidents for the Accounting departments of the parent corporation and the company that was acquired. You decide to create a group on the domain used by the parent corporation. Which one of the following options should you select for group scope?

   A. Domain local

   B. Global

   C. Distribution

   D. Universal

4. You have just created a new group on a Windows 2003 domain controller. Which of the following properties can be configured for an Active Directory group?

   A. Logon hours

   B. Logon computers

   C. Logon scripts

   D. Whom the group is managed by

5. You recently hired a new employee to help manage file backups and restores for the Windows Server 2003 computers within the Sales department. You create an account for a user named Jackie, who will be managing the backups and restores. You want to allow Jackie to back up and restore the file system, but you do not want her to be able to access the file system. To which of the following groups should you assign Jackie?

   A. Server Operators

   B. Backup Operators

   C. Administrators

   D. Replicator

6. You are the network administrator for a medium-sized network. Your company develops applications that will be used on Windows Server 2003 platforms. You run a test lab that has Windows Server 2003 on member servers within several workgroups. You hire a user named Affie to help you run and manage tests. You have just added Affie to the Server Operators group on your Windows 2003 domain. Which of the following tasks will Affie be able to complete based on this group membership? (Choose all that apply.)

   A. Create users and groups.

   B. Delete users and groups.

   C. Create network shares.

   D. Create network printers.

7. You are the network administrator of a small Windows 2003 network. One of your users has come to you because he can't remember the password he uses to log on to your Windows Server 2003 domain. Which utility should you use to change a user's password?

   A. Password Manager

   B. Password Administrator

   C. The Setpass utility

   D. The Active Directory Users And Computers utility

8. You have just installed a new Windows 2003 domain. You need to create 1000 initial user accounts. You would like to create the accounts as quickly as possible and do not want to use the Windows GUI utilities. Which of the following command-line utilities will allow you to automate the creation of users through scripting?

   A. `Dsadd`

   B. `Adduser`

   C. `Useradd`

   D. `Usrmgr`

9. You are the administrator for a medium-sized company. You support the Finance group, which contains 20 financial analysts. You want to configure the user profiles for each of the financial analysts so that they see a consistent desktop each time they log on. The financial analysts should not be able to modify their user profiles. Which of the following options should you use to create a mandatory profile for these users?

   A. Configure the `Ntuser.dat` file for the user profiles as read-only.

   B. Only allow the users Read permission to the `Ntuser.dat` file.

   C. Rename the `Ntuser.dat` file to `Ntuser.man`.

   D. Configure the user profiles as mandatory through Control Panel ➢ System, Advanced Properties tab.

10. You are the network administrator for a large company. As a part of your security policy you have configured your group policy as follows:

    Account Lockout Threshold: 3

    Account Lockout Duration: 60 minutes

    Reset Account Lockout Counter: 30 minutes

    You get a call on Monday morning from a user named Blair who tells you that she changed her password on Friday afternoon. When she tried to log on, she could not remember her password and after three attempts, she was locked out of her computer, even through she now remembers what her password is. What course of action should you take?

    A. Tell Blair to wait 30 minutes and then try to log on again.

    B. Tell Blair to wait 60 minutes and then try to log on again.

    C. Use the Group Policy Object utility to unlock Blair's account.

    D. Use the Active Directory Users And Computers utility to unlock Blair's account.

11. You are the network administrator of a small company. You have a Windows 2003 domain. You have two user accounts. You use the Kdonald-Admin account, which is a member of the Domain Admins group, for administrative purposes and the Kdonald account for regular user access. You want to ensure that your network is as secure as possible. Which of the following options will allow you to perform administrative tasks through the Active Directory Users And Computers utility without exposing your network to possible security attacks?

A. Log on to the domain as Kdonald-Admin to complete the administrative tasks and immediately log out and log on as Kdonald when you are done with the administrative tasks.

B. While logged on as Kdonald, right-click the Active Directory Users And Computers utility and select the Run As option. Specify that you want to run the utility as Kdonald-Admin.

C. Remove Kdonald-Admin from the Domain Admins group and make him a member of the Account Operators group.

D. Use the `Adduser` command-line utility with the `/user=Kdonald-Admin` switch.

12. You are the network administrator of a large corporation. You are planning to deploy a Windows 2003 network. You will be using Windows Server 2003 domain controllers with Active Directory. Your client computers will be using a variety of operating systems. Which of the following operating systems will need to have computer accounts created through the Active Directory? (Choose all that apply.)

A. Windows 95

B. Windows 98

C. Windows Me

D. Windows NT 4 Workstation

E. Windows NT 4 Server

F. Windows 2000 Professional

G. Windows XP Home Edition

H. Windows XP Professional

I. Windows Server 2003 member servers

13. You are the network administrator for a Fortune 500 company. Your company recently purchased another company and you need to integrate the new company's domain into your Active Directory structure. As a part of the integration, you need to rename all of the user accounts so that they meet the naming standards specified by corporate policy. Which of the following command-line utilities can be used to automate renaming Active Directory objects?

A. `Dsadd`

B. `Dsmod`

C. `Dsget`

D. `Dsmove`

14. You are the network administrator for a large company. One of your users, Debbie, recently returned from a three-month maternity leave. While Debbie was on leave, no one used her Windows XP Professional computer. When Debbie attempted to log on to her computer, she received an error because her computer's password had expired. What should you do?

A. Reset her computer account through the Active Directory Users And Computers utility.

B. Reset her computer account through Computer Management.

C. Change the group policy setting for Assign New Computer Password for her computer.

D. Log on to her computer running Safe Mode and run the `Setpass` command-line utility.

15. You are the system administrator for a large company. You want to create a database that contains all of the employees' addresses and phone numbers. All of the data you need is currently configured within the Active Directory. You already have a listing of all of the usernames. Which of the following command-line utilities should you use to extract user property data from the Active Directory?

A. `Dsadd`

B. `Dsmod`

C. `Dsget`

D. `Dsquery`

Answers to Review Questions

1. D.   If no user profile is specified in the Profile tab of the user's Properties, the user will use the locally stored profile on the local computer that is created by default the first time the user logs on. If a user needs to have a user profile that can be accessed from any computer, you would configure roaming profiles.

2. B.   If you create an Active Directory account, you can limit logon hours by clicking the Logon Hours button in the Account tab of the user Properties dialog box.

3. D.   Universal groups are used to logically organize global groups and appear in the Global Catalog (a search engine that contains limited information about every object in the Active Directory). Universal groups can contain users from anywhere in the domain tree or forest, other universal groups, and global groups.

4. D.   Logon hours, logon computers, and logon scripts can be managed only on a per-user basis. You can configure who manages a group in an Active Directory forest.

5. B.   The members of the Backup Operators group have rights to back up and restore the file system, even if the file system is NTFS and they have not been assigned permissions to the file system. However, the members of Backup Operators can access the file system only through the Backup utility. To be able to directly access the file system, they must have explicit permissions assigned. By default, there are no members of the Backup Operators local group.

6. C, D.   The Server Operators group members can administer domain servers. Administration tasks include creating, managing, and deleting shared resources, starting and stopping services, formatting hard disks, backing up and restoring the file system, and shutting down domain controllers.

7. D.   To set up and manage domain user accounts, you use the Active Directory Users And Computers utility. Right-click the user whose password you want to change and select Reset Password.

8. A.   Most of the tasks in Windows 2003 that can be completed through GUI utilities can also be completed through command-line utilities. The Dsadd User command is used to create users.

9. C.   You can create mandatory profiles for a single user or a group of users. The mandatory profile is stored in a file named Ntuser.man. A user with a mandatory profile can set different Desktop preferences while logged on, but those settings will not be saved when the user logs off.

10. D.   If you configure account lockout policies, you can unlock the account by unchecking the Account Is Locked Out checkbox through the user's Properties in the Active Directory Users And Computers utility. This option is active only when a computer has been locked out based on account lockout settings.

11. B.   The Run As option allows you to use a secondary logon process to log on to a computer using administrative credentials in order to perform a specific task. For security purposes, it is recommended that you use the Run As option when performing administrative tasks rather than logging into a computer or domain with an administrative account. You can use the Run As option through most Windows programs, some Control Panel items, and the Microsoft Management Console (MMC). You can also use the Run As option with command-line utilities.

12. D, E, F, H, I.   Any computers that are running Windows NT, Windows 2000, Windows XP Professional, or Windows Server 2003 require a computer account when added to an Active Directory domain. You manage computer accounts through the Active Directory Users And Computers utility.

13. D.   The Dsmove command-line utility is used to rename or move a single object within the Active Directory. When you use the Dsmove command-line utility, you specify the object's distinguished name, then the new name of the object (if you are changing the object's name) and the new location of the object.

14. A.   As a part of Active Directory security, computer accounts are assigned passwords that are changed every 30 days. This process is transparent to the user. If the computer password is reset and the computer crashes and is restored from a backup that contains an outdated computer password, the user who uses the computer will not be able to log on to the domain. In this case you will need to reset the computer account, which is done through the Active Directory Users And Computers utility.

15. C.   The Dsget command-line utility is used to display the selected properties of a specified object within the Active Directory. Each Dsget command has a unique set of parameters associated with the specified object.

Chapter

4

Managing Disks

MICROSOFT EXAM OBJECTIVES COVERED IN THIS CHAPTER:

✓ **Manage basic disks and dynamic disks.**

✓ **Optimize server disk performance.**

- Implement a RAID solution.
- Defragment volumes and partitions.

✓ **Monitor file and print servers. Tools might include Task Manager, Event Viewer, and System Monitor.**

- Monitor disk quotas.

✓ **Perform system recovery for a server.**

- Restore data from shadow copy volumes.

When you install Windows Server 2003, you choose how your disks are initially configured. Through Windows Server 2003's utilities and features, you can change your configuration and perform disk-management tasks.

Another factor in disk management is choosing how your physical drives are configured. Windows Server 2003 supports basic disks and dynamic disks. When you install Windows Server 2003 or upgrade from Windows NT, the drives are configured as basic storage. Windows 2000, Windows XP Professional, and Windows Server 2003 support dynamic storage. Windows Server 2003 dynamic storage supports the creation of simple, spanned, striped, mirrored, and RAID-5 volumes. Once you decide how your disks should be configured, you implement the disk configurations through the Disk Management utility. This utility allows you to view and manage your physical disks and volumes. In this chapter, you will learn how to manage both types of storage and how to upgrade from basic storage to dynamic storage. You can also manage your disks through the `DiskPart` command-line utility.

The other disk-management features covered in this chapter are data compression, disk quotas, shadow copies, data encryption, disk defragmentation, and disk cleanup. You will also learn how to troubleshoot disk devices and volumes.

 The procedures for many disk-management tasks are the same for both Windows Server 2003 and Windows XP Professional. The main difference is that Windows XP Professional does not support mirrored volumes or RAID-5 volumes.

Configuring Disk Storage

Windows Server 2003 supports two types of disk storage: basic disks and dynamic disks. Basic disks are backward compatible with MS-DOS and all Windows operating systems. Dynamic disks can only be accessed by Windows 2000, Windows XP Professional, and Windows Server 2003. The following sections describe the basic storage and dynamic storage configurations.

 You can convert a basic disk to a dynamic disk in Windows Server 2003 without losing any data, as described in the "Upgrading a Basic Disk to a Dynamic Disk" section later in this chapter. However, you cannot convert a dynamic disk to a basic disk without first deleting all of the volumes contained on the disk.

Basic Disks

Basic disks are used with MS-DOS and all versions of Windows. They consist of primary and extended partitions. The first partition on a basic disk for an x86-based computer is called the Master Boot Record (MBR) disk. The MBR disk contains the partition table for the disk, and the master boot code, which is used to locate the files needed to boot the operating system.

Basic disks can have up to four primary partitions. A *primary partition* is a portion of a physical disk that appears to the operating system as a separate physical disk. With the MBR disk, you can have four primary partitions or three primary partitions and one extended partition. With *extended partitions* you create one or more logical drives, each of which uses a unique drive letter.

If you are using an Itanium-based computer, the disks use GUID Partition Table (GPT). With GPT, you can have up to 128 primary partitions per disk (also known as volumes) and the volumes can be up to 18EB (exabytes).

At the highest level of disk organization, you have a physical hard drive. You cannot use space on the physical drive until you have logically partitioned the physical drive. A *partition* is a logical definition of hard drive space.

Advantages of using multiple partitions on a single physical disk are:

- You can allocate the space however you want. For example, if you had a 20GB physical drive and you created two primary partitions, you could allocate the space 5GB to drive C: to store the operating system files and 15GB to drive D: to store data files.

- Each partition can have a different file system. For example, the C: drive might be FAT32 and the D: drive might be NTFS. Multiple partitions also make it easier to manage security requirements.

Dynamic Disks

Dynamic disks were a new feature in Windows 2000 and are used with Windows XP and Windows Server 2003. Dynamic disks are a physical disk type that provides disk support that is not available through basic disks. Dynamic disks are divided into dynamic *volumes*. Dynamic volumes cannot contain partitions or logical drives, and they are only accessible through Windows 2000, Windows XP, and Windows Server 2003 systems.

Windows Server 2003 dynamic storage supports five dynamic volume types: simple volumes, spanned volumes, striped volumes, mirrored volumes, and RAID-5 volumes. These are similar to disk configurations that were used with Windows NT 4. When you install or upgrade to Windows Server 2003 from Windows NT Server 4, you are using basic storage, and you can't add volume sets. Fortunately, you can upgrade from basic storage to dynamic storage, as explained in the "Upgrading a Basic Disk to a Dynamic Disk" section later in this chapter.

To set up dynamic storage, you create or upgrade a disk to a dynamic disk. Then you create dynamic volumes within the dynamic disk. You create dynamic storage with the Windows 2003 Disk Management utility or the Diskpart command-line utility. Both utilities are covered later in this chapter.

In the following sections you will learn about simple volumes, spanned volumes, striped volumes, mirrored volumes, and RAID-5 volumes in greater detail.

Simple Volumes

A *simple volume* contains space from a single dynamic drive. The space from the single drive can be contiguous or noncontiguous. Simple volumes are used when you have enough disk space on a single drive to hold your entire volume. Figure 4.1 illustrates two simple volumes on a physical disk.

FIGURE 4.1 Two simple volumes

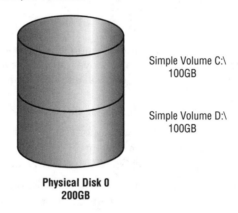

Simple Volume C:\
100GB

Simple Volume D:\
100GB

Physical Disk 0
200GB

Spanned Volumes

Spanned volumes consist of disk space on two or more dynamic drives; up to 32 dynamic drives can be used in a spanned volume configuration. Spanned volume sets are used to dynamically increase the size of a dynamic volume. When you create spanned volumes, the data is written sequentially, filling space on one physical drive before writing to space on the next physical drive in the spanned volume set. Typically, administrators use spanned volumes when they are running out of disk space on a volume and want to dynamically extend the volume with space from another hard drive.

You do not need to allocate the same amount of space to the volume set on each physical drive. This means that you could combine a 100GB volume on one physical drive with three 75GB volumes on other dynamic drives, as shown in Figure 4.2.

Because data is written sequentially, you do not see any performance enhancements with spanned volumes, as you do with striped volumes (discussed next). The main disadvantage of spanned volumes is that if any drive in the spanned volume set fails, you lose access to all of the data in the spanned set.

FIGURE 4.2 A spanned volume set

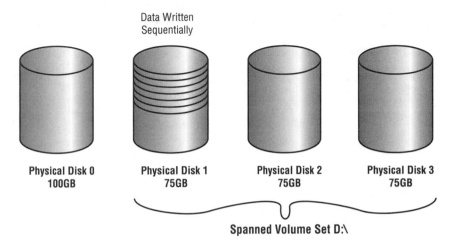

Data Written
Sequentially

Physical Disk 0
100GB

Physical Disk 1
75GB

Physical Disk 2
75GB

Physical Disk 3
75GB

Spanned Volume Set D:\

Striped Volumes

Striped volumes store data in equal stripes between two or more (up to 32) dynamic drives, as illustrated in Figure 4.3. Since the data is written sequentially in the stripes, you can take advantage of multiple I/O performance and increase the speed at which data reads and writes take place. Typically, administrators use striped volumes when they want to combine the space of several physical drives into a single logical volume and increase disk performance.

FIGURE 4.3 A striped volume set

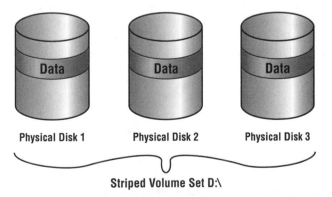

Data

Data

Data

Physical Disk 1

Physical Disk 2

Physical Disk 3

Striped Volume Set D:\

The main disadvantage of striped volumes is that if any drive in the striped volume set fails, you lose access to all of the data in the striped set.

Mirrored Volumes

Mirrored volumes are copies of two simple volumes stored on two separate physical drives, as illustrated in Figure 4.4. In a mirrored volume set, you have a primary drive and a secondary drive. The data written to the primary drive is mirrored to the secondary drive. Mirrored volumes provide fault tolerance—if one drive in the mirrored volume fails, the other drive still works without any interruption in service or loss of data.

FIGURE 4.4 A mirrored volume set

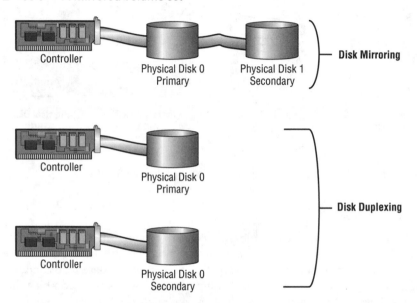

Another advantage of mirrored volumes is enhanced disk-read performance, because the drive head closest to the sector being read is accessed for the operation. However, there is some reduction in disk-write performance, because one disk controller needs to write to two separate drives. To improve write performance and also increase your system's fault tolerance, you can use a variation of mirroring called duplexing. In duplexing, you add another disk controller, which is also illustrated in Figure 4.4. (Windows Server 2003 does not distinguish between mirroring and duplexing, essentially viewing both configurations as mirrored volumes.)

The system and boot partition can exist on a mirrored volume set.

The main disadvantage of mirrored volumes is high overhead. All of your data is written to two locations. For example, if you mirrored a 100GB drive, you would need two 100GB disks (a total of 200GB of storage space), but you would not be able to store more than 100GB of data on your system.

RAID-5 Volumes

RAID-5 volumes are similar to striped volumes in that they stripe the data over multiple disk channels. In addition, RAID-5 volumes place a parity stripe across the volume. (*Parity* is a mathematical calculation performed on the data that provides information that can be used to rebuild data on failed drives.) If a single drive within the volume set fails, the parity information stored on the other drives can be used to rebuild the data on the failed drive. RAID-5 volumes require at least three physical drives (up to a maximum of 32 drives), using an equal amount of free space on all of the drives, as illustrated in Figure 4.5.

FIGURE 4.5   A RAID-5 volume set

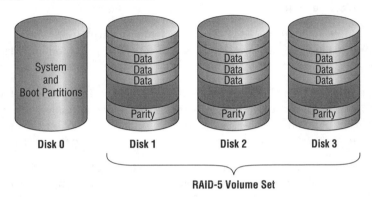

WARNING

Unlike with mirrored volumes, the system and boot partition cannot exist on a RAID-5 volume.

The main advantages of RAID-5 volumes are that they are fault tolerant and provide good performance because this configuration uses multiple disk I/O channels. The other advantage of RAID-5 volumes is that they require less disk space for fault tolerance than mirrored volumes need. A mirrored volume set uses half of the volume set to store the mirror. A RAID-5 volume set requires only the storage space of one drive in the volume set to store the parity information. For example, if you have three 100GB drives in a RAID-5 volume set, 100GB of the volume set is used to store parity information, and the remaining 200GB can store data. If your volume set contained five 100GB drives, you could use 400GB for data and 100GB for storing parity information.

The main disadvantage of a RAID-5 volume is that once a drive fails, system performance suffers until you rebuild the RAID-5 volume. This is because the parity information must be recalculated through memory to reconstruct the missing drive. If more than one drive fails, the RAID-5 volume becomes inaccessible. At that point, you must restore your data from your backup media.

TIP

As a best practice, mirrored and RAID-5 volumes should use identical hard drives (same manufacturer, model, and size) within the volume set. You should also purchase a spare drive that matches the drive set to facilitate recovery in the event of disk failure.

🌐 Real World Scenario

Selecting Fault Tolerance for Mission-Critical Servers

You are the network administrator of a large company. You need to install a Windows Server 2003 server that will be used as a database server. This is a mission-critical server and must be as reliable as possible. One of your tasks is to plan the disk configuration.

In this case you would most likely use a hardware implementation of RAID. When you purchase a high-end server, it is typically configured with drive arrays that can be configured to use RAID that is implemented as a hardware solution.

The difference between software RAID and hardware RAID is that software RAID is implemented solely through the software and requires no special hardware. Hardware implementations of RAID use special disk controllers and specific drives. When you install and configure the server, the manufacturer of the server typically provides software that is used to configure the RAID array.

Hardware implementations of RAID are more expensive to initially deploy than software implementations of RAID. However, RAID that is implemented through hardware is more fault-tolerant, faster, and is easier to recover from failure than the software RAID offered through Windows Server 2003.

For your disk configuration, you decide to buy a high-end server that supports RAID with hot-swappable drives, with an extra drive installed that can be used as an online spare. This allows you to have fault tolerance and speedy recovery in the event of disk failure.

Using the Disk Management Utility

The *Disk Management utility* is a graphical tool for managing disks and volumes within the Windows Server 2003 environment. In order to have full permissions to use the Disk Management utility, you should be logged on with Administrative privileges. To access the utility, select Start ➢ Administrative Tools ➢ Computer Management. Expand the Storage folder to see the Disk Management utility. The Disk Management utility's opening window is shown in Figure 4.6.

You can also access the Disk Management utility by right-clicking My Computer, selecting Manage, expanding Computer Management, expanding Storage, and selecting Disk Management. As an alternative, you can add Disk Management as an MMC snap-in.

The main window shows the following information:

- The volumes that are recognized by the computer
- Layout, either a partition or a volume

- The type of partition, either basic or dynamic
- The type of file system used by each partition
- The status of the partition and whether or not the partition contains the system or boot partition
- The capacity, or amount of space, allocated to the partition
- The amount of free space remaining on the partition
- The amount of overhead associated with the partition
- Whether the volume is configured for fault tolerance

FIGURE 4.6   The Disk Management window

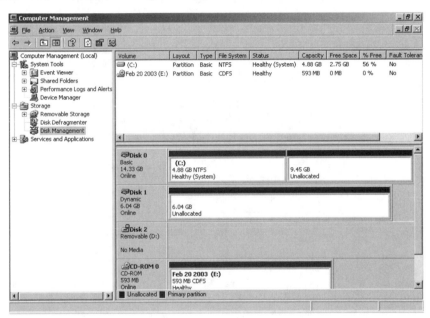

In the following sections, you will learn how to access the Disk Management utility and use it to manage basic tasks, basic storage, and dynamic storage, as well as troubleshoot disk management.

Managing Basic Tasks

With the Disk Management utility, you can perform a variety of basic tasks:

- View disk and volume properties
- Add a new disk
- Create partitions and volumes
- Upgrade a basic disk to a dynamic disk
- Change a drive letter and path
- Delete partitions and volumes

These tasks are covered in detail in the following sections.

Viewing Disk and Volume Properties

To view the properties of a disk, right-click the drive in the lower half of the Disk Management main window and choose Properties from the pop-up menu. This brings up the disk Properties dialog box, as shown in Figure 4.7.

FIGURE 4.7   The disk Properties dialog box

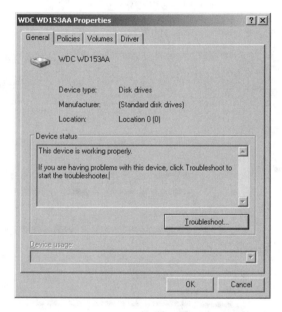

This dialog box displays four tabs: General, Policies, Volumes, and Driver.

The General tab contains information regarding the device type (disk drive, DVD/CD-ROM, or unknown), the manufacturer of the device, and the location of the device. You can also see the device status, which is whether the device is working properly; if it is not, you can use a troubleshooter to help identify the problem.

The Policies tab of the disk Properties dialog box is used to configure whether the computer will use write-caching and safe removal. Write-caching is a feature that is used to boost performance, but if there is a power outage or the computer is shut down unexpectedly, there could be a loss of data.

The Volumes tab of the disk Properties dialog box is used to list all of the volumes that have been created on the disk. You can see the Disk ID number, the type (basic or dynamic), the status (online or offline), the partition style (for example, Master Boot Record), the capacity, the unallocated space (free space), and the reserved space.

The Driver tab of the disk Properties dialog box displays the driver associated with the disk drive. From this screen you can view the driver properties or update the driver, roll back to a previous driver, or uninstall the disk driver. You cannot roll back to a previous driver unless that driver was working correctly.

Viewing Volume and Local Disk Properties

On a dynamic disk, you manage volume properties. On a basic disk, you manage local disk properties. Volumes and local disks perform the same function, and the options discussed in the following sections apply to both. The examples are based on a dynamic disk using a simple volume. If you are using basic storage, you will view the local disk properties rather than the volume properties.

To view the properties of a volume, right-click the volume in the upper half of the Disk Management main window and choose Properties. This brings up the volume Properties dialog box, as shown in Figure 4.8.

FIGURE 4.8   The volume Properties dialog box

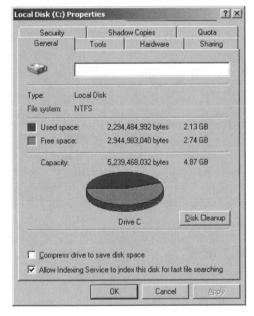

In the dialog box, the volume properties are organized on seven tabs (four for FAT16 or FAT32 volumes):

- General
- Tools
- Hardware
- Sharing
- Security
- Shadow Copies
- Quota

 The Security, Shadow Copies, and Quota tabs appear only for NTFS volumes.

These tabs are covered in detail in the following sections.

Configuring General Properties

The information on the General tab of the volume Properties dialog box gives you a general idea of how the volume is configured. This dialog box shows the label, type, file system, used and free space, and capacity of the volume. The label is shown in an editable text box, and you can change it if desired. The space allocated to the volume is shown in a graphical representation as well as in text form.

> The volume or local disk label is for informational purposes only. For example, depending on its use, you might give a volume a label like APPS or ACCTDB.

The Disk Cleanup button starts the Disk Cleanup utility, which allows you to delete unnecessary files and free up disk space. This utility is covered in more detail later in this chapter in the "Using the Disk Cleanup Utility" section.

Accessing Tools

The Tools tab of the volume Properties dialog box, shown in Figure 4.9, provides access to three tools:

- Click the Check Now button to run the Check Disk utility. You would check the volume for errors if you were experiencing problems accessing the volume or if the volume had been open during a system restart that had not gone through a proper shutdown sequence. The Check Disk utility is covered later in this chapter in the "Troubleshooting Disk Devices and Volumes" section.

- Click the Defragment Now button to run the Disk Defragmenter utility. This utility defragments files on the volume by storing files in a contiguous manner on the hard drive. Defragmentation is covered in detail later in this chapter in the "Defragmenting Disks" section.

- Click the Backup Now button to run the Backup Wizard. This Wizard steps you through backing up the files on the volume. Backup procedures are covered in Chapter 10, "Performing System Recovery Functions."

Viewing Hardware Information

The Hardware tab of the volume Properties dialog box, shown in Figure 4.10, lists the hardware associated with the disk drives that are recognized by the Windows Server 2003 operating system. The bottom half of the dialog box shows the properties of the device highlighted in the top half of the dialog box.

For more details about a hardware item, highlight it and click the Properties button in the lower-right corner of the dialog box. This brings up a Properties dialog box for the item. (Figure 4.7 shows an example of the disk drive Properties dialog box.) With luck, your device status will report that "This device is working properly." If the device is not working properly, you can click the Troubleshooter button to bring up a troubleshooting Wizard to help you discover what the problem is.

FIGURE 4.9   The Tools tab of the volume Properties dialog box

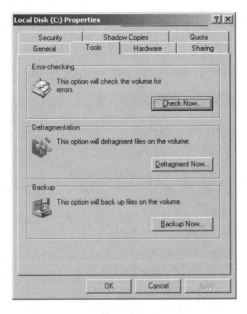

FIGURE 4.10   The Hardware tab of the volume Properties dialog box

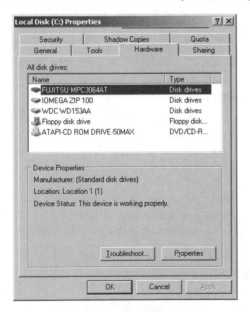

Sharing Volumes

The Sharing tab of the volume Properties dialog box, shown in Figure 4.11, allows you to specify whether or not the volume is shared. By default, all volumes are shared. The share name is the drive letter followed by a $ (dollar sign). The $ indicates that the share is hidden. These volumes are accessible only by users with administrative rights. From this dialog box, you can set the user limit, permissions, and offline settings and create a new share. Sharing and offline files are covered in Chapter 5, "Accessing Files and Folders."

FIGURE 4.11   The Sharing tab of the volume Properties dialog box

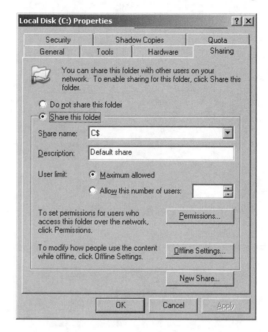

Configuring Security Options

The Security tab of the volume Properties dialog box, shown in Figure 4.12, appears only if the volume is NTFS. The Security tab is used to add or remove users and groups and set NTFS permissions for the volume. Managing file system security is covered in Chapter 5.

Setting Quotas

Like the Security tab, the Quota tab of the volume Properties dialog box appears only if the volume is NTFS. Through this tab, you can limit the amount of space users can use within the volume. Quotas are covered in detail later in this chapter in the "Setting Disk Quotas" section.

Enabling Shadow Copies

The Shadow Copies tab will appear if the volume is NTFS. This tab allows you to enable shadow copies, which are copies of files taken at different points in time that can be restored in the event that a file is accidentally deleted or overwritten, or if you want to compare a current version of a file with a previous version of the same file. Shadow copies are covered in detail later in this chapter in the "Using Shadow Copies" section.

FIGURE 4.12   The Security tab of the volume Properties dialog box

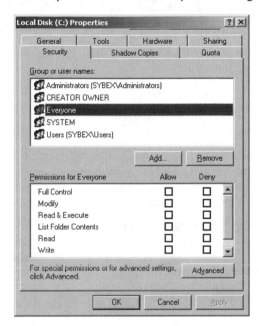

Adding a New Disk

To increase the amount of disk storage you have, you can add a new disk. This is a fairly common task that you will need to perform as your application programs and files grow larger. How you add a disk depends on whether your computer supports the hot swapping of drives. *Hot swapping* is the ability to add new hard drives while the computer is turned on. Most medium-to high-end servers with hardware RAID support hot swapping.

If your computer does not support hot swapping, you need to shut down the computer before you add a new disk. Then add the drive according to the manufacturer's directions. When you're finished, restart the computer. The new drive should now be listed in the Disk Management utility.

When you start the Disk Management utility, you will be prompted to write a signature to the disk so that it will be recognized by a Windows Server 2003. By default, the new drive will be configured as a dynamic disk.

If your computer does support hot swapping, you don't need to turn off your computer first. Just add the drive according to the manufacturer's directions. Then, open the Disk Management utility and select Action ➢ Rescan Disks. The new drive should appear in the Disk Management utility; if it does not, use Device Manager to "Scan for hardware changes."

Creating Partitions and Volumes

If you have unallocated (free) space on a basic disk and you want to create a logical drive, you create a partition. If you have unallocated space on a dynamic disk and you want to create a logical drive, you create a volume. The processes for creating partitions and volumes are described in Exercise 4.1.

We will create a partition in Exercise 4.1.

Creating a Partition

1. Select Start ➢ Administrative Tools ➢ Computer Management. Expand the Storage folder to see the Disk Management utility.

2. Right-click an area of free space and choose the New Partition option from the pop-up menu.

3. The Welcome To The New Partition Wizard dialog box appears. Click the Next button to continue.

4. The Select Partition Type dialog box appears. In this dialog box, select the type of partition you want to create: primary, extended, or logical drive (you will only see logical drive as an active choice if you have already created an extended partition). Click the Primary Partition radio button, then click the Next button.

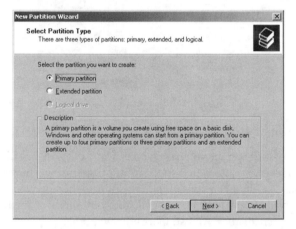

5. The Specify Partition Size dialog box appears. Here, you can specify the maximum partition size, up to the amount of free disk space that is recognized. In this exercise, use whatever free space you have and then click the Next button.

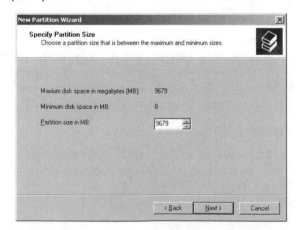

6. The Assign Drive Letter Or Path dialog box appears. Through this dialog box, you can specify a drive letter, mount the partition as an empty folder, or choose not to assign a drive letter or drive path. If you choose to mount the volume as an empty folder, you can have an unlimited number of volumes, negating the drive-letter limitation. In this exercise, accept the default drive letter, then click the Next button.

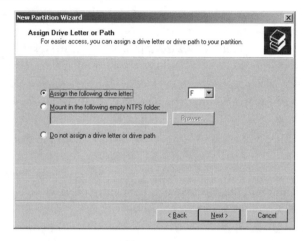

7. The Format Partition dialog box appears. This dialog box allows you to choose whether or not you will format the partition. If you choose to format the volume, you can format it as FAT32 or NTFS. You can also select the allocation unit size, enter a volume label (for informative purposes), specify a quick format, or choose to enable file and folder compression. Specifying a quick format is risky, because it will not scan the disk for bad sectors (which is done in a normal format operation). In this exercise, accept the default value to format as NTFS (leave the other settings as their defaults) and click the Next button.

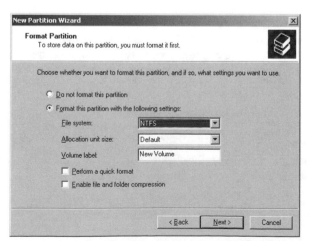

8. The Completing The Create Partition Wizard dialog box appears. Verify your selections. If you need to change any of them, click the Back button to reach the appropriate dialog box. Otherwise, click the Finish button.

The process for creating partitions (on basic disks) and creating volumes (on dynamic disks) is very similar. You right-click an area of free space on a dynamic disk and select the Create Volume option, and the Create Volume Wizard starts. This Wizard displays a series of dialog boxes to guide you through the process of creating a partition:

- The Select Volume Type dialog box allows you to select the type of volume you want to create. Options include simple volume, spanned volume, striped volume, mirrored volume, or RAID-5 volume.

- The Select Disks dialog box allows you to select the disks and the size of the volume that is being created.

- The Assign Drive Letter or Path dialog box allows you to assign a drive letter or a drive path. There is also an option to not assign a drive letter or path, but if you choose this option, users will not be able to access the volume.

- The Format Volume dialog box lets you specify whether or not you want to format the volume. If you choose to format the volume, you can select the file system, allocation unit size, and volume label. You can also choose to perform a quick format and to enable drive compression (which makes the drive a compressed drive).

Upgrading a Basic Disk to a Dynamic Disk

To take advantage of the features offered by Windows 2003 dynamic disks, you must upgrade your basic disks to dynamic disks.

WARNING　Upgrading disks with data from basic disks to dynamic disks is a one-way process (although you can convert empty dynamic disks back to basic disks). If you have a dynamic disk that contains data and you decide to revert to a basic disk, you must first delete all volumes associated with the drive.

The following steps are required to convert a basic disk to a dynamic disk on a basic disk that has an existing volume. If the disk is empty, then you can convert it using steps 1 through 3.

1. In the Disk Management utility, right-click the drive you want to convert and select the Convert To Dynamic Disk option, as shown in Figure 4.13.

2. The Convert To Dynamic Disk dialog box appears, as shown in Figure 4.14. Select the disk that you want to upgrade and click the OK button.

FIGURE 4.13   Selecting the Convert To Dynamic Disk option

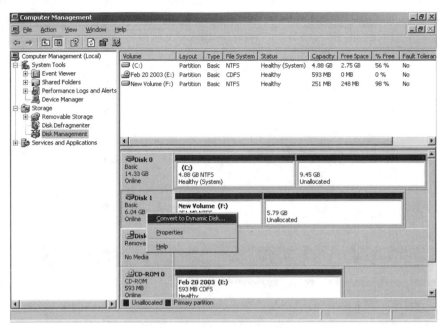

FIGURE 4.14   The Convert To Dynamic Disk dialog box

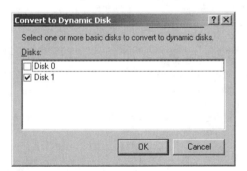

3. The Disks To Convert dialog box appears, as shown in Figure 4.15. Click the Convert button.

4. A confirmation dialog box warns you that you will no longer be able to boot previous versions of Windows from this disk. Click the Yes button to continue.

5. The next confirmation dialog box warns you that any file systems mounted on the disk will be dismounted. Click the Yes button to continue.

6. An information dialog box tells you that a reboot is required to complete the upgrade. Click the OK button. Your computer will restart, and the disk-upgrade process is complete.

FIGURE 4.15   The Disk To Convert dialog box

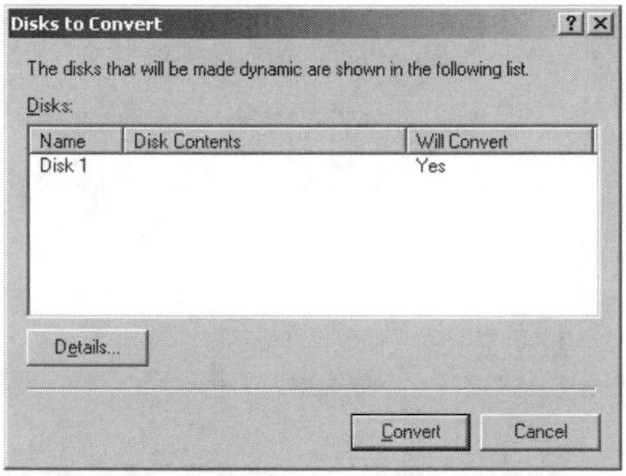

You will upgrade a basic disk to a dynamic disk in Exercise 4.2.

EXERCISE 4.2

Converting a Basic Disk to a Dynamic Disk

1.   Select Start ➤ Administrative Tools ➤ Computer Management. Expand the Storage folder to see the Disk Management utility. Click on the Disk Management utility.

2.   Right-click Disk 0 and select Convert to Dynamic Disk.

3.   The Convert to Dynamic Disk dialog box appears. Verify that Disk 0 is selected and click the OK button.

4.   The Disks To Convert dialog box appears. Click the Convert button.

5.   A confirmation dialog box warns you that you will no longer be able to boot previous versions of Windows from this disk. Click the Yes button to continue.

6.   The next confirmation dialog box warns you that any file systems mounted on the disk will be dismounted. Click the Yes button to continue.

7.   An information dialog box tells you that a reboot is required to complete the upgrade. Click the OK button. Your computer will restart, and the disk-upgrade process is complete.

Changing the Drive Letter and Paths

Suppose that you have drive C: assigned as your first partition and drive D: assigned as your CD drive. You add a new drive and partition it as a new volume. By default, the new partition is assigned as drive E:. If you want your logical drives to appear before the CD drive, you can use the Disk Management utility's Change Drive Letter And Paths option to rearrange your drive letters.

When you need to reassign drive letters, right-click the volume you want to change the drive letter on and choose the Change Drive Letter And Paths option, as shown in Figure 4.16. This brings up the Change Drive Letter And Paths For *Drive:* dialog box, as shown in Figure 4.17. Click the Edit button to access the Edit Drive Letter Or Paths dialog box. Use the drop-down list next to the Assign A Drive Letter option to select the drive letter you want to assign to the volume. Finally, confirm the change when prompted.

FIGURE 4.16   Selecting the Change Drive Letter And Paths option

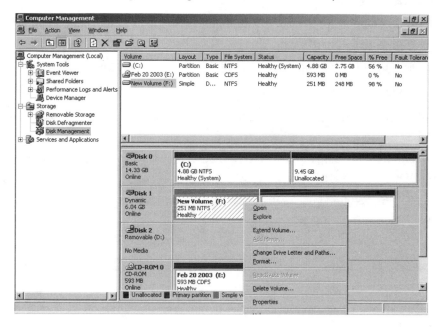

FIGURE 4.17   The Change Drive Letters And Paths dialog box

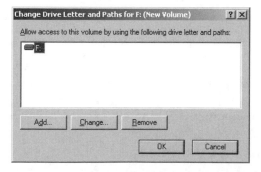

In Exercise 4.3, you will edit the drive letter of the partition you created in Exercise 4.1. Since your computer has a CD drive, your hard drive partition is C: and your CD drive is most likely D: with the new partition you created in Exercise 4.1 defined as E:. In this exercise, you will modify your drive letter settings so that the partitions are C: and D: and the CD-ROM drive is E. If your computer is using a configuration that has more drives, you will need to modify the exercise based on your configuration. The goal of this exercise is to ensure that your volumes are defined as C: and D:.

Editing a Drive Letter

1. Select Start ➢ Administrative Tools ➢ Computer Management. Expand Computer Management, then Storage, then click Disk Management.

2. Right-click your CD drive and select Change Drive Letter And Paths.

3. In the Change Drive Letter And Paths dialog box, click the Change button.

4. In the Edit Drive Letter Or Path dialog box, select a new drive letter L: and click the OK button.

5. In the confirmation dialog box, click the Yes button to confirm that you want to change the drive letter.

6. Right-click the partition you created in Exercise 4.1 and select Change Drive Letter And Paths.

7. In the Change Drive Letter And Paths dialog box, click the Change button.

8. In the Edit Drive Letter Or Path dialog box, select a new drive letter D: and click the OK button.

9. In the confirmation dialog box, click the Yes button to confirm that you want to change the drive letter.

10. Right-click your CD drive and select Change Drive Letter And Paths.

11. In the Change Drive Letter And Paths dialog box, click the Change button.

12. In the Change Drive Letter Or Path dialog box, select a new drive letter E: and click the OK button.

13. In the confirmation dialog box, click the Yes button to confirm that you want to change the drive letter.

Deleting Partitions and Volumes

You would delete a partition or volume if you wanted to reorganize your disk or make sure that data would not be accessed. Once you delete a partition or volume, it is gone forever.

To delete a partition or volume, in the Disk Management window, right-click the partition or volume and choose the Delete Volume (or Delete Partition) option. You will see a dialog box warning you that all the data on the partition or volume will be lost, as shown in Figure 4.18. Click Yes to confirm that you want to delete the volume or partition.

FIGURE 4.18   Delete Primary Partition dialog box

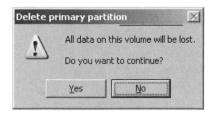

Managing Basic Storage

The Disk Management utility offers limited support for managing basic storage. You can create, delete, and format partitions on basic drives. The process for creating, deleting, and formatting partitions is very similar to the process used to create, delete, and format volumes with dynamic storage.

You also can delete volume sets and stripe sets that were created through Windows NT. Most other disk-management tasks require that you upgrade your drive to dynamic disks. (The upgrade process was described earlier in this chapter, in the "Upgrading a Basic Disk to a Dynamic Disk" section.)

Managing Dynamic Storage

As noted earlier in this chapter, a dynamic disk can contain simple, spanned, striped, mirrored, or RAID-5 volumes. Through the Disk Management utility, you can create volumes of each type. You can also create an extended volume, which is the process of adding disk space to a single simple volume. The following sections describe these disk-management tasks.

Creating Extended Volumes

When you create an extended volume, you are taking a single simple volume and adding more disk space to the volume from free space that exists on the same physical hard drive. When the volume is extended, it is seen as a single drive letter. In order to extend a volume, the simple volume must be formatted as NTFS. You cannot extend a system or boot partition. You also cannot extend volumes that were originally created as basic disk partitions and then converted to a dynamic disk.

An extended volume assumes that you are only using one physical drive. A spanned volume assumes that you are using two or more physical drives.

The following steps are used to create an extended volume:

1. In the Disk Management utility, right-click the volume you want to extend and choose the Extend Volume option.

2. The Extend Volume Wizard starts. Click the Next button.

3. The Select Disks dialog box appears, as shown in Figure 4.19. Select the disk that you want to use for the extended volume from the Available list, click the Add button, and then click the Next button.

FIGURE 4.19 The Select Disks dialog box

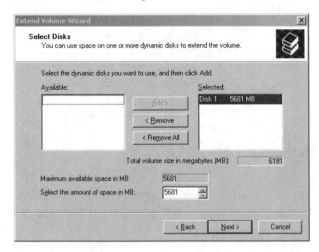

4. The Completing The Extend Volume Wizard dialog box appears. Click the Finish button.

WARNING   Once a volume is extended, no portion of the volume can be deleted without losing data on the entire set.

 Real World Scenario

Adding Disk Space to a Volume in a Pinch

You are the network administrator of a large company. You manage a database server called \ACCTDB that stores all of the accounting information for your company. The volume that stores the data for the database is 100GB. You monitor the free space for the volume and realize that you have less than 5% of free space for the volume. The server is due to be upgraded and you have ordered new server hardware that includes a drive array of 300GB that will store the database. However, the new server will not arrive for another month due to budgeting restrictions.

You need to ensure that the database does not report "out of disk space" errors in the upcoming month, while you are waiting to upgrade the server hardware. You have access to another 100GB drive, which is the designated spare drive for the current server.

You decide to add the second 100GB drive to the server and create an extended volume. You back up all of the current data, add the second drive, and create an extended volume. None of the current data is lost, and you can now store up to 200GB of data. This is not a good long-term solution, because if either drive fails, you lose access to all of the data. However, this solution is a good short-term option until the new server hardware arrives.

Creating Spanned Volumes

When you create a spanned volume, you are forming a new volume from scratch that includes space from two or more physical drives, up to a maximum of 32 drives. You can create spanned volumes that are formatted as FAT, FAT32, or NTFS. In order to create a spanned volume, you must have at least two drives installed on your computer and each drive must contain unallocated space.

The following steps are used to create a spanned volume:

1. In the Disk Management utility, right-click an area of unallocated space on one of the drives that will be part of the spanned volume and select New Volume from the pop-up menu.

2. The New Volume Wizard starts. Click the Next button.

3. The Select Volume Type dialog box appears, as shown in Figure 4.20. Select the Spanned radio button and click the Next button.

FIGURE 4.20   The Select Volume Type dialog box

Only the options that are supported by your computer's hardware will be available in the Select Volume Type dialog box.

4. The Select Disks dialog box appears. By default, the disk that you originally selected to create the spanned volume is selected. You need to select at least one other dynamic disk by highlighting the disk and clicking the Add button. The disks that you select appear in the Selected Dynamic Disks list box, as shown in Figure 4.21. When you have added all of the disks that will make up the spanned volume, click the Next button.

5. The Assign Drive Letter Or Path dialog box appears. Specify a drive letter, mount the volume at an empty folder that supports drive paths, or choose not to assign a drive letter or drive path. Then click the Next button.

6. The Format Partition dialog box appears. You can choose whether or not you will format the partition, and if so, what file system will be used. After you've made your choice, click the Next button.

FIGURE 4.21 The Select Disks dialog box for spanned volumes

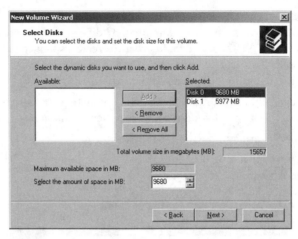

7. The Completing The Create Volume Wizard dialog box appears, offering you the opportunity to verify your selections. If you need to make changes, click the Back button. If the configuration is correct, click the Finish button. In the Disk Management window, you will see that the spanned volume consists of two or more drives that share a single drive letter, in this case F:, as in the example shown in Figure 4.22. Notice that in this example, the disks that make up the spanned volume are unequal in size.

FIGURE 4.22 A spanned volume shown in the Disk Management utility

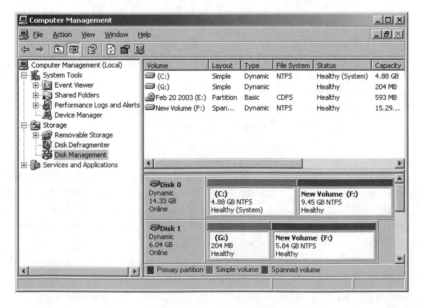

Once a spanned volume is created, no portion of the volume can be deleted without losing the data on the entire set.

Creating Striped Volumes

When you create a striped volume, you are forming a new volume that combines free space on 2 to 32 drives into a single logical partition. Data in the striped volume is written across all drives in 64KB stripes. (Data in spanned and extended volumes is written sequentially.) In order to create a striped volume, you must have at least two drives installed on your computer, and each drive must contain unallocated space. The stripe cannot contain the system or boot volumes. The free space on all drives must be equal in size.

The following steps are used to create a striped volume:

1. In the Disk Management utility, right-click an area of unallocated space on one of the drives that will be a part of the striped volume set and select Create Volume from the pop-up menu.

2. The Create Volume Wizard starts. Click the Next button.

3. The Select Volume Type dialog box appears. Select the Striped radio button and click the Next button.

4. The Select Disks dialog box appears. By default, the disk that you originally selected to create the striped volume is selected. You need to select at least one other dynamic disk by highlighting the selected disk and clicking the Add button. The disks that you select appear in the Selected Dynamic Disks list box. When you have added all of the disks that will make up the striped volume, click the Next button.

5. The Assign Drive Letter Or Path dialog box appears. Specify a drive letter, mount the volume at an empty folder that supports drive paths, or choose not to assign a drive letter or drive path. Then click the Next button.

6. The Format Partition dialog box appears. You can choose whether or not you will format the partition, and if so, what file system will be used. After you've made your choice, click the Next button.

7. The Completing the Create Volume Wizard dialog box appears, offering you the opportunity to verify your selections. If you need to make changes, click the Back button. If the configuration is correct, click the Finish button. In the Disk Management window, you will see that the striped volume consists of two or more drives that share a single drive letter, as in the example shown in Figure 4.23. Notice that the disks that make up the striped volume are equal in size.

Once a striped volume is created, no portion of the volume can be deleted without losing the data on the entire set.

FIGURE 4.23   A striped volume shown in the Disk Management utility

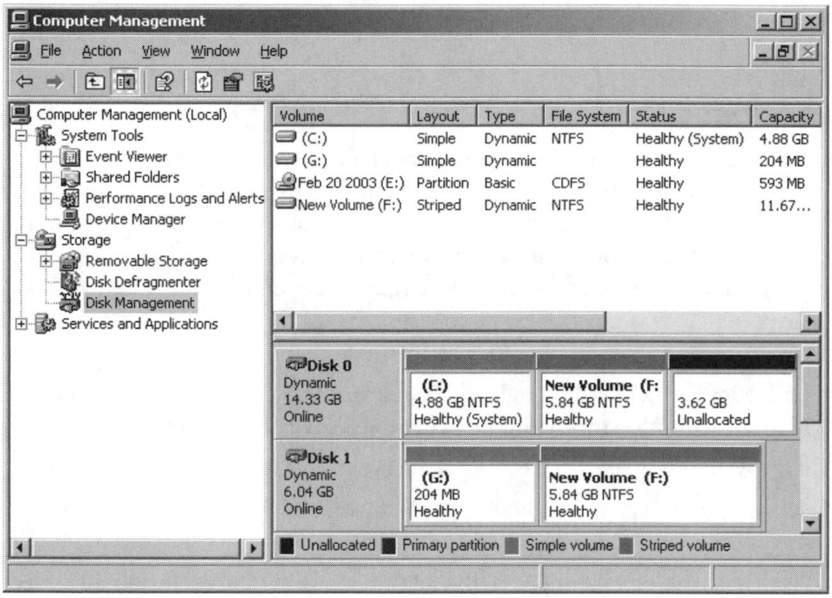

Creating Mirrored Volumes

When you create a mirrored volume, you are setting up two physical drives that contain volumes that mirror each other. You create mirrored volumes from areas of free space on the two drives. In order to create a mirrored volume, you must have at least two drives installed on your computer and each drive must contain unallocated space. Mirrored volumes require that the space on each drive used for the mirror set be equal in size.

In the following steps, you will learn how to create a mirrored volume. You can follow these steps if you have at least two dynamic disks configured on your computer and they both contain unallocated space.

Note that you can only perform this exercise on a dynamic disk.

1. Select Start ➢ Administrative Tools ➢ Computer Management. Expand Computer Management, then Storage, then click Disk Management.

2. In the Disk Management utility, right-click an area of unallocated space on one of the drives that will be a part of the mirrored volume set and select New Volume.

3. When the New Volume Wizard starts, click the Next button.

4. In the Select Volume Type dialog box, select the Mirrored radio button. Then click the Next button.

5. In the Select Disks dialog box, select the second dynamic disk to be part of the mirrored volume set and click the Add button. Then click the Next button.

6. In the Assign Drive Letter or Path dialog box, accept the default assignment of the next available drive letter and click the Next button.

7. In the Format Partition dialog box, you can choose whether or not you will format the partition, and if so, what file system will be used. For this exercise, select the Format This Volume As Follows radio button and format the file system with NTFS. Then click the Next button.

8. In the Completing The Create Volume Wizard dialog box, verify that the configuration is correct and click the Finish button. You will now see the mirrored volume in the Disk Management window (in this example, drive F:).

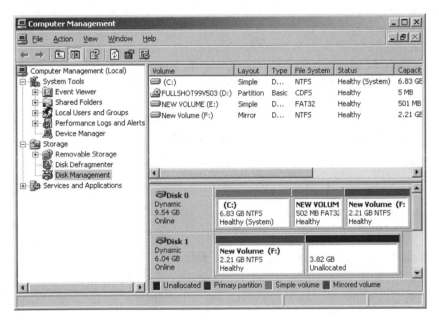

Creating RAID-5 Volumes

When you create a RAID-5 volume, you are creating a new volume that combines free space on 3 to 32 physical drives. The volume will contain stripes of data and parity information for increased performance and fault tolerance. You must choose at least three physical disks (not including the system or boot volume) that will be part of the RAID-5 volume. The free space on all the drives must be equal in size.

The following steps are used to create a RAID-5 volume:

1. In the Disk Management utility, right-click an area of unallocated space on one of the drives that will be a part of the RAID-5 volume set and select Create Volume from the pop-up menu.

2. The Create Volume Wizard starts. Click the Next button.

3. The Select Volume Type dialog box appears. Select the RAID-5 radio button and click the Next button.

4. The Select Disks dialog box appears. By default, the disk that you originally selected to create the RAID-5 volume is selected. Select at least two other dynamic disks by highlighting

each disk and clicking the Add button. The disks that you select appear in the Selected Dynamic Disks list box. When you have finished adding the disks that will make up the RAID-5 volume, click the Next button.

5. The Assign Drive Letter Or Path dialog box appears. Specify a drive letter, mount the volume at an empty folder that supports drive paths, or choose not to assign a drive letter or drive path. Then click the Next button.

6. The Format Partition dialog box appears. You can choose whether or not you will format the partition, and if so, what file system will be used. After you've made your choices, click the Next button.

7. The Completing The Create Volume Wizard dialog box appears. If you need to make changes, click the Back button. If the configuration is correct, click the Finish button. In the Disk Management window, you will see that the RAID-5 volume consists of three or more drives that share a single drive letter.

Troubleshooting Disk Management

The Disk Management utility can be used to troubleshoot disk errors through a set of status codes; however, if a disk will not initialize, no status code will be displayed. Disks will not initialize if there is not a valid disk signature.

In the following sections, you will learn how to interpret Disk Management status codes and how to troubleshoot disks that fail to initialize.

Using Disk Management Status Codes

The main window of the Disk Management utility displays the status of disks and volumes. The following list contains the possible status codes and a description of each code; these are very useful in troubleshooting disk problems:

Online   Indicates that the disk is accessible and that it is functioning properly. This is the normal disk status.

Online (Errors)   Only used with dynamic disks. Indicates that I/O errors have been detected on the dynamic disk. One possible fix for this error is to right-click the disk and select Reactivate Disk in an attempt to return the disk to Online status. This fix will work only if the I/O errors were temporary. You should immediately back up your data if you see this error and suspect that the I/O errors are not temporary.

Healthy   Specifies that the volume is accessible and functioning properly.

Healthy (At Risk)   Used to indicate that a dynamic volume is currently accessible, but I/O errors have been detected on the underlying dynamic disk. This option is usually associated with Online (Errors) for the underlying disk.

Offline or Missing   Only used with dynamic disks. Indicates that the disk is not accessible. This can occur if the disk is corrupt, the disk's data/power cable is disconnected, or the hardware has failed. If the error is not caused by hardware failure or major corruption, you may be able to re-access the disk by using the Reactivate Disk option to return the disk to Online status.

If the disk was originally offline and then the status changed to Missing, it indicates that the disk has become corrupt, been powered down, or was disconnected.

Unreadable   Can occur on basic or dynamic disks. Indicates that the disk is inaccessible and might have encountered hardware errors, corruption, or I/O errors, or that the system disk configuration database is corrupt. This message may also appear when a disk is spinning up while the Disk Management utility is rescanning the disks on the computer.

Failed   Can be seen with basic or dynamic volumes. Specifies that the volume can't be started. This can occur because the disk is damaged or the file system is corrupt. If this message occurs with a basic volume, you should check the underlying disk hardware. If the error occurs on a dynamic volume, verify that the underlying disks are Online.

Unknown   Used with basic and dynamic volumes. Occurs if the boot sector for the volume becomes corrupt—for example, from a virus. This error can also occur if no disk signature is created for the volume.

Incomplete   Occurs when you move some, but not all, of the disks from a multi-disk volume. If you do not complete the multi-volume set, then the data will be inaccessible.

Foreign   Can occur if you move a dynamic disk from one computer to another computer running Windows 2000 (any version), Windows XP Professional, or Windows Server 2003 to your Windows Server 2003 computer. This error is caused because configuration data is unique to computers where the dynamic disk was created. You can correct this error by right-clicking the disk and selecting the option Import Foreign Disks. Any existing volume information will then be visible and accessible. You see an example of a Foreign error in Figure 4.24.

FIGURE 4.24   Example of a Foreign Status Code

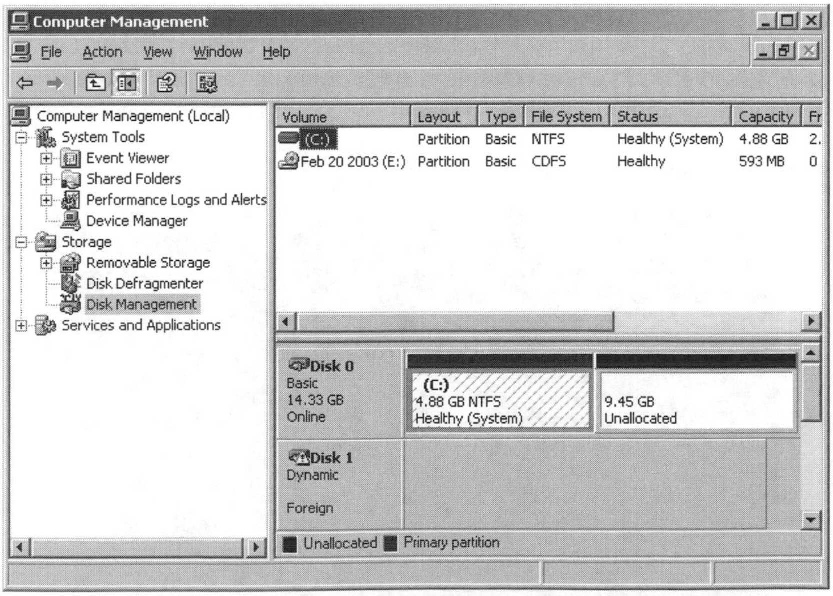

Troubleshooting Disks That Fail to Initialize

When you add a new disk to your computer in Windows Server 2003, the disk does not initially contain a disk signature, which is required for the disk to be recognized by Windows Server 2003. Disk signatures are at the end of the sector marker on the Master Boot Record (MBR) of the drive. When you install a new drive and run the Disk Management utility, a wizard starts and lists all new disks that have been detected. The disk signature is written through this process. If you cancel the wizard before the disk signature is written, you will see the disk status Not Initialized.

To initialize a disk, you right-click the disk you want to initialize and select the Initialize Disk option. If you are running a 32-bit edition of Windows Server 2003, you will write the disk signature to the MBR of the drive. If you are using an Itanium-based computer and are using a 64-bit edition of Windows Server 2003, you can write the signature to the MBR or the GUID Partition Table (GPT).

In an Itanium based computer the MBR disk can be converted to a GPT disk.

Using the *DiskPart* Command-Line Utility

The DiskPart command-line utility can be used to manage disks, partitions, and volumes from a command prompt or through the use of automated scripts.

When you execute Diskpart from a command prompt, you start the DiskPart utility and you will see the following prompt:

DISKPART>

You can then list available objects through the List Disk, List Partition, or List Volume commands. The List Partition only displays the partitions on a disk that has been focused (explained shortly). An example of List Disk and List Partition is shown in Figure 4.25.

FIGURE 4.25   DiskPart command-line utility

```
Command Prompt - diskpart                                    _ □ x
Microsoft Windows [Version 5.2.3718]
(C) Copyright 1985-2002 Microsoft Corp.

C:\Documents and Settings\Administrator>diskpart

Microsoft DiskPart version 5.2.3718
Copyright (C) 1999-2001 Microsoft Corporation.
On computer: SERVER2003

DISKPART> list disks

Microsoft DiskPart version 5.2.3718

DISK        - Prints out a list of disks.
PARTITION   - Prints out a list of partitions on the current disk.
VOLUME      - Prints out a list volumes.

DISKPART> list volumes

Microsoft DiskPart version 5.2.3718

DISK        - Prints out a list of disks.
PARTITION   - Prints out a list of partitions on the current disk.
VOLUME      - Prints out a list volumes.

DISKPART>
```

You can then select the disk, volume, or partition you want to manage by selecting the object through the Select command (for example, Select Disk, Select Volume, or Select Partition). It is called focus when you select an object and any commands that are executed will be executed on the focused object. For example, if you have two physical disks on your server and you execute List Disks, you will see Disk 0 and Disk 1. If you want to set the focus to Disk 1, you would execute:

Select Disk 1

Then you would execute:

List Disks

After you select a disk, notice that Disk 1 will have an * next to it, which indicates that Disk 1 is the current focus.

The options that can be used with DiskPart (version 5.2.3) are defined in Table 4.1.

TABLE 4.1   DiskPart Command-Line Options

Option	Description
Add	Used to add a mirror to a simple volume.
Active	Used to specify which partition should be marked as the active partition. The active partition is used to boot the operating system. If you mark the wrong partition as active, your computer will not boot.
Assign	Assigns a drive letter or mount to the focused volume. You cannot assign drive letters to system volumes, paging file volumes, boot volumes, OEM partitions, or any GPT partition other than a basic data partition.
Break	Used with mirroring to break a mirror set.
Clean	Used to remove or clear all existing configuration information for the specified disk.
Convert	Converts between different disk formats (basic, dynamic, GPT, MBR)
Create	Creates a new partition or volume.
Delete	Used to remove or delete the specified object.
Detail	Displays details about the selected volume or disk.
Exit	Exits the DiskPart utility.
Extend	Used to extend the specified volume.

TABLE 4.1   DiskPart Command-Line Options *(continued)*

Option	Description
Help	Displays a list of commands that can be used with DiskPart and a short explanation of each command.
Import	Imports a disk group from a foreign source to the local disk group.
List	Use List Disk, List Partition, or List Volume to see all of the specified objects listed, as well as information about each object, and the status of each object.
Online	Used if you have a disk that is currently offline, to make the disk online.
Rem	Used with scripting to mark the text within the script as a remark, so no action is taken.
Remove	Removes the specified drive letter or mount point.
Rescan	Forces a manual scan for any new drives or volumes.
Retain	Used in conjunction with unattended installations to prepare a simple volume to be used as a system or boot volume.
Select	Moves the focus to the specified disk, partition, or volume.

Recovering from Disk Failure

If your disk fails, you will need to implement a recovery process. If your failure occurred on a simple, extended, spanned, or striped volume, you will need to restore your data from your last backup using the Windows Backup utility.

     The Windows Backup utility is described in detail in Chapter 10.

When a disk in a mirrored or RAID-5 volume set fails, you can't miss it—you will see a system error and an error in Event Viewer (which is covered in Chapter 10). In the Disk Management utility, the failed volume will be indicated by the description Failed Redundancy. If the disk that failed was part of a mirrored volume set, you need to remove and re-create the failed volume. If the disk was part of a RAID-5 volume set, you need to repair the volume.

The following sections describe how to recover from mirrored and RAID-5 volume failures.

Recovering from a Mirrored Volume Failure

To recover from a mirrored volume failure, you need to remove the volume that failed and then re-create the volume. You can perform both of these tasks through the Disk Management utility.

If a drive fails in a mirrored volume set that contains only data (it does not contain your system or boot partition), take the following steps:

1. In the Disk Management utility, right-click the failed mirrored volume (marked as Failed Redundancy) and choose Remove Mirror from the pop-up menu.

2. The Remove Mirror dialog box appears. Select the disk that will be removed from the mirrored volume and click the Remove Mirror button.

3. You will see a dialog box asking you to confirm that you want to remove the mirror. Click the Yes button. The remaining drive will become a simple volume.

4. Remove the failed hard drive from the computer and replace the drive, or use a spare drive.

5. Use the Disk Management utility to re-create the mirrored volume, as described in the "Creating Mirrored Volumes" section earlier in this chapter.

If a drive fails in a mirrored volume set that contains the boot partition, you must first determine whether the failed drive is the primary drive (the one with the original data) or the secondary drive (the one with the mirrored data) in the set. If the secondary drive failed, you can remove the failed drive, replace it, and then re-create the mirrored volume, just as you do to recover from a failed mirrored volume set containing only data (described in the previous section).

If the primary drive fails and it contains the boot partition, then recovery becomes more complex, because the `Boot.ini` file, which is used during the Windows 2003 boot process, contains the location of the boot partition. If this file points to the failed partition, Windows Server 2003 will not boot. To recover from this type of failure, you will need a Windows Server 2003 boot disk with a `Boot.ini` file that points to the secondary drive in the mirrored set. (The `Boot.ini` file and the process for creating a Windows Server 2003 boot disk are covered in Chapter 10.) Then you can follow the same steps as you would to recover from a failed data volume (described in the previous section).

If you have at least two dynamic disks configured on your computer and have created a mirrored volume, you can follow the steps in Exercise 4.4 to learn how to recover from a mirror failure where hot swapping is not supported.

EXERCISE 4.4

Recovering from a Mirrored Volume Failure

1. Power down your computer and remove the data cable from the second drive that you configured in the mirrored volume set.

2. Restart your server.

EXERCISE 4.4 *(continued)*

---

3. In the Disk Management utility, right-click the failed mirrored volume (marked as Failed Redundancy) and choose Remove Mirror.

4. In the Remove Mirror dialog box, select the disk that will be removed from the mirrored volume and click the Remove Mirror button.

5. In the next dialog box, click Yes to confirm that you want to remove the mirror.

6. Power down your computer and reconnect the data cable on your second drive. Restart and log on as Administrator.

7. Re-create the mirrored volume (discussed in "Creating Mirrored Volumes," above).

Recovering from a RAID-5 Volume Failure

If a drive in a RAID-5 volume set fails, you will still be able to access your volume set; however, your system performance will degrade significantly, and you will need to re-create the missing data through the parity information.

In Exercise 4.5, you will recover from a RAID-5 volume failure.

EXERCISE 4.5

Recovering from a RAID-5 Volume Failure

1. Replace the failed hardware.

2. Open the Disk Management utility, right-click the failed RAID-5 volume set (marked as Failed Redundancy) and choose Repair Volume from the pop-up menu.

3. The Repair RAID-5 Volume dialog box appears. Choose the drive that you have replaced and click the OK button to regenerate the RAID-5 volume set.

Managing Data Compression

Data compression is the process of storing data in a form that takes less space than uncompressed data does. If you have ever "zipped" or "packed" a file, you have used data compression. With Windows Server 2003, data compression is available only on NTFS partitions.

Both files and folders in the NTFS file system can be compressed or uncompressed. Files and folders are managed independently, which means that a compressed folder could contain uncompressed files, and an uncompressed folder could contain compressed files.

Access to compressed files by DOS or Windows applications is transparent. For example, if you access a compressed file through Microsoft Word, the file will be uncompressed automatically when it is opened, and then automatically compressed again when it is closed.

Data compression is only available on NTFS partitions. If you copy or move a compressed folder or file to a FAT partition (or a floppy disk), Windows 2003 will automatically uncompress the folder or file.

You implement compression through the Windows Explorer utility. Compression is an advanced attribute of a folder's or file's properties.

You will compress folders and files in Exercise 4.6. This exercise assumes that you have completed Exercise 4.1.

EXERCISE 4.6

Compressing Folders and Files

1. Select Start ➢ Windows Explorer.

2. In Windows Explorer, create a folder on the D: drive called **Test** and copy some files to the Test folder.

3. Right-click the folder and select Properties. In the General tab of the folder Properties dialog box, note the value listed for Size On Disk. Then click the Advanced button.

4. In the Advanced Attributes dialog box, check the Compress Contents To Save Disk Space option. Then click the OK button. In the folder Properties dialog box, click the Apply button.

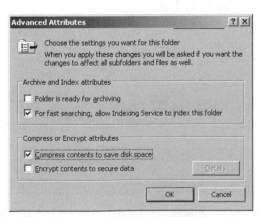

5. In the Confirm Attribute Changes dialog box, select Apply Changes To This Folder, Sub-folders and Files (if this dialog box does not appear, click the Apply button in the folder Properties dialog box to display it). Then click the OK button.

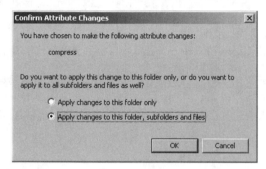

6. In the General tab of the folder Properties dialog box, note the value that now appears for Size On Disk. This size should have decreased because you compressed the folder.

You can specify that compressed files be displayed in a different color from the uncompressed files. To do so, in Windows Explorer, select Tools ➤ Folder Options ➤ View. Under Files And Folders, check the Show Encrypted Or Compressed NTFS Files In Color option. Compressed files will display in blue and encrypted files will display in green.

Setting Disk Quotas

Suppose that you have a server with an 18GB drive that is mainly used for users' home folders, and you start getting "out of disk space" error messages. On closer inspection, you find that a single user has taken up 10GB of space by storing multimedia files that she has downloaded from the Internet. This type of problem can be avoided through the use of disk quotas.

Disk quotas are used to specify how much disk space a user is allowed on specific NTFS volumes. You first specify disk quotas for all users, and then you can limit disk space on a per-user basis.

Before you administer disk quotas, you should be aware of the following aspects of disk quotas:

- Disk quotas can be specified only for NTFS volumes.

- Disk quotas apply only at the volume level, even if the NTFS partitions reside on the same physical hard drive.

- Disk usage is calculated on file and folder ownership. When a user creates, copies, or takes ownership of a file, that user is the owner of the file.

- When a user installs an application, the free space that the application will see is based on the disk quota availability, not the actual amount of free space on the volume.

- Disk quota space used is based on actual file size. There is no mechanism to support or recognize file compression.

Disk quotas are not applied to the local domain Administrator account or members of the local domain Administrators group. If an administrator from a trusted domain stores data on a drive with a quota, the administrator account from the trusted domain's file ownership is charged against the quota. A trusted administrator is not exempt from quotas.

 Real World Scenario

Using Disk Quotas to Manage Disk Space

You are the network administrator of a large company. You manage a server called \SalesData that stores user data for the 20 sales account managers. The \SalesData server has a share called Users, and underneath the Users share, each user has a folder that corresponds to their logon name. The \SalesData\Users share is on an NTFS volume on a 200GB drive.

Some of the sales account managers have been downloading large video files from the Internet, which is causing your disk to report that its free space is low. You determine that each sales account manager can safely store all of his or her business data with 5GB of disk space.

You decide to implement disk quotas and set warnings for the users at 4GB and restrict them from using more than 5GB of disk space. This will prevent individual users from using excessive disk space since it is shared among many users. If you determine that a specific user requires more disk space for business purposes, you can set higher disk quota limits on a per-user basis.

The following sections describe how to configure and monitor disk quotas.

Configuring Disk Quotas

You configure disk quotas through the NTFS volume Properties dialog box. This dialog box was discussed in detail earlier in the chapter in the "Managing Basic Tasks" section. You learned that you can access the volume Properties dialog box in the Disk Management utility by right-clicking the drive letter and selecting Properties from the pop-up menu. Another way to access this dialog box is from Windows Explorer—just right-click the drive letter in the listing and select Properties. In the volume Properties dialog box, click the Quota tab to see the dialog box shown in Figure 4.26. When you open the Quota tab, you will see that disk quotas are disabled by default.

FIGURE 4.26   The Quota tab of the volume Properties dialog box

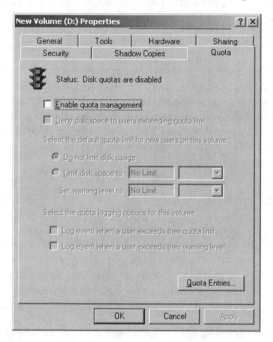

The options that can be configured through the Quota tab are described in Table 4.2.

TABLE 4.2   Disk Quota Configuration Options

Option	Description
Enable Quota Management	Specifies whether quota management is enabled for the volume.
Deny Disk Space To Users Exceeding The Quota Limit	Specifies that users who exceed their disk quota will not be able to override their disk allocation. Those users will receive "out of disk space" error messages.
Select The Default Quota Limit For New Users On This Volume	Allows you to define quota limits for new users. Options include not limiting disk space, limiting disk space, and specifying warning levels.
Select The Quota Logging Options For This Volume	Specifies whether events that relate to quotas will be logged. You can enable logging events for users exceeding quota limits or users exceeding warning limits.

Notice the traffic light icon in the upper-left corner of the Quota tab. The traffic light indicates the status of disk quotas, as follows:

- A red light specifies that disk quotas are disabled.

- A yellow light specifies that Windows Server 2003 is rebuilding disk quota information.

- A green light specifies that the disk quota system is enabled and active.

The next sections describe how to set quotas for all new users as default quotas and how to set quotas for a specific user.

Setting Default Quotas

When you set default quota limits for new users on a volume, the quotas apply only to users who have not yet created files on that volume. This means that users who already own files or folders on the volume will be exempt from the quota policy. It is also important to note that the data stored before the quota is set is not counted against the quota limit. Users who have not yet created a file on the volume will be bound by the quota policy.

To set the default quota limit for new users, access the Quota tab of the Volume Properties dialog box and check the Enable Quota Management checkbox. Click the Limit Disk Space To radio button and enter a number in the first box next to the option. In the drop-down list in the second box, specify whether disk space is limited by KB (kilobytes), MB (megabytes), GB (gigabytes), TB (terabytes), PB (petabytes), or EB (exabytes). If you choose to limit disk space, you can also set a warning level, so that users will be warned if they come close to reaching their limit. Ensure that Deny Disk Space To Users Exceeding Quota Limit is checked or the users will be allowed to exceed the quota limit you set.

If an administrator from a trusted domain stores data on a drive with a quota, the administrator's file ownership is charged against the quota. A trusted administrator is not exempt from quotas.

Setting an Individual Quota

You can also set quotas for individual users. There are several reasons for setting quotas this way:

- You can allow a user who routinely updates your applications to have unlimited disk space, while restricting other users.

- You can set warnings at lower levels for a user who routinely exceeds disk space.

- You can apply the quota to users who already had files on the volume before the quota was implemented. The previously stored files will not count against the quota, but any newly owned files will.

To set an individual quota, click the Quota Entries button in the bottom-right corner of the Quota tab. This brings up the dialog box shown in Figure 4.27.

FIGURE 4.27   Quota Entries For New Volume dialog box

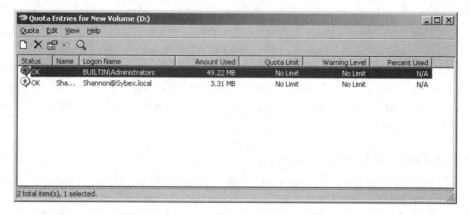

To modify a user's quota, double-click that user. This brings up the dialog box shown in Figure 4.28. Here you can specify whether or not the user's disk space should be limited, the limit, and the warning level.

FIGURE 4.28   Quota Settings For user dialog box

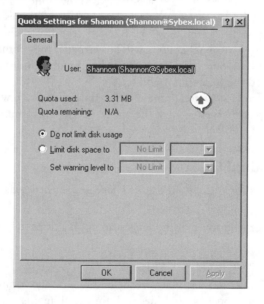

 You can also modify the quotas of several users at once by pressing Ctrl and clicking to highlight several users and selecting Quota ➢ Properties.

In Exercise 4.7, you will set a default quota limit on your D: drive. This exercise assumes that you have completed Exercise 4.1.

EXERCISE 4.7

Applying Default Quota Limits

1. Use the Active Directory Users And Computers utility to create two new users: Shannon and Dana. (See Chapter 3, "Managing Users, Groups, and Computers," for details on creating user accounts.) Deselect the User Must Change Password At Next Logon option for each user.

2. Share the D:\Test folder that you created in Exercise 4.6 by right-clicking the folder and selecting Sharing And Security. From the Sharing tab, click the Share This Folder radio button. Click the Permissions button. Highlight the Everyone group and check the Full Control, Allow checkbox. Click the Apply button, then the OK button. From the Sharing tab, click the OK button.

3. Modify the NTFS permissions of the Test folder by right-clicking the folder and selecting Sharing And Security. Click the Security tab. Select the Users group and in Permissions for Users check the Full Control, Allow checkbox. Click the Apply button, then the OK button.

4. From your Windows Professional computer, log on to your domain as Shannon. If you do not have access to a Windows XP Professional computer, see the note below for modifying this exercise to be run from your domain controller.

5. From the Windows XP Professional computer, select Start All Programs ➢ Accessories ➢ Windows Explorer. From Windows Explorer, select Tools ➢ Map Network Drive. Use the Browse button to select your domain controller and the Test share you created in Step 2 of this exercise. Click the OK button, then the Finish button.

6. The share will open. Use Windows Explorer to copy some new files to this folder.

7. From your Windows 2003 domain controller (where you should be logged on as Administrator) select Start ➢ Windows Explorer.

8. In Windows Explorer, expand My Computer. Right-click Local Disk (D:) and select Properties. In the Local Disk Properties dialog box, select the Quota tab. Check the Enable Quota Management checkbox and the Deny Disk Space To Users Exceeding Quota Limit checkbox. Click the Limit Disk Space to radio button. Specify 5MB as the limit. Specify the Set Warning Level To value as 4MB. Click the Apply button.

9. Click the Quota Entries button. You will notice that Shannon has used disk space. Note the Amount Used, Quota Limit, and Warning Level settings for Shannon.

10. From the Windows XP Professional computer, log off as Shannon and log on as Dana. Map a network drive to the Test folder that was shared on your domain controller. Copy some files to the Test share.

11. From your Windows Server 2003 domain controller, you should be on the Quota Entries For New Volume (D:) dialog box. Select View ➢ Refresh.

EXERCISE 4.7 *(continued)*

---

12. Note that Dana appears on the list and that the quota limits were applied to his user account.

13. Leave all dialog boxes open; you will continue to manage disk quotas in Exercise 4.8.

 If you do not have a Windows XP Professional computer installed as a part of your practice network, you can still see how quotas will be applied using your Windows Server 2003 domain controller. However, the default security settings do not allow regular users to log on interactively at a server. You can change this setting through Start ➤ Administrative Tools ➤ Domain Controller Security Policy. Expand Local Policies, then User Rights Assignment. Double-click Allow Log On Locally and click the Add User Or Group button. In the Add User Or Group dialog box, type in **Everyone** and click the OK button. In the Security Policy Setting dialog box, click the OK button. Close any open dialog boxes.

In Exercise 4.8, you will configure the quotas for individual users. This exercise assumes that you have completed Exercise 4.7.

EXERCISE 4.8

Applying Individual Quota Limits

1.   From the Quota tab, click the Quota Entries button.

2.   Double-click user Dana to bring up his Quota Settings dialog box. Notice that Dana has limited disk space (because he first created files on the volume after disk quotas were applied). Click the Do Not Limit Disk Usage radio button. Click the Apply button and then click the OK button.

3.   Double-click user Shannon to bring up his Quota Settings dialog box. Click the Limit Disk Space To radio button and specify the limit as 100MB. Set the warning level to 95MB. Click the Apply button and then click the OK button.

Monitoring Disk Quotas

If you implement disk quotas, you will want to monitor disk quotas on a regular basis. Monitoring allows you to check the disk usage by all the users who own files on the volume with the quotas applied.

It is especially important to monitor quotas if you have specified that disk space should be denied to users who exceeded their quota limit. Otherwise, some users may not be able to get their work done. For example, suppose that you have set a limit for all users on a specific volume. Your boss tries to save a file she has been working on all afternoon, but she gets an "out of disk space" error message because she has exceeded her disk quota. While your intentions in setting up and using disk quotas were good, the boss is still cranky.

You monitor disk quotas through the Quota Entries dialog box that appears when you click the Quota Entries button in the Quota tab of the volume Properties dialog box, as shown in Figure 4.27.

The dialog box shows the following information:

- The status of the user's disk quota. Status icons include:
    - A green arrow in a dialog bubble indicates the status is OK.
    - An exclamation point in a yellow triangle indicates the warning threshold has been exceeded.
    - An exclamation point in a red circle indicates the user threshold has been exceeded.
- The name and logon name of the user who has stored files on the volume
- The amount of disk space the user has used on the volume
- The user's quota limit
- The user's warning level
- The percent of disk space the user has used in relation to their disk quota

You can also manage disk quotas from the command-line utility Fsutil. You use Fsutil quota to manage disk quotas. For example: fsutil quota enforce C: will enable quotas even though they were not enabled on the Quota tab. You use Fsutil behavior to specify the frequency with which disk quota events are written to the system log.

Using Shadow Copies

Shadow copies are used to create copies of shared folders and files at specified points in time. The advantages of using shadow copies are:

- You can recover files that have been accidentally deleted.
- You can recover files that have been overwritten and you want to access a previous version of the file.
- You can use file comparison to see the differences between a current version of a file and a previous version of a file.

In order to use shadow copies, you must configure the volume that the shared folders exist on and deploy Shadow Copies Of Shared Folders software to the client computers. This allows a client to access a Previous Versions tab in the Properties dialog box of the shared folder or file.

Note that there is a limit of 64 shadow copies that can be created for a volume. When there are more than 64 shadow copies, the oldest shadow copy is deleted.

Real World Scenario

Using Shadow Copies for Fault Tolerance

You are the network administrator of a large company. You manage a server called \SalesData that stores user data for the 20 sales account managers. The \SalesData server has a share called \Data that is accessed by all of the sales account managers. The SalesData\Data share is on an NTFS volume on a 200GB drive.

All of the sales account managers have Full Control NTFS and share permissions for the Data share. In the past you have had problems with data accidentally being deleted or overwritten. In order to restore the previous data, you have had to restore the data from the tape backups you make on a daily basis, which is a time-consuming process.

You decide to enable shadow copies on the \SalesData\Data share and on each client computer. You train the users on how shadow copies work and can be accessed. Now when a user needs to access a previous version of a file, they can do it without administrative intervention.

In the following sections, you will learn how to configure shadow copies on a Windows Server 2003 computer and a client computer.

  Shadow copies should not be considered an alternative to regular backups.

Configuring the Server for Shadow Copies

You configure shadow copies at the volume level. The volume must be NTFS. You can't specify that only specific folders or files will be configured as shadow copies. In order to host shadow copies, the volume that will be configured should have at least 100MB of free volume space. The default maximum amount allocated is 10% of the volume's free disk space.

You can configure a NTFS volume for shadow copies through Windows Explorer or Disk Management (in the following example, we are using Windows Explorer). The steps to enable shadow copies are as follows:

1. Select Start ➢ Windows Explorer.

2. Right-click the drive you want to enable shadow copies on and select Properties. Click the Shadow Copies tab to display the dialog box shown in Figure 4.29.

FIGURE 4.29 Shadow Copies tab

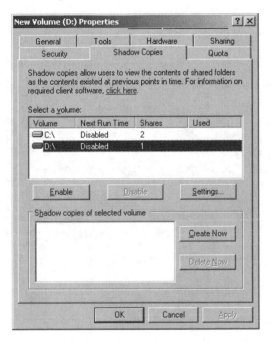

3. Click the drive you want to enable shadow copies on and click the Enable button.

4. The Enable Shadow Copies dialog box will appear, as shown in Figure 4.30, and will inform you that Windows will use the default schedule and settings for the selected shadow volume. Click the Yes button to continue.

FIGURE 4.30 Enable Shadow Copies dialog box

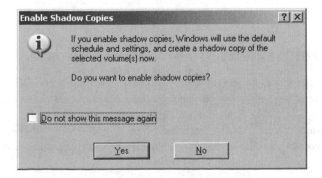

Once you have enabled shadow copies, you can configure the settings for the shadow copies by clicking the Settings button from the Shadow Copies tab. This brings up the Settings dialog box shown in Figure 4.31.

FIGURE 4.31 Settings dialog box

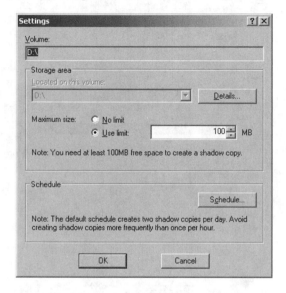

The options that can be set through the Settings dialog box include:

- Defining the storage area for the shadow copies (by default this is on the drive that shadow copies have been enabled on, but you can specify a different volume for storage)

- The maximum size (amount of space) that can be used for the shadow copy

- The schedule that will be used to create the shadow copies (by default shadow copies are created Monday thru Friday, twice a day, at 7:00 A.M. and 12:00 P.M.)

You can force a shadow copy to be created by clicking the Create Now button within the Shadow Copies tab. You can disable shadow copies by clicking the Disable button in the Shadow Copies tab.

Configuring the Client for Shadow Copies

You can configure the Client for Shadow Copies on Windows XP and Window Server 2003 computers. In order to use shadow copies the client must install the Shadow Copies of Shared Folders software. Windows Server 2003 computers have this software installed in the *windir*\system32\clients\twclient folder. You can distribute this software through group policy, or you can create a share to let the clients download and install the client software.

In Exercise 4.9, you will configure shadow copies and use shadow copies.

EXERCISE 4.9

Using Shadow Copies

The following steps should be completed from your Windows Server 2003 domain controller.

1. From your Windows Server 2003 domain controller, select Start ➢ Windows Explorer.

2. Right-click your D: drive and select Properties. Click the Shadow Copies tab.

3. Click your D: drive and click the Enable button.

4. The Enable Shadow Copies dialog box will appear; click the Yes button to continue.

5. Click the Create Now button to create shadow copies.

6. From Windows Explorer, select C:\Windows\System32\clients and right-click the twclient folder. Select Sharing And Security and then select the Sharing tab. Click the Share This Folder radio button and click the OK button.

The following steps should be completed from your Windows XP Professional computer.

7. Log on as the Administrator of your domain from your Windows XP Professional computer.

8. Access Windows Explorer and map a drive to the twclient share you created on your Windows Server 2003 domain controller. From the twclient share, open the x86 folder. Click on twcli32 to install Previous Versions Client Setup. When the software is installed, click the Finish button.

The following steps should be completed from your Windows Server 2003 domain controller.

9. From Windows Explorer, create a folder on your D: drive called **Shadows**. Within the Shadows folder, create a text file called **Data.txt** with text within the file noting that this is a part of test 1. Share the Shadows folder and set the share security so that the Everyone group is allowed Full Control permission.

10. From Windows Explorer, right-click your D: drive and select Properties. Click the Shadow Copy tab and click Create Now to create a shadow copy.

The following steps should be completed from your Windows XP Professional computer.

11. Access Windows Explorer and map a drive to the Shadows share you created on your Windows Server 2003 domain controller. From the Shadows folder, edit the Data.txt file and save the changes.

12. To access the shadow copy of Data.txt, right-click Data.txt and select Properties. You will see a tab for Previous Versions. You can click the View, Copy, or Restore buttons based on what you want to do with the shadow copy. Click the Restore button and the successful completion dialog box will appear.

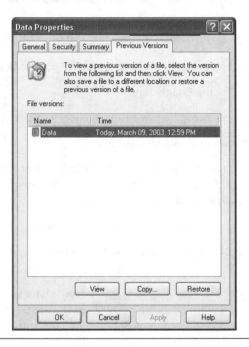

Listed below are some additional facts about shadow copies:

- Mounted drives are not included when shadow copies are taken.
- Do not use shadow copies on dual-boot computers. The older version may be corrupted and unusable when the computer is booted to any OS other than Windows Server 2003.
- Using a volume on a separate disk is recommended for improved performance. This is highly recommended for production file servers.
- Do not schedule shadow copies to occur more often than once per hour.
- You must delete the shadow copies scheduled task prior to deleting the volume that is shadowed. Otherwise, the next time the schedule executes, an Event ID of 7001 will occur.
- When you restore a file, the file's permissions will be retained.
- When you recover a file that was deleted, the file permissions will become the directory's default permissions.
- You cannot edit the contents of a shadowed copy until it is restored.

Managing Data Encryption with EFS

Data encryption is a way to increase data security. Encryption is the process of translating data into code that is not easily accessible. Once data has been encrypted, you must have a key to decrypt the data. Unencrypted data is known as plain text or clear text, and encrypted data is known as cipher text.

The *Encrypting File System (EFS)* is a technology used by Windows 2000, Windows XP Professional, and Windows Server 2003 to store encrypted files on NTFS partitions. Encrypted files add an extra layer of security to your file system. A user with the proper key can transparently access encrypted files. A user without the proper key is denied access. If the user who encrypted the files is unavailable, you can use the *data recovery agent (DRA)* to provide the proper key to decrypt folders or files.

In the following sections you will learn about the new EFS features in Windows Server 2003, how to create and manage DRAs, how to recover encrypted files, and how to use the Cipher utility.

New EFS Features in Windows Server 2003

The functionality of EFS has been improved in Windows Server 2003. The enhanced and new features include:

- Automatic color-coding of encrypted files in green text, so you can easily identify files that have been encrypted

- Support so that offline folders can also be encrypted

- A shell user interface (UI) that is used to support encrypted files for multiple users

- Improved performance and reliability

- New security features that better protect EFS data

- Improved recovery policy

Encrypting and Decrypting Folders and Files

To use EFS, a user specifies that a folder or file on an NTFS partition should be encrypted. The encryption is transparent to that user, who has access to the file. However, when other users try to access the file, they will not be able to unencrypt the file—even if those users have Full Control NTFS permissions. Instead, they will receive an error message.

To encrypt a folder or a file, take the following steps:

1. Select Start ➤ Windows Explorer.
2. In Windows Explorer, find and select the folder or file you wish to encrypt.
3. Right-click the folder or file and select Properties from the pop-up menu.
4. In the General tab of the folder or file Properties dialog box, click the Advanced button.
5. The Advanced Attributes dialog box appears. Check the Encrypt Contents To Secure Data check-box. Then click the OK button. From the folder Properties dialog box, click the Apply button.

6. In the Confirm Attribute Changes dialog box (if this dialog box does not appear, click the Apply button in the folder Properties dialog box to display it), select Apply Changes To This Folder, Subfolders And Files. Then click the OK button.

7. Notice that the folder is displayed through Windows Explorer in green, which indicates the folder or file is encrypted.

To decrypt folders and files, repeat these steps, but uncheck the Encrypt Contents To Secure Data option in the Advanced Attributes dialog box.

In Exercise 4.10, you will use EFS to encrypt a folder. This exercise assumes that you have completed Exercise 4.1.

EXERCISE 4.10

Using EFS to Manage Data Encryption

1. Use the Active Directory Users And Computers utility to create the new user **Lauren**. (See Chapter 3 for details on creating user accounts.) Deselect the User Must Change Password At Next Logon option for this user and make her a member of the Administrators group.

2. Select Start ➢ Windows Explorer.

3. In Windows Explorer, create a folder on the D: drive called **Secret**. Create a file within the Secret folder called **Payroll.txt** and add some text to the file. Right-click the folder and select Properties.

4. In the General tab of the folder Properties dialog box, click the Advanced button.

5. In the Advanced Attributes dialog box, check the Encrypt Contents To Secure Data option. Then click the OK button. Then click the Apply button.

6. In the Confirm Attribute Changes dialog box (if this dialog box does not appear, click the Apply button in the folder Properties dialog box to display it), select Apply Changes To This Folder, Subfolders And Files. Then click the OK button.

7. Log off as Administrator and log on as Lauren.

8. Open Windows Explorer and attempt to access one of the files in the folder you encrypted. You should receive an error message stating that access is denied, even though Lauren is a member of the Administrators group.

9. Log off as Lauren and log on as Administrator.

Understanding Data Recovery Agents

If the user who encrypted the folders or files is unavailable to decrypt the folders or files when they're needed, you can use the data recovery agent (DRA) to access the encrypted files. DRAs are implemented differently depending on the version of your operating system and the configuration of your computer:

- For Windows 2000 Professional and Windows 2000 Server computers, a DRA was mandatory, and EFS could not be used if a DRA was not in place. For Windows 2000 Professional computers that were installed as a part of the Active Directory, the domain Administrator user account is automatically assigned the role of the DRA. If the Windows 2000 Professional computer is a part of the Active Directory and is logged onto the local machine, then the local Administrator account is automatically assigned the role of DRA.

- For Windows XP Professional computers or Windows Server 2003 computers that are a part of a Windows 2000 or a Windows 2003 Active Directory domain, the domain Administrator user account is automatically assigned the role of DRA.

- For Windows XP Professional computers that are installed as stand-alone computers or if the computer is a part of a workgroup, there is no default DRA assigned.

 You should use extreme caution when using EFS on a stand-alone Windows XP Professional computer. If the user who encrypts the files is unavailable, there is no default recovery process, and all access to the files will be lost.

In the next section you will learn how to create a DRA.

Creating a DRA

In order to be designated as a DRA, a user must have a certificate that will be used to access encrypted files. To create a certificate for the user who will be the DRA, you should log on as that user, and execute the following command:

`Cipher /R:filename`

You will then be asked to type in the password to protect your .pfx, followed by a request to retype the password.

The /R switch is used to generate two files, one with a .pfx extension and one with a .cer extension. The .pfx file is used for data recovery and the .cer file includes a self-signed EFS recovery agent certificate. The .cer file (self-signed public key certificate) can then be imported into the local security policy and the .pfx file (private key) can be stored in a secure location.

Once you have created the public and private keys to be used with EFS, you can specify the DRA through Group Policy, using the following steps:

1. Select Start ➢ Administrative Tools ➢ Active Directory Users And Computers.

2. Right-click the domain that you want to add the DRA to and select Properties.

3. Click the Group Policy tab to access the dialog box shown in Figure 4.32 and click the Edit button.

FIGURE 4.32   Group Policy tab for domain Properties

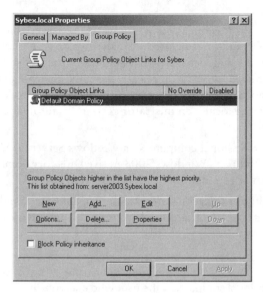

4.   From the Group Policy Editor dialog box, select Computer Configuration ➢ Windows Settings ➢ Security Settings ➢ Public Key Policies ➢ Encrypting File System, as shown in Figure 4.33.

FIGURE 4.33   Group Policy for Encrypting File System

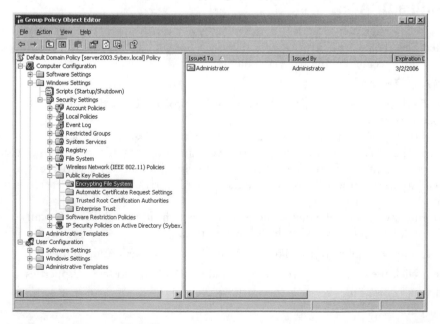

5. Right-click Encrypting File System and select New ➤ Data Recovery Agent.

6. The Add Recovery Agent Wizard will start. Click the Next button.

7. The Select Recovery Agents dialog box will appear, as shown in Figure 4.34.

FIGURE 4.34   Select Recovery Agents

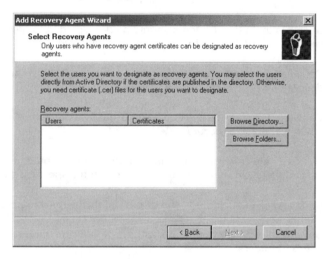

8. From the Select Recovery Agents dialog box, click the Browse Folders button. Use the Browse button to find the `.cer` file that was created with the `Cipher /R:filename` command. Click the Open button.

9. You will see a dialog box stating that Windows cannot determine if this certificate has been revoked. Click the Yes button to install this certificate and then click the Next button.

10. The Completing the Add Recovery Agent Wizard will appear. Click the Finish button. You will now see the specified user configured as a DRA.

Recovering Encrypted Files

If the DRA has the private key to the DRA certificate (that was created through `Cipher /R:filename`), the DRA can decrypt files in the same manner as the user who originally encrypted the file. Once the encrypted files are opened by a DRA, they are available as unencrypted files, and can be stored as either encrypted or unencrypted files.

Using the *Cipher* Utility

Cipher is a command-line utility that can be used to encrypt files on NTFS volumes. The syntax for the `Cipher` command is as follows:

```
Cipher /command parameter filename
```

Table 4.3 lists the command parameters associated with the `Cipher` command.

TABLE 4.3 Cipher Command Parameters

Parameter	Description
/e	Specifies that files or folders should be encrypted. Any files that are subsequently added to the folder will be encrypted.
/d	Specifies that files or folders should be decrypted. Any files that are subsequently added to the folder will not be encrypted.
/s:*dir*	Specifies that subfolders of the target folder should also be encrypted or decrypted based on the option specified.
/I	Causes any errors that occur to be ignored. By default, the Cipher utility stops whenever an error occurs.
/f	Forces all files and folders to be encrypted or decrypted, regardless of their current state. Normally, if a file is already in the specified state, it is skipped.
/q	Runs Cipher in quiet mode and displays only the most important information.
/a	Specifies that you want the operation you are executing to be applied to all files and folders.
/h	By default, files with hidden or system attributes are omitted from display. This option specifies that hidden and system files should be displayed.
/r	Used to generate a recovery agent key and certificate for use with EFS.

In Exercise 4.11, you will use the Cipher utility to encrypt files. This exercise assumes that you have completed Exercise 4.10.

EXERCISE 4.11

Using the Cipher Utility

1. Select Start ➢ Command Prompt.

2. In the Command Prompt dialog box, type **D:** and press Enter to access the D: drive.

3. From the D:\> prompt, type **cipher**. You will see a list of folders and files and the state of encryption. The folder you encrypted in Exercise 4.10 will be indicated by an E.

4. Type **MD TEST** and press Enter to create a new folder named **Test**.

5. Type **cipher /e test** and press Enter. You will see a message verifying that the folder was encrypted.

Using the Disk Defragmenter Utility

Data is normally stored sequentially on the disk as space is available. Fragmentation naturally occurs as users create, delete, and modify files. The access of noncontiguous data is transparent to the user. However, when data is stored in this manner, the operating system must search through the disk drive to access all of the pieces of a file. This slows down data access.

Disk defragmentation rearranges the existing files so that they are stored contiguously, which optimizes access to those files. The disk must have at least 15% free space, as the free space is used for sorting the files during the defragmentation process. In Windows Server 2003, you use the *Disk Defragmenter utility* to defragment your disk.

To access the Disk Defragmenter utility, select Start ➢ All Programs ➢ Accessories ➢ System Tools ➢ Disk Defragmenter. The main Disk Defragmenter window, shown in Figure 4.35, lists each volume, the file system used, capacity, free space, and percent of free space.

FIGURE 4.35   The main Disk Defragmenter window

Volume	Session Status	File System	Capacity	Free Space	% Free Space
(C:)		NTFS	4.88 GB	2.71 GB	55 %
New Volume (D:)		NTFS	499 MB	394 MB	78 %

Estimated disk usage before defragmentation:

Estimated disk usage after defragmentation:

Analyze   Defragment   Pause   Stop   View Report

■ Fragmented files ■ Contiguous files □ Unmovable files □ Free space

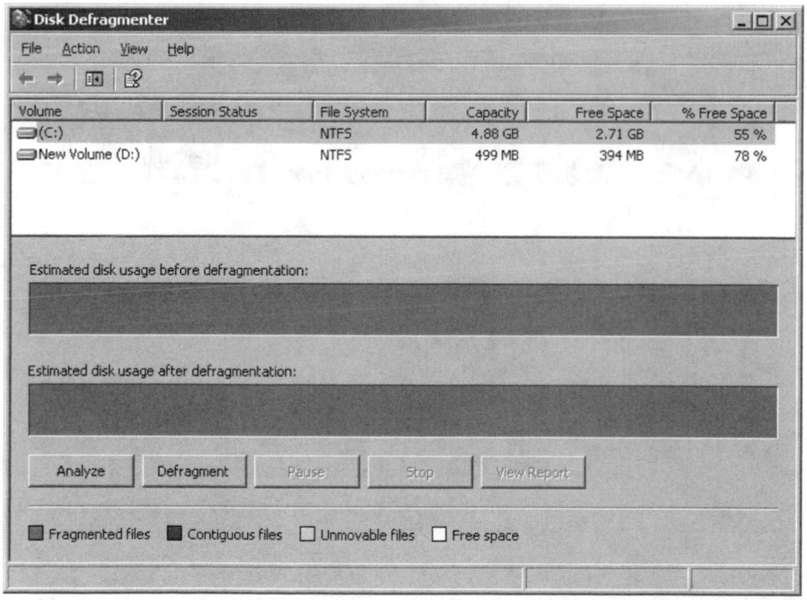

Along with defragmenting disks, this utility can analyze your disk and report on the current file arrangement. Analyzing and defragmenting disks are covered in the following sections.

You can only defragment local disks. You can't use Computer Management to defragment a remote computers disk.

Analyzing Disks

To analyze a disk, open the Disk Defragmenter utility, select the drive to be analyzed, and click the Analyze button on the bottom-left side of the window. When you analyze a disk, the Disk Defragmenter utility checks for fragmented files, contiguous files, system files, and free space. The results of the analysis are shown in the Analysis display bar that is color-coded as follows:

Fragmented files   Red

Contiguous files   Blue

System files   Green

Free space   White

Even though you can't see the colors, you can get an idea of what this Analysis bar looks like in Figure 4.36.

FIGURE 4.36   The Disk Defragmenter Analysis bar

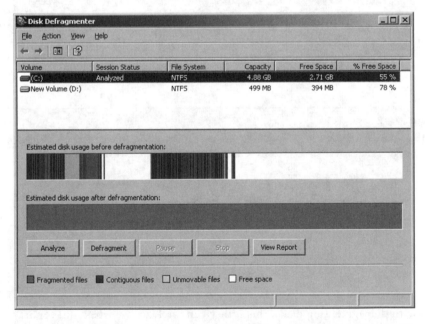

The disk analysis also produces a report, which is displayed when you click the View Report button. The report contains the following information:

▪   Whether or not the volume needs defragmenting

- Volume information that includes general volume statistics, volume fragmentation, file fragmentation, page file fragmentation, directory fragmentation, and master file table (MFT) fragmentation
- A list of the most fragmented files

Defragmenting Disks

To defragment a disk, open the Disk Defragmenter utility, select the drive to be defragmented, and click the Defragment button (to the right of the Analyze button at the bottom of the window). Defragmenting causes all files to be stored more efficiently in contiguous space. When defragmentation is complete, you can view a report of the defragmentation process.

You will use the Disk Defragmenter utility in Exercise 4.12 to analyze and defragment a disk.

EXERCISE 4.12

Analyzing and Defragmenting Disks

1. Select Start ➤ All Programs ➤ Accessories ➤ System Tools ➤ Disk Defragmenter.

2. Highlight the C: drive and click the Analyze button.

3. When analysis is complete, click the View Report button to see the analysis report. Record the following information:

    > Volume size: _____
    > Cluster size: _____
    > Used space: _____
    > Free space: _____
    > Volume fragmentation—Total fragmentation: _____
    > File fragmentation—Total fragmented files: _____

4. Click the Defragment button.

5. When defragmentation is complete, click the Close button.

Using the Disk Cleanup Utility

The *Disk Cleanup utility* identifies areas of disk space that can be deleted to free additional hard disk space. Disk Cleanup works by identifying temporary files, Internet cache files, and unnecessary program files.

In Exercise 4.13, you will run the Disk Cleanup utility.

EXERCISE 4.13

Using the Disk Cleanup Utility

1. Select Start ➤ All Programs ➤ Accessories ➤ System Tools ➤ Disk Cleanup. The Disk Cleanup Select Drive dialog box asks you to select the drive you want to clean up. In this exercise, select the C: drive and click OK.

2. The Disk Cleanup utility will run and calculate the amount of disk space you can free up. After the analysis is complete, the Disk Cleanup dialog box appears, as shown below. This dialog box lists files that are suggested for deletion and shows how much space will be gained by deleting those files. In this exercise, leave all the boxes checked and click OK.

3. You will be asked to confirm the deletions. Click Yes. The Disk Cleanup utility will delete the files and automatically close the Disk Cleanup dialog box.

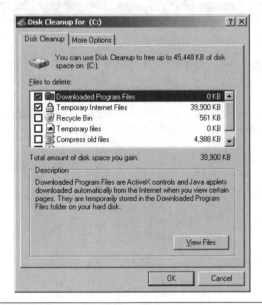

Troubleshooting Disk Devices and Volumes

If you are having trouble with your disk devices or volumes, you can use the *Check Disk utility*. This utility detects bad sectors, attempts to fix file system errors, and scans for and attempts to recover bad sectors.

File system errors can be caused by a corrupt file system or by hardware errors. There is no way to fix hardware errors through software. If you have software errors, the Check Disk utility will help you find them. You can choose the Automatically Fix File System Errors and Scan For And Attempt Recovery Of Bad Sectors options. If you have excessive hardware errors, you should replace your disk drive.

In Exercise 4.14, you will run the Check Disk utility.

EXERCISE 4.14

Using the Check Disk Utility

1. Select Start ➤ Administrative Tools ➤ Computer Management. Expand Computer Management, then Storage, then click Disk Management.

2. Right-click the D: drive and choose Properties.

3. Click the Tools tab, then click the Check Now button.

4. In the Check Disk dialog box, check both of the disk options checkboxes. Then click the Start button.

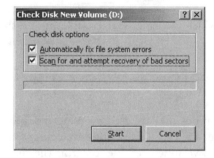

5. When you see the Disk Check Complete dialog box, click the OK button and close any open dialog boxes.

If the system cannot gain exclusive access to the partition, the check will be executed the next time the system is restarted. You cannot gain exclusive access to partitions or volumes that contain the system or boot partition.

Summary

In this chapter, you learned about managing disks with Windows Server 2003. We covered the following topics:

- Disk storage configurations, which can be basic disks or dynamic disks

- The Disk Management utility, which is used to manage routine tasks, basic storage, and dynamic storage
- Shadow copies
- Data compression, which is used to store files in a compressed format that uses less disk space
- Disk quotas, which are used to limit the amount of disk space that users can have on an NTFS partition
- How to use shadow copies to maintain copies of files based on a schedule you define for historical purposes
- Data encryption, which is implemented through the Encrypting File System (EFS) and provides increased security for files and folders
- Adding DRAs to recover encrypted files
- Disk defragmentation, which is accomplished through the Disk Defragmenter utility and allows you to store files contiguously on your hard drive for improved access speeds
- The Disk Cleanup utility, which is used to free disk space by removing unnecessary files
- The Check Disk utility, which can be used to troubleshoot disk errors

Exam Essentials

Understand the disk configurations that are used by Windows 2003. Define the differences between basic and dynamic disks. Be able to configure options such as simple, spanned, striped, mirrored, and RAID-5 volumes. Be able to define the characteristics of each volume configuration.

Be able to recover from disk failure. List the steps that would be used to recover from failure for disks that are spanned, striped, mirrored, or configured as RAID-5.

Define and set data compression. Define the requirements for disk compression and be able to configure data compression.

Set and manage disk quotas. Be able to specify the purpose of disk quotas, and successfully set disk quotas.

Protect data by using EFS. Be able to encrypt data with EFS and also recover data that is encrypted in the event that the user who encrypted the data is unavailable.

Key Terms

Before you take the exam, be certain you are familiar with the following terms:

basic disks

Check Disk utility

Cipher

data recovery agent (DRA)

Disk Cleanup utility

disk defragmentation

Disk Defragmenter utility

Disk Management utility

disk quotas

dynamic disks

Encrypting File System (EFS)

extended partitions

hot swapping

mirrored volumes

parity

partition

primary partition

RAID-5 volumes

shadow copies

simple volume

spanned volumes

striped volumes

volumes

Review Questions

1. You are the network administrator for a small company. One of your engineers stores large CAD files on a server called \Engineering in a folder called C:\Drawings. The C:\ drive is running out of space, and you want to maximize space as much as possible until you can add another hard drive to the server. The C: partition is on a basic disk, and is configured to use the NTFS file system. You would like to use disk compression. What process would you use to compress the folder?

    A. Within Disk Management, Volume Properties, click the Advanced tab, check the box Compress Contents To Save Disk Space.

    B. Within Disk Management, Folder Properties, Select C:\Drawings, click the Advanced tab, check the box Compress Contents To Save Disk Space.

    C. Right-click C:\Drawings, select Properties, click the Advanced tab, check the box Compress Contents To Save Disk Space.

    D. You can't compress data that is stored on basic disks, so the disk must be converted to a dynamic disk before you can compress the files.

2. You are the network administrator for a large network. There is an accounting server called \Accounting. On the \Accounting server there is a folder called C:\Payroll. This folder is located on an NTFS partition, but the Accounting manager would like to set up additional security. He thinks that he has properly configured EFS, but wants you to verify that EFS is working. Which of the following command-line utilities can you use to display the current encryption state of the files in the C:\Payroll folder?

    A. `Cipher`

    B. `EFSStatus`

    C. `DIR /EFS`

    D. `DIR /encryption`

3. You are the network administrator for a large network. There is an accounting server called \Accounting. On the \Accounting server there is a folder called C:\Payroll. This folder is located on an NTFS partition, but the Accounting manager would like to set up additional security. What step should he take to enable file encryption?

    A. Within Disk Management, Volume Properties, click the Advanced tab, check the box Encrypt Contents To Secure Data.

    B. Within Disk Management, Folder Properties, Select C:\Payroll, click the Advanced tab, check the box Encrypt Contents To Secure Data.

    C. Right-click C:\Payroll, select Properties, click the Advanced tab, check the box Encrypt Contents To Secure Data.

    D. When you are in the C:\Payroll folder, from the command prompt execute the command `Cipher /d*.*`

4. You are the manager of a large network. Your Engineering department uses a server called \Engineering. The server has a 40GB hard drive that stores all of the company's engineering data. You want to add additional fault tolerance to the drive in case of failure and add a second drive so that you can use disk mirroring. When you right-click the new free space within Disk Management, you do not see any option to create a new volume or a mirrored volume. What action should you take to create a mirrored volume on both of the drives?

   A. Make sure that the drive you want to convert is formatted as NTFS 4.

   B. Make sure that the drive you want to convert is formatted as NTFS 5.

   C. Convert both drives to enhanced disks.

   D. Convert both drives to dynamic disks.

5. Your Windows Server 2003 hosts the company's data files on a 20GB hard drive. Users are complaining that access to the files has slowed down over the past six months. You verify that the average access, size, and number of files has remained fairly constant. What should you do to improve access speeds?

   A. Defragment the disk.

   B. Configure the volume with EFS.

   C. Upgrade the disk to a dynamic disk.

   D. Compress the data files.

6. You are preparing to install a Windows Server 2003 that will act as a domain controller. You are trying to determine what disk configuration will be used by the server. Which of the following disk configurations could you use to store the system or boot partition? (Choose all that apply.)

   A. Simple volume

   B. Striped volume

   C. Mirrored volume

   D. RAID-5 volume

7. Brad is the Accounting manager and has encrypted the C:\Payroll folder on his computer, which is a part of the San Jose domain. His appendix bursts, and he is not able to process the company's payroll. His assistant, Carrie, can process the payroll if she can access the C:\Payroll files. All of the data encryption settings are at default settings. What is the easiest option for accessing the encrypted files?

   A. Log on as the domain Administrator and you will be able to access the encrypted file normally.

   B. Logon as the local Administrator, access the folder and use the command-line utility Cipher /u *.*.

   C. While logged in as Administrator, access the Disk Management utility, and for the volume, clear the Encrypt Contents To Secure Data checkbox.

   D. Backup the encrypted folder using Windows Backup, restore the folder on a computer where you are logged in as the Administrator, access the folder's Properties dialog box, within the Advanced tab clear the Encrypt Contents To Secure Data checkbox.

8. You are the network administrator of a large network. You are preparing a disaster recovery plan that will be used in the event of hardware failure. As part of your recovery plan, you have decided to implement disk mirroring on your Windows Server 2003. You create a boot disk with a modified `boot.ini` file that will be used in the event of a disk failure within the mirrored volume set. Under what circumstance would you need to use a Windows Server 2003 boot disk with an edited `boot.ini` file in the event of a drive failure in a mirrored volume?

   A. If the primary drive in a data mirror volume fails

   B. If the secondary drive in a data mirror volume fails

   C. If the primary drive that contains the boot partition in a mirror volume fails

   D. If the secondary drive that contains the boot partition in a mirror volume fails

9. You are the network administrator of a large network. You manage the \SalesDataserver, which is used by the Sales department. The Sales users tend to store large files on the \SalesData server on the \SalesData\Data share, which is located on the D: drive of the \SalesData server. The D: drive is constantly running out of disk space. You have identified the problem as resulting from two users, Larry and Moe, who store large and outdated files on a regular basis. You decide you want to impose disk quotas. You configure quotas for the D: drive on the \SalesData server as shown in the following exhibit. Larry is already using 4.9GB of disk space on the D: drive. When he copies a 250MB file to the \SalesData\Data share, the file copy is successful. Why?

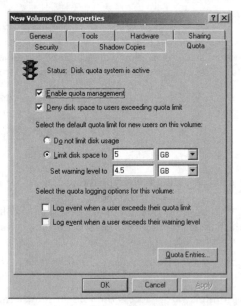

   A. Disk quotas are only applied to files copied after the disk quota was applied.

   B. Larry is a member of the Server Operators group, and disk quotas are not applied to members of the Server Operators group.

   C. If a user already has files on a volume and disk quotas are applied, then the existing user is not bound by disk quotas.

   D. The partition must be configured as FAT32, so quota limits will not be applied.

10. You are installing Windows Server 2003 on a computer with the configuration shown in the following exhibit. You want to make sure that you use the maximum amount of disk space with the fastest access. What configuration should you use?

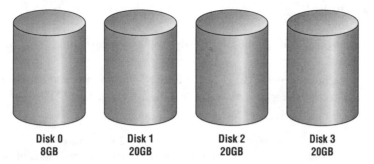

Disk 0	Disk 1	Disk 2	Disk 3
8GB	20GB	20GB	20GB

  A. Install Windows Server 2003 on the 8GB drive. Create a spanned volume set with the three remaining drives.

  B. Install Windows Server 2003 on the 8GB drive. Create a striped volume set with the three remaining drives.

  C. Install Windows Server 2003 on the 8GB drive. Create a RAID-3 volume set with the three remaining drives.

  D. Install Windows Server 2003 on the 8GB drive. Create a RAID-5 volume set with the three remaining drives.

11. You have a server that contains a single 36GB hard drive. The server stores a database that must be accessed as a single drive letter. You are starting to receive messages that the disk is almost out of space. The server supports hot swapping and there is a hot-swappable drive bay on your server. You purchase an identical 36GB drive and want to add it to your server. You back up the data on your hard drive. Which of the following options will allow you to overcome your disk-space shortage with the least amount of downtime?

  A. Shut down the server and add the disk to the computer. Restart the computer and create a striped volume set.

  B. Shut down the server and add the disk to the computer. Restart the computer and create a spanned volume set.

  C. Add the disk to the computer, rescan the disks, and create a striped volume set.

  D. Add the disk to the computer, rescan the disks, and create a spanned volume set.

12. You have a mirrored volume set on your Windows Server 2003 computer. You open Disk Management and realize that the secondary drive in the mirror set has failed. You make a full backup at the end of each day. Which of the following courses of action should you take?

  A. Remove the mirror, replace the failed drive, and recreate the mirrored set.

  B. Replace the failed drive, right-click the mirrored set, and choose to regenerate the mirrored set.

  C. Replace the failed drive, right-click the mirror set, and choose to repair the volume. On the drive you replaced, select to regenerate the mirrored set.

  D. Replace the failed drive, rescan the disks, and restore the volume set from tape backup.

13. You have a RAID-5 volume set on your Windows Server 2003 computer. You open Disk Management and realize one of the drives in the RAID-5 set has failed. Which of the following courses of action should you take?

A. Remove the RAID-5 volume set, replace the failed drive, and re-create the RAID-5 volume set.

B. Replace the failed drive, right-click the RAID-5 volume set, and choose to reactivate the mirrored set.

C. Replace the failed drive, right-click the RAID-5 volume set, and choose to repair the volume. On the drive you replaced, select to regenerate the RAID-5 set.

D. Replace the failed drive and select to rescan the disks.

14. You have a striped volume set on your Windows Server 2003. One of the drives in the striped volume set fails. You create a full backup of your server each night. Which of the following courses of action should you take?

A. Remove the striped set, replace the failed drive, and re-create the striped set.

B. Replace the failed drive, right-click the striped set, and choose to regenerate the striped set.

C. Replace the failed drive, right-click the striped set, and choose to repair the volume. On the drive you replaced, select to regenerate the striped set.

D. Replace the failed drive, re-create and format the stripe set, and restore the volume set from tape backup.

15. You are the network administrator for the Wacky Widgets Corporation. You manage a server called \AcctData that is used to store all of the data for the accounting department. The D: drive for the \AcctData stores all of the data that is used for forecasting of sales information. This data changes on a daily basis. Sometimes the analysts need to access data from a historical standpoint that may have been modified. You decided to implement shadow copies on the \AcctData D: drive and configure the server as shown in the following exhibit:

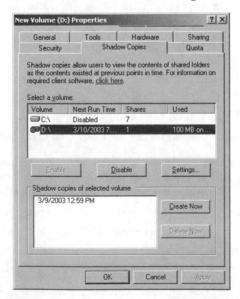

You have an analyst named Dietrich who is using Windows XP Professional; when he tries to access a shadow copy from the \AcctData server, he sees the following screen:

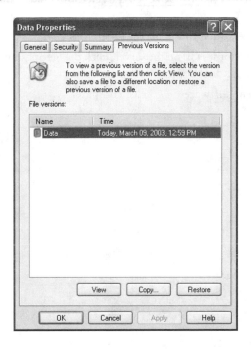

You have an analyst named Curtis who is using Window XP Professional; when he tries to access a shadow copy from the \AcctData server, he sees the following screen:

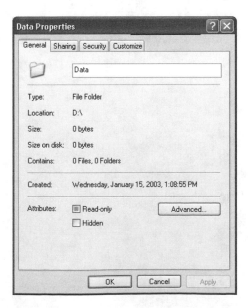

What needs to be done so that Curtis can access shadow copies from his computer?

- **A.** Edit the registry entry HKEY_LOCAL_COMPUTER\SOFTWARE\Shadow Copies\Enable to a value of 1.
- **B.** Curtis needs to be added to the Server Operators group.
- **C.** From the Shadow Copies tab on the server, click the Settings button to specify that Curtis is allowed to use shadow copies.
- **D.** Install the twclient software on Curtis' computer.

Answers to Review Questions

1. C.   As long as the partition is NTFS you can set compression for the folder, through the Advanced tab of the folder's Properties by checking the box Compress Contents To Save Disk Space.

2. A.   The `Cipher` command is used to display the current status of file encryption. It can also be used to encrypt and decrypt files. EFS can also be managed through the Windows Explorer utility.

3. C.   As long as the partition is NTFS, you can set EFS for the folder through the Advanced tab of the folder's properties by checking the box Encrypt Contents To Secure Data. You could use the `Cipher` command-line utility, but it would require the `/e` option for encryption.

4. D.   When you mirror a volume, the drive can contain FAT or NTFS partitions, but the drive must be defined as a dynamic disk rather than a basic disk. If the disk is configured as a basic disk you will not see an option to create a mirrored set.

5. A.   If the files have become fragmented, you can improve disk access by defragmenting the drive. You should periodically defragment disks as a part of server maintenance.

6. A, C.   You cannot put the system or boot partition on a striped or RAID-5 volume. Simple volumes and mirrored volumes can contain the system or boot partition.

7. A.   If the user who encrypted the data is not available, and the computer is a part of the domain, the domain Administrator account is automatically configured as the data recovery agent (DRA) and the DRA can access the files normally.

8. C.   You only need to use an edited `boot.ini` file when the primary drive that contains the boot partition in a mirror set fails. If any other drive in a mirror set fails, the `boot.ini` file will still point to the correct location of the Windows Server 2003 operating system files.

9. A.   Disk quotas can only be applied to NTFS volumes. If disk quotas are applied to a volume after users have already stored files on that volume, those files will not count against the quota. You will need to manually configure quota limits for all users who created files on the volume prior to disk quotas being enabled.

10. B.   You should create a striped volume set if you want to maximize the amount of storage and increase performance. A spanned volume set will not increase performance, and a RAID-5 volume set will not maximize space. Windows Server 2003 does not support RAID-3.

11. D.   Since the computer supports hot swapping and you have a hot-swappable drive bay, you can add the disk to the computer and rescan the disk without shutting down the computer. You can then create a spanned volume set. Striped volume sets can only be created from new space and can't be created with existing data.

12. A.   If a mirrored set fails, you right-click the mirrored volume in Disk Management and remove the mirror. You cannot tell which drive failed until the mirror set is removed. Then you select the disk that has failed. The remaining disk will become a simple volume. Replace the failed drive, and then use Disk Management to recreate the mirrored volume. If you restore the set from backup, you will lose any of the data that had been created or edited since the last backup.

13. C.   If a drive in a RAID-5 volume set fails, you should take the following steps to re-create the data through the parity on your other drives: Replace the failed hardware. Open the Disk Management utility, right-click the failed RAID-5 volume set (marked as failed redundancy), and choose Repair Volume from the pop-up menu. In the Repair RAID-5 Volume dialog box, choose the drive that has been replaced and click OK to regenerate the RAID-5 volume set.

14. D.   Since a striped set is not fault tolerant, if any drives in the set fail, you will need to re-create the striped set and restore your data from your backups.

15. D.   You can configure the Client for Shadow Copies on Windows XP and Window Server 2003 computers. In order to use shadow copies, the client must install the Shadow Copies of Shared Folders software. Windows Server 2003 computers have this software installed in the \\windir\ system32\clients\twclient folder. You can distribute this software through group policy, or you can create a share to let the clients download and install the client software.

Accessing Files and Folders

MICROSOFT EXAM OBJECTIVES COVERED IN THIS CHAPTER:

✓ **Configure access to shared folders.**

- Manage shared folder permissions.

✓ **Configure file system permissions.**

- Verify effective permissions when granting permissions.

- Change ownership of files and folders.

✓ **Troubleshoot access to files and shared folders.**

Local access defines what access a user has to local resources. You can limit local access by applying NTFS permissions to files and folders.

A powerful feature of networking is the ability to allow network access to local folders. In Windows Server 2003, it is very easy to share folders. You can also apply security to shared folders in a manner that is similar to applying NTFS permissions. Once you share a folder, users with appropriate access rights can access the folders through a variety of methods.

To effectively manage both local and network resource access and troubleshoot related problems, you should understand how local and share permissions are applied. You should also know the most common problems relating to resource access and how to troubleshoot resource access problems.

In this chapter, you will learn how to manage local and network access to resources, including how to configure NTFS permissions and network share permissions.

Managing Local Access

The two common types of file systems used by local partitions are FAT (which includes FAT16 and FAT32) and NTFS. FAT partitions do not support local security; NTFS partitions do support local security. This means that if the file system on the partition that users access is configured as a FAT partition, you cannot specify any security for the file system once a user has logged on. However, if the partition is NTFS, you can specify the access level each user has to specific folders and files on the partition, based on the user's logon name and group associations.

NTFS permissions control access to NTFS folders and files. You configure access by allowing or denying NTFS permissions to users and groups. NTFS permissions are usually cumulative, based on group memberships if the user has been allowed access. However, if the user has been denied access through user or group memberships, those permissions override allowed permissions.

Windows Server 2003 offers five levels of NTFS permissions:

Full Control   This permission allows the following rights:

- Traverse folders and execute files (programs) in the folders. The ability to traverse folders allows you to access files and folders in lower subdirectories, even if you do not have permissions to access specific portions of the directory path.

- List the contents of a folder and read the data in a folder's files.

- See a folder's or file's attributes.
- Change a folder's or file's attributes.
- Create new files and write data to the files.
- Create new folders and append data to files.
- Delete subfolders and files.
- Delete files.
- Compress files.
- Change permissions for files and folders.
- Take ownership of files and folders.

If you select the Full Control permission, all permissions will be checked by default, and can't be unchecked. If you uncheck any lower level permission (such as Read), the Full Control Allow checkbox will be automatically unchecked.

Modify   This permission allows the following rights:

- Traverse folders and execute files in the folders.
- List the contents of a folder and read the data in a folder's files.
- See a file's or folder's attributes.
- Change a file's or folder's attributes.
- Create new files and write data to the files.
- Create new folders and append data to files.
- Delete files.

If you select the Modify permission, the Read & Execute, List Folder Contents, Read, and Write permissions will be checked by default, and can't be unchecked.

Read & Execute   This permission allows the following rights:

- Traverse folders and execute files in the folders.
- List the contents of a folder and read the data in a folder's files.
- See a file's or folder's attributes.

If you select the Read & Execute permission, the List Folder Contents and Read permissions will be checked by default, and can't be unchecked.

List Folder Contents   This permission allows the following rights:

- Traverse folders.
- List the contents of a folder.
- See a file's or folder's attributes.

Read   This permission allows the following rights:

- List the contents of a folder and read the data in a folder's files.

- See a file's or folder's attributes.
- View ownership.

Write   This permission allows the following rights:

- Overwrite a file.
- View file ownership and permissions.
- Change a file's or folder's attributes.
- Create new files and write data to the files.
- Create new folders and append data to files.

Any user with Full Control access can manage the security of a folder. However, in order to access folders, a user must have physical access to the computer as well as a valid logon name and password. By default, regular users can't access folders over the network unless the folders have been shared. Sharing folders is covered in the "Managing Network Access" section later in this chapter.

When a folder is created on a Windows Server 2003 NTFS volume, the default permissions are as follows:

- Administrators group has Full Control (default permission inherited from the root folder, unless root folder permissions have been modified).

- System group has Full Control (default permission inherited from the root folder, unless root folder permissions have been modified).

- Users group has Read & Execute, List Folder Contents, and Read (default permission inherited from the root folder, unless root folder permissions have been modified).

Default NTFS permissions have changed significantly from Windows NT and Windows 2000, which by default assigned the Everyone group Full Control permissions.

In Exercise 5.1, you will create a directory structure that will be used throughout the exercises in this chapter.

EXERCISE 5.1

Creating a Directory and File Structure

1. Select Start ➢ Windows Explorer.

2. In Windows Explorer, expand My Computer, then Local Disk (D:). Select File ➢ New ➢ Folder and name the new folder **Data**.

3. Double-click the Data folder to open the folder. Select File ➢ New ➢ Folder and name the new folder **WP Docs**.

4. Double-click the Data folder, select File ➤ New ➤ Folder, and name the new folder **SS Docs**.

5. Confirm that you are still in the Data folder. Select File ➤ New ➤ Text Document. Name the file **Doc1.txt**.

6. Double-click the WP Docs folder. Select File ➤ New ➤ Text Document. Name the file **Doc2.txt**.

7. Double-click the SS Docs folder. Select File ➤ New ➤ Text Document. Name the file **Doc3.txt**. Your structure should look like the one shown below.

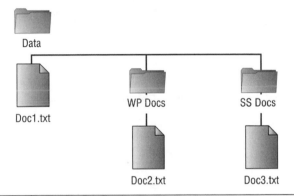

In the following sections you will learn how to apply NTFS permissions, understand how effective permissions are applied, how to control permission inheritance, understand ownership and security descriptors, determine permissions for copied or moved files, and use folder and file auditing.

Applying NTFS Permissions

You apply NTFS permissions through Windows Explorer. Right-click the file or folder that you want to control access to and select Properties from the pop-up menu. This brings up the folder or file Properties dialog box. Figure 5.1 shows a folder Properties dialog box.

The process for configuring NTFS permissions for folders and files is the same. The examples in this chapter use a folder, because NTFS permissions are most commonly applied at the folder level.

The tabs in the file or folder Properties dialog box depend on the options that have been configured for your computer. For files and folders on NTFS partitions or volumes, the dialog box will contain a Security tab, which is where you configure NTFS permissions. (The Security tab is not present in the Properties dialog box for files or folders on FAT partitions, because FAT partitions do not support local security.) The Security tab lists the users and groups that have been assigned permissions to the folder (or file). When you click a user or group in the top half of the dialog box, you see the permissions that have been allowed or denied for that user or group in the lower half of the dialog box, as shown in Figure 5.2.

FIGURE 5.1 The folder Properties dialog box

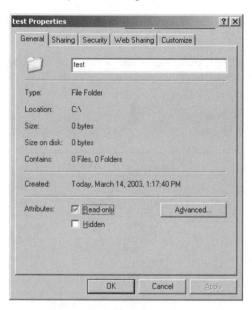

FIGURE 5.2 The Security tab of the folder Properties dialog box

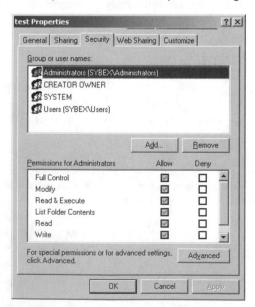

To apply NTFS permissions, take the following steps:

1. In Windows Explorer, right-click the file or folder that you want to control access to, select Properties from the pop-up menu, and click the Security tab of the Properties dialog box. (You could also select the Sharing And Security option as opposed to Properties to access the Security tab of a folder's properties.)

2. Click the Add button to open the Select Users, Computers, Or Groups dialog box, shown in Figure 5.3.

FIGURE 5.3   The Select Users or Groups dialog box

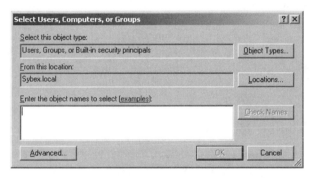

3. In the Enter The Object Names To Select area of the Select Users, Computers, Or Groups dialog box, type in the name of the user or group you want to apply NTFS permissions for and click the OK button. Complete this step for each additional user or group you want to manage NTFS permissions for.

4. You return to the Security tab of the folder Properties dialog box. Highlight each user or group in the top list box individually and specify the NTFS permissions that should be applied. When you are finished, click the OK button.

 Through the Advanced button of the Security tab, you can configure more granular NTFS permissions, such as Traverse Folder/Execute File and Read Attributes permissions.

To remove the NTFS permissions for a user, computer, or group, highlight the user, computer, or group you wish to remove in the Security tab and click the Remove button. Note that if the permissions are being inherited, you must remove the permissions at the level at which they were applied or you must first uncheck the Allow Inheritable Permissions From Parent To Propagate To This Object And All Child Objects checkbox (by clicking the Advanced button from the Security tab) before removing the permissions.

 Be careful when you remove NTFS permissions. Unlike when you delete most other types of items in Windows Server 2003, you won't be asked to confirm the removal of NTFS permissions.

Understanding How Effective Permissions Are Applied

To determine a user's *effective permissions* (the rights the user actually has to a file or folder), add all of the permissions that have been allowed through the user's assignments based on that user's username and group associations. After you determine what the user is allowed, you subtract any permissions that have been denied the user through the username or group associations.

As an example, suppose that user Marilyn is a member of the Accounting and Execs groups. The following assignments have been made:

Accounting Group Permissions

Permission	Allow	Deny
Full Control		
Modify		
Read & Execute	✓	
List Folder Contents	✓	
Read	✓	
Write		

Execs Group Permissions

Permission	Allow	Deny
Full Control		
Modify		
Read & Execute		
List Folder Contents		
Read		
Write	✓	

To determine Marilyn's effective permissions, you combine the permissions that have been assigned. The result is that Marilyn's effective permissions are Read & Execute, List Folder Contents, Read, and Write.

As another example, suppose that user Dan is a member of the Sales and Temps groups. The following assignments have been made:

Sales Group Permissions

Permission	Allow	Deny
Full Control		
Modify		
Read & Execute	✓	
List Folder Contents	✓	
Read	✓	
Write		✓

Temps Group Permissions

Permission	Allow	Deny
Full Control		
Modify		
Read & Execute	✓	
List Folder Contents	✓	
Read	✓	
Write	✓	

To determine Dan's effective permissions you start by seeing what Dan has been allowed through his combined group memberships: Read & Execute, List Folder Contents, Read, and Write permissions. You then remove anything that he is denied: Write permissions. In this case, Dan's effective permissions are Read & Execute, List Folder Contents, and Read.

Windows Server 2003 includes an option for calculating permissions that are granted to a specific user or group. The domain is queried to determine what domain and local groups the user has membership in. The calculation is based on the permissions that have been granted to a user or group directly for an NTFS object as well as any permissions that have been inherited from parent objects. Any permissions that are denied are then removed.

The Effective Permissions tool assumes that the user will be logged onto the computer locally. It does not determine what the effective permissions will be if the user is accessing the resource over a share or logs in remotely or through Terminal Services, which can add additional layers of security.

To calculate a user or groups Effective Rights, click the Advanced button from the Security tab of the folder's properties you want to query. Then click the Effective Permissions tab in the Advanced Security Settings dialog box. You will see the dialog box shown in Figure 5.4. From that dialog box, you click the Select button and in the Select User Or Group dialog box, enter the user or group name you want to view effective permissions for. The effective permissions for that user or group will then be displayed.

FIGURE 5.4   The Effective Permissions dialog box

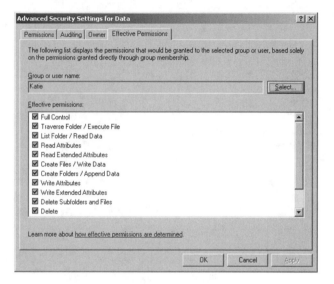

 By default, the Everyone group is listed with NTFS permissions. Previous to Server 2003, the Everyone group contained all users. With Server 2003 the Everyone group no longer includes Anonymous Logon. In Domain Security Policy or local policies, anonymous users can be added to the Everyone group. The setting is: Network access: Let Everyone permissions apply to anonymous users.

In Exercise 5.2, you will configure NTFS permissions based on the preceding examples. This exercise assumes you have completed Exercise 5.1.

EXERCISE 5.2

Configuring NTFS Permissions

1. Using the Active Directory Users And Computers utility, create two users: **Marilyn** and **Dan**. (See Chapter 3, "Managing Users, Groups, and Computers," for details on using the Active Directory Users And Computers utility.) Deselect the User Must Change Password At Next Logon option.

2. Using the Active Directory Users And Computers utility, create four global security groups: **Accounting**, **Execs**, **Sales**, and **Temps**. Add Marilyn to the Accounting and Execs groups, and add Dan to the Sales and Temps groups.

3. Select Start ➢ Windows Explorer. Expand the D:\Data folder you created in Exercise 5.1.

4. Right-click the Data folder, select Properties, and click the Security tab.

5. In the Security tab of the folder Properties dialog box, highlight the Users group and click the Remove button. You see a dialog box telling you that you cannot remove Users because it is inheriting permissions from a higher level. Click the OK button.

6. Click the Advanced button. Deselect the Allow Inheritable Permissions From The Parent To Propagate To This Object And All Child Objects checkbox, and click Copy in the Security dialog box in case you need to restore the permissions later. Click OK to exit the Advanced Security Settings dialog box. Now remove the Users group from the Security tab of the folder Properties dialog box.

7. Configure NTFS permissions for the Accounting group by clicking the Add button. In the Select Users Or Groups dialog box, enter **Accounting; Execs; Sales; Temps**, and click the OK button.

8. In the Security tab, highlight each group and check the Allow or Deny checkboxes to add permissions as follows:

   ▪ For Accounting, allow Read & Execute (List Folder Contents and Read will automatically be allowed) and Write.

   ▪ For Execs, allow Read.

   ▪ For Sales, allow Modify (Read & Execute, List Folder Contents, Read, and Write will automatically be allowed).

   ▪ For Temps, deny Write.

9. Click the OK button to close the folder Properties dialog box.

10. You will see a Security dialog box cautioning you about the deny entry. Click the Yes button to continue.

11. Log off as Administrator and log on as Marilyn. Access the D:\Data\Doc1 file, make changes, and then save the changes. Marilyn's permissions will allow these actions.

12. Log off as Marilyn and log on as Dan. Access the D:\Data\Doc1 file, make changes, and then save the changes. Dan's permissions will allow Dan to open the file but not to save any changes.

13. Log off as Dan and log on as Administrator.

Controlling Permission Inheritance

Directory structures are organized in a hierarchical manner. This means that you are likely to have subfolders in the folders that you apply permissions to. In Windows Server 2003, by default, parent folder permissions are applied to any files and any subfolders in that folder. These are called *inherited permissions*.

You can specify how permissions will be inherited from parent containers within the directory structure to child objects within the directory structure by clicking the Advanced button from the folder's Properties dialog box. This brings up the Advanced Security Settings dialog box shown in Figure 5.5.

FIGURE 5.5   The Advanced Security Settings dialog box

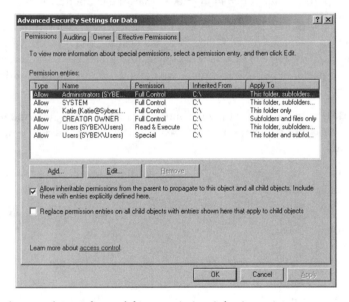

The options that can be configured for permission inheritance are:

- Allow inheritable permissions from the parent to propagate to this object and all child objects. Include these with entries explicitly defined here.

- Replace permission entries on all child objects with entries shown here that apply to child objects.

If an Allow or a Deny checkbox in the Permission list in the Security tab has a shaded check mark, this indicates that the permission was inherited from an upper-level folder. If the check mark is not shaded, it indicates that the permission was applied at the selected folder. This is known as an explicitly assigned permission. It is useful to see inherited permissions so that you can more easily troubleshoot permissions.

To minimize administration and simplify troubleshooting of folder permissions, you should assign permissions at higher-level folders within the directory structure and use inheritable permissions to propagate the permissions to all child objects within the directory structure.

Understanding Ownership and Security Descriptors

When an object is initially created on an NTFS partition, an associated security descriptor is created. A security descriptor contains the following information:

- The user or group that owns the object
- The users and groups that are allowed or denied access to the object
- The users and groups whose access to the object will be audited

After an object is created, the owner (creator) of the object has full permissions to change the information in the security descriptor, just as members of the Administrators group can. You can view the owner of an object from the Security tab of the specified folder's Properties and clicking the Advanced button, then click the Owner tab to see who the owner of the object is, as shown in Figure 5.6. From this dialog box you can change the owner of the object.

FIGURE 5.6   The Owner tab of the Advanced Security Settings dialog box

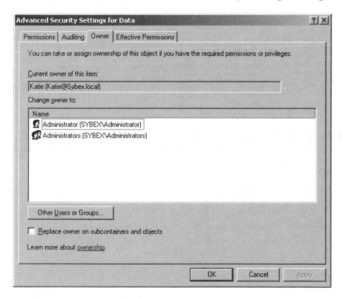

While the owner of an object can set the permissions of an object so that the Administrator can't access the object, the Administrator or any member of the Administrators group can take ownership of an object, and thus manage the object's permissions. When you take ownership of an object, you can specify whether you want to replace the owner on subdirectories and objects within the object. If the Administrators group no longer has permissions to the folder you are taking ownership of, you will also have the option to replace the existing permissions so that the Administrator will have Full Control permission to the folder. If you replace permissions, all existing permissions will be deleted.

From a command prompt, you can see who the owner of a directory is by typing **dir /q**.

Real World Scenario

Using the Take Ownership Option

You are the administrator of a large network. The manager of the Accounting department, Michael, set up a series of files and folders with a high level of security. Michael was the owner of these and all of the associated files and folders. When he set up NTFS security for his files and folders, he removed access for everyone, including the Administrators group. Michael recently left the company, and Kevin has been hired to take over the accounting manager's job. When Kevin tries to access Michael's files, he can't. When you log on as Administrator, you also can't access any of the files.

In this case, you should access the Owner tab of the parent folder for the files and folders and simply add Kevin. Kevin will automatically become the owner. You should ensure that you check the Replace Owner On Subcontainers And Objects option, and Kevin will now have Full Control permissions to the folder, subfolders, and files within that folder hierarchy.

In Exercise 5.3, you will configure NTFS permissions as a regular user and block access to a folder for all other users. You will then use the Take Ownership option to access the file as a member of the Administrators group.

EXERCISE 5.3

Using Take Ownership

1. Using the Active Directory Users And Computers utility, create a user named **Aaron**. (See Chapter 3 for details on using the Active Directory Users And Computers utility.) Deselect the User Must Change Password at Next Logon option.

2. Log on as Aaron and select Start ➢ My Computer.

3. Open the D: drive and select File ➢ New ➢ Folder and name the new folder **Aaron's Data**.

4. Create a text file called **Secret.txt** in D:\Aaron's Data.

5. Right-click Aaron's Data, select Properties, and click the Security tab.

6. In the Security tab of the folder Properties dialog box, highlight the Users group and click the Remove button. You see a dialog box telling you that you cannot remove Users because this group is inheriting permissions from a higher level. Click the OK button.

7. Click the Advanced button. Deselect the Allow Inheritable Permissions From The Parent To Propagate To This Object And All Child Objects checkbox, and click Copy in the Security dialog box in case you need to restore the permissions later. Click OK to exit the Advanced Security Settings dialog box. Now remove the Users group and the Administrators group from the Security tab of the folder Properties dialog box. Click OK.

8.   Log off as Aaron and log on as Administrator.

9.   Try to access D:\Aaron's Data\Secret.txt. When you click D:\Aaron's Data, you will get an Access Is Denied error message. Click the OK button.

10. Right-click the Aaron's Data folder, select Properties, and click the Security tab. You may see a message that you do not have permission to view or edit the current permission settings for the folder but you can take ownership or change auditing settings. Click the OK button.

11. Click the Advanced button and select the Owner tab. Click on the Administrator account and check the box Replace Owner On Subcontainers And Objects and click the OK button.

12. A Security dialog box will appear notifying you that you do not have permissions to read the contents of the directory and asking you if you want to replace the directory permissions so that you are granted Full Control permission. Click the Yes button to replace all permissions. You will now have Full Control permission to the Aaron's Data folder and the Secret.txt file.

Determining NTFS Permissions for Copied or Moved Files

When you copy or move NTFS files, the permissions that have been set for those files might change. The following guidelines can be used to predict what will happen:

- If you move a file from one folder to another folder on the same NTFS volume, the file will retain the original NTFS permissions.

- If you move a file from one folder to another folder between different NTFS volumes, the file is treated as a copy and will have the same permissions as the destination folder.

- If you copy a file from one folder to another folder (on the same volume or on a different volume), the file will have the same permissions as the destination folder.

- If you copy or move a folder or file to a FAT partition, it will not retain any NTFS permissions.

Using Folder and File Auditing

If you have configured a partition or volume as NTFS, you can take advantage of an additional security feature called *auditing*. Auditing allows you to track the success or failure of folder and file access. In order to use auditing, two options must be configured:

- Configure the computer to enable auditing for object access.

- Configure the events that you want to audit on the specific NTFS folder or file.

After you configure auditing, you view the results through the Event Viewer utility's Security log.

In the following sections you will learn how to set audit policy, configure NTFS auditing, and view results from folder and file auditing.

Setting Audit Policy

To enable folder and file auditing, you must first enable auditing for object access. This setting is either enabled or disabled for the entire computer. You enable object access from Administrative Tools ➢ Domain Security Policy, then click Local Policies, Audit Policy, Audit Object Access, and then configure success and/or failure, as shown in Figure 5.7. By default, object access is not active. To configure auditing using Active Directory, you must be a member of the Domain Admins group or the Enterprise Admins group or be delegated the right. To set an audit policy on the local machine, you must be a member of the local Administrators group.

FIGURE 5.7 Domain Security Policy Setting—Audit Object Access

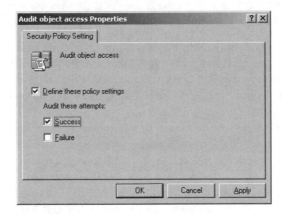

Configuring NTFS Auditing

You can configure only folder and file auditing on NTFS partitions. When you configure auditing, you must specify which users and groups are being tracked through auditing, which folders and/or files are being audited, and what types of events you want to audit for success or failure. To enable folder or file auditing, take the following steps:

1. Within the NTFS partition, right-click the folder or file you want to configure.

2. Select Properties, then click the Security tab.

3. Within the Security tab, click the Advanced button.

4. Click the Auditing tab, then click the Add button.

5. The Select User, Computer, Or Group dialog box will appear. Enter the users, computers, or groups you want to audit and click the OK button.

6. The Auditing Entry For Data dialog box will appear, as shown in Figure 5.8. Specify the events that will be audited. You can also choose to Apply These Auditing Entries To Objects And/Or Containers Within This Container Only. You can select Successful or Failed for the following events:

   - Full Control
   - Traverse Folder/Execute File

- List Folder/Read Data
- Read Attributes
- Read Extended Attributes
- Create Files/Write Data
- Create Folders/Append Data
- Write Attributes
- Write Extended Attributes
- Delete Subfolders and Files
- Delete
- Read Permissions
- Change Permissions
- Take Ownership

Once you make your selections, click the OK button.

FIGURE 5.8   Auditing Entry for folder

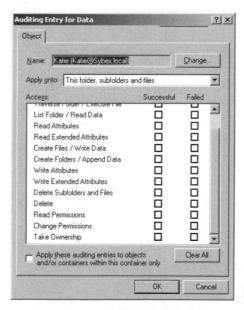

Viewing the Results of Folder and File Auditing

Once you have enabled auditing, you can view the results of auditing through Event Viewer. To view the results of auditing, access Event Viewer through Administrative Tools ➤ Event Viewer, then click on the Security Log. A key icon indicates that a successful event occurred, while a lock icon indicates that a failed event occurred.

Real World Scenario

Tracking Folder and File Access

Suppose you are the network administrator of a server called HR. Several managers have access to a folder called C:\Reports with Full Control access. There has recently been a problem where reports that are copied to the network share are disappearing. You want to track who is accessing the files and when.

In order to track folder and file access, you would enable auditing for the Everyone group on the C:\Reports folder. Select Successful and Failed events for Delete Subfolders And Files. If you want to track Read access, select List Folder/Read Data for the Everyone group.

Then, if files or folders are manipulated in a malicious way, you can track exactly what access occurred in the Security log stored within Event Viewer. The drawback to auditing is that, depending on the amount of data you are tracking, auditing can be very processor intensive. If there is frequent access, log files can also become cumbersome very quickly.

By being able to audit folders and files you, as a network administrator, can track any access to a folder or file on any NTFS partition or volume.

Managing Network Access

Sharing is the process of allowing network users to access a folder, called a *shared folder*, located on a Windows Server 2003 computer. A network share provides a single location to manage shared data used by many users. Sharing also allows an administrator to install an application once, as opposed to installing it locally at each computer, and to manage the application from a single location.

In the following sections you will learn how to create shared folders, configure share permissions, and manage shares with the Shared Folders utility.

Creating Shared Folders

To share a folder on a Windows Server 2003 member server, you must be logged on as a member of the Administrators or Power Users group. To share a folder on a Windows Server 2003 domain controller or a computer that is part of a domain, you must be logged on as a member of the Administrators or Server Operators group. You enable and configure sharing through the Sharing tab of the folder Properties dialog box, as shown in Figure 5.9.

When you share a folder, you can configure the options listed in Table 5.1.

If you share a folder and then decide that you do not want to share it, just select the Do Not Share This Folder radio button in the Sharing tab of the folder Properties dialog box.

FIGURE 5.9   The Sharing tab of the folder Properties dialog box

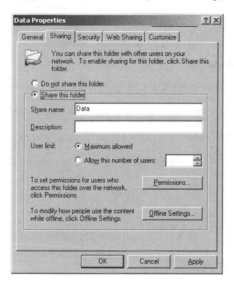

TABLE 5.1   Shared Folder Options

Option	Description
Do Not Share This Folder	Specifies that the folder is available only through local access
Share This Folder	Specifies that the folder is available through local access and network access
Share Name	Specifies a descriptive name by which users will access the folder
Description	Allows you to enter more descriptive information about the share (optional)
User Limit	Allows you to specify the maximum number of connections to the share at any one time
Permissions	Allows you to configure how users will access the folder over the network
Offline Settings	Specifies how folders are cached when the folder is offline

In Windows Explorer, you can easily tell that a folder has been shared by the hand icon under the folder.

In Exercise 5.4, you will create a shared folder.

EXERCISE 5.4

Creating a Shared Folder

1. Select Start ➤ Windows Explorer. Expand My Computer, and then expand Local Disk (D:).

2. Select File ➤ New ➤ Folder and name the new folder **Share Me**.

3. Right-click the Share Me folder, select Properties, and click the Sharing tab.

4. In the Sharing tab of the folder Properties dialog box, click the Share This Folder radio button.

5. Type **Test Shared Folder** in the Share Name text box.

6. Type **This is a comment for a shared folder** in the Description text box.

7. Under User Limit, click the Allow This Number Of Users radio button and specify 5 users.

8. Click the OK button to close the dialog box.

Configuring Share Permissions

You can control users' access to *shared folders* by assigning *share permissions*. Share permissions are less complex than NTFS permissions and can be applied only to folders (unlike NTFS permissions, which can be applied to folders and files).

To assign share permissions, click the Permissions button in the Sharing tab of the folder Properties dialog box. This opens the Share Permissions dialog box, as shown in Figure 5.10.

FIGURE 5.10 The Share Permissions dialog box

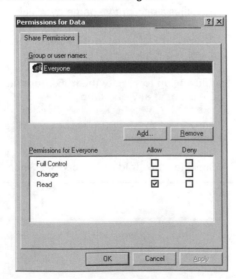

You can assign three types of share permissions:

- The Full Control share permission allows full access to the shared folder. When the Full Control permission is assigned, the Change and Read permissions are checked as well.

- The Change share permission allows users to change data in a file or to delete files.

- The Read share permission allows a user to view and execute files in the shared folder.

Read is the default permission on shared folders for the Everyone group. In previous versions of Windows, the default permission for the Everyone group was Full Control.

 Shared folders do not use the same concept of inheritance as NTFS folders. If you share a folder, there is no way to block access to lower-level resources through share permissions.

In Exercise 5.5, you will apply share permissions to a folder. This exercise assumes that you have completed the other exercises in this chapter.

EXERCISE 5.5

Applying Share Permissions

1. Select Start ➢ Windows Explorer. Expand My Computer, then expand Local Disk (D:).

2. Right-click the Share Me folder, select Sharing And Security, and click the Permissions button.

3. In the Share Permissions dialog box, highlight the Everyone group and click the Remove button. Then click the Add button.

4. In the Select Users, Computers, Or Groups dialog box, enter **Dan; Marilyn** and then click the OK button.

5. Click user Marilyn and check the Allow box for the Full Control permission.

6. Click user Dan and check the Allow box for the Read permission.

7. Click the OK button to close the dialog box, and click OK again to close the folder Properties dialog box.

Managing Shares with the Shared Folders Utility

Shared Folders is a computer management utility for creating and managing shared folders on the computer. The Shared Folders window displays all of the shares that have been created on the computer, the user sessions that are open on each share, and the files that are currently open, listed by user.

To access Shared Folders, select Administrative Tools ➢ Computer Management, expand System Tools, and then expand Shared Folders.

In the following sections you will learn how to use the Shared Folders utility to view shares, create new shares, view share sessions, and view open files.

Viewing Shares

When you select Shares in the Shared Folders utility, you see all of the shares that have been configured on the computer. Figure 5.11 shows an example of a Shares listing.

FIGURE 5.11   The Shares listing in the Shared Folders window

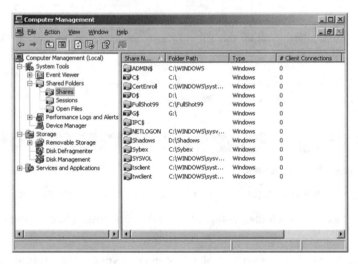

Along with the shares that you have specifically configured, you will also see the Windows Server 2003 special shares, which are shares created by the system automatically to facilitate system administration. A share that is followed by a dollar sign ($) indicates that the share is hidden from view when users access utilities such as My Network Places and browse network resources. The following special shares may appear on your Windows Server 2003 computer, depending on how the computer is configured:

- The *drive_letter*$ share is the share for the root of the drive. By default, the root of every drive is shared. For example, the C: drive is shared as C$.

On Windows Server 2003 member servers and Windows XP Professional computers, only members of the Administrators and Backup Operators groups can access the *drive_letter*$ share. On Windows Server 2003 domain controllers, members of the Administrators, Backup Operators, and Server Operators groups can access this share.

- The ADMIN$ share points to the Windows Server 2003 system root (for example, C:\Windows).

- The IPC$ share allows remote administration of a computer and is used to view a computer's shared resources. (IPC stands for interprocess communication.)

- The PRINT$ share is used for remote printer administration. This share will appear only if a printer has been defined on the server.

- The FAX$ share is used by fax clients to cache fax cover sheets and documents that are in the process of being faxed. This share will appear only if a fax device has been configured on the server.

Creating New Shares

In Shared Folders, you can create new shares through the following steps:

1. Right-click the Shares folder and select New Share from the pop-up menu.

2. The Share A Folder Wizard starts. Click the Next button. The Share A Folder Wizard dialog box will appear, as shown in Figure 5.12. Specify the folder that will be shared (you can use the Browse button to select the folder). Click the Next button.

FIGURE 5.12   The Folder Path dialog box

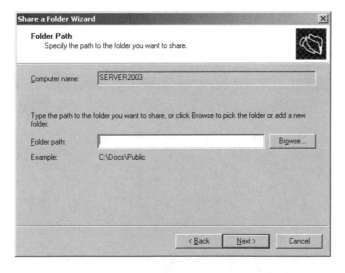

3. The Name, Description, And Settings dialog box appears, as shown in Figure 5.13. You can specify the Share Name (by default the folder name), the Description, and the Offline Setting options (whether the files in the folder are available for offline access). Once you make your selections, click the Next button.

FIGURE 5.13   The Name, Description, And Settings dialog box

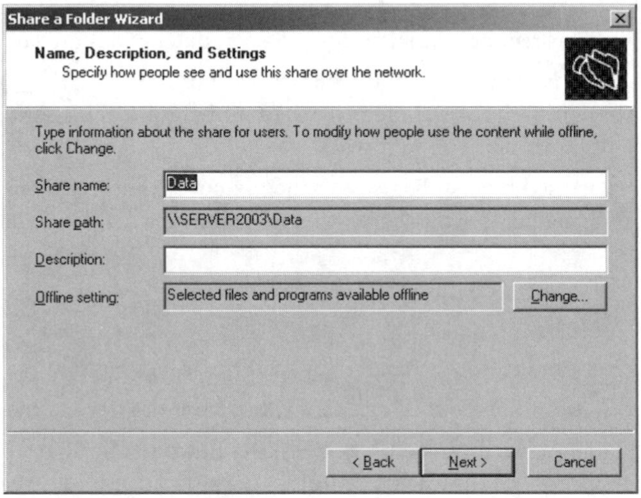

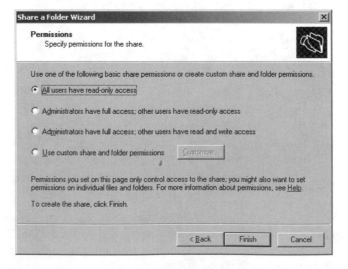

4. The Permissions dialog box for assigning share permissions appears, as shown in Figure 5.14. You can select from one of the predefined permissions assignments or customize the share permissions. After you specify the permissions that will be assigned, click the Finish button.

FIGURE 5.14   Assigning share permissions

5. The Sharing Was Successful Statement dialog box appears. This dialog box verifies that the folder has been shared successfully. Click the Close button.

You can stop sharing a folder by right-clicking the share and selecting Stop Sharing from the pop-up menu. You will be asked to confirm that you want to stop sharing the folder.

Viewing Share Sessions

When you select Sessions in the Shared Folders utility, you see all of the users who are currently accessing shared folders on the computer.

The Sessions listing includes the following information:

- The username that has connected to the share
- The computer name that the user has connected from
- The client operating system that is used by the connecting computer
- The number of files that the user has open
- The amount of time that the user has been connected
- The amount of idle time for the connection
- Whether or not the user has connected through Guest access

Viewing Open Files in Shared Folders

When you select Open Files in the Shared Folders utility, you see a list of all the files that are currently open from shared folders.

The Open Files listing shows:

- The path and files that are currently open
- The username that is accessing the file
- The operating system used by the user who is accessing the file
- Whether or not any file locks have been applied (file locks are used to prevent two users from opening the same file and editing it at the same time)
- The open mode that is being used (such as read or write)

Local and Network Resource Access

Local and network security work together. The most restrictive access between the two will determine what a user can do. For example, if the local folder is NTFS and the Everyone group has been assigned the Full Control permission and the local folder is shared and the share permissions are set so that only the Sales group had been assigned the Read permission, then only the Sales group can access that shared folder via Read permission.

Conversely, if the local NTFS permissions allow only the Managers group the Read permission to a local folder, and that folder has been shared with permissions allowing the Everyone group Full Control permission, only the Managers group can access the folder with Read permissions, because Read is the more restrictive permission between the two security settings.

Another example: Suppose that you have set up the NTFS and share permissions for the D:\Data folder as shown in Figure 5.15. Jose is a member of the Sales group and wants to access the D:\Data folder. If he accesses the folder locally, he will be governed by only the NTFS security, so he will have the Modify permission. However, if Jose accesses the folder from another workstation through the network share, he will be governed by the more restrictive share permission, Read.

FIGURE 5.15   Local and network security govern access.

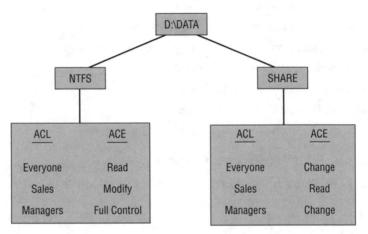

As another example, suppose that Chandler is a member of the Everyone group. He wants to access the D:\Data folder. If he accesses the folder locally, he will have Read permission. If he accesses the folder remotely via the network share, he will still have Read permission. Even though the share permission allows the Everyone group the Change permission to the folder, the more restrictive permission (in this case, the NTFS permission Read) will be applied.

Troubleshooting NTFS and Shared Folder Access

If you are having problems with NTFS permissions or can't access a shared resource, the following list defines common problems and solutions, which can facilitate the troubleshooting process:

A user can access a resource locally but can't access the same resource over the network even though it has been shared.   Effective permissions are based on permissions that have been applied to NTFS and the share permissions. The user must have NTFS and share permissions that allow access to the requested folder. Verify that the user is not a member of any group that has been assigned Deny permission(s) for the share.

A user can access a local folder with more permissions than they have been explicitly assigned through user or group memberships.   The user may be inheriting permissions from a parent container. Calculate effective permissions by clicking the Advanced button from the Security tab of the folder properties you want to query. Then click the Effective Permissions tab in the Advanced Security Settings dialog box. From that dialog box, you click the Select button, and in the Select User, Computer, Or Group dialog box, enter the user or group name you want to view effective permissions for. The Effective permissions for that user or group will then be displayed. If the permissions are displayed as shaded out, you know the user's permissions are being inherited from a parent container.

When attempting to set NTFS permissions, there is no Security tab in the folder's Properties dialog box.   The volume that the folder is located on is not NTFS.

When attempting to configure a share, there is no Share tab in the folder's Properties dialog box.   You are logged in as a user who does not have appropriate rights to create a share.

You stop sharing the C$ drive and it keeps reappearing.   This share will reappear when the Server service is stopped and restarted.

Summary

In this chapter, you learned about managing access to files and folders. We covered the following topics:

- Local access management, which involves assigning NTFS permissions
- Network access management, which includes creating shared folders, assigning share permissions, and accessing network resources
- How resources are accessed when local NTFS permissions and network share permissions have been applied
- Common problems for accessing local or shared folders and how to troubleshoot each problem

Exam Essentials

Be able to define local NTFS security options and be able to configure local security.   Be able to list NTFS permissions and understand how they work together when combined (especially Deny permissions). Know who can manage NTFS permissions and how they are applied.

Create network shares and apply share permissions.   Know what group memberships can create network shares and be able to configure and apply share permissions.

Understand how NTFS and share permissions interact with each other.   Be able to specify how NTFS permissions and share permissions interact and determine what the effective permissions are, based on user and group memberships.

Know how to troubleshoot common errors for accessing local and network resources.   Be able to troubleshoot access problems. Common problems include incorrectly configured rights or insufficient permissions to complete administrative tasks.

Key Terms

Before you take the exam, be certain you are familiar with the following terms:

effective permissions

inherited permissions

NTFS permissions

share permissions

shared folder

shared folders

Review Questions

1. You are currently logged in to the \Sales server as an Administrator. You want to add additional security to the D:\Data folder. When you attempt to set permissions, you see the following dialog box that does not display a Security tab. What is the most likely reason for this?

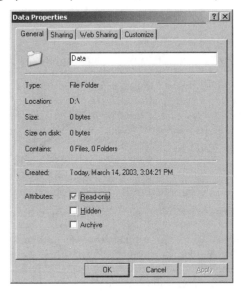

   A. The partition is not configured as NTFS.

   B. Your account has been assigned No Access rights through the user account or through group membership.

   C. You need to be logged on as a member of the Server Operators group.

   D. The folder has already been encrypted with EFS.

2. You are the network administrator for a large corporation and your job is to support the Accounting department. Your company has a server called \Acct, which contains a folder called C:\Reviews. All of the Accounting Managers have permission to create files in this folder. Due to the sensitive nature of the data stored in the C:\Reviews folder, you want to monitor any access to this folder. You configure the folder's Properties For Auditing Success And Failure for Read access for the Everyone group. When you check the Event Viewer Security log after a week, no events are logged even though you know that users have accessed files within the folder. What is the most likely error?

   A. You have not started the Auditing service.

   B. You did not enable auditing for Object Access through the Domain Security policy.

   C. Auditing can only occur on dynamic disks, and the disk is configured as a basic disk.

   D. You did not restart the server after configuring auditing.

3. You are the network administrator for all of the Windows Server 2003 member servers in the Sales and Marketing departments. You are in the process of installing a new server called \Sales-Data. You have specified that all volumes will be formatted as NTFS and what directory structure will be used. When you initially create the directory structure, what NTFS permissions will be applied by default? (Choose all that apply.)

    A. Administrators group has Full Control.

    B. System group has Full Control.

    C. Everyone group has Full Control.

    D. Users group has Read & Execute, List Folder Contents, and Read.

4. You are the network administrator for a large corporation, in charge of running the Help Desk. You have just created a folder called C:\Data on the \TechSupport server. The server has subfolders called C:\Data\Calls and C:\Data\Comp. What is the default permission that will be applied to subfolders when you apply NTFS permissions to parent folders?

    A. Full Control

    B. Read

    C. Whatever permissions are applied to the parent folder

    D. You are prompted to specify what permissions should be applied.

5. You are the network administrator for a small company and manage the Test Lab. Your \Test server has C:, D:, and E: volumes. You want to see all of the shares that have been created on the server for all volumes. Which utility can be used to quickly view all of the folders that have been shared on a Windows Server 2003 computer?

    A. Shared Folders

    B. File Manager

    C. Windows Explorer

    D. Share Manager

6. You are the network administrator of a medium-sized company. Your network consists of a single Windows Server 2003 domain with a Windows Server 2003 domain controller and 250 client workstations running Windows XP Professional. As a member of the Domain Admins group, you want to be able to remotely manage any of the Windows XP Professional computers within the domain. Which special share allows remote administration of a computer and is used to view a computer's shared resources?

    A. ADMIN$

    B. WINNT$

    C. IPC$

    D. NET$

7. Elisa is a member of the Sales and Sales Temps groups. The following NTFS permissions have been applied to the D:\Sales folder:

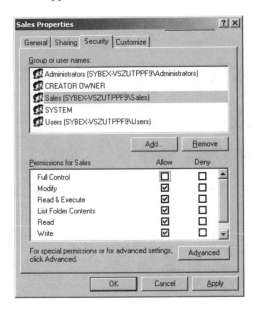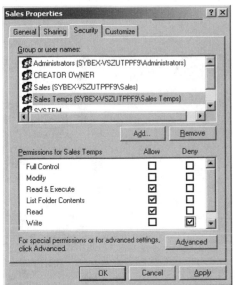

What will Elisa's effective permissions be to the D:\Sales folder? (Choose all that apply.)

A. Modify

B. Read & Execute

C. List Folder Contents

D. Read

E. Write

8. Rashid is the network administrator for a small company. He is managing a server called \Sales and is assigning NTFS permissions to the D:\Data folder for the Managers group. He wants the Managers group to be able to list the contents of the folder and read the data in the folder's files. He does not want anyone from the group to change or delete any of the data. Which NTFS permission should he apply?

A. Full Control

B. Modify

C. Read

D. Write

9. Marcus has assigned the NTFS Read permission to the Managers group for the D:\Data folder as shown in the following exhibit. What will be the default right assigned to the Managers group for the D:\Data\2003 subfolder?

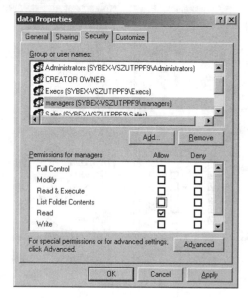

A. Full Control

B. Modify

C. Read

D. Write

10. Marty is planning on copying the `Test.txt` file from the D:\Data folder to the D:\Test folder. The D: drive is NTFS. The `Test.txt` file currently has Modify permission applied for the Users group. The D:\Test folder has the Write permission applied for the Users group. What permission will the `Test.txt` file have after it has been copied?

A. Full Control

B. Modify

C. Read

D. Write

11. Lynne is planning on moving the `Test.txt` file from the D:\Data folder to the D:\Test folder. The D: drive is NTFS. The `Test.txt` file currently has Modify permission applied for the Users group. The D:\Test folder has the Write permission applied for Users. What permission will the `Test.txt` file have after it has been moved?

A. Full Control

B. Modify

C. Read

D. Write

12. Dustin is planning on moving the `Test.txt` file from the D:\Data folder to the E:\Test folder. The D: and E: drives are NTFS. The `Test.txt` file currently has Modify permission applied for the Users group. The E:\Test folder has the Write permission applied for Users. What permission will the `Test.txt` file have after it has been moved?

   A. Full Control

   B. Modify

   C. Read

   D. Write

13. You have asked Dietrich to help with server management by creating a network share on a Windows Server 2003 member server called \MIS. When he logs on to the \MIS member server and tries to create a share, he sees the following exhibit. You want him to be able to create shares on the server. Which of the following groups could you add Dietrich's user account to so that he would have permissions to create network shares? (Choose all that apply.)

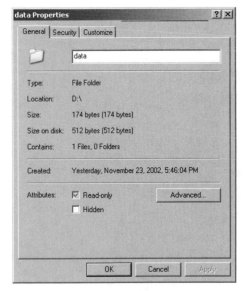

   A. Power Users on the local accounts database

   B. Power Operators on the local accounts database

   C. Server Operators on the domain that the computer is a part of

   D. Administrators on the local accounts database or the domain that the computer is a part of

14. Maria needs to disconnect all users that are connected to the APPS share. Which of the following utilities can she use to see which users are currently connected to the share?

   A. Shared Folders

   B. File Manager

   C. Windows Explorer

   D. Server Manager

15. You are the network administrator for a small company. You manage a Windows Server 2003 domain that includes a Windows Server 2003 domain controller and two Windows Server 2003 member servers. One of your users reports that they can't access a local NTFS resource called \Sales-Data. When you try to access the NTFS resource, you realize that all of the permissions for the Administrators group have been removed. You want to determine who the current owner of the folder is before you make any changes. Which of the following options can be used to display the current owner?

A. `Dir /q`

B. `Dir /o`

C. `ListDir /b`

D. `ListDir /o`

Answers to Review Questions

1. **A.**   If you are logged in as Administrator and do not see a Security tab on the folder's Property page, then the most likely problem is that the partition is not formatted as NTFS.

2. **B.**   In order to support folder, file, and print auditing, you must be on an NTFS partition, or the option to configure security and auditing will not even appear. In order to support auditing, you must enable auditing for Object Access through the computer's Domain Security policy. Then you enable auditing through the folder or file Properties.

3. **A, B, D.**   When a folder is created on a Windows Server 2003 NTFS volume, the default permissions are as follows: Administrators group has Full Control (default permission inherited from the root folder, unless root folder permissions have been modified), System group has Full Control (default permission inherited from the root folder, unless root folder permissions have been modified), Users group has Read & Execute, List Folder Contents, and Read (default permission inherited from the root folder, unless root folder permissions have been modified).

4. **C.**   When you apply NTFS permissions to a folder with subfolders, the default is to allow inheritable permissions to propagate from the parent to this object. This means that whatever permissions have been applied to the parent folder will be automatically applied to subfolders.

5. **A.**   The Shared Folders utility displays all of the folders that have been shared. You can see shared folders through Windows Explorer, but the process is more time-consuming and will not display hidden folders.

6. **C.**   The IPC$ (Interprocess Communication) special share is used for remote administration of a computer and to view a computer's shared resources.

7. **B, C, D.**   Elisa's effective permission will be Read & Execute, List Folder Contents, and the Read permissions. She will not have Modify access since the Write permission was explicitly denied for the Sales Temp Group.

8. **C.**   The Managers group should be assigned the most restrictive permission that will still allow the members to read the data in the D:\Data folder, which is the NTFS Read permission.

9. **C.**   In Windows Server 2003, a parent folder's permissions are applied to any files or subfolders in that folder by default. This means that by default, the D:\Data\2003 subfolder will inherit the parent folder's NTFS permissions, and the Managers group will inherit the Read permission.

10. **D.**   If you copy a file from one folder to another folder (on the same volume or on a different volume), the file will have the same permissions as the destination folder.

11. **B.**   If you move a file from one folder to another folder on the same NTFS volume, the file will retain the original NTFS permissions.

12. **D.**   If you move a file from one folder to another folder between different NTFS volumes, the file is treated as a copy and will have the same permissions as the destination folder.

13. A, C, D.   To share a folder on a Windows Server 2003 member server, you must be logged on as a member of the Administrators or Power Users group or be a member of the Server Operators group for the domain that the computer belongs to.

14. A.   When you select Sessions in the Shared Folders utility, you see all of the users who are currently accessing shared folders on the computer.

15. A.   You can view the Owner tab from Advanced folder Properties or you can view ownership through the command-line `Dir /q`. Users who are familiar with command-line utilities can sometimes perform tasks more quickly with command-line utilities than through their GUI equivalents.

Chapter

6

Managing Web Services

MICROSOFT EXAM OBJECTIVES COVERED IN THIS CHAPTER:

✓ **Manage a Web server.**

- Manage Internet Information Services (IIS).
- Manage security for IIS.

Windows Server 2003 comes with Internet Information Services (IIS) 6.0, which allows you to create and manage websites. This software provides a wide range of options for configuring the content, performance, and access controls for your websites.

In this chapter, you will learn how to install Internet Information Services and how to configure and manage website properties. You will learn how to create a new website. You will also learn about the IIS metabase and how to back it up. The final section of the chapter includes tips for troubleshooting problems with website access.

Benefits of Using IIS

Windows Server 2003 includes IIS 6.0, which is web server software that provides integrated, reliable, secure, and scalable software for creating and managing internal corporate websites and external websites on the Internet.

The benefits and features of IIS include:

- IIS is fully integrated and designed to work with Windows Server 2003.

- Each website is isolated and functions as a self-contained worker process. This promotes reliability, since an application that may not be functioning properly on one website can't adversely affect another website that is hosted on the same IIS server.

- For security purposes, IIS 6.0 is not installed by default. IIS offers a variety of security features that protect the IIS site and reduce the possibility of security breaches from external threats.

- IIS uses a new kernel-mode driver for HTTP parsing and cacheing. The kernel-mode driver is tuned for scalability and throughput, which increases the number of sites that an IIS server can host and the number of concurrent active worker processes that the IIS server can host.

- IIS can be managed in a variety of options including IIS Manager, administration scripts, or editing of IIS configuration files.

- IIS supports web developers by supporting the latest web standards, which include XML, SOAP, and IPv6.

Key IIS Services

IIS is made up of several key services. The following list describes the main IIS services:

World Wide Web Service   The World Wide Web (WWW) service is used to publish Web services and connect HTTP requests from IIS clients to IIS websites.

Hypertext Transfer Protocol   *Hypertext Transfer Protocol (HTTP)* is used to create content for websites as well as to navigate websites.

File Transfer Protocol   *File Transfer Protocol (FTP)* is used to copy files to and from remote computer systems using the Transmission Control Protocol (TCP). The TCP protocol is designed to support accurate and reliable data transfer. FTP requires an FTP server and an FTP client. IIS allows you to create and manage an FTP server.

Simple Mail Transfer Protocol   *Simple Mail Transfer Protocol (SMTP)* is used on the Internet to route e-mail between transfer agents. SMTP does not provide e-mail server capabilities. For full e-mail services, you need an e-mail application such as Microsoft Exchange Server.

Network News Transfer Protocol   *Network News Transfer Protocol (NNTP)* is used to distribute network news messages to NNTP servers and to NNTP clients (news readers) on the Internet. News articles are stored on an NNTP server in a central database where they can be indexed, retrieved, and posted.

IIS Admin Service   The IIS Admin Service manages the IIS metabase. The IIS metabase is a special database that contains all of the settings and configuration data for IIS. The IIS Admin Service manages the IIS metabase by updating the Windows Server 2003 Registry with the settings for the WWW service, FTP, SMTP, and NNTP.

IIS Security

Before you connect your website to the Internet, you should first plan and implement a security strategy that will meet the requirements of your website.

Some of the main considerations are:

- Does your site require anonymous access?

- How is your current Windows 2003 user security defined?

- Do you want to limit access to your website to specific host addresses or network addresses?

- Do you require Secure Sockets Layer (SSL) for encryption and authentication?

These questions are explored in the following sections.

Access Control for Anonymous Access

In order to access IIS, you must be logged in with a valid Windows 2003 user account. If you choose to allow anonymous access, your users will access your website through a user account called IUSR_*computername*. This user account is created when you install IIS, and can be viewed and managed through Active Directory Users And Computers.

The IUSR_*computername* user account is limited in that it only has guest access permissions (this account is added to the local group Guests on the computer that has IIS installed). The IUSR_*computername* account is restricted so that it can only log on locally to the IIS server and is not able to access other computers within the Windows 2003 domain. The use of the IUSR_*computername* user account allows anonymous users to access your web server without needing a unique Windows 2003 username and password.

Access Control for Users and Groups

One way you can control website access is to eliminate anonymous access. In this case, you force users to be authenticated as valid Windows 2003 users.

When users log on to your website through a valid Windows 2003 user account, you can specify that one of the following authentication methods be used:

- Integrated Windows Authentication
- Digest Authentication For Windows Domain Servers
- Basic Authentication (Password Is Sent In Clear Text)
- .NET Passport Authentication

Each of these authentication methods is covered in more detail in the "Authentication And Access Control" section of this chapter.

Access Control through Host and Network

It is possible to allow or deny website access to specific IIS services based on IP address and host names. When you define IP address restrictions, they can be set to grant or deny access.

If you grant access by default, you specify that access is allowed for all users, except those with the specific IP addresses or domain names that are explicitly defined.

If you deny access by default, you specify that access is denied for all users, except those with the specific IP addresses or domain names that are explicitly defined.

Using SSL for Encryption and Authentication

One way to ensure that you have a secure communication channel when communicating with a website via the Internet is to take advantage of Secure Sockets Layer (SSL).

SSL provides the following advantages:

- There is a secure path created between the client and the web server so that data can't be diverted to another computer.
- Because data is encrypted, even if it could be diverted to another computer, the diverting computer would not be able to decrypt the data.
- The encryption ensures that the data is delivered intact and that it has not been tampered with in any way.

SSL works through the combination of public and private keys. This is illustrated in the following example. Kevin wants to order a Roadrunner Demolition Kit from the Acme Corporation. He wants to pay by credit card, but does not want to send the credit card number over the Internet in an unsecured manner. The following process would use SSL services:

1. Kevin would access the Acme Corporation's website. When he started the payment transaction, his computer would request a copy of Acme's public key. This key could be generated from Acme or a trusted third-party security organization.

2. Kevin's credit card information would be encrypted using the public key that was provided by Acme.

3. The data would be transmitted from Kevin's computer to the Acme website.

4. At the Acme website, the corresponding Acme private key would be used to decrypt the data that contained Kevin's credit card number.

Installing IIS

In this section, you will learn how to install IIS. In order to install IIS, the following requirements must be met:

- The server must be using the TCP/IP protocol and your server must be configured with an IP address.

- If you will be publishing your web server on the Internet, you must have Internet connectivity.

- You must be logged in with Administrative rights to install IIS.

It is also recommended that you have a Domain Name System (DNS) server installed (or configure a point to a DNS server through TCP/IP properties), which is a hierarchical database that contains mappings of DNS domain names to IP addresses. You should also consider installing IIS on an NTFS volume, which will allow you to configure additional security.

To install IIS, follow these steps:

1. Select Start ➢ Control Panel ➢ Add or Remove Programs.

2. The Add Or Remove Programs dialog box will appear. Click Add/Remove Windows Components.

3. The Windows Components dialog box will appear, which is the start of the Windows Components Wizard. Highlight Application Server and then click the Details button.

4. The Application Server dialog box will appear, as in Figure 6.1. Check the box for Internet Information Services (IIS) and ASP .NET. Click the OK button.

5. In the Windows Components dialog box, click the Next button.

6. The Insert Disk dialog box will appear. Insert the Windows Server 2003 distribution CD and click the OK button.

7. The Completing The Windows Components Wizard dialog box will appear. Click the Finish button.

FIGURE 6.1   The Application Server dialog box

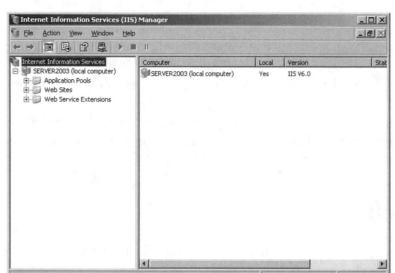

The following directories are installed as a part of IIS:

- \Inetpub
- *Windir*\Help\IisHelp
- *Windir*\System32\Inetsrv

These directories all contain user content and cannot be moved.

Configuring and Administering IIS

By default, IIS is installed and configured in highly secure mode, which allows you to serve only static content. You must manually enable the features of IIS that you want to use. Examples of features include Active Server Pages (ASP), ASP .NET Internet Server Application Programming Interface (ISAPI), and Common Gateway Interface (CGI).

The IIS console can be launched through Administrative Tools ➢ Internet Information Services (IIS) Manager or by running the Inetmgr command.

Because IIS is installed in highly secure mode, you must first "unlock" it by taking the following steps:

1. Select Start ➢ Administrative Tools ➢ Internet Information Services (IIS) Manager. You will see the dialog box shown in Figure 6.2.

2. Expand your server name. Expand the Web Service Extensions directory. You will see the Web Service Extensions listed on the right-hand side of the dialog box, as shown in Figure 6.3. Select each Web Service Extension that you want to enable and click Allow.

FIGURE 6.2   Internet Information Service (IIS)

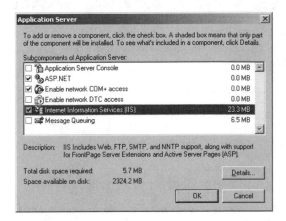

FIGURE 6.3   Web Service Extensions

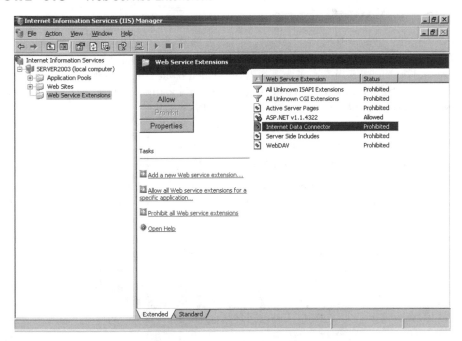

In Exercise 6.1, you will enable Web Service Extensions.

EXERCISE 6.1

Enabling Web Service Extensions

1.   Select Start ➢ Administrative Tools ➢ Internet Information Services (IIS) Manager.

EXERCISE 6.1 *(continued)*

2. Expand your server name. Expand the Web Service Extensions directory. From Web Service Extensions listed on the right-hand side of the dialog box, select Active Server Pages and click Allow.

3. Select ASP .NET v1.1.4322 and click Allow.

4. Select Internet Data Connector and click Allow.

5. Select Server Side Includes and click Allow.

6. Select WebDAV and click Allow.

In the following sections you will learn how to create a new website and how to configure websites. You will also learn how to configure default website properties.

Creating a New Website

IIS allows you to host multiple websites on a single computer. Creating a web (or FTP) site using IIS Manager does not create the actual site content, but merely creates a directory structure and configuration files. Content is published by adding it to the directory structure for a website, or by pointing that website to the physical location of the content files. To create a new website, take the following steps from the IIS console:

1. Right-click the Web Sites folder under the web server and select New ➢ Web Site from the pop-up menu.

2. The Web Site Creation Wizard starts. Click the Next button.

3. The Web Site Description dialog box appears, as shown in Figure 6.4. Type a descriptive name for your site and click the Next button.

FIGURE 6.4   Web Site Description dialog box

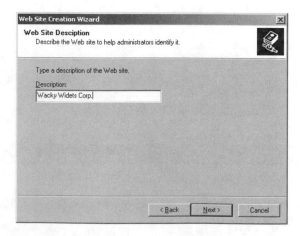

4. The IP Address And Port Settings dialog box appears, as shown in Figure 6.5. This allows you to host a different website on each IP address your computer has. You must pick an IP address that is not being used by another website. You can specify the IP address, TCP port, and host header for the website. Host headers are used to route requests to the proper website (when a computer hosts multiple websites). Configure the settings, then click the Next button.

FIGURE 6.5   The IP Address and Port Settings dialog box

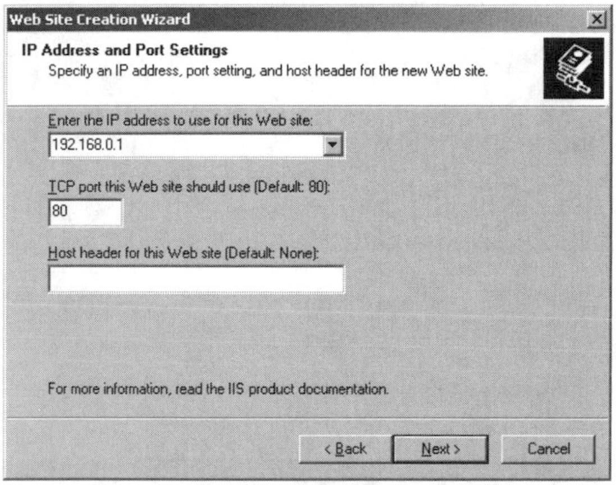

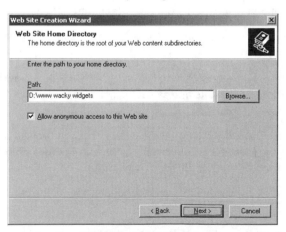

5. The Web Site Home Directory dialog box appears, as shown in Figure 6.6. Enter the path (such as D:\My Site) that will be used for the home directory. You can also specify whether anonymous access will be allowed for the website. Click the Next button.

FIGURE 6.6   Web Site Home Directory dialog box

6. The Web Site Access Permissions dialog box appears, as shown in Figure 6.7. Configure permissions (permissions are covered in the "Local Path and Permissions" section of this chapter), then click the Next button.

FIGURE 6.7 Web Site Access Permissions dialog box

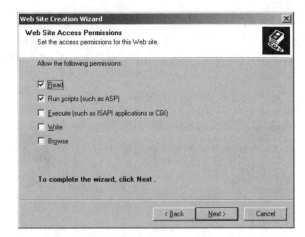

7. The Web Site Creation Wizard will tell you that you have successfully completed the Web Site Creation Wizard. Click the Finish button.

In Exercise 6.2 you will create a new website.

EXERCISE 6.2

Creating a New Web Site

1. Select Start ➢ Administrative Tools ➢ Internet Information Services (IIS) Manager.

2. Right click Web Sites and select New ➢ Web Site.

3. The Web Site Creation Wizard starts. Click the Next button.

4. The Web Site Description dialog box appears. Under Description type **Practice Web Site** and click the Next button.

5. The IP Address And Port Settings dialog box appears. Click the arrow for Enter The IP Address To Use For This Web Site and select the IP address of your Windows Server 2003 server. Click the Next button.

6. The Web Site Home Directory dialog box appears. Click the Browse button. Select Local Disk (C:) and click the Make New Folder button. Type in **Practice Web Site** for the home directory and click the OK button. Click the Next button.

7. The Web Site Access Permissions dialog box appears. Accept the default settings and click the Next button.

8. The Web Site Creation Wizard will tell you that you have successfully completed the Web Site Creation Wizard. Click the Finish button.

Now that you have created a website, you can configure and manage it as described in the following sections.

Configuring Websites

Each website hosted on the IIS server can be individually configured through its Properties dialog box, accessed by right-clicking the site and choosing Properties from the pop-up menu.

The website Properties dialog box has eight tabs with options for configuring and managing your website. The options on these tabs are described briefly in Table 6.1 and in more detail in the following sections.

TABLE 6.1   The Website Properties Dialog Box Tabs

Tab	Description
Web Site	Settings include website identification, connections, and logging
Performance	To configure performance tuning options, including bandwidth throttling and limits on connections to the website
ISAPI Filters	To set ISAPI (Internet Server Application Programming Interface) filters
Home Directory	To configure the content location, access permissions, and application settings
Documents	To set the default document users see when they access the site, as well as the option to enable a document footer
Directory Security	To configure authentication and access control (including anonymous access), IP address and domain name restrictions, and secure communications
HTTP Headers	To enable content expiration, custom HTTP headers, content ratings, and MIME types
Custom Errors	To configure a custom error message for a given HTTP error number

Each of the website property tabs is covered in more detail in the following sections.

Setting Website Properties

The Web Site tab (see Figure 6.8) includes options for identifying the website, controlling connections, and enabling logging.

FIGURE 6.8   The website Properties dialog box

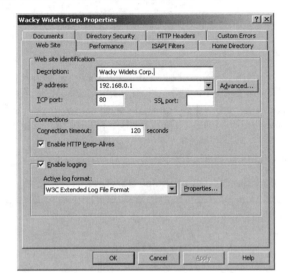

Website Identification

The description of the website appears in the Internet Information Services console. By default, the website description is the same as the name of the website. You can change the description in the Description text box.

You also configure the IP address that is associated with the site. The IP address must already be configured for the computer. If you leave the IP address at the default setting of All Unassigned, all of the IP addresses that are assigned to the computer and have not been assigned to other websites will be used.

The TCP port specifies the port that will be used to respond to HTTP requests. By default, HTTP uses TCP port 80. There are some secure environments in which the TCP port is changed to prevent malicious attacks. In this instance, it is necessary to change the port number on the client. Otherwise the client will send HTTP requests on port 80 while the server is listening for HTTP requests on a different port, and you will have a breakdown in communication.

> Common ports that are used by IIS and can be modified for additional security include FTP on port 21, Telnet on port 23, and HTTP on port 80.

Connections

The Connection Timeout is used to specify how long an inactive user can remain connected to the website before the connection is automatically terminated.

Enable HTTP Keep-Alives allows a client to maintain an open connection with the server, as opposed to opening a new connection for each HTTP request the client makes. This is an option that enhances server performance, but may degrade client performance. This option keeps the connection open, thus reducing the number of client connection attempts. Another concern with this setting is security. The longer the connection is open, the greater the chance the connection can be tapped.

Enable Logging

Logging can be enabled on the Web Site tab by checking the Enable Logging option. There are four log file formats, which you can configure to suit any third-party tracking software used to measure and chart website performance counters. This option is enabled by default.

The log file formats that are supported through IIS are:

- Microsoft IIS Log File Format
- NCSA Common Log File Format
- ODBC Logging
- W3C Extended Log File Format

For each log format you can click the Properties button to configure more specific logging properties. For example, if you select Microsoft IIS Log File Format and click the Properties button, you can configure options for the log schedule and log file directory, as shown in Figure 6.9.

FIGURE 6.9   Microsoft IIS Log File Format Logging Properties dialog box

Setting Performance Options

The Performance tab, shown in Figure 6.10, allows you to enable bandwidth throttling and limit the total website connections. IIS 6 no longer has options for performance tuning or process throttling, because the new application architecture enables these processes to be controlled on a more granular kernel level.

Bandwidth Throttling

Bandwidth is defined as the total capacity of your transmission media. IIS allows you to limit how much network bandwidth can be used by a given website. This is called *bandwidth throttling*, and it prevents a particular website from hogging bandwidth and adversely affecting the performance of the other sites on the web server. When bandwidth throttling is enabled, IIS sets it to 1024 bytes per second (minimum); the maximum is 32,767 bytes per second.

FIGURE 6.10   The Performance tab of the website Properties dialog box

Website Connections

You can allow unlimited user connections to the website (the default), or you can control the number of connections. To specify a connection limit, select the Connections Limited To radio button and enter the maximum number of connections allowed.

Setting ISAPI Filters

Internet Server Application Programming Interface (ISAPI) filters monitor HTTP requests and respond to specific events as defined through the filter. When an event triggers a filter, the request is redirected to specific ISAPI applications, which are then run. ISAPI filters are commonly used to manage customized logon authentication. The ISAPI Filters tab is shown in Figure 6.11. Filters are applied in the order in which they are listed in the list box.

Configuring Home Directory Options

The Home Directory tab, shown in Figure 6.12, includes options for the content location, access permissions, and application settings.

The home directory for the default website is C:\Inetpub\wwwroot.

FIGURE 6.11   The ISAPI Filters tab of the website Properties dialog box

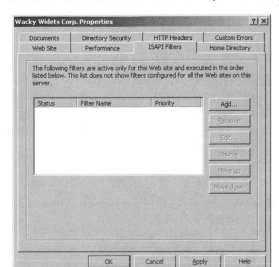

FIGURE 6.12   The Home Directory tab of the website Properties dialog box

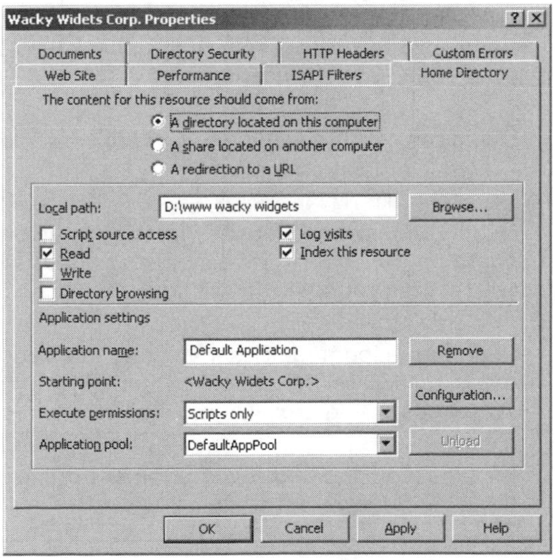

Content

The home directory points to the location of the website content. Radio buttons offer three choices for the location of the home directory:

- A Directory Located On This Computer

- A Share Located On Another Computer
- A Redirection To A URL

Local Path and Permissions

The local path points to the location of the home directory from the perspective of the web server. For instance, it may be a local directory such as F:\inetpub\wwwroot, or it may be a share on another server such as \\server2\webshare.

Access permissions define what access users have to the website. By default, users have only Read access, and Log Visits and indexing are enabled. Table 6.2 details the many security implications of each of the access permissions.

TABLE 6.2   Access Permissions

Option	Description
Script Source Access	Users can access source code for scripts, such as ASP (Active Server Pages) applications, if the user has either Read or Write permissions. Use with caution!
Read	Users can read or download files located in your home folder. This is used if your folder contains HTML files. If your home folder contains CGI applications or ISAPI applications, this option is unnecessary, and you should uncheck it so that users can't download your application files.
Write	Users can modify or add to your web content. This access should be granted with extreme caution.
Directory Browsing	Users can view the website directory structure. This option is not commonly used because it exposes your directory structure to users who access your website without specifying a specific HTML file.
Log Visits	Enables the logging of user visits to the website. In order to effectively log access, the Enable Logging box in the Web Site tab of the Properties dialog box also must be checked.
Index This Resource	Enables indexing of the home folder for use with the Microsoft Indexing Service.

Web service access permissions and NTFS permissions work together. The more restrictive of the two permissions will be the effective permission. It is recommended that you control permissions solely through NTFS permissions.

Application Settings

"Application," in this context, refers to a root directory for an executable application. The Application Name setting is the name of the root directory that contains the files and subdirectories of an executable application.

The Execute Permissions option enables an administrator to restrict or enable access as follows:

- None restricts access to static files such as HTML or image files
- Scripts Only prevents the user from running executables
- Scripts And Executables lifts all restrictions so that all file types can be either accessed or executed

Note that in IIS 6 you can set the Application Pool associated with this home directory.

Setting a Default Document

The Documents tab, shown in Figure 6.13, allows you to specify the default document users will see when they access your website unless they specify a document. Under most circumstances, the default document functions as the website's home page.

FIGURE 6.13 The Documents tab of the website Properties dialog box

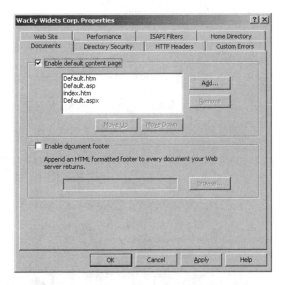

You can enable multiple documents in a preferred order. The order provides options for fault tolerance in the event that a document cannot be found—for instance, if `default.htm` was moved or renamed, `default.asp` (the second page in the order) will be used.

You can also enable document footers. A document footer is an HTML-formatted footer appended to every document the web server returns to a client.

Setting Directory Security

The Directory Security tab, shown in Figure 6.14, includes options for authentication and access control, IP address and domain name restrictions, and secure communications.

FIGURE 6.14   The Directory Security tab of the website Properties dialog box

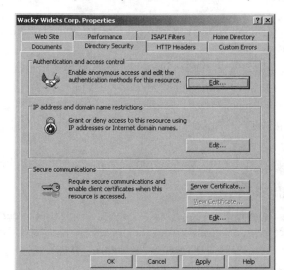

Authentication and Access Control

To enable anonymous access and edit the authentication methods used by this web resource, click the Edit button to the right of Authentication And Access Control section of the dialog box. This brings up the Authentication Methods dialog box, as shown in Figure 6.15.

FIGURE 6.15   The Authentication Methods dialog box

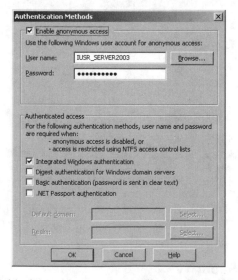

If your website is available for public use, you will most likely allow anonymous access. If you enable anonymous access, by default your computer will use the IUSR_*computername* user

account to allow this access. It is advisable to apply NTFS permissions to the web content in order to limit access from the Anonymous user account. You also have the option of using a different Windows user account for anonymous access.

There are four choices in the Authenticated access section of the Authentication Methods dialog box:

- The Integrated Windows Authentication option employs a cryptographic exchange between the web server and the user's Internet Explorer web browser to confirm the user's identity.

- The Digest Authentication For Windows Domain Servers option works only with Active Directory accounts and sends a hash value rather than a clear-text password. It works across proxy servers and other firewalls. Digest authentication requires Windows 2000 or later client computers.

- The Basic Authentication (Password Is Sent In Clear Text) option requires a Windows 2000 or Windows Server 2003 user account. If anonymous access is disabled or the anonymous account tries to access data that the account does not have permission to access, the system will prompt the user for a valid Windows 2000 user or Windows Server 2003 user account. With this method, all passwords are sent as clear text. You should use this option with extreme caution since it poses a security risk.

- The .NET Passport Authentication option is a new web authentication service that lets users of your site create a single sign-in name and password for simplified, secure access to all .NET Passport-enabled websites and services.

IP Address and Domain Name Restrictions

To control access to files, directories, and websites based on IP addresses or domain names, click the Edit button in the IP Address And Domain Name Restrictions section of the Directory Security tab. This brings up the dialog box shown in Figure 6.16.

FIGURE 6.16   The IP Address and Domain Name Restrictions dialog box

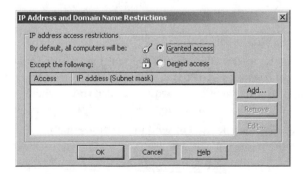

In the IP Address And Domain Name Restrictions dialog box, you can specify whether all computers will be granted or denied access and then specify exceptions. Each exception can be based on its IP address, subnet, or domain name (this requires DNS reverse lookup capabilities).

Secure Communications

Secure communications enable you to increase the security of your website by using certificates. When you click on Server Certificate, the Web Server Certificate Wizard is launched. Server Certificates are required to establish a Secure Sockets Layer (SSL) connection. An SSL connection is indicated by HTTPS: in the address bar of a browser. If a browser is using Basic Authentication, it is highly recommended that this authentication method be secured with SSL.

Configuring HTTP Headers

The HTTP Headers tab, shown in Figure 6.17, allows you to configure values that will be returned to web browsers in the HTML headers of the web pages.

FIGURE 6.17   The HTTP Headers tab of the website Properties dialog box

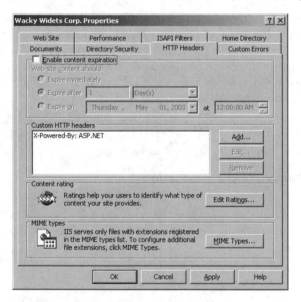

You can configure four options:

- If your website contains information that is time-sensitive, you can enable content expiration. You can set content to expire immediately, after a specified number of minutes, or on a specific date. This helps the client's web browser to determine whether it should use a cached copy of a requested page or request an updated copy of the web page from the website.

- Custom HTTP headers may be used to send instructions that may not be supported by the HTML specification that is currently in use.

- Content ratings allow you to specify appropriate restrictions if a site contains violence, sex, nudity, or adult language. Most web browsers can then be configured to block objectionable material based on how the content rating has been defined.

- MIME (Multipurpose Internet Mail Extensions) maps are used to configure web browsers so that they can view files that have been configured with different formats. MIME allows the mapping of a file extension to the application that will open that file.

Specifying Custom Error Messages

If the web browser encounters an error, it will automatically display a message specific to that error number. Through the Custom Errors tab, shown in Figure 6.18, you can customize the error message that is generated. It's as easy as creating an .HTM file, which you then map to a specific HTTP error number.

FIGURE 6.18   The Custom Errors tab of the web server Properties dialog box

In Exercise 6.3, you will manage the properties of the website you created in Exercise 6.2.

EXERCISE 6.3

Managing Websites

1. Select Start ➢ Administrative Tools ➢ Internet Information Services (IIS) Manager.

2. Expand your server name and expand Web Sites. Right-click Practice Web Site and select Properties.

3. On the Web Site tab, in the Connection Timeout option, specify **1200** seconds.

4. Click the Performance tab. Select the Connections Limited To option and specify 500 connections.

5. Click the Home Directory tab. Under the Execute Permissions option, select Scripts And Executables.

6. Click the OK button to close the Default Web Site Properties dialog box.

Configuring Default Website Properties

You can configure master properties for all websites created on a specific computer running IIS. This allows you to centrally manage all website properties. If you have websites that were configured before you set the master properties, you have the option to replace the existing configurations with the master properties. New websites will automatically inherit the master properties that you have configured.

To configure website master properties:

1. From Internet Information Services (IIS) Manager, right-click the Web Sites folder and select Properties.

2. The Web Site Properties dialog box will appear. Configure each property tab that contains properties that can be configured as default settings for all websites.

3. If you have already created websites, you will see an Inheritance Overrides dialog box that will allow you to select any child nodes of the website that you want to override existing settings for.

Once you've created a new website, it will inherit master properties. New settings in the website will override master properties.

IIS Backup

Windows Server 2003 stores most configuration information in the registry. IIS stores information in a metabase, which is a hierarchical database and is specific to IIS. In order to backup the IIS metabase you must have administrative rights.

You can create a metabase backup of IIS through the Internet Information Services (IIS) Manager through the following steps:

1. Right-click the server you want to backup and select All Tasks ➢ Backup/Restore Configuration, as shown in Figure 6.19.

FIGURE 6.19 Internet Information Services (IIS) Manager Backup/Restore Configuration option dialog box

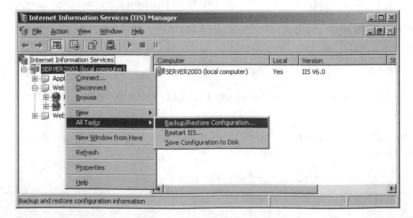

2. The Configuration Backup/Restore dialog box will appear, as shown in Figure 6.20. You will notice that an initial backup and automatic backups are created for you. To manually create a backup, click the Create Backup button.

FIGURE 6.20   Configuration Backup/Restore dialog box

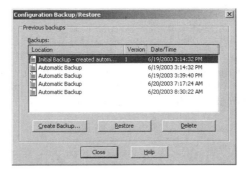

3. The Configuration Backup dialog box will appear, as shown in Figure 6.21. You should type in a Configuration Backup Name. You can also choose Encrypt Backup Using Password, which encrypts the backup and requires the password that is supplied to be used when you restore the metabase. Once you have completed the information in this dialog box, click the OK button.

FIGURE 6.21   Configuration Backup dialog box

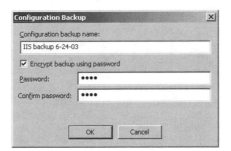

4. The Configuration Backup Name you specified will now be listed in the Configuration Backup/Restore dialog box (shown in Figure 6.20).

5. To restore the IIS metabase, you would click on the previous backup that you want to restore in the Configuration/Backup Restore dialog box and click the Restore button. If you choose to restore the metabase it will delete all of the current settings and stop all IIS services. Once the metabase is restored, the IIS services will be automatically restarted.

Troubleshooting IIS

In the event that users can't properly access your IIS server, you may need to troubleshoot IIS access. The following sections cover common troubleshooting techniques that are associated with IIS.

Pinging Your Server

If your web browser returned either the Cannot Find Server error or the Page Cannot Be Displayed error, then use the `ping` command to verify that:

- The name resolution server resolves your IIS web server's name to its IP address
- Your server responds to network requests from a remote computer

A Request Timed Out error indicates that the web server is not responding to network requests or there is some kind of network failure between the remote computer and the server.

An Unknown Host error may indicate a name resolution problem. Try to ping your server by IP address to determine whether this is the case.

If the server responds when you ping it by IP address but not by name, then you have a name resolution problem.

Verifying the Location of Content Pages

If you receive either the Under Construction or the Site You Are Trying To Reach Does Not Currently Have A Default Page error, you need to verify and/or change the location of your default website. By default, the files for your default website are located at *systemroot:*\inetpub\ wwwroot. Check the location of the home folder and also the default document configuration.

Verifying Permissions

If a specific user or group of related users cannot access the website, there are several things you should verify:

- If Anonymous access is enabled, verify the Windows account in use. Ensure that a password has not been set on this account. If one has, users will have to know it to access the site.
- Check to see if access has been denied due to IP restrictions.
- Check NTFS permissions on the home folder.

Restarting IIS

If you receive a Page Cannot Be Displayed Error, you may need to restart IIS if you cannot locate the source of the problem by using the `ping` command. Your options include starting or stopping any website on your IIS server or restarting the World Wide Web (WWW) Publishing service, which restarts IIS at the server level. Note that when you restart the WWW Publishing service, all sites running from the designated computer are affected. Only members of the local Administrator group can restart the WWW Publishing service.

In the IIS console, right-click the website that you want to restart. Note that the pop-up menu enables you to stop, start, or pause services for the website. When the site is stopped, you will see (Stopped) next to the site name in the IIS Manager. Start the server again.

Summary

In this chapter, you learned how to create, administer, and troubleshoot websites using IIS 6. We covered the following topics:

- How to install IIS. You add IIS and its optional components through the Add or Remove Programs icon in Control Panel.

- The security issues that should be addressed before you install IIS.

- How to create a new website. A single computer can host multiple websites.

- How to configure and administer IIS. The website Properties dialog box contains eight tabs full of options for your website.

- How to configure the master properties, which can be applied to all websites configured on an IIS server.

- How to create a backup of the IIS metabase, which is a hierarchical database containing all of the IIS settings.

- How to troubleshoot IIS errors and access problems. Depending on the nature of the problem, you can verify network access and name resolution, verify a website's content directory, check the access permissions, and restart IIS.

Exam Essentials

Know how to install and configure a web server.   Know how to install and configure IIS. Know which protocols are used to support different services. Know what security issues should be addressed for IIS. Be able to configure IIS security.

Troubleshoot web access problems.   List the common problems that cause users access problems and be able to correct them.

Key Terms

Before you take the exam, be certain you are familiar with the following terms:

bandwidth throttling

File Transfer Protocol (FTP)

Hypertext Transfer Protocol (HTTP)

Internet Server Application Programming Interface (ISAPI) filters

Network News Transfer Protocol (NNTP)

Simple Mail Transfer Protocol (SMTP)

Review Questions

1. When user Becky tries to browse to the intranet site via a link she created on her desktop, she gets the error "The site you are trying to reach does not currently have a default page." Other users in her department can browse to the site. How can you fix the problem?

   A. Enable Anonymous access for all users.

   B. Set the proxy server to bypass local traffic.

   C. Set Becky's browser to bypass the proxy server for local traffic.

   D. Set the Properties for the intranet site to Enable Default Content Page.

2. You are a system administrator setting up an intranet so that your users can easily locate and download the documents they need from multiple departments. You also want to make it easy for users to share files with a web browser interface. IIS is already installed. Which of the following additional services should you install to give your users the functionality that they desire?

   A. SNMP.

   B. FTP.

   C. HTTP.

   D. None of the above; all of the functionality is already included in the default IIS installation.

3. You are the administrator of a company with remote offices throughout the U.S. You want to configure services to disseminate corporate information through articles that clients can browse and search. You also want clients to have the ability to post their own articles. Of the following IIS services, which can be used to provide this functionality?

   A. SNMP

   B. NNTP

   C. FTP

   D. HTTP

   E. TCP/IP

4. None of your users can access the default.htm page on the corporate intranet. The error they get is "The page cannot be displayed." Which of the following is not a valid troubleshooting step in this scenario?

   A. Try to ping the web server by name and IP address.

   B. Stop and start the website.

   C. Restart the WWW Publishing service.

   D. Change the Windows user account for anonymous access back to IUSR_*computername*.

5. What is one way you can secure your web server against malicious attacks via HTTP?

   A. Defend the bandwidth threshold in the web server Properties.

   B. Change the anonymous access privileges to use the Windows Server 2003 Guest account.

   C. Reconfigure the website to listen for clients on TCP port 10000.

   D. Set an ISAPI filter with a rule to deny all HTTP traffic.

6. You have a corporate intranet that uses IIS services. You want to allow users the fastest access possible to the server. Which website option should you configure if you want users to maintain open connections with the server for faster access?

   A. HTTP Keep-Alives

   B. HTTP Connections Open

   C. HTTP Heartbeat

   D. HTTP Keep-Aways

7. You have an IIS server that hosts two external websites, ABCCORP.com and XYZCORP.com. You want to ensure that neither site is able to use too much of the available bandwidth. Which website performance option is used to specify how much network bandwidth will be available to the website?

   A. Bandwidth management

   B. Bandwidth allocation

   C. Bandwidth pipeline

   D. Bandwidth throttling

8. What is the default home directory for the first website created by IIS?

   A. *systemroot*:\wwwroot

   B. *systemroot*:\inetpub\www

   C. *systemroot*:\iis\wwwroot

   D. *systemroot*:\inetpub\wwwroot

9. The AcmeToyStore Corporation is configuring a website using IIS. This website will allow the public to access the company's online toy catalog. Which of the following directory security options should be configured?

   A. Anonymous access

   B. Basic access

   C. Remote access

   D. Public access

10. You have a corporate website that will be used by local and remote users. You want to ensure that security is maintained and you want users to log on to the website with either Windows 2000 or Windows 2003 user accounts and passwords. Which of the following website authentication methods require the user to present a valid Windows 2000 or Windows 2003 user account and password? (Choose all that apply.)

A. Basic authentication

B. Digest authentication for Windows domain servers

C. Integrated Windows authentication

D. Anonymous access

11. Chuck has specified that his website will use anonymous access. Users are not able to access his website. Which user account should he confirm is properly configured?

A. IUSR_*computername*

B. IUSR_IIS

C. IUSR_Anonymous

D. IIS_Anonymous

12. Your website's home page lists a special offer that expires at the end of the month. How can you configure IIS so that users don't find out about the promotion after it's over?

A. Configure HTTP Keep-Alives

B. Configure Content Expiration

C. Configure HTML Header Forwarding

D. Configure HTTP Expiration

13. Jayda manages her company's internal website. She wants users to contact her directly if they receive error 404: Not found. She creates a custom error file with the message "Error: Contact Jayda at (415) 555-1234." What steps must she take?

A. Create a file with a .ERR extension. Save it to the \inetpub directory.

B. Create a file with a .MSG extension. Save it to the \wwwroot directory.

C. Create a file with an .HTM extension. Save it to the *systemroot*:\help\iisHelp\common\ directory.

D. Create a file with either an .HTM or a .MSG extension. Save it to the *systemroot*:\help\ iisHelp\common\ directory.

14. When Kyle accesses his company's internal network, he does not see a list of the documents in the website's home folder. Since this is an internal site, the managers decide that users should be able to access a directory list. Which option should be configured?

A. Directory Browsing

B. File Lists

C. Display Contents Of Folder

D. DOS-style Directory Listing

15. You are the system administrator at a web hosting company. A particular company's website, www.FREERAZOR.com, gets a sudden increase in traffic due to a one-day special promotion they advertised. There is so much traffic to the site that it is disrupting access for all of the other websites hosted on that web server. What options can you configure to relieve the access and congestion problems for the rest of the websites on the web server? (Choose two.)

    A. In the website's Properties, limit the network bandwidth available to FREERAZOR.COM.

    B. In the web server's Properties, limit the network bandwidth available to FREERAZOR.COM.

    C. In the website's Properties, enable content expiration for FREERAZOR.COM. Indicate that website content should expire immediately.

    D. In the website's Properties, limit the number of website connections allowed to FREERAZOR.COM.

    E. In the web server's Properties, change the virtual directory for FREERAZOR.COM to point to its mirror site on a separate server.

Answers to Review Questions

1. D.   The error message "The site you are trying to reach does not currently have a default page" indicates that no default content page is configured in the Documents tab of the website's Properties. Without a default content page specified, no content can be sent to a client who does not indicate a specific page. The users who could browse to the site successfully were most likely pointing not just to the site, but to a specific page on the site, which would circumvent the error.

2. B.   The File Transfer Protocol (FTP) is used to transfer files between two TCP/IP hosts. IIS 6 does not install FTP services by default, so you must install FTP separately.

3. B.   The Network News Transfer Protocol (NNTP) is used to provide newsgroup services between NNTP servers and NNTP clients.

4. D.   This error indicates a connection or service problem, so options A through C are all valid troubleshooting options. The error has nothing to do with which Windows account is being used for anonymous access, so D is wrong.

5. C.   By default, TCP port 80 is used by IIS websites. For increased security, you can change the default TCP port used for HTTP traffic from port 80 to a unique port number. Note that clients must have their browser settings reconfigured to communicate with the web server via this unique port number.

6. A.   HTTP Keep-Alives are used to maintain open connections between the server and web clients. If this option is not selected, a new connection is opened for each client request. This option speeds up client requests, and minimizes server load.

7. D.   Bandwidth throttling is used to specify the maximum bytes per second (B/S) that the website can consume.

8. D.   The default website's home directory is *systemroot*:\inetpub\wwwroot.

9. A.   If the public will access your website, you should configure anonymous access. This will allow users to access your website using the IUSR_*computername* user account.

10. A, B, C.   If you configure your website to use basic authentication, digest authentication for Windows domain servers, or integrated Windows authentication, the user will be prompted for a Windows 2000 or Windows 2003 username and password.

11. A.   If your website is available for public use, you will most likely use anonymous access. If you allow anonymous access, by default your computer will use the IUSR_*computername* user account. You can limit the access the Anonymous user account has by applying NTFS permissions to your web content.

12. B.   If your website contains information that is time-sensitive, you can configure Content Expiration to make sure clients always get the most up-to-date pages delivered to them. You can set the content to expire immediately, after a specified number of minutes, or on a specific date. The web browser determines whether it should use a cached copy of a requested page or whether it should request an updated copy of the web page from the website.

13. C.   To create a custom error message, Jayda should create an .HTM file, which can then be mapped to a specific HTML error. By default, these files appear in the *systemroot*:\help\ iisHelp\common\ directory.

14. A.   The Directory Browsing option exposes your directory structure to users who access your website without specifying a specific HTML file.

15. A, D.   To relieve the access and congestion problems for the other websites on the same server, you can employ bandwidth throttling to limit the network bandwidth available to FREERAZOR.COM. You can also limit the number of connections allowed, which will ease the congestion problems.

Chapter

7

Managing Printing

MICROSOFT EXAM OBJECTIVES COVERED IN THIS CHAPTER:

✓ **Troubleshoot print queues.**

✓ **Monitor file and print servers. Tools might include Task Manager, Event Viewer, and System Monitor.**

- Monitor print queues.

The process of creating, managing, and deleting printers is fairly easy. When you connect a Plug and Play printer to a Windows Server 2003, it is typically recognized through the Found New Hardware Wizard. You can also manually configure printers through the Add New Printer Wizard, which will walk you through the process of installing and configuring your printer.

Each printer has an associated set of print properties, which allows you to exercise full control over how the printer is set up. For example, you can determine whether the printer is shared, whether it will use advanced features such as print pooling, and which users and groups can access the printer. In addition to using the Windows GUI utilities for print management, you can also use command-line utilities and Windows Script Host printing scripts that are included with Windows Server 2003. You will learn about printer properties and how to manage and configure them in this chapter.

You will also learn about Windows Server 2003's support for a variety of Windows print clients and non-Windows print clients. Print support is included for Unix clients, NetWare clients, and Macintosh clients.

It is also important to understand how to manage printers and print servers, which we will discuss later in this chapter. You can manage printers and print documents locally or remotely. Some of the options that can be managed for the print server include creating customized forms and specifying the location of the print spool folder.

This chapter will also show you how to monitor print queue status. You can monitor printing through the System Monitor utility, which allows you to track print queue–related counters such as how many pages have been printed and how many "out of paper" errors have occurred. You can use the Performance Logs And Alerts utility to proactively alert you when print queue events are under or over specified alert thresholds.

Finally, this chapter will focus on how to troubleshoot common printing-related problems. The modular nature of Windows printing allows you to easily identify what component is having problems and needs troubleshooting.

The printing processes used by Windows Server 2003 and Windows XP Professional are the same.

Setting Up Printers

Before you can access your physical print device under Windows Server 2003, you must first create a logical printer. After you create printers, you may need to delete or rename printers. These tasks are covered in the following sections.

If you have a Plug and Play printer that has a driver included with the Windows Server 2003 distribution CD, the printer will be recognized once it is attached to the Windows Server 2003 computer, and the Found New Hardware Wizard will automatically start and walk you through the process of installing your printer.

You can also manually create a printer using the Add Printer Wizard, which guides you through all of the steps. In order to create a new printer in Windows Server 2003, you must be logged on as a member of the Administrators or Power Users (for a member server) or Server Operators (for a server configured as a domain controller) group. You can create a *local printer*, which is a print device that is directly attached to the local computer, or a *network printer*, which is a print device that is attached to another computer on the network or a print device that has its own network card and attaches directly to the network.

The computer on which you run the Add Printer Wizard and create the printer automatically becomes the *print server* for that printer. The print server manages all of the printers that have been created on the computer. As the print server, the computer must have enough processing power to support incoming print jobs and enough disk space to hold all of the print jobs that will be queued.

To manually create a new local printer or network printer, take the following steps:

1. Select Start ➢ Printers And Faxes.

2. Click the Add Printer icon. The Add Printer Wizard will start. Click the Next button to continue.

3. The Local Or Network Printer dialog box appears. Choose Local Printer Attached To This Computer if you have a printer directly attached to computer, or choose A Network Printer, Or A Printer Attached To Another Computer if you have a printer attached to a network. If the printer is attached to the local computer, you can select Automatically Detect And Install My Plug And Play Printer. This option will automatically scan your computer for a Plug and Play printer and try to automatically install it for you. Once you make your selections, click the Next button.

4. If your printer is automatically detected, you may see the Found New Hardware Wizard, which will lead you through the process of installing the software driver. The driver may be on the CD (the installation CD that comes with the print device), on the Internet, or included with the drivers that ship with Windows Server 2003 and are already digitally signed.

5. The Print Test Page dialog box appears. If the print device is attached to your computer, you should print a test page to verify that everything is configured properly. Otherwise, you should skip this step. Click the Next button to continue.

6. The Completing The Add Printer Wizard dialog box appears. This gives you a chance to verify that all of the printer settings have been set correctly. If there are any problems, click the Back button to make corrections. If everything is configured properly, click the Finish button.

7. The new Printer will be shown in the Printer And Faxes window. By default, the printer will be shared.

If you are used to configuring printers from previous versions of Windows, you will notice that printers that are automatically detected have less setup involved. By default in Windows Server 2003, printers are automatically named based on the print driver that is installed. In addition, printers are automatically shared by default. In previous versions of Windows, this was a part of the setup process and was not automated.

In Exercise 7.1, you will see how printers are created with the Add Printer Wizard when the print device is not automatically detected. In this exercise, you will manually create two local printers—one to share and one that will not be shared. You will manually specify their print device configuration.

EXERCISE 7.1

Creating Printers

Adding the First Printer

1. Select Start ➤ Printers And Faxes.

2. Click the Add Printer icon. The Add Printer Wizard will start. Click the Next button to continue.

3. In the Local Or Network Printer dialog box, select the Local Printer Attached To This Computer radio button. Make sure that the Automatically Detect And Install My Plug And Play Printer checkbox is not checked (unless you have a print device attached to your computer) and click the Next button.

4. In the Select The Printer Port dialog box, select the Use The Following Port radio button, select LPT1 in the list box, and click the Next button.

5. In the Install Printer Software dialog box, choose HP in the Manufacturer list box and HP OfficeJet Pro 1170Cxi in the Printers list box. Then click the Next button.

6. In the Name Your Printer dialog box, leave the default name of HP OfficeJet Pro 1170Cxi and click the Next button.

7. In the Printer Sharing dialog box, select the Share As radio button and type **HPOJPro** in the Share Name text box. Then click the Next button.

8. In the Location And Comment dialog box, type **Training Room** in the Location text box and **Color Printer** in the Comment text box. Click the Next button.

9. In the Print Test Page dialog box, select the No radio button to skip printing a test page and click the Next button.

10. In the Completing The Add Printer Wizard dialog box, click the Finish button.

Adding the Second Printer

11. In the Printers And Faxes Control Panel, click the Add Printer icon.

12. When the Add Printer Wizard starts, click the Next button to continue.

13. In the Local Or Network Printer dialog box, select the Local Printer Attached To This Computer radio button. Make sure that Automatically Detect And Install My Plug And Play Printer is not checked (unless you have a print device attached to your computer) and click the Next button.

14. In the Select The Printer Port dialog box, select the Use The Following Port radio button, select LPT2 in the list box, and click the Next button.

15. In the Install Printer Software dialog box that appears, choose HP in the Manufacturer list box and HP LaserJet 4Si in the Printers list box. Then click the Next button.

16. In the Name Your Printer dialog box, leave the default name of HP LaserJet 4Si and click the Next button.

17. In the Printer Sharing dialog box, select the Do Not Share This Printer radio button and click the Next button.

18. In the Print Test Page dialog box, select No to skip printing a test page and click the Next button.

19. In the Completing The Add Printer Wizard dialog box, click the Finish button.

Managing Printer Properties

Printer properties allow you to configure options such as the printer name, whether or not the printer is shared, and printer security. To access the printer Properties dialog box, open the Printers And Faxes folder, right-click the printer you want to manage, and choose Properties from the pop-up menu.

The printer Properties dialog box has a minimum of six tabs: General, Sharing, Ports, Advanced, Security, and Device Settings. The following sections describe the properties on these tabs.

The Properties dialog boxes for some printers will contain additional tabs to allow advanced configuration of the printer. For example, if you install an HP DeskJet 970Cse printer, its Properties dialog box will have additional tabs for Color Management and Services.

Configuring General Properties

The General tab of the printer Properties dialog box, shown in Figure 7.1, contains information about the printer. It also lets you set printing preferences and print test pages.

FIGURE 7.1   The General tab of the printer Properties dialog box

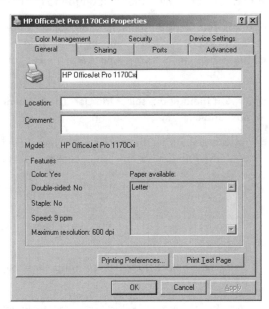

The name of the printer, the location of the printer, and comments about the printer shown here reflect your entries when you set up the printer. You can add or change this information in the text boxes.

Beneath the Comment box, you see the model of the printer. The items listed in the Features section of the dialog box depend on the model and driver you are using. The following are some examples of printer features:

- Color printing support
- Double-sided printing support
- Stapling support
- The maximum number of pages that can be printed per minute (ppm)
- The maximum resolution for the printer, in dots per inch (dpi)

At the bottom of the dialog box, you see the Printing Preferences and Print Test Page buttons. Their functions are described in the following sections.

Setting Printing Preferences

Clicking the Printing Preferences button opens the Printing Preferences dialog box, which allows you to specify the layout of the paper, page order, and paper source. This dialog box has Layout and Paper Quality tabs, as well as an Advanced button that allows you to configure more printer options.

Layout Settings

The Layout tab of the Printing Preferences dialog box, shown in Figure 7.2, allows you to specify the orientation and page order. Your choices for the Orientation setting are Portrait (vertical) or Landscape (horizontal).

FIGURE 7.2   The Layout tab of the Printing Preferences dialog box

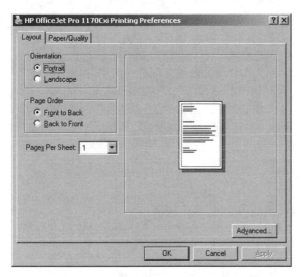

The Page Order setting specifies whether you want page 1 of the document to be on the top of the stack (Front to Back) or on the bottom of the stack (Back to Front).

The Pages Per Sheet setting determines how many pages should be printed on a single page. You might use this feature if you were printing a book and wanted two pages to be printed side by side on a single page.

Paper/Quality Settings

The Paper/Quality tab of the Printing Preferences dialog box allows you to configure properties that relate to the paper and quality of a print job. The options that are available depend on the features of your printer. For example, a printer may have only one option, such as Paper Source. For an HP OfficeJet Pro Cxi printer, you can configure Paper Source, Media, Quality Settings, and Color options, as shown in Figure 7.3.

If you are using a color ink jet printer, you can save ink and speed up the time it takes your documents to print by selecting to print documents using the Draft setting in Black & White mode.

FIGURE 7.3   The Paper/Quality tab of the Printing Preferences dialog box

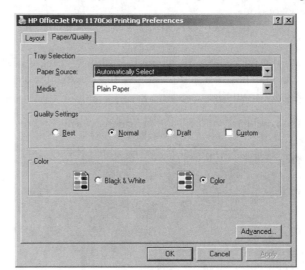

Advanced Settings

Clicking the Advanced button in the lower-right corner of the Printing Preferences dialog box opens the Advanced Options dialog box, as shown in Figure 7.4. Here, you can configure printer options such as Paper/Output, Graphic, Document Options, and Printer Features. The availability of these options depends on the specific print driver you are using.

FIGURE 7.4   The Advanced Options dialog box

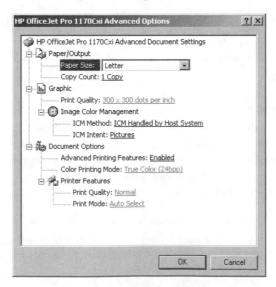

Printing a Test Page

The Print Test Page button at the bottom of the General tab of the printer Properties tab allows you to print a test page. This option is especially useful in troubleshooting printing problems. For example, you might use the Print Test Page option in a situation where no print driver is available for a print device and you want to try to use a compatible print driver. If the print job doesn't print or doesn't print correctly (it might print just one character per page, for example), you will know that the print driver isn't compatible.

Configuring Sharing Properties

The Sharing tab of the printer Properties dialog box, shown in Figure 7.5, allows you to specify whether the printer will be configured as a local printer or as a shared network printer. If you choose to share the printer, you also need to specify a share name, which will be seen by the network users. You can also select List In The Directory, which will publish the shared printer within Active Directory. This allows users to search Active Directory for printers with specific properties—for example, the ability to sort and staple or print in color.

FIGURE 7.5   The Sharing tab of the printer Properties dialog box

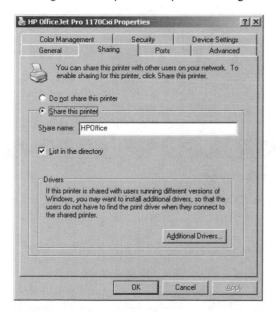

The other option that can be configured through the Sharing tab is driver support for print clients other than Windows Server 2003 clients. This is a significant feature of Windows Server 2003 print support, because it allows you to specify print drivers for additional clients to automatically download. By default, the only driver that is loaded is the Intel driver for Windows 2000, Windows Server 2003, and Windows XP. To provide the additional drivers for the clients, click the Additional Drivers button at the bottom of the Sharing tab. This opens the Additional Drivers dialog box, as shown in Figure 7.6.

FIGURE 7.6 The Additional Drivers dialog box

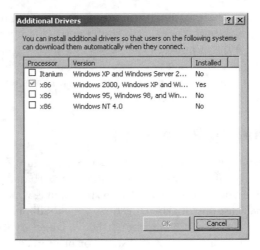

Windows Server 2003 supports adding print drivers for the following platforms:

- Itanium Windows XP or Windows Server 2003
- $x86$ Windows 2000, Windows XP, or Windows Server 2003 (default)
- $x86$ Windows 95, Windows 98, or Windows Millennium Edition
- $x86$ Windows NT 4

In Exercise 7.2, you will share an existing printer. This exercise assumes that you have completed Exercise 7.1.

EXERCISE 7.2

Sharing an Existing Printer

1. Select Start ➢ Printers And Faxes, right-click HP LaserJet 4Si, and choose Properties.

2. Click the Sharing tab.

3. Click the Shared As radio button. Accept the default value, HPLaserJ, and click the OK button.

4. Click the Apply button, then click the OK button to close the dialog box.

Once a printer has been shared, users with the Print permission can connect to the network printer through their network connection. To connect to a network printer, from My Computer open My Network Places (from the pull-down Address bar), expand Entire Network, expand Microsoft Windows Network, then Workgroup or the domain, then the computer name. Finally, click the printer to connect to it.

Configuring Port Properties

The Ports tab, shown in Figure 7.7, allows you to configure all of the ports that have been defined for printer use. A port is defined as the interface that allows the computer to communicate with the print device. Windows Server 2003 supports local ports (or physical ports) and standard TCP/IP ports (or *logical ports*). Local ports are used when the printer attaches directly to the computer. In the case where you are running Windows Server 2003 in a small workgroup, you would likely run printers attached to the local port LPT1.

FIGURE 7.7 The Ports tab of the printer Properties dialog box

Standard TCP/IP ports are used when the printer is attached to the network by installing a network card in the printer. The advantage of network printers is that they are faster than local printers and can be located anywhere on the network. When you specify a TCP/IP port, you must know the IP address of the network printer.

Along with deleting and configuring existing ports, you can also set up printer pooling and redirect print jobs to another printer, as described in the next sections.

The Enable Bidirectional Support option on the Ports tab will be available if your printer supports this feature. It allows the printer to communicate with the computer. For example, your printer may be able to send informative printer errors and status (text or verbal) messages.

Printer Pooling

Printer pools are used to associate multiple physical print devices with a single logical printer, as illustrated in Figure 7.8. You would use a printer pool if you had multiple physical printers in the same location that were the same type and could use a single print driver. The advantage of using a printer pool is that the first available print device will print your job. This is useful in situations where there is a group of print devices shared by a group of users, such as a secretarial pool.

FIGURE 7.8 Printer pooling

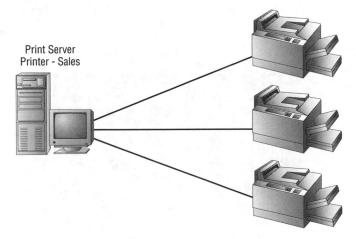

Print Server
Printer - Sales

To configure a printer pool, click the Enable Printer Pooling checkbox at the bottom of the Ports tab and then check all of the ports that the print devices in the printer pool will attach to. If you do not select the Enable Printer Pooling option, you can select only one port per printer.

> All of the print devices within a printer pool must be able to use the same print driver.

Redirecting Print Jobs to Another Printer

If your print device fails, you can redirect all of the jobs that are scheduled to be printed to that print device to another print device that has been configured as a printer. For this redirection to work, the new print device must be able to use the same print driver as the old print device.

To redirect print jobs, click the Add Port button in the Ports tab, highlight Local Port, and choose New Port. In the Port Name dialog box, type the UNC name of the printer that you want to redirect the jobs to, in the format *computername**printer_sharename*.

Configuring Advanced Properties

The Advanced tab of the printer Properties dialog box, shown in Figure 7.9, allows you to control many characteristics of the printer. You can configure the following options:

- The availability of the printer
- The priority of the printer
- The driver the printer will use

- The spooling properties
- How documents are printed
- The printing defaults
- The print processor that will be used
- The separator page

FIGURE 7.9 The Advanced tab of the printer Properties dialog box

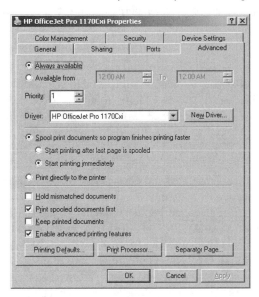

These options are covered in the following sections.

Printer Availability

Availability, or scheduling, specifies when a printer will service jobs. Usually, you control availability when you have multiple printers that use a single print device. By default, the Always Available radio button in the Advanced tab is selected, so that users can use the printer 24 hours a day. To limit the printer's availability, select the Available From radio button and specify the range of time when the printer will be available.

 Real World Scenario

Using Printer Availability to Manage Printing

You have a printer defined for the Accounting department. Typically users send small jobs to the printer, but during the month-end closing, there are several reports generated for archival purposes that are several hundred pages in length. Users who send short jobs to the printer complain about long waits while the archival reports are being printed.

Printer availability can be used to manage this situation. For example, you could schedule the large jobs to print only during a specified time, say between 10:00 P.M. and 4:00 A.M. To set this up, you would create two printers on the same port, such as printers named ACCT and REPORTS on the LPT1 port. (Both printers are on the same port since the same physical print device services them.) Configure ACCT to always be available. Configure REPORTS to be available only from 10:00 P.M. to 4:00 A.M. You would then instruct your users to send short jobs to ACCT and long jobs to REPORTS, with the understanding that print jobs sent to REPORTS print only during the specified hours. Since the long jobs are for archival purposes only, the delay should not matter.

Printer Priority

Priority is another option that you might configure if you have multiple printers that use a single print device. When you set priority, you specify how jobs are directed to the print device. For example, you might use this option when two groups share a printer and you need to control the priority in which print jobs are serviced by the print device. In the Advanced tab of the printer Properties dialog box, you can set the priority value to a number from 1 to 99, with 1 as the lowest priority and 99 as the highest priority.

As an example, suppose that a single print device is used by the accounting department. The managers in the accounting department always want their print jobs to print before the jobs created by the other workers in the accounting department. To configure this arrangement, you could create a printer called MANAGERS on port LPT1 with a priority of 99. You would then create a printer on port LPT1 called WORKERS with a priority of 1. Through the Security tab of the printer Properties dialog box, you would allow only managers to use the MANAGERS printer and allow the other accounting users to use the WORKERS printer. (Security tab options are covered later in this chapter.) When the Print Manager (which is responsible for polling the print queue for print jobs and directing the print jobs to the correct port) is polled for print jobs, it would always send the higher-priority print jobs before the lower-priority print jobs.

Print Driver

The Driver setting in the Advanced tab shows which driver is associated with your printer. If you have configured multiple printers on the computer, you can select any of the installed drivers. Clicking the New Driver button starts the Add Printer Driver Wizard, which allows you to update or add new print drivers.

Spooling

When you configure spooling options, you specify whether print jobs are spooled or sent directly to the printer. Spooling means that print jobs are saved to disk in a queue before they are sent to the printer. Consider spooling as the traffic controller of printing—it keeps all of the print jobs from trying to print at the same time.

By default, spooling is enabled, with printing beginning immediately. Your other option is to wait until the last page is spooled before printing. An analogy for these choices is the actions you can take in a grocery store cashier line. Let's say you have an entire cart full of groceries and the guy behind you has only a few things. Even if you've started loading your groceries onto the belt, as long as the cashier hasn't started with your items, you can choose to let the person with fewer items go before you, or you can make him wait. If the cashier has already started totaling your groceries, then you don't have that choice. Windows Server 2003 spooling options allow you to configure your print environment for similar situations.

In the Advanced tab, you can leave the Start Printing Immediately option selected, or you can choose the Start Printing After Last Page Is Spooled option. If you choose the latter option, a smaller print job that finishes spooling first will print before your print job, even if your job started spooling before it did. If you specify Start Printing Immediately, the smaller job will need to wait until your print job is complete.

The other main option is to Print Directly To The Printer, which bypasses spooling altogether. This option doesn't work well in a multi-user environment, where multiple print jobs are sent to the same device. However, it is useful in troubleshooting printer problems. If you can print to a print device directly, but you can't print through the spooler, then you know that your spooler is corrupt or has other problems. You also use the Print Directly To The Printer option to print from DOS.

Print Options

The Advanced tab contains checkboxes for four print options:

- The Hold Mismatched Documents option is useful when you're using multiple forms with a printer. By default, this feature is disabled, and jobs are printed on a first-in-first-out (FIFO) basis. For example, you might enable this option if you need to print on both plain paper and certificate forms. Then all the jobs with the same form will print first. Forms are discussed in more detail later in this chapter in the "Managing Print Servers" section.

- The Print Spooled Documents First option specifies that the spooler print jobs that have completed spooling before large jobs that are still spooling, even if the large print job that is still spooling has a higher priority. By default, this option is enabled, which increases printer efficiency.

- The Keep Printed Documents option specifies that print jobs should not be deleted from the print spooler (queue) when they are finished printing. You normally want to delete the print jobs as they print, because saving print jobs can take up a lot of disk space. By default, this option is disabled.

- The Enable Advanced Printing Features option specifies that any advanced features that your printer supports, such as Page Order and Pages Per Sheet, should be enabled. By default, this option is enabled. You would disable these features if there were compatibility problems. For example, if you are using the driver for a similar print device that does not support all of the features of the print device that the driver was written for, you should disable the advanced printing features.

Enabling the Keep Printed Documents option can be useful if you need to identify the source or other attributes of a finished print job. For example, this option helped track down a person who had been sending nasty notes to a co-worker. The workers knew that the notes were being printed on the company laser printer. Since the print queue was on an NTFS volume, the administrator enabled the Keep Printed Documents option and was able to identify the offender through the owner attribute of the file.

Printing Defaults

The Printing Defaults button in the lower-left corner of the Advanced tab calls up the Printing Preferences dialog box (see Figure 7.2, earlier in this chapter). This is the same dialog box that appears when you click the Printing Preferences button in the General tab of the printer Properties dialog box, and its options were covered in the "Configuring General Properties" section earlier in this chapter.

Print Processor

Print processors are used to specify whether Windows Server 2003 needs to do additional processing to print jobs, and if so, receives and alters the print job based on the data type so that the print job prints properly. The WinPrint print processor is installed and used by Windows Server 2003 by default. The WinPrint print processor supports several data types.

By default, almost all Windows-based applications use the EMF (enhanced metafile) standard to send jobs to the printer. The EMF standard uses the RAW data type, which tells the print processor that the print job does not need to be altered prior to printing. It is possible for software vendors to develop custom print processors if custom data types are required. However, this is very uncommon, and normally the print processor is left at default settings and administrator configuration is not required.

The data types supported by Windows Server 2003 WinPrint print processor are listed in Table 7.1.

TABLE 7.1   WinPrint Print Processor Data Types Supported by Windows Server 2003

Print Processor Data Type	Description
RAW	Makes no changes to the print document
RAW (FF appended)	Makes no changes to the print document except to always add a form-feed character
RAW (FF Auto)	Makes no changes to the print document except to try to detect whether a form-feed character needs to be added
NT EMF 1.00*x*	Generally spools documents that are sent from other Windows clients
TEXT	Interprets all of the data as plain text, and the printer will print the data using standard text commands

To modify your Print Processor settings, click the Print Processor button at the bottom of the Advanced tab to open the Print Processor dialog box, shown in Figure 7.10. You would generally edit the print processor in this dialog box, unless you had loaded an alternate print processor and were otherwise directed by the custom application that you are using.

FIGURE 7.10   The Print Processor dialog box

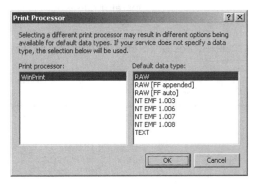

Separator Pages

Separator pages are used at the beginning of each document to identify the user who submitted the print job. If your printer is not shared, a separator page is generally a waste of paper. If the printer is shared by many users, the separator page can be useful for distributing finished print jobs.

To add a separator page, click the Separator Page button in the lower-right corner of the Advanced tab of the printer Properties dialog box. This opens the Separator Page dialog box, shown in Figure 7.11. Click the Browse button to locate and select the separator page file that you want to use. Windows Server 2003 supplies the separator files listed in Table 7.2, which are stored in the *Windir*\System32 folder.

FIGURE 7.11   The Separator Page dialog box

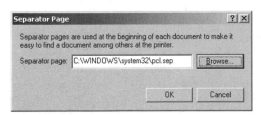

TABLE 7.2   Separator Page Files

Separator Page File	Description
pcl.sep	Used to send a separator page on a dual-language HP printer after switching the printer to PCL (Printer Control Language), which is a common printing standard

TABLE 7.2   Separator Page Files *(continued)*

Separator Page File	Description
pscript.sep	Does not send a separator page, but switches the computer to PostScript printing mode
sysprint.sep	Used by PostScript printers to send a separator page
sysprintj.sep	Same as sysprint.sep, but with support for Japanese characters

In Exercise 7.3, you will configure some advanced printer properties. This exercise assumes you have completed Exercise 7.2.

EXERCISE 7.3

Managing Advanced Printer Properties

1. Select Start ≻ Printers And Faxes, right-click HP LaserJet 4Si, and select Properties.

2. Click the Advanced tab.

3. Click the Available From radio button and specify that the printer is available from 12:00 A.M. to 6:00 A.M.

4. Click the Start Printing After Last Page Is Spooled radio button.

5. Click the Separator Page button. In the Separator Page dialog box, click the Browse button and choose the sysprint.sep file. Click the Open button, then click the OK button in the Separator Page dialog box.

6. Click the OK button to close the printer Properties dialog box.

Security Properties

You can control which users and groups can access Windows Server 2003 printers by configuring the print permissions. In Windows Server 2003, you can allow or deny access to a printer. If you deny access, the user or group will not be able to use the printer. Deny permissions override allow permissions.

You assign print permissions to users and groups through the Security tab of the printer Properties dialog box, as shown in Figure 7.12. The print permissions that can be assigned are defined in Table 7.3.

FIGURE 7.12   The Security tab of the printer Properties dialog box

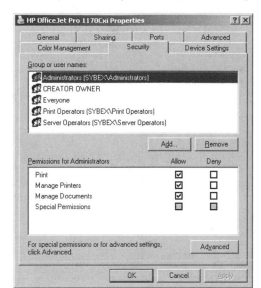

TABLE 7.3   Print Permissions

Print Permission	Description
Print	Allows a user or group to connect to a printer and send print jobs to the printer.
Manage Printers	Allows administrative control of the printer. With this permission, a user or group can pause and restart the printer, change the spooler settings, share or unshare a printer, change print permissions, and manage printer properties.
Manage Documents	Allows users to manage documents by pausing, restarting, resuming, and deleting queued documents. Users cannot control the status of the printer.
Special Permissions	By clicking the Advanced Tab in Print Permissions you can manage Special Permissions, which allows you to apply permissions to the printer or documents only.

By default, whenever a printer is created, default print permissions are assigned. The default permissions are normally appropriate for most network environments. Table 7.4 shows the default print permissions that are assigned.

TABLE 7.4   Default Print Permissions

Group	Print	Manage Printers	Manage Documents
Administrators	✓	✓	✓
Creator Owner			✓
Everyone	✓		
Print Operators	✓	✓	✓
Server Operators	✓	✓	✓

On a Windows Server 2003 server configured as a member server, you would see the Power Users group in place of the Server Operators group in the print permissions list.

Print Permission Assignment

Usually, you can accept the default print permissions, but you might need to modify them for special situations. For example, if your company bought an expensive color laser printer for the marketing department, you probably wouldn't want to allow general access to that printer. In this case, you would deselect the Allow checkbox for the Everyone group, add the Marketing group to the Security tab list, and then allow the Marketing group the Print permission.

To add print permissions, take the following steps:

1.   In the Security tab of the printer Properties dialog box, click the Add button.

2.   The Select Users, Computers, Or Groups dialog box appears. Enter the user or group name that you want to assign print permissions to and click the Add button. After you specify all of the users you want to assign permissions to, click the OK button.

3.   Highlight the user or group and select Allow or Deny access for the Print, Manage Printers, and Manage Documents permissions. Click the OK button when you are finished assigning permissions.

To remove an existing group from the permissions list, highlight the group and click the Remove button. That group will no longer be listed in the Security tab and cannot be assigned permissions.

In Exercise 7.4, you will assign print permissions. This exercise assumes that you have completed Exercise 7.1.

EXERCISE 7.4

Assigning Print Permissions

1. From your Windows Server 2003 domain controller, using the Active Directory Users And Computers utility, create two users named **Kim** and **Jennifer**. (See Chapter 3, "Managing Users, Groups, and Computers," for details on using the Active Directory Users And Computers utility.) Deselect the User Must Change Password At Next Logon option.

2. Using the Active Directory Users And Computers utility, verify that you have a group named **Execs**. (See Chapter 3 for details on creating groups.) Place Kim in the Execs group.

3. Select Start ➢ Printers And Faxes, right-click HP LaserJet 4Si, and select Properties.

4. Click the Security tab and click the Add button.

5. In the Select Users, Computers, Or Groups dialog box, type in **Execs**. Click the OK button to continue.

6. In the Security tab, highlight the **Execs** group. By default, the Allow checkbox should be selected for the Print permission. Leave the default setting. Highlight the **Everyone** group and click the Remove button. Click OK to close the Printer Properties dialog box and save the changes.

7. From your Windows XP Professional computer logon as Kim to your Windows 2003 domain.

8. Select Start ➢ Printers And Faxes and click Add a Printer.

9. The Add Printer Wizard will start. Click the Next button.

10. In the Local or Network Printer dialog box, select the A Network Printer, Or A Printer Attached To Another Computer radio button and click the Next button.

11. In the Specify A Printer dialog box, select the Find A Printer In The Directory radio button and click the Next button.

12. The Find Printers dialog box will appear. Click the Find Now button. The HP OfficeJet Pro 1170Cxi printer will be listed. Select the HP OfficeJet Pro 1170Cxi printer and click the OK button.

13. The Completing The Add Printer Wizard dialog box will appear. Click the Finish button.

14. From your Windows XP Professional computer, log on as Jennifer to your Windows Server 2003 domain.

15. Select Start ➢ Printers And Faxes and click Add a Printer.

16. The Add Printer Wizard will start, click the Next button.

17. In the Local Or Network Printer dialog box, select the A Network Printer, Or A Printer Attached To Another Computer radio button and click the Next button.

EXERCISE 7.4 *(continued)*

18. In the Specify A Printer dialog box, select the Find A Printer In The Directory radio button and click the Next button.

19. The Find Printers dialog box will appear. Click the Find Now button. The HP OfficeJet Pro 1170Cxi printer will be listed. Select the HP OfficeJet Pro 1170Cxi printer and click the OK button. Because Jennifer does not have permissions to the printer, you will see a Connect To *yourservername* dialog box that will allow you to specify a username and password that has permissions to the printer. Click the Cancel button, then click Cancel again to exit out of the Add Printer Wizard.

If you do not have a Windows XP Professional computer installed as a part of your practice network, you can still see how print permissions will be applied using your Windows Server 2003 domain controller. However, the default security settings do not allow regular users to log on interactively at a server. You can change this setting through Start ➤ Administrative Tools ➤ Domain Controller Security Policy. Expand Local Policies, then User Rights Assignment. Double-click Allow Log On Locally and click the Add User Or Group button. In the Add User Or Group dialog box, type in **Everyone** and click the OK button. In the Security Policy Setting dialog box, click the OK button. Close any open dialog boxes.

Advanced Settings

The advanced settings accessed from the Security tab allow you to configure permissions, auditing, and owner properties, and view effective printing permissions. Clicking the Advanced button in the lower-right corner of the Security tab opens the Advanced Security Settings dialog box, shown in Figure 7.13. This dialog box has four tabs:

- The Permissions tab lists all of the users and groups that have been given permission to the printer, the permission that has been granted, whether the permission was inherited, and whether the permission applies to documents or to the printer.

- The Auditing tab allows you to keep track of who is using the printer and what type of access is being used. You specify what users or groups will be audited. You can then track the success or failure of six events: Print, Manage Printers, Manage Documents, Read Permissions, Change Permissions, and Take Ownership.

- The Owner tab shows the owner of the printer (the user or group who created the printer), which you can change if you have the proper permissions. For example, if the print permissions excluded the Administrator from using or managing the printer, and the print permissions needed to be reassigned, an Administrator could take ownership of the printer and then reapply print permissions.

- The Effective Permissions tab allows you to select a user or group and view their effective permissions for the print device.

FIGURE 7.13   The Advanced Security Settings dialog box

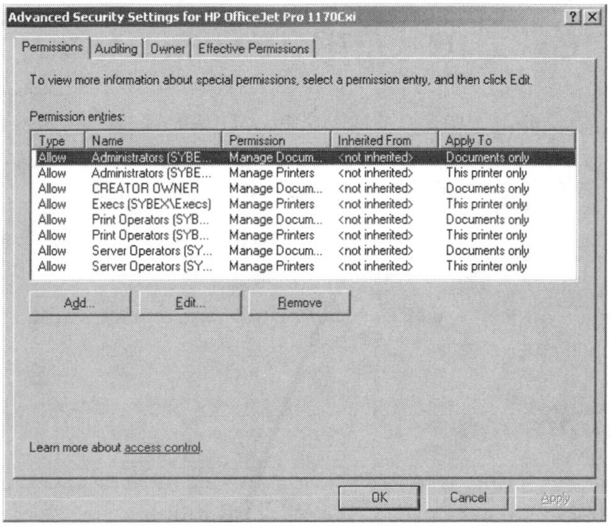

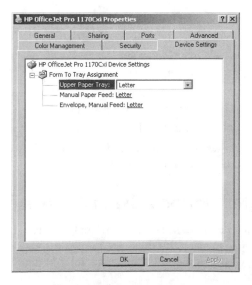

Device Settings Properties

The properties that you see on the Device Settings tab of the printer Properties dialog box depend on the printer and print driver that you have installed. You might configure these properties if you want to manage which forms are associated with tray assignments. For example, you could configure the upper tray to use letterhead and the lower tray to use regular paper. An example of the Device Settings tab for an HP OfficeJet Pro 770Cxi printer is shown in Figure 7.14.

FIGURE 7.14   The Device Settings tab of the printer Properties dialog box

Managing Printing through Command-Line Utilities and Scripts

In addition to managing your printers through the GUI interface you access through Printers And Faxes, you can also manage printing through command-line utilities and scripts.

The command-line utilities that are related to printing include:

- `Print`
- `Net Print`

The command-line utilities, as well as other print management scripts, are discussed in the following sections.

The *Print* Command

The `Print` command-line utility is used to print a text file or to display the contents of a print queue. The syntax used with the `Print` command is as follows:

`Print [/D:printer] [Drive:][Path] Filename`

The `/D:` option can be a port—for example, LPT1, LPT2, or COM1—or a network printer using the queue name `\\ComputerName\PrinterShareName`. If you are not on the drive that the file you want to print is on, you use the `Drive:` option to specify the logical or physical drive the file you want to print is located on. If you are not within the directory path that the file you want to print is on, you use the `Path:` option to specify the directory that the file you want to print is located on. `Filename` specifies the file that you want to print.

The *Net Print* Command

The `Net Print` command-line utility is used to display information about the specified print queue or to control a specific print job. The syntax used with the `Net Print` command is as follows:

`Net Print \\ComputerName\PrinterShareName`

You specify the computer that has shared the printer through `ComputerName` and the name of the shared printer though `PrinterShareName`.

You can manage a print job using the following syntax:

`Net Print [\\ComputerName] JobNumber [/hold | /release | /delete`

`JobNumber` is the job you want to manage, and the `/hold`, `/release`, or `/delete` options specify what action should be applied to the print job.

Managing Printer Options Using Scripts

Windows Server 2003 comes with several scripts that can be used to automate print management. If you have an understanding of using Windows Script Host through the `Cscript` command-line utility and how scripting works, you can automate several printing-related tasks. The scripts are located in the *Windir*\System32 folder and are executed through a command prompt using the Cscript command-line utility.

The scripts that can be used in conjunction with printing are defined in Table 7.5.

TABLE 7.5   Printing-Related Scripts Defined

Print Script	Description
Prncnfg.vbs	Used to view printer configuration, configure a printer, or rename a printer
Prndrvr.cfg	Used to list, view, or add print drivers
Prnqctl.vbs	Used to list, resume, or cancel print jobs
Prnjobs.vbs	Used to manage print queues by pausing or resuming a printer, clearing a print queue, or printing a test page
Prnmngr.vbs	Used to add, delete, or list printer connections; can also be used to obtain or set the default printer
Prnport.vbs	Used to list, add, or delete TCP/IP ports or set port configuration

Supporting Non-Windows Print Clients

The Windows Server 2003 print environment allows you to support Unix, NetWare, and Macintosh clients that want to print to Windows Server 2003 print devices. The requirements for configuring these options are defined in the following sections.

Support for Unix Clients

Unix clients send print jobs to printers via the Line Printer Remote (LPR) utility. This utility is installed on Unix clients and allows them to print files to computers that are running the Line Printer Daemon (LPD) service. Windows Server 2003 allows a Unix client to send print jobs to Windows Server 2003 printers if the following options have been configured:

1. The appropriate print driver must be available to the Unix client for the print device that the client will attach to. This is loaded at the client, as Windows Server 2003 print servers do not store Unix print drivers.

2. Verify that the Windows Server 2003 print server is using TCP/IP. The Unix client should automatically be using the TCP/IP protocol.

3. Verify that the Unix client is using a Request for Comment (RFC)–compliant version of LPR. Some versions of Unix do not use an RFC-compliant LPR. If this is the case, the client will not be able to print to Windows Server 2003.

4. Install Print Services for Unix on the Windows Server 2003 or Windows XP Professional client. Verify that the service is started and is configured to start automatically through Services.

5. Once Print Services for Unix is installed, install an LPR port. In the Name Or Address Of Server Providing LPD, you will need to provide the DNS name or IP address of the host for the printer you are adding.

6. From the Unix client, connect to the Windows Server 2003 printer using the LPR utility. The syntax used with LPR is dependent on the version of Unix you are using. This command is typical of how the LPR syntax is used:

```
lpr -S computername or ipaddress -P printsharename
```

If you want to send a document from a Windows XP Professional client to a Unix host that is using LPD, then the Windows XP Professional computer must have Print Services for Unix installed.

Support for NetWare Clients

If you want NetWare clients to be able to print to Windows Server 2003 print devices, you must install a separate product called File and Print Services for NetWare (NWLink IPX/SPX is required to support File and Print Services for NetWare) on the Windows Server 2003 print server. When this product is installed, the Windows Server 2003 server emulates a NetWare server. This software does not require any changes to the NetWare client's configuration.

Windows Server 2003 ships with Gateway Services for NetWare (GSNW). While File and Print Services for NetWare allows NetWare clients to access Windows Server 2003 resources, GSNW is used to allow Windows Server 2003 clients to access NetWare resources.

Support for Macintosh Clients

In order to allow Macintosh clients to print to a Windows Server 2003 printer, you must install Print Services for Macintosh on the Windows Server 2003 print server. To install this, follow these steps:

1. In Control Panel, select Add Or Remove Programs and then Add/Remove Windows Components.

2. Select Other Network File And Print Services and click the Details button.

3. Select Print Services For Macintosh. This software allows the Windows Server 2003 server to emulate an AppleTalk device.

No other configuration changes are required for the Macintosh client.

Windows Server 2003 Itanium versions do not support Print Services for Macintosh.

Managing Printers and Print Documents

Administrators or users with the Manage Printers permission can manage how the printer services print jobs and the print documents in a *print queue*. The print queue is a special folder on the print server that holds all of the print jobs until they are printed. When you manage a printer, you manage all of the documents in a queue. When you manage print documents, you manage specific documents.

As you would expect, you manage printers and print documents from the Printers And Faxes folder (select Start ➤ Printers And Faxes). The following sections describe the printer management and print document management options, as well as how to manage printers remotely.

Managing Printers

To manage a printer, right-click the printer you want to manage. From the pop-up menu, shown in Figure 7.15, select the appropriate option for the area you want to manage. Table 7.6 describes these options.

FIGURE 7.15   The printer management options

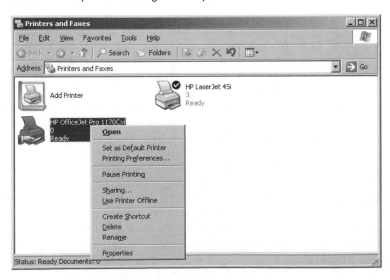

TABLE 7.6   Printer Management Options

Option	Description
Set As Default Printer	Allows you to specify the default printer that will be used when the user does not send a job to a specific printer (you will only see this option if the computer is configured to access multiple printers).
Printing Preferences	Opens the Printing Preferences dialog box (see Figure 7.2), which allows you to configure printer settings for page layout and paper quality. You can also access this dialog box through the General tab of the printer Properties dialog box, as described earlier in this chapter.
Pause Printing	Pauses the printer. Print jobs can be submitted to the printer, but they will not be forwarded to the print device until you resume printing (by unchecking this option). You might use this option if you need to troubleshoot the printer or maintain the print device.
Sharing	Allows the printer to be shared or unshared.
Use Printer Offline	Pauses the printer. Print documents will remain in the print queue, even if you restart the computer.
Create Shortcut	Used to create a shortcut to access the printer.
Delete	Removes the printer. You might use this option if you no longer need the printer, if you want to move the printer to another print server, or if you suspect the printer is corrupt and you want to delete and re-create it.
Rename	Allows you to rename the printer. You might use this option to give a printer a more descriptive name or a name that follows naming conventions.
Properties	Allows you to access the printer properties for additional configuration.

Managing Print Documents

As an Administrator or a user with the Manage Printers or Manage Documents permission, you can manage print documents within a print queue. For example, if a user has sent the same job multiple times, you might need to delete the duplicate print jobs.

To manage print documents, in the Printers And Faxes folder double-click the printer that contains the documents to open a dialog box with information about the documents in its print queue. Select Document from the menu bar to access the pull-down menu of options that you can use to manage documents, as shown in Figure 7.16. These menu options are described in Table 7.7.

FIGURE 7.16 The Document menu options

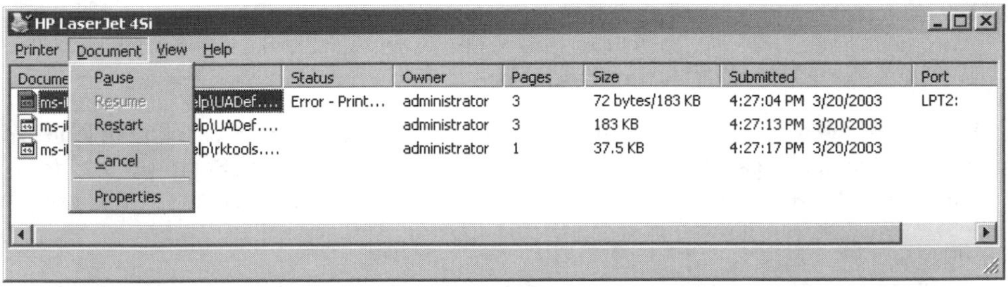

TABLE 7.7 Document Management Options

Option	Description
Pause	Places the printing of this document on hold
Resume	Allows the document to print normally (after it has been paused)
Restart	Resends the job from the beginning, even if it has already partially printed
Cancel	Deletes the job from the print spooler
Properties	Opens the document Properties dialog box, which allows you to set options such as user notification when a print job is complete, document priority, document printing time, page layout, and paper quality

In Exercise 7.5, you will manage printers and print documents. This exercise assumes you have completed the other exercises in this chapter.

EXERCISE 7.5

Managing Printers and Print Documents

1. Select Start ➤ Printers And Faxes, right-click HP LaserJet 4Si, and select Pause Printing.

2. Select Start ➤ All Programs ➤ Accessories ➤ Notepad.

3. Create a new text file and then select File ➤ Save As. In the Save As dialog box, save the file in the default location, My Documents, as **PrintMe.txt**. Click the Save button.

4. While still in Notepad, select File ➤ Print. Select HP LaserJet 4Si and click the Print button. Repeat this step two more times so that you have sent a total of three print jobs. Close Notepad.

5. Select Start ➤ Printers And Faxes ➤ HP LaserJet 4Si. At the top of the window, you will see that the status of the printer is Paused.

EXERCISE 7.5 *(continued)*

6. Right-click one of the print jobs in the print queue and select Cancel. The print job will be deleted after you confirm the cancellation.

7. Right-click one of the print jobs in the print queue and select Properties. The print job Properties dialog box appears. Change Notify from Administrator to Kim. Set the Priority from 1 to 99. For Schedule, select Only From 12:00 A.M. to 4:00 A.M. Then click the OK button.

8. Close all of the dialog boxes.

Managing Printers Remotely

Windows Server 2003 uses a stronger default level of security compared to previous versions of Windows operating systems. By default, remote printer management is not available. You can configure a printer so that it can be managed remotely through the following process:

1. Select Start ➢ Administrative Tools ➢ Active Directory Users And Computers.

2. Right-click your domain and select Properties.

3. The domain Properties dialog box will appear. Click the Group Policy tab, then click the Edit button.

4. Expand Computer Configuration, Administrative Templates, Printers to view all of the Printer Policies, as shown in Figure 7.17.

FIGURE 7.17 Group Policy Printing Policies

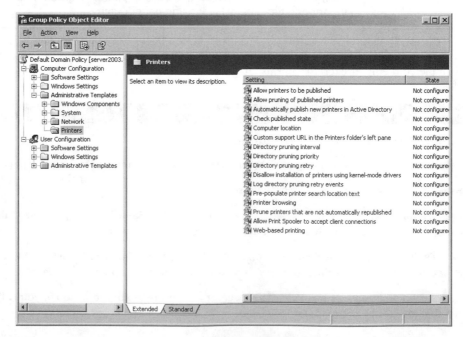

5.   Double-click the Allow Print Spooler To Accept Client Connections option. The Allow Print Spooler To Accept Client Connection Properties dialog box will appear, click the Enabled radio, then the Apply button.

6.   Stop and restart the print spooler for the change to take effect.

You can then remotely manage a printer (assuming you have the appropriate print permissions) through My Network Places and double-clicking the printer you want to manage.

If you make changes to group policy and the settings are not updates, you can refresh the group policy settings through the Gpupdate command-line utility. Gpupdate replaces the Secedit /refreshpolicy option that was used in Windows 2000.

Managing Print Servers

A print server is the computer on which printers have been defined. When you send a job to a network printer, you are actually sending it to the print server first.

You can manage print servers by configuring their properties. To access the Print Server Properties dialog box, open the Printers And Faxes folder and select File ➢ Server Properties. The Print Server Properties dialog box contains Forms, Ports, Drivers, and Advanced tabs. The properties on each of these tabs are discussed in the following sections.

Configuring Form Properties

If your printer has support for multiple trays and you use a different kind of paper in each tray, you will want to configure forms and assign them to specific trays. The Forms tab of the Printer Server Properties dialog box, shown in Figure 7.18, allows you to create and manage forms for a printer. Forms can be given any description and are configured primarily based on size.

To add a new form, take the following steps:

1.   In the Forms tab, select the Create A New Form option.

2.   Type the form name in the Form Name text box.

3.   Specify the form measurements in the Form Description area.

4.   Click the Save Form button.

You associate a form with a specific printer tray through the printer Properties dialog box, rather than through the Printer Server Properties dialog box. In the Device Settings tab of the printer Properties dialog box (see Figure 7.14 earlier in the chapter), under Form To Tray Assignment, select the paper tray that you will associate with the form. Then choose the form that will be used with the paper tray from the drop-down list.

FIGURE 7.18   The Forms tab of the Print Server Properties dialog box

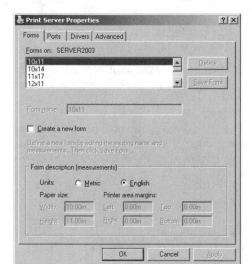

Configuring Print Server Port Properties

The Ports tab of the Printer Server Properties dialog box, shown in Figure 7.19, is very similar to the Ports tab of the printer Properties dialog box. The properties you can configure for ports were described in the "Configuring Port Properties" section earlier in this chapter. The difference between the two Ports tabs is that the one in the Print Server Properties dialog box is used to manage all of the ports for the print server, rather than the ports for a particular print device.

FIGURE 7.19   The Ports tab of the Print Server Properties dialog box

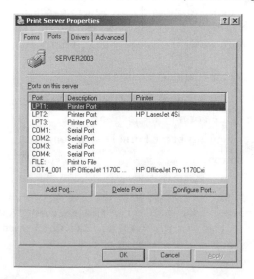

Configuring Driver Properties

The Drivers tab of the Print Server Properties dialog box, shown in Figure 7.20, allows you to manage the print drivers installed on the print server. For each print driver, the tab shows the name, the environment that the driver was written for (for example, *x*86 or Itanium), and the operating system platforms that the driver supports.

FIGURE 7.20   The Drivers tab of the Print Server Properties dialog box

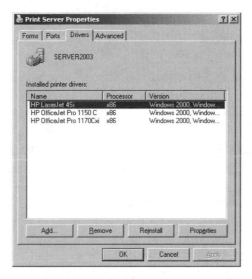

Using the options on the Drivers tab, you can add, remove, and update print drivers. To see a print driver's properties, select the driver and click the Properties button. A print driver's properties include:

- Name
- Version
- Processor
- Language monitor
- Default data type
- Driver path

Configuring Print Server Advanced Properties

The Advanced tab of the Print Server Properties dialog box, shown in Figure 7.21, allows you to configure the spool file, spooler event logging, and notifications about remote documents. You can set these:

- The spool file or hard disk location where the print files wait until they can be serviced by the print device (by default, the print spool folder is located in the *Windir*\system32\ spool\PRINTERS folder)

- Whether Error, Warning, and Information events are logged in Event Viewer (Event Viewer is covered in Chapter 10)

- Whether the print server will beep if there are errors when remote documents are printed

- Whether notification should be sent to the print server when remote documents are printed

- Whether the computer, as opposed to the user, should be notified when remote documents are printed

FIGURE 7.21   The Advanced tab of the Print Server Properties dialog box

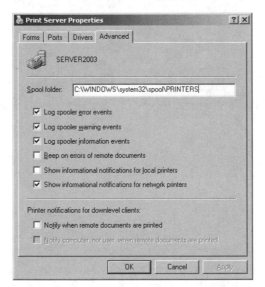

Monitoring Print Queue Status

You can monitor print queue status through the System Monitor utility. System Monitor is used to track performance-related counters for many computer objects. You monitor print queue status through the System Monitor utility using the following process:

1. Select Start ➢ Administrative Tools ➢ Performance.

2. The Performance dialog box will appear and the System Monitor utility will be selected by default, as shown in Figure 7.22.

3. Click the Add button (which looks like a Plus sign) to access the Add Counters dialog box, and then select the Print Queue Performance Object, as shown in Figure 7.23.

4. From the Add Counters dialog box, you can specify the computer you want to monitor (local computer or remote computer), the Performance Object you want to track (in this case Print Queue), the counters you want to track, and whether you want to track all instances or selected instances of the counters. All Instances will show all data from all the print queues that are defined on the computer. Selected Instances allow you to track data from individual print queues.

FIGURE 7.22   System Monitor utility

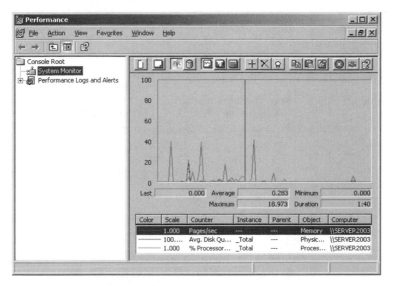

FIGURE 7.23   Add Counters dialog box

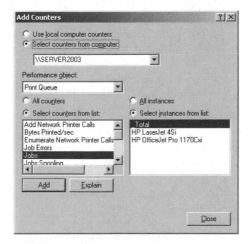

You monitor the print queue through the Print Queue performance object. The counters that can be specified for the Print Queue performance object are defined in Table 7.8.

TABLE 7.8   Print Queue Counters Defined

Print Queue Counter	Description
Add Network Printer Calls	This counter specifies how many print servers have added shared network printers to the print server. The number is cumulative from when the server was last started.

TABLE 7.8   Print Queue Counters Defined *(continued)*

Print Queue Counter	Description
Bytes Printed/Sec	The number of bytes, in real time, that have been printed on a print queue per second.
Enumerate Network Printer Calls	Specifies how many browser requests have been made to the print server from network browse lists. The number is cumulative from when the server was last started.
Job Errors	The total number of job errors that have been reported by the print queue. The number is cumulative from when the server was last started.
Jobs	Specifies the current number of print jobs that are pending in the print queue.
Job Spooling	Specifies the current number of print jobs that are being spooled to the print queue.
Max Jobs Spooling	Specifies the peak number of print jobs that have been stored in the print queue since the server was last started.
Max References	Specifies the peak number of open jobs (references) that have been sent to the printer since the server was last started.
Not Ready Errors	Shows the number of "printer not ready" errors that have been generated by the print queue. The number is cumulative from when the server was last started.
Out of Paper Errors	Shows the number of "out of paper" errors that have been generated by the print queue. The number is cumulative from when the server was last started.
References	The current (real-time) number of open jobs (references) for the printer.
Total Jobs Printed	Used to display how many print jobs have printed successfully since the server was last started.
Total Pages Printed	Used to display how many pages have printed successfully since the server was last started.

The System Monitor utility is covered in greater detail in Chapter 9, "Optimizing Windows Server 2003."

In Exercise 7.6, you will use the System Monitor utility to monitor print queue status.

EXERCISE 7.6

Monitoring Print Queue Status

1. Select Start ➤ Administrative Tools ➤ Performance.

2. From System Monitor, click the Add button (button that looks like a plus sign).

3. The Add Counters dialog box will appear.

4. Select the Print Queue Performance Object from the pull-down menu.

5. Click the All Counters radio button and the Add button. Click the Close button.

6. Minimize the Performance dialog box and send some print jobs to your print queues.

7. Maximize the Performance dialog box to view the print queue activity.

In addition to monitoring print queue events through the System Monitor utility, you can create alerts for managing print queue events through the Performance Logs And Alerts utility.

 Real World Scenario

Using System Monitor to Track Printing Usage and Problems

You are the network administrator for a Fortune 500 company. As part of your job, you need to create budgets for maintenance and new purchases for printers. Through the Help Desk, you are able to track and monitor how many tickets are created for printer maintenance. In addition, you want to track each print queue for the number of errors that are generated and how many pages are printed per printer on a monthly basis. You also want to track each printer to determine how long each print queue is during peak hours and whether users have to wait to get their print jobs.

You decide to use System Monitor to track print queue errors and usage. You include this information with your maintenance and new equipment reports to show actual usage.

Setting Alerts for Print Queue Events

The Performance Logs And Alerts utility can be used to create alerts that notify the administrator when certain counters are over or under a specified value. For example, the administrator can be alerted when the print queue reports an "out of paper" error or there are print job errors.

In the following example, an alert will be created whenever the Print Queue has more than five "out of paper" errors.

1. Select Start ➢ Administrative Tools ➢ Performance.

2. Expand Performance Logs And Alerts. Right-click Alerts and select New Alert Settings.

3. The New Alert Setting dialog box will appear. Give your alert setting a name and click the Next button.

4. The alert setting dialog box will appear, as shown in Figure 7.24. You will see three tabs: General, Action, and Schedule.

FIGURE 7.24   General tab of Alert Settings dialog box

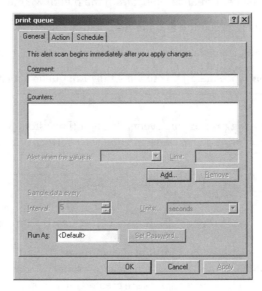

5. In the General tab, specify a comment for the alert setting (optional) and specify the counters you want to track by clicking the Add button.

6. The Add Counters dialog box will appear. In this example, you would pick the Print Queue Performance Object and the Out Of Paper Errors counter, then click the Printer's instance, click the Add button, and click the Close button.

7. You will be returned to the General tab; the counter should be displayed in the Counters listing. Select Alert When The Value Is: Over and the Limit is 5. Set the Sample Data Every field to an Interval of 5 and a Unit of Minutes.

8. Click the Action tab. You will see the dialog box shown in Figure 7.25. From the Action tab, you specify what happens when an alert is generated. You can specify Log An Entry In The Application Event Log, Send A Network Message To (a specified user), Start Performance Data Log, and/or Run This Program. In this example, we are configuring Log An Entry In The Application Event Log and Send A Network Message To Administrator. When you are done, click the Apply button.

FIGURE 7.25   Action tab of Alert Settings dialog box

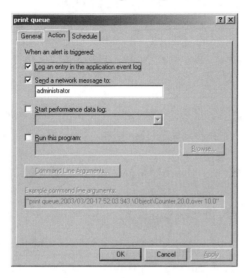

9. Click the Schedule tab. You will see the dialog box shown in Figure 7.26. From the Schedule tab, you specify whether a scan should be executed manually or at a specified date and time. You also specify when the scan should be stopped and whether a new scan should begin when an alert scan finishes.

FIGURE 7.26   Schedule tab of Alert Settings dialog box

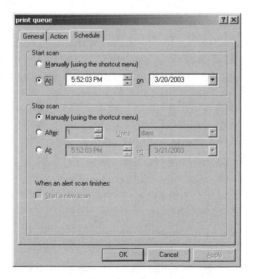

The Performance Logs And Alerts utility is covered in greater detail in Chapter 9.

Troubleshooting Printing

There are many causes for printing-related errors. In order to troubleshoot printing errors, you need to first identify the general cause of the problem. General print errors can be caused by the following:

- The printing device itself has an error.
- There is a failed physical connection between the print device and the network.
- One of the print components—for example, the print queue of the print server—is not configured properly or has an error.
- There is a problem with the network or network protocols.
- Lack of driver support.
- If some users can print but others can't, you should also check if the users who can't print have appropriate print permissions.

Based on the modularity of the Windows print environment, if you are having problems during any of the following stages, you can logically troubleshoot each print component as follows:

The print device is initially set up.   Verify that the print device is in a ready state and that you can successfully print a test page from the local printer setup process.

The printer is created through Windows Server 2003 and the printer is shared.   When the printer is being created, verify that you are logged in as an administrator or a member of the Server Operators group. Make sure that when the printer was created, the proper driver was loaded. Verify that all client drivers that are needed are loaded. Create another printer using the Add Printer Wizard to see if the problem is a corrupt logical printer.

A network client is attempting to connect to the print share.   Determine whether the problem is with a specific client or all clients. If the problem is with all clients, then it is likely that the problem is with the logical printer or the print server. Verify that the print spooler service is running and that the printer is shared. If the problem is with a specific client, verify that all client drivers that are needed are loaded and that the client has print permissions for the print share they are attempting to access. Verify that there are no group policy settings that are causing the lack of access. Make sure that all of the network connections for the clients are properly configured.

The client sends a print job to the print queue.   If the client is sending graphics, make sure the printer driver supports all of the graphic settings. See if another client can successfully send the same print job. Try to send the print job from another application (if possible) or to another printer (if possible).

The print job is sent from the print queue to the print server and the print job is spooled. Verify that there is enough space on the drive that contains the print queue to hold all of the spooled print jobs. If the print job is using the EMF standard, print using the RAW standard.

The print server redirects the print jobs to the physical print device.   Verify that the physical print device is in a ready state. Make sure the physical print device is connected to the network. Verify that the network settings are properly configured if the device is a network printer.

Summary

In this chapter, you learned how to manage printing with Windows Server 2003. We covered the following topics:

- How to create local and network printers
- Printer properties, which include general properties, sharing properties, port properties, advanced properties, security properties, and device settings
- How to manage printers through the Windows Server 2003 GUI interface or through command-line utilities or the use of the Cscript utility using script files
- Support that is included for non-Windows clients
- Print management tasks, such as setting default printers and canceling all print documents
- Document management tasks, such as pausing, resuming, and canceling print documents
- How to manage print server properties, which include form, port, driver, and advanced properties
- How to monitor print queue status through the System Monitor utility and the Performance Logs And Alerts utility
- How to troubleshoot common printing problems

Exam Essentials

Be able to set up and manage printers   Know how to install and configure Windows Server 2003 printers for general properties, sharing properties, port properties, advanced properties, and security properties.

Know how to support non-Windows clients   Support Unix, NetWare, and Macintosh clients so that they can submit print jobs to Windows Server 2003 printers.

Manage printers and print documents   Know how to manage printers and print documents and be able to troubleshoot print problems.

Manage print servers   Know the options that are used to configure print servers as opposed to individual printers and when it is appropriate to configure each option.

Monitor print queues   Be able to monitor print queues through the System Monitor utility and the Performance Logs And Alerts utility.

Be able to troubleshoot Windows Server 2003 printing   Be able to isolate what part of the print process is not working and be able to successfully troubleshoot and resolve common printing problems.

Key Terms

Before you take the exam, be certain you are familiar with the following terms:

local printer	print queue
logical ports	print server
network printer	printer pools
print processors	separator pages

Review Questions

1. Your company uses Windows Server 2003 with Active Directory. Within the network, there are a variety of clients, including Unix clients. One of the Windows Server 2003 member servers on your network is configured as a print server with a printer called ColorLaser. You have a Unix client that wants to submit jobs to the printer. The Unix client has obtained the proper Unix print driver for the print device. Which of the following options must be configured on the Windows Server 2003 print server to support printing from the Unix client?

   A. Install the DLC protocol.

   B. Install File and Print Sharing for Unix clients.

   C. Install Print Services for Unix.

   D. If TCP/IP is already installed, no further configuration is required.

2. You have a Unix client who is trying to print a document to a Windows Server 2003 printer, but is unsuccessful. You verify that the Windows Server 2003 print server is properly configured to support Unix printing. You also verify that other Unix clients are able to send print jobs to the Windows Server 2003 printer. What option should you check on the Unix client's computer that is unable to print?

   A. Verify that the Unix client is using a RFC-compliant version of LPR.

   B. Verify that the Unix client is using a RFC-compliant version of LPD.

   C. Verify that the Unix client has File and Print Services for Microsoft Networks installed.

   D. Verify that the Unix client has File and Print Services for Unix clients installed.

3. Your network uses Windows Server 2003 with Active Directory and a NetWare 4 network with NetWare clients. You have several Windows Server 2003 printers configured that the NetWare clients would like to access. Which of the following options must be installed in order for the NetWare clients to send print jobs to Windows Server 2003 printers?

   A. Install GSNW on the Windows Server 2003 print servers.

   B. Install GSNW on the NetWare clients.

   C. Install File and Print Services for NetWare on the Windows Server 2003 print servers.

   D. Install File and Print Services for NetWare on the NetWare clients.

4. Your company has an HP LaserJet 4050. You have created a printer called HP LaserJet 4050 Series PCL for use with the print device. Your users print documents on letter-sized paper and legal-sized paper. You configure the paper trays as shown in the first exhibit. You also configure the Advanced printer properties for the printer as shown in the second exhibit. The users' computers are configured to send print jobs to the appropriate print tray based on the document type they are printing. You have left the printer's security settings at the default values. What is the result of your configuration?

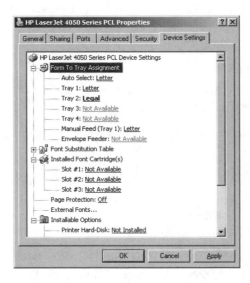 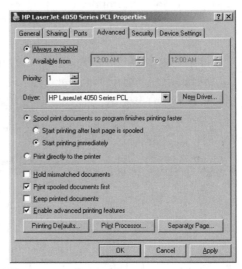

    A. Letter-sized jobs will always print first.

    B. Legal-sized jobs will always print first.

    C. You need to configure print permissions before this scenario will work.

    D. Everything is set up properly, and jobs will be printed in the order that they are spooled, regardless of the form you use.

5. You are the network administrator for a large company. You manage all of the Windows Server 2003 computers, client computers, and printers for the corporate headquarters. Your network users are complaining that it is taking a long time for jobs to print from the ExecPrinter print device. The print device is a high-speed printer and you are trying to determine whether the bottleneck is being caused by the network connection or by the print device itself. How can you track how much throughput is being processed by the print device?

    A. Track the Print Queue object, Bytes Printed/Sec counter in Performance Monitor.

    B. Track the Print Queue object, Bytes Printed/Sec counter in System Monitor.

    C. Track the Print Queue object, Total Pages Printed/Minute counter in Performance Monitor.

    D. Track the Print Queue object, Total Pages Printed/Minute counter in System Monitor.

6. Your network has a print device that is used by 20 people in the accounting department. Most of the print jobs are between one and 10 pages. However, at the end of the month, several print jobs that average 300 pages are sent to the print device. When these large print jobs are generated, you receive complaints about how long people are waiting for their shorter print jobs. What is the best solution to this problem?

    A. Specify two groups, Accountants and Reports. Create two printers that will point to the same print device called AcctPrinter and ReportPrinter. Assign the AcctPrinter priority 99 and the ReportPrinter priority 1. Specify that print jobs that are more than 50 pages be sent to the ReportPrinter printer.

    B. Create two printers that will point to the same print device called AcctPrinter and ReportPrinter. Configure the AcctPrinter so that it is available 24 hours a day and the ReportPrinter so that it is only available during off-peak hours. Instruct users to send the long print jobs to the ReportPrinter.

    C. Specify that users should submit long print jobs only when they are ready to leave for the day, so that their print jobs will print during off-peak hours.

    D. Specify that long print jobs be submitted, then placed on hold until you leave for the day, at which time they can be released.

7. Your network has a network print device that is used by 20 people in the accounting department. The accounting department has two managers, and the rest of the department is staff level. The managers have complained that sometimes they have a long wait before their print jobs are printed. They want their print jobs to always go to the top of the print queue. What is the best solution to this problem?

    A. Specify two groups, Managers and Accountants. Create two printers that will point to the same print device called ManagerPrinter and AcctPrinter. Assign the ManagerPrinter priority 99 and the AcctPrinter priority 1. Tell the regular accounting staff to send their print jobs to the AcctPrinter and the managers to send their print jobs to the ManagerPrinter.

    B. Specify two groups, Managers and Accountants. Create two printers that will point to the same print device called ManagerPrinter and AcctPrinter. Assign Print permission to the Managers group with a priority of 99. Assign Print permission to the Accountants group with a priority of 1.

    C. Specify two groups, Managers and Accountants. Create two printers that will point to the same print device called ManagerPrinter and AcctPrinter. Assign the Manager-Printer priority 99 and the AcctPrinter priority 1. Remove the Print permission from the Everyone group on the ManagerPrinter and assign the Managers group Print permission. Tell the regular accounting staff to send their print jobs to the AcctPrinter and the managers to send their print jobs to the ManagerPrinter.

    D. Specify two groups, Managers and Accountants. Create one printer called AcctPrinter. Assign the Manage Documents permission to the Managers group and leave the Everyone group with Print permission. Instruct the managers to send their jobs to the AcctPrinter and through their Manage Documents permission, place their print jobs at the top of the print queue.

8. You have users who need to print documents on letter-sized paper, legal-sized paper, and envelopes. Your print device has three paper trays and you have loaded each tray with the three types of paper that will be used. Where within the printer properties do you configure each type of paper to be associated with a different form?

   A. In the Forms tab of the Print Server Properties dialog box

   B. In the Advanced tab of the Print Server Properties dialog box

   C. In the Forms tab of the printer Properties dialog box

   D. In the Advanced tab of the printer Properties dialog box

9. You have a print device that has failed. The print device services a printer called AcctLaser1 that is located on Server1. You want to redirect the print jobs that would normally be sent to the AcctLaser1 printer to a printer called AcctLaser2 that is located on Server2. You do not want the users to need to change any of their configuration settings. What should you do?

   A. In the AcctLaser1 port properties, create a new port that is redirected to \\Server1\ AcctLaser1. Specify that AcctLaser1 will use this port.

   B. In the AcctLaser1 port properties, create a new port that is redirected to \\Server2\ AcctLaser2. Specify that AcctLaser1 will use this port.

   C. In the AcctLaser2 port properties, create a new port that is redirected to \\Server1\ AcctLaser1. Specify that AcctLaser1 will use this port.

   D. In the AcctLaser2 port properties, create a new port that is redirected to \\Server2\ AcctLaser2. Specify that AcctLaser1 will use this port.

10. You are the network administrator for a large company. You manage all of the Windows Server 2003 computers, client computers, and printers for the corporate headquarters. Several of the users in the Sales department have complained that it is taking a long time for print jobs to print because there are always print jobs printing ahead of them. The Sales department has five printers and the Marketing department has four printers. Each of the print devices has one logical printer created for the print device. You want to track print usage on all nine printers to see how much usage each printer experiences and whether you need to reallocate the printer resources. Which of the following options will best allow you to determine resource usage for each printer? (Choose the two best answers.)

    A. Track the Print Queue object, Bytes Printed/Sec counter in Performance Monitor.

    B. Track the Print Queue object, Total Jobs printed counter in System Monitor.

    C. Track the Print Queue object, Total Pages Printed/Minute counter in Performance Monitor.

    D. Track the Print Queue object, Jobs counter in System Monitor.

    E. Track the Print Queue object, Jobs Spooling counter in Performance Monitor.

    F. Track the Print Queue object, Total Pages Printed counter in System Monitor.

11. Bart sits near the network printers and is competent to manage network printing. You have decided to grant Bart the Manage Printers print permission for the AcctLaser printer. Which of the following tasks will Bart be able to accomplish? (Choose all that apply.)

   A. Pause or restart the printer.

   B. Change spooler settings.

   C. Create a new printer.

   D. Share or unshare the printer.

12. You are the network administrator for a large company. You manage all of the Windows Server 2003 computers, client computers, and printers for the corporate headquarters. One of your printers, ExecPrinter, is a color laser printer that uses very expensive consumables. You suspect that the printer is being heavily used for non-business purposes. You want to track every time a user sends a print job to this printer and what user sent the job. Which feature should you configure to track these events?

   A. Configure auditing for Print events on the printer.

   B. Configure auditing for Access events on the printer.

   C. Track usage through the System Monitor utility.

   D. Track usage through the Performance Logs And Alerts utility.

13. You are the network administrator for a large company. You manage all of the Windows Server 2003 computers, client computers, and printers for the corporate headquarters. One of the printers, SalesLaser, is not printing properly. You determine that the problem is not specific to a single user. You are now trying to determine whether the problem is with the physical print device or with the logical printer and spool file. Which of the following options will allow you to bypass the print spooler and print directly to the printer?

   A. In the General tab of the printer Properties dialog box, select Bypass Network Printing.

   B. In the Advanced tab of the printer Properties dialog box, select Bypass Network Printing.

   C. In the General tab of the printer Properties dialog box, select Print Directly To The Printer.

   D. In the Advanced tab of the printer Properties dialog box, select Print Directly To The Printer.

14. You have a new print device that attaches to the network through a network card that is installed in the print device. Which port should you specify for this device when you create the printer?

   A. Printer port

   B. Serial port

   C. Network port

   D. Standard TCP/IP port

15. You are the network administrator of a large company. You manage all of the Windows Server 2003 computers, client computers, and printers for the corporate headquarters. One of the printers is not accepting print jobs. You suspect that the print queue may be on a folder of a volume that is running out of disk space. As a part of the troubleshooting process, you want to track print jobs as they are being sent to the print spool folder. What is the default location of the print server's spool folder?

A. *Windir*\Spool

B. *Windir*\System32\Spool

C. *Windir*\system32\spool\PRINTERS

D. *Windir*\System32\Spool\Print Server

Answers to Review Questions

1. C. In order to support Unix print clients, you must install Print Services for Unix on the Windows Server 2003 print server. You should also verify that the service is started and is configured to start automatically through Services.

2. A. Verify that the Unix client is using an Request for Comments (RFC)–compliant version of LPR. Some versions of Unix do not use an RFC–compliant LPR. If this is the case, the client will not be able to print to a Windows Server 2003 printer.

3. C. If you want NetWare clients to be able to print to Windows Server 2003 print devices, you must install a separate product called File and Print Services for NetWare (NWLink IPX/SPX is required to support File and Print Services for NetWare) on the Windows Server 2003 print servers. When this product is installed, the Windows Server 2003 print server emulates a NetWare server. This software does not require any changes to the NetWare client's configuration.

4. D. Because you have multiple paper trays, and everything is configured properly, jobs will be printed as they are spooled, regardless of the form you are using. If your printer had only one print tray, then you would have to manually manage switching paper trays.

5. B. You can monitor print queue status through the System Monitor utility. System Monitor is used to track performance-related counters for many computer objects. Specifically, you can track Bytes Printed/Sec. This will allow you to see how quickly a specific print queue is processing and printing data.

6. B. You want users to be able to easily submit jobs and have those jobs automatically print at the correct time. This can be accomplished by creating two printers that are configured with different availability. You can then instruct users to send long print jobs to the printer that has availability configured for off-peak business hours.

7. C. Option A is a possible answer, but this does not prevent members of the Accountants group from sending their print jobs to the ManagerPrinter. In option C, you manage the print permissions so that only members of the Managers group can send print jobs to the ManagerPrinter. Since this printer is configured with a higher priority, its print jobs will always be serviced before jobs from the AcctPrinter.

8. A. You create new forms through the Print Server Properties dialog box. After you create the forms, you associate them with the printer through the Device Settings tab of the printer Properties dialog box.

9. B. In this case, you are redirecting the jobs from AcctLaser1 to AcctLaser2. You must modify the port properties on AcctLaser1 to point to AcctLaser2, which is \\Server2\AcctLaser2.

10. D, F. You can monitor print queue status through the System Monitor utility. System Monitor is used to track performance-related counters for many computer objects. Specifically, you should track the Total Pages Printed counter, which will tell you how busy each printer is, and the Jobs counter, which will tell you how many jobs are in the queue over a time period.

11. A, B, D.   A user or group with the Manage Printers permission has administrative control of the printer. With this permission, a user or group can pause and restart the printer, change the spooler settings, share or unshare a printer, change print permissions, and manage printer properties.

12. A.   When you access advanced security properties, you'll see the Auditing tab, which allows you to keep track of who is using the printer (by auditing the group Everyone) and what type of access is being used. You can track the success or failure of six events: Print, Manage Printers, Manage Documents, Read Permissions, Change Permissions, and Take Ownership. You could track how many pages were being printed through the System Monitor utility, but it would not show you what user was sending the print jobs.

13. D.   In the Advanced tab of the printer Properties dialog box, you can specify how you will spool print documents or whether you will print directly to the printer. If you can print directly to the printer, then you know the problem is with the print queue or the print spool as opposed to the physical print device.

14. D.   For a network printer, you create a standard TCP/IP port based on the TCP/IP address of the network device.

15. C.   When you access the Advanced tab of the Print Server Properties dialog box, you will see that the default location of the spool folder is *Windir*\system32\spool\PRINTERS. If a print queue is not accepting print jobs because the volume is out of disk space, you can specify another location for the spool folder.

Chapter

8

Administering Terminal Services

MICROSOFT EXAM OBJECTIVES COVERED IN THIS CHAPTER:

✓ **Troubleshoot Terminal Services.**

  ▪ Diagnose and resolve issues related to Terminal Services security.

  ▪ Diagnose and resolve issues related to client access to Terminal Services.

✓ **Manage servers remotely.**

  ▪ Manage a server by using Terminal Services remote administration mode.

In some network environments, it is not feasible to upgrade every client to the latest, most full-featured Windows client software. There are many reasons why a company may choose not to upgrade older computers or replace them with new computers that are powerful enough to run the latest Microsoft Windows desktop operating system and applications. Terminal Services supports networks with older client computers by allowing just about any Windows-based computer or terminal to use Terminal Services servers to handle the entire computing load for every Terminal Services client. Terminal Services can also be used for remote administration. Through Terminal Services, technical staff can perform administrative tasks on remote servers and clients with ease.

Terminal Services does require a certain amount of planning. You should make sure that the computer you use as the Terminal Services server is powerful enough to handle all of the users who will be connected to it and that your clients are able to run the client software. You also need to purchase and configure all of the proper licenses that are required to run Terminal Services.

After you have planned your Terminal Services configuration, you can begin deploying the server and client software. Terminal Services includes a configuration utility, a management utility, and a client creator tool for managing the server and clients.

In this chapter, you will learn how Terminal Services works and how to install, configure, manage, and troubleshoot Terminal Services servers and clients.

Understanding Terminal Services

The main function of a Terminal Services server is to enable what are known as *thin clients* to run application sessions directly on a Windows Server 2003. Thin clients are usually devices with simple hardware configurations, often legacy desktops, which lack the hardware resources to run the latest Microsoft Windows operating system or applications. Terminal Services turns Microsoft Windows Server 2003 into a multi-user operating system, in which multiple clients can access the server simultaneously. Such clients often include legacy personal computers, Windows CE–based handheld PCs (H/PCs), or traditional terminal clients. The term *Windows-based terminal* (*WBT*) broadly describes a class of thin-client terminal devices that can gain access to servers running a multi-user Windows operating system, such as Windows Server 2003 running Terminal Services.

In a Terminal Services environment, the only data transmitted across the wire is video, keystroke, and mouse output. The Terminal Services server executes applications and processes all information locally and sends only the data response back to the Terminal Services client. This approach allows clients to run much more powerful applications than they could run locally, as well as minimizing network bandwidth utilization between the server and client.

Clients can access Terminal Services over a local area connection or a wide area connection (for example, through a Virtual Private Network connection).

Some of the clients that can act as Terminal Services clients include:

- MS-DOS-based clients
- Windows for Workgroups clients, version 3.11 or later
- Windows-based terminals (Windows CE devices)
- Macintosh clients (with third-party software)
- Unix clients (with third-party software)

In the following sections you will learn about Terminal Services modes, benefits of Terminal Services, Terminal Services enhancements in Windows Server 2003, and Terminal Services components.

Terminal Services Modes

Terminal Services can serve either of two functions:

- *Terminal Server mode* delivers powerful user applications to computers that may be unable to run such applications locally because of hardware or other limitations.
- *Remote Desktop For Administration mode* allows administrators to perform administrative tasks on remote servers and clients from a centralized console.

Terminal Server Mode

In Terminal Server mode, the Terminal Services server enables administrators to deploy and manage enterprise applications from a central location. The server's graphical user interface is transmitted to the remote client (the thin client), and the client sends keyboard and mouse signals to the server. Users log on through any client on the network and can see only their individual session. Terminal Services manages unique client sessions transparently. Many different types of hardware devices can run the thin client software, including Windows-based terminals and computers.

You can deploy applications by installing them directly on the server or you could use Group Policy and Active Directory to publish Windows Installer application packages to a Terminal Services server or a group of Terminal Services servers. Applications can be installed by an Administrator—only on a per-server basis, and only if the appropriate Group Policy setting is enabled.

It is necessary to use a license server; each client computer that will connect to the Terminal Services server must have a Terminal Services Client Access License as well as a Client Access License for the appropriate version of Microsoft Windows. Terminal Server licensing is covered in detail in the section "Determining Proper Licensing Requirements," later in this chapter.

In Windows 2000, Terminal Server mode was called Application Server mode.

Remote Desktop For Administration Mode

The Remote Desktop For Administration mode gives system administrators the ability to remotely administer any Windows Server 2003 server over any TCP/IP connection. The administrator can access administrative graphical utilities even if the local computer they are using does not have a Windows-based operating system. Some of the tasks that can be administered include file and print sharing, edits to the Registry, and performance monitoring.

In Windows 2000, Remote Desktop For Administration mode was called Remote Administration mode.

You can use Remote Desktop For Administration mode in conjunction with Terminal Server mode to support up to two concurrent remote administration sessions. In Windows 2000, you could not use Application Server mode and Remote Desktop For Administration mode concurrently.

Benefits of Terminal Services

Terminal Services offers many benefits that could make it the most advantageous solution for your network, including:

Wider deployment of advanced desktop operating systems Rather than installing a full version of the latest Microsoft Windows client operating system on every Desktop, you can deploy Terminal Services instead. Computers whose hardware might not be supported by the full version of a new operating system can still take advantage of many of its features.

Simultaneous operation of both the thin client software and a stand-alone operating system With Terminal Services, network users can continue to use their existing computer systems, but they can also enjoy the benefits of the Windows Server 2003 environment.

Simplified application deployment Instead of installing and updating applications on every machine in the network, the administrator can install and update one copy on the Terminal Services server. This ensures that every user has access to the latest version of the application.

Remote administration of the server Terminal Services allows you to administer the server remotely. This is especially useful in enterprise environments with many servers in diverse locations. Support is included for two remote sessions, which can be used for collaboration between administrators.

Terminal Services includes many features that make it easy to use and manage. These features are described in Table 8.1.

TABLE 8.1   Terminal Services Features

Feature	Description
Multiple logon support	Users can log on multiple times simultaneously, either from many clients or from one client, and can log on to multiple servers as well. This allows users to perform several tasks at the same time.
Roaming disconnect support	A user can disconnect from a session without logging off. The session remains active while disconnected, allowing the user to reconnect at another time or from another client.
Performance enhancements	Enhanced use of caching improves performance significantly.
Clipboard redirection	Users can cut and paste between applications on the local computer and applications on the Terminal Services server.
Automated local printer support	Printers attached to clients are automatically added and reconnected.
Security	The logon process is encrypted, and administrators can specify the number of logon attempts and the connection time of individual users. Data transmitted between the server and client can be encrypted at three levels (low, medium, or high) depending on your security needs.
Session remote control	Two users can view the same session concurrently. This allows support personnel to diagnose problems or train users.
Network load balancing	Terminal Services can evenly distribute client connections across a group of servers, thus alleviating the load on any one server.
Windows-based terminals	Windows-based terminals that run on a modified version of Windows CE and Remote Desktop Protocol are available.
Client Connection Manager	This utility creates an icon on the Desktop that allows quick connectivity to servers for either single program or full Desktop access.
Terminal Services Licensing	This tool helps administrators track clients and their licenses.
Dfs support	Users can connect to a Distributed file system (Dfs) share. Administrators can host a Dfs share from a Terminal Services server.
Terminal Services Manager	This tool is used by administrators to query and manage sessions, users, and processes.
Terminal Services Configuration	This tool is used to create, modify, and delete sessions.

TABLE 8.1 Terminal Services Features *(continued)*

Feature	Description
Integration with local users and groups and the Active Directory	Administrators can create Terminal Services accounts in much the same way as they create regular user accounts.
Integration with System Monitor	System performance characteristics of Terminal Services can be tracked by System Monitor.
Messaging support	Administrators can send messages to clients.
Remote administration	Users with appropriate permissions can remotely manage all aspects of a Terminal Services server.
Configurable session timeout	Administrators can configure how long a session can remain either active or idle before disconnecting it.

Terminal Services Improvements and Enhancements for Windows Server 2003

The following features and improvements have been made for Terminal Services in Windows Server 2003:

Improved scalability   Terminal Services supports more users on high-end servers compared to the number of users that could be supported in Windows 2000. There is also support for network load balancing.

New Remote Desktop For Administration Mode   In Windows 2000, remote administration was implemented directly through the Terminal Services server. In Windows Server 2003, this component has been modularized and is implemented through Remote Desktop For Administration mode.

New Remote Desktop Connection   Remote Desktop Connection replaces the Terminal Services Client that was used to make remote connections to the server. Remote Desktop Connection uses an improved user interface, allows users to easily save connection settings, and control the Remote Desktop environment (referred to as Experience).

Terminal Services Components

Terminal Services consists of three components: the Terminal Services server, the Remote Desktop Protocol, and the Terminal Services client. The Terminal Services server communicates with the Terminal Services client using the Remote Desktop Protocol. We will look at each of these components in the following sections.

The Terminal Services Server

Most Terminal Services operations take place on the *Terminal Services server* (or Terminal Server). Applications are run on the server. The Terminal Services server sends only screen information to the client and receives only mouse and keyboard input. The server must keep track of the active sessions, and this process is completely transparent to the clients. The data itself is considered very secure because it is stored solely on the server and not on the client.

The Remote Desktop Protocol

When you install Terminal Services, the *Remote Desktop Protocol (RDP)* is automatically installed. RDP is the only connection that needs to be configured in order for clients to connect to the Terminal Services server. You can configure only one RDP connection per network adapter.

You use the Terminal Services Configuration tool to configure the properties of the RDP connection. You can set encryption settings and permissions, and limit the amount of time client sessions can remain active.

The Terminal Services Client

The *Terminal Services client* (or Terminal client) uses thin-client technology to establish a connection with the server and display the graphical user interface information that it receives from the server. This process requires very little overhead on the client's part, and it can be run on older machines that would not otherwise be able to use newer applications.

The Terminal Services client uses Remote Desktop Connection (RDC), which is the latest client software used by Terminal Services. The software that ships with Windows Server 2003 and Windows XP Professional uses Remote Desktop Protocol (RDP) 5.2, which makes significant improvements and enhancements over previous versions of Terminal Services client software.

Planning the Terminal Services Configuration

Before you can use Terminal Services, you need to determine which applications will be shared and what kind of hardware you will be using. The requirements for running a Terminal Services server are more substantial than for those servers running Windows Server 2003 without Terminal Services, especially if you are using it to run applications on the server.

You must also consider the extent and cost of licensing a Terminal Services configuration. Each client that will connect to the Terminal Services server must have a special Terminal Services client license.

In the following sections you will learn how to determine client applications and the hardware requirements for Terminal Services servers.

Determining Client Applications

Applications used with Terminal Services are installed on a per-computer basis, rather than a per-user basis. They must be available to every user who accesses the Terminal Services server.

Administrators can install applications on the Terminal Services server directly or from a remote session.

Terminal Services tends to require extra system resources to manage all of the client traffic. You should be aware of certain program characteristics that might inordinately tax the server. Intel-based programs running on Alpha machines, video-intensive applications, MS-DOS applications, and bits of code that are continuously running (such as automatic spell checkers) can drain system resources. You should limit access to these types of programs to only those users who really need them, and turn off any optional application features that might burden the server unnecessarily.

The Windows Server 2003 operating system uses a 32-bit environment (for *x*86-based computers) or a 64-bit environment (for Itanium-based computers). In order to run 16-bit applications, Windows Server 2003 must employ a system called Windows On Windows (WOW), which consumes copious system resources. Using 16-bit applications can reduce the number of users that a single processor can handle by 40 percent and can increase the amount of memory required for each user by 50 percent. Obviously, it's best to use 32-bit applications whenever possible.

You cannot run 16-bit applications on the 64-bit version of Windows 2003. Running 32-bit applications on the 64-bit platform will result in significantly reduced performance.

Determining Hardware Requirements

You will need a computer that can handle the Terminal Services loads for your Terminal Services server. The requirements for Terminal Services clients are minimal.

The hardware requirements for a Terminal Services server depend on how many clients will be connecting concurrently and the usage requirements of the clients. The following are some guidelines:

- A Terminal Services server requires at least a Pentium processor and 128MB RAM (256MB RAM to perform adequately). You should also provide an additional 10MB to 20MB RAM per client connection, depending on the applications the clients will be using. A Terminal Services server shares executable resources among users, so memory requirements for additional users running the same application are less than the requirements for the first user to load the program.

- You should use a high-performance bus architecture such as EISA, MCA, or PCI, with PCI being preferred since it is the highest performance architecture. The ISA (AT) bus cannot move enough data to support the kind of traffic that is generated by a typical Terminal Services installation.

- You should consider using a SCSI disk drive, preferably one that is compatible with Fast SCSI, Ultra WideFast, SCSI-2, or Ultra160 SCSI. For the best performance, you should use a SCSI disk with RAID, which significantly reduces disk-access time by placing data on multiple disks.

- Because many users will be accessing the Terminal Services server simultaneously, you should use a high-performance network adapter. The best solution would be to install two adapters in your machine and dedicate one to RDP traffic only.

The Terminal Services client runs well on a variety of machines, including:

- Windows-based terminal devices (embedded)

- Intel and Alpha-based computers running Windows for Workgroups 3.11, Windows 95, Windows 98, Windows Me, Windows CE, Windows NT 3.1, 3.5, and 3.51, Windows NT 4, Windows 2000, Windows XP, or Windows Server 2003

- Macintosh OS-X (with third-party software)

- Unix-based computers (with third-party software)

Installing Terminal Services Server

The Terminal Services server controls all of the thin clients that are connected to it. All Terminal Services operations actually take place on the Terminal Services server. The clients are nothing more than dumb terminals that display information sent from the server and send mouse and keyboard information to the server.

You install Terminal Services through the Add Or Remove Programs applet in Control Panel. Exercise 8.1 steps you through the process.

EXERCISE 8.1

Installing a Terminal Services Server

1. Select Start ➤ Control Panel ➤ Add Or Remove Programs.

2. In the Add Or Remove Programs window, click Add/Remove Windows Components.

3. The Windows Components Wizard will automatically start. Check the Terminal Server checkbox and click the Next button.

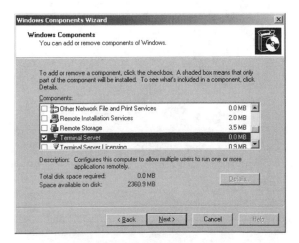

4. The Terminal Server Setup page will appear. You'll be presented with information notifying you that certain applications may not work properly after installing Terminal Services in Terminal Server mode and that you will need to have Terminal Server Licensing configured within 120 days. Click the Next button.

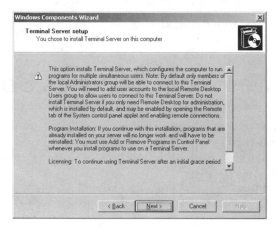

5. The Terminal Server Setup page for security settings will appear. You can select Full Security or Relaxed Security. Select the Relaxed Security option and click the Next button to continue.

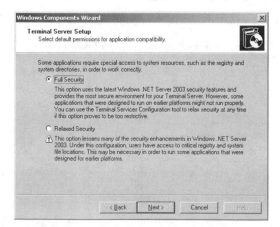

6. The appropriate files will be copied from the Windows Server 2003 distribution CD. The Completing The Windows Components Wizard page will appear. Click the Finish button.

7. The System Settings Change page will appear. This prompts you to reboot the computer. Click Yes to reboot now.

After you install Terminal Services, three new items are added to the Administrative Tools program group:

- Terminal Services Configuration
- Terminal Services Manager
- Terminal Server Licensing

The following sections describe how to configure and manage Terminal Services with the Terminal Services Configuration and Terminal Services Manager utilities. You will also learn how to license Terminal Services.

Using the Terminal Services Configuration Utility

With the *Terminal Services Configuration utility* (TSCC.msc), you can change the properties of the RDP-Tcp (Remote Desktop Protocol–Transmission Control Protocol) connection that is created when you install Terminal Services. You can also add new connections with this utility. To open Terminal Services Configuration, select Start ➢ Administrative Tools ➢ Terminal Services Configuration. The main Terminal Services Configuration window is shown in Figure 8.1.

FIGURE 8.1   The Terminal Services Configuration window

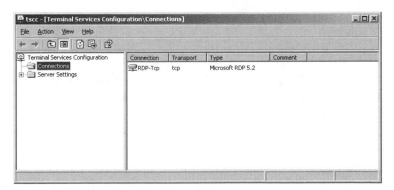

In the following sections you will learn how to manage Terminal Services connections, Terminal Services server settings, and Terminal Services user settings through the Terminal Services Configuration utility.

Configuring and Managing Terminal Services Connections

To configure the properties for a specific connection, select the Connections folder, right-click the connection (for example, RDP-Tcp) in the Terminal Services Configuration window, and select Properties from the pop-up menu. This opens the RDP-Tcp Properties dialog box. This dialog box has eight tabs: General, Logon Settings, Sessions, Environment, Remote Control, Client Settings, Network Adapter, and Permissions. The options on these tabs are described in the following sections.

Configuring General Properties

The General tab, shown in Figure 8.2, shows the connection type and transport protocol. In this tab, you can also specify a comment for the connection, select the encryption level that will be used, and choose whether or not standard Windows authentication will be used. If another authentication package has been installed on the server (besides Windows authentication), you would have the option of selecting standard Windows authentication as opposed to the authentication method that had been installed on the server.

FIGURE 8.2   The General tab of the RDP-Tcp Properties dialog box

Terminal Services uses the standard RSA RC4 encryption method when transferring data between the server and clients. You can change the level of encryption depending on your needs. The Encryption Level drop-down list has four choices:

- The Low setting encrypts data sent from the client to the server, but not from the server to the client, using a 56-bit encryption key.

- The Client Compatible setting encrypts data between the server and the client at the highest security level that can be negotiated between the server and the client. This encryption level is used with environments that support a mixture of Windows 2000 and higher and older legacy clients.

- The High setting secures data traveling in both directions. This encryption level uses a 128-bit key. If a client does not support 128-bit encryption, they will not be able to connect to the Terminal Services server.

- The FIPS Compliant setting uses Federal Information Processing Standard (FIPS) to encrypt data that is sent between the server and the client. If you enable FIPS compliance through the group policy setting System Cryptography: Use FIPS Compliant Algorithms For Encryption, Hashing, And Signing, then this option will be enabled by default and you will not be able to change the security setting for the Terminal Services connection.

Windows XP Professional and Windows XP Professional with SP1 do not support the FIPS Compliant level and cannot connect to a Windows Server 2003 server using remote assistance.

Configuring Logon Settings

The Logon Settings tab, shown in Figure 8.3, allows you to specify whether the client will provide logon information or whether the logon information will be pre-configured for the User Name, Domain, Password, and Confirm Password. You can also specify whether the user will always be prompted for a password even if the user has configured their password for automatic logon.

FIGURE 8.3   The Logon Settings tab of the RDP-Tcp Properties dialog box

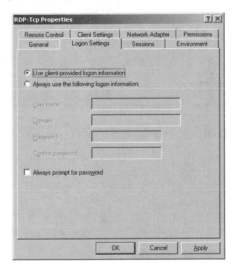

Configuring Sessions Settings

The Sessions tab, shown in Figure 8.4, allows you to configure the following option:

- The first Override User Settings selection is used to override user settings that have been configured for a user through the Active Directory Users And Computers utility. You can choose to end a disconnected session, active session, or idle session based on how long the session has been disconnected, active, or idle (time can be never, by minutes, or by days).

- The second Override User Settings selection is used to override user settings that have been configured for a user through the Active Directory Users And Computers utility. You can specify that when a session limit is reached or a connection is broken, you want to disconnect from the session or end the session. A disconnected session is saved on the server, and the disconnected user can reconnect from any client without losing any data. Ending a session closes all of the user's applications immediately, usually resulting in lost data.

- The third Override User Settings selection is used to override user settings that have been configured for a user through the Active Directory Users And Computers utility. You can allow a reconnection from any client or from a previous client.

FIGURE 8.4 The Sessions tab of the RDP-Tcp Properties dialog box

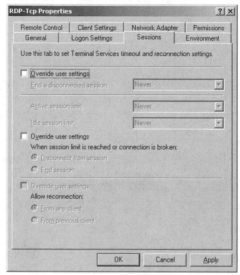

Configuring Environment Settings

The Environment tab, shown in Figure 8.5, allows you to override the settings that are created in the Active Directory Users And Computers utility or client settings that are configured in the Client Connection Manager. When this option is selected, you can configure a specific program to start when the user logs on.

FIGURE 8.5 The Environment tab of the RDP-Tcp Properties dialog box

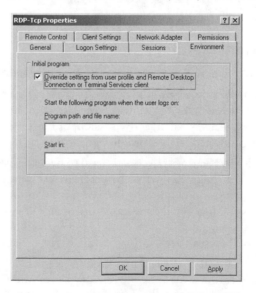

Configuring Remote Control Options

Remote control allows you to view or control a user's session from another session. You cannot control a session from the Terminal Services server console.

The Remote Control tab, shown in Figure 8.6, allows you to configure the following options:

- Use Remote Control With Default User Settings

- Do Not Allow Remote Control

- Use Remote Control With The Following Settings (with this option you can configure Require User's Permission, which allows you to configure whether the user can only view the session or can interact with the session).

FIGURE 8.6   The Remote Control tab of the RDP-Tcp Properties dialog box

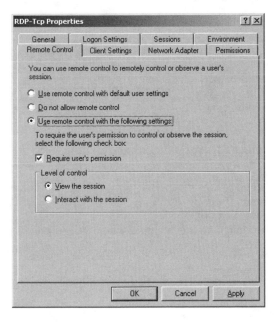

 You can access a session for remote control management through the Terminal Services Manager utility, as described in "Using Remote Desktop For Administration," later in this chapter.

Configuring Client Settings

The Client Settings tab, shown in Figure 8.7, allows you to configure connection settings and specify which options are disabled.

FIGURE 8.7   The Client Settings tab of the RDP-Tcp Properties dialog box

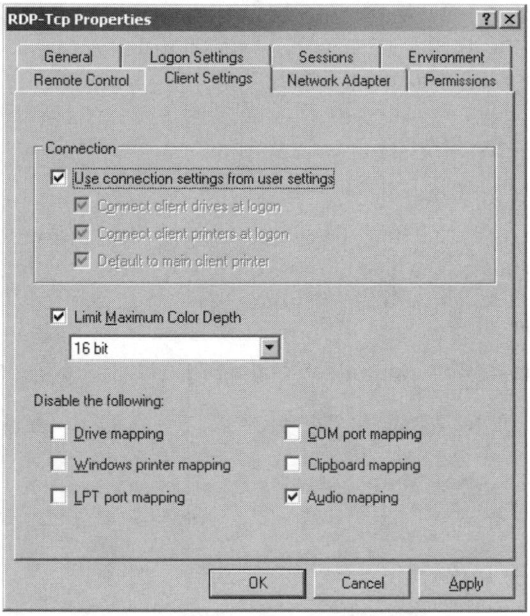

By default, mappings that a user sets in a session are lost when the user logs off. Terminal Services Configuration allows you to automatically restore the user's mappings every time he or she logs on. Users can map drives and connect to Windows printers, and can set the main client printer as the default. You can also specify whether you want to limit maximum color depth for the Terminal Services client.

In addition, you can specify whether the following options are disabled:

- Drive mapping
- Windows printer mapping
- LPT port mapping
- COM port mapping
- Clipboard mapping
- Audio mapping

Configuring the Network Adapter

The Network Adapter tab, shown in Figure 8.8, allows you to specify the network adapter that will service Terminal Services clients. You can also allow unlimited connections or set the maximum number of connections that can be made. You might choose to limit connections to conserve your server's resources and improve its ability to service clients.

FIGURE 8.8   The Network Adapter tab of the RDP-Tcp Properties dialog box

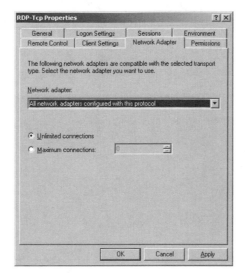

Configuring Connection Permissions

The Permissions tab, shown in Figure 8.9, allows you to configure permissions that allow or deny Terminal Services server access to users and groups. The specific permissions you can set are:

- Full Control, which allows:
  - Query Information, which queries sessions and servers for information
  - Set Information, which configures connection properties
  - Remote Control, which allows you to view or control another session
  - Logon, which logs on to a Terminal Services session
  - Logoff, which logs off another user from a session
  - Message, which sends a message to another session
  - Connect, which connects to another session
  - Disconnect, which disconnects another session
  - Virtual Channels, which uses virtual channels to provide access from a server program to client devices
- User Access, which allows:
  - Query Information, which queries sessions and servers for information
  - Logon, which logs on to a Terminal Services session
  - Connect, which connects to another session
  - Message, which sends a message to another session
- Guest Access, which allows:
  - Logon, which logs on to a Terminal Services session

- Special Permissions allow you to create a customized combination of permissions, which can be set through the Advanced button

By default, the RDP-Tcp connection that is installed with Terminal Services assigns Full Control to Administrators and User Access to Users.

FIGURE 8.9   The Permissions tab of the RDP-Tcp Properties dialog box

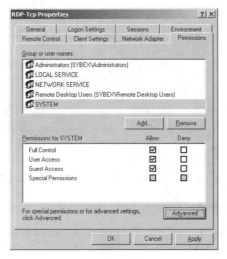

You can set specific permissions by clicking the Advanced button in the Permissions tab, which accesses the Advanced Security Settings For RDP-Tcp dialog box shown in Figure 8.10. Then click the name (the user or group) you want to set permissions for and click the Edit button. You will see the Permission Entry For RDP-Tcp dialog box (shown in Figure 8.11), which allows you to set customized Terminal Services permissions.

FIGURE 8.10   The Advanced Security Settings For RDP-Tcp dialog box

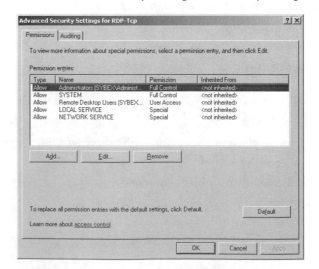

FIGURE 8.11   The Permission Entry For RDP-Tcp dialog box

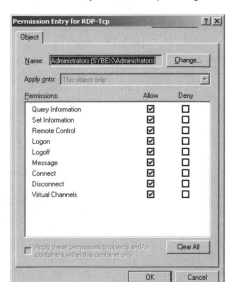

Managing Server Settings

Through the Terminal Services Configuration utility, you can also configure settings that apply to the Terminal Services server. When you click the Server Settings folder in the Terminal Services Configuration, as shown in Figure 8.12, you see configuration options defined in Table 8.2.

FIGURE 8.12   The Terminal Services Configuration\Server Settings window

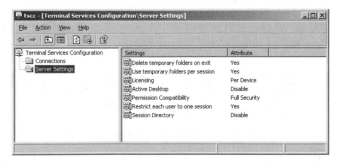

TABLE 8.2   Terminal Services Server Settings

Setting	Value	Description
Delete Temporary Folders On Exit	Yes/No	Specifies whether or not temporary folders are deleted after a session ends.

TABLE 8.2 Terminal Services Server Settings *(continued)*

Setting	Value	Description
Use Temporary Folders Per Session	Yes/No	Specifies whether or not temporary folders should be created for each session.
Licensing	Enable/Disable	Specifies whether you are using the Per Device or the Per User Licensing Mode. If you enable licensing, a license is required for each device that connects to the Terminal Services server.
Active Desktop	Enable/Disable	Turns on or off the Active Desktop. Disabling the Active Desktop conserves server resources, since the Active Desktop configuration is not passed between the Terminal Services server and the Terminal Services client.
Permission Compatibility	Full Security or Relaxed Security	Specifies whether you are using Full Security or Relaxed Security for clients accessing the Terminal Services server. Some applications may not work properly with Full Security.
Restrict Each User To One Session	Enabled/Disable	Specifies that, to conserve server resources, a user can only use a single session.
Session Directory	Enable/Disable Session Directory	Stores user session information in a Session Directory, which is used to reconnect to disconnected servers if the Terminal Services server is a part of a server cluster.

In Exercise 8.2, you will use the Terminal Services Configuration utility to configure the Terminal Services server you installed in Exercise 8.1.

EXERCISE 8.2

Configuring a Terminal Services Server

1. Select Start ➤ Administrative Tools ➤ Terminal Services Configuration.

2. In the Terminal Services Configuration window, expand the Connections folder and then right-click the RDP-Tcp connection and select Properties.

3. In the General tab of the RDP-Tcp Properties dialog box, select High from the Encryption Level drop-down list.

4. Click the Sessions tab. Check the first Override User Settings checkbox and specify 15 minutes for the Idle Session Limit option.

5. Click the Remote Control tab. Click the Use Remote Control With The Following Settings radio button and select the Interact With The Session radio button.

6. Click the OK button to close the RDP-Tcp Properties dialog box.

Managing Terminal Services Users

You can also configure properties that apply to users on a per-user basis through user Properties in the Active Directory Users And Computers utility. If you want these properties to apply to all of the users on a connection, use Terminal Services Configuration to override the individual user settings.

To set Terminal Services properties for an Active Directory user, open the Active Directory Users And Computers utility, open the folder that contains the user you want to manage (for example, the Users folder), and double-click the user account. Four of the tabs in the Active Directory user Properties dialog box contain properties that relate to Terminal Services:

- The Environment tab, shown in Figure 8.13, contains options for configuring the user's Terminal Services startup environment. This allows you to specify programs that should be started at logon and any devices that the client should connect to at logon.

FIGURE 8.13   The Environment tab of the Active Directory user Properties dialog box

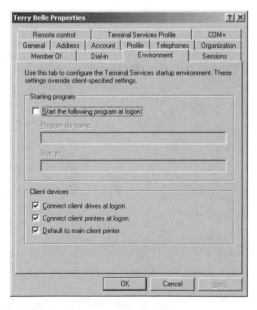

- The Sessions tab, shown in Figure 8.14, allows you to configure Terminal Services timeout and reconnection settings.

FIGURE 8.14   The Sessions tab of the Active Directory user Properties dialog box

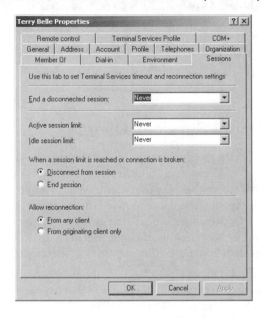

- The Remote Control tab, shown in Figure 8.15, allows you to configure Terminal Services remote control settings. You can configure whether remote control will be enabled and whether remote control access requires the user's permission.

FIGURE 8.15   The Remote Control tab of the Active Directory user Properties dialog box

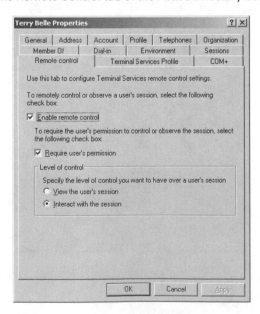

- The Terminal Services Profile tab, shown in Figure 8.16, allows you to set up a Terminal Services user profile. You can also specify the location of the Terminal Services home directory that will be used by the user.

FIGURE 8.16   The Terminal Services Profile tab of the Active Directory user Properties dialog box

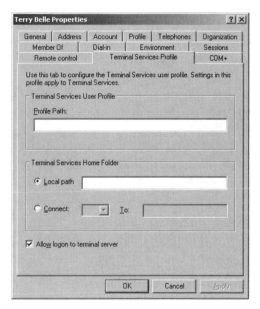

Using the Terminal Services Manager Utility

The *Terminal Services Manager utility* allows you to manage and monitor users, sessions, and processes that are connected to or running on any Terminal Services server on the network. With this utility, you can perform the following tasks:

- Display information about servers, sessions, users, and processes
- Connect to and disconnect from sessions
- Monitor sessions
- Reset sessions
- Send messages to users
- Log off users
- Terminate processes

To open Terminal Services Manager, select Start ≻ Administrative Tools ≻ Terminal Services Manager. The main Terminal Services Manager window is shown in Figure 8.17. The navigation pane on the left displays the domains, servers, and sessions. The details pane on the right has tabs that display information about the selected item in the navigation pane.

FIGURE 8.17   The Terminal Services Manager window

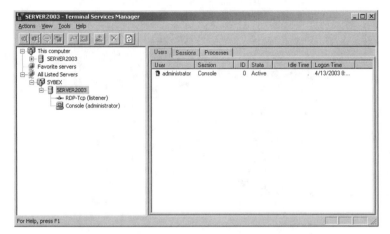

The options on the Actions menu allow you to perform several actions on sessions and processes. Most of these actions require special permissions. The Actions menu options are described in Table 8.3.

TABLE 8.3   Terminal Services Manager Actions Menu Options

Action	Description	Permission Required
Connect	Allows a user to connect to a session from another session. This option can be used only from a session; it cannot be used from the console.	Full Control or User Access
Disconnect	Disconnects a user from a session. The session is saved, and all running applications continue to run.	Full Control
Send Message	Allows a user to send a message to any or all sessions.	Full Control or User Access
Remote Control	Allows a user to use the session to view or control another user's session. Sessions cannot be controlled from the console.	Full Control
Reset	Immediately ends a session. Any unsaved data will be lost.	Full Control

TABLE 8.3   Terminal Services Manager Actions Menu Options *(continued)*

Action	Description	Permission Required
Status	Displays information about a session, such as bytes sent and received.	Full Control or User Access
Log Off	Logs off a user from a session.	Full Control
End Process	Ends a process on a session. This is useful if a program has crashed and is no longer responding.	Full Control

Using Terminal Services Licensing

Terminal Services uses its own licensing method. A Terminal Services client must receive a valid license from a Terminal Services *license server* before logging on to a Terminal Services server to run applications. For remote administration, two concurrent client sessions are allowed automatically; you do not need to receive a license from a license server.

You can enable Terminal Services Licensing when you install Windows Server 2003 or later, through the Add or Remove Programs icon in Control Panel. When you enable Terminal Services Licensing, you can select between two types of license servers:

- An enterprise license server can serve Terminal Services servers on any Windows Server 2003 or Windows 2000 domain, but cannot serve workgroups or Windows NT 4 domains.

- A domain license server can serve only Terminal Services servers that are in the same domain. In Windows Server 2003 or 2000 domains, domain license servers must be installed on domain controllers. In workgroups or Windows NT 4 domains, domain license servers can be installed on any member server.

In order to deploy Terminal Services, you will be required to obtain server and client licenses. The licenses you may need are described in Table 8.4.

TABLE 8.4   Terminal Services Licenses

License	Description
Windows Server 2003 license	This server license is included when you purchase Windows Server 2003.
Windows Server 2003 Client Access license	This license is required for all computers or Terminal Services clients that connect to a Windows Server 2003 server. This license is required by all connecting computers to use file, print, and other network services, regardless of whether they are using Terminal Services.

TABLE 8.4   Terminal Services Licenses *(continued)*

License	Description
Windows Server 2003 Terminal Services Client Access license	Every Terminal Services client needs to have a Windows Terminal Services Client Access license in addition to a Windows Server 2003 Client Access license. This license provides each Terminal Services client the right to connect to a Terminal Services server and run applications on the server.
Windows Terminal Services Internet Connector license	This license can be purchased and used separately from the client access licenses described above. This license allows up to 200 clients to connect anonymously from the Internet. This is useful for providing Windows-based applications to the public without porting them to a web-based format.
Work At Home Windows Terminal Services Client Access license	This license is required for users who want to use Terminal Services to access the Windows Desktop and applications from home. You can purchase a Work At Home Windows Terminal Services Client Access license for each Terminal Services Client Access license owned. The Work At Home license includes a Windows Server Client Access license, but does not include application licenses, which must be purchased separately.

The first time a client attempts to log on to the Terminal Services server, the server will recognize that the client has not been issued a license and will locate a license server to issue a license to the client. This license is a digitally signed certificate that will remain with the client forever and cannot be used by any other client.

Before you can begin using a license server, you must activate it through the Microsoft Clearinghouse using the Terminal Services Licensing tool.

You can configure Terminal Services Licensing through the following steps:

1. Select Start ➢ Control Panel ➢ Add Or Remove Programs.

2. Click the Add/Remove Windows Components option.

3. The Windows Components Wizard starts. Check the Terminal Services Licensing checkbox and click the Next button.

4. The Terminal Services Licensing Setup dialog box appears, as shown in Figure 8.18. Specify whether the license server will be available for your entire enterprise, or for your domain or workgroup. You can accept the default location for where the license database server should be stored or select an alternate location. Click the Next button.

5. If your Windows Server 2003 distribution CD is not already in the CD-ROM drive, you will be prompted to insert the Windows Server 2003 distribution CD so that the necessary files can be copied.

6. The Completing The Windows Components Wizard dialog box appears. Click the Finish button. Close the Add/Remove Windows Components window.

FIGURE 8.18 Terminal Services Licensing Setup dialog box

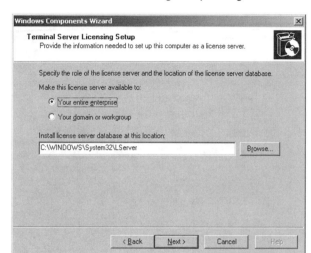

7. Select Start ➤ Administrative Tools ➤ Terminal Services Licensing.

8. The Terminal Server Licensing utility starts, as shown in Figure 8.19. Note that even though you have installed a license server, it is not activated by default. Right-click your license server and select Activate Server.

FIGURE 8.19 The Terminal Server Licensing window

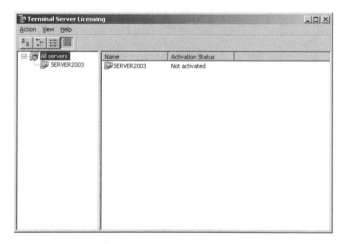

9. The Terminal Server License Activation Wizard will start. Click the Next button.

10. The Connection Method dialog box appears, as shown in Figure 8.20. You can choose to connect to the Microsoft Clearinghouse by one of three methods: Automatic, Web Browser, or Telephone. In this example, we will connect by telephone. Select the Telephone option and click the Next button.

FIGURE 8.20 Connection Method dialog box

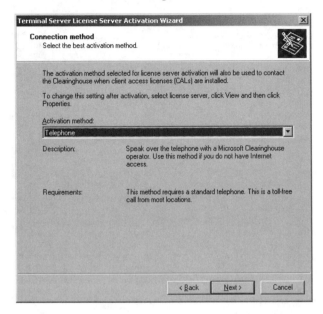

11. The Country/Region Selection dialog box appears. Select your country or region and click the Next button.

12. The License Server Activation dialog box appears see Figure 8.21. Type in the license number provided by Microsoft (or leave this blank and provide a valid number within 120 days). Click the Next button, then Finish.

FIGURE 8.21 License Server Activation dialog box

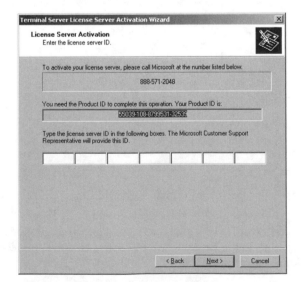

> While you are waiting for the registration process to complete, you can issue temporary 120-day licenses to clients who need to use Terminal Services immediately.

After a license server is activated, you can begin installing *client license key packs*. The key packs are sets of client licenses that the license server distributes to your clients. You install key packs either at the end of the license server activation process or, later, by right-clicking a license server in the Terminal Services Licensing tool and selecting Install Licenses (this option will not be active if the license server has not been activated). Terminal Services Licensing will contact Microsoft (requires an Internet connection) and request the number of keys that you specify. Microsoft will send the keys to the license server, and the keys will be available for use immediately after they are received by the license server.

Running Applications on the Terminal Services Server

When you have configured Terminal Services in Terminal Server mode, the Terminal Services clients you have installed will be able to access the applications running on the Terminal Services server. The following sections describe how to install applications on your Terminal Services server as well as how to configure applications for multi-session use.

Installing Applications

The Registry and .ini file mapping support that is built into Terminal Services allows programs to run correctly in Terminal Services, even if they were not designed to run in a multi-user environment. Terminal Services automatically replicates the .ini files and Registry settings from the system to each user if the application is installed properly. It places the .ini files in the user's home folder, or if no home folder is specified, in the *Windir*\Documents and Settings*Username* folder. Registry settings are moved from HKEY_LOCAL_MACHINE\SOFTWARE\ Microsoft\WindowsNT\CurrentVersion\Terminal Server\Install\Software to HKEY_ CURRENT_USER\Software.

To install applications on a Terminal Services server, use the Add Or Remove Programs icon in Control Panel. Add Or Remove Programs automatically runs the change user command, which ensures that the .ini files and Registry entries are replicated and the program you install will work properly for all Terminal Services clients. You should install the applications on an NTFS partition, so that you can set permissions for your programs.

If you need to install applications after your Terminal Services server is up and running, you should make sure that all of the users have ended their sessions. You can send a message to every session notifying them of the impending shutdown so that users have a chance to save their work.

It is essential that you test your application from at least two clients before allowing users access to the Terminal Services server. This gives you the chance to test your programs before users can access them, reducing the number of errors that might occur. Some programs need to be fine-tuned before they can be run in multi-session mode. This is explained in more detail in the next section.

Configuring Application Sharing

Terminal Services allows several users to simultaneously run the same program. Because of this, applications that are run with Terminal Services must be configured for multi-session use. Most of the time, you will not need to perform any extra steps for a program to run correctly with Terminal Services server. However, you might need to configure certain applications for multi-session use.

In the following sections you will learn about compatibility scripts and per-user data.

Compatibility Scripts

Most well-known applications have been tested for use with Terminal Services. Some of these applications require *compatibility scripts* that should be run after the program is installed to achieve the best performance on a Terminal Services server. These scripts can be found in *Windir*\Application Compatibility Scripts\Install. The compatibility scripts may include notes on specific script capabilities and instructions on modifying them for custom installations. You can edit compatibility scripts in Notepad.

Windows Server 2003 comes with three application compatibility scripts by default:

- `Eudora4.cmd`, for Eudora 4.0

- `Msvs6.cmd`, for Microsoft Visual Studio 6.0

- `Outlk98.cmd`, for Microsoft Outlook 98

Per-User Data

Each user is given an HKEY_CURRENT_USER Registry key, which stores user-specific data. There is also a Registry key called HKEY_LOCAL_MACHINE, which stores information that is shared among users. Unfortunately, applications that assume one computer equals one user also assume that they can store user-specific data in HKEY_LOCAL_MACHINE. They also assume that they can store any file-based information, such as user preferences, in the System folder or the program directory. You should always make sure that any per-user data is stored in HKEY_CURRENT_USER, in the user's home folder, or in a user-specified folder. Any global data should always be stored in either HKEY_LOCAL_MACHINE or in a specific location on the disk that is write protected, such as the System folder.

Problems can arise when programs need to store user-specific data in either the Registry or in a file. This data could consist of path information, such as to a mailbox, or per-user preference settings, such as enabling background spell checking. If all of this data is stored in one location, the users will need to either use the same settings or readjust their settings every time they log on. If one user updates the settings, the changes will affect every other user.

Another problem is that programs sometimes update files in the *Windir* folder. Administrators have write access to the *Windir* folder, but most users do not. You will know that write access to this folder is necessary if a program executes properly for an Administrator but not for other users. You can audit all write operations and see which ones fail in order to detect and remedy the problem.

 Real World Scenario

Maximizing Terminal Services in Terminal Server Mode

You have installed Terminal Services in Terminal Server mode. Your users are complaining that performance is much slower than expected. Before you resort to a hardware upgrade on the Terminal Services server, consider the following options that can improve the performance between a Terminal Services server and a Terminal Services client. These options would be configured on the Terminal Services server.

- Minimize the use of animated graphics. This includes graphics and the animated Microsoft Office Assistant.

- When configuring the desktop appearance, do not use bitmap files for wallpaper, and set wallpaper to None. Select a single color for the display appearance. Do not use screen savers.

- Disable the smooth scrolling option.

- Do not use Active Desktop.

Avoid the use of DOS or Windows 16-bit applications. Use Windows 32-bit applications, if possible.

Using Remote Desktop For Administration

Remote Desktop For Administration is integrated by default with Windows Server 2003 and does not require you to install a Terminal Services server. With Windows 2000 Server Terminal Services, remote access required you to install a Terminal Services server using Remote Administration mode. By integrating Remote Desktop For Administration into the Windows Server 2003 kernel, no additional disk space is required to host the service and there is minimal impact on server performance. Typically, Remote Desktop For Administration uses 2MB of server memory and has negligible processor usage.

Terminal Services remote administration enables administrators to remotely perform such tasks as file sharing, managing users and groups, and editing the Registry. Remote administration allows up to two concurrent connections to the Terminal Services server, but does not require additional Terminal Services client licenses.

In the following sections, you will learn how to enable Remote Desktop For Administration and how to make a Remote Desktop For Administration connection from a client computer.

Enabling Remote Desktop For Administration

While Remote Desktop For Administration is installed by default, it is not enabled by default. To enable Remote Desktop For Administration, select Start ➤ Control Panel ➤ System, and click the Remote tab, as shown in Figure 8.22. Under Remote Desktop, ensure that Allow Users To Connect Remotely To Your Computer is checked and click the OK button.

FIGURE 8.22   Remote tab of System Properties

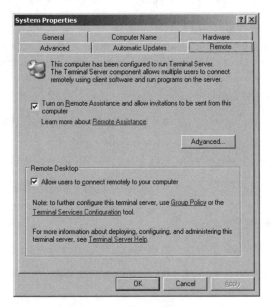

Connecting with Remote Desktop For Administration from a Client Computer

You use Remote Desktop Connection (RDC) to make a Remote Desktop For Administration connection. This software uses TCP/IP and is designed for high and low bandwidth networks. RDC is supported on the following client platforms:

- Windows for Workgroups with MS-TCP/IP-32
- Windows 95, Windows 98, Windows Me, Windows NT, Windows 2000, Windows XP Professional, and Windows Server 2003
- Windows CE-based handheld devices
- Windows CD-based terminals

RDC is installed by default on Windows XP Professional and Windows Server 2003 computers. For other clients, you can install the software by creating a share on the *Windir*\System32\Clients\ Tsclient\Win32 folder and then running the Setup program.

Remote Desktop is covered in greater detail in Chapter 10, "Performing System Recovery Functions."

Troubleshooting Terminal Services

If you are having trouble with Terminal Services, there are several things you can troubleshoot. Possible problems you might encounter include:

Installed applications do not work properly on Terminal clients.   You may encounter this problem if the application was installed before Terminal Services was installed. To fix this problem, uninstall the application, and then reinstall it using the Add or Remove Programs icon in Control Panel.

Terminal Services is installed on a domain controller, and the Administrator can log on to the Terminal Services server but regular users can't.   Verify that users have the Log On Locally user right.

Terminal Services is working in Terminal Server mode and after a period of time no users can access the Terminal Services server.   If you are using Terminal Server mode, you can only use temporary licenses for 120 days. If you do not complete the Terminal Services licensing process, no users will be able to connect to the Terminal Services server after the temporary license period has expired.

Sometimes users can access the Terminal Server and sometimes they can't.   If you are using Terminal Services in Terminal Server mode, use Terminal Services Configuration to see if the number of connections has been limited.

Users are unable to connect to the Terminal Services server.   Verify that the Terminal Services server and the Terminal Services client are configured to use compatible encryption levels. If you suspect that the client can't connect due to encryption settings, configure the Terminal Services server to use Client Compatible encryption.

When using remote control, the user can view the remote session, but can't interact with the remote session.   Check the Remote Control settings through Terminal Services Configuration to verify that the Level Of Control is set to Interact With The Session instead of View The Session.

Summary

In this chapter, you learned about Terminal Services. We covered these topics:

- The features and benefits of Terminal Services, including rapid deployment, application sharing, and remote administration.
- Planning for Terminal Services deployment, including hardware requirements, licensing requirements, and client application requirements
- Installing a Terminal Services server

- Managing Terminal Services with the Terminal Services Configuration and Terminal Services Manager utilities
- How to license a Terminal Services server
- Installing applications and configuring application sharing on a Terminal Services server
- Remotely administering a server through Terminal Services
- How to troubleshoot Terminal Services

Exam Essentials

Understand the primary purpose of Terminal Services.   Know what a thin client is and how Terminal Services can be used to support a wide variety of client types.

List and describe the components of Terminal Services.   Know the function and requirements for the Terminal Services server and the Terminal Services clients. Understand the function of the Remote Desktop Protocol.

Be able to install and configure Terminal Services for use as an terminal server.   List the utilities and options that are used to install and configure Terminal Services as an application server. Be able to configure applications for use with Terminal Services.

Know how to install and configure Terminal Services client software.   Know where the client software is located and know the options for deploying client software to different Terminal Services clients.

Be able to manage servers remotely through Terminal Services.   Configure Terminal Services for remote administration. Know what options can be remotely managed.

Know how to troubleshoot Terminal Services.   Know the common causes of Terminal Services errors and how they can be corrected.

Key Terms

Before you take the exam, be certain you are familiar with the following terms:

client license key packs	Terminal Server mode
compatibility scripts	Terminal Services client
license server	Terminal Services Configuration utility
remote control	Terminal Services Manager utility
Remote Desktop For Administration	Terminal Services server
Remote Desktop Protocol (RDP)	thin clients

Review Questions

1. You are running an application on a Terminal Services server from a Terminal Services client. The application is not saving user preferences properly. What is most likely the problem?

   A. The application was installed by running `Setup.exe`, and therefore is not properly configured.

   B. There is a bug in the program that is affecting only the saving of user preferences.

   C. You have not activated the license server.

   D. The application was not installed using Control Panel, Add Or Remove Programs, and therefore did not replicate the `.ini` files and Registry entries for each user.

2. For security and performance reasons, you want any user who has remained idle for 15 minutes to be disconnected from the Terminal Services server. Furthermore, if that user does not reconnect within 15 minutes, you want her session to be terminated. Which of the following options accomplishes the objective with the least amount of administrative effort?

   A. Create a security group called TSUsers and set the appropriate session-related settings for the group.

   B. Specify the appropriate session-related settings for each user account.

   C. Configure an alert in System Monitor to notify you each time the user reaches her limit, then take appropriate action.

   D. Configure the session-related settings for the Terminal Services connection.

3. Your network is configured with the clients shown in the following diagram. Based on your network, which of the clients will run as Terminal Services clients without having to install third-party software? (Choose all that apply.)

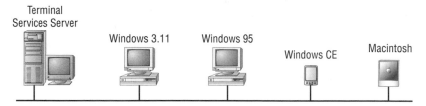

   A. Windows 3.11 clients

   B. Windows CE devices

   C. Windows 95 clients

   D. Macintosh computers

4. You are the network administrator of a large company. You have configured your Windows Server 2003 member server as a Terminal Services server. You want to enable clients to access a share on the Terminal Services server in order to install the Terminal Services client software. Which folder is the correct location of the Terminal Services client software?

   A. *Windir*\\Services\\Clients\\TS

   B. *Windir*\\Clients\\Tsclients

   C. *Windir*\\System32\\Clients\\Tsclient

   D. \\Clients\\TS\\Win32

5. You are the network administrator of a large company. You have configured your Windows Server 2003 member server as a Terminal Services server. You want to disable drive mapping for all users on a particular Terminal Services server. Where should you configure this setting?

   A. In the Client Settings tab of the Domain Users group Properties dialog box

   B. In the Client Settings tab of the TSUsers group Properties dialog box

   C. In the Environment tab of the TSUsers group Properties dialog box

   D. In the Client Settings tab of the RDP-Tcp connection Properties dialog box

6. You are upgrading the hardware on a server in preparation for installing Windows Server 2003 with Terminal Services. How much extra RAM should you allow for each user connection to the Terminal Services server?

   A. 2MB

   B. 10–20MB

   C. 256KB

   D. 25MB

7. You are the lead network administer for your company. Your network consists of Windows 2000 Servers and Windows Server 2003 servers. With several hundred users, many of whom are remote, you have implemented Terminal Services on 12 of the Windows Server 2003 servers. You want to enable the HelpDesk security group to perform administrative tasks on the Terminal Services servers. How can you best achieve this objective?

   A. Create a GPO, link it to the HelpDesk group, and enable all relevant Terminal Services policies.

   B. Create a remote access policy with the appropriate permissions and define a filter so that it applies only to the HelpDesk group.

   C. In the Properties page of the HelpDesk group, assign Administrative control.

   D. Assign the HelpDesk group the appropriate permissions for the connection on each Terminal Services server.

8. You are the network administrator of a large company. You have configured your Windows Server 2003 member server as a Terminal Services server. Which of the following utilities enables the administrator to interact with users' sessions, with the users' permission?

   A. Terminal Services Client Manager

   B. Terminal Services Configuration

   C. Terminal Services Manager

   D. Terminal Services Administration

9. You can log on to the Terminal Services server as Administrator. When you tried to log on to Terminal Services as a regular user, you received an error message that reported that you could not log on interactively. What is the most likely cause of this problem?

   A. You need to grant the users Read permission to the Tcp-RDP protocol.

   B. You need to grant the users Full Control permission to the Tcp-RDP protocol.

   C. You need to grant the users the Log On Locally user right.

   D. You need to grant the users the Allow Interactive Logon user right.

10. You have a user who is connected to the Terminal Services application server. The session seems to have hung and you want to manually disconnect the user. Which utility should you use?

   A. Terminal Services Client Creator

   B. Terminal Services Configuration

   C. Terminal Services Manager

   D. Terminal Services Licensing

11. You are the network administrator of a large company. You have configured your Windows Server 2003 member server as a Terminal Services server. Which of the following utilities can be used to view all of the users who are currently connected to the Terminal Services server?

   A. Terminal Services Client Manager

   B. Terminal Services Configuration

   C. Terminal Services Manager

   D. Terminal Services Administration

12. You are the network administrator of a large company. You have configured your Windows Server 2003 member server as a Terminal Services server. One of your Terminal Services users complains that the application he is using has stopped responding. What should you do?

   A. In Terminal Services Manager, click the session that is having the problem. In the Processes tab, end the process that has stopped responding.

   B. In Terminal Services Manager, disconnect the session that is having the problem.

   C. In Terminal Services Manager, reset the session that is having the problem.

   D. Run the application compatibility script for the program.

13. You are the System Administrator of a manufacturing company that uses a proprietary procurement application that is constantly being updated by the software vendor. Instead of managing the application on the users' local computers, you decide to deploy the application through Terminal Services in Terminal Server mode. You want members of the IT group to be able to remotely manage and troubleshoot any application problems that the users may have. Which action should you take to enable the IT department to do this?

    A. Grant the IT group Read permission to the RDP-Tcp protocol.

    B. Grant the IT group Full Control permission to the RDP-Tcp protocol.

    C. Add the IT group to the built-in TS-Operators group.

    D. Add the IT group to the built-in TS-Admins group.

14. Clients are complaining that they are not able to access the Terminal Services server. You want to verify that the service required by the Terminal Services server is running properly. Which of the following services is required for use with Terminal Services?

    A. RDP-Tcp

    B. NetBEUI

    C. TS-Tcp

    D. RTS-Tcp

15. You are attempting to connect to a Windows Server 2003 domain controller using remote administration. When you attempt to connect to the server you receive an error message because the number of concurrent connections has been exceeded. How many concurrent connections are supported by Terminal Services remote administration mode?

    A. 1

    B. 2

    C. 3

    D. 4

Answers to Review Questions

1. D.   You should always use the Add Or Remove Programs icon in Control Panel to install applications on a Terminal Services server. This ensures that your applications will be properly configured for all users.

2. D.   Session-related settings for Terminal Services users can be configured on a per-user basis on the Sessions tab in each user's Properties page, or on a per-server basis on the Sessions tab in the connection's Properties page, which will override the user-specific settings. In this scenario, you want the settings to apply to any given user, so D is the best choice.

3. A, B, C.   Terminal Services can run on Macintosh-based computers, but this requires third-party software. Windows-based computers can use the client software provided with Windows Server 2003 Terminal Services.

4. C.   The Terminal Services client software is located in the *Windir*\System32\Clients\Tsclient folder on the Terminal Services server.

5. D.   To disable the drive mapping option for all users, you should configure the setting in the Properties dialog box (Client Settings tab) for the RDP-Tcp connection. You can also configure this setting on a per-user basis in the Client Settings tab of the user Properties dialog box.

6. B.   Terminal Services is a memory-intensive application. Each user connection will require between 10 and 20MB of RAM on the server. You should add 20MB of additional RAM for each user who is running three or more applications simultaneously.

7. D.   Each Terminal Services connection can be configured with unique permission sets for specific user groups via the Permissions tab in its Properties page.

8. B.   Through the Remote Control tab of Terminal Services Configuration, you can configure the connection property to allow you to interact with user sessions.

9. C.   When you install Terminal Services on a domain controller, you will have to grant regular users the Log On Locally user right. Otherwise users will receive an error message that they cannot log on interactively. Installing Terminal Services on a domain controller is not recommended, for both load and security reasons.

10. C.   You manage sessions and servers with the Terminal Services Manager utility.

11. C.   You can manage and access Terminal Services sessions through the Terminal Services Manager utility.

12. A.   You can end processes on a per-session basis in Terminal Services Manager. Disconnecting the session would not end any of the processes associated with the session, and ending the session could result in data loss if the session was running any other applications. Application compatibility scripts would not help in this instance.

13. B.   You configure Terminal Services permissions through the Terminal Services Configuration utility. You can grant the IT group the Full Control permission to the RDP-Tcp protocol, and this will enable them to manage the users' Terminal Services sessions.

14. A.   The Remote Desktop Protocol–Transmission Control Protocol (RDP-Tcp) service is used by all Terminal Services connections.

15. B.   Terminal Services remote administration enables administrators to remotely perform such tasks as file sharing, managing users and groups, and editing the Registry. Remote administration allows up to two concurrent connections to the Terminal Services server, but does not require additional Terminal Services client licenses.

Chapter

9

Optimizing Windows Server 2003

MICROSOFT EXAM OBJECTIVES COVERED IN THIS CHAPTER:

✓ **Monitor and analyze events. Tools might include Event Viewer and System Monitor.**

✓ **Monitor system performance.**

✓ **Monitor file and print servers. Tools might include Task Manager, Event Viewer, and System Monitor.**

- ▪ Monitor server hardware for bottlenecks.

✓ **Monitor and optimize a server environment for application performance.**

- ▪ Monitor memory performance objects.
- ▪ Monitor network performance objects.
- ▪ Monitor process performance objects.
- ▪ Monitor disk performance objects.

Monitoring system performance is an important administrative task. You can create baselines, determine trends, test configuration changes or fine-tune efforts, and use alerts for problem notification.

The main utilities for managing system performance are System Monitor and Performance Logs And Alerts. System Monitor is used to view information in real-time format or to view data from a log that was previously created. Performance Logs And Alerts is used to create counter logs, trace logs, and alerts. You can also manage system performance through command-line utilities.

The main subsystems that should be monitored on a Windows Server 2003 computer are memory, processor, processes, disk subsystem, and the network subsystem. For each subsystem, you should know the key counters to monitor and how to tune and upgrade the subsystem. You should also know how to create a baseline report that monitors all key subsystem counters.

The System tool's Advanced tab in Control Panel allows you to configure performance-related settings for visual effects, processor scheduling, memory usage, and the page file.

The Task Manager utility is also used to view and manage system performance options. You can view and manage applications, processes, and performance settings, view network usage, and perform some network user management.

All of these topics are covered throughout this chapter.

Using the Event Viewer to monitor and analyze events is covered in more detail in Chapter 10, "Performing System Recovery Functions."

Determining System Performance

To have an optimized system, you must monitor its performance. The tools for monitoring Windows Server 2003 are System Monitor, Performance Logs And Alerts, and Task Manager. With these tools, you can track memory activity, processor activity, the disk subsystem, the network subsystem, and other computer subsystems. The monitoring tools allow you to assess your server's current health and determine what it requires to improve its present condition.

You access System Monitor and Performance Logs And Alerts through the Performance console, which is accessed through Start ➢ Administrative Tools ➢ Performance.

With System Monitor and Performance Logs And Alerts, you can perform the following tasks:

- Create baselines
- Identify system bottlenecks
- Determine trends

- Test configuration changes or tuning efforts
- Create alert thresholds

Each of these tasks is discussed in the following sections.

Creating Baselines

A *baseline* is a snapshot of how your system is currently performing. Suppose that your computer's hardware has not changed over the last six months, but the computer seems to be performing more slowly now than it did six months ago. If you have been using the Performance Logs And Alerts utility and taking baseline logs, as well as noting the changes in your workload, you can more easily determine what resources are causing the system to slow down.

You should create baselines at the following times:

- When the system is first configured without any load
- At regular intervals of typical usage
- Whenever any changes are made to the system's hardware or software configuration

Baselines are particularly useful for determining the effect of changes that you make to your computer. For example, if you are adding more memory to your computer, you should take baselines before and after you install the additional memory to determine the effect of the change. Along with hardware changes, system configuration modifications also can affect your computer's performance, so you should create baselines before and after you make any changes to your Windows Server 2003 configuration.

For the most part, Windows Server 2003 is a self-tuning operating system. If you decide to tweak the operating system, you should take baselines before and after each change. If you do not notice a performance gain after the tweak, you should consider returning the computer to its previous configuration, because some tweaks may cause more problems than they solve.

You create baselines by using the Performance Logs And Alerts utility to create a baseline counters log file. This process is described in the "Creating Baseline Reports" section later in this chapter.

Identifying System Bottlenecks

A *bottleneck* is a system resource that is inefficient compared with the rest of the computer system as a whole. The bottleneck can cause the rest of the system to run slowly.

Common causes of bottlenecks include:

- A resource is being overused and additional resources need to be allocated to the system, or the resource needs to be upgraded.
- If you have multiple instances of a resource, the workload may not be evenly balanced and needs to be manually balanced.

- A specific application is using excessive system resources, in which case the application should be updated or replaced.

- A resource might not be working properly and be causing unnecessary workload, in which case the resource needs to be reconfigured or replaced.

You need to pinpoint the cause of a bottleneck in order to correct it. Consider a system that has a Pentium 166 processor with 128MB of RAM. If your applications are memory-intensive, and lack of memory is your bottleneck, then upgrading your processor will not eliminate the bottleneck. By using System Monitor, you can measure the performance of the various parts of your system, which allows you to identify system bottlenecks in a scientific manner. You will learn how to set counters to monitor your network and spot bottlenecks in the "Using System Monitor" section later in this chapter.

Determining Trends

Many of us tend to manage situations reactively instead of proactively. With reactive management, you focus on a problem when it occurs. With proactive management, you take steps to avoid the problem before it happens. In a perfect world, all management would be proactive.

System Monitor and Performance Logs And Alerts are great tools for proactive network management. If you are creating baselines on a regular basis, you can identify system trends. For example, if you notice average CPU utilization increasing 15 percent every month, you can assume that within the next six to twelve months, you're going to have a problem. Before performance becomes so slow that your system is not responding, you can upgrade the hardware.

Testing Configuration Changes or Tuning Efforts

When you make configuration changes or tune your computer, you may want to measure the effects of those changes. When making configuration changes, the following recommendations apply:

- Make only one change at a time. If you are making configuration changes for tuning, and you make multiple changes at one time, it is difficult to quantify the effect of each individual change. In addition, some changes may have a negative impact that, if you have made multiple changes, may be difficult to identify.

- Repeat monitoring with each individual change you make. This will help you determine whether additional tuning is required.

- As you make changes, check the Event Viewer log files. Some performance changes will generate events within Event Viewer that should be reviewed.

 Event Viewer is covered in more detail in Chapter 10.

- If you suspect that network components are affecting performance, compare the performance of the network version with a version that runs locally.

Using Alerts for Problem Notification

The Performance Logs And Alerts utility provides another tool for proactive management in the form of *alerts*, which are used to notify the administrator when specified system events take place. Through Performance Logs And Alerts, you can specify alert thresholds (when a counter reaches a specified value) and have the utility notify you when these thresholds are reached.

For example, you could specify that if your logical disk has less than 10 percent of free space, you want to be notified. Once alerted, you can add more disk space or delete unneeded files before you run out of disk space. You will learn how to create alerts in the "Using Performance Logs And Alerts" section later in this chapter.

Performance Updates in Windows Server 2003

Most of the utilities and features for monitoring system performance are the same in Windows 2000 Server and Windows Server 2003. However, Windows Server 2003 has made the following improvements compared to Windows 2000 Server:

- Several command-line utilities have been added that correspond to the GUI utility, System Monitor. The new command-line utilities are Logman, Relog, Tracerpt, and Typeperf.

- System Monitor has been enhanced so that if you have created several log files, they can be viewed simultaneously.

- Performance Logs And Alerts has been enhanced so that it can now store log files greater than 1GB, new file formats are supported, and performance data can be appended to an existing file. You can also log data directly to a SQL database using an Open DataBase Connectivity (ODBC) connection.

Using System Monitor

The *System Monitor* utility (Figure 9.1) is used to collect and measure the real-time performance data for a local or remote computer on the network. Through *System Monitor*, you can view current data or data from a log file. When you view current data, you are monitoring real-time activity. When you view data from a log file, you are importing a log file from a previous session.

System Monitor enables you to do the following tasks:

- Collect data from your local computer or remote computers on the network. You can collect data from a single computer or multiple computers concurrently.

- View data as it is being collected in real time, or historically from collected data.

- Have full control over the selection of what data will be collected, by selecting which specific objects and counters will be collected.

- Choose the sampling parameters that will be used, meaning the time interval that you want to use for collecting data points and the time period that will be used for data collection.

FIGURE 9.1 System Monitor

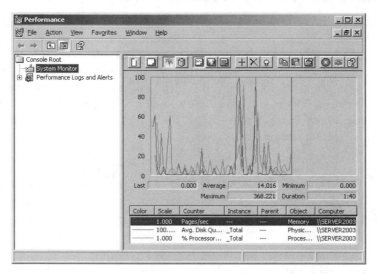

- Determine the format in which data will be viewed, in Graph, Histogram, or Report views.
- Create HTML pages for viewing data.
- Create specific configurations for monitoring data that can then be exported to other computers for performance monitoring.

In the following sections you will learn about System Monitor security groups, using the System Monitor toolbar, how System Monitor is organized, how to add counters in System Monitor, the counters that are added by default, how to select the appropriate view in System Monitor, and how to manage System Monitor properties.

System Monitor Security Groups

In order to use System Monitor, you must be a member of one of the following groups:

- Administrators
- Server Operators
- Performance Log Users
- Performance Monitor Users

The Performance Log Users and Performance Monitor Users groups are new security groups in Windows Server 2003, so we will look at them here:

Performance Log Users   A security group that allows members to manage performance-related counters through System Monitor, or logs and alerts through Performance Logs And Alerts, on a local server or on a remote computer without having to be a member of the Administrators or Server Operators group.

Performance Monitor Users   A security group that allows members to view performance-related counters through System Monitor, or logs and alerts through Performance Logs And Alerts, on a local server or on a remote computer without having to be a member of the Administrators or Server Operators group.

Once you are logged in as a user who has rights to use System Monitor, you can complete common administrative tasks (such as creating baselines or monitoring performance data) using the System Monitor toolbar.

The Administrators and Server Operators groups are covered in Chapter 3, "Managing Users, Groups, and Computers."

Using the System Monitor Toolbar

The main functionality of System Monitor is provided through the toolbar at the top of the main dialog window, or through keystroke combinations. The buttons for the toolbar, each associated function, and the keystroke alternatives are defined in Table 9.1.

TABLE 9.1   System Monitor Toolbar Functions and Keystrokes

Button	Function	Associated Keystrokes
	New Counter Set	Ctrl+E
	Clear Display	Ctrl+D
	View Current Activity	Ctrl+T
	View Log Data	Ctrl+L
	View Graph	Ctrl+G
	View Histogram	Ctrl+B
	View Report	Ctrl+R
	Add	Ctrl+I

TABLE 9.1   System Monitor Toolbar Functions and Keystrokes *(continued)*

Button	Function	Associated Keystrokes
✕	Delete	Delete
💡	Highlight	Ctrl+H
📋	Copy Properties	Ctrl+C
📋	Paste Counter List	Ctrl+V
📋	Properties	Ctrl+Q
⊗	Freeze Display	Ctrl+F
📷	Update Data	Ctrl+U
📖	Help	F1

Organization of System Monitor

System Monitor allows you to track performance-related data about your computer using a hierarchical structure for specifying what should be tracked. When you click the Add button on the System Monitor toolbar, the Add Counters dialog box appears (see Figure 9.2), which shows how counters are added based on:

The local computer or counters from another computer   By default, any counters that are added to System Monitor track the local computer. However, you can specify that you want to track counters on a remote computer. This option allows you to track performance data for several computers within a single System Monitor session.

Performance object   Windows Server 2003 organizes system resources that affect system performance into categories called performance objects. The sum of all of the performance objects represents your system. Depending on the configuration of your server, you will see different performance objects listed. Examples of performance objects include Paging File, Memory, Process, and Processor.

All counters or specific counters   Each performance object has an associated set of counters. Counters are used to track specific information regarding the performance object. For example, the performance object Memory allows you to track counters for Page Reads/sec and Page Writes/sec.

All instances or selected instances   Each performance object can consist of one or more instances. Performance objects such as Memory and Cache will always have one instance. Performance objects such as Print Queue or Processor can have multiple instances if you have more than one print queue or processor installed on your computer. By using the instance option, you can track data for all instances—e.g., all print queues—or specific instances— e.g., the Laser print queue.

FIGURE 9.2   Add Counters dialog box

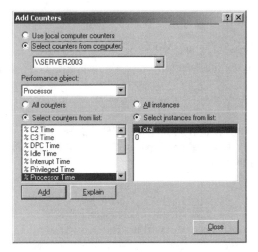

System Monitor Default Counters

When you first start System Monitor, you will see that three counters are tracked by default (as opposed to previous versions of Windows, which did not track any counters by default). The default counters that are tracked contain some of the most useful performance data and include:

- Memory > Pages/Sec
- PhysicalDisk > Avg. Disk Queue Length
- Processor > Processor Time

You will learn about counters in the "Managing System Performance" section of this chapter.

In this book, we use the format *performance object > counter*. For example, Memory > Pages/Sec denotes the Memory performance object and the Pages/ Sec counter.

Each counter is listed at the bottom of the System Monitor utility (as shown in Figure 9.1). The fields just above the counter list will contain data, based on the counter that is highlighted in the list, as follows:

- The Last field displays the most current data.

- The Average field shows the average of the counter.

- The Minimum field shows the lowest value that has been recorded for the counter.

- The Maximum field shows the highest value that has been recorded for the counter.

- The Duration field shows how long the counter has been tracking data.

Adding Counters

To add additional counters to System Monitor, use the following steps:

1. In System Monitor, click the Add button on the toolbar. This brings up the Add Counters dialog box.

 To see information about a specific counter, select it and click the Explain button in the Add Counters dialog box. System Monitor will display text regarding the highlighted counter.

2. In the Add Counters dialog box, select the Use Local Computer Counters radio button to monitor the local computer. Alternatively, select the Select Counters From Computer radio button and choose a computer from the drop-down list to select counters from a specific computer. You can monitor remote computers if you have Administrative permissions on that computer. This option is useful when you do not want the overhead of System Monitor running on the computer you are trying to monitor.

3. Select the performance object from the drop-down list.

4. Select the All Counters radio button to track all the associated counters, or select the Select Counters From List radio button and choose specific counters from the list box below.

 You can select multiple counters of the same performance object by pressing Shift and clicking contiguous counters or pressing Ctrl and clicking noncontiguous counters.

5. Select the All Instances radio button to track all the associated instances, or select the Select Instances From List radio button and choose specific instances from the list box below.

6. Click the Add button to add the counters for the performance object.

7. Repeat steps 2 through 6 to specify any additional counters you want to track. When you are finished, click the Close button.

Selecting the Appropriate View

By clicking the appropriate button in the System Monitor toolbar, you can see your data in three views. For each view, you can view real-time data by clicking the Current Activity button on the System Monitor toolbar, or you can view data that was previously collected and saved in a file by clicking the Log Data button. The three views you can select are:

Graph view   The Graph view, shown in Figure 9.1, is the default view used with System Monitor. This view is useful for viewing a small number of counters in a graphical format. The main advantage of graph view is that you can see how the data has been tracked during the defined time period. When you start to track a large number of counters, it can be difficult to view the data in graph form.

Histogram view   The Histogram view, shown in Figure 9.3, shows System Monitor data in bar graph form. This view is useful for viewing large amounts of data. However, it only shows performance for the current period. You do not see a record of performance over time, as you do with the graph view.

FIGURE 9.3   The Histogram view in System Monitor

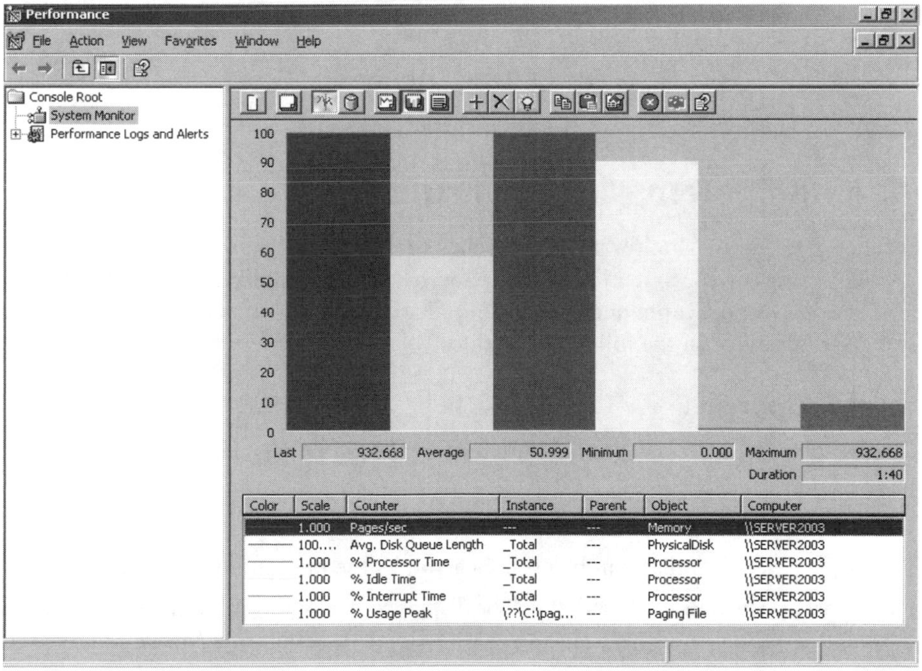

Report view   The Report view, shown in Figure 9.4, is used to list all of the counters that are being tracked through System Monitor in a logical report. The data that is displayed is for the current session. Watching these numbers in real time, you'll notice the numbers are constantly jumping up and down. The advantage of this view is that it allows you to easily track large numbers of counters in a real-time manner.

FIGURE 9.4   The Report view in System Monitor

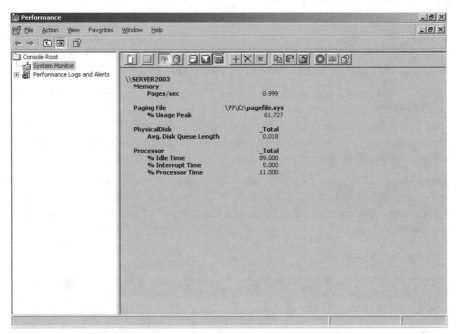

Managing System Monitor Properties

To configure the System Monitor properties, click the Properties button on the System Monitor toolbar. This brings up the System Monitor Properties dialog box. This dialog box has five tabs: General, Source, Data, Graph, and Appearance. The properties you can configure on each of these tabs are described in the following sections.

General Properties

The General tab of the System Monitor Properties dialog box (see Figure 9.5) contains the following options:

- The view that will be displayed: Graph, Histogram, or Report
- The display elements that will be used: Legend, Value bar, and/or Toolbar
- The report and histogram data that will be displayed: Default (for reports or histograms, this is current data; for logs, this is average data), Current, Minimum, Maximum, or Average
- The appearance: Flat or 3D
- The border: None or Fixed Single
- How often the data is updated, in seconds (1 second is the default)
- Whether duplicate counter instances are allowed

FIGURE 9.5   The General tab of the System Monitor Properties dialog box

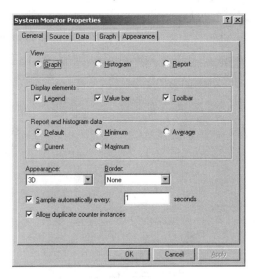

Source Properties

The Source tab, shown in Figure 9.6, allows you to specify the data source. This can be current activity, or it can be data that has been collected in a log file. If you import data from a log file, you can specify the time range that you wish to view.

FIGURE 9.6   The Source tab of the System Monitor Properties dialog box

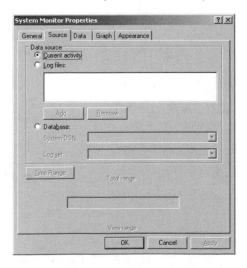

Data Properties

The Data tab, shown in Figure 9.7, lets you specify the counters that you wish to track. You can add and remove counters by clicking the Add and Remove buttons. You can also select a specific counter and define the color, scale, width, and style (for example, solid line or line of dashes) that are used to represent the counter in the graph.

FIGURE 9.7   The Data tab of the System Monitor Properties dialog box

Graph Properties

The Graph tab, shown in Figure 9.8, contains the following options, which can be applied to the Report or Histogram view:

- A title

- A vertical axis label

- Whether you will show a vertical grid, a horizontal grid, and/or vertical scale numbers

- The minimum and maximum numbers for the vertical scale

FIGURE 9.8   The Graph tab of the System Monitor Properties dialog box

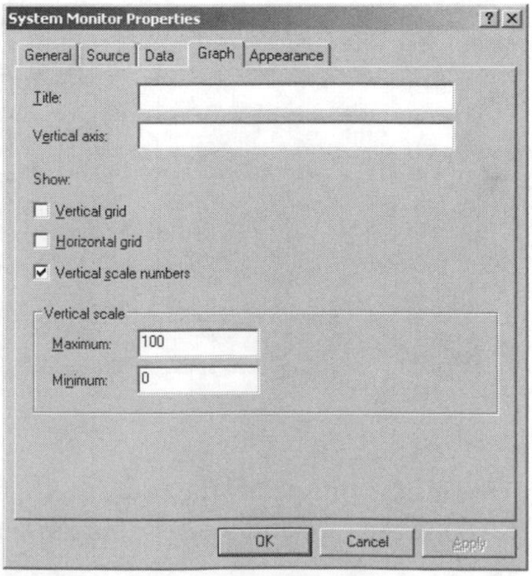

Appearance Properties

The Appearance tab, as shown in Figure 9.9, has options for customizing the appearance of the System Monitor display. You can choose the background color that will be used by System Monitor and the fonts that System Monitor will use.

FIGURE 9.9 The Appearance tab of the System Monitor Properties dialog box

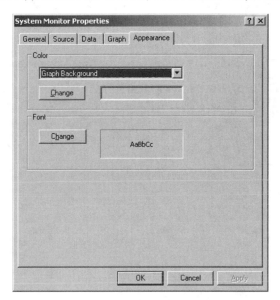

Using Command-Line Utilities for System Monitoring

Windows Server 2003 added new command-line utilities that allow you to manage system monitoring. The command-line utilities related to system monitoring are:

Logman Used to manage and schedule performance monitoring sessions.

Relog Used to extract the performance data that has been collected as a counter log and convert the data to text-TSV format (tab-delimited text), text-CSV format (comma-delimited text), binary format, or SQL format so that the data can be exported into a spreadsheet or database.

Tracerpt Used to process data that has been collected through an event trace provider and create a trace analysis report and a CSV file for the events that have been collected.

Typeperf Takes performance counter data that is in the current command window and writes it to a counter data log file.

Using Performance Logs And Alerts

Through *Performance Logs And Alerts*, you can create counter logs and trace logs, and you can define alerts. After you've created logs, you can view log files with System Monitor or export the data to a spreadsheet or database.

You access Performance Logs And Alerts through Start ➢ Administrative Tools ➢ Performance. Expand Performance Logs And Alerts, as shown in Figure 9.10. You can then define new counter logs, trace logs, and alerts, as described in the following sections.

FIGURE 9.10 The expanded Performance Logs And Alerts snap-in

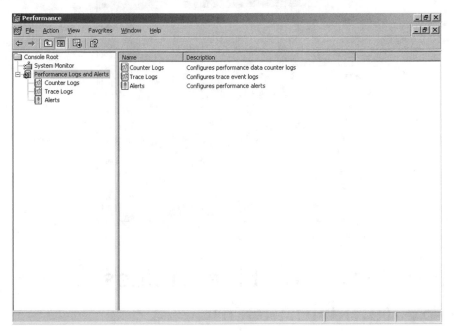

Creating a Counter Log

Counter logs record data about hardware usage and the activity of system services. You can configure logging to occur manually or on a predefined schedule.

To create a counter log, take the following steps:

1. Expand Performance Logs And Alerts, right-click Counter Logs, and select New Log Settings from the pop-up menu.

2. The New Log Settings dialog box appears, as shown in Figure 9.11. Type in a name for the log file. For example, you might give the log a name that indicates its type and the date (Counter*mmddyy*). Then click the OK button.

FIGURE 9.11   The New Log Settings dialog box

3. The counter log file Properties dialog box appears. You can configure counter log properties as follows:

   - In the General tab, shown in Figure 9.12, you can specify the objects and counters you want to track in the log and the interval for sampling data. Click the Add Objects button and select each object you want to add and click the Add button. You can select multiple counters by holding down the Ctrl key (for non-contiguous counters) or the Shift key (for your selected objects, all counters for that object will be monitored) while clicking the mouse to make your selections. If you only want to monitor specific counters, then you would add individual counters through the Add Counters button.

FIGURE 9.12   The General tab of the counter log file Properties dialog box

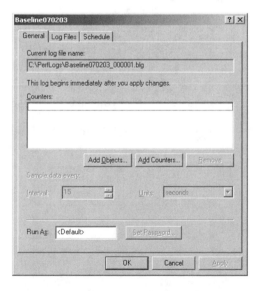

   - In the Log Files tab, shown in Figure 9.13, you can configure what type of log file will be created. You can select from Text File (Comma Delimited), Text File (Tab Delimited), Binary File, Binary Circular File, or SQL Database. The type of file you create will be based on the application that you will use to analyze the data. For example, if you will track data through a SQL database, then you would select SQL Database. If you were to export the data to Excel, you would probably use comma delimited. Other custom applications might require you to use a binary file. You can also choose to add a comment or overwrite an existing log file. If you click the Configure button, you can specify the location of the log file, the filename, and the log file size (either maximum limit based on available disk space or a predefined limit). This option can only be accessed if you have already selected objects or counters.

FIGURE 9.13   The Log Files tab of the counter log Properties dialog box

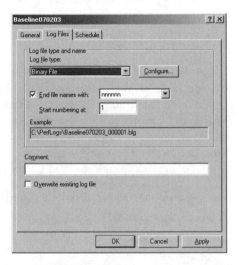

- In the Schedule tab, shown in Figure 9.14, you can specify when the log file will start, when the log file will stop, and what action should be taken, if any, when the log file is closed. This option can only be accessed if you have already selected objects or counters.

FIGURE 9.14   The Schedule tab of the counter log Properties dialog box

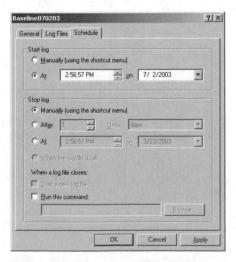

4. When you are finished configuring the counter log file properties, click the OK button. The log will be created and will record the activity for the counters you specified.

Creating a Trace Log

Trace logs measure data continuously as opposed to measuring data through periodic samples. Trace logs are also used to track data that is collected by the operating system or programs. For example, you could specify that you want to trace the creation or deletion of processes or threads.

To create a trace log, take the following steps:

1. Expand Performance Logs And Alerts, right-click Trace Logs, and select New Log Settings from the pop-up menu.

2. The New Log Settings dialog box appears. Type in a name for the log file, such as the type of log and the date (Trace*mmddyy*), and click the OK button.

3. The trace log file Properties dialog box appears. You can configure trace log properties as follows:

    ▪   In the General tab, shown in Figure 9.15, you can select which system events you want to track. For example, you can check the Process Creations/Deletions and Thread Creations/Deletions checkboxes. You can also specify which nonsystem providers you want to track.

FIGURE 9.15   The General tab of the trace log file Properties dialog box

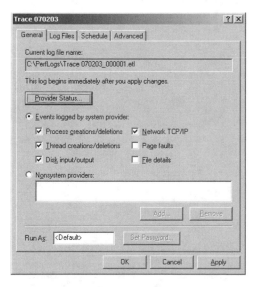

▪   In the Log Files tab, shown in Figure 9.16, you can configure the log file type, which can be Circular Trace File or Sequential Trace File. If you click the Configure button, you can specify the location, filename, and log file size.

▪   In the Schedule tab, shown in Figure 9.17, you can configure when the log file will start, when the log file will stop, and what action should be taken, if any, when the log file is closed.

FIGURE 9.16 The Log Files tab of the trace log file Properties dialog box

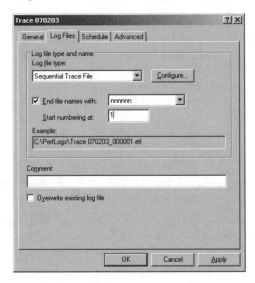

FIGURE 9.17 The Schedule tab of the trace log file Properties dialog box

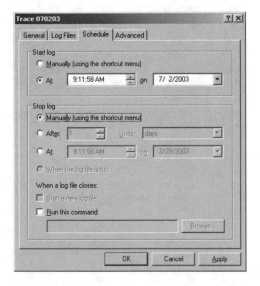

- In the Advanced tab, shown in Figure 9.18, you can configure the buffer settings for the log file. By default, the log service will save the trace file to memory and then transfer the data to the log file.

4. When you are finished configuring the trace file properties, click the OK button. The log will be created and will record the activity for the system events you specified.

FIGURE 9.18   The Advanced tab of the trace log file Properties dialog box

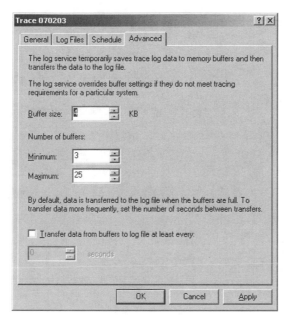

Creating an Alert

Alerts can be generated when a specific counter exceeds or falls below a specified value. You can configure alerts so that a message is sent, a program is run, or a more detailed log file is generated.

To create an alert, take the following steps:

1. Expand Performance Logs And Alerts, right-click Alerts, and select New Alert Settings from the pop-up menu.

2. The New Alert Settings dialog box appears. Type in a name for the alert file and click the OK button.

3. The alert file Properties dialog box appears. You can configure alert properties as follows:

   - In the General tab, shown in Figure 9.19, you can select which counters you want to track by clicking the Add button. When you add a counter, you must specify that the alert be generated when the counter is under or over a certain value. You can also set the interval for sampling data and, under Run As, the user account that will be used to generate the alert.

   - In the Action tab, shown in Figure 9.20, specify what action should be taken if an alert is triggered. You can choose to log an entry in the application event log, send a network message, start another performance data log, and/or run a specific program (and specify command-line parameters for the program).

FIGURE 9.19   The General tab of the alert Properties dialog box

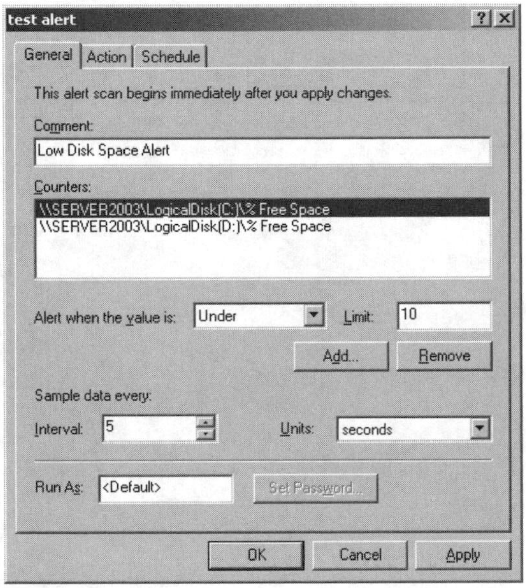

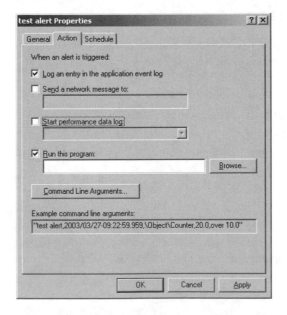

FIGURE 9.20   The Action tab of the alert Properties dialog box

- In the Schedule tab, shown in Figure 9.21, you can configure when scans of the counters you have defined will start and stop.

4. When you are finished configuring the alert properties, click the OK button.

FIGURE 9.21   The Schedule tab of the alert Properties dialog box

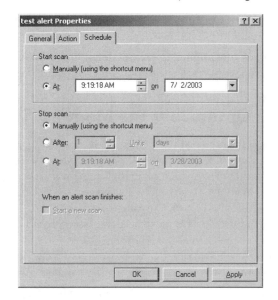

Managing System Performance

By analyzing data, you can determine whether any resources are placing an excessive load on your computer that is resulting in a system slowdown. Some of the causes of poor system performance include:

- A resource is insufficient to handle the load that is being placed upon it, and it may need to be upgraded, or additional components may be required. For example if the processor is the bottleneck, you can upgrade the processor or add an additional processor to the server.

- If a resource has multiple instances, the resources may not be evenly balancing the workload, and the workload may need to be balanced over the multiple instances more effectively.

- A resource might be malfunctioning. In this case, the resource should be repaired or replaced.

- A specific program might be allocated resources improperly or inefficiently, in which case the program needs to be rewritten or another application should be used.

- A resource might be configured improperly and be causing excessive resource usage, and need to be reconfigured.

  The five main subsystems that should be monitored are:

- The memory subsystem

- The processor subsystem

- The processes subsystem
- The disk subsystem
- The network subsystem

Each of these subsystems is examined in greater detail in the following sections, as well as how to create a baseline report to track the important counters for each subsystem.

Monitoring and Optimizing the Memory Subsystem

When a program or process is required by the operating system, the first place the operating system looks for the program or process is in the physical memory. If the program or process is not in physical memory, the system will look in logical memory (the page file). If the program or process is not in logical memory, the system will need to retrieve the program or process from the hard disk. It has been estimated that it can take from 100,000 to 1,000,000 times longer to access information from the hard disk than to access it from physical RAM.

Memory is the most likely cause of system bottlenecks. If you have no idea what is causing a system bottleneck, memory is usually a good place to start checking. To determine how memory is being used, there are two areas you need to examine:

- Physical memory, which is the physical RAM you have installed on your computer. You can't have too much memory. It's actually a good idea to have more memory than you think you will need just to be on the safe side. As you've probably noticed, each time you add or upgrade applications, you require more system memory.

- The *page file*, which is logical memory that exists on the hard drive. If you are experiencing excessive paging (swapping between the page file and physical RAM), it's a clear sign that you need to add more memory.

For example, suppose that the accounting department has just started using a new accounting application that runs on the accounting manager's local computer. The accounting manager complains that this application is slow, and he says that he needs a new computer. You decide to use System Monitor to determine why the computer is responding so slowly. You see that the processor utilization is low, and that the system is using excessive paging. Based on this information, you determine that the account manager's computer will work with the application, but it needs a memory upgrade.

In the following sections you will learn about the key counters to track for memory management, managing the page file, and tuning and upgrading the memory subsystem.

Key Counters to Track for Memory Management

The following are the three most important counters for monitoring memory:

Memory > Available Mbytes   Measures the amount of physical memory that is available to run processes on the computer. If this number is less than 4MB, you should add more memory.

Memory > Pages/Sec (added to System Monitor by default)   Shows the number of times that the requested information was not in memory and the request had to be retrieved from disk.

This counter's value should be below 10. For optimal performance, this counter's value should be between 4 and 5.

Paging File > %Usage   Indicates how much of the allocated page file is currently in use. If this number is consistently over 70 percent, you may need to add more memory. This number could also be artificially high if the paging file was not properly sized and was set too low.

These counters work together to show what is happening on your system, so you should use the Paging File > %Usage counter value in conjunction with the Memory > Available Bytes and Memory > Pages/Sec counters to determine how much paging is occurring on your computer.

These counters work together to show what is happening on your system. Use the Paging File > %Usage counter value in conjunction with the Memory > Available MBytes and Memory > Pages/Sec counters to determine how much paging is occurring on your computer.

If you suspect that one of your applications has a memory leak and is not reallocating memory properly, you should monitor the following counters:

- Memory > Available Bytes
- Memory > Committed Bytes
- Process > Private Bytes (for the application you suspect is leaking memory)
- Process > Working Set (for the application you suspect is leaking memory)
- Process > Handle Count (for the application you suspect is leaking memory)
- Memory > Pool Nonpaged Bytes
- Memory > Pool Nonpaged Allocs

Managing the Windows Server 2003 Page File

Typically, if your computer is experiencing excessive paging, the best way to optimize memory is to add more physical memory. However, there are some other options for managing the paging file for better performance. They include:

- Spreading the page file across multiple hard disks, which allows the disk I/O associated with paging to be spread over multiple disk I/O channels, for faster access.
- If you have sufficient disk space, increasing the size of the page file. By default, Windows Server 2003 creates a page file (`pagefile.sys`) that is 1.5 times the amount of physical memory that has been installed on your computer. You would want to consider increasing the page file size if the Paging File > %Usage counter was near 100%.

The main counters for tracking page file usage are:

- Paging File > %Usage
- Paging File > %Usage Peak (bytes)

WARNING   If a paging file reaches the maximum size, the user will see a warning displayed, and the system might halt. This is another reason to monitor the page file and increase the size.

You will learn how to view and manage the page file later in this chapter in the "Using the System Tool in Control Panel" section. Only Administrators can manage this option.

Tuning and Upgrading the Memory Subsystem

If you suspect that you have a memory bottleneck, the following options can be used to tune or upgrade memory:

- Increase the amount of physical memory that is installed on the computer.
- If your computer has multiple disk channels, create multiple page files across the disk channels.
- Verify that your paging file is sized correctly.
- Try to run less memory-intensive applications.
- Try to avoid having your paging file on the same partition as the system files.

In Exercise 9.1, you will monitor your computer's memory subsystem.

EXERCISE 9.1

Monitoring System Memory

1. Select Start ➢ Administrative Tools ➢ Performance. System Monitor will open by default.

2. In the System Monitor window, click the Add button on the toolbar.

3. In the Add Counters dialog box, select the following performance objects and counters:

   - Select Memory from the Performance Object drop-down list, select Available MBytes in the counter list box, and click the Add button.

   - Select Paging File from the Performance Object drop-down list, select %Usage in the counter list box, and click the Add button.

4. Click the Close button. You should see a graph showing how your computer's memory is being used.

5. To generate some activity, select Start ➢ Help And Support. Close Help And Support. Open and close Help And Support. You should have seen that the first time you opened Help And Support, your Memory > Pages/Sec counter spiked, and the second time you accessed Help, the spike was much lower. This is because the first time you accessed the program, it needed to be retrieved from disk; the second time you accessed this program, it was already in memory.

6. Note the Paging > %Usage counter. If this counter is below 99 percent, you are not using excessive paging.

7. Note the Memory > Available MBytes counter. If this counter is above 4MB, you should have sufficient RAM.

8. Leave System Monitor open, because you will use this utility again in Exercise 9.2.

Monitoring and Optimizing the Processors Subsystem

Although processors are usually not the source of bottlenecks, you should still monitor this subsystem to make sure that processor utilization is at an efficient level. If your Windows Server 2003 computer has multiple processors, you can monitor them through System Monitor and configure them through Task Manager.

In the following sections you will learn about the key counters to track for the processor subsystem and how to tune and upgrade the processor subsystem.

Key Counters to Track for Processor

You can track processor utilization through the Processor and System objects to determine whether a processor bottleneck exists. The following are the three most important counters for monitoring the system processor:

Processor > %Processor Time (added to System Monitor by default)   Measures the time that the processor spends responding to system requests. If this value is consistently above an average of 85 percent, you may have a processor bottleneck.

Processor > Interrupts/Sec   Shows the average number of hardware interrupts the processor receives each second. If this value is more than 1000 on a Pentium-class computer, you might have a problem with a program or hardware that is generating spurious interrupts.

System > Processor Queue Length   Used to determine whether a processor bottleneck is due to high levels of demand for processor time. If a queue of two or more items exists, a processor bottleneck is indicated.

If you suspect that a processor bottleneck is due to excessive hardware I/O requests, or improperly configured IRQs, then you should also monitor the System > File Control Bytes/Sec counter.

Tuning and Upgrading the Processor Subsystem

If you suspect that you have a processor bottleneck, you can try the following solutions:

- Use applications that are less processor-intensive.
- Upgrade your processor.
- If your computer supports multiple processors, add one. You can also use processor affinity to help manage processor-intensive applications.

In Exercise 9.2, you will monitor your computer's processor.

EXERCISE 9.2

Monitoring the System Processor

1. If System Monitor is not already open, select Start ➢ Administrative Tools ➢ Performance.

2. In the System Monitor window, click the Add button on the toolbar.

3. In the Add Counters dialog box, select the following performance objects and counter:

    ▪ Select Processor from the Performance Object drop-down list, select Interrupts/Sec in the counter list box, and click the Add button.

4. Click the Close button. You should see these counters added to your graph.

5. Note the Processor > %Processor Time counter (which was added by default). If this counter's average is below 85 percent, you do not have a processor bottleneck.

6. Note the Processor > Interrupts/Sec counter. If this counter is below 1000 on a Pentium computer, you do not have any processes or hardware that are generating excessive interrupts.

7. Leave System Monitor open, because you will use this utility again in Exercise 9.5.

Using Multiple Processors

Windows Server 2003 supports multiple processors. The number of processors that can be supported is based on the version of Windows Server 2003, as follows:

▪ Windows Server 2003 Web edition can support up to two processors.

▪ Windows Server 2003 Standard edition can support up to four processors.

▪ Windows Server 2003 Enterprise edition can support up to eight processors.

▪ Windows Server 2003 Datacenter edition can support up to 32 processors on an x-86-based computer and up to 64 processors on an Itanium-based computer.

If your computer is capable of supporting multiple processors, you should follow the computer manufacturer's instructions for installing the additional processors. This usually involves updating the processor's driver to a driver that supports multiple processors through the Upgrade Device Driver Wizard.

Once you install your second processor, you can monitor the processors through the System Monitor utility, as described in the previous section. You can verify that multiple processors are recognized by the operating system, as well as configure multiple processors, through the Task Manager utility. You can access the Task Manager utility through the Windows Security dialog box by pressing Ctrl+Alt+Delete or you can right-click an empty space on the taskbar and select Task Manager.

To configure multiple processors, you can associate each processor with specific processes that are running on the computer. This is called *processor affinity*. Once you have two or more processors installed on your computer, you can set processor affinity. We will do this in Exercise 9.3.

Configuring Multiple Processors

1. Press Ctrl+Alt+Delete to access the Windows Security dialog box. Click the Task Manager button.

2. The Task Manager dialog box opens. Click the Processes tab to see a list of all the processes that are currently running on your computer.

3. Right-click the process you want to associate with a specific processor and select Processor Affinity from the pop-up menu. This option will only appear if your server has two or more processors installed.

4. The Processor Affinity dialog box appears. Specify the processor that this process will use and click the OK button.

5. Close the Task Manager utility.

Task Manager is covered in greater detail in the "Using Task Manager" section later in this chapter.

Monitoring and Optimizing the Processes Subsystem

If you suspect that an application or process is consuming a large share of resources, you can monitor specific processes through the Process performance object. For example, suppose that you are running an application called abc.exe and you want to track how much of the processor's time is spent servicing this application and how many bytes of the page file are allocated to this application.

In the following sections you will learn about the key counters to track for the processes subsystem and how to tune and upgrade the processes subsystem.

Key Counters to Track for Processes

To collect this information, you should add the following counters to System Monitor (for a graph) or Performance Logs And Alerts (for a log):

Process > %Processor Time   This counter specifies the amount of time that the process threads were being processed by the processor. If your processor utilization is high, you can determine which process is using the most processor time through this counter.

Process > Page File Bytes   This counter shows how much of the page file is being used by the process in bytes. If your page file usage is high, you can determine which process is using excessive page file memory through this counter.

By default, all DOS and Windows 16-bit applications run in a process called ntvdm.exe, which stands for NT Virtual DOS Machine. By default, DOS applications will run in separate ntvdm sessions. If you run 16-bit Windows applications, they will run in a single ntvdm session. Within System Monitor, you will see the DOS and Windows 16-bit applications listed as ntvdm.

Tuning and Upgrading the Processes Subsystem

If you suspect that you have a process bottleneck, you can try the following solutions:

- Upgrade the application that is using excessive processor or memory allocation and see if the upgraded application handles processor and memory requests more efficiently.

- Replace processor- or memory-intensive applications with applications that use fewer resources.

- Upgrade hardware resources to support processor- or memory-intensive applications.

Monitoring and Optimizing the Disk Subsystem

Disk access is the amount of time it takes your disk subsystem to retrieve data that is requested by the operating system. The two factors that determine how quickly your disk subsystem will respond to system requests are the average disk access time on your hard drive and the speed of your disk controller. On writes, the OS writes only to the controller. Therefore, high-speed writes mandate a very fast controller. On reads, the data is accessed from the disk to the controller. Therefore, on reads the disk access speed is critical. Using high-speed disk controllers and drives in a stripe set, you can attain a disk access time of approximately 5.1 to 6.4 milliseconds.

In the following sections you will learn about the key counters to track for the disk subsystem and how to tune and upgrade the disk subsystem.

Key Counters to Track for the Disk Subsystem

You can monitor the PhysicalDisk object, which is the sum of all logical drives on a single physical drive, or you can monitor the LogicalDisk object, which represents a specific logical disk. The following are the most important counters for monitoring the disk subsystem:

PhysicalDisk > %Disk Time   Shows the amount of time the physical disk is busy because it is servicing read or write requests. If the disk is busy more than 90 percent of the time, you will improve performance by adding another disk channel and splitting the disk I/O requests between the channels.

PhysicalDisk > Current Disk Queue Length   Indicates the number of outstanding disk requests that are waiting to be processed. This value should be less than 2. A value greater than 2 indicates a disk bottleneck.

PhysicalDisk > Disk Reads/sec and Physical Disk > Disk Writes/Sec   This value is dependent on the specified transfer rate as defined by the hard drive manufacturer. As an example, Ultra Wide SCSI disks can typically handle 50 to 70 I/O requests per second.

PhysicalDisk > %Free Space   This counter tracks how much free space is available on the hard drive. It is a way to track disk space usage proactively so users do not experience "out of disk space" errors. It is recommended that this value be set at 15%.

These counters can be tracked for both the PhysicalDisk object and the LogicalDisk object.

Tuning and Upgrading the Disk Subsystem

If you suspect that you have a disk subsystem bottleneck, the first thing you should check is your memory subsystem. If you do not have enough physical memory, it can cause excessive paging, which in turn affects the disk subsystem. If you do not have a memory problem, you can try the following solutions to improve disk performance:

- Use faster disks and controllers.
- Use disk striping to take advantage of multiple I/O channels.
- Balance heavily used files on multiple I/O channels.
- Add another disk controller for load balancing.
- Use Disk Defragmenter to consolidate the files on the disk and optimize disk access.

In Exercise 9.4, you will monitor your disk subsystem.

EXERCISE 9.4

Monitoring the Disk Subsystem

1. If System Monitor is not already open, select Start ➤ Administrative Tools ➤ Performance.

2. In the System Monitor window, click the Add button on the toolbar.

3. In the Add Counters dialog box, select the following performance objects and counters:

    - Select PhysicalDisk from the Performance Object drop-down list, select %Disk Time from the counter list box, and click the Add button.

    - Select PhysicalDisk from the Performance Object drop-down list, select Current Disk Queue Length from the counter list box, and click the Add button.

    - Select LogicalDisk from the Performance Object drop-down list, select %Idle Time from the counter list box, and click the Add button.

4. Click the Close button. You will see these counters added to your graph.

5. To generate some activity, open and close some applications and copy some files between your domain controller and the member server.

6. Note the PhysicalDisk > %Disk Time counter. If this counter's average is below 90 percent, you are not generating excessive requests to this disk.

EXERCISE 9.4 *(continued)*

7. Note the PhysicalDisk > Current Disk Queue Length counter. If this counter's average is below 2, you are not generating excessive requests to this disk.

8. Leave System Monitor open, because you will use this utility again in Exercise 9.5.

You can monitor your logical disk's amount of free disk space through the LogicalDisk > %Free Space counter. This counter can also be used as an alert. For example, you might set an alert to notify you when the LogicalDisk > %Free Space counter on your C: drive is under 10 percent.

Monitoring and Optimizing the Network Subsystem

Windows Server 2003 does not have a built-in mechanism for monitoring the entire network. However, you can monitor and optimize the traffic that is generated on the specific Windows Server 2003 computer. You can monitor the network interface (your network card), and you can monitor the network protocols that have been installed on your computer.

In the following sections you will learn about the key counters to track for the network subsystem and how to tune and upgrade the network subsystem.

Key Counters to Track for the Network Subsystem

The following are two of the counters that are useful for monitoring the network subsystem:

Network Interface > Bytes Total/Sec Measures the total number of bytes that are sent or received from the network interface and includes all network protocols.

TCPv4 > Segments/Sec Measures the number of bytes that are sent or received from the network interface and includes only the TCP protocol.

Normally, you monitor and optimize the network subsystem from a network perspective rather than from a single computer. For example, you can use a network protocol analyzer to monitor all of the traffic on the network to determine if the network bandwidth is acceptable for your requirements or if the network bandwidth is saturated.

Tuning and Upgrading the Network Subsystem

The following suggestions can help to optimize and minimize network traffic:

- Use only the network protocols you need. For example, use TCP/IP and don't use NWLink and NetBEUI.

- If you need to use multiple network protocols, place the most commonly used protocols higher in the binding order.

- Use network cards that take full advantage of your bus width. For example, use 32-bit cards instead of 16-bit cards.

- Use faster network cards. For example, use 100Mbps Ethernet instead of 10Mbps Ethernet.

In Exercise 9.5, you will monitor your network subsystem.

EXERCISE 9.5

Monitoring the Network Subsystem

1. If System Monitor is not already open, select Start ➢ Administrative Tools ➢ Performance.

2. In the System Monitor window, click the Add button on the toolbar.

3. In the Add Counters dialog box, select the following performance objects and counters:

    - Select Network Interface from the Performance Object drop-down list, select Bytes Total/Sec in the counter list box, and click the Add button.

    - Select TCPv4 from the Performance Object drop-down list, select Segments/Sec from the counter list box, and click the Add button.

4. Click the Close button. You should see these counters added to your graph.

5. To generate some activity, copy some files between your domain controller and the member server.

6. Note the Network Interface > Bytes Total/Sec and TCPv4 > Segments/Sec counters. These numbers are cumulative. Use them in your baselines to determine network activity.

7. Leave your console open, because you will use it again in Exercise 9.6.

Creating Baseline Reports

As explained earlier in this chapter, baselines show how your server is performing at a certain time. By taking baselines at regular intervals and also whenever you make any changes to the system's configuration, you can monitor your server's performance over time.

You can create baselines by setting up a counter log file in the Performance Logs And Alerts utility. In Exercise 9.6, you will create a baseline report for your computer.

EXERCISE 9.6

Creating a Baseline Report

1. If the System Monitor is not already open, select Start ➢ Administrative Tools ➢ Performance.

2. Expand Performance Logs And Alerts.

3. Right-click Counter Logs and select New Log Settings.

4. In the New Log Settings dialog box, type **Counter*mmddyy*** (replace *mmddyy* with the current month, date, and year) as the log name. The log file will be stored in the C:\PerfLogs folder by default. Click the OK button.

5. In the General tab of the counter log Properties dialog box, click the Add button and add the following counters:

   - Memory > Available Mbytes

   - Memory > Pages/Sec

   - Paging File > %Usage

   - Processor > %Processor Time

   - Processor > Interrupts/Sec

   - PhysicalDisk > %Disk Time

   - PhysicalDisk > Current Disk Queue Length

   - Network Interface > Bytes Total/Sec

   - TCPv4 > Segments/Sec

6. Set the interval for sampling data to five seconds.

7. Click the Log Files tab. Uncheck the End File Names With checkbox. This will prevent the filename from being appended with *mmddhh* (month/day/hour). Click the OK button to close the Properties dialog box and start the log file.

8. To generate system activity, start and stop some applications, copy a few files, and run a screen saver for one to two minutes.

9. To view your log file, open System Monitor. Click the View Log File Data button on the toolbar.

10. In the open file dialog box, select C:\PerfLogs\Countermmddyy and click the Open button.

11. Add the counters from the log file you created to see the data that was collected in your log.

Using the System Tool in Control Panel

The System Tool in Control Panel can be used to manage performance options for your computer. The performance-related options that can be configured through the System Tool include how visual settings affect performance, how processor resources are allocated, how system memory is allocated, and how the paging file is configured.

To access these options, select Start ≻ Control Panel ≻ System. Select the Advanced tab, and then for Performance, click the Settings button. You will see two tabs, Visual Effects and Advanced.

From the Visual Effects tab, shown in Figure 9.22, you can specify how performance is tuned based on the visual effects you choose to use with your user interface. The selections for visual effect settings include:

- Let Windows Choose What's Best For My Computer

- Adjust For Best Appearance

- Adjust For Best Performance

- Custom (which allows you to specifically configure several options relating to appearance that effect system performance)

FIGURE 9.22 The Visual Effects tab of the Performance Options dialog box

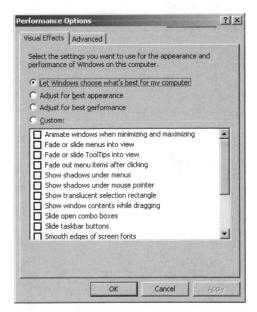

If you click the Advanced tab, you will see the dialog box shown in Figure 9.23. From the Advanced tab, you can configure:

- Processor Scheduling, which allows you to optimize the processor time for running programs or background services

- Memory Usage, which allows you to optimize memory for programs or system cache

- Virtual Memory, which is used to configure the paging file

If you click the Change button within the Virtual Memory section of the Advanced tab, you can manage the page file, as shown in Figure 9.24.

FIGURE 9.23   The Advanced Tab of the System Tool

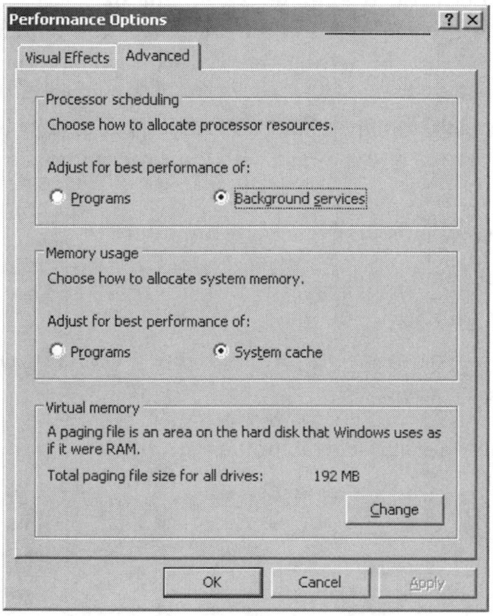

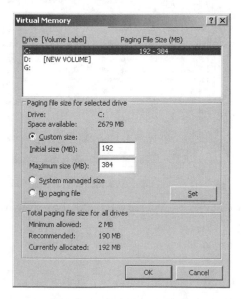

FIGURE 9.24   Virtual Memory dialog box

When Windows is initially installed, the page file, pagefile.sys, is set to 1.5 times the amount of physical memory. You can optimize the page file by moving it from the drive that contains the system partition or by splitting it over multiple disk I/O channels.

In order to make changes to the System Tool, you must be logged on to the local computer with administrative rights.

Using Task Manager

The *Task Manager* utility shows the applications and processes that are currently running on your computer, as well as CPU and memory usage information. To access Task Manager, press Ctrl+Alt+Delete and click the Task Manager button. Alternatively, right-click an empty area in the Taskbar and select Task Manager from the pop-up menu.

You can use Task Manager to manage application, process, performance, networking, and user tasks. We will look at all these in the following sections.

Managing Application Tasks

The Applications tab of the Task Manager dialog box, shown in Figure 9.25, lists all of the applications that are currently running on the computer. For each task, you will see the name of the task and the current status (running, not responding, or stopped).

FIGURE 9.25   The Applications tab of the Task Manager dialog box

From the application tab, you can manage application tasks as follows:

- To close an application, select it and click the End Task button at the bottom of the dialog box. This option is especially useful for closing applications that have stopped responding.
- To make the application window active, select it and click the Switch To button.

- To start an application, click the New Task button to bring up the Create New Task dialog box. Type in the name of the program or click the Browse button to select the program you wish to start and click the OK button.

Managing Process Tasks

The Processes tab of the Task Manager dialog box, shown in Figure 9.26, lists all of the processes that are currently running on the computer. This is a convenient way to get a quick look at how your system is performing. Unlike using System Monitor, you don't need to first configure the collection of this data; it's gathered automatically.

FIGURE 9.26   The Processes tab of the Task Manager dialog box

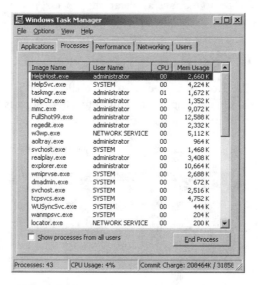

For each process, you will see the image (process) name, the username associated with the process that is running, the amount of CPU utilization that the process is using, and the amount of memory being used by the process.

From the Processes tab, you can organize the listing and control processes as follows:

- To organize the processes based on usage, click the column headings. For example, if you click the CPU column, the listing will start with the processes that use the most CPU resources. If you click the CPU column a second time, the listing will be reversed.

- To manage a process, right-click it and choose an option from the pop-up menu. You can choose to end the process, end the process tree, or set the priority of the process, as described in the following sections. If your computer has multiple processors installed, you can also set processor affinity, as described in the "Using Multiple Processors" section earlier in the chapter.

- To customize the counters that are listed, select View ➢ Select Columns. This brings up the Select Columns dialog box, shown in Figure 9.27, where you can select the information that you want to see listed on the Processes tab.

FIGURE 9.27   The Select Columns dialog box

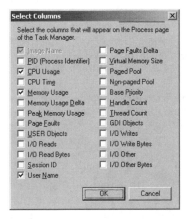

The counters that can be tracked through the Process page of the Task Manager are listed in Table 9.2.

TABLE 9.2   Task Manager Process Counters

Counter	Description
Image Name	The name of the process, as displayed through Task Manager.
PID (Process Identifier)	Unique numerical identifier used to identify a process through Task Manager.
CPU Usage	The percent of time used by the process since the last update.
CPU Time	Time in seconds, used by the process since it was started.
Memory Usage	Number of kilobytes currently in use by the current working set of a process.
Memory Usage Delta	Change in memory (in kilobytes) used since the last update.
Peak Memory Usage	Peak amount of memory used since the process was started.
Page Faults	Number of times the software tried to read from memory and had to get the requested information from disk.
USER Objects	Number of user objects currently used by a process. User objects include windows, menus, cursors, icons, and other internal objects.
I/O Reads	The number of read input/output (I/O) events that have been generated by the process.
I/O Read Bytes	The number of bytes that have been generated by I/O read events.

TABLE 9.2 Task Manager Process Counters *(continued)*

Counter	Description
Session ID	This option is used by Terminal Services and lists the Terminal Services ID that owns the process.
User Name	This option will only appear when Terminal Services is installed, and lists the name of the user whose Terminal Service session created the process.
Page Faults Delta	Number of page faults since the last update.
Virtual Memory Size	Amount of virtual memory that has been allocated to a process.
Paged Pool	Amount of virtual memory that is being served by physical memory.
Non-Paged Pool	Amount of virtual RAM that is being processed from disk.
Base Priority	Order in which the threads of a process are scheduled for the processor.
Handle Count	Number of object handles used by a specific process.
Thread Count	Number of threads generated for the current process.
GDI Objects	Number of objects that have been generated by the process from the Graphics Driver Interface (GDI) library of application programming interfaces (APIs).
I/O Writes	Number of write I/O events that have been generated by the process.
I/O Write Bytes	Number of bytes that have been generated by I/O write events.
I/O Other	Number of I/O operations that are not read or write events—for example, network or other device I/O.
I/O Other Bytes	Number of bytes that have been generated by I/O other events.

 Real World Scenario

Using Task Manager to Monitor Processes

Your Windows Server 2003 is primarily used as an applications server running an application called ABC.EXE. Users are complaining that when they access this application, it is slow to respond. You check the processor utilization through Task Manager and see that it is averaging 95 percent.

Your server has an empty slot for an extra processor. However, before you add the second processor, you want to verify that the ABC.EXE application is multithreaded. If the application uses a single thread, then it will only be processed on a single processor. If the application is multithreaded, then it can take advantage of multiple processors.

To verify how many threads are being used by a process, run Task Manager while the process is running. Click the Processes tab and from View, choose Select Columns. Verify that Thread Count is selected. When you click OK, you can see the number of threads that have been generated by the process.

In the following sections you will learn how to stop processes and how to manage process priority.

Stopping Processes

You may need to stop a process that isn't executing properly. To stop a specific process, select the process you want to stop in the Task Manager's Processes tab and click the End Process button. Task Manager displays a Warning dialog box. Click the Yes button to terminate the process.

If you right-click a process, you can end the specific process or you can use the option End Process Tree. The End Process Tree option ends all processes that have been created either directly or indirectly by the process.

Some of the common processes that can be managed through Task Manager are listed in Table 9.3.

TABLE 9.3 Common Processes

Process	Description
System Idle Process	A process that runs when the processor is not executing any other threads
smss.exe	Session Manager subsystem
csrss.exe	Client-server runtime server service
mmc.exe	Microsoft Management Console program (used to track resources used by MMC snap-ins such as System Monitor)
Explorer.exe	Windows Explorer interface
ntvdm.exe	MS-DOS and Windows 16-bit application support

Managing Process Priority

You can manage process priority through the Task Manager utility or through the start command-line utility.

To change the priority of a process that is already running, use the Processes tab of Task Manager. Right-click the process you want to manage and select Set Priority from the pop-up menu. You can select from Realtime, High, AboveNormal, Normal, BelowNormal, and Low priorities.

To start applications and set their priority at the same time, use the start command. The options that can be used with the start command are listed in Table 9.4.

TABLE 9.4   Options for the start Command-Line Utility

Option	Description
/low	Starts an application in the idle priority class.
/normal	Starts an application in the normal priority class.
/high	Starts an application in the high priority class.
/realtime	Starts an application in the real-time priority class.
/abovenormal	Starts an application in the above normal priority class.
/belownormal	Starts an application in the below normal priority class.
/min	Starts the application in a minimized window.
/max	Starts the application in a maximized window.
/separate	Starts a Windows 16-bit application in a separate memory space.
/shared	Starts a Windows 16-bit application in a shared memory space.

The syntax that is used with the Start command-line utility is:

Start /option(s) [Filename]

An example of starting the abc.exe Windows 16-bit application using the Start command-line utility in a separate memory space using above normal priority would be:

Start /separate /abovenormal abc.exe

WARNING   Running a process-intensive application in the real-time priority class can significantly impact Windows Server 2003 performance.

In Exercise 9.7, you will manage your computer's processes.

Managing Computer Processes

1. Right-click an empty space on your Taskbar and select Task Manager from the pop-up menu.

2. In the Applications tab, click the New Task button.

3. In the Create A New Task dialog box, type **Calc** and click the OK button.

4. Click the Processes tab. Right-click calc.exe and select Set Priority, then Low. In the Task Manager Warning dialog box, click the Yes button to continue.

5. Right-click calc.exe and select End Process. In the Task Manager Warning dialog box, click the Yes button.

Managing Performance Tasks

The Performance tab of the Task Manager dialog box, shown in Figure 9.28, provides an overview of your computer's CPU and memory usage. This is similar to the information that System Monitor tracks.

FIGURE 9.28   The Performance tab of the Task Manager dialog box

The Performance tab shows the following information:

- CPU usage, real-time and history graph. CPU usage indicates, in a percentage format, how much of the processor time was used processing system or user requests.

- Page file usage, real-time and history graph. Page file usage shows how much of your paging file is being used. If this number is high, you should add memory or increase the size of your paging file.

- Totals for handles, threads, and processes. A handle is a value that is used to identify a resource (for example, a file or Registry key). A thread is a discrete object within a process that is used to execute instructions generated by the application. Multithreaded applications can take advantage of multiple processors. A process is an executable program or service—for example, System Monitor.

- Physical memory statistics, which include how much physical memory is installed, how much physical memory is currently available, and how much system cache memory (from the page file) is available.

- Commit charge memory statistics. Commit charge memory is all of the memory (physical memory and page file memory) that has been allocated to the operating system and any applications that are running.

- Kernel memory statistics. Kernel memory is memory used by the operating system kernel and device drivers. Paged memory is from the page file and nonpaged memory is physical memory.

Managing Networking Tasks

The Networking tab of the Task Manager dialog box, as shown in Figure 9.29, provides you with an overview of the adapters that are being used by the server, the percentage of network utilization for each adapter, the link speed (for example, 100Mbps Ethernet), and the current status of the adapter.

FIGURE 9.29   The Networking tab of the Task Manager dialog box

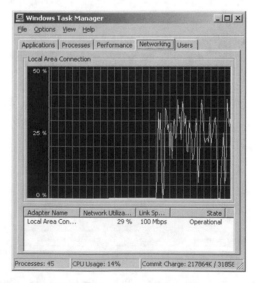

Through the graph, you can see the percentage of network utilization (or bandwidth) that is in use for the specified adapter. If the server has two or more network adapters, you can see the traffic being generated on each adapter. If the network utilization is consistently high, you should tune your network subsystem, as described earlier in this chapter.

Managing Network Users

The Users tab of the Task Manager dialog box, as shown in Figure 9.30, provides you with a list of all users who are currently connected to the server. For each user, you can see:

- The name of the user who is currently logged on
- The numeric ID that is used to uniquely identify the session number of the computer
- The current status of the session, either Active or Disconnected
- The name of the client computer that the user is using, if applicable

   If you click on a specific user, you can disconnect the user, log the user off, or send the user a message using the associated buttons at the bottom of the Users tab dialog box.

FIGURE 9.30   The Users tab of the Task Manager dialog box

Summary

In this chapter, you learned about Windows Server 2003 optimization. We covered the following topics:

- How to determine what system performance is and why it is important to track system performance
- The performance updates that have been added to System Monitor and Performance Logs And Alerts in Windows Server 2003
- How to use the System Monitor utility and the Performance Logs And Alerts utility to track and monitor your system's performance

- How to track system performance data using command-line utilities
- How to monitor and optimize memory, the processor, processes that are running on the server, the disk subsystem, and the network subsystem, and how to create a system baseline
- How to use the System Tool in Control Panel to optimize system performance
- How to use the Task Manager utility to view and manage running applications and processes, to get an overview of CPU and memory usage, to view network bandwidth, and to manage network users

Exam Essentials

Be able to monitor and troubleshoot Windows Server 2003 performance.   Know how to track Windows Server 2003 performance events and issues with System Monitor, Performance Logs And Alerts, and command-line utilities. Know how to track and identify performance problems related to memory, the processor, the disk subsystem, and the network subsystem. Be able to correct system bottlenecks once they are identified.

Be able to manage processes.   Know how to manage processes including identifying which resources are used by a process, how to stop and start processes, and how to assign priorities to processes.

Be able to use the Task Manager utility.   Know which performance monitoring options can be viewed and managed through the Task Manager utility. Be able to use Task Manager to quickly identify common system bottlenecks.

Key Terms

Before you take the exam, be certain you are familiar with the following terms:

alerts	Performance Logs And Alerts
baseline	processor affinity
bottleneck	System Monitor
page file	Task Manager

Review Questions

1. You are the network administrator of a medium-sized company. You manage a Sales Server that is primarily used as an application server. Your server has been running for several months with no problems. Yesterday you installed a new application called ABC Application. Today your users are complaining that access to the other applications on the server is very slow. You use Task Manager, and under the Processes tab you see that the abc.exe application has a fairly high CPU utilization. You then use Task Manager to end ABC Application, but the processor utilization is still very high. You restart ABC Application. Which of the following actions should you take?

    A. Right-click the ABC process through Task Manager and select End Process Tree.

    B. Use Service Manager to stop the ABC process.

    C. Right-click the ABC process through Application Manager and select End All Child Processes.

    D. Use Control Panel, Applications to end the ABC process.

2. Peter is the system administrator for a medium-sized company. He has used the Performance Logs And Alerts utility to create a baseline log file for all of the Windows Server 2003 servers that he manages. Peter would like to take the data that has been collected and create a database that includes the log files from all servers for analysis. Which of the following command-line utilities can be used to extract the data and save it in SQL format?

    A. Typeperf

    B. Tracerpt

    C. Logman

    D. Relog

3. Dave is the system administrator for a medium-sized company. He is currently using the System Monitor utility to view memory usage, processor usage, and disk subsystem usage for the Sales department's Windows Server 2003 member server. Dave suspects that he has identified a memory bottleneck. He wants to send a copy of the data he has collected to another system administrator for a second opinion before he orders more memory for the server. Which of the following command-line utilities can he use to create a data log file based on the information that is currently displayed through System Monitor?

    A. Typeperf

    B. Tracerpt

    C. Logman

    D. Relog

4. Tomisa is using ABC Application on her Windows Server 2003 member server. After she added the application, she noticed that the processor utilization was very high. Tomisa knew that the application was processor intensive, so she installed it on a server that has the capability to support two processors. Tomisa wants to install a second processor on her server, but wants to verify that the application is multithreaded before she performs the upgrade. Based on the following exhibit, which of the following columns should she enable for monitoring process-related events?

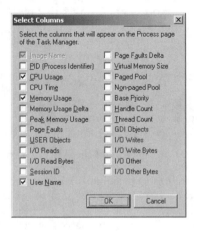

A. USER Objects

B. Base Priority

C. Thread Count

D. GDI Objects

5. Vadim works for a Fortune 500 company. He is in charge of all of the servers used by the Finance department. One of the servers is used primarily as a database server. He wants to add about 20% more load to the server and wants to see how much processing the server is currently handling over a two-week period before he adds the additional load. He wants to create a report that will sample the system every five minutes for a specified set of performance monitoring counters. Which of the following utilities should he use?

A. Performance Monitor

B. System Monitor

C. Performance Logs And Alerts

D. Report Manager

6. Brad wants to track what effect running a new application will have on his Windows Server 2003 member server. He decides to use lab resources to run tests of how system resources are affected when the new application is running. Before the application is installed and running, he starts System Monitor with counters added for each major subsystem. Next, he will start the application and run a program that will simulate usage of the application. Which of the following views in System Monitor will allow Brad to watch the counters over a period of time so that he can see the effect that the application has on the server's performance?

A. Graph

B. Histogram

C. History

D. Report

7. You are the network administrator for a computer book publisher. You have a user named Jeff who uses a Windows XP Professional computer that is a part of the Sybex domain. He executes a program called `abc.exe` that is located on a Windows Server 2003 member server called Editing. When he executes this program, it seems to be running slowly. He calls you to notify you of the problem. You suspect that the application is improperly allocating memory. You ask Jeff to quit the application as quickly as possible in order to restore the server to its normal operating environment. When Jeff attempts to quit the application, it seems to hang. Which of the following options can he use to stop the `abc.exe` program?

A. Performance Logs And Alerts

B. System Monitor

C. Performance Monitor

D. Task Manager

8. You are in charge of all of the Marketing servers, which are all running Windows Server 2003 and are configured as member servers. One of the servers is used primarily as an applications server. One of the users needs to access some historical data that was created using a legacy application that has not been updated. The user has the data stored on tape, but the application is currently not available on any of the corporate servers. He asks you to reload the legacy application so he can access the data. You agree to reload the application, but are concerned that it may place a significant load on the server and want to monitor its impact on the server. You install and run the `xyz.exe` application, which is the only 16-bit Windows application now running on the server. You now want to track the processor usage for this application in System Monitor. When you check System Monitor, you see no listing for `xyz.exe`. Which process should you track?

A. `xyz.exe`

B. `ntvdm`

C. `win16`

D. `wow`

9. You have a Windows Server 2003 member server that is used as a database server. The database is very write intensive. You notice that the system performance on the server has been steadily declining over the past month. You decide to use System Monitor to determine what the bottleneck is. After analysis, you discover that you have a disk subsystem bottleneck on your Windows Server 2003. Which of the following options *cannot* be used to optimize disk performance to help alleviate the bottleneck?

    A. Use faster disks and controllers.

    B. Balance heavily used files on multiple I/O channels.

    C. Use disk striping.

    D. Use online volume growth.

10. You are the network administrator of a medium-sized company. You run several Windows 16-bit applications on your Windows Server 2003 member server called App Server. When you try to track resource usage for the applications, they are all listed as a single `ntvdm` session. You want to run the `1234.exe` Windows 16-bit application in its own memory space so that you can track resource usage for this specific application. Which of the following command-line options could be used to start the DOS `1234.exe` program in its own memory space?

    A. `start /separate 1234.exe`

    B. `run /separate 1234.exe`

    C. `start /min 1234.exe`

    D. `run /min 1234.exe`

11. Kelly wants to run the `lala.exe` program on Windows Server 2003. She notices that when this program is run at the server, the server slows down significantly. Which of the following utilities can she use to set the priority of the `lala.exe` program to low?

    A. Performance Monitor

    B. System Monitor

    C. Task Manager

    D. Service Manager

12. You are the network manager of a medium-sized company. You use the Task Manager utility as a way of quickly monitoring processor and memory usage whenever you directly access a server. Which process is used in Task Manager to indicate that a process is running when the processor is not executing any other threads?

    A. System Idle Process

    B. Processor Free Time

    C. Processor Idle Time

    D. Processor Available

13. You are the network administrator for a medium-sized company. You have noticed that your e-mail server, which is configured as a Windows Server 2003 member server, is performing sluggishly. You have been steadily adding users and applications to the server over the last six months. You suspect that you may have a memory bottleneck and want to determine how much of the paging file is currently in use. Which of the following System Monitor counters should you use if you want to determine how much of the allocated page file is currently in use?

A. Memory > %Paging File

B. Memory > Pages/Sec

C. Paging File > %Usage

D. Paging File > Pages/Sec

14. Dave has two processors in his Windows Server 2003. The server primarily acts as an applications server. One of the applications is called `1234.exe`. Dave wants to configure the application so that it always runs on the second processor. Which of the following utilities can be used to set processor affinity for the `1234.exe` application?

A. Performance Monitor

B. System Monitor

C. Task Manager

D. Service Manager

15. You are an applications developer and you want to perform testing on the application you have written to work with Windows Server 2003. You want to verify what priority your application is using. Based on the following exhibit, which of the following columns should you enable for monitoring which priority processes are being used?

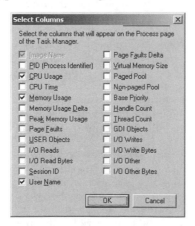

A. PID

B. CPU Time

C. Base Priority

D. GDI Objects

Answers to Review Questions

1. **A.** Through Task Manager, when you right-click a process you can end the specific process or you can use the option End Process Tree. The End Process Tree option ends all processes that have been created either directly or indirectly by the process. Sometimes the child processes are actually creating the processor or memory bottleneck.

2. **D.** The Relog command-line utility is used to extract the performance data that has been collected as a counter log and convert the data to text-TSV format (tab-delimited text), text-CSV format (comma-delimited text), binary format, or SQL format so that the data can be exported into a spreadsheet or database.

3. **A.** The Typeperf command-line utility takes performance counter data that is in the current command window and writes it to a counter data log file.

4. **C.** Thread Count is used to display how many threads are associated with an application. If an application is not multithreaded, it will not be able to be processed on multiple processors.

5. **C.** The Performance Logs And Alerts utility is used to create reports, which can then be viewed with the System Monitor utility. He can then compare the baseline he creates before he adds the additional load to the server with the baseline he creates after the additional load is added. This will allow him to tune or upgrade the server if necessary.

6. **A.** The only System Monitor view that allows you to see how the data is being tracked over time is the Graph view. If he used the Histogram or Report view, the data would be displayed as a real-time value.

7. **D.** Task Manager can be used to stop applications or processes that are currently running on the computer, even if they have stopped responding to normal application requests.

8. **B.** When you are running Windows 16-bit applications, they are automatically executed in a shared memory space called ntvdm, which stands for NT Virtual DOS Machine. If you run DOS applications, each DOS application will run in a separate ntvdm session.

9. **D.** You can improve disk performance by using faster disks and controllers, by using disk striping to take advantage of multiple I/O channels, by balancing heavily used files in multiple I/O channels, and by adding another disk controller for load balancing.

10. **A.** You use the start command to start new applications. The /separate switch is used to start Windows 16-bit applications in their own memory space. By default, Windows 16-bit applications run in a shared memory space.

11. **C.** The Processes tab of Task Manager can be used to manage process priorities. To change the priority of a process that is already running, right-click the process you want to manage and select Set Priority. You can select from Realtime, High, AboveNormal, Normal, BelowNormal, and Low priorities.

12. **A.** The System Idle Process is used to specify that the processor is not executing any other threads. If the System Idle Process is a high value, then the processor is available to process requests.

13. C.   The Paging File > %Usage counter indicates how much of the allocated page file is currently in use. If this number is consistently over 70 percent, you may need to add more memory or increase the size of the paging file.

14. C.   The Processes tab of Task Manager can be used to set processor affinity for processes on a server with more than one processor. Right-click the process you want to associate with a specific processor and select Processor Affinity.

15. C.   The Base Priority option is used to display the priority that the current process is using. You can change the process priority through Task Manager.

Chapter

10

Performing System Recovery Functions

MICROSOFT EXAM OBJECTIVES COVERED IN THIS CHAPTER:

✓ **Monitor and analyze events. Tools might include Event Viewer and System Monitor.**

✓ **Manage servers remotely.**

- Manage a server by using Remote Assistance.
- Manage a server by using available support tools.

✓ **Perform system recovery for a server.**

- Implement Automated System Recovery (ASR).
- Back up files and System State data to media.
- Configure security for backup operations.

✓ **Manage backup procedures.**

- Verify the successful completion of backup jobs.
- Manage backup storage media.

✓ **Recover from server hardware failure.**

✓ **Restore backup data.**

✓ **Schedule backup jobs.**

System recovery is the process of making your computer work again in the event of failure. The benefit of having a disaster recovery plan is that when you expect the worst to happen and you are prepared for it, you can easily recover from most system failures.

One utility that you can use to diagnose system problems is Event Viewer. Through the Event Viewer utility, you can see logs that list events related to your operating system and applications.

If your computer will not boot, an understanding of the Window Server 2003 boot process will help you identify the area of failure and correct the problem. You will learn about the startup process that is used in *x*86-based systems and in Itanium-based systems. You should know the steps in each stage of the boot process, the function of each boot file, and how to edit the Boot.ini file.

When you have problems starting Windows Server 2003, you can press F8 when prompted during the boot sequence. This calls up the Windows Server 2003 Advanced Options menu. This menu includes several special boot options, such as Safe Mode and Last Known Good Configuration, which are useful for getting your system started so you can track down and correct problems.

Some of the new features of system recovery in Windows Server 2003 include Driver Rollback, which allows you to easily roll back to a previously used driver. System Restore allows you to create and use restore points to return your operating system to a previous configuration.

Startup and Recovery options are used to specify how the operating system will react in the event of system failure. For example, you can specify whether or not the system should automatically reboot and whether or not administrative alerts should be sent.

Backups are the best protection you can have against system failure. You can create backups through the Windows Backup utility. The Windows Backup utility offers options to run the Backup and Restore Wizard. Windows Backup also allows you to create an Automated System Recovery backup that is used to restore critical Windows operating system files. You can schedule the backup jobs as an automated process.

Another option that experienced administrators can use to recover from a system failure is the Recovery Console. The Recovery Console boots your computer so that you have limited access to FAT16, FAT32, and NTFS volumes.

Windows Server 2003 supports Remote Desktop and Remote Assistance. Remote Desktop allows you to take remote control access of a remote computer. Remote Assistance is used to request assistance from an expert user.

In this chapter, you will learn how to use the Windows Server 2003 system recovery functions. We'll begin with an overview of the techniques you can use to protect your computer and recover from disasters.

Safeguarding Your Computer and Recovering from Disaster

One of the worst events you will experience is a computer that won't boot. An even worse experience is discovering that there is no recent backup for that computer.

The first step in preparing for disaster recovery is to expect that a disaster will occur at some point and take proactive steps to plan your recovery before the failure. The following are some of the preparations you can make:

- Perform regular system backups.

- Use virus-scanning software.

- Perform regular administrative functions, such as monitoring the logs in the Event Viewer utility.

If you can't start Windows Server 2003, there are several options and utilities that can be used to identify and resolve Windows errors. The following is a broad list of troubleshooting options:

- If you have recently made a change to your server's configuration by installing a new device driver or application and Windows Server 2003 will not load properly, you can use the Last Known Good Configuration, roll back the driver, or use System Restore to restore a previous system configuration.

- If you can boot your computer to Safe Mode, and you suspect that you have a system conflict, you can temporarily disable applications, processes, or services, or uninstall software.

- If your computer will not boot to Safe Mode, then you can use the Recovery Console to replace corrupted files or perform other recovery options manually. For example, on an *x*86 system, you should verify that the Boot.ini settings are correct. On an Itanium-based computer, you would verify that the NVRAM startup settings are correct.

- If necessary, you can use Windows Backup to restore operating system files and data files from backup media. You can also use Automated System Recovery in conjunction with Windows Backup to reformat the system partition and restore operating system files from backup media you previously created.

Table 10.1 summarizes the Windows Server 2003 recovery tools and techniques.

TABLE 10.1   Windows Server 2003 Recovery Techniques

Recovery Technique	When to Use
Event Viewer	If the Windows Server 2003 operating system can be loaded through normal or Safe Mode, one of the first places to look for hints about the problem is Event Viewer. Event Viewer displays System, Security, and Application logs. You may also see other logs based on how the server is configured.

TABLE 10.1   Windows Server 2003 Recovery Techniques *(continued)*

Recovery Technique	When to Use
Safe Mode	This is generally your starting point for system recovery. Safe Mode loads the absolute minimum of services and drivers that are needed to boot Windows Server 2003. If you can load Safe Mode, you should be able to troubleshoot devices or services that keep Windows Server 2003 from loading normally.
Last Known Good Configuration	You can use this option if you made changes to your computer and are now having problems. Last Known Good Configuration is an Advanced Options menu item that you can select during startup. It loads the configuration that was used the last time the computer booted successfully. This option will not help if you have hardware errors or if you logged on after the error occurred.
Driver Rollback	Allows you to roll back to a driver that was a previously known good driver.
System Restore	System Restore is used to create a series of restore points that can be used to restore your operating system to a previous date and time.
Windows Backup	You should use this utility to safeguard your computer. Through the Backup utility, you can back up the system or parts of the system, and restore data from backups that you have made. The Backup utility is also used with Automated System Recovery to recover operating system files in the event they are missing or corrupt.
Recovery Console	You can use this option if none of the other options or utilities works. The Recovery Console starts Windows Server 2003 without the graphical interface and allows the administrator limited capabilities, such as adding or replacing files and starting and stopping services.

All of these Windows Server 2003 recovery techniques are covered in detail in this chapter.

Using Event Viewer

Whenever events occur on a Windows Server 2003 computer, an event is logged through the Event Log Service. You can use the *Event Viewer* utility to view the events that are logged. The information that is tracked includes hardware and software events and monitored security events. The most common use for viewing event logs is for troubleshooting system problems or monitoring the computer for potential problems.

The information that is tracked is stored in three types of log files:

- The *System log* tracks events that are related to the Windows Server 2003 operating system.

- The *Security log* tracks events that are related to Windows Server 2003 auditing.
- The *Application log* tracks events that are related to applications that are running on your computer.

 On Windows Server 2003 domain controllers, Event Viewer also includes Directory Service, DNS Server, and File Replication Service logs. Depending on how your server is configured, you may also have other Event Viewer logs.

You can access Event Viewer by selecting Start ➢ Administrative Tools ➢ Event Viewer. Alternatively, right-click My Computer, select Manage from the pop-up menu, and access Event Viewer under System Tools. From Event Viewer, select the log you want to view. Figure 10.1 shows Event Viewer with the System log displayed.

FIGURE 10.1   A System log in Event Viewer

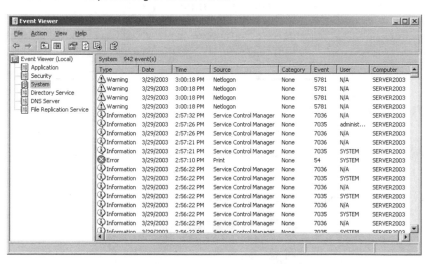

In the log file, you will see all of the events that have been recorded. By default, you see the oldest events at the bottom of the screen and the newest events at the top of the screen. This can be misleading in troubleshooting, since one error can precipitate other errors. You should always resolve the oldest errors first. To change the default listing order, click one of the three logs and select View ➢ Oldest First.

The following sections describe how to view events and manage logs, how to set log file properties, and how to manage event logs from command-line utilities.

Reviewing Event Types

The Event Viewer logs display five event types, denoted by their icons. Table 10.2 describes each event type.

TABLE 10.2 Event Viewer Log Events

Icon	Event Type	Description
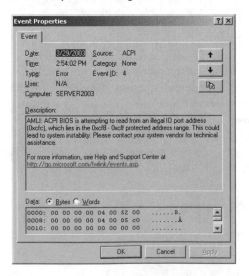	Information	Informs you of the occurrence of a specific action, such as the system shutting down or starting. *Information events* are logged for informative purposes.
	Warning	Indicates that you should be concerned with the event. *Warning events* may not be critical in nature but may be indicative of future errors.
	Error	Indicates the occurrence of an error, such as a driver failing to load. You should be very concerned with *Error events*.
	Success Audit	Indicates the occurrence of an event that has been audited for success. For example, a *Success Audit event* is a successful logon when system logons are being audited.
	Failure Audit	Indicates the occurrence of an event that has been audited for failure. For example, a *Failure Audit event* is a failed logon due to an invalid username and/or password when system logons are being audited.

Getting Event Details

Clicking an event in an Event Viewer log file brings up the Event Properties dialog box, which shows details about the event. An example of the Event Properties dialog box for an Error event is shown in Figure 10.2. Table 10.3 describes the information that appears in this dialog box.

FIGURE 10.2 The Event Properties dialog box

TABLE 10.3   Event Properties Dialog Box Items

Item	Description
Date	The date that the event was generated
Time	The time that the event was generated
Type	The type of event that was generated: Information, Warning, Error, Success Audit, or Failure Audit
User	The name of the user that the event is attributed to, if applicable (not all events are attributed to a user)
Computer	The name of the computer on which the event occurred
Source	The software that generated the event (e.g., operating system components or drivers)
Category	The source that logged the event (this field will say None until this feature has been fully implemented in Windows Server 2003)
Event ID	The event number specific to the type of event that was generated (e.g., a print error event has the event ID 45)
Description	A detailed description of the event
Data	The binary data generated by the event (if any; some events do not generate binary data) in hexadecimal bytes or Word format (programmers can use this information to interpret the event)

Managing Log Files

Over time, your log files will grow, and you will need to decide how to manage them. You can clear a log file for a fresh start. You may want to save the existing log file before you clear it, to keep that log file available for future reference or further analysis.

To clear all log file events, right-click the log you wish to clear and choose Clear All Events from the pop-up menu. Then specify whether or not you want to save the log before it is cleared.

If you just want to save an existing log file, right-click that log and choose Save Log File As. Then specify the location and name of the file.

To open an existing log file, right-click the log you wish to open and choose Open Log File. Then specify the name and location of the log file and click the Open button.

Setting Log File Properties

Each Event Viewer log has two sets of properties associated with it:

- General properties control items such as the log filename, its maximum size, and the action to take when the log file reaches its maximum size.
- Filter properties specify which events are displayed.

To access the log Properties dialog box, right-click the log you want to manage and select Properties from the pop-up menu. The following sections describe the properties available on the General and Filter tabs of this dialog box.

General Properties

The General tab of the log Properties dialog box, shown in Figure 10.3, displays information about the log file and includes options to control its size. Table 10.4 lists the properties on the General tab.

FIGURE 10.3   The General tab of the System Log Properties dialog box

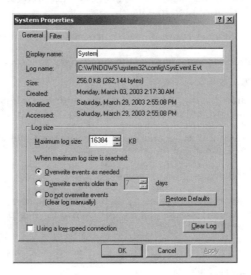

TABLE 10.4   General Log Properties

Property	Description
Display Name	Allows you to change the name of the log file. For example, if you are managing multiple computers and want to distinguish the logs for each computer, you can make the names more descriptive (e.g., DATA-Application and ROVER-Application).
Log Name	Displays the path and filename of the log file.
Size	Displays the current size of the log file.
Created	Specifies the date and time that the log file was created.
Modified	Specifies the date and time that the log file was last modified.
Accessed	Specifies the date and time that the log file was last accessed.

TABLE 10.4   General Log Properties *(continued)*

Property	Description
Maximum Log Size	Allows you to specify the maximum size that the log file can grow to. You can use this option to prevent the log file from taking up excessive disk space.
When Maximum Log Size Is Reached	Allows you to specify what action will be taken when the log file reaches the maximum size (if a maximum size is specified). You can choose to overwrite events as needed (on a first-in-first-out basis), overwrite events that are over a certain age, or specify that events should not be overwritten (which means that you would need to clear log events manually).
Using A Low-Speed Connection	Specifies that you are monitoring the log file of a remote computer and that you connect to that computer through a low-speed connection.

The Clear Log button in the General tab of the log Properties dialog box clears all log events.

Filter Properties

The Filter tab of the log Properties dialog box, shown in Figure 10.4, allows you to control which events are listed in the log. For example, if your system generates a large number of log events, you might want to set the Filter properties so that you can track specific events. You can filter log events based on the event type, source, category, ID, users, computer, or specific time period. Table 10.5 lists the properties on the Filter tab.

FIGURE 10.4   The Filter tab of the log Properties dialog box

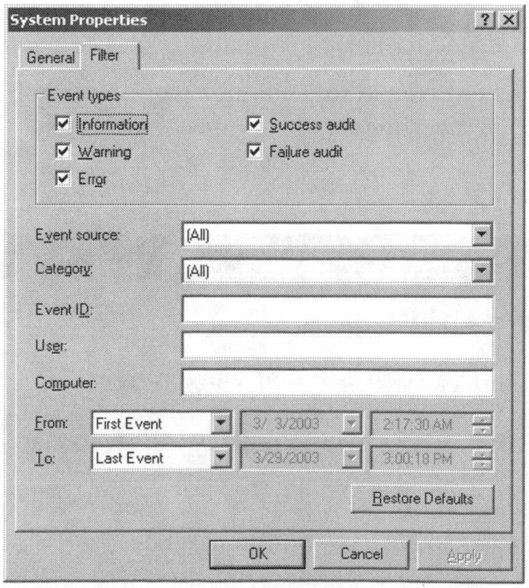

TABLE 10.5 Filter Properties for Logs

Property	Description
Event Types	Allows you to list only the specified event types (Warning, Error, Success Audit, or Failure Audit). By default, all event types are listed.
Event Source	Allows you to filter events based on the source of the event. The drop-down box lists the software that might generate events, such as Application Popup and DHCP. By default, events triggered by all sources are listed.
Category	Allows you to filter events based on the category that generated the event. The drop-down box lists the event categories. By default, events in all categories are listed.
Event ID	Allows you to filter events based on a specific event number.
User	Allows you to filter events based on the user who caused the event to be triggered.
Computer	Allows you to filter events based on the name of the computer that generated the event.
From-To	Allows you to filter events based on the date and time that the events were generated. By default, events are listed from the first event to the last event. To specify specific dates and times, select Events On from the drop-down list and select dates and times.

In Exercise 10.1, you will view events in Event Viewer and set log properties.

 All of the exercises in this chapter can be done from either a Windows Server 2003 member server or domain controller.

EXERCISE 10.1

Using the Event Viewer Utility

1. Select Start ≻ Administrative Tools ≻ Event Viewer.

2. Click System in the left pane of the Event Viewer window to display the System log events.

3. Double-click the first event in the right pane of the Event Viewer window to see its Event Properties dialog box. Click the Cancel button to close the dialog box.

4. Right-click System in the left pane of the Event Viewer window and select Properties.

5. Click the Filter tab. Clear all the check marks under Event Types except those in the Warning and Error checkboxes, then click the OK button. You should see only Warning and Error events listed in the System log.

6. To remove the filter, return to the Filter tab of the log Properties dialog box, click the Restore Defaults button at the bottom of the dialog box, and click the OK button. You will see all of the event types listed again.

7. Right-click System and select Clear All Events.

8. You see a dialog box asking if you want to save the System log before clearing it. Click the Yes button. Specify the path and filename for the log file, then click the Save button. All the events should be cleared from the System log.

If your server is connected to the Internet, you can get information on error messages and event logs from Start ➤ Help And Support; under Support Tasks, click on Error And Event Log Messages.

Using Command-Line Utilities to Manage Event Logs

There are several command-line utilities that can be used to manage event logs. The following list defines the commands that are associated with managing event logs and a description of what each command is used for.

Eventvwr   Eventvwr is used to execute Event Viewer.

Eventcreate   Eventcreate is used to create a customized application or system event log. You can create event logs based on specific events (error, warning, or information).

Eventquery   Eventquery is used to query one or more event logs for specific events or event properties. You can use a filter with the query to include or exclude information such as event type, user who generated the event, or the category of the event.

Eventtriggers   Eventtriggers is used to configure or display an event trigger. For example, you could create an event trigger that monitors the percentage of free disk space and, when the number is below 10%, starts the Disk Cleanup utility.

Understanding the Windows Server 2003 Boot Process

When you are diagnosing a server error, you first need to determine whether the error is occurring when Windows Server 2003 is loading, when Windows Server 2003 is running, or when Windows Server 2003 is shutting down. Some of the problems that cause system failure are related to the Windows Server 2003 boot process. The boot process starts when you turn on your computer and ends when you log on to Windows Server 2003.

There are many reasons why you might have startup failures. Some errors can be easily corrected, while others might require you to reinstall Windows Server 2003. Some of the errors that occur during the startup process are related to:

- User error in configuration

- Application errors

- Hardware failures—for example, the hard drive is failing

- Virus activity, which could damage or delete files or corrupt the Master Boot Record (MBR), partition table, or boot sector

- Incompatible or improperly configured hardware

- Corrupt or missing system files

Depending on whether your server is using an *x*86-based processor or an Itanium-based processor, the boot process will be slightly different. The following sections review the boot process for each respective platform. You will also learn how to create a `Boot.ini` file and how to create a Windows Server 2003 boot disk, which can both be used with the *x*86-based platform during the Windows Server 2003 boot process. You will also learn about the NVRAM Startup setting, which is associated with the Itamium-based startup process.

Reviewing the *x*86-Based Boot Process

If you are running Windows Server 2003 on an *x*86-based platform, the boot process consists of six major stages: the pre-boot sequence, the boot sequence, kernel load, kernel initialization, logon, and Plug and Play detection. Many files are used during these stages of the boot process. The following sections describe the steps in each boot process stage, the files used, and the errors that might occur.

Finding the Boot Process Files

Most of the boot process files reside in the root of the system partition. In the Windows Server 2003 documentation, you will see the terms *system partition* and *boot partition*. The system partition is the computer's active partition where the files needed to boot the operating system are stored. This is typically the C: drive. The boot partition refers to the partition where the system files are stored. You can place the system files anywhere. The default folder for the system files is \Windows (unless your Windows Server 2003 computer was upgraded; then it will use the same folder name as the operating system that was upgraded) and is referred to as the variable *Windir*. The system partition and boot partition can be on the same partition or on different partitions.

File attributes are used to specify the properties of a file. Examples of file attributes are System (S), Hidden (H), and Read-only (R). This is important to know because, by default, System and Hidden files are not listed in Windows Explorer or through a standard Dir command. If you look for these files but don't see them, they may just be hidden. You can turn on the display of System and Hidden files in Windows Explorer by selecting Tools ➢ Folder Options and clicking the View tab. In this dialog box, select the Show Hidden Files And Folders option, and verify that the Hide File Extensions For Known File Types and Hide Protected Operating System Files (Recommended) options are unchecked.

The Pre-Boot Sequence

A normal boot process begins with the pre-boot sequence, in which your computer starts up and prepares to boot the operating system.

The computer will search for a boot device based on the boot order that was configured in the computer's CMOS settings. If the boot device is defined as the hard drive that contains the Windows Server 2003 system partition, then during the pre-boot sequence, your computer accesses the Ntldr file. This file is used to control the Windows Server 2003 boot process until control is passed to the Ntoskrnl file for the boot sequence. The Ntldr file is located in the root of the system partition. It has the file attributes of System, Hidden, and Read-only.

Steps in the Pre-Boot Sequence

The pre-boot sequence consists of the following steps:

1. When the computer is powered on, it runs a power-on self-test (POST) routine. The POST detects the processor you are using, how much memory is present, what hardware is recognized, and what BIOS (Basic Input/Output System) your computer is using. The system also enumerates and configures hardware devices at this point.

2. The BIOS points to the boot device, and the *Master Boot Record (MBR)* is loaded. The MBR is located on the first sector of the hard disk. It contains the partition table and master boot code, which is executable code used to locate the active partition.

3. The MBR points to the active partition. The active partition is used to specify the partition that should be used to boot the operating system. This is normally the C: drive. Once the MBR locates the active partition, the boot sector is loaded into memory and executed.

4. As part of the Windows Server 2003 installation process, the Ntldr file is copied into memory and executed. The boot sector points to the Ntldr file, and this file executes. The Ntldr file is used to initialize and start the Windows Server 2003 boot process.

Possible Errors during the Pre-Boot Sequence

If you see errors during the pre-boot sequence, they are probably not related to Windows Server 2003, since the operating system has not yet been loaded. Table 10.6 lists some common causes for errors during the pre-boot stage.

TABLE 10.6   Common Pre-Boot Errors

Symptom	Possible Cause
Improperly configured hardware	If the POST cannot recognize your hard drive, the pre-boot stage will fail. This error is most likely to occur in a computer that is still being initially configured. If everything has been working properly and you have not made any changes to your configuration, a hardware error is likely.
Corrupt MBR	Viruses that are specifically designed to infect the MBR can corrupt it. You can protect your system from this type of error by using virus-scanning software. Also, most virus-scanning programs can correct an infected MBR.
No partition is marked as active	This can happen if you used the Fdisk utility and did not create a partition from all of the free space. If the partition is FAT16 or FAT32 and on a basic disk, you can boot the computer to DOS or Windows 9x with a boot disk, run Fdisk, and mark a partition as active. If you created your partitions as a part of the Windows Server 2003 installation and have dynamic disks, marking an active partition is done for you during installation.
Corrupt or missing Ntldr file	If the Ntldr file does not execute, it may have been corrupted or deleted (by a virus or malicious intent). You can restore this file through Automated System Recovery or a Windows Server 2003 boot disk, both of which are covered later in this chapter.
SYS program run from DOS or Windows 9x after Windows Server 2003 installation	The Ntldr file may not execute because the SYS program was run from DOS or Windows 9x after Windows Server 2003 was installed. If you have done this, the only solution is to reinstall Windows Server 2003.

The Boot Sequence

When the pre-boot sequence is completed, the boot sequence begins. Ntldr switches the CPU to protected mode, which is used by Windows Server 2003, and starts the appropriate file systems. The contents of the Boot.ini file are read and the information is used to build the initial boot menu selections. When Windows Server 2003 is selected, Ntdetect.com gathers the computer's basic hardware configuration data and passes the collected information back to Ntldr. The system also checks to see if more than one hardware profile is detected; if so, the hardware profile selection menu will be displayed as a part of the startup process. In the next step of the boot sequence, your server's firmware is checked for ACPI compatibility. If your computer is ACPI compatible, then ACPI features will be loaded into the server.

Along with the Ntldr file, which was described in the previous section, the following files are used during the boot sequence:

Boot.ini   Used to build the operating system menu choices that are displayed during the boot process. It is also used to specify the location of the boot partition. This file is located in the root of the system partition. It has the file attributes of System and Hidden.

Bootsect.dos   An optional file that is loaded if you choose to load an operating system other than Windows Server 2003, Windows 2000, or Windows NT. It is used only in dual-boot or multi-boot computers. This file is located in the root of the system partition. It has the file attributes of System and Hidden.

Ntdetect.com   Used to detect any hardware that is installed and add that information about the hardware to the Registry. This file is located in the root of the system partition. It has the file attributes of System, Hidden, and Read-only.

Ntbootdd.sys   An optional file that is used when you have a Small Computer Standard Interface (SCSI) adapter with the onboard BIOS disabled. (This option is not commonly implemented.) This file is located in the root of the system partition. It has the file attributes of System and Hidden.

Ntoskrnl.exe   Used to load the Windows Server 2003 operating system. This file is located in *Windir*\System32 and has no file attributes.

Steps in the Boot Sequence

The boot sequence consists of the following steps:

1. For the initial boot loader phase, Ntldr switches the processor from real mode to 32-bit flat memory mode and starts the appropriate mini file system drivers. Mini file system drivers are used to support your computer's file systems and include FAT16, FAT32, and NTFS.

2. For the operating system selection phase, the computer reads the Boot.ini file. If you have configured your computer to dual-boot or multi-boot and Windows Server 2003 recognizes that you have choices, a menu of operating systems that can be loaded is built. If you choose an operating system other than Windows Server 2003, Windows 2000, or Windows NT, the Bootsect.dos file is used to load the alternate operating system, and the Windows Server 2003 boot process terminates.

3. If you choose a Windows Server 2003 operating system, the Ntdetect.com file is used to perform hardware detection. Any hardware that is detected is added to the Registry, in the HKEY_LOCAL_MACHINE key. Some of the hardware that Ntdetect.com will recognize includes communication and parallel ports, the keyboard, the floppy disk drive, the mouse, the SCSI adapter, and the video adapter.

4. Control is passed to Ntoskrnl.exe to start the kernel load process.

Possible Errors during the Boot Sequence

Table 10.7 lists some common causes for errors during the boot stage.

TABLE 10.7 Common Boot Errors

Symptom	Possible Cause
Missing or corrupt boot files	If Ntldr, Boot.ini, Bootsect.dos, Ntdetect.com, or Ntoskrnl.exe is corrupt or missing (by a virus or malicious intent), the boot sequence will fail. You will see an error message that indicates which file is missing or corrupt. You can restore these files through Automated System Recovery.
Improperly configured Boot.ini file	If you have made any changes to your disk configuration and your computer will not restart, chances are your Boot.ini file is configured incorrectly. The Boot.ini file is covered in detail later in the chapter.
Unrecognizable or improperly configured hardware	If you have serious errors that cause Ntdetect.com to fail, you should resolve the hardware problems. If your computer has a lot of hardware, remove all of the hardware that is not required to boot the computer. Add each piece of hardware one at a time and boot the computer. This will help you identify which piece of hardware is bad or is conflicting for a resource with another device.

The Kernel Load Sequence

All of the information that is collected by Ntdetect.com, is passed to Ntoskrnl.exe. In the kernel load sequence, the Hardware Abstraction Layer (HAL), computer control set, Registry information, and low-level device drivers are loaded. The Ntoskrnl.exe file, which was described in the previous section, is used during this stage.

The kernel load sequence consists of the following steps:

1. The Ntoskrnl.exe file is loaded and initialized.

2. The HAL is loaded. The HAL is what makes Windows Server 2003 portable to support different platforms; for example, there are separate HALs for ACPI and non-ACPI computers.

3. The control set that the operating system will use is loaded. The control set is used to control system configuration information, such as a list of device drivers that should be loaded.

4. Low-level device drivers, such as disk drivers, are loaded.

If you have problems loading the Windows Server 2003 kernel, you will most likely need to reinstall the operating system.

The user will see a progress indicator at the bottom of the screen during the kernel load sequence.

The Kernel Initialization Sequence

In the kernel initialization sequence, the HKEY_LOCAL_MACHINE\HARDWARE Registry and Clone Control set are created, device drivers are initialized, and high-order subsystems and services are loaded.

The kernel initialization sequence consists of the following steps:

1. Once the kernel has been successfully loaded, the Registry key HKEY_LOCAL_MACHINE\ HARDWARE is created. This Registry key is used to specify the hardware configuration of hardware components when the computer is started.

2. The Clone Control set is created. The Clone Control set is an exact copy of the data that is used to configure the computer and does not include changes made by the startup process.

3. The device drivers that were loaded during the kernel load phase are initialized.

4. Higher-order subsystems and services are loaded.

If you have problems during the kernel initialization sequence, you might try to boot to the Last Known Good configuration, which is covered in the "Using Advanced Startup Options" section later in this chapter.

The Logon Sequence

In the logon sequence, the user logs on to Windows Server 2003 and any remaining drivers and services are loaded.

The logon sequence consists of the following steps:

1. After the kernel initialization is complete, the Log On To Windows dialog box appears. At this point, you type in a valid Windows Server 2003 username and password.

2. The service controller executes and performs a final scan of HKEY_LOCAL_MACHINE\ SYSTEM\CurrentControlSet\Services to see if there are any remaining services that need to be loaded.

If logon errors occur, they are usually due to an incorrect username or password or to the unavailability of a DNS server or a domain controller to authenticate the request (if the computer is a part of a domain). See Chapter 3, "Managing Users, Groups, and Computers," for more information about troubleshooting user authentication problems.

Errors can also occur if a service cannot be loaded. If a service fails to load, you will see a message in the System Log of Event Viewer. Using the Event Viewer utility was covered earlier in this chapter.

Plug and Play Device Detection Phase

If Windows Server 2003 has detected any new devices during the startup process, they will automatically be assigned system resources. If the device is Plug and Play and the needed driver can be obtained from the Driver.cab file, they are extracted. If the needed driver files are not found, the user will be prompted to provide them. Device detection occurs asynchronously with the initial user logon process when the system is started.

Editing the *Boot.ini* File

If you are using an *x*86-based system, then it is critical that the `Boot.ini` file be configured properly. This file is created during the Windows Server 2003 installation and is stored in the system root partition. The `Boot.ini` file contains the information required by `Ntldr` to create and display the boot startup menu. The information that is contained in the `Boot.ini` file includes:

- The path to the boot partition
- Descriptive text that should be displayed on the boot startup menu
- Optional parameters for managing computer startup
- Optional support for multiple boot configurations if other Microsoft operating systems have been installed in separate partitions

The `Boot.ini` file contains two main sections for configuration: the boot loader and operating systems. Options that are configured in the boot loader section are applied to all Windows installations on the computer. Settings in the operating system section are applied only to the specific Windows installation that is referenced within the operating systems section.

The following is an example of text that you might see in a `Boot.ini` file:

```
[Boot Loader]
timeout=30
default=multi(0)disk(0)rdisk(0)partition(1) \Windows
[operating systems]
multi(0)disk(0)rdisk(0)partition(1) \Windows="Microsoft Windows Server 2003"
/fastdetect
```

If you only have one operating system installed, and one entry under the operating systems section, then that option will be installed by default and you will not see a boot loader menu presented when the operating system is started.

In the following sections, you will learn about the boot loader configuration options, ARC naming conventions, `Boot.ini` operating system parameters, how to edit the `Boot.ini` file, and how to replace a damaged or missing `Boot.ini` file.

Boot Loader Configuration Options

The parameters that can be configured within boot loader include `timeout=` and `default=`. The `timeout` setting is used when the startup menu contains more than one operating system. In the event that more than one operating system exists, `timeout` specifies how long the boot startup menu will be displayed. The `default` option specifies the default operating system that will be loaded in the event that no selection is made.

If you set `timeout=0`, then `Ntldr` will automatically load the default operating system selection, and no boot startup menu will be displayed. If you set `timeout=-1`, then `Ntldr` will display the boot startup menu indefinitely until the user makes an operating system selection manually.

ARC Naming Conventions

In the Boot.ini file, the ARC path is used to specify the location of the boot partition within the disk channel. ARC names are made up of the information shown in Table 10.8.

TABLE 10.8   ARC Naming Conventions

ARC Path Option	Description
Multi (w) or scsi (w)	Identifies the type of disk controller that is being used by the system. The multi option is used by IDE controllers and SCSI adapters that use the SCSI BIOS. The scsi option is used by SCSI adapters that do not use the SCSI BIOS. The number (w) represents the number of the hardware adapter you are booting from (disks and controllers always begin at 0).
disk (x)	Indicates which SCSI adapter you are booting from if you use the scsi option. If you use multi, this setting is always 0.
Rdisk (y)	Specifies the number of the physical disk to be used. In an IDE environment, it is the ordinal of the disk attached to the controller and will always be a 0 or a 1. On a SCSI system, this is the ordinal number of the SCSI drive.
partition (z)	Specifies the partition number that contains the operating system files. The first partition is always 1.

As an example, suppose the Boot.ini file contained the following line:

```
multi(0)disk(0)rdisk(0)partition(1)\Windows= "Microsoft Windows Server 2003"
```

This indicates that the boot partition is in the following location:

- multi(0) is an IDE controller or a SCSI controller with the BIOS enabled.
- disk(0) is 0 since the multi option was used.
- rdisk(0) specifies that the first disk on the controller is being used.
- partition(1) specifies that the system partition is on the first partition.
- \Windows indicates the folder that is used to store the system files.
- "Microsoft Windows Server 2003 Server" is what the user sees in the boot menu.

If you use the SCSI or Signature syntax with a disk controller with disabled firmware, you will be required to use Ntbootdd.sys. Ntbootdd.sys is a storage controller device driver and resides on the startup partition at the root (it is the SCSI driver).

You might also see the Signature() syntax. Signature is similar to SCSI and is implemented when you have added drive controllers to your computer through Plug and Play associated with ATA or SCSI hard disks. The Signature syntax also indicates that the Ntbootdd.sys file is required to access the boot partition and one or both of the following conditions exist: Windows Server 2003 was installed on a disk partition that was greater than 7.8GB and the ending cylinder was higher than 1024 for the partition, so the system firmware or the BIOS for the startup controller can't gain access to the partition by using extended Interrupt 13 calls, and/or (2) the hard disk controller's BIOS has Interrupt 13 calls disabled or does not support them. If either requirement is not met, the Ntbootdd.sys file is required for boot partition access. Depending on the controllers you are using, the Signature option may increase the time it takes Windows Server 2003 to boot.

Boot.ini Operating System Parameters

When you edit your Boot.ini file, you can add switches or options that allow you to control how the operating system is loaded. Table 10.9 defines the Boot.ini switches.

TABLE 10.9   Boot.ini Switches

Switch	Description
/3GB	Used for *x*86-based systems to specify that the operating system can allocate up to 3GB of virtual address space for applications and 1GB for the kernel and executive components. The application must be designed to take advantage of the additional memory allocation. This switch only applies to Windows Server 2003 Enterprise or Datacenter editions when more than 4GB of memory is installed.
/basevideo	Boots the computer using a standard VGA video driver (640x480 resolution with 16 colors). This option is used when you change your video driver and then cannot use the new driver due to video corruption. You boot the computer using the /basevideo switch and then you can remove, update, or roll back the video driver to proper settings. Remember to remove the /basevideo switch after you load the correct driver.
/baudrate	Used in conjunction with kernel debugging. Specifies the baud rate that can be used, and must be used in conjunction with the /debug parameter. Settings can range from 9600Kbps (for modems) to 115,200bps for null modem cables.
/bootlog	Used to enable boot logging. The file that is created is called *systemroot*\Ntbtlog.txt.

TABLE 10.9   Boot.ini Switches *(continued)*

Switch	Description
/burnmemory=*number*	This option specifies the amount of memory in megabytes that Windows Server 2003 can't use. This parameter is used to confirm performance problems that are related to RAM depletion.
/crashdebug	Used to load the kernel debugger when the Windows Server 2003 operating system is loaded. However, the kernel debugger will remain active until a Stop error occurs. This parameter is used to debug random stop kernel errors.
/debug	Specifies that the kernel debugger should be loaded with Windows Server 2003.
/debugport={*com1, com2, or 1394*}	Used with the kernel debugger and specifies what communication port will be used for kernel debugging.
/dsrepair	Used with Directory Services Restore mode.
/fastdetect=com*x*	Keeps the computer from scanning a com port on power up.
/maxmem:*number*	Specifies the maximum amount of RAM that is recognized. This option is sometimes used in test environments where you want to analyze performance using different amounts of memory or if you are trying to identify a faulty memory component. This switch cannot be used in 64-bit versions of Windows Server 2003 that have more than 4GB RAM.
/noguiboot	Boots Windows Server 2003 without loading the GUI. With this option, a command prompt appears after the boot process ends.
/nodebug	This option disables the kernel debugger.
/minimal	Loads the operating system with the minimal services to simplify the configuration as much as possible, but still uses the Windows interface. This switch does not load any network support.
/minimal(alternateshell)	Loads the operating system with the minimal services to simplify the configuration as much as possible using a command prompt instead of the Windows interface.
/network	Loads Safe Mode with minimal services, but includes support for networking.
/numproc=*number*	If your server is using multiple processors, this option allows you to specify how many processors will be used.

TABLE 10.9 Boot.ini Switches *(continued)*

Switch	Description
/pcilock	This option applies only to *x86*-based systems and prevents the operating system from dynamically assigning hardware I/O and IRQs to PCI devices.
/safeboot:*parameter*	Forces a start in Safe Mode using one of the safeboot parameters such as Safe Mode With Networking or Safe Mode With Command Prompt. Safe Mode options are covered in greater detail later in this chapter.
/sos	Used to display the name of each device driver as it is loaded. This is useful in troubleshooting if a driver is failing to load.

Editing the *Boot.ini* File

The following options can be used to edit the Boot.ini file:

- Bootcfg.exe
- System Configuration Utility
- Control Panel
- Text editor (such as Notepad.exe)

 You should always make a copy of the Boot.ini before editing it. Improper edits can cause the operating system to not load.

Editing the *Boot.ini* File with *Bootcfg.exe*

The Bootcfg.exe is a new command-line tool for viewing and editing the Boot.ini file with Windows XP Professional or Windows Server 2003 though a command-line interface or through the Recovery Console.

Bootcfg works by scanning the hard disk for the Windows NT, Windows 2000, Windows XP, or Windows Server 2003 operating systems. Based on what the scan finds, the Boot.ini file can be rebuilt or a new Boot.ini file can be created if the file is missing or corrupt.

The following command-line switches can be used in conjunction with the Bootcfg utility.

- /query is used to query and view the [boot loader] and [operating systems] sections of the Boot.ini file
- /copy makes a copy of existing boot entries for the [operating systems] section of the Boot.ini file
- /delete is used to delete an entry from an existing boot entry in the [operating systems] section of the Boot.ini file

Editing the *Boot.ini* File with the System Configuration Utility

One of the easiest ways to edit the `Boot.ini` file is with the System Configuration utility. To access the System Configuration Utility, you select the Run dialog box and type **Msconfig**, then click the BOOT.INI tab to show the dialog box shown in Figure 10.5.

FIGURE 10.5   The BOOT.INI tab of the System Configuration Utility

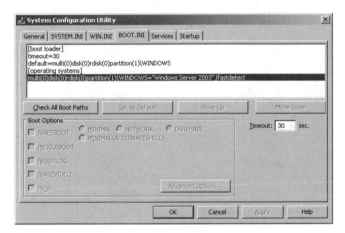

When editing the `Boot.ini` file with the System Configuration Utility, there is an option called Check All Boot Paths that will check all lines in your `Boot.ini` file to see if anything has been misconfigured.

Editing the *Boot.ini* File with Control Panel

Some of the options within the `Boot.ini` file can be edited through the System applet in Control Panel. To access these settings, select Start ➢ Control Panel ➢ System. From System, select the Advanced tab, then select Settings under Startup And Recovery (see Figure 10.6).

The `Boot.ini` options that can be configured through Startup and Recovery options include:

- The default operating system that will be selected if no user selection is made
- The number of seconds (timeout value) that the boot loader menu will be displayed when the system is started
- The number of seconds that the recovery options will be displayed when needed

By clicking the Edit button, you can view or edit the `Boot.ini` file through the Notepad text editor.

Editing the *Boot.ini* File with a Text Editor

Because the `Boot.ini` file is marked with the System and Hidden attributes, it is not normally seen through Windows Explorer or the DOS DIR command. After you turn off the System and Hidden attributes, you can edit the `Boot.ini` file with a standard text editor.

FIGURE 10.6 The Startup And Recovery dialog box

Replacing a Damaged *Boot.ini* File

If you can't start Windows Server 2003 on an *x*86-based system because the `Boot.ini` file is damaged or missing, the following repair techniques can be used: Automatic or Manual.

Automatic Recovery

The `Bootcfg` command in conjunction with the Recovery Console to rebuild a missing or corrupt `Boot.ini` file. The `Bootcfg` that is used within Recovery Console is similar to the `Bootcfg` command-line utility. The Automatic Recovery Utility is covered in greater detail later in this chapter. To use Automatic Recovery, you would take the following actions:

1. Start the Recovery Console.

2. At the Recovery Console prompt, type **bootcfg /rebuild**.

3. Windows Server 2003 will then scan the hard disk on your computer and rebuild the `Boot.ini` file.

Manual Recovery

To use the Recovery Console to create a new `Boot.ini` file manually, you would take the following steps:

1. Start the Recovery Console.

2. At the Recovery Console prompt, type **map**.

3. A list will appear containing all of the hard disk and partition information for Windows Server 2003 and any other Windows operating systems that are detected. This information can be used to correct or build a `Boot.ini` file using a text editor, such as Notepad. You

will not be able to edit the file while in Recovery Console, since Recovery Console does not support text editing. You could edit the file on another computer, then replace it through Recovery Console.

> The Recovery Console is covered in more detail in the "Using the Recovery Console" section.

Creating the Windows Server 2003 Boot Disk

After you create a *Windows Server 2003 boot disk*, you can use it to boot to the Windows Server 2003 server operating system using an *x*86-based processor in the event of a Windows Server 2003 server boot failure.

> The Boot.ini file on the Windows Server 2003 server boot disk contains a specific configuration that points to the computer's boot partition. This might keep a Windows Server 2003 boot disk that was made on one computer from working on another computer.

In Exercise 10.2, you will create a Windows Server 2003 boot disk.

EXERCISE 10.2

Creating a Windows Server 2003 Boot Disk

1. Put a blank floppy disk in your floppy drive.

2. Select Start ➤ Windows Explorer.

3. In Windows Explorer, expand My Computer, right-click 3 1/2 Floppy (A:), and select Format. Accept all of the default options and click the Start button.

4. You see a dialog box warning you that all the data will be lost. Click the OK button.

5. When you see the Format Complete dialog box, click the OK button, then click the Close button to close the Format dialog box.

6. Select Start ➤ Command Prompt.

7. In the Command Prompt dialog box, type **cd **, then type **ATTRIB** and press Enter. You see all of the files at the root of the C: drive. Note the file attributes of the Ntldr, Ntdetect.com, and Boot.ini files.

8. Type **ATTRIB NTLDR –S –H –R** and press Enter.

9. Type **COPY NTLDR A:** and press Enter.

10. Type **ATTRIB NTLDR +S +H +R** and press Enter.

11. Repeat steps 8 through 10 for the Ntdetect.com and Boot.ini files, to remove the file attributes, copy the file, and replace the file attributes. If you have a SCSI adapter with the BIOS disabled, you will also need to copy the Ntbootdd.sys file.

12. Verify that all of the files are on the boot disk by typing **DIR A:**.

13. Type **Exit** to close the Command Prompt dialog box.

14. To test your Windows Server 2003 boot disk, select Start ≻ Shut Down ≻ Restart and click the OK button.

15. Label your Windows Server 2003 boot disk and put it in a safe place.

If the Boot.ini file for the computer has been edited, you will need to update the Boot.ini file on your Windows Server 2003 boot disk.

Reviewing the Itanium Boot Process

If you are using an Itanium-based computer for Windows Server 2003, the following boot process would be used:

1. Power-on self-test phase

2. Initial startup and the boot manager phase

3. Kernel load phase

4. Device drivers and service initialization phase

5. Logon phase

6. Plug and Play device detection phase

The Itanium boot process phases that differ from those occurring with *x*86-based systems are covered in the following sections.

 The process for loading device drivers and service initialization, and the process for Plug and Play device detection, is similar to the process used by *x*86-based systems.

Power-On Self-Test Phase

Itanium-based computers use a Power-on self-test (POST) process that is similar to *x*86-based systems. However, instead of using a BIOS, Itanium-based systems use the Extensible Firmware Interface (EFI), which is a new model for defining the interface between the operating system and the platform's firmware. The EFI performs rudimentary hardware checks and specifies and verifies what devices will be used to start the computer.

Initial Startup and the Boot Manager Phase

When the POST is complete, the boot manager, which is a part of the EFI, specifies which EFI drivers should be used, the EFI tool set that will be available to the user, and the EFI startup options that should be displayed. Depending on your Itanium-based system, the boot manager features will vary, and you should check the manufacturer's documentation for managing options such as performing system recovery tasks, restoring the boot manager startup window, and updating system firmware.

When Windows Server 2003 is started, the boot manager will perform the following tasks:

- Read the EFI configuration settings, which specify the boot order sequence, stored in non-volatile memory (NVRAM). Settings in NVRAM are saved even when the computer is turned off and are the equivalent of CMOS settings on *x*86-based systems.

- Initialize the drivers that are needed to start Windows Server 2003. The configuration for storage devices, and any other required devices, is also stored in NVRAM. Device detection is also performed. Some of the devices that might be detected at this stage include:
  - Drive controllers (ATA or SCSI)
  - Storage devices
  - Keyboard
  - Video adapters
  - Network adapters

- Determine where the EFI system partition image has been stored. The EFI system partition holds the files required to start Windows Server 2003. The EFI system partition must be a minimum of 100MB and a maximum of 1000MB. The remaining system files for the *Windir* folder (the \\Windows folder by default) must be stored on another partition.

- Locates the *Windir* folder and the directories that contain the Windows Server 2003 files.

- Locates and starts the loader file, which is called IA64ldr.efi. The IA64ldr.efi file is responsible for starting the 64-bit Windows kernel.

 The Boot.ini, Ntdetect.com, and Ntldr files are not used on Itanium-based systems.

Kernel Load Phase

Instead of using the Ntldr file to load the kernel, Itanium-based systems use the IA64ldr.efi file to load the kernel (Ntoskrnl.exe) and the HAL into memory.

Managing NVRAM Startup Settings

As noted previously, $x86$-based computers use the `Boot.ini` file to track ARC paths for Windows startup. Itanium-based systems use NVRAM settings and the EFI boot manager to build the Windows Server 2003 boot options. These settings can be managed through the `Bootcfg.exe` and `Nvrboot.efi` utilities.

`Bootcfg.exe` is used to change the startup parameters in NVRAM. `Nvrboot.efi` is a menu-driven utility and is used to restore boot manager setup options.

Using Advanced Startup Options

The Windows Server 2003 advanced startup options can be used to troubleshoot errors that keep Windows Server 2003 server from successfully booting.

To access the Windows Server 2003 advanced startup options, press the F8 key when prompted during the beginning of the Windows Server 2003 server boot process. This will bring up the Windows Server 2003 Advanced Options menu, which allows you to boot Windows Server 2003 with the following options:

- Safe Mode
- Safe Mode With Networking
- Safe Mode With Command Prompt
- Enable Boot Logging
- Enable VGA Mode
- Last Known Good Configuration
- Directory Services Restore Mode
- Debugging Mode
- Boot Normally

 If Windows Server 2003 starts without displaying the Startup Menu, you should press F8 after the firmware POST process ends and before Windows Server 2003 displays graphical output to access the Advanced Options menu.

Each of these advanced startup options is covered in the following sections.

Starting in Safe Mode

When your computer will not start, one of the basic troubleshooting techniques is to simplify the configuration as much as possible. This is especially important when you do not know the cause of your problem and you have a complex configuration. After you have simplified your configuration, you determine whether the problem is in the basic configuration or is a result of your more complex configuration. If the problem is in the basic configuration, you have a starting point for troubleshooting. If the problem is not in the basic configuration, you proceed to restore each configuration option you removed, one at a time. This helps you to identify what is causing your error.

If Windows Server 2003 will not load, you can attempt to load the operating system through *Safe Mode*. When you run Windows Server 2003 in Safe Mode, you are simplifying your Windows configuration as much as possible. Safe Mode loads only the drivers and services needed to get the computer up and running. The items loaded with Safe Mode include basic system files and drivers for the mouse (unless you have a serial mouse), monitor, keyboard, hard drive, standard video driver, and default system services. Safe Mode is considered a diagnostic mode, so you do not have access to all of the features and devices in Windows Server 2003 that you have access to when you boot normally, including networking capabilities. A computer booted to Safe Mode will show *Safe Mode* in the four corners of your Desktop.

> When you start your computer in Safe Mode, the following Registry hive is loaded: HKEY_LOCAL_MACHINE\SYSTEM\CurrentControlSet\Control\SafeBoot\Minimal. When you start your computer in Safe Mode With Networking, the following Registry hive is loaded: HKEY_LOCAL_MACHINE\SYSTEM\CurrentControlSet\Control\SafeBoot\Network.

If you boot to Safe Mode, you should check all of your hardware and software settings in Control Panel to try to determine why Windows Server 2003 server will not boot properly. After you take steps to fix the problem, attempt to boot to Windows Server 2003 server normally.

In Exercise 10.3, you will boot your computer to Safe Mode.

EXERCISE 10.3

Booting Your Computer to Safe Mode

1. If your computer is currently running, select Start ➢ Shutdown ➢ Restart. You will need to specify a comment for the Shutdown Event Tracker and click the OK button.

2. At the Operating System Selection screen, press the F8 key to access the Windows Server 2003 Advanced Options menu. If you do not see the Operating System Selection screen, press F8 after the firmware POST process, before Windows Server 2003 displays graphical output.

3. Highlight Safe Mode and press Enter. Select Windows Server 2003 and press Enter. Then log on as Administrator.

4. When you see the Desktop dialog box letting you know that Windows Server 2003 is running in Safe Mode, click the OK button.

5. Try accessing network resources in Windows Explorer. You should see an error message stating that you are unable to browse the network (because you are in Safe Mode). Click OK to close the error dialog box.

6. Select Start ➢ Administrative Tools ➢ Computer Management, then click on Device
    Manager. Look in Device Manager to see if any devices are not working properly.

7. Don't restart your computer yet; you will do this as a part of the next exercise.

Enabling Boot Logging

Boot logging creates a log file that tracks the loading of drivers and services. When you choose
the *Enable Boot Logging* option from the Advanced Options menu, Windows Server 2003
loads normally, not in Safe Mode. This allows you to log all of the processes that take place during a normal boot sequence.

This log file can be used to troubleshoot the boot process. When logging is enabled, the log file
is written to *Windir*\ntbtlog.txt. A sample of the ntbtlog.txt file is shown in Figure 10.7.

FIGURE 10.7   The Windows Server 2003 boot log file

In Exercise 10.4, you will create and access a boot log file.

Using Boot Logging

1. Start your computer. (If your computer is currently running, select Start ➢ Shutdown ➢
    Restart and specify a comment for the Shutdown Event Tracker).

2. At the Operating System Selection screen, press the F8 key to access the Windows
    Advanced Options menu. If you do not see the Operating System Selection screen, press F8
    after the firmware POST process, before Windows Server 2003 displays graphical output.

3. Highlight Enable Boot Logging and press Enter. Select Windows Server 2003 and press
    Enter. Then log on as Administrator.

4. Select Start ➢ Windows Explorer.

5. In Windows Explorer, expand My Computer, then C:. Open the \Windows folder and double-click ntbtlog.txt.

6. Examine the contents of your boot log file.

The boot log file is cumulative. Each time you boot to any Advanced Options menu mode (except Last Known Good Configuration), you are writing to this file. This allows you to make changes, reboot, and see if you have fixed any problems. If you want to start from scratch, you should manually delete this file and reboot to an Advanced Options menu selection that supports logging.

Using Last Known Good Configuration

The *Last Known Good Configuration* option boots Windows Server 2003 using the Registry information that was saved the last time the computer was successfully booted. You would use this option to restore configuration information if you have improperly configured the computer and have not successfully rebooted the computer. When you use the Last Known Good Configuration option, you lose any system configuration changes that were made since the computer last successfully booted.

Using Other Advanced Options Menu Modes

The other selections on the Advanced Options menu work as follows:

- The *Safe Mode With Networking* option is the same as the Safe Mode option, but it adds all networking features. You might use this mode if you need networking capabilities in order to download drivers or service packs from a network location.

- The *Safe Mode With Command Prompt* option starts the computer in Safe Mode, but instead of loading the Windows Server 2003 graphical interface, it loads a command prompt. Experienced troubleshooters use this mode.

- The *Enable VGA Mode* option loads a standard VGA driver without starting the computer in Safe Mode. You might use this mode if you changed your video driver, did not test it, and tried to boot to Windows Server 2003 with a bad driver that would not allow you to access video. Enable VGA Mode bails you out by loading a default driver, providing access to video so that you can properly install (and test!) the correct driver for your computer.

When you boot to any Safe Mode, you automatically use VGA Mode.

- The *Directory Services Restore Mode* option is used by Windows Server 2003 computers that are configured as domain controllers to restore the Active Directory. This option is not available on Windows Server 2003 computers that are installed as member servers. This option is used if you need to restore System State data on a domain controller or restore the Active Directory service database.

- The *Debugging Mode* option runs the Kernel Debugger, if that utility is installed. The Kernel Debugger is an advanced troubleshooting utility.

- The *Boot Normally* option boots to Windows Server 2003 in the default manner. This option is on the Advanced Options menu in case you hit F8 during the boot process, but really wanted to boot Windows Server 2003 normally.

 Windows Server 2003 handles startup options in a slightly different way than Windows NT 4 does. In Windows NT 4, the boot loader menu shows an option to load VGA mode, which appears each time you restart the computer. In Windows Server 2003, this has been moved to the Advanced Options menu to present the user with a cleaner boot process. Also, in Windows NT 4, you need to press the spacebar as a part of the boot process to access the Last Known Good Configuration option.

Boot.ini Switches Used with Advanced Options Menu Modes

When you select an Advanced Options menu mode, the following switches are applied at startup. These switches were defined in Table 10.9.

- Safe Mode uses `/safeboot:minimal /sos /bootlog /noguiboot`

- Safe Mode With Networking uses `/safeboot:network /sos /bootlog /noguiboot`

- Safe Mode With Command Prompt uses `/safeboot:minimal(alternateshell) /sos /bootlog /noguiboot`

- Enable Boot Logging uses `/bootlog`

- Enable VGA Mode uses `/basevideo`

- Directory Services Restore Mode (domain controllers only) uses `/safeboot:dsrepair /sos`

- Debugging Mode uses `/debug`

Using Driver Rollback

Windows XP Professional and Windows Server 2003 offer a new feature called Driver Rollback. You would use Driver Rollback if you installed or upgraded a driver and you encountered problems that you did not have with the previous driver. Some of the problems with drivers relate to the following errors:

- Use of unsigned drivers

- Resource conflicts
- Badly written drivers

The following steps would be used to roll back a driver:

1. Select Start ➤ Control Panel ➤ System.
2. From System, select the Hardware tab, then select Device Manager.
3. Expand the category for the device driver you want to roll back—for example, a network card—then double-click the device and select the Driver tab, as shown in Figure 10.8. From the Driver tab, click the Roll Back Driver option.

FIGURE 10.8 Driver tab of a device's Properties in Device Manager

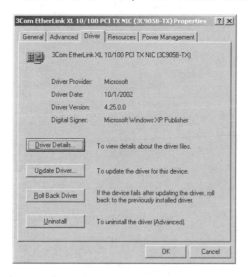

4. You will be prompted to confirm that you want to overwrite the current driver; click the Yes button. The rollback process will proceed, or you will be notified that an older driver was not available for rollback.

The System Properties dialog box can be opened from the Start menu by selecting Run and then typing in `sysdm.cpl`.

Using Startup and Recovery Options

The Startup and Recovery options are used to specify the default operating system that is loaded and specify which action should be taken in the event of system failure. You can access the Startup and Recovery options from your Desktop by right-clicking My Computer, selecting Properties from the pop-up menu, clicking the Advanced tab, and then clicking the Startup And Recovery Settings button. Alternatively, select Start ➤ Control Panel ➤ System. From System, select the Advanced tab, then select Settings under Startup And Recovery. You will see the dialog box shown in Figure 10.9.

FIGURE 10.9 The Startup And Recovery dialog box

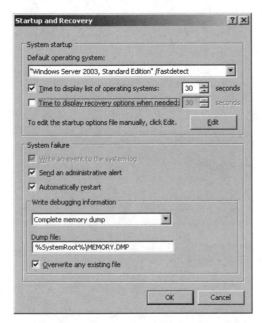

The options that can be specified through the Startup And Recovery dialog box are described in Table 10.10.

TABLE 10.10 Startup and Recovery Options

Option	Description
Default Operating System	Specifies the operating system that is loaded by default if no selection is made from the operating system selection menu (if your computer dual-boots or multi-boots and an operating system selection menu appears during bootup). By default, this option is set to Microsoft Windows Server 2003.
Time To Display The List of Operating Systems	Specifies how long the operating system selection menu is available before the default selection is loaded (if your computer dual-boots or multi-boots and an operating system selection menu appears during bootup). By default, this option is set to 30 seconds.
Time To Display Recovery Options When Needed	If the system detects an error and the system automatically starts system recovery options, the number of seconds that the recovery options will be displayed.

TABLE 10.10   Startup and Recovery Options *(continued)*

Option	Description
Write An Event To The System Log	Specifies that an entry is made in the System log any time a system failure occurs. By default, this option is enabled, which allows you to track system failures.
Send An Administrative Alert	Specifies that a pop-up alert message will be sent to the Administrator any time a system failure occurs. By default, this option is enabled, so the Administrator is notified of system failures.
Automatically Restart	Specifies that the computer will automatically reboot in the event of a system failure. By default, this option is enabled, so the system restarts after a failure without intervention. You would disable this option if you wanted to examine the blue screen for analysis.
Write Debugging Information	Specifies that debugging information (a memory dump) is written to a file. You can choose not to create a dump file or to create a small memory dump (64KB) file, a kernel memory dump file, or a complete memory dump file. Complete memory dump files require free disk space equivalent to your memory size and a page file that is at least as large as your memory with an extra 2MB. The default setting is to write debugging information to a complete memory dump.
Overwrite Any Existing File	If you create dump files, allows you to create a new dump file that overwrites the old dump file or to keep all dump files each time a system failure occurs. This option is selected by default.

In Exercise 10.5, you will access the Startup and Recovery options and make changes to the settings.

EXERCISE 10.5

Using Startup and Recovery Options

1. Select Start, right-click My Computer, and choose Properties. Click the Advanced tab and then click the Startup And Recovery Settings button.

2. Change the Time To Display List Of Operating Systems option from 30 seconds to 10 seconds.

3. In the Write Debugging Information section, choose (None) from the drop-down list.

4. Click the OK button to close the Startup And Recovery dialog box.

Using the Backup Utility

The *Backup utility* allows you to create and restore backups. Backups protect your data in the event of system failure by storing the data on another medium, such as another hard disk or a tape. If your original data is lost due to corruption, deletion, or media failure, you can restore the data using your backup.

The types of data that can be backed up with the Backup utility include System State data and user data and applications. System State data is data related to the configuration of the Windows Server 2003 operating system. User data and applications are the data that have been created and stored on the computer.

By default, users can back up their own data and any data that they have Read permission to. Users can restore their own data to any folder that they have Write permission to. Users who are members of the Administrators, Server Operators, or Backup Operators group can back up or restore any files on the server, regardless of file and folder permissions, since these groups have the Backup Files And Directories and Restore Files And Directories user rights.

In the following sections you will learn how to use the Backup utility, including the following topics:

- Using the Backup Wizard
- Managing System State data
- Configuring backup options
- Scheduling backup jobs
- Using the Restore Wizard
- Using Automated System Recovery

Using the Backup Wizard

The Backup utility allows you to manually configure backup and restore sessions or to automate the process through the use of wizards. The *Backup Wizard* takes you through all of the steps that are required for a successful backup.

Before you start the Backup Wizard, you should be logged on as a member of the Administrators, Server Operators, or Backup Operators groups.

To use the Backup Wizard, take the following steps:

1. Select Start ➤ All Programs ➤ Accessories ➤ System Tools ➤ Backup.

2. The Welcome To The Backup Utility Advanced Mode dialog box appears. In this example the backup is being performed through the Backup Wizard, so you will need to click the Wizard Mode option to use simplified settings for the backup. The Welcome To The Backup Or Restore Wizard will start, as shown in Figure 10.10. Click the Next button.

FIGURE 10.10   The Welcome To The Backup Or Restore Wizard page

3. The Backup Or Restore page appears, as shown in Figure 10.11. Ensure that the Back Up Files And Settings option is selected and click the Next button.

FIGURE 10.11   Backup Or Restore page

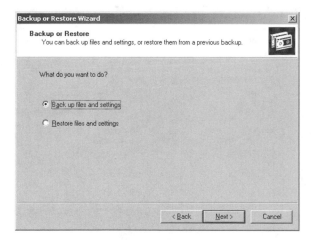

4. The What To Back Up page appears, as shown in Figure 10.12. This dialog box allows you to select what you will back up. You can select All Information On This Computer or Let Me Choose What To Back Up. If you choose what will be backed up, you can choose to back up just selected files, drives, or network data; or back up only the System State data. System State data includes system configuration information, as explained in the next section. For this example, select Let Me Choose What To Back Up and click the Next button.

5. The Items To Back Up page appears, as shown in Figure 10.13. Check the items that you want to back up and click the Next button.

FIGURE 10.12 What To Back Up page

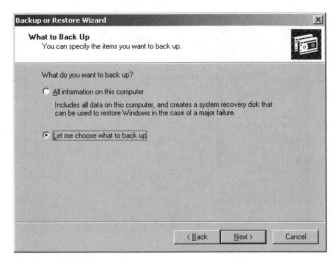

FIGURE 10.13 The Items To Back Up page

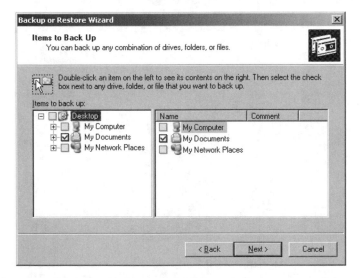

6. The Backup Type, Destination, And Name page appears, as shown in Figure 10.14. You can either type in the backup media or filename, or click the Browse button to locate it. Clicking the Browse button brings up the Open dialog box. Select the drive, give your backup a filename (for example, you might use the date as the filename), and click the Open button. You return to the Backup Type, Destination, and Name page. When your backup media or filename path is correct, click the Next button.

7. The Completing The Backup Or Restore Wizard page appears. If all of the information is correct, click the Finish button.

FIGURE 10.14   The Backup Type, Destination, And Name page

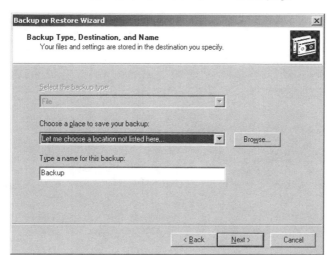

Clicking the Advanced button in the Completing The Backup Or Restore Wizard page brings up a dialog box that allows you to specify the type of backup: Normal, Copy, Incremental, Differential, or Daily. These backup types are discussed in the "Selecting a Backup Type" section later in this chapter.

8. During the backup process, the wizard displays the Backup Progress dialog box, as shown in Figure 10.15. Once the backup process is complete, you can click the Report button in this dialog box to see details of the backup session. Figure 10.16 shows an example of a backup report.

FIGURE 10.15   The Backup Progress dialog box

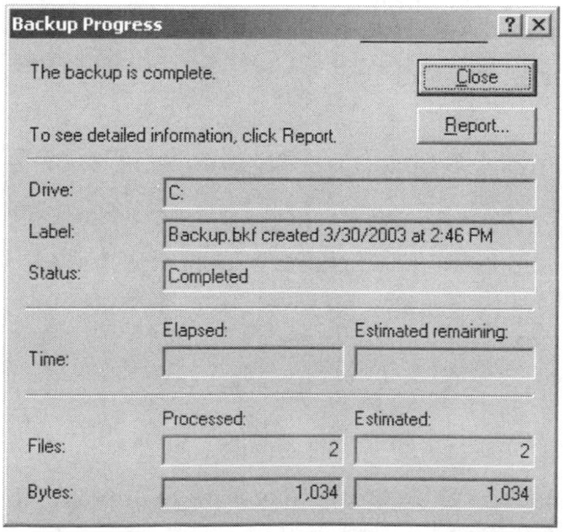

FIGURE 10.16   An example of a backup report

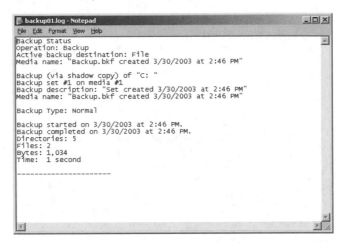

In Exercise 10.6, you will use the Backup Wizard. You will need a blank, formatted, high-density floppy disk for this exercise.

EXERCISE 10.6

Using the Backup Wizard

1. Create a folder on your D: drive called **DATA**. Create some small text files in this folder. The size of all of the files combined should not exceed 1MB.

2. Select Start ➢ All Programs ➢ Accessories ➢ System Tools ➢ Backup.

3. The Welcome To The Backup Utility Advanced Mode dialog box appears. Click Wizard Mode. The Welcome to the Backup Or Restore Wizard page appears. Click the Next button.

4. The Backup Or Restore page appears. Ensure that the Back Up Files And Settings option is selected and click the Next button.

5. The What To Back Up page appears. Select Let Me Choose What To Back Up and click the Next button.

6. In the Items To Back Up dialog box, select My Computer, expand D:, and check the DATA folder. Click the Next button.

7. In the Backup Type, Destination, And Name page, select Let Me Choose A Location Not Listed Here from the Choose A Place To Save Your Backup pull-down menu and click the Browse button. In the Open dialog box, select Floppy (A:). For the filename, enter the date (in the *mmddyy* format). Then click the Open button.

8. In the Backup Type, Destination, And Name page, click the Next button.

9. The Completing The Backup Or Restore Wizard page appears. If all of the information is correct, click the Finish button.

10. When the Backup Wizard completes, click the Report button in the Backup Progress dialog box. This will show the backup log in a Notepad window. Close this window when you are finished viewing the report.

11. Close all of the Backup Wizard dialog boxes.

Managing System State Data

System State data refers to a collection of system-specific configuration information. You can manage the availability of System State data by using the Backup utility to back up this information on a regular basis.

On a Windows Server 2003 member server, System State data consists of the Registry, the COM+ Class Registration database, and the system boot files. If the server is configured as a certificate server, System State data will also include the Certificate Services database. On Windows Server 2003 domain controller, System State data also includes the Active Directory services database and the SYSVOL directory, which is a shared directory that stores the server copy of the domain's public files.

To backup System State data, you take the following steps:

1. Select Start ➤ All Programs ➤ Accessories ➤ System Tools ➤ Backup.

2. You will see the Welcome To The Backup Utility Advanced Mode dialog box shown in Figure 10.17.

FIGURE 10.17 Welcome To The Backup Utility Advanced Mode dialog box

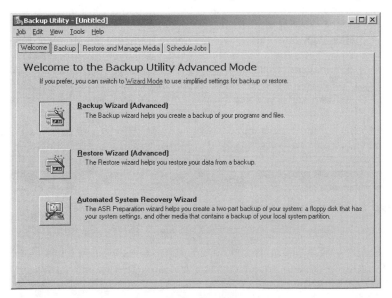

3. Click the Backup Wizard (Advanced) button. The Welcome To The Backup Wizard dialog box will appear. Click the Next button to continue.

4. On the What To Back Up page, select the Only Back Up The System State Data radio button, as shown in Figure 10.18, and click the Next button.

FIGURE 10.18 The What To Back Up page

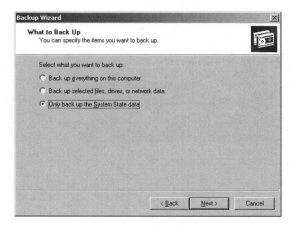

5. In the Backup Type, Destination, And Name dialog box, select the location of your backup media and click the Next button.

6. The Completing The Backup Wizard dialog box will appear. If all of the information is correct, click the Finish button.

If you need to restore System State data on a domain controller, you should restart your computer with the advanced startup option Directory Services Restore Mode. This allows the Active Directory directory service database and the SYSVOL directory to be restored. If the System State data is restored on a domain controller that is a part of a domain where data is replicated to other domain controllers, you must perform an authoritative restore. For an authoritative restore, you use the Ntdsutil.exe command, then restart the computer.

If you have a backup device attached to your computer, you can follow the steps in Exercise 10.7 to back up your System State data. This information will not fit on a single floppy disk.

EXERCISE 10.7

Backing Up System State Data

1. Select Start ➤ All Programs ➤ Accessories ➤ System Tools ➤ Backup.

2. The Welcome To The Backup Utility Advanced Mode dialog box will appear, click the button for Backup Wizard (Advanced). The Welcome To The Backup Wizard dialog box will appear. Click the Next button to continue.

3. On the What To Back Up Page, select the Only Back Up the System State Data option and click the Next button.

4. In the Backup Type, Destination, And Name dialog box, select the location of your backup media (for example, D:\Backup) and click the Next button.

5. The Completing The Backup Wizard dialog box will appear. If all of the information is correct, click the Finish button.

6. When the backup is complete, click the Report button in the Backup Progress dialog box.

7. The backup log appears in a Notepad window. Close this window when you are finished viewing the report.

8. Close all of the Backup dialog boxes.

Configuring Backup Options

You can configure more specific backup configurations by selecting backup options. To access the backup options, start the Backup utility in Advanced mode (as described above) and select Tools ➢ Options. This brings up the Options dialog box. This dialog box has five tabs with options for controlling the backup and restore processes: General, Restore, Backup Type, Backup Log, and Exclude Files. The options on these tabs are covered in the following sections.

Configuring General Backup Options

The General tab, shown in Figure 10.19, contains options for configuring backup sessions. Table 10.11 describes these options.

FIGURE 10.19   The General tab of the Options dialog box

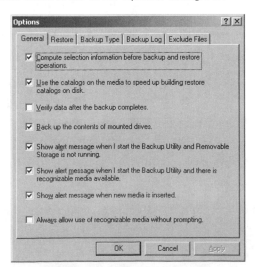

TABLE 10.11 General Backup Options

Option	Description
Compute Selection Information Before Backup And Restore Operations	Estimates the number of files and bytes that will be backed up or restored during the current operation and displays this information prior to the backup or restore operation
Use The Catalogs On The Media To Speed Up Building Restore Catalogs On Disk	Specifies that you want to use an on-media catalog to build an on-disk catalog that can be used to select which folders and files will be restored during a restore operation
Verify Data After The Backup Completes	Makes sure that all data has been backed up properly
Back Up The Contents Of Mounted Drives	Specifies that the data should be backed up on mounted drives; otherwise, only path information on mounted drives is backed up
Show Alert Message When I Start The Backup Utility And Removable Storage Is Not Running	Notifies you if Removable Storage is not running (when you are backing up to tape or other removable media)
Show Alert Message When I Start The Backup Utility And There Is Recognizable Media Available	Notifies you when you start Backup if new media have been added to the Removable Storage import pool
Show Alert Message When New Media Is Inserted	Notifies you when new media are detected by Removable Storage
Always Allow Use Of Recognizable Media Without Prompting	Specifies that if new media are detected by Removable Storage, that media should be directed to the Backup media pool

Configuring Restore Options

The Restore tab of the Options dialog box, shown in Figure 10.20, contains three options that relate to how files are restored when the file already exists on the computer:

- Do Not Replace The File On My Computer (Recommended)
- Replace The File On Disk Only If The File On The Disk Is Older
- Always Replace The File On My Computer

Selecting a Backup Type

The Backup Type tab, shown in Figure 10.21, allows you to specify the default backup type that will be used. You should select the type of backup based on the following:

- How much data you are backing up

- How quickly you want to be able to perform the backup
- The number of tapes you are willing to use in the event that you need to perform a restore operation

FIGURE 10.20   The Restore tab of the Options dialog box

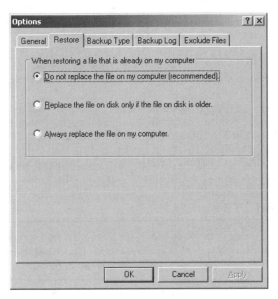

FIGURE 10.21   The Backup Type tab of the Options dialog box

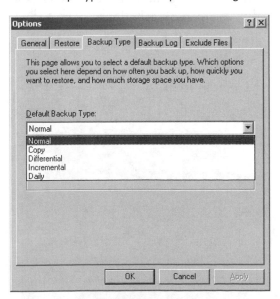

Table 10.12 describes the backup type options.

TABLE 10.12 Backup Type Options

Option	Description
Normal	Backs up all files and sets the archive bit as marked for each file that is backed up. Requires only one tape set for the restore process.
Copy	Backs up all files and does not set the archive bit as marked for each file that is backed up. Requires only one tape set for the restore process.
Differential	Backs up only the files that have not been marked as archived and does not set the archive bit for each file that is backed up. Requires the last normal backup set and the last differential tape set for the restore process.
Incremental	Backs up only the files that have not been marked as archived and sets the archive bit for each file that is backed up. Requires the last normal backup set and all of the incremental tapes that have been created since the last normal backup for the restore process.
Daily	Backs up only the files that have been changed today and does not set the archive bit for each file that is backed up. Requires each daily backup and the last normal backup set for the restore process.

Setting Backup Log Options

The Backup Log tab, shown in Figure 10.22, allows you to specify the amount of information that is logged during the backup process. Table 10.13 list the backup log options.

FIGURE 10.22 The Backup Log tab of the Options dialog box

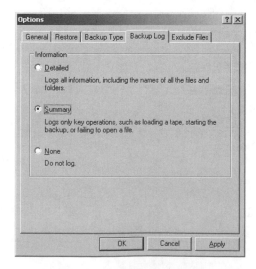

TABLE 10.13   Backup Log Options

Option	Description
Detailed	Logs all information, including the names of the folders and files that are backed up
Summary	Logs only key backup operations, such as starting the backup
None	Specifies that a log file will not be created

Excluding Files

The Exclude Files tab of the Options dialog box, shown in Figure 10.23, allows you to explicitly exclude specific files during the backup process. For example, you might choose to exclude the page file or application files.

FIGURE 10.23   The Exclude Files tab of the Options dialog box

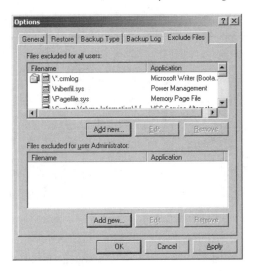

Scheduling Backup Jobs

The Backup utility allows you to schedule backup jobs on a specified schedule. You can choose from the following options:

- Once, which means the backup job will only be run one time based on the specified date and time
- Daily, which allows you to schedule a backup job to run at the specified time on a recurring daily basis
- Weekly, which is used to schedule a backup job to run on the specified day at the specified time on a recurring weekly basis

- Monthly, which is used to schedule a backup job to run on the specified day of the month at the specified time on a recurring monthly basis

- At System Startup, which schedules a backup job to run each time the system is started

- At Logon, which schedules a backup job to run each time the job's owner logs on locally at the computer

- When Idle, which will trigger a backup job to be run when the server has been idle for the specified number of minutes

You can schedule backup jobs when the backup job is initially created or through the Scheduled Jobs tab of the Backup utility, as shown in Figure 10.24.

FIGURE 10.24   The Schedule Jobs tab of the Backup utility

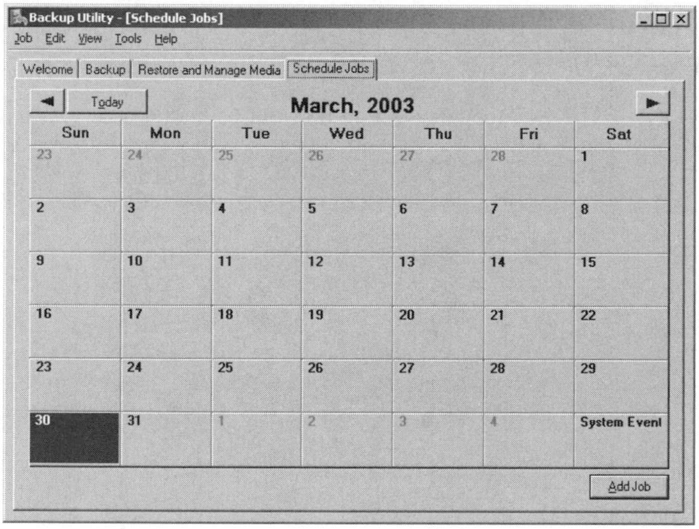

To schedule a job through the Schedule Jobs tab, you would take the following steps:

1. Click the Add Job button in the lower right-hand corner of the Schedule Jobs tab.

2. The Welcome To The Backup Wizard page will appear. Click the Next button.

3. The What To Back Up page will appear. You can specify the following: Back Up Everything On This Computer; Back Up Selected Files, Drives, Or Network Data; or Only Back Up The System State Data. In this example, we will only back up selected files, so the Back Up Selected Files, Drives, Or Network Data option is selected. Click the Next button.

4. The Items To Back Up page will appear. Select what items you will back up and click the Next button.

5. The Backup Type, Destination, And Name page will appear. Select the location for your backup and click the Next button.

6. The Type Of Backup page will appear. You can select from Normal, Copy, Incremental, Differential, or Daily backup type. Make your selection and click the Next button.

7. The How To Back Up page will appear, as shown in Figure 10.25. You can select options for Verify Data After Backup; Use Hardware Compression, If Available; and Disable Volume Shadow Copy. Once you make your selections, click the Next button.

 Shadow copies, which are used in conjunction with the Backup Utility, are covered in Chapter 4, "Managing Disks."

FIGURE 10.25 How To Back Up page

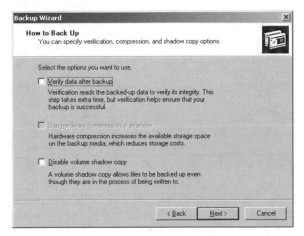

8. The Backup Options page will appear, as shown in Figure 10.26. You can select from Append This Backup To The Existing Backups or Replace The Existing Backups. If you are replacing existing backups, you can also select Allow Only The Owner And The Administrator Access To The Backup Data And To Any Backups Appended To This Medium option. Make your selection and click the Next button.

FIGURE 10.26 Backup Options page

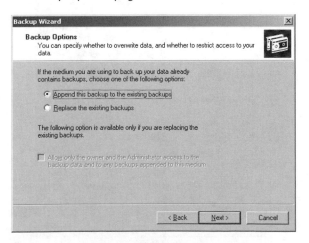

9. The When To Back Up page will appear, as shown in Figure 10.27. You can specify that the backup should be run now or later. To schedule a backup job, verify that the Later radio button is selected. Give the job a name in the Job Name field and then click the Set Schedule button.

FIGURE 10.27   When To Back Up page

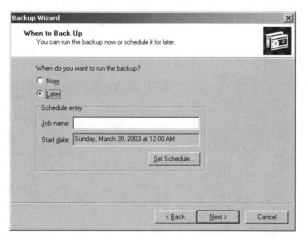

10. The Schedule tab of the Schedule Job dialog will appear, as shown in Figure 10.28. You can configure the scheduled task to run daily, weekly, monthly, once (the default selection), at system startup, at logon, or when idle. Start Time allows you to specify what time the backup should start. The middle of the dialog box will show you options about the schedule based on the Schedule Task option you select. The Advanced button is used to configure scheduling options such as when the schedule will start, when it will end, and how often the schedule should be repeated.

FIGURE 10.28   Schedule tab of Schedule Job dialog box

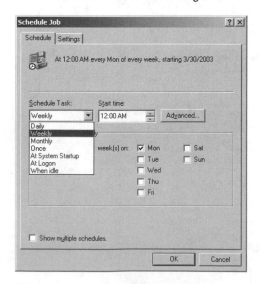

11. Click the Settings tab, as shown in Figure 10.29, to set additional settings related to the scheduled job. The Settings tab allows you to configure options such as what action should be taken when the scheduled task is completed, configuration for idle time if you chose the option to schedule backups when the computer has been idle for the specified amount of time, and power management options. Once you make your selections, click the OK button.

FIGURE 10.29 Settings tab of Schedule Job dialog box

12. The Set Account Information dialog will appear, as shown in Figure 10.30. This dialog box is used to configure the username and password of the user account that will be used to run the scheduled backup job. Specify the username in the Run As dialog box and type and confirm the password for the user. Click the OK button. Click the Next button.

FIGURE 10.30 Set Account Information dialog box

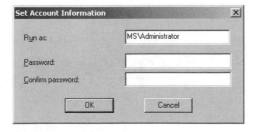

13. The Completing The Backup Wizard page will appear. Click the Finish button.

Once you have created scheduled backup jobs, they will be listed on the Scheduled Jobs tab of the Backup utility and in Scheduled Tasks in Control Panel.

Now that you have backed up a job and learned how to schedule a job, the next task is to be able to restore backup jobs.

Using the Restore Wizard

Having a complete backup won't help you if your system fails unless you can successfully restore that backup. To be sure that you can restore your data, you should test the restoration process before anything goes wrong. You can use the *Restore Wizard* for testing purposes, as well as when you actually need to restore your backup.

To use the Restore Wizard, take the following steps:

1. Select Start ≻ All Programs ≻ Accessories ≻ System Tools ≻ Backup.

2. The Welcome To The Backup Utility Advanced Mode dialog box appears. Click Wizard Mode. The Welcome To The Backup Or Restore Wizard dialog box appears. Click the Next button.

3. The Backup Or Restore page appears. Select the Restore Files And Settings option and click the Next button.

4. The What To Restore page appears. This page allows you to select which backup session you will restore, as shown in Figure 10.31. Select the backup session you want to restore by selecting the appropriate label from the Backup Identification Label, then select the directories and files you want to restore. Click the Next button.

FIGURE 10.31   The What To Restore page

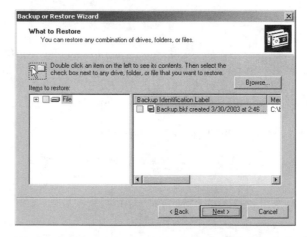

5. The Completing The Backup Or Restore Wizard page appears. If all of the information is correct, click the Finish button.

 Clicking the Advanced button in the Completing The Backup Or Restore Wizard dialog box brings up a dialog box that allows you to specify the type of backup: Normal, Copy, Incremental, Differential, or Daily. These backup types were discussed in the "Selecting a Backup Type" section earlier in this chapter. You can also specify an alternate location where the files should be restored.

NTFS data must be restored to a NTFS partition to maintain permissions. Active Directory data must be restored to its original location.

6. During the restore process, the wizard displays the Restore Progress dialog box. Once the restore process is complete, you can click the Report button to verify that all files were successfully restored.

In Exercise 10.8, you will use the Restore Wizard. You will need to have completed Exercise 10.7 to do this exercise.

EXERCISE 10.8

Using the Restore Wizard

1. Select Start ➢ All Programs ➢ Accessories ➢ System Tools ➢ Backup.

2. The Welcome To The Backup Utility Advanced Mode dialog box appears. Click Wizard Mode. The Welcome To The Backup Or Restore Wizard page appears. Click the Next button.

3. The Backup Or Restore page appears. Select the Restore Files And Settings option and click the Next button.

4. The What To Restore page appears. Select the session you created in Exercise 10.7, and specify the files you want to restore. Click the Next button.

5. The Completing The Backup Or Restore Wizard page appears. If all of the information is correct, click the Finish button.

6. During the restore process, the Wizard displays the Restore Progress dialog box. Once the restore process is complete, you can click the Report button to verify that all files were successfully restored.

Using Automated System Recovery

Windows XP Professional and Windows Server 2003 now include a new feature in the Backup utility called Automated System Recovery. *Automated System Recovery (ASR)* is used for system recovery in the event of system failure. It is a two-part system recovery that consists of an ASR backup component and an ASR restore component. The system information that is backed up by ASR includes System State data, system services, and disk configuration information (information about basic and dynamic disks and the file signature associated with each disk). You create ASR backups with the Automated System Recovery Wizard through the Backup utility. This utility is used only to back up system data and your local system partition. It does not back up folders and files.

When you use the ASR Restore process, the following information is restored:

- Disk recovery configuration information including disk signatures, volumes, and partition for all disks used to start the computer

- A simplified version of Windows
- The copy of the system partition (containing the system state data) that was backed up through the ASR backup component

You should only use the Automated System Recovery Wizard for system recovery after you have tried to boot the computer to Safe Mode and used the Last Known Good Configuration option. You should always try the easier and less invasive methods of recovery before trying more complex recovery options. ASR is used to recover a system when none of the other recovery features work. Example, you power up the computer to a black screen. It is highly recommended that critical machines use the ASR feature.

If you are using FAT16 volumes, ASR will only support volumes up to 2.1GB. If you have a FAT16 partition that is over 2.1GB, you should convert them to NTFS if you want to use ASR.

In Exercise 10.9, you will create an Automated System Recovery backup. You will need some form of backup media, a 1.44MB floppy disk, and your Windows Server 2003 distribution CD.

EXERCISE 10.9

Using the Automated System Recovery Wizard

Create an Automated System Recovery Backup

1. Select Start ➢ All Programs ➢ Accessories ➢ System Tools ➢ Backup. Click the Advanced Mode link to open the main Backup utility screen.

2. From the Welcome tab, click the Automated System Recovery Wizard button.

3. The Automated System Recovery Preparation Wizard will start. Click the Next button to continue.

4. The Backup Destination page will appear. Specify the location of your backup media (which should not be on the system or boot partition) and click the Next button. This process may take 30 minutes or longer, as the system partition is being backed up. Click the Finish button.

5. The Backup Utility dialog box will appear and you will be prompted to insert a blank 1.44MB floppy diskette into drive A:. Click the OK button.

6. The Backup Utility dialog box will prompt you to remove the diskette and label it Windows Automated System Recovery Disk for Backup.bkf created *mm/dd/yyyy* at *h:mm*. Label the diskette and click the OK button.

Perform an Automated System Recovery Restore

7. Boot your computer using the Windows Server 2003 CD. During the boot process, you may need to press a specified key (based on your computer's BIOS) to boot the computer from CD.

8. Press F2 when prompted during the text-mode portion of the Windows Server 2003 Setup process to initiate the recovery process. You will be prompted to insert the ASR floppy disk. Insert the disk and press any key.

9. You have only a few seconds to cancel the recovery by hitting the Esc key. Otherwise, the system reformats the C drive automatically. After the format is complete, the Automated System Recovery Wizard begins an installation process very similar to the initial Windows Server 2003 installation.

10. After the Windows Server 2003 files are copied to the hard drive and the computer reboots, the Windows Server 2003 setup procedure continues. During this procedure, the Automated System Recovery Wizard appears automatically and prompts you for the backup location. Select the correct backup location to complete the wizard and continue with the normal setup process. At the end of the Automated System Recovery process, the Backup utility will open automatically and restore the system.

The Ntbackup command-line utility can be used to back up and restore Windows Server 2003 data using command-line switches. Ntbackup only supports backing up of folders unless you create a backup selection file. It is also important to note that Ntbackup does not allow you to back up data based on wildcards (for example, *.doc). You can use Ntbackup to schedule backup jobs. If you run the Ntbackup command without any command-line switches, it opens the Backup and Restore Wizard.

Using the Recovery Console

If your computer will not start, and you have tried to boot to Safe Mode and the Last Known Good Configuration with no luck, there's one more option you can try. The *Recovery Console* is an option designed for administrators and advanced users. It allows you limited access to FAT16, FAT32, and NTFS volumes without starting the Windows Server 2003 graphical interface. Through the Recovery Console, you can perform the following tasks:

- Copy, replace, or rename operating system files and folders. You might do this if missing or corrupt files caused the boot failure.

- Enable or disable the loading of services when the computer is restarted. If a particular service may be keeping the operating system from booting, you could disable the service. If a particular service is required for successful booting, you want to make sure that service loading was enabled.

- Repair the file system boot sector or the MBR. You would use this option if a virus damaged the system boot sector or the MBR.

- Create and format partitions on the drives. You might use this option if your disk utilities will not delete or create Windows Server 2003 partitions. Normally, you use a disk-partitioning utility for these functions.

 The Recovery Console can only be used on *x*86-based servers and is not supported on Itanium-based computers.

In the following sections, you will learn how to access and use the Recovery Console.

Starting the Recovery Console

You can start the Recovery Console from the Windows Server 2003 CD, or alternatively, you can add the Recovery Console to the Windows Server 2003 startup options, but you need to configure this prior to the failure. Each of these options is covered in the following sections.

Starting the Recovery Console with the Windows Server 2003 CD

To access the Recovery Console from the Windows Server 2003 CD, take the following steps:

1. Restart your computer using the Windows Server 2003 CD.

2. Follow the prompts until you get to the Welcome To Setup screen. From this screen, press R to repair a Windows Server 2003 installation using Recovery Console.

3. Select the installation you want to use and press Enter.

4. At the prompt, type in the local Administrator password, and the Recovery Console will start.

Adding the Recovery Console to Windows Server 2003 Startup

You can add the Recovery Console to the Windows Server 2003 server startup options so it will be available in the event of a system failure. This option is only available on *x*86-based computers. This configuration takes about 7MB of disk space to hold the CMDCONS folder and files. To set up this configuration, take the following steps:

1. Insert the Windows Server 2003 CD into your CD-ROM drive. You can disable auto-play by pressing the Shift key as the CD is read. From a command prompt, change to the CD drive letter (example: D:) then change the directory to the I386 folder by typing **CD I386**. In the \I386 folder, type **WINNT32 /CMDCONS**.

2.   The Windows Server 2003 Setup dialog box appears, asking you to confirm that you want to install the Recovery Console. Click the Yes button.

3.   The installation files will be copied to your computer. Then you will see a dialog box letting you know that the Recovery Console has been successfully installed. Click the OK button to continue.

The next time you restart your computer, you will see an option for the Microsoft Windows Server 2003 Recovery Console.

In Exercise 10.10, you will add the Recovery Console to the Windows Server 2003 startup options. You will need the Windows Server 2003 CD for this exercise.

EXERCISE 10.10

Adding the Recovery Console to the Windows Server 2003 Setup

1.   Insert the Windows Server 2003 CD in your CD-ROM drive. Hold down the Shift key as the CD is read to prevent auto-play.

2.   Select Start ≻ Command Prompt.

3.   Change the drive letter to your CD-ROM drive.

4.   From the CD drive letter prompt ($x:\>$), type **CD I386** and press Enter.

5.   From $x:\I386>$, type **WINNT32 /CMDCONS**.

6.   In the Windows Server 2003 Setup dialog box, click the Yes button to confirm that you want to install the Recovery Console.

7.   After the installation files are copied to your computer, a dialog box appears to let you know that the Recovery Console has been successfully installed. Click the OK button.

8.   Shut down and restart your computer. In the startup selection screen, select the option for Microsoft Windows Server 2003 Recovery Console.

9.   At the prompt, press the Enter key to close the Recovery Console. Your computer will restart normally.

Using the Recovery Console

After you add the Recovery Console, you can access it by restarting your computer. In the operating system selection menu, you will see an option for Microsoft Windows Server 2003 Recovery Console. Select this option to start the Recovery Console.

The Recovery Console presents you with a command prompt and very limited access to system resources. This keeps unauthorized users from using the Recovery Console to access sensitive data. The following are the only folders you can access through the Recovery Console:

▪   The root folder

▪   The *Windir* folder and the subfolders of the Windows Server 2003 installation

- The CMDCONS folder
- Removable media drives such as CD-ROM drives

If you try to access any other folders besides the ones listed above, you will receive an "access denied" error message.

In the Recovery Console, you cannot copy files from a local hard disk to a floppy disk. You can only copy files from a floppy disk or CD to a hard disk, or from one hard disk to another hard disk. This is for security purposes.

 You should use the Recovery Console with extreme caution. Improper use may cause even more damage than the problems you are trying to fix. For example, you could delete or overwrite files that are normally protected by the operating system.

If your computer dual-boots with other Windows Server 2003 operating systems, the first option you must specify is which Windows Server 2003 operating system you will log on to. A legend is provided that designates the operating system to select based on a simple numeric. For example; 1: C:\Windows would appear, and you would enter a 1 to select this OS. Next, you must specify the local Administrator password for the system you are logging on to.

When the Recovery Console starts, you can use the commands listed in Table 10.14.

TABLE 10.14 Commands Available with the Recovery Console

Command	Description
ATTRIB	Used to set file attributes. You can set file attributes for Read-only (R), System (S), Hidden (H), or Compressed (C).
BATCH	Used to execute commands in a specified input file.
BOOTCFG	Used to view or configure Boot.ini settings.
CHDIR (or you can use CD)	Used to navigate the directory structure. If executed without a directory name, the current directory is displayed. (CHDIR and CD work the same way.)
CLS	Used to clear any text that is currently displayed on the console.
CHKDSK	Used to check the disk and display a disk status report.
COPY	Used to copy a single file from one location to another. COPY does not support wildcards and does not copy files to removable media (such as floppy disks).
DELETE (or DEL)	Used to delete a single file. Wildcards are not supported. (DELETE and DEL work the same way.)

TABLE 10.14 Commands Available with the Recovery Console *(continued)*

Command	Description
DIR	Used to display lists of files and subdirectories in the current directory.
DISABLE	Used to disable Windows Server 2003 system services and drivers.
DISKPART	Used to manage disk partitions. If executed without a command-line argument, a user interface is displayed.
ENABLE	Used to enable Windows Server 2003 system services and drivers.
EXIT	Used to quit the Recovery Console and restart the computer.
EXPAND	Used to expand compressed files such as CABs.
FIXBOOT	Used to write a new boot sector onto the computer's system partition.
FIXMBR	Used to repair the MBR of the computer's boot partition.
FORMAT	Used to prepare a disk for use with Windows Server 2003 by formatting the disk as FAT16, FAT32, or NTFS.
HELP	Used to display help information for Recovery Console commands.
LISTSVC	Used to list all available services and drivers on the computer, as well as the current status of each service and driver.
LOGON	If the computer is configured for dual-booting or multi-booting, used to log on to other installations as the local administrator.
MAP	Used to display the current drive-letter mappings.
MKDIR (or MD)	Used to create new directories. (MKDIR and MD work the same way.)
MORE	Used to display a text file on the console screen. (Same as TYPE.)
NET	Used to access Net services command, for example: Net Use or Net Share.
RENAME (REN)	Used to rename a single file. (RENAME and REN work the same way.)
RMDIR (or RD)	Used to delete directories. (RMDIR and RD work the same way.)
SYSTEMROOT	Used to specify that the current directory is the system root.
TYPE	Used to display a text file on the console screen. (Same as MORE.)

In Exercise 10.11, you will use the Recovery Console. This exercise assumes that you completed Exercise 10.10 to add the Recovery Console to the Windows Server 2003 startup options.

EXERCISE 10.11

Using the Recovery Console

1. Restart the computer. In the operating system selection menu, select the Microsoft Windows Server 2003 Recovery Console option.

2. Select the Windows Server 2003 installation you want to manage and press Enter. (If the computer has been configured as specified in this book, this will be option 1.)

3. Enter the local Administrator password and press Enter. You see the C:\Windows> prompt.

4. Type DIR and press Enter to see a current listing of available files and folders. In the listing, you can press Enter to scroll down line by line or the spacebar to scroll continuously.

5. Type CD .. and press Enter to move to the root of the C: drive. You see the C:\> prompt.

6. Type DIR Boot.ini and press Enter to see the file attributes of the Boot.ini file.

7. Type MORE Boot.ini and press Enter to see the contents of the Boot.ini file.

8. Type LISTSVC and press Enter (continuously) to see a list of all the services and drivers.

9. Type EXIT to exit the Recovery Console and restart your computer.

 Real World Scenario

The Last-Ditch Effort

You have just installed a new CD-RW device to your server. As you are loading the driver, your server hangs. You restart the computer, and it still won't boot. You attempt to start your server in Safe Mode, but even Safe Mode will not load. Before you panic, you should attempt to fix the problem through the Recovery Console.

To use the Recovery Console to fix this problem you would take the following steps: First, restart the computer using the Recovery Console. Once in the Recovery Console, use LISTSVC to obtain the exact spelling of the driver and then enter disable *driver_name*. This will disable the new driver you loaded that is causing the computer to hang. Restart the computer; it will boot. Use Device Manager to remove the driver.

Using Remote Desktop and Remote Assistance

Remote Desktop allows you to remotely take control of a Windows Server 2003 server from another location. For example, you could access a server located in a remote office from your company's corporate headquarters. *Remote Assistance* is used to request assistance from another user. For example, if you were having problems troubleshooting your Windows Server 2003 server, you could ask a remote administrator to walk you through the troubleshooting process.

You will learn more about Remote Desktop and Remote Assistance in the following sections.

Using Remote Desktop

Remote Desktop allows you to take control of a remote computer's keyboard, video, and mouse. This tool does not require that someone collaborate with you on the remote computer. While the remote computer is being accessed, it remains locked and any actions that are performed remotely will not be visible on the monitor that is attached to the remote computer. Remote Desktop is used in the following situations:

- For troubleshooting computers within an organization that are in a remote location but are connected to the central network through a direct network connection, secure Virtual Private Network (VPN), or remote access
- To allow Help Desk administrators within a network to remotely troubleshoot organizational computers
- To allow remote access to organizational computers without security concerns that unauthorized users are viewing the remote computer's monitor and watching what actions are being performed remotely

In the following sections you will learn:

- The Remote Desktop restrictions
- The minimum set of requirements for Remote Desktop
- How to configure the computer that will be accessed remotely
- How to configure the computer that will be used to access the remote computer
- How to customize a remote Desktop session
- How to start a remote Desktop session
- How to end a remote Desktop session

Remote Desktop Restrictions

Remote Desktop uses all of the inherent security features of Windows Server 2003. In addition, Remote Desktop imposes these security features:

- Remote Desktop is designed to be used for accessing internal domain computers. If the computer that you want to access is outside your organization's firewall, then you will need to use Internet proxy software or Microsoft Internet Security and Acceleration Server client software.

- If you want to establish a session from a computer via the Internet to your company's internal network, you must first establish a secure VPN connection to the internal network you wish to access.

- Remote Desktop can't be used to create a connection between two computers directly connected to the Internet.

- There is no option for simultaneous remote and local access to the Windows Server 2003 Desktop. If a computer will be accessed remotely, Windows Server 2003 will prompt the local user that they need to be logged off before the computer can be accessed remotely.

Remote Desktop Requirements

To use Remote Desktop, the following requirements must be met:

- Windows XP Professional or Windows Server 2003 must be running on the computer that will be accessed remotely.

- The computer that will access the remote computer must be running Windows 95 or higher and have Remote Desktop client software installed and configured.

- There must be an IP connection between the two computers that will be used to establish a Remote Desktop session.

Configuring a Computer for Remote Access

You enable a computer to be accessed remotely through Control Panel. To enable remote access, select Start ➢ Control Panel ➢ System. Click the Remote tab. Within the Remote tab of System Properties, check Allow Users To Connect Remotely To This Computer, as shown in Figure 10.32. To enable Remote Desktop, you must be logged on to the computer as an administrator or a member of the Administrators group.

FIGURE 10.32 The Remote tab of the System Properties dialog box

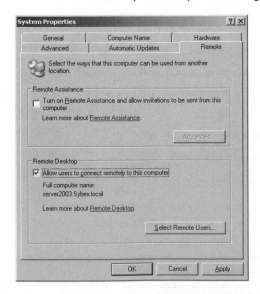

By default, only members of the Administrators group can access a computer that has been configured to use Remote Desktop. To enable other users to access the computer remotely, click the Select Remote Users button shown in Figure 10.32. This brings up the Remote Desktop Users dialog box, shown in Figure 10.33, and allows you to specify which users can access the remote computer by selecting users through the Add or Remove buttons.

FIGURE 10.33   The Remote Desktop Users dialog box

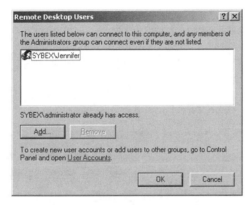

 When you enable remote access to a computer, the changes will take effect immediately. By default, members of the local or domain Administrators group will have Remote Desktop permissions. Members of the Administrators groups can end a local user's session without permission. Non-administrative users who are granted Remote Desktop permissions can't end a local user's session if the local user refuses the session.

Configuring the Remote Desktop Client Software

The Remote Desktop Connection client software is used to control a Windows Server 2003 computer remotely. This software is installed by default on computers running Windows XP Home Edition, Windows XP Professional, and Windows Server 2003.

To configure the Remote Desktop Connection, you would click Start ➤ All Programs ➤ Accessories ➤ Communications ➤ Remote Desktop Connection, which displays the dialog box shown in Figure 10.34.

FIGURE 10.34   The Remote Desktop Connection dialog box

To configure the Remote Desktop Connection options, you would click the Options button in the Remote Desktop Connection dialog box. You will see the Remote Desktop Connection options.

The options that can be configured for the client that is initiating the Remote Desktop Connection include General, Display, Local Resources, Programs, and Experience. Each of these options is covered in more detail in the following sections.

General

The General tab, as shown in Figure 10.35, is used to configure Logon Settings, which specifies the computer you will connect to, the username, password, and domain for the user who will remotely connect to the server, and whether you want to save the current settings or bypass the current settings and open an existing saved connection settings file.

FIGURE 10.35 The General tab of the Remote Desktop Connection options dialog box

Display

The Display tab, as shown in Figure 10.36, is used to configure the remote desktop size, the color settings you want to use, and whether to display the connection bar when in Full Screen Mode.

Local Resources

The Local Resources tab, as shown in Figure 10.37, is used to configure the Remote Computer sound (choices are Bring to This Computer, Do Not Play, and Leave At Remote Computer), the keyboard (specifies how Windows key combinations are applied), and which local devices you want to connect to (disk drives, printers, and serial ports).

FIGURE 10.36   The Display tab of the Remote Desktop Connection options dialog box

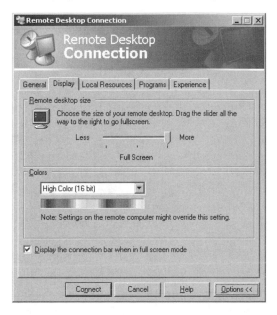

FIGURE 10.37   The Local Resources tab of the Remote Desktop Connection options dialog box

Programs

The Programs tab, as shown in Figure 10.38, is used to specify whether you want to start a program when the remote connection is made. If you choose to start a program on connection, you can configure the Program Path And File Name and the Start In The Following Folder options.

FIGURE 10.38 The Programs tab of the Remote Desktop Connection options dialog box

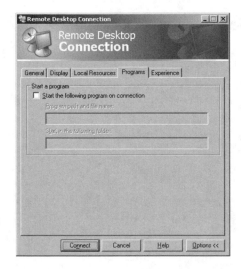

Experience

The Experience tab, as shown in Figure 10.39, is used to specify performance options for your connection. You can specify the maximum connection speed and the following options:

- Desktop Background
- Show Contents Of Window While Dragging
- Menu And Window Animation
- Themes
- Bitmap Caching

FIGURE 10.39 The Experience tab of the Remote Desktop Connection options dialog box

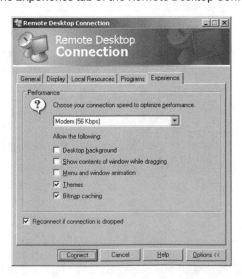

If you connect through a modem, you can increase performance by disabling options such as Desktop Background and Menu And Window Animation, and enabling Bitmap Caching.

Starting a Remote Desktop Session

Once you have configured the computer that will be accessed remotely and have configured the Remote Desktop Connection client software, you are ready to start a Remote Desktop session. You start a session through the following steps:

1. Select Start ➢ All Programs ➢ Accessories ➢ Communications ➢ Remote Desktop Connection. You could also use the command-line utility MSTSC to start the Remote Desktop connection. This will bring up the Remote Desktop Connection dialog box that was shown in Figure 10.34.

2. In the Computer field, type in the name of the computer you wish to access. Remote Desktop must be enabled on this computer and you must have permissions to access the computer remotely.

3. Click the Connect button.

4. The Log On To Windows dialog box will appear. Type in your username, password, and domain name, and click OK.

5. The Remote Desktop Connection window will open, and you will now have complete control of the remote machine.

Once a computer has been accessed remotely, it will be locked. No one at the local site will be able to use the local computer without a password. In addition, no one at the local site will be able to see the work that is being done on the computer remotely.

Ending a Remote Desktop Session

Once you have a Remote Desktop Connection, you will see a modified taskbar at the top of your remote connection that displays the computer name that you are connected to. Click the × to close the Remote Desktop Connection.

In Exercise 10.12, you will remotely access your Windows Server 2003 domain controller from your Windows XP Professional computer.

EXERCISE 10.12

Using Remote Desktop Connection

1. From your Windows Server 2003 domain controller, select Start ➢ Control Panel ➢ System and click the Remote tab.

2. Within the Remote tab of System Properties, check Allow Users To Connect Remotely To This Computer.

3. From your Windows XP Professional computer, log on to the domain as Administrator.

4. Select Start ➢ All Programs ➢ Accessories ➢ Communications ➢ Remote Desktop Connection and click the Options button.

5. In the General tab, type in the name of your Windows Server 2003 domain controller in the Computer field. Use the Administrator username and configure your password and domain in the Password and Domain fields.

6. Click the Experience tab. Select Desktop Background, Themes, and Bitmap Caching from the Allow The Following list.

7. Click the Connect button at the bottom of the Remote Desktop Connection dialog box.

8. The Log On To Windows dialog box will appear. Verify that the Administrator name and password are entered and click the OK button.

9. The Remote Desktop Connection will appear. You can manage any task from the remote session. When you are done, click the × button at the top of the screen in the modified taskbar.

Using Remote Assistance

Remote Assistance provides a mechanism for requesting help for x86-based computers through Windows Messenger and an e-mail client. To use Remote Assistance, the computer requesting help and the computer providing help must be using Windows XP or Windows Server 2003 and both computers must have interconnectivity. Common examples of when you would use Remote Assistance include:

- When you are diagnosing problems that are difficult to explain or reproduce. By using Remote Assistance, you can remotely view the computer and the remote user can show you what the error is or step you through processes that caused the error to occur.

- When an inexperienced user needs to perform a complex set of instructions. Instead of asking the inexperienced user to complete the task, you can use Remote Assistance to take control of the computer and complete the tasks yourself.

In the following sections you will learn more about:

- Differences between Remote Desktop and Remote Assistance

- Options for establishing remote connections

- Enabling Remote Assistance

- How users request remote assistance

- How administrators respond to remote assistance requests

- Administrator-initiated remote assistance

- Limitations of Remote Assistance invitations

- Security and Remote Assistance

Differences Between Remote Desktop and Remote Assistance

The key differences between the Remote Desktop utility and the Remote Assistance utility are:

- With Remote Desktop, there is only one connection at a time. With Remote Assistance, the expert is able to establish a concurrent session with the user at the remote computer.

- Remote Assistance requires the user at the remote computer to authorize access. Remote Desktop does not require administrators to seek permission before they establish a remote session.

- With Remote Assistance, both computers have to be running Windows XP or Windows Server 2003.

Options for Establishing Remote Assistance

The following options can be used to establish remote connections:

- A Local Area Network connection between the expert's computer and the novice's computer

- An Internet connection between the expert's computer and the novice's computer

- Connection via the Internet when the expert computer is behind a firewall and the novice computer is just connected to the Internet

- Connection via the Internet when the expert computer is behind a firewall and the novice computer is also behind a firewall

 If the Remote Assistance connections are made through a firewall, the firewall may need to be configured to open TCP Port 3389.

Enabling Remote Assistance

You can enable Remote Assistance through the following steps:

1. Select Start ➤ Control Panel ➤ System.

2. Click the Remote tab and select the Turn On Remote Assistance And Allow Invitations To Be Sent From This Computer checkbox, as shown in Figure 10.40.

If you click the Advanced button from the Remote tab, you can set configuration options for the maximum number of days, hours, or minutes that invitations will remain open, as shown in Figure 10.41.

Requesting Remote Assistance

If a user requires remote assistance, they send an invitation. In the following example, a user who is at a Windows Server 2003 domain controller is asking a user who is logged in at a Windows XP Professional computer for help. The following steps are used to request remote assistance:

1. Notify the person providing assistance that you will be sending a Remote Assistance invitation. Notification methods might include e-mail, instant messaging, or a telephone call. Give the person providing assistance the password that will be used for the Remote Assistance session.

FIGURE 10.40 The Remote Tab of the System Properties dialog box

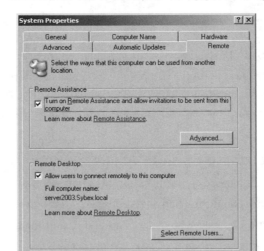

FIGURE 10.41 The Remote Assistance Settings dialog box

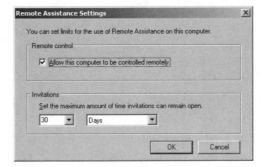

2. Select Start ➢ Help and Support.

3. From the Help And Support Center window, under Support Tasks, click the Remote Assistance option, as shown in Figure 10.42.

4. From the Remote Assistance window, shown in Figure 10.43, select Invite Someone To Help You.

5. You will be asked to specify how you want to contact the person providing assistance. You can specify Windows Messenger or e-mail (for example, using Outlook or Outlook Express).

6. Click Send Invitation to send the invitation. You can specify the invitation delivery method, the length of time until the invitation expires, and whether to use the optional password protection feature.

FIGURE 10.42   Help And Support Center window

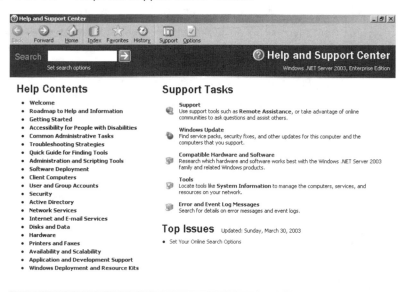

FIGURE 10.43   Remote Assistance window

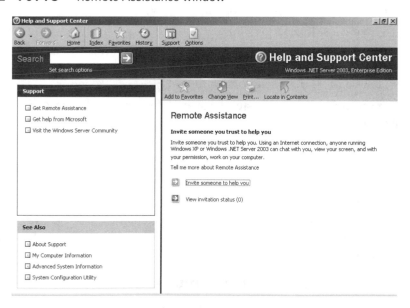

Responding to Remote Assistance Requests

When you receive a Remote Assistance invitation, you would use the following steps to respond:

1. Receive the Remote Assistance invitation via e-mail or Instant Messenger.

2. Open the invitation and double-click the attachment that is used to start the session. If a password has been configured, provide the appropriate password.

3. The user seeking assistance will see an acceptance message on their screen and be prompted to verify that you be allowed to view the remote screen and chat with them.

4. The user seeking assistance should confirm the acceptance message; a terminal window will appear on your monitor, displaying the user's computer Desktop.

5. You will then be able to manipulate remotely the user's computer by using the Take Control option, after the user approves the interaction by clicking the Allow Expert Interaction button that they see in the Remote Assistance window.

 The person who requested remote assistance can terminate the session at any time by clicking the Stop Control button in the Remote Assistance window.

Initiating a Remote Assistance Session

Administrators can also initiate a remote assistance session through the Offer Remote Assistance feature. By default, this option is disabled, but can be enabled through Group Policy by taking the following actions:

1. Select Start ➢ Run and in the Run dialog box, type **gpedit.msc**.

2. Expand Local Computer Policy ➢ Computer Configuration ➢ Administrative Templates.

3. Expand System, then Remote Assistance.

4. In the details pane, double-click Offer Remote Assistance and check the Enabled checkbox. Under Helpers, click the Show button. Click the Add button, type in the names of any users that are allowed to offer Remote Assistance, and click the OK button.

Once Offer Remote Assistance is enabled, you can offer remote assistance to a user through the following steps:

1. Inform the user that you will be offering remote assistance.

2. From the Help And Support Center dialog box, under the Support Tasks list, select Remote Assistance, then Offer Remote Assistance.

3. Follow the instructions for providing the name or IP address of the user's computer.

4. The user will see a prompt that you—the network administrator—would like to view the screen, chat with them in real time, and work on their computer. The user then accepts your assistance request.

Reuse of Remote Assistance Invitations

If both of the following conditions are met, a Remote Assistance ticket can be used more than once:

-   The invitation ticket can't be expired.

-   The IP address of the computer cannot have changed since the ticket was issued. Such a change can occur if a user connects to the Internet through an ISP that assigns dynamic IP addresses each time the user connects to the Internet.

Security and Remote Assistance

You need to keep the following security concerns in mind when authorizing Remote Assistance:

- If a user clicks the Allow Expert Interaction button, then the person providing expert assistance will have all of the security privileges that the local user has.

- If you allow a user outside of your organization to access your computer, you should have them connect via a VPN account. If they connect through the network firewall, then TCP Port 3389 must be opened, which may be considered a security risk.

Summary

In this chapter, you learned about the Windows Server 2003 system recovery options and utilities. We covered the following topics:

- Basic techniques that you can use to safeguard your computer and plan for disaster recovery

- The Event Viewer utility, including how to view the details of an event and manage log files

- The Windows Server 2003 boot process, including the steps in a normal boot, the Boot.ini file, and how to create a Windows Server 2003 boot disk

- Advanced startup options, including Safe Mode, Enable Boot Logging, Last Known Good Configuration, and additional options for booting in special modes

- Startup and Recovery options, which are used to specify what action Windows Server 2003 should take in the event of system failure

- The Windows Backup utility, which includes a Backup Wizard and Restore Wizard, Automated System Recovery, and the option to schedule backups

- The Recovery Console, which is a special boot process that allows you limited access to your file system for replacement of files or specifying which services should be started or disabled the next time the computer is booted

- The Remote Desktop and Remote Assistance features that are used to remotely control a computer or to ask for help from a remote user

Exam Essentials

Be able to use the Event Viewer.   Know how to access the Event Viewer and understand which events are stored in each of the Event Viewer logs.

Manage the Windows Server 2003 boot process.   List the files required within the Windows Server 2003 boot process. Be able to troubleshoot the boot process in the event of failure. Know the options that are configured within Boot.ini and how the Boot.ini file is configured. Be able to recover the boot files in the event of corruption.

Use the Windows Server 2003 advanced startup options. List the Windows Server 2003 Advanced Startup Options and under what circumstances it is appropriate to use each one.

Use the Windows Server 2003 Backup utility. Be able to use the Windows Server 2003 Backup utility to perform system backups and restores. Understand what information is backed up through the System State data option of backup. Be able to restore System State data on a Windows Server 2003 domain controller. Understand the backup schemes, the amount of data backed up by each scheme, and the number of tape sets that are required to execute a restore based on the backup scheme used. Be able to create an Automated System Recovery backup and know how to perform an Automated System Recovery restore. Know how to schedule backups to run on a specified schedule.

Use the Recovery Console. Know when it is appropriate to use the Recovery Console. Be able to install and use the Recovery Console.

Use Remote Control and Remote Desktop. Be able to troubleshoot Windows Server 2003 computers remotely through the use of Remote Control and Remote Desktop. Know the requirements for configuring these options and how they are used.

Key Terms

Before you take the exam, be certain you are familiar with the following terms:

Application log	Last Known Good Configuration
Automated System Recovery (ASR)	Master Boot Record (MBR)
Backup utility	Recovery Console
Backup Wizard	Remote Assistance
Boot Normally	Remote Desktop
Debugging Mode	Restore Wizard
Directory Services Restore Mode	Safe Mode
Driver Rollback	Safe Mode With Command Prompt
Enable Boot Logging	Safe Mode With Networking
Enable VGA Mode	Security log
Error events	Success Audit event
Event Viewer	System log
Failure Audit event	Warning events
Information events	Windows Server 2003 boot disk

Review Questions

1. You are the administrator for a large Windows Server 2003 network using Active Directory. You have delegated administrative control on several of your domains and want to track the changes that are made to the Active Directory. You enable auditing for Active Directory events. When performing maintenance on the domain controllers, which of the following command-line utilities can be used to view all of the Success Audits and Failure Audits that have occurred within your event logs?

   A. Eventcreate

   B. Eventfilter

   C. Eventquery

   D. Eventmanage

2. You are the network administrator of a medium-sized company. You have a third-party utility that is used to manage the Active Directory. Before you install the application, you backup your domain controller's System State data and the Active Directory database using the Backup Utility. After you install the third-party application, you realize that one of your domains is corrupt. You remove the application and want to restore the Active Directory database. When you try to perform an authoritative restore of the Active Directory database and information that was backed up through the Backup utility, you are unable to restore the Active Directory service database. Which of the following actions should you take? (Choose all that apply.)

   A. Restore the ERD.

   B. Restore the System State data using your ASR backup.

   C. Perform an authoritative restore with the Ntdsutil utility and restart the computer.

   D. Boot the computer to Recovery Console Mode and perform an authoritative restore of the Active Directory.

   E. Restart the computer using the Advanced Startup Option Directory Services Restore Mode.

3. You are the network administrator for a large company. One of your responsibilities is ensuring that all of the Windows Server 2003 domain controllers and member servers get backed up on a regular basis. You create a schedule that specifies that all servers will be backed up every day at 1:00 A.M. You want to automate the process using batch files. Which of the following command-line utilities can be used in conjunction with the batch files to manage the scheduled backups?

   A. Backupschedule

   B. Backup /schedule

   C. Winbackup

   D. Ntbackup

4. You are the network administrator for the XYZ Corporation and are located at the corporate headquarters in New York. Your network is configured behind a firewall that is configured for maximum security. You have a remote user who works out of their home in London and who accesses your network through the Internet. The remote user reports that they are having problems with their Windows XP Professional configuration. Within your corporate network, you use Remote Assistance to help local users with problems. Users within the network can use Remote Assistance successfully. However, when your remote user requests Remote Assistance, it does not work properly. What is the most likely problem?

    A. The firewall is blocking the request and you need to open TCP Port 9833.

    B. The firewall is blocking the request and you need to open TCP Port 8976.

    C. The firewall is blocking the request and you need to open TCP Port 3389.

    D. The firewall is blocking the request and you need to open TCP Port 7760.

5. You are the network administrator of the Wacky Widgets Corporation. You need to install a custom application on a Windows Server 2003 member server. The application requires that you manually edit the Registry to add a key and edit another key. When you attempt to restart the server, it hangs between starting to load and accessing the logon screen. Which recovery option should you try first?

    A. Boot the computer in Safe Mode and fix the Registry settings.

    B. Boot the computer with the Last Known Good Configuration option.

    C. Use the last full backup you made to restore the server.

    D. Use the ERD that was created when the server was installed to restore the Registry.

6. You are the administrator of a large network. You are responsible for managing all of the Windows Server 2003 servers within the Sales domain. When you boot the Sales-Data server, you see an error message pop up on the server console, but you accidentally clear the screen before you can read the entire message. What can you do?

    A. Check the log file *Windir*\nterrors.txt.

    B. Check the log file *Windir*\errors.txt.

    C. Check the Event Viewer log files.

    D. Check the Windows Diagnostics log files.

7. You are the network administrator for a large company. Your responsibilities include managing all of the servers for the Sales department. When you attempt to start your Windows Server 2003 servers, your computer hangs during the boot process. What troubleshooting step should you take first?

    A. Attempt to start Windows Server 2003 using Safe Mode.

    B. Attempt to start Windows Server 2003 using the ERD.

    C. Use the Windows Server 2003 Setup Boot Disks to start the computer.

    D. Restore your server using your latest system backup.

8. You are the network administrator for a large network. You just received an updated driver for your disk controller. After you update the driver, your computer won't restart. Since the computer won't start, you can't use the Driver Rollback option. You decide to use the Last Known Good Configuration option. How can you access the Last Known Good Configuration option?

   A. Press the spacebar when prompted during the boot sequence.

   B. Access the Advanced Options menu by pressing F8 when prompted during the boot sequence.

   C. Access the Advanced Options menu by pressing F6 when prompted during the boot sequence.

   D. There is no Last Known Good Configuration option in Windows Server 2003.

9. You have configured your Windows Server 2003 computer with Certificate Server. Which option should be configured in Windows Backup to ensure that all of the Certificate Server files are properly backed up?

   A. Back up *Windir*\Certificate.

   B. Back up *Windir*\System32.

   C. Back up *Windir*\CertServices.

   D. Back up the System State data.

10. You are using Windows Server 2003 Backup. You configure the backup program to back up the System State data. Which of the following options is not considered System State data?

   A. Registry

   B. The boot partition

   C. COM+ Class Registration database

   D. System boot files

11. You recently added a new partition to your hard drive. When you restart Windows Server 2003, you get an error that `Ntoskrnl.exe` is missing or corrupt. Which file is most likely the problem and needs to be updated?

   A. `Ntoskrnl.exe`

   B. `Boot.ini`

   C. `Ntbootdd.sys`

   D. `Bootsect.dos`

12. You have a SCSI adapter with the BIOS enabled. It is the only adapter in your computer. The adapter has two physical drives attached. The second drive contains the system boot partition. It is located on the first partition on the drive. What is the ARC path to the boot partition?

   A. `scsi(0)disk(1)rdisk(0)partition(1)`

   B. `scsi(1)disk(0)rdisk(1)partition(1)`

   C. `multi(0)disk(0)rdisk(1)partition(1)`

   D. `multi(0)disk(1)rdisk(0)partition(1)`

13. You are the network administrator for a large network. One of your responsibilities is managing all of the accounting servers. One of your servers has become infected with a virus and you suspect that some of the system operating system files have become corrupt. Which of the following system recovery techniques should you use to recover system operating system files?

A. Use the ERD.

B. Use Automated System Recovery.

C. Use System Restore.

D. Use Driver Rollback.

14. You are the network administrator for a large network. You are responsible for all of the servers in the IT department. One of the servers has extremely large disk drives and your tape backup system will not accommodate backing up all of the data at once. You want to back up any data that has changed each day. Which of the following backup options backs up only the files that have not been marked as archived and sets the archive bit for each file that is backed up?

A. Copy

B. Differential

C. Incremental

D. Normal

15. You have chosen to use the differential backup method. You perform a full backup on Friday. On Monday, Tuesday, and Wednesday you perform differential backups. Early Thursday morning, the server fails. Within the following exhibit, drag and drop the tapes on the server that will be used to restore the server backup.

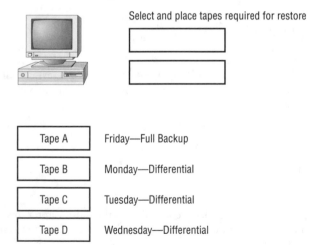

Answers to Review Questions

1. C. `Eventquery` is used to query one or more event logs for specific events or event properties. You can use a filter with the query to include or exclude information such as event type, the user who generated the event, or the category of the event. In this case, `Eventquery` could be used to query event types based on Success Audit or Failure Audit.

2. C, E. If you need to restore System State data on a domain controller, you must restart your computer with the advanced startup option Directory Services Restore Mode. This allows the Active Directory service database and the SYSVOL directory to be restored. If the System State data is restored on a domain controller that is a part of a domain where data is replicated to other domain controllers, you must perform an authoritative restore. For an authoritative restore, you use the `Ntdsutil.exe` command, then restart the computer. There is no ERD (Emergency Repair Disk) in Windows Server 2003.

3. D. The `Ntbackup` command-line utility can be used to back up and restore Windows Server 2003 data. You can use `Ntbackup` to schedule backup jobs.

4. C. If the Remote Assistance connections are made through a firewall, the firewall will need to be configured to open TCP Port 3389.

5. B. You use the Last Known Good Configuration if you made changes to your computer and are now having problems. Last Known Good Configuration is an Advanced Options menu item that you can select during startup. It loads the configuration that was used the last time the computer booted successfully.

6. C. Whenever you see errors in Windows Server 2003, you should check Event Viewer. Event Viewer will show you important information about your computer (including detailed information about error messages).

7. A. When you troubleshoot your computer, you should try the most simple solutions first. In this case, try to boot your computer to Safe Mode. Safe Mode starts the server with the minimum number of services and drivers. If you can boot to Safe Mode, you can start troubleshooting. If this doesn't work, you can attempt more drastic measures.

8. B. In Windows NT 4, you access the Last Known Good Configuration option by pressing the spacebar when prompted during the boot sequence. In Windows Server 2003, the Last Known Good Configuration option is in the Advanced Options menu, which you access by pressing F8 during the boot sequence.

9. D. On Windows Server 2003 computers, System State data includes the Certificate Services database if the server is configured as a Certificate Server. You can back up and restore System State data through the Windows Backup utility.

10. B. On any Window Server 2003 computer, System State data consists of the Registry, the COM+ Class Registration database, and the system boot files. This data can be backed up and restored with the Windows Backup utility.

11. B.   The Boot.ini file is used to point to the location of the Windows Server 2003 boot partition. If you have recently modified your partitions, then it is likely that the ARC path to your boot partition needs to be updated.

12. C.   In this case, you use multi, because the adapter is SCSI with the BIOS enabled. You only use scsi when you have a SCSI adapter with the BIOS disabled. With the multi option, disk is always 0. Rdisk refers to the number of the drive that you are using. The first drive is 0; the second drive is 1. Partition refers to the partition in the physical drive, and the first partition is 1.

13. B.   Windows XP Professional and Windows Server 2003 now include a new feature in Windows Backup called Automated System Recovery (ASR). ASR is used to recover from system partition damage. ASR works by allowing you to back up operating system files onto backup media and hard disk configuration settings to a floppy disk. After you have backed up your system settings, you can restore your operating system files by booting to the Windows Server 2003 CD and during text-mode, when prompted, pressing F2 to run Automated System Recovery, then following the screen instructions that appear.

14. C.   Incremental backups are used to back up only the files that have not been marked as archived and set the archive bit for each file that is backed up. This option requires the last normal backup and all of the incremental tapes that have been created since the last normal backup for the restore process.

15. With differential backups, you only need to restore the last full backup and the last differential tape.

Select and place tapes required for restore

Tape A

Tape D

Glossary

A

ACPI   See *Advanced Configuration and Power Interface*.

Active Directory (AD)   A directory service available with the Windows 2000 Server and Windows Server 2003 platforms. The Active Directory stores information in a central database and allows users to have a single user account (called a *domain user account* or *Active Directory user account*) for the network.

Active Directory user account   A user account that is stored in the Windows 2000 or Windows 2003 *Active Directory*'s central database. An Active Directory user account can provide a user with a single user account for a network. Also called a *domain user account*.

Active Directory Migration Tool (ADMT)   A graphical utility used to import users, groups, and computer accounts from a Windows NT 4.0 domain or a Windows 2000 domain to a Windows 2003 domain.

AD   See *Active Directory*.

adapter   Any hardware device that allows communications to occur through physically dissimilar systems. This term usually refers to peripheral cards that are permanently mounted inside computers and provide an interface from the computer's bus to another medium, such as a hard disk or a network.

Administrator   A Windows Server 2003 special user account that has the ultimate set of security permissions and can assign any permission to any user or group.

Administrators group   A Windows Server 2003 local built-in group that consists of *Administrator accounts*.

ADMT   See *Active Directory Migration Tool*.

Advanced Configuration and Power Interface (ACPI)   A specification that controls the amount of power given to each device attached to the computer. With ACPI, the operating system can turn off peripheral devices when they are not in use.

alerts   A system-monitoring feature that is generated when a specific *counter* exceeds or falls below a specified value. Through the *Performance Logs and Alerts* utility, administrators can configure alerts so that a message is sent, a program is run, or a more detailed log file is generated.

Anonymous Logon group   A Windows Server 2003 *special group* that includes users who access the computer through anonymous logons. Anonymous logons occur when users gain access through special accounts, such as the IUSR_*computername* and TsInternetUser user accounts. Normally, a password is not required, so that anyone can log on.

Application log   A log that tracks events that are related to applications running on the computer. The Application log can be viewed in the *Event Viewer* utility.

ASR   See *Automated System Recovery*.

audit policy   A Windows Server 2003 policy that tracks the success or failure of specified security events.

Authenticated Users group   A Windows Server 2003 *special group* that includes users who access the Windows Server 2003 operating system through a valid username and password.

authentication   The process required to log on to a computer locally or to Active Directory. Authentication requires a valid username and a password that exists in the local accounts database or in Active Directory. A ticket will be created if the information presented matches the account in the database.

Automated System Recovery (ASR)   A process used for system recovery in the event of system failure. It is a two-part process that utilizes a backup component and a restore component. The system information that is backed up by ASR includes *System State data*, system services, and disk configuration information (information about basic and dynamic disks and the file signature associated with each disk).

Automatic Update   Used to extend the functionality of *Windows Update* by automating the process of updating critical files. With Automatic Update, you can specify whether you want updates to be automatically downloaded and installed or whether you just want to be notified when updates are available.

B

backup   The process of writing all the data contained in online mass-storage devices to offline mass-storage devices for the purpose of safekeeping. Backups are usually performed from hard disk drives to tape drives. Also referred to as archiving.

Backup Operators group   A Windows Server 2003 built-in group that includes users who can backup and restore the *file system*, even if the file system is *NTFS* and they have not been assigned permissions to the file system. The members of the Backup Operators group can access the file system only through the *Backup utility*. To be able to directly access the file system, the user must have explicit permissions assigned.

backup type   A *backup* choice that determines which files are backed up during a backup process. Backup types include *normal backup*, *copy backup*, *incremental backup*, *differential backup*, and *daily backup*.

Backup utility   The Windows Server 2003 utility used to run the *Backup Wizard*, the *Restore Wizard*, and the *Automated System Recovery* Wizard.

Backup Wizard   A wizard that is used to perform backup operations. The Backup Wizard is accessed through the *Backup utility*.

bandwidth throttling   A technology that allows you to limit how much network bandwidth can be used by a given website. It prevents a particular website from hogging bandwidth and adversely affecting the performance of the other sites on the web server.

base memory   Also called memory, it refers to the reserved area in memory where devices can store data so that the processor can directly access that data.

baseline   A snapshot record of a computer's current performance statistics that can be used for performance analysis and planning purposes.

basic disk   A disk-storage system supported by Windows Server 2003 that consists of *primary partitions* and *extended partitions*.

Batch group   A Windows Server 2003 *special group* that includes users who log on as a user account that is only used to run a batch job.

boot   The process of loading a computer's operating system. Booting usually occurs in multiple phases, each successively more complex, until the entire operating system and all its services are running. Also called bootstrap. The computer's BIOS must contain the first level of booting.

Boot.ini   A file accessed during the Windows Server 2003 *boot* sequence. The `Boot.ini` file is used to build the operating system menu choices that are displayed during the boot process. It is also used to specify the location of the *boot partition*.

Boot Normally   A Windows Server 2003 Advanced Options menu item used to boot Windows Server 2003 normally.

boot partition   The *partition* that contains the system files. The system files are located in C:\Windows by default.

BOOTSECT.DOS   An optional file that is loaded if the user chooses to load an operating system other than Windows Server 2003. This file is used only in *dual-booting* or multi-booting computers.

bottleneck   A system *resource* that is inefficient compared with the rest of the computer system as a whole. The bottleneck can cause the rest of the system to run slowly.

C

cacheing   A speed-optimization technique that keeps a copy of the most recently used data in a fast, high-cost, low-capacity storage device rather than in the device on which the actual data resides. Cacheing assumes that recently used data is likely to be used again. Fetching data from the cache is faster than fetching data from a slower, larger storage device. Most cacheing algorithms also copy data that is most likely to be used next and perform *write-back cacheing* to further increase speed gains.

CAL   See *Client Access License*.

CDFS   See *CD-ROM File System*.

CD-ROM File System (CDFS)   A *file system* used by Windows Server 2003 to read the files on a CD-ROM.

central processing unit (CPU)   The main *processor* in a computer.

certificate authentication   A security authentication process that uses a special authentication credential, called a certificate. A certificate is a digital signature that is issued by a certificate authority. When a client and server are configured to use certificate authentication, they must both present a valid certificate for mutual authentication.

Check Disk utility   A Windows Server 2003 utility that checks a hard disk for errors. Check Disk (chkdsk) attempts to fix file-system errors and scans for and attempts to recover bad sectors.

CIPHER   A command-line utility that can be used to encrypt and decrypt files on NTFS volumes.

cipher text   Encrypted data. Encryption is the process of translating data into code that is not easily accessible. Once data has been encrypted, a user must have a password or key to decrypt the data. Unencrypted data is known as plain text or clear text.

client   A computer on a network that subscribes to the services provided by a server.

Client Access License (CAL)   A special license for each device or user that enables access to Windows Server 2003 servers. CALs are used with the *Per Seat licensing* mode.

client license key packs   A set of client licenses used by the Terminal Services *license server* to distribute licenses to your *Terminal Services clients*.

compatibility scripts   A script used by applications that require modifications before they can be run with Terminal Services.

compression   The process of storing data in a form using special algorithms that takes less space than the uncompressed data.

Computer accounts   Accounts stored in the Active Directory that are used to uniquely identify, authenticate, and manage computers within the domain.

container   An *Active Directory* object that holds other Active Directory objects. *Domains* and *Organizational Units* are examples of container objects.

Control Panel   A Windows Server 2003 utility that allows users to change default settings for operating system services to match their preferences. The *Registry* contains the Control Panel settings.

CONVERT   A command-line utility used to convert a *partition* or *volume* from *FAT16* or *FAT32* to the *NTFS* file system.

copy backup   A *backup type* that backs up selected folders and files but does not set the archive bit (indicating that the file has been backed up).

counter   A performance-measuring tool used to track specific information regarding a system resource, called a performance object. All Windows Server 2003 system resources—such as Cache, Memory, Paging File, Process, and Processor—are tracked as performance objects. Each performance object has an associated set of counters. Counters are selected in the *System Monitor* utility.

CPU   See *central processing unit*.

Creator group   The Windows Server 2003 *special group* (rather than an individual user) that created or took ownership of an object. When a regular user creates an object or takes ownership of an object, the username becomes the *Creator Owner group*. When a member of the *Administrators group* creates or takes ownership of an object, the Administrators group becomes the Creator group.

Creator Owner group   The Windows Server 2003 *special group* that includes the account that created or took ownership of an object. The account, usually a user account, has the right to modify the object, but cannot modify any other objects that were not created by the user account.

D

daily backup   A *backup type* that backs up all of the files that have been modified on the day that the daily backup is performed. The archive attribute is not set (indicating that the files have been backed up) on the files that have been backed up.

data compression   The process of storing data in a form using special algorithms that takes less space than the uncompressed data.

data encryption   The process of translating data into code that is not easily accessible to increase security. Once data has been encrypted, a user must have a password or key to decrypt the data. Data encryption adds an additional layer of security in remote communications, by encrypting all of the data that is sent and adding security to the logon authentication process.

data recovery agent (DRA)   A special recovery agent that provides access to encrypted files, used if the user who encrypted the folders or files is unavailable to decrypt them when they're needed.

Debugging Mode   A Windows Server 2003 Advanced Option menu item that runs the Kernel Debugger. The Kernel Debugger is an advanced software troubleshooting utility.

Desktop   A directory that the background of the Windows Explorer shell represents. By default, the Desktop includes objects that contain the local storage devices and available network shares. Also a key operating part of the Windows graphical interface.

device driver   Software that allows a specific piece of hardware to communicate with the Windows Server 2003 operating system.

Device Manager   A Windows Server 2003 utility used to view information about the computer's hardware configuration and set configuration options.

DHCP   See *Dynamic Host Configuration Protocol*.

DHCP server   A server configured to provide *DHCP* clients with all of their *Internet Protocol (IP)* configuration information automatically.

differential backup   A *backup type* that copies only the files that have been changed since the last *normal backup* (full backup), and does not reset the archive bit (indicating that the file has been backed up).

Digital Versatile Disc (DVD)   A disk standard that supports 4.7GB of data per disk. One of DVD's strongest features is compatibility with CD-ROM technology in personal computers, so that a DVD drive can play CD-ROMs. Formerly known as Digital Video Disk.

Direct Memory Access (DMA)   Enables a direct access device to transfer data directly to and from RAM by temporarily disabling the CPU's ability to transfer data across its external bus.

Directory Services Restore Mode   A Windows Server 2003 Advanced Option menu item that is used by Windows Server 2003 computers that are configured as *domain controllers* to restore the *Active Directory*. This option is not available on Windows Server 2003 computers that are installed as *member servers*. This option is used if you need to restore *System State data* on a domain controller or restore the Active Directory service database.

Disk Cleanup utility   A Windows Server 2003 utility used to identify files that can be deleted to free additional hard disk space. Disk Cleanup works by identifying temporary files, Internet cache files, and unnecessary program files.

disk defragmentation   The process of rearranging the existing files on a disk so that they are stored contiguously, which optimizes access to those files.

Disk Defragmenter utility   A Windows Server 2003 utility that performs *disk defragmentation*.

Disk Management utility   A Windows Server 2003 graphical tool for managing disks, *partitions*, and *volumes*.

disk partitioning   The process of creating logical *partitions* on the physical hard drive.

disk quotas   A Windows Server 2003 feature used to specify how much disk space a user is allowed to use on specific *NTFS volumes*. Disk quotas can be applied to all users or to specific users.

Distribution group   A logical group of users who have common characteristics, for example a group of Sales users. Applications and e-mail programs (for example, Microsoft Exchange) can use distribution groups for sending data as opposed to sending data to individual users.

DMA   See *Direct Memory Access*.

DNS   See *Domain Name System*.

domain   In Microsoft networks, an arrangement of client and server computers referenced by a specific name that shares a single security permissions database. On the Internet, a domain is a named collection of hosts and subdomains, registered with a unique name by the InterNIC.

domain controller   A Windows Server 2003 computer that is configured to store the domain database, commonly referred to as *Active Directory*.

domain local groups A type of group used to assign permissions to resources. Domain local groups can contain user accounts, *universal groups*, and *global groups* from any domain in the tree or forest. A domain local group can also contain other domain local groups from its own local domain.

domain name A name such as sybex.com that identifies one or more *IP addresses*. Domain names are used in browser address bars to identify particular web pages.

Domain Name System (DNS) The *TCP/IP* network service that translates fully qualified domain names (or host names) into *IP addresses*.

Domain Name System (DNS) server An Internet host dedicated to the function of translating fully qualified domain names into *IP addresses*.

domain user account A user account that is stored in the Windows 2000 Server or Windows Server 2003 *Active Directory*'s central database. A domain user account provides a user with access to domain-based resources. Also called an Active Directory user account.

DRA See *Data Recovery Agent*.

drive letter A single letter assigned as an abbreviation to a mass-storage *volume* available to a computer.

driver A program that provides a software interface to a hardware device. Drivers are written for the specific devices they control, but they present a common software interface to the computer's operating system, allowing all devices of a similar type to be controlled as if they were the same.

driver rollback An option that allows you to restore a previously used driver after a driver has been upgraded. This option provides an easy mechanism for restoring a driver if the upgraded driver does not work properly.

driver signing A digital imprint that is Microsoft's way of guaranteeing that a driver has been tested and will work properly in a computer.

dual-booting The process of allowing a computer to *boot* more than one operating system.

DVD See *Digital Versatile Disc*.

dynamic disk A Windows Server 2003 disk-storage technique. A dynamic disk is divided into dynamic *volumes*. Dynamic volumes cannot contain *partitions* or *logical drives*, and they are not accessible through DOS. You can size or resize a dynamic disk without restarting Windows Server 2003. Dynamic disks are accessible only to Windows 2000, Windows XP, and Windows Server 2003 computers.

Dynamic Host Configuration Protocol (DHCP) A method of automatically assigning *IP addresses* to client computers on a network.

dynamic storage A Windows Server 2003 disk-storage system that is configured as *volumes*. Windows Server 2003 dynamic storage supports *mirrored volumes*, *simple volumes*, *spanned volumes*, *RAID-5 volumes*, and *striped volumes*.

E

EB   See *exabyte*.

effective permissions   The permissions that a user actually has to a file or folder. To determine a user's effective permissions, add all of the permissions that have been allowed through the user's assignments based on that user's username and group associations. Then subtract any permissions that have been denied the user through the username or group associations.

EFS   See *Encrypting File System*.

Enable Boot Logging   A Windows Server 2003 Advanced Options menu item that is used to create a log file that tracks the loading of *drivers* and *services*.

Enable VGA Mode   A Windows Server 2003 Advanced Options menu item that loads a standard VGA driver without starting the computer in *Safe Mode*.

Encrypting File System (EFS)   The Windows Server 2003 technology used to store encrypted files on *NTFS partitions*. Encrypted files add an extra layer of security to the *file system*.

encryption   The process of translating data into code that is not easily accessible to increase security. Once data has been encrypted, a user must have a password or key to decrypt the data.

Error event   An *Event Viewer* event type that indicates the occurrence of an error, such as a driver failing to load.

Event Viewer   A Windows Server 2003 utility that tracks status information about the computer's hardware and software, as well as security events. This information is stored in multiple log files dependent upon the configuration of the server. The minimum number of logs is three: the *Application log*, the *Security log*, and the *System log*.

Everyone   A Windows Server 2003 *special group* that includes anyone who could possibly access the computer. The Everyone group includes all of the users (including *Guests*) who have been defined on the computer.

exabyte (EB)   A computer storage measurement equal to 1024 *petabytes*.

extended partition   In basic storage, a *logical drive* that allows you to allocate the logical partitions however you wish. Extended partitions are created after a *primary partition* has been created.

F

Failure Audit event   An *Event Viewer* entry that indicates the occurrence of an event that has been audited for failure, such as a failed logon when someone enters an invalid username and/or password.

FAT16   The 16-bit version of the *File Allocation Table (FAT)* system, which was widely used by DOS and Windows 3.*x*. The file system is used to track where files are stored on a disk. Most operating systems support FAT16.

FAT32 The 32-bit version of the *File Allocation Table (FAT)* system, which is more efficient and provides more safeguards than *FAT16*. Windows 95 OSR2, Windows 98, Windows XP, and Windows Server 2003 all support FAT32. Windows NT does not support FAT32.

fault tolerance Any method that prevents system failure by tolerating single faults, usually through hardware redundancy.

File Allocation Table (FAT) The *file system* used by *MS-DOS* and available to other operating systems such as Windows (all versions) and OS/2. FAT, now known as *FAT16*, has become something of a mass-storage compatibility standard because of its simplicity and wide availability. FAT has fewer fault-tolerance features than the *NTFS* file system and can become corrupted through normal use over time.

file attributes Information stored along with the name and location of a file in a directory entry. File attributes show the status of a file, such as system, archived, hidden, and read-only. Different operating systems use different file attributes to implement services such as sharing, *compression*, and *security*.

file system A software component that manages the storage of files on a mass-storage device by providing services that can create, read, write, and delete files. File systems impose an ordered database of files on the mass-storage device. Storage is arranged in *volumes*. File systems use hierarchies of directories to organize files.

File Transfer Protocol (FTP) A simple Internet protocol that transfers complete files reliably from an FTP server to a client running the FTP client. FTP provides a simple, low-overhead method of transferring files between computers but cannot perform browsing functions. Users must know the *Uniform Resource Locator (URL)* of the FTP server to which they wish to attach.

fragmentation A process that naturally occurs as users create, delete, and modify files. The access of noncontiguous data is transparent to the user; however, when data is stored in this manner, the operating system must search through the disk to access all the pieces of a file. This slows down data access.

FTP See *File Transfer Protocol*.

G

GB See *gigabyte*.

GDI See *Graphical Device Interface*.

gigabyte (GB) A computer storage measurement equal to 1024 *megabytes*.

global group A type of group used to organize users who have similar network access requirements. A global group is simply a container of users. Global groups can contain users and global groups (in native mode) from the local domain.

GPO See *Group Policy Object*.

Graphical User Interface (GUI)   A computer shell program that represents mass-storage devices, directories, and files as graphical objects on a screen. A cursor driven by a pointing device such as a mouse manipulates the objects.

Graphical Device Interface (GDI)   The programming interface and graphical services provided to *Win32* for programs to interact with graphical devices such as the screen and printer.

group   Security entities to which users can be assigned membership for the purpose of applying a broad set of group permissions to the user. By managing permissions for groups and assigning users to groups, rather than assigning permissions to users, administrators can more easily manage security.

Group Policy Object (GPO)   A set or sets of rules for managing client configuration settings that pertain to desktop lockdowns and the launching of applications. GPOs are data structures that are attached in a specific hierarchy to selected Active Directory Objects. You can apply GPOs to sites, domains, or organizational units.

group scope   Used to determine if the group is limited to a single domain or if the group can span multiple domains. Group scopes are used to assign permissions to resources.

group type   Used to organize users, computers, and other groups into logical objects that are used for management purposes.

Guest   A Windows Server 2003 user account created to provide a mechanism to allow users to access the computer even if they do not have a unique username and password. This account normally has very limited privileges on the computer. This account is disabled by default.

Guests group   A Windows Server 2003 built-in group that has limited access to the computer. This group can access only specific areas. Most administrators do not allow Guest account access because it poses a potential security risk.

GUI   See *Graphical User Interface*.

H

HAL   See *Hardware Abstraction Layer*.

hard disk drive   A mass-storage device that reads and writes digital information magnetically on disks that spin under moving heads. Hard disk drives are precisely aligned and should not be removed, except for maintenance. They are an inexpensive way to store *gigabytes* of computer data permanently. Hard disk drives also store the applications and user data installed on a computer.

Hardware Abstraction Layer (HAL)   A Windows Server 2003 service that provides basic input/output services such as timers, interrupts, and multiprocessor management for computer hardware. The HAL is a *device driver* for the CPU/motherboard circuitry that allows different families of computers to be treated the same by the Windows Server 2003 operating system.

Hardware Compatibility List (HCL)   A list of all of the hardware devices supported by Windows Server 2003. Hardware on the HCL has been tested and verified as being compatible with Windows Server 2003.

hardware profile   A file that stores a hardware configuration for a computer. Hardware profiles are useful when a single computer (for instance, a laptop that can be docked or undocked) has multiple hardware configurations.

HCL   See *Hardware Compatibility List*.

HelpServices group   The *HelpServices group* has special permissions needed to support the computer through Microsoft Help Services.

home folder   A folder where users normally store their personal files and information. A home folder can be a local folder or a network folder.

host   An Internet server. A host is a node that is connected to the Internet.

hot swapping   The ability of a device to be plugged into or removed from a computer while the computer's power is on.

HTML   See *HyperText Markup Language*.

HTTP   See *HyperText Transfer Protocol*.

hyperlink   A link within text or graphics that has a web address embedded in it. By clicking the link, a user can jump to another web address.

HyperText Markup Language (HTML)   A textual data format that identifies sections of a document such as headers, lists, hypertext links, and so on. HTML is the data format used on the World Wide Web for the publication of web pages.

HyperText Transfer Protocol (HTTP)   An Internet protocol that transfers HTML documents over the Internet and responds to context changes that happen when a user clicks a *hyperlink*.

I

IE   See *Internet Explorer*.

IIS   See *Internet Information Services*.

incremental backup   A *backup type* that backs up only the files that have changed since the last normal or incremental backup. It sets the archive attribute (indicating that the file has been backed up) on the files that are backed up.

Information event   An *Event Viewer* entry that informs you that a specific action has occurred, such as when a system shuts down or starts.

inherited permissions   Parent folder permissions that are applied to (or inherited by) files and subfolders of the parent folder. In Windows Server 2003, the default is for parent folder permissions to be applied to any files or subfolders in that folder.

Intel architecture   A family of microprocessors descended from the Intel 8086, itself descended from the first microprocessor, the Intel 4004. The Intel architecture is the dominant microprocessor family. It was used in the original IBM PC microcomputer adopted by the business market and later adapted for home use.

Interactive group   A Windows Server 2003 *special group* that includes all the users who use the computer's resources locally.

interactive logon   A *logon* when the user logs on from the computer where the user account is stored on the computer's local database. Also called a *local logon*.

interactive user   A user who physically logs on to the computer where the user account resides (rather than logging on over the network).

Internet Explorer (IE)   A World Wide Web browser produced by Microsoft and included with Windows 9*x*, Windows Me, Windows NT 4, Windows 2000, Windows XP, and Windows Server 2003.

Internet Information Services (IIS)   Software that serves Internet higher-level protocols such as *HTTP* and *FTP* to clients using web browsers. The IIS software that is installed on a Windows Server 2003 computer is a fully functional web server and is designed to support heavy Internet usage.

Internet Printing Protocol (IPP)   A Windows Server 2003 protocol that allows users to print directly to a *Uniform Resource Locator (URL)*. Printer- and job-related information are generated in *HTML* format.

Internet printer   A Windows Server 2003 feature that allows users to send documents (print requests) to a physical printer via the Internet.

Internet Protocol (IP)   The Network layer protocol upon which the Internet is based. IP provides a simple connectionless packet exchange. Other protocols, such as TCP, use IP to perform their connection-oriented (or guaranteed delivery) services.

Internet Server Application Programming Interface (ISAPI) filters   Used to monitor *HTTP* requests and respond to specific events as defined through the filter. When an event triggers a filter, the request is redirected to specific ISAPI applications, which are then run.

Internet Services Manager   A Windows Server 2003 utility used to configure the protocols that are used by *Internet Information Services (IIS)*.

internetwork   A network made up of multiple network segments that are connected with a device, such as a router. Each network segment is assigned a network address. Network layer protocols build routing tables that are used to route packets through the network in the most efficient manner.

interprocess communications (IPC)   A generic term describing any manner of client/server communication protocol. IPC mechanisms provide a method for the client and server to trade information.

interrupt request (IRQ)   A hardware signal from a peripheral device to the microcomputer indicating that it has input/output (I/O) traffic to send. If the microprocessor is not running a more important service, it will interrupt its current activity and handle the interrupt request. IBM PCs have 16 levels of interrupt request lines.

intranet   A privately owned network based on the *TCP/IP* protocol suite.

I/O memory   A memory address called an I/O address, which is stored as a part of I/O memory (called I/O in Windows Server 2003). The address acts like a mailbox that the processor uses to send instructions to the device.

IP   See *Internet Protocol.*

IP address   A four-byte number that uniquely identifies a computer on an *Internet Protocol (IP) internetwork.*

IPC   See *interprocess communications.*

IPCONFIG   A command used to display the computer's *Internet Protocol (IP)* configuration.

IPP   See *Internet Printing Protocol.*

IRQ   See *interrupt request.*

K

kernel   The core process of a preemptive operating system, consisting of a multitasking scheduler and the basic security services. Depending on the operating system, other services such as virtual memory drivers may be built into the kernel. The kernel is responsible for managing the scheduling of *threads* and *processes.*

L

Last Known Good Configuration option   A Windows Server 2003 Advanced Options menu item used to load the control set that was used the last time the computer was successfully booted.

License Logging service   A service used to track and manage licenses associated with Windows Server 2003.

license server   A special server used with Terminal Services that distributes and accounts for Terminal Services licenses to *Terminal Services clients.*

local group   A group that is stored on the local computer's accounts database. These are the groups that administrators can add users to and manage directly on a Windows Server 2003 computer.

local logon   A *logon* when the user logs on from the computer where the user account is stored on the computer's local database. Also called an interactive logon.

local printer   A printer that uses a *physical port* and that has not been shared. If a printer is defined as local, the only users who can use the printer are the local users of the computer that the printer is attached to.

local security   Security that governs a local or interactive user's ability to access locally stored files. Local security can be set through *NTFS permissions*.

local user profile   A profile created the first time a user logs on, stored in the Documents and Settings folder. The default user profile folder's name matches the user's logon name. This folder contains a file called NTUSER.DAT and subfolders with directory links to the user's *Desktop* items.

logical drive   An allocation of disk space on a hard drive, using a *drive letter*. For example, a 50GB logical drive could be partitioned into two logical drives: a C: drive, which might be 20GB, and a D: drive, which might be 30GB.

logical port   A port that connects a device directly to the network. Logical ports are used with printers by installing a network card in the printers.

logical printer   The software interface between the physical printer (the *print device*) and the operating system. Also referred to as just a *printer* in Windows Server 2003 terminology.

logoff   The process of closing an open session with a Windows Server 2003 computer or Windows domain.

logon   The process of opening a session with a Windows Server 2003 computer or a network by providing a valid authentication consisting of a user account name and a password. After logon, network resources are available to the user according to the user's assigned *permissions*.

logon script   A command file that automates the *logon* process by performing utility functions such as attaching to additional server resources or automatically running different programs based on the user account that established the logon.

M

mandatory profile   A *user profile* created by an administrator and saved with a special extension (.man) so that the user cannot modify the profile in any way. Mandatory profiles can be assigned to a single user or a group of users.

mapped drive   A shared network folder associated with a drive letter. Mapped drives appear to users as local connections on their computers and can be accessed through a drive letter using My Computer.

Master Boot Record (MBR)   A record used in the Windows Server 2003 *boot* sequence to point to the active *partition*, which is the partition used to boot the operating system. This is normally the C: drive. Once the MBR locates the active partition, the boot sector is loaded into memory and executed.

MB   See *megabyte*.

MBSA   See *Microsoft Baseline Security Analyzer*.

MBR   See *Master Boot Record*.

megabyte (MB)   A computer storage measurement equal to 1024 kilobytes.

megahertz   One million cycles per second. The internal clock speed of a microprocessor is expressed in megahertz (MHz). A 2.4 GHz processor would be 2400 MHz.

member server   A Windows Server 2003 server that has been installed as a non-domain controller and joined to a domain. This allows the server to operate as a file, print, and application server without the overhead of account administration.

memory   Any device capable of storing information. This term is usually used to indicate volatile *random-access memory (RAM)* capable of high-speed access to any portion of the memory space, but incapable of storing information without power.

MHz   See *megahertz*.

Microsoft Baseline Security Analyzer (MBSA)   A utility, downloadable from the Microsoft website, used to ensure that you have the most current security updates.

Microsoft Disk Operating System (MS-DOS)   A 16-bit operating system designed for the 8086 chip that was used in the original IBM PC. MS-DOS is a simple program loader and *file system* that turns over complete control of the computer to the running program and provides very little service beyond file system support and the services provided by the BIOS.

Microsoft Management Console (MMC)   A console framework for management applications. The MMC provides a common environment for *snap-ins*.

Mirrored volumes   A volume set that consists of copies of two simple volumes stored on two separate physical partitions. A mirrored volume set contains a primary volume and a secondary volume. The data written to the primary volume is mirrored to the secondary volume. Mirrored volumes provide fault tolerance, because if one volume in the mirrored volume fails, the other volume still works without any interruption in service or loss of data.

MMC   See *Microsoft Management Console*.

MS-DOS   See *Microsoft Disk Operating System*.

MSINFO32   A command-line utility that provides the same functionality as the *System Information utility*.

My Computer   The folder used to view and manage a computer. My Computer provides access to all local and network drives, as well as to *Control Panel*.

My Documents   The default storage location for documents that are created. Each user has a unique My Documents folder.

My Network Places   The folder that provides access to shared resources, such as local network resources and web resources.

N

NetBEUI   See *NetBIOS Extended User Interface*.

NetBIOS   See *Network Basic Input/Output System*.

NetBIOS Extended User Interface (NetBEUI)   A simple Network layer transport protocol developed to support *NetBIOS* installations. NetBEUI is not routable, and so it is not appropriate for larger networks. NetBEUI is the fastest transport protocol available for Windows Server 2003.

NET USE   A command-line utility used to map network drives.

network adapter   The hardware used to connect computers (or other devices) to the network.

Network Basic Input/Output System (NetBIOS)   A client/server *interprocess communications (IPC)* service developed by IBM in the early 1980s. NetBIOS presents a relatively primitive mechanism for communication in client/server applications, but its widespread acceptance and availability across most operating systems make it a logical choice for simple network applications. Many of the network IPC mechanisms in Windows Server 2003 are implemented over NetBIOS.

Network Configuration Operators group   A Windows Server 2003 *special group* whose members have some administrative rights to manage the computer's network configuration.

Network group   A Windows Server 2003 *special group* that includes the users who access a computer's resources over a network connection.

Network News Transfer Protocol (NNTP)   A protocol used to distribute network news messages to NNTP servers and to NNTP clients (news readers) on the Internet. News articles are stored on an NNTP server in a central database where they can be indexed, retrieved, and posted.

network printer   A *printer* that is available to local and network users. A network printer can use a *physical port* or a *logical port*.

New Technology File System (NTFS)   A secure, transaction-oriented file system developed for Windows NT and used by Windows 2000, Windows XP, and Windows Server 2003. NTFS offers features such as *local security* on files and folders, *data compression*, *disk quotas*, and *data encryption*.

NNTP   See *Network News Transfer Protocol*.

normal backup   A *backup type* that backs up all selected folders and files and then marks each file that has been backed up as archived.

NTBOOTDD.SYS   A file accessed in the Windows Server 2003 *boot* sequence. NTBOOTDD.SYS is an optional file (the *SCSI* driver) that is used when the computer has a SCSI adapter with the on-board *BIOS* disabled.

NTDETECT.COM   A file accessed in the Windows Server 2003 *boot* sequence. NTDETECT.COM is used to detect any hardware that is installed and add information about the hardware to the *Registry*.

NTFS   See *New Technology File System.*

NTFS permissions   Permissions used to control access to *NTFS* folders and files. Access is configured by allowing or denying NTFS permissions to users and groups.

NTLDR   A file used to control the Windows Server 2003 *boot* process until control is passed to the NTOSKRNL.EXE file.

NTOSKRNL.EXE   A file accessed in the Windows Server 2003 *boot* sequence. NTOSKRNL.EXE is used to load the Windows Server 2003 *kernel.*

NTUSER.DAT   The file that is created for a *user profile.*

NTUSER.MAN   The file that is created for a *mandatory profile.*

O

offline files and folders   A Windows Server 2003 feature that allows network folders and files to be stored on Windows clients. Users can access network files even if the network location is not available.

optimization   Any effort to reduce the workload on a hardware component by eliminating, obviating, or reducing the amount of work required of that hardware component through any means. For instance, file *cacheing* is an optimization that reduces the workload of a hard disk drive by reducing the number of requests sent to the hard disk drive.

organizational unit (OU)   In *Active Directory*, an organizational unit is a generic folder used to create a collection of objects. An OU can represent a department, division, location, or project group. Used to ease administration of AD objects and as a unit to which group policy can be deployed.

OU   See *organizational unit.*

owner   The user associated with an *NTFS* file or folder who is able to control access and grant permissions to other users.

P

page file   Logical memory that exists on the hard drive. If a system is experiencing excessive paging (swapping between the page file and physical RAM), it needs more memory.

parity   Within disk management, a mathematical calculation performed on the data that is stored on a special part of the disk. In the event of disk failure, the parity calculations are used to rebuild data on failed drives.

partition   A section of a hard disk that can contain an independent *file system* volume. Partitions can be used to keep multiple operating systems and file systems on the same hard disk.

PB   See *petabyte*.

PCI   See *Peripheral Component Interconnect*.

Performance Logs and Alerts   A Windows Server 2003 utility used to log performance-related data and generate *alerts* based on performance-related data.

Peripheral Component Interconnect (PCI)   A high-speed, 32/64-bit bus interface developed by Intel and widely accepted as the successor to the 16-bit Industry Standard Architecture (ISA) interface. PCI devices support input/output (I/O) throughput about 40 times faster than the ISA bus.

permissions   Security constructs used to regulate access to resources by username or group affiliation. Permissions can be assigned by administrators to allow any level of access, such as read-only, read/write, or delete, by controlling the ability of users to initiate object services.

Per Seat licensing   A client licensing mode used by enterprise environments. This mode requires that you purchase a *Client Access License (CAL)* for each device or user. Each client is licensed at the client side to access as many servers as needed.

Per Server licensing   A licensing mode for client licensing. In this mode, the server must be licensed for each concurrent connection.

petabyte (PB)   A computer storage measurement that is equal to 1024 *terabytes*.

physical port   A serial (COM) or parallel (LPT) port that connects a device, such as a printer, directly to a computer.

PING   A command used to send an Internet Control Message Protocol (ICMP) echo request and echo reply to verify that a remote computer is available.

Plug and Play   A technology that uses a combination of hardware and software to allow the operating system to automatically recognize and configure new hardware without any user intervention.

policies   General controls that enhance the *security* of an operating environment. In Windows Server 2003, policies affect restrictions on password use and rights assignments, and determine which events will be recorded in the *Security log*.

port address   Each device has a memory address called an I/O address, which is stored as a part of *I/O memory* (called I/O in Windows Server 2003). The address acts like a mailbox that the processor uses to send instructions to the device. The I/O address is also commonly called the device's port address.

POST   See *Power-On Self-Test*.

Power-On Self-Test (POST)   A part of the Windows Server 2003 *boot* sequence. The POST detects the computer's *processor*, how much memory is present, what hardware is recognized, and whether the *BIOS* is standard or has *Plug and Play* capabilities.

primary partition   A part of *basic storage* on a disk. The primary partition is the first partition created on a hard drive. The primary partition uses all of the space that is allocated to the partition. This partition is usually marked as active and is the partition that is used to *boot* the computer.

print device   The actual physical printer or hardware device that generates printed output.

print driver   The specific software that understands a *print device*. Each print device has an associated print driver.

print processor   The process that determines whether a print job needs further processing once that job has been sent to the *print spooler*. The processing (also called *rendering*) is used to format the print job so that it can print correctly at the *print device*.

print queue   A directory or folder on the *print server* that stores the print jobs until they can be printed. Also called a *print spooler*.

print server   The computer on which the printer has been defined. When a user sends a print job to a *network printer*, it goes to the print server first.

print spooler   A directory or folder on the *print server* that stores the print jobs until they can be printed. Also called a *print queue*.

printer   In Windows Server 2003 terminology, the software interface between the physical printer (see *print device*) and the operating system.

printer pool   A configuration that allows one printer to be used for multiple *print devices*. Printer pooling can be used when multiple printers use the same *print driver* (and are normally in the same location since you don't know which print device will service the print job). With a printer pool, users can send their print jobs to the first available printer.

priority   A level of execution importance assigned to a *thread*. In combination with other factors, the priority level determines how often that thread will get computer time according to a scheduling algorithm.

process   A running program containing one or more *threads*. A process encapsulates the protected memory and environment for its threads.

processor   A circuit designed to automatically perform lists of logical and arithmetic operations. Unlike microprocessors, a processor may be designed from discrete components rather than be a monolithic integrated circuit.

processor affinity   The association of a *processor* with specific *processes* that are running on the computer. Processor affinity is used to configure processes across multiple processors.

product activation   Microsoft's way of reducing software piracy. Unless you have a volume corporate license for Windows Server 2003 or are using a 64-bit version of Windows Server 2003 (which does not use product activation), you will need to perform post-installation activation. This can be done online or through a telephone call.

protocol An established rule of communication adhered to by the parties operating under it. Protocols provide a context in which to interpret communicated information. Computer protocols are rules used by communicating devices and software services to format data in a way that all participants understand.

R

RAID-5 volume A volume configuration that stripes data over multiple disk channels and places a *parity* stripe across the volume for fault tolerance.

RAM See *random-access memory*.

random-access memory (RAM) Integrated circuits that store digital bits in massive arrays of logical gates or capacitors. RAM is the primary memory store for modern computers, storing all running software processes and contextual data.

RDP See *Remote Desktop Protocol*.

real-time application A *process* that must respond to external events at least as fast as those events can occur. Real-time *threads* must run at very high priorities to ensure their ability to respond in real time.

Recovery Console A Windows Server 2003 option for recovering from a failed system. The Recovery Console starts Windows Server 2003 without the graphical interface and allows the administrator limited capabilities, such as adding or replacing files and enabling and disabling services.

Regedit A Windows program, the *Registry Editor*, which is used to edit the *Registry*.

Registry A database of settings required and maintained by Windows Server 2003 and its components. The Registry contains all of the configuration information used by the computer. It is stored as a hierarchical structure and is made up of keys, hives, and value entries.

Registry Editor The utility used to edit the Windows Server 2003 *Registry*. You can use the REGEDIT command-line utility to access the Registry Editor.

Remote Assistance A mechanism for requesting help for *x*86-based computers through Windows Messenger and e-mail, or by sending a file requesting help.

Remote Control Allows you to view or control a user's session from another session.

Remote Desktop A tool for Windows Server 2003 that allows you to take control of a remote computer's keyboard, video, and mouse.

Remote Desktop for Administration A Terminal Services mode that allows administrators to perform administrative tasks on remote servers and clients from a centralized console.

Remote Desktop Protocol (RDP) A connection that needs to be configured in order for clients to connect to the Terminal Services server. You can configure only one RDP connection per network adapter.

Remote Desktop Users group A special group automatically created on Windows Server 2003 computers that is used in conjunction with the Remote Desktop service.

Removable Storage A Windows Server 2003 utility used to track information on removable storage media, which include CDs, DVDs, tapes, and jukeboxes containing optical discs.

rendering The process that determines whether a print job needs further processing once that job has been sent to the spooler. The processing is used to format the print job so that it can print correctly at the *print device*.

Replicator group A Windows Server 2003 built-in group that supports directory replication, which is a feature used by domain servers. Only *domain user accounts* that will be used to start the replication service should be assigned to this group.

resource Any useful service, such as a *shared folder* or a *printer*.

Restore Wizard A wizard used to restore data. The Restore Wizard is accessed through the *Backup utility*.

roaming profile A *user profile* that is stored on a network share. Users can access their roaming profiles from any location on the network.

S

Safe Mode A Windows Server 2003 Advanced Options menu item that loads the absolute minimum of *services* and *drivers* that are needed to start Windows Server 2003. The drivers that are loaded with Safe Mode include basic files and drivers for the mouse (unless a serial mouse is attached to the computer), monitor, keyboard, hard drive, standard video driver, and default system services. Safe Mode is considered a diagnostic mode. It does not include networking capabilities.

Safe Mode with Command Prompt A Windows Server 2003 Advanced Options menu item that starts Windows Server 2003 in *Safe Mode*, but instead of loading the graphical interface, it loads a command prompt.

Safe Mode with Networking A Windows Server 2003 Advanced Options menu item that starts Windows Server 2003 in *Safe Mode*, but adds networking features.

SCSI See *Small Computer System Interface*.

security The measures taken to secure a system against accidental or intentional loss, usually in the form of accountability procedures and use restriction—for example, through *NTFS permissions* and *share permissions*.

security group   A logical group of users who need to access specific resources. Security groups are listed in Discretionary Access Control Lists (DACLs) to assign permissions to resources.

security identifier (SID)   A unique code that identifies a specific user or group to the Windows Server 2003 security system. SIDs contain a complete set of *permissions* for that user or group.

Security log   A log that tracks events that are related to Windows Server 2003 auditing. The Security log can be viewed through the *Event Viewer* utility.

separator page   A page used at the beginning of each document to identify the user who submitted the print job. When users share a printer, separator pages can be useful for distributing print jobs.

service   A *process* dedicated to implementing a specific function for another process. Most Windows Server 2003 components are services used by user-level applications.

Service group   A Windows Server 2003 *special group* that includes users who log on as a user account that is only used to run a *service*.

service pack   An update to the Windows Server 2003 operating system that includes bug fixes and enhancements.

Services utility   A Windows Server 2003 utility used to manage the *services* installed on the computer.

shadow copies   Used to create copies of shared folders and files at specified points in time.

share   A *resource* such as a folder or printer shared over a network.

shared folder   A folder on a Windows Server 2003 computer that network users can access.

Shared Folders utility   A Windows Server 2003 utility for managing *shared folders* on the computer.

share permissions   Permissions used to control access to shared folders. Share permissions can only be applied to folders, as opposed to *NTFS permissions*, which are more complex and can be applied to folders and files.

shortcut   A quick link to an item that is accessible from a computer or network, such as a file, program, folder, printer, or computer. Shortcuts can exist in various locations including the *Desktop* and the *Start menu*, or within folders.

SID   See *security identifier*.

Simple Mail Transfer Protocol (SMTP)   An Internet protocol for transferring mail between Internet hosts. SMTP is often used to upload mail directly from the client to an intermediate host, but can only be used to receive mail by computers constantly connected to the Internet.

simple volume   A *dynamic disk* volume that contains space from a single disk. The space from the single disk can be contiguous or noncontiguous. Simple volumes are used when the computer has enough disk space on a single drive to hold an entire volume.

site license server   A special server that is responsible for managing all of the Windows licenses for the site.

Small Computer System Interface (SCSI)   A high-speed, parallel-bus interface that connects hard disk drives, CD-ROM drives, tape drives, and many other peripherals to a computer. SCSI is the mass-storage connection standard among all computers except IBM compatibles, which use SCSI or IDE.

smart card   A special piece of hardware with a microchip, used to store public and private keys, passwords, and other personal information securely. Can be used for other purposes, such as telephone calling and electronic cash payments.

SMTP   See *Simple Mail Transfer Protocol.*

snap-in   An administrative tool developed by Microsoft or a third-party vendor that can be added to the *Microsoft Management Console (MMC)* in Windows Server 2003.

Software Update Services (SUS)   This is used to deploy a limited version of *Windows Update* to a corporate server, which in turn provides the Windows updates to client computers within the corporate network. This allows clients that are limited to what they can access through a firewall to still keep their Windows operating systems up-to-date.

spanned volume   A *dynamic disk* volume that consists of disk space on 2 to 32 dynamic drives. Spanned volume sets are used to dynamically increase the size of a dynamic volume. With spanned volumes, the data is written sequentially, filling space on one physical drive before writing to space on the next physical drive in the spanned volume set.

special group   A group used by the Windows Server 2003, in which membership is automatic if certain criteria are met. Administrators cannot manage special groups.

spooler   A service that buffers output to a low-speed device such as a printer, so the software outputting to the device is not tied up waiting for the device to be ready.

Start menu   A Windows Server 2003 *Desktop* item, located on the *Taskbar*. The Start menu contains a list of options and programs that can be run.

stripe set   A single *volume* created across multiple hard disk drives and accessed in parallel for the purpose of optimizing disk-access time. *NTFS* can create stripe sets.

striped volume   A *dynamic disk* volume that stores data in equal stripes between 2 to 32 dynamic drives. Typically, administrators use striped volumes when they want to combine the space of several physical drives into a single logical volume and increase disk performance.

subnet mask   A number mathematically applied to *IP addresses* to determine which IP addresses are a part of the same subnetwork as the computer applying the subnet mask.

Success Audit event   An *Event Viewer* entry that indicates the occurrence of an event that has been audited for success, such as a successful logon.

Support_*xxxxxxx*   Microsoft uses the Support_*xxxxxxx* account for the Help and Support Service. This account is disabled by default.

SUS See *Software Update Services*.

System Configuration Utility A utility that allows the administrator to see and edit configuration information about the computer. You access this utility through the `Msconfig` command-line utility.

System group A Windows Server 2003 *special group* that is used when the system accesses specific functions as a user, that process becomes a member of the System group.

System Information utility A Windows Server 2003 utility used to collect and display information about the computer's current configuration.

System log A log that tracks events that relate to the Windows Server 2003 operating system. The System log can be viewed through the *Event Viewer* utility.

System Monitor A Windows Server 2003 utility used to monitor real-time system activity or view data from a log file.

system partition The active *partition* on an *x*86-based computer that contains the hardware-specific files used to load the Windows Server 2003 operating system.

System State data A set of data that is critical to the operating system booting and includes the *Registry*, the COM+ registration database, and the system boot files.

T

Task Manager A Windows Server 2003 utility that can be used to start, end, or prioritize applications. The Task Manager shows the applications and *processes* that are currently running on the computer, as well as *CPU* and *memory* usage information. You can also view network utilization and manage network users.

Taskbar A Windows Server 2003 *Desktop* item, which appears across the bottom of the screen by default. The Taskbar contains the *Start menu* and buttons for any programs, documents, or windows that are currently running on the computer. Users can switch between open items by clicking the item in the Taskbar.

TB See *terabyte*.

TCP See *Transmission Control Protocol*.

TCP/IP See *Transmission Control Protocol/Internet Protocol*.

TCP/IP port A *logical port* used when a printer is attached to the network by installing a network card in the printer. Configuring a TCP/IP port requires the IP address of the network printer.

terabyte (TB) A computer storage measurement that equals 1024 *gigabytes*.

Terminal Server mode Used with Terminal Services to deliver powerful user applications to computers that may be unable to run such applications locally because of hardware or other limitations.

Terminal Server User group   A Windows Server 2003 *special group* that includes users who log on through Terminal Services.

Terminal Services client   A client of a *Terminal Services server*. It uses *thin client* technology to establish a connection with the server and display the graphical user interface information that it receives from the server.

Terminal Services Configuration utility   A Windows Server 2003 Terminal Services utility that is used to change the properties of the RDP-Tcp (Remote Desktop Protocol-Transmission Control Protocol) connection that is created when you install Terminal Services. You can also add new connections with this utility.

Terminal Services Manager utility   A Windows Server 2003 Terminal Services utility that allows you to manage and monitor users, sessions, and processes that are connected to or running on any *Terminal Services server* on the network.

Terminal Services server   A special type of server running Terminal Services that executes applications and processes all information locally and sends only the data response back to the *Terminal Services client*.

thin client   Devices with simple hardware configurations, often legacy desktops, which lack the hardware resources to run the latest Microsoft Windows operating system or applications.

thread   A list of instructions running in a computer to perform a certain task. Each thread runs in the context of a *process*, which embodies the protected memory space and the environment of the threads. Multithreaded processes can perform more than one task at the same time.

Transmission Control Protocol (TCP)   A Transport layer protocol that implements guaranteed packet delivery using the *Internet Protocol (IP)* protocol.

Transmission Control Protocol/Internet Protocol (TCP/IP)   A suite of Internet protocols upon which the global Internet is based. TCP/IP is a general term that can refer either to the *TCP* and *IP* protocols used together or to the complete set of Internet protocols. TCP/IP is the default protocol for Windows Server 2003.

Troubleshooting Wizards   A series of Windows Server 2003 wizards that are used to guide the user through a set of troubleshooting questions related to a specific piece of hardware.

U

UMA   See *Upper Memory Area*.

UNC   See *Universal Naming Convention*.

Uniform Resource Locator (URL)   An Internet standard naming convention for identifying resources available via various *TCP/IP* application protocols. For example, `http://www.microsoft.com` is the URL for Microsoft's World Wide Web server site, and `ftp://gateway.dec.com` is a popular *FTP* site. A URL allows easy hypertext references to a particular resource from within a document or mail message. A URL always has the *domain* name on the right and the *host* name on the left.

uninterruptible power supply (UPS)   An emergency power source that can provide a limited amount of power to a computer in the event of a power outage.

universal groups   A special type of group used to logically organize global groups and appear in the Global Catalog (a search engine that contains limited information about every object in the Active Directory). Universal groups can contain users (not recommended) from anywhere in the domain tree or forest, other universal groups, and *global groups*.

Universal Naming Convention (UNC)   A multivendor, multiplatform convention for identifying shared resources on a network. UNC names follow the naming convention *computername*\ *sharename*.

Universal Serial Bus (USB)   An external bus standard that allows USB devices to be connected through a USB port. USB supports transfer rates up to 12Mbps. A single USB port can support up to 127 devices.

upgrade   A method for installing Windows Server 2003 that preserves existing settings and preferences when converting to the newer operating system.

Upgrade Report   A report generated by the Windows Server 2003 Setup program when upgrading to Windows Server 2003 from a previous operating system. The report summarizes any known compatibility issues that you might encounter during the upgrade. The Upgrade Report can be saved as a file or printed.

Upper Memory Area   Memory that is typically located in the upper area of RAM memory.

UPS   See *uninterruptible power supply*.

URL   See *Uniform Resource Locator*.

USB   See *Universal Serial Bus*.

user profile   A directory that stores a user's *Desktop* configuration and other preferences. A user profile can contain a user's Desktop arrangement, program items, personal program groups, network and printer connections, screen colors, mouse settings, and other personal preferences. Administrators can create *mandatory profiles*, which cannot be changed by the users, and *roaming profiles*, which users can access from any computer they log on to.

user right policies   Policies that control the rights that users and groups have to accomplish network tasks.

username   A user's account name in a logon authenticated system.

Users group   A Windows Server 2003 built-in group that includes end users who should have very limited system access. After a clean install of Windows Server 2003, the default settings for this group prohibit users from compromising the operating system or program files. By default, all users who have been created on the computer, except the *Guest* account, are members of the Users group.

V

video adapter   The hardware device that outputs the display to the monitor.

virtual memory   A *kernel* service that stores memory pages not currently in use on a mass-storage device to free occupied memory for other uses. Virtual memory hides the memory-swapping process from applications and higher-level services.

volume   A storage area on a Windows Server 2003 *dynamic disk*. Dynamic volumes cannot contain *partitions* or *logical drives*. Windows Server 2003 dynamic storage supports five dynamic volume types: *mirrored volumes*, *simple volumes*, *spanned volumes*, *striped volumes*, and *RAID 5 volumes*. Dynamic volumes are accessible only to Windows 2000, Windows XP, and Windows Server 2003.

W

Warning event   An *Event Viewer* entry that indicates that you should be concerned with an event. The event may not be critical in nature, but it is significant and may be indicative of future errors.

web browser   An application that makes *HTTP* requests and formats the resultant *HTML* documents for users. Most web browsers understand all standard Internet protocols.

Win16   The set of application services provided by the 16-bit versions of Microsoft Windows: Windows 3.1 and Windows for Workgroups 3.11.

Win32   The set of application services provided by the 32-bit versions of Microsoft Windows: Windows 95, Windows 98, Windows Me, Windows NT, Windows 2000, Windows XP, and Windows Server 2003.

Windows 9x   The 32-bit Windows 95 and Windows 98 versions of Microsoft Windows for medium-range, *x*86-based personal computers. This system includes peer networking services, Internet support, and strong support for older DOS applications and peripherals.

Windows Backup   The utility used to access the *Backup Wizard*, the *Restore Wizard*, and *Automated System Recovery* options.

Windows Internet Name Service (WINS)   A network service for Microsoft networks that provides Windows computers with the *IP address* for specified *NetBIOS* computer names. WINS facilitates browsing and intercommunication over *TCP/IP* networks.

Windows NT   The predecessor to Windows 2000 that is a 32-bit version of Microsoft Windows for powerful Intel, Alpha, PowerPC, or MIPS-based computers. These operating systems include Windows NT 3.1, Windows NT 3.5, Windows NT 3.51, and Windows NT 4 and include peer networking services, server networking services, Internet client and server services, and a broad range of utilities.

Windows Update   A utility that attaches to the Microsoft website through a user-initiated process and allows the Windows users to update their operating systems by downloading updated files (critical and non-critical software updates).

Windows Server 2003 boot disk   A disk that can be used to *boot* to the Windows Server 2003 operating system in the event of a Windows Server 2003 boot failure.

Windows XP Professional   The current version of the Windows operating system for high-end desktop environments. Windows XP Professional integrates the best features of Windows 98, Windows Me, and Windows 2000 Professional, and supports a wide range of hardware, has an easier-to-use operating system, and results in a reduced cost of ownership.

WINS   See *Windows Internet Name Service.*

WINS server   The server that runs *WINS* and is used to resolve *NetBIOS* computer names to *IP addresses.*

WMI Control   A Windows Server 2003 utility that provides an interface for monitoring and controlling system resources. WMI stands for Windows Management Instrumentation.

write-back cacheing   A cacheing optimization wherein data written to the slow store is cached until the cache is full or until a subsequent write operation overwrites the cached data. Write-back cacheing can significantly reduce the write operations to a slow store because many write operations are subsequently obviated by new information. Data in the write-back cache is also available for subsequent reads. If something happens to prevent the cache from writing data to the slow store, the cache data will be lost.

write-through cacheing   A cacheing optimization wherein data written to a slow store is kept in a cache for subsequent rereading. Unlike *write-back cacheing*, write-through cacheing immediately writes the data to the slow store and is therefore less optimal but more secure.

Index

Note to the reader: Throughout this index **boldfaced** page numbers indicate primary discussions of a topic. *Italicized* page numbers indicate illustrations.

Q

R

X

Y

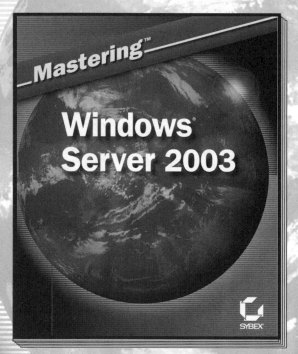

TELL US WHAT YOU THINK!

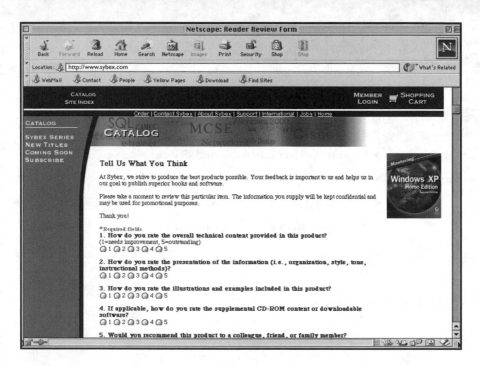

Your feedback is critical to our efforts to provide you with the best books and software on the market. Tell us what you think about the products you've purchased. It's simple:

1. Go to the Sybex website.
2. Find your book by typing the ISBN or title into the Search field.
3. Click on the book title when it appears.
4. Click **Submit a Review.**
5. Fill out the questionnaire and comments.
6. Click **Submit.**

With your feedback, we can continue to publish the highest quality computer books and software products that today's busy IT professionals deserve.

www.sybex.com

Sybex Offers the Complete Solution

MCSA/MCSE: Windows Server 2003 Environment Management and Maintenance Study Guide
ISBN 0-7821-4260-5 • $49.99

MCSA/MCSE: Windows XP Professional Study Guide, Second Edition
ISBN 0-7821-4241-9 • $49.99

MCSA: Windows 2003 Core Requirements
ISBN 0-7821-4264-8 • $119.99

The **Microsoft Certified Systems Administrator (MCSA)** will put you on the path to manage and maintain the computing environment of medium- to large-sized companies.

MCSA 2003 Track

Choose ONE Client OS Requirement

Exam #	Exam
70-210	Installing, Configuring and Administering Microsoft Windows 2000 Professional
70-270	Installing, Configuring and Administering Windows XP Professional

2 Network Operating System Requirements

Exam #	Exam
70-290	Managing and Maintaining a Microsoft Windows Server 2003 Environment
70-291	Implementing, Managing, and Maintaining a Microsoft Windows Server 2003 Network Infrastructure

Choose ONE Elective

Exam #	Exam
70-086	Implementing and Supporting Microsoft Systems Management Server 2.0
70-228	Installing, Configuring, and Administering Microsoft Internet Security and Acceleration (ISA) 2000
70-228	Installing, Configuring and Administering SQL Server 2000
	CompTIA A+ and Network+ combo
	CompTIA A+ and Server+ combo

For a list of all Sybex products that will help prepare you for any of the MCSA exams, visit **www.sybex.com**.